Organizational Wrongdoing

Organizational Wrongdoing is an essential companion to understanding the causes, processes, and consequences of misconduct at work. With contributions from some of the world's leading management theorists, past theories on misconduct are critically evaluated, and the latest research is introduced, expanding the boundaries of our knowledge and filling in gaps highlighted in previous studies. A wide range of unethical, socially irresponsible, and illegal behaviors are discussed, including cheating, hyper-competitive employee actions, and financial fraud. Further, multiple levels of analysis are considered, ranging from individual-to organizational field-wide processes. By providing a contemporary overview of wrongdoing and misconduct, this book provides solid and accessible foundations for established researchers and advanced students in the fields of behavioral ethics and organizational behavior.

DONALD PALMER is Professor of Organizational Behavior at the University of California, Davis. He is the former Editor of *Administrative Science Quarterly* (2002–2008) and the recipient of the *Journal of Management Inquiry* Scholar Award 2005. His book *Normal Organizational Wrongdoing* won the Academy of Management, Social Issues in Management Division, Best Book Award and was a finalist for the Academy of Management's George R. Terry Award.

KRISTIN SMITH-CROWE is Associate Professor of Organizational Behavior in the Questrom School of Business at Boston University, USA. She serves on the editorial boards of the *Academy of Management Review, Organizational Behavior and Human Decision Processes*, and *Organization Science*.

ROYSTON GREENWOOD is the Telus Professor of Strategic Management at the University of Alberta, Canada, and Professorial Fellow at the University of Edinburgh, UK. In 2010, he was elected a Fellow of the

Academy of Management and in 2013 was selected as that year's Honorary Member by the European Group for Organization Studies (EGOS). He received the Distinguished Scholar Award from the Organization & Management Theory Division of the Academy of Management in 2014.

CAMBRIDGE COMPANIONS TO MANAGEMENT

Cambridge Companions to Management provide an essential resource for academics, graduate students, and reflective business practitioners seeking cutting-edge perspectives on managing people in organizations. Each *Companion* integrates the latest academic thinking with contemporary business practice, dealing with real-world issues facing organizations and individuals in the workplace, and demonstrating how and why practice has changed over time. World-class editors and contributors write with unrivalled depth on managing people and organizations in today's global business environment, making the series a truly international resource.

Organizational Wrongdoing

Key Perspectives and New Directions

Edited by

DONALD PALMER
Graduate School of Management, University of California, Davis

KRISTIN SMITH-CROWE
Questrom School of Business, Boston University

ROYSTON GREENWOOD
University of Alberta and University of Edinburgh

CAMBRIDGE
UNIVERSITY PRESS

CAMBRIDGE
UNIVERSITY PRESS

University Printing House, Cambridge CB2 8BS, United Kingdom

One Liberty Plaza, 20th Floor, New York, NY 10006, USA

477 Williamstown Road, Port Melbourne, VIC 3207, Australia

314-321, 3rd Floor, Plot 3, Splendor Forum, Jasola District Centre, New Delhi - 110025, India

79 Anson Road, #06-04/06, Singapore 079906

Cambridge University Press is part of the University of Cambridge.

It furthers the University's mission by disseminating knowledge in the pursuit of
education, learning and research at the highest international levels of excellence.

www.cambridge.org
Information on this title: www.cambridge.org/9781107541658

© Cambridge University Press 2016

First published 2016
First paperback edition 2019

A catalogue record for this publication is available from the British Library

Library of Congress Cataloging in Publication data
Palmer, Donald, 1951– editor. | Smith-Crowe, Kristin,
editor. | Greenwood, Royston, editor.
Organizational wrongdoing / edited by Donald Palmer,
Kristin Smith-Crowe, Royston Greenwood.
New York : Cambridge University Press, 2016. |
Series: Cambridge companions to management
LCCN 2016015479 | ISBN 9781107117716 (hardback)
LCSH: Organizational change. | BISAC: BUSINESS &
ECONOMICS / Organizational Behavior.
LCC HD58.8 .O7566 2016 | DDC 302.3/5–dc23
LC record available at https://lccn.loc.gov/2016015479

ISBN 978-1-107-11771-6 Hardback
ISBN 978-1-107-54165-8 Paperback

Contents

Figures

Tables

Contributors

MICHEL ANTEBY is Associate Professor of Organizational Behavior at Boston University's Questrom School of Business, USA. He received a joint PhD in management from New York University and in sociology from EHESS (France). His research looks at how people relate to their work, their occupations, and the organizations they belong to. He is the author of two monographs: *Moral Gray Zone: Side-Production, Identity, and Regulation in an Aeronautic Plant* and *Manufacturing Morals: The Values of Silence in Business School Education.*

BLAKE E. ASHFORTH is the Horace Steele Arizona Heritage Chair at Arizona State University, USA. He received his PhD from the University of Toronto, Canada. His research concerns the ongoing dance between individuals and organizations, including identity and identification, socialization and newcomer adjustment, and the links among individual-, group-, and organization-level phenomena.

JAMES N. BARON is the William S. Beinecke Professor of Management and Professor of Sociology (by courtesy) at Yale University, USA. He previously was on the faculty of Stanford's Graduate School of Business. He is the author or coauthor of numerous publications in leading journals in management, sociology, economics, and psychology. His research interests include economic sociology; organizations; stratification and inequality; work, labor markets, and careers; human resource management; and entrepreneurial companies.

DOLLY CHUGH is a tenured Associate Professor in the Management and Organizations Department at New York University's Stern School of Business, USA. Her research focuses on the psychological constraints on the quality of decision-making with ethical import, a phenomenon known as "bounded ethicality." She is particularly interested in unintentional forms of unethical behavior and biased behavior. She holds an MBA from the Harvard Business School and a PhD in social psychology/organizational behavior from Harvard University, USA.

MARCO CLEMENTE is a postdoctoral researcher at the Institute of Strategy at Aalto University, Finland, and is affiliated with the Society & Organizations Research Center at HEC Paris, where he received his PhD. His current research focuses on both the social construction and the consequences of organizational misconduct and scandals. His research has appeared in the *Academy of Management Review*. Prior to joining academia, Marco was marketing manager at Procter & Gamble.

RODOLPHE DURAND is Professor of Strategy and Director of the Society & Organizations Research Center at HEC Paris. His primary research interests concern the social and institutional sources of competitive advantage and organizational performance, and his recent works feature the social, normative, and strategic underpinnings of organizational conformity and deviance.

JAMES FAULCONBRIDGE is Professor of Transnational Management at Lancaster University Management School, UK. His research focuses on the professions and, in particular, the globalization of professional services. Over the past decade James has completed extensive qualitative research in several professional service sectors, including advertising, architecture, executive search, and law. His research has been funded by the UK's Research Councils, the British Academy, and the US Sloan Foundation. He has published extensively in leading journals, including in *Economic Geography, Environment and Planning A*, the *Journal of Economic Geography*, the *Journal of Management Studies, Organization Studies*, and *Work, Employment and Society*. James co-authored the books *The Globalization of Advertising* and *The Globalization of Executive Search*, and co-edited the books *International Business Travel in the Global Economy* and *The Business of Global Cities*.

CLAUDIA GABBIONETA is Senior Lecturer in Accounting at Newcastle University Business School, UK. She has done extensive research on corporate corruption and professional misconduct. Her recent work on the subject has been published in *Accounting, Organization and*

Society (under the title "The influence of the institutional context on corporate illegality") and in the *Journal of Professions and Organization* (under the title "Sustained corporate corruption and processes of institutional ascription within professional networks"). She is currently investigating the antecedents of professionals' involvement in cases of corporate corruption.

ROYSTON GREENWOOD is the Telus Professor of Strategic Management at the University of Alberta, Canada, and Professorial Fellow at the University of Edinburgh, UK. He received his PhD from the University of Birmingham, UK. In 2010, Greenwood was elected a Fellow of the Academy of Management and in 2013 was selected that year's Honorary Member by the European Group for Organization Studies (EGOS). He received the Distinguished Scholar Award from the Organization & Management Theory Division of the Academy of Management in 2014.

HENRICH R. GREVE is Professor of Entrepreneurship at INSEAD, Singapore. His research focuses on misconduct and social judgment, diffusion processes with adverse consequences, and organizational learning from experience through mechanisms like performance and problemistic search. His current research also examines organizations creating institutional legacies in local communities. He is a past associate editor of *Administrative Science Quarterly* and *Organization Science*. His recent work includes "The thin red line between success and failure: path dependence in the diffusion of innovative production technologies," published in *Strategic Management Journal* (coauthored with Marc-David Seidel).

JARED D. HARRIS is a faculty member at the University of Virginia's Darden School of Business, USA, and a Senior Fellow at Darden's Olsson Center for Applied Ethics. In the Darden curriculum, Jared teaches both the required MBA strategy course and the required MBA business ethics course. His research centers on the interplay between ethics and strategy and has been published in *Strategic Management Journal, Academy of Management Review, Organization Science, Journal of Business Venturing, Business Ethics Quarterly*, and *Journal of Business Ethics*. Insights from this research have been highlighted in the *New York Times*, the *Washington Post*, and *The New Yorker*, as well as other media outlets in the United States, Canada, Germany, India, Portugal, and the United Kingdom. His academic career follows a distinguished business career, first in consulting at several global public accounting firms, followed by a stint as a Chief Financial Officer (CFO) for a small technology startup.

DADAO HOU is a PhD student in sociology at Texas A&M University, USA. His areas of research include sociology of organizations, political sociology, and political economy. His dissertation research examines the financialization of the US economy and the political economy of US financial regulations since the late 1970s. He holds a master's degree in sociology from the Chinese University of Hong Kong and bachelor's degrees in mathematical statistics and sociology from Peking University, China.

MARY C. KERN is an Associate Professor of Management at Baruch College and the Graduate Center at the City University of New York. She received her BBA from the University of Notre Dame, USA, and her PhD from Northwestern University, USA. Her research and publications focus on negotiation and decision-making behavior, with specific emphasis on the impact of cognitive and social blinders.

MARISSA D. KING is an Associate Professor of Organizational Behavior at the Yale School of Management, USA. Her research analyzes the spatial and temporal dimensions of innovation and social learning. To understand how large-scale social transformations arise from local social networks, she has studied cases ranging from the rise in autism prevalence during the past decade to the organizational foundations of the antislavery movement in the late 19th century.

DONALD LANGE is Associate Professor and the Lincoln Professor of Management Ethics at Arizona State University, USA. His PhD is from the University of Texas, Austin, USA. His research interests include individual- and situational-level drivers of good and bad behavior, antecedents and outcomes of reputation, and the nature of social (ir)responsibility.

IAN LARKIN is Assistant Professor of Strategy at the Anderson School of Management, University of California, Los Angeles, USA. He received his PhD from the University of California, Berkeley, USA, and was a faculty member at Harvard Business School for six years. He researches incentive system design, with an emphasis on the unexpected and often deleterious effects that formal reward systems have on employee motivation and performance. His research has been published in leading management and economics journals.

RYANN MANNING is a PhD student in organizational behavior and sociology at Harvard University, USA. Her research focuses on emotion, culture, and ambiguity in organizational life. She received her Master in Public Policy and Master of Arts in Sociology degrees from Harvard University, and prior to her doctoral studies, she worked as a researcher and manager in international development and global health.

YURI MISHINA is Assistant Professor of Organizational Behavior/ Strategy in the Department of Management at Imperial College Business School, UK. His research examines how the top management team and stakeholder belief systems influence a firm's strategic choices and outcomes. His research has been published in the *Academy of Management Journal, Organization Science*, and *Strategic Management Journal*, and he is an International Research Fellow of the Oxford University Centre for Corporate Reputation.

CELIA MOORE is an Associate Professor in the Department of Management and Technology at Bocconi University in Milan, Italy. Her research focuses on how organizational contexts affect how we construe, and therefore facilitate, morally problematic behavior. Her work has appeared in leading journals, including the *Academy of Management Annals, Journal of Applied Psychology*, and *Journal of Personality and Social Psychology*. Before receiving her PhD from the University of Toronto, she was a Senior Associate at Catalyst, a research and advisory organization that works with business to advance women.

DANIEL MUZIO is a Professor of Professions and Organization at the University of Newcastle. He has previously worked at the universities of Lancaster, Leeds, and Manchester. He has also held visiting professorships at the Said Business School, Oxford; Alliance MBS, The University of Manchester; Cass Business School, London;

The University of Law, London; and Luiss Guido Carli in Rome. His research interests include the organization and management of professional services firms, the sociology of the professions, and the role of professions in institutional change processes. Daniel has published in several leading management and social sciences journals, including *Organization Studies, Sociology, Journal of Management Studies, Human Relations*, and the *Journal of Economic Geography*. He is an associate editor of the *Journal of Management Studies* and a founding editor of the *Journal of Professions and Organization*, a co-editor of the *Oxford Handbook of Professional Services Firms* (2015) and a director of the research group on Professions, Work and Organization at the University of Newcastle.

DONALD PALMER is Professor of Management in the Graduate School of Management at the University of California, Davis. He received his PhD in sociology from Stony Brook University, USA. Palmer was an Associate Editor of *Administrative Science Quarterly* from 2000 to 2002 and Editor of the journal from 2003 to 2008. He is the author of *Normal Organizational Wrongdoing*, which won the 2013 Academy of Management (AOM) Social Issues in Management Division best book award and was a finalist for the 2013 AOM All-Academy (George R. Terry) best book award.

LAMAR PIERCE is Associate Professor of Organization and Strategy at the Olin Business School at Washington University in St. Louis and Academic Director of the Masters of Science in Leadership at the Brookings Institution in Washington, DC. He is the winner of the Harrington Foundation Fellowship from the University of Texas and the Olin Award for Research from Washington University, and he serves as Chief Academic Advisor for CivicScience. Lamar's research on employee productivity and misconduct has featured in major newspapers and on National Public Radio. His work has been published in major journals in organizational behavior, strategy, psychology, marketing, operations, political science, and business ethics. He holds a PhD from the Haas School of Business at the University of California, Berkeley.

TIMOTHY G. POLLOCK is the Farrell Professor of Entrepreneurship in the Smeal College of Business at the Pennsylvania State University. His research focuses on how reputation, celebrity, social capital, media accounts, and power influence corporate governance and strategic decision-making in entrepreneurial firms and the social construction of entrepreneurial markets. He has published articles in all of the top management journals, including the *Academy of Management Journal, Academy of Management Review, Administrative Science Quarterly, Organization Science,* and the *Strategic Management Journal.* His research has also won numerous awards. Tim is a former Associate Editor for the *Academy of Management Journal* and an International Research Fellow of the Oxford Centre for Corporate Reputation.

JOSEPH PORAC is Professor of Business Leadership at Stern School of Business, New York University. His research examines how social and cognitive processes shape organizational and interorganizational action. His work includes research into the sociopolitical aspects of corporate governance, the formation of markets, and the consequences of scandals.

JO-ELLEN POZNER is an Assistant Professor at the Leavey School of Business, Santa Clara University. She holds a PhD in management (Kellogg School of Management, Northwestern University), an MBA in finance and management (New York University), an MA in international economics (Johns Hopkins University), and a BSFS in economics (Georgetown University). Her research focuses on organizational misconduct, with a particular emphasis on the consequences of organizational wrongdoing on individuals; corporate governance; social and identity movements; and institutional change. She has published in outlets, including the *American Journal of Sociology,* the *Annals of the Academy of Management, Strategic Organization,* and *Organization Studies.*

MICHAEL G. PRATT is the O'Connor Family Professor in the Carroll School of Management at Boston College. He earned his PhD from the University of Michigan and has previously taught at the University of Illinois, Urbana–Champaign. His research interests are problem-centered and cross-level and include how people connect to their organizations, professions, and work. In addressing these research interests, he utilizes various methods, including ethnography and grounded theory, and draws heavily from theories of identity and identification, meaning, emotion, intuition, and culture (e.g., artifacts). His research has appeared in numerous outlets, including the *Academy of Management Annual Review, Academy of Management Journal, Academy of Management Review, Administrative Science Quarterly, Organizational Research Methods, Organization Science, Research in Organizational Behavior*, and in numerous edited books. He is currently an associate editor of the *Administrative Science Quarterly*.

HARLAND PRECHEL is Professor of Sociology at Texas A&M University. His research examines the relationship between political and economic conditions and corporate change. His current research program examines the effects of corporations' organizational and political-legal arrangements on financial malfeasance and environmental pollution. He is a former editor of *Research in Political Sociology*. His articles have appeared in *American Sociological Review, Social Forces, Social Problems*, and elsewhere.

YEONJI SEO is a PhD student in the Management and Organization Department of the Pennsylvania State University Smeal College of Business. She received her MS in strategy and international management from Seoul National University and BA in international studies from Ewha Womans University. Her research interests are in the areas of corporate social responsibility and the social evaluations of firms, including their reputation, image, legitimacy, and celebrity. Her current projects focus on how external stakeholders' perceptions influence strategic choices of a firm in newly developed categories.

KRISTIN SMITH-CROWE is an Associate Professor of Organizational Behavior in the Questrom School of Business at Boston University, USA. She earned her PhD in psychology from Tulane University, USA. She studies behavioral ethics in organizations and is especially interested in experiences of moral emotions and moral ambiguity. Her research has appeared in the *Academy of Management Annals*, the *Academy of Management Review, Organizational Behavior and Human Decision Processes*, the *Journal of Applied Psychology, Organization Science*, and *Research in Organizational Behavior*.

OLAV SORENSON is the Frederick Frank '54 and Mary C. Tanner Professor of Management and Professor of Sociology (by courtesy) at

Yale University. Prior to his current position, he held professorships at the University of Toronto, London Business School, UCLA, and the University of Chicago. He has published research on a range of subjects, including economic geography, social networks, entrepreneurship, industry evolution, corporate strategy, and the sociology of science and technology.

DAPHNE TEH is a PhD candidate at INSEAD, Singapore. She does research on issues related to legitimacy loss and focuses on understanding how networks and social influence affect the occurrence of organizational misconduct. Daphne also explores how audiences respond to low legitimacy and make sense of ambiguous situations. Together with Henrich Greve and Ji-Yub Kim, she recently published "Ripples of fear: the diffusion of a bank panic" in *the American Sociological Review*. Currently, Daphne does research on how cultural industries manage the lack of legitimacy during the process of emergence.

ABHIJEET K. VADERA is an Assistant Professor of Organisational Behaviour and Human Resources at Singapore Management University. He earned his PhD from the University of Illinois, Urbana–Champaign, USA, and previously taught at the Indian School of Business. His research focuses on examining the antecedents, processes, and consequences of constructive (e.g., whistle-blowing, creativity) as well as destructive (e.g., workplace crimes, white-collar crime) deviance. He has presented his work at several academic conferences and has published in several top journals such as the *Academy of Management Journal, Organization Science, Journal of Management, Business Ethics Quarterly*, and *Journal of Business Ethics*.

CHRISTOPHER B. YENKEY is an Assistant Professor of Organizations and Strategy at the University of Chicago Booth School of Business. He earned his PhD in sociology from Cornell University in 2011. Yenkey served as a visiting scholar in 2008 at the Institute for Economic Affairs in Nairobi, Kenya, and was Associate Director of Cornell's Center for the Study of Economy and Society from 2010 to 2011. His research on trust and market development has been published in *Administrative Science Quarterly* and was awarded the William H. Newman Best Dissertation Paper Award from the Academy of Management in 2011.

TENG ZHANG is a PhD candidate in the Management Department of the University of Utah David Eccles School of Business. He received his MA in communication from the University of Maryland, College Park, USA, and BA in English from Xi'an Jiaotong University, China. His research interests are in the areas of behavioral ethics, conflict and negotiation, and power and status in the workplace. His dissertation examines the effects of intuition on ethical decision-making.

Foreword

In the 1987 film *Wall Street*, written and directed by Oliver Stone, the main character Gordon Gekko says "Greed, for lack of a better word is good. Greed is right; greed works. Greed clarifies, cuts through, and captures the essence of the evolutionary spirit." This rationalization of wrongdoing – exemplified by Enron, Arthur Andersen, WorldCom, and so on, and some very recent examples as well (e.g., Libor rigging of inter-bank interest rates by banks, VW car emissions scandal) – makes this book a timely reminder of misconduct in the workplace and its consequences for individuals, businesses, and society. The volume editors, Donald Palmer, Kristin Smith-Crowe, and Royston Greenwood, have put together the latest research by some of the most prominent academics and scholars in the field, to highlight "a wide range of unethical, socially irresponsible, and illegal behaviors" engaged in by senior executives and others in a variety of organizations for personal gain, or to enhance their promotion, or to cover up their incompetence or lack of goal achievement, and so on.

The book explores some of the following issues: the limitations and imbalances of theory and research on organizational wrongdoing, workplace morality, market enablers to wrongdoing (an historical review), trust and mistrust, a boundaries perspective of professional misconduct, social networks and organizational wrongdoing, compensation and employee misconduct, the consequences of misconduct, the media portrayal of wrongdoing, and other very important topics.

Although business wrongdoing has been around since trade began, through the Industrial Revolution to the conglomerates of today, the "big data age" and media scrutiny have more quickly highlighted corporate corruption. Now that the light is able to shine on these events, we are more able to explore organizational wrongdoing and business ethics than in the past. This volume provides the science and informed debate on where we go from here in creating more ethical workplaces. As Plato said, "there are not many very good or very bad people, but the great majority are something between the two." We need to create more ethical organizational cultures for the majority.

Sir Cary L. Cooper, CBE, Manchester Business School, University of
Manchester, UK
Jone Pearce, University of California, Irvine, USA
Series editors

1 | The imbalances and limitations of theory and research on organizational wrongdoing

DONALD PALMER, KRISTIN SMITH-CROWE,
AND ROYSTON GREENWOOD

This volume is devoted to exploring the causes, processes, consequences, and nature of wrongdoing in and by organizations. Such conduct, hereafter for convenience referred to as *organizational misconduct* and *organizational wrongdoing*, includes a wide range of behaviors – violations of criminal, civil, and administrative law; transgressions of explicit industry and professional codes; and contraventions of less codified organizational rules, social norms, and ethical principles. Given their apparent greater incidence and scale in recent years, it is not surprising that these behaviors have received increasing attention in scholarly circles, in practitioner communities, and among the general public as of late. Moreover, and contrary to previous work, recent scholarship has adopted a range of perspectives and elaborated its focus and concerns to include aspects of wrongdoing previously ignored. This introduction outlines how recent scholarship contributes to the renaissance of management scholarship on organizational misconduct.

The dearth of theory and research on organizational wrongdoing

Kenneth Boulding (1958), in his review of the first two volumes of *Administrative Science Quarterly*, identified the study of misconduct in and by organizations as an object of inquiry that was of enduring importance to management practitioners and society but that was receiving scant attention from the journal's contributors. Since Boulding's early assessment, other observers have periodically lamented management scholars' neglect of organizational misconduct relative to other topics of apparently greater interest, such as organizational efficiency and effectiveness (Brief 2000; Hinings and Greenwood 1982). This lack of attention to misconduct in and by organizations implicitly conveys the assumption that organizational wrongdoing is rare and peripheral to organizational functioning.

At the dawn of the new century, though, a series of episodes of organizational wrongdoing received massive media attention, including incidents at Enron, Arthur Andersen, Tyco, and WorldCom in the United States, Barclays Bank in the United Kingdom, Parmalat in Italy, Satyam in India, as well as incidents of misconduct at a large number of multi-national financial institutions implicated in the recent global financial crisis and in international governance organizations such as the world soccer Fédération Internationale de Football Association (FIFA). These affairs likely received extensive media attention partly because new forms of media (most importantly, forms of media made possible by the expansion of the Internet) were emerging that facilitated the dissemination and amplification of news about misconduct. Regardless, the attention these episodes received contributed to the perception that organizational misconduct is increasing in frequency, scale, and complexity, suggesting systemic causes and precipitating catastrophic consequences.

In the wake of these scandals, psychologists began to explore the ways in which human cognition is structured so as to make errors in ethical decision-making perhaps inevitable (Chugh, Banaji, and Bazerman 2005). At the same time, management theorists drawing on sociological insights began to focus on how wrongdoing can become "normalized" in organizations (Ashforth et al. 2004; Brief et al. 2001; Vaughan 1996). Reflecting these developments, some management theorists began to conceptualize organizational wrongdoing more generally as a normal phenomenon (cf. Palmer 2013). Viewing organizational wrongdoing in and by organizations as a normal phenomenon implies not only that misconduct is frequent but also that it is associated with the same processes that give rise to right-doing (e.g., human cognition and efficient and effective organizational processes).

The theme that wrongdoing is a normal phenomenon is picked up in this volume most obviously by Larkin and Pierce (Chapter 10) in their analysis of compensation systems. They maintain that even the most well-conceived compensation systems are likely to simultaneously facilitate the performance of efficient, inefficient, and even wrongful behavior. It is also evident in Ashforth and Lange's (Chapter 11) analysis of organizational saints, which argues that individuals and organizations with strong moral self-concepts will tend to both exhibit superior moral behavior and be susceptible to ethical lapses. In addition, it is reflected in Vadera and Pratt's (Chapter 12) assertion that employees' over-identification with an organization's mission can both advance its mission and facilitate misconduct on its behalf. It is further evident in Pollock, Mishina, and Seo's (Chapter 9) observation that firm celebrity and infamy are in the eyes of the beholder and that nonconformity can be seen in a positive or negative light. It is also evident in Muzio, Faulconbridge, Gabbioneta, and Greenwood's (Chapter 6) analysis of professional service firms that shows how misconduct can be inadvertently accepted because of embedded professional norms. Interestingly, though these examples span levels of analysis, for the most part organizational wrongdoing has often been considered from a micro perspective – the emphasis has been upon individual behavior, reflecting an implicit assumption that it is individuals rather than organizations that are motivated to act inappropriately. We discuss this literature next.

The predominant use of the micro lens to understand the causes of misconduct

Psychologists and those approaching the study of organizations from a psychological perspective were the first to pursue the subject of organizational wrongdoing in a sustained fashion. Their work, which appeared as early as the 1970s, tended to assume that organizational participants are rational and explored why people chose to engage in unethical or ethical behavior (e.g., Jones 1991). They focused on three factors: the attributes of the decision-maker (e.g., their gender or cognitive moral development), the nature of the ethical dilemma (e.g., its moral intensity), and the character of the decision context (e.g., its embeddedness in strong governance and cultural restraints). More recent years have seen a shift in thinking, with psychologists considering how inherent human cognitive processes put all organizational participants at risk of perpetrating unethical behavior. This later work explicitly assumes that people's rationality is bounded and explores the universal biases and framing effects that compromise all individuals' attempts to behave ethically, regardless of personal characteristics, decision attributes, or decision contexts (Bazerman and Tenbrunsel 2011).

This individual-level research, which was given a boost by the highly publicized business scandals mentioned above, has generated a large corpus of findings that enhance our understanding of wrongdoing (for reviews, see Treviño, Weaver, and Reynolds 2006; Tenbrunsel and Smith-Crowe 2008; Treviño, den Nieuwenboer, and Kish-Gephart 2014). This research is represented in this volume by Chugh and Kern's (Chapter 16) analysis of the factors that facilitate ethical learning in organizations. It is also represented in Smith-Crowe and Zhang's (Chapter 2) discussion of the outcomes studied by ethical decision-making scholars and the opportunities for expanding the range of outcomes considered. However, this research, as with micro work more generally, has been criticized for failing to pay sufficient attention to the organizational context (Brief and Smith-Crowe 2015; Porter 1996; Staw in press) and the wider institutional context (Gabbioneta et al. 2013). The psychological perspective fails to take into account the collective character of much misconduct in and by organizations – that is, the fact that much organizational wrongdoing involves multiple interacting individuals, situated within a larger social context.

Theory and research advanced from the meso and macro levels are well positioned to fill this gap in our understanding of wrongdoing in and by organizations. By their very nature they provide ways to conceptualize and parameterize the small-group, organizational, and institutional contexts in which misconduct often occurs. As a result, meso and macro perspectives are enjoying increased attention. Indicative of this trend, misconduct in and by organizations is increasingly referred to as *corruption*, to telegraph the degree to which it is a group- and organizational- as opposed to an individual-level phenomenon. To date, though, the full promise of the meso and macro vantage points is yet to be realized. We discuss the nature of this deficit next.

The relative underdevelopment of meso and macro theory and research on the causes of organizational wrongdoing

Although meso and macro theory and research possess the promise to expand our understanding of misconduct in and by organizations, and for this reason are enjoying increased vitality, research to date has been largely restricted to two theoretical approaches. The first approach focuses on the ways economic incentives and opportunities can motivate misconduct (Becker 1968) – specifically the extent to which governance regimes fail to detect misconduct and swiftly and significantly punish it when detected (Fama 1980). The second approach focuses on sociological incentives and opportunities that can motivate misconduct and on the cultural prescriptions that can endorse it. Some of this work holds that organizational actors pursue misconduct when they experience performance strain – that is, when performance aspirations cannot be reached (Simpson 1986; Staw and Szwajkowski 1975). Some holds that organizational actors pursue misconduct when their cultural environments endorse wrongdoing (Sims and Brinkmann 2003). These two approaches are frequently presented in tandem, as exemplified by McKendall and Wagner's (1997) often cited study of financial fraud.[1]

Without a doubt, economic theory provides fundamental insights about the causes of misconduct. Larkin and Pierce's (Chapter 10) analysis of the way compensation systems can motivate wrongdoing represents a direct extension of this line of inquiry. Similarly, theory about performance strain and culture provide crucial insights about the causes of organizational wrongdoing as well. But, recently management scholars have begun to draw on other meso and macro theories to develop an enhanced understanding of the causes of misconduct. Institutional theory (Gabionetta et al. 2013), political economy (Prechel and Morris 2010), social network analysis (Palmer and Yenkey 2015), status and reputation approaches (Mishina et al. 2010), social interaction perspectives (Ashforth and Anand 2003), and organizational identification theory (Vadera and Pratt 2013) are just a few of the alternative meso and macro perspectives that have been exploited to develop a deeper understanding of the causes of organizational wrongdoing in recent years.

A glance at the table of contents of this volume will reveal how this expanded meso and macro theoretical focus is manifest in this volume. Prechel and Hou (Chapter 4) use the political economy lens to provide a chronological account of how the complexity of legislative changes and regulatory shifts arising from corporate lobbying have given rise to

---

[1] This formulation has so dominated the literature on accounting and financial fraud, that it has been adopted by the American Society of Fraud Examiners (ASFE) as the definitive explanation of fraud, known as the "fraud triangle" (the corners of which are motivation, opportunity, and rationalization).

"structural holes" that provide opportunities for financial wrongdoing. Yenkey draws on some of this work to examine stockbroker fraud in Kenya (Chapter 5). Muzio, Faulconbridge, Gabbioneta, and Greenwood draw on institutional theory as it has been applied to the professions to explore the causes of misconduct in professional service firms (Chapter 6). Baron, King, and Sorenson (Chapter 7), drawing on multiple meso- and macro-level theories, analyze the causes of scientific misconduct, a form of organizational wrongdoing of paramount importance to our field, but which has so far almost completely been overlooked by management scholars (see Furman, Jensen, and Murray [2012] for a rare exception). Palmer and Moore (Chapter 8) critically review research on the way in which social networks can facilitate organizational misconduct. Pollock, Mishina, and Seo (Chapter 9) extend their work on celebrity firms to explore how high-profile firms can fall from grace. Finally, Vadera and Pratt (Chapter 12) extend their analysis of how organizational identification and disidentification can give rise to misconduct by drawing on role theory to explore how the occupancy of multiple roles can mitigate tendencies to engage in organizational crime.

The predominant focus on the *causes* of misconduct

Traditionally, theory and research on wrongdoing in and by organizations, whether pursued from a micro, meso, or macro vantage point, have focused on the *causes* of organizational misconduct (e.g., Kish-Gephart, Harrison, and Treviño 2010). Further, most of this work has focused on the *initiation* of misconduct, the factors that cause organizational participants or organizations to embark on a wrongful course of action. Such a focus implicitly treats the proliferation, evolution, and maintenance of misconduct as unproblematic. There is some older research on the consequences of misconduct, but the vast majority of this work focuses exclusively on the legal and stock market penalties to which detected wrongdoers are exposed. As such, it ignores the wide range of noneconomic consequences to which detected perpetrators (and those to whom they are related) can be exposed.

Recently, research has expanded beyond this traditional focus (Greve, Palmer, and Pozner 2010). Some theorists have offered process theories of corruption, which analyze how misconduct diffuses and proliferates among individuals within organizations (Ashforth and

Anand 2003; Brief et al. 2001; Palmer 2008; Smith-Crowe and Warren 2014). Others have explored how misconduct diffuses and proliferates within organizations and among organizations in a field (Baker and Faulkner 2003; Gabbioneta et al. 2013; Mohliver 2012). Further, a handful of researchers have begun to explore the structure and impact of misconduct (Baker and Faulkner 1993, 2004), as well as the non-economic penalties suffered not only by wrongdoers but by those individuals and organizations related in some way to them (Jonsson, Greve, and Fujiwara-Greve 2009; Pozner 2008). Coming from a fundamentally different angle, but also focused on the consequences of morally relevant behavior, psychologists have considered the potentially negative effects stemming from *moral* behavior. Research on moral licensing (see Mullen and Monin [in press] for a review) suggests that an individual's moral behavior may actually license subsequent immoral behavior. This paradoxical consequence can happen either because the individual banked moral credits that can be subsequently spent or because the initial behavior provides the person with a moral credential, influencing his or her perception such that subsequent actions are seen in a more moral light.

This expanded substantive focus is evident in the chapters included in this volume, most obviously in Greve and Teh's (Chapter 13) analysis of the consequences that can befall organizations discovered to have engaged in misconduct, Pozner and Harris's (Chapter 14) analysis of the consequences that can befall individuals associated with delinquent organizations, and Ashforth and Lange's (Chapter 11) analysis of the moral pitfalls of individuals having a moral self-concept. But it is also evident in Palmer and Moore's (Chapter 8) discussion of social network explanations of misconduct, Yenkey's (Chapter 5) pointed analysis of victims' reactions to stockbroker fraud in Kenya, and Vadera and Pratt's (Chapter 12) consideration of the dark side of organizational identification.

The provincialism of theory and research on organizational wrongdoing

Management scholars periodically lament that the bulk of theory and research in our field is produced by scholars located in developed societies, especially North America and more narrowly the United

States, and that it focuses on people and organizations located in these societies (cf. Graham et al. 2011). As Palmer (2006: 550) noted,

> Boulding (1958) contended that the first two volumes of *ASQ* did not pay sufficient attention to organizations located outside the U.S. Forty years later, Hickson (1996) summarized research by Usdiken and Pasadeos (1995) showing that organizational scholarship was more developed in North America than elsewhere and that while organization scholars in other parts of the world frequently cited their colleagues in North America, the reverse did not often happen ... Augier, March, and Sullivan (2005) later provided a brief history of the evolution of organization studies in Anglophone North America, suggesting that, to all extents and purposes, this history was coterminous with the development of the field as a whole.

Moreover, broader disciplinary work is similarly limited. For instance, Henrich, Heine, and Norenzayan (2010) argued that research on WEIRD people (those who are Western, educated, industrialized, rich, and democratic) is not sufficiently generalizable to be a basis for an understanding of human psychology. They claim that this population is in fact weird – that these are "some of the most psychologically unusual people on Earth" (29).

Some headway has been made toward addressing these biases. For example, the journal *Organization Studies* was founded in 1980 with the explicit intention of providing a home for research conducted by non-North American scholars focused on non-North American organizations. Further, *Management and Organization Review* was established in 2005 to provide similar opportunities for scholars located in and focused on the Chinese context. Moreover, there has been an explicit attempt to internationalize the editorial boards of several of the more prestigious management journals in order to make them more receptive to non-US scholarship. The list of "best papers" for these journals indicates the recent success of this strategy (Greenwood, 2016).

Our volume continues this effort. It includes contributions from authors hailing from the United Kingdom (Celia Moore, Yuri Mishina, James Faulconbridge, and Daniel Muzio), France (Rudy Durand), Italy (Claudia Gabionetta and Marco Clemente), and Singapore (Henrich Greve, Daphne Teh, and Abhijeet Vadera). Further, it includes contributions that focus on people and organizations around the globe. Yenkey's (Chapter 5) focus is on financial fraud in Kenya, while Clemente, Durand, and Porac's (Chapter 15) focus is on misconduct in Italian soccer. Both Muzio, Faulconbridge, Gabbioneta, and Greenwood's (Chapter 6) analysis of misconduct in professional firms and Greve and Teh's (Chapter 13) analysis of the consequences of misconduct consider examples of misconduct from around the globe. Finally, Manning and Anteby (Chapter 3) rely on examples of paralegals and nurses in West African nations who struggle to justify the line between right and wrong.

The uncritical treatment of the definition of organizational wrongdoing

Traditionally, in the meso and macro literatures, management scholars have considered the definition of wrongdoing to be unproblematic. In the micro literature, definitions are rarely given, though when they do appear, they are consistent with those found in the macro and meso literatures, where misconduct is defined in highly general terms, such as the violation of ethical principles, social norms, administrative rules, or civil and criminal law. In this respect, wrongdoing is generally operationalized as behaviors that authors assume readers will accept as fitting these broad definitions and that will be uncontroversial.

In the case of micro studies, researchers analyze lying, cheating, and the inequitable allocation of communal resources. In the case of meso studies, researchers analyze uncooperative and aggressive behavior. In the case of macro studies, researchers analyze legal indictments and prosecutions for financial fraud, environmental pollution, and other crimes.

This approach overlooks an important component of wrongdoing recognized by the classic sociologist Emile Durkheim and his intellectual descendants (Becker 1963; Black 1998) – that in order for a behavior to constitute wrongdoing and for a perpetrator to assume the status of wrongdoer, another actor must label the behavior and perpetrator as such. The implication of this insight is that in order to understand the causes of misconduct, one must understand not only the behavior of those who perpetrate behavior considered wrongful but also the behavior of those who seek to label behavior as "wrongful" (Palmer 2013, Chapter 11). To be fair, some macro scholars recognize this fact. But most who do primarily view it from a methodological standpoint – that is, as leading to the underestimation or biased measurement of wrongdoing in a population or sample that can only be overcome through the use of sophisticated measurement techniques (cf. Prechel and Morris 2010; Palmer and Yenkey 2015). It is only very recently that some management scholars have begun to theorize and study the process by which behaviors and perpetrators are labeled as "wrongdoing" and "wrongdoers" (Graffin et al. 2013).

The sociological view of wrongdoing can be contrasted with a more psychologically grounded view, which considers the evolutionary basis and innateness of human moral capacity. For instance, Bloom (2013) argues that we are born with a sense of right and wrong and with a capacity for compassion and empathy, though certainly we do not arrive as fully formed moral beings. His argument is built to some extent on evidence from other fields showing commonalities across cultures and species, but he focuses largely on evidence from developmental psychology, including three-month-olds preferring good puppets to bad puppets and one-year-olds punishing bad puppets. This innateness perspective is evident in the influential moral foundations theory (Graham et al. 2011), which holds that humans subscribe to at least five moral foundations, each connected to an evolution-based origin story. Theoretically, this perspective raises important questions, including the extent to which our sense of right and wrong is malleable versus entrenched and which aspects of the moral domain might be more hardwired and what might be more learned.

Several of the chapters included in this volume contribute to a more critical consideration of the definitional problem. Manning and Anteby (Chapter 3) approach the issue from a micro perspective, examining how organizational participants establish the line between acceptable and unacceptable moral behavior in the places where they work. Smith-Crowe and Zhang (Chapter 2) recognize a burgeoning conversation in the micro literature on the constructed definition of wrongdoing, focusing on examples of more developed conversations from elsewhere (such as that on moral foundations theory) to suggest both how the conversation could be carried forward and why micro scholars should care whether it is. Clemente, Durand, and Porac (Chapter 15) approach the issue from a macro perspective, examining the role that the media plays in scandalizing behavior that it considers wrongful and, in so doing, activates more formally constituted social control agents to suppress the behavior.

The restricted derivation of practical implications from theory and research on organizational misconduct

Finally, management scholars periodically lament the seeming disconnect between organization theory and research on the one hand and practical prescriptions for organizational improvement on the other (Pfeffer and Sutton 2006). This deficit is particularly evident in the domain of wrongdoing in and by organizations. As indicated above, since the turn of the century, theory and research on misconduct in and by organizations have enjoyed a renaissance. But while many business schools and organizations devote attention to misconduct, their approach to it is mired in theory that is out of step with recent scholarly developments.

Most business schools offer courses on governance, the primary objective of which is to convey means of organizing that inhibit the capacity of superiors, peers, and especially subordinates to engage in misconduct. Most organizations institute compliance systems, which have the same objective. This approach implicitly assumes that misconduct is perpetrated by the "other guy" or gal, who needs to be watched closely and controlled tightly (in Muzio et al.'s terms in Chapter 6, the "bad apple"). But this assumption flies in the face of logic and empirical evidence. If it is only the other person who is at risk of engaging in misconduct and everyone wishes to control the other person, then wrongdoing should be relatively rare, which it is not.

Most business schools also offer ethics courses, the primary objective of which is to educate students on philosophical approaches to misconduct and the secondary objective of which is to exhort students to take ethical criteria into account when making business decisions. Many organizations adopt a similar approach, promulgating ethical codes and purporting to evaluate employees according to their adherence to them. The primary objective of these efforts implicitly assumes that organizational participants are rational actors, capable of sophisticated ethical reasoning and (importantly) of acting on that reasoning. The secondary objective assumes that ethical behavior is a matter of will – in common parlance, of the strength of one's moral compass. But research suggests that organizational participants are far from fully rational. It also suggests that an organizational participant's moral compass, however strong, is often no match for the magnetic pull of the many contextual factors that shape attitudes and behavior in organizations.

In the last several years, though, a small number of management scholars who study misconduct have begun to develop the practical implications of their ideas (Bazerman and Tenbrunsel 2011). The final chapter in our volume pushes this practical project forward. Chugh and Kern (Chapter 16) suggest that an understanding of the formidable organizational forces that can cause organizational participants to jettison their moral selves and behave in ways inconsistent with their closely held values is insufficient to overcome those forces. They maintain that it is also necessary that organizational participants cultivate a growth mindset and that organizations foster a safe environment, in which individuals can learn from the moral lapses and in this way improve the ethicality of their behavior.

Conclusion

This volume is motivated by the fundamental belief that misconduct in and by organizations is both common and highly consequential not only for organizations, the participants who constitute them, and the people and organizations that populate their environments but also for the fundamental institutions of society – not least, the market system, which rests upon the assumption of trust. It is inspired by recent management scholarship that builds upon and goes beyond early work on organizational misconduct. And it consists of original chapters that extend recent scholarship on the subject. Our hope is that this volume will inspire other management theorists to take up the challenge of conducting research on misconduct in and by organizations and, in doing so, provide insights that will push the field forward.

References

Ashforth, B. E. and Anand, V. 2003. "The normalization of corruption in organizations," *Research in Organizational Behavior* 25: 1–52.
Ashforth, B. E., Anand, V., and Joshi, M. 2004. "Business as usual: The acceptance and perpetuation of corruption in organizations," *Academy of Management Executive* 18(2): 39–53.
Augier, M., March, J. G., and Sullivan, B. N. 2005. "Notes on the evolution of a research community: Organization studies in anglophone North America, 1945–2000," *Organization Science* 16: 85–95.

Baker, W. E. and Faulkner, R. R. 1993. "The social organization of conspiracy: Illegal networks in the heavy electrical equipment industry," *American Sociological Review* 58: 837–860.

Baker, W. E. and Faulkner, R. R. 2003. "Diffusion of fraud: Intermediate economic crime and investor dynamics," *Criminology* 41: 1173–1206.

Baker, W. E. and Faulkner, R. R. 2004. "Social networks and loss of capital," *Social Networks* 26: 91–111.

Bazerman, M. and Tenbrunsel, A. 2011. *Blind Spots: Why We Fail to Do What's Right and What to Do about It*. Princeton: Princeton University Press.

Becker, G. S. 1968. "Crime and punishment: An economic approach," *Journal of Political Economy* 76: 169–217.

Becker, H. S. 1963. *Outsiders: Studies in the Sociology of Deviance*. New York: Free Press.

Black, D. 1998. *The Social Structure of Right and Wrong*. New York: Academic Press.

Bloom, P. 2013. *Just Babies: The Origins of Good and Evil*. New York: Broadway Books.

Boulding, K. E. 1958. "Evidences for an administrative science: A review of the *Administrative Science Quarterly*, volumes 1 and 2," *Administrative Science Quarterly* 3(1): 1–22.

Brief, A. P. 2000. "Still servants of power," *Journal of Management Inquiry* 9: 342–351.

Brief, A. P., Bertram, R. T., and Dukerich, J. M. 2001. "Collective corruption in the corporate world: Toward a process model," in M. E. Turner (ed.), *Groups at Work: Advances in Theory and Research*: 471–499. Hillsdale, NJ: Lawrence Erlbaum and Associates.

Brief, A. P. and Smith-Crowe, K. 2015. "Organizations matter," in A. G. Miller (ed.), *The Social Psychology of Good and Evil* (2nd edn.). New York: Guilford Press.

Chugh, D., Banaji, M., and Bazerman, M. 2005. "Bounded ethicality as a psychological barrier to recognizing conflicts of interest," in D. Moore, D. Cain, G. Loewenstein, and M. Bazerman (eds.), *Conflicts of Interest: Challenges and Solutions in Business, Law, Medicine, and Public Policy*. New York: Cambridge University Press.

Fama, E. F. 1980. "Agency problems and the theory of the firm," *Journal of Political Economy* 88: 288–307.

Furman, L. F., Jensen, K., and Murray, F. 2012. "Governing knowledge in the scientific community: Exploring the role of retractions in biomedicine," *Research Policy* 41(2): 276–290.

Gabbioneta, C., Greenwood, R., Mazzola, P., and Minoja, M. 2013. "The influence of institutional context on corporate illegality," *Accounting, Organizations, and Society* 38: 484–504.

Graffin, S. D., Bundy, J., Porac, J. F., Wade, J. B., and Quinn, D. P. 2013. "Falls from grace and the hazards of high status: The 2009 British MP expense scandal and its impact on parliamentary elites," *Administrative Science Quarterly* 58(3): 313–345.

Graham, J., Nosek, B. A., Haidt, J., Iyer, R., Koleva, S., and Ditto, P. H. 2011. "Mapping the moral domain," *Journal of Personality and Social Psychology* 101: 366–385.

Greenwood, R. 2016 "OMT, then and now," *Journal of Management Inquiry*, 25 (1): 27-33.

Greve, H. R., Palmer, D., and Pozner, J.-E. 2010. "Organizations gone wild: The causes, processes, and consequences of organizational misconduct," *The Academy of Management Annals* 4(1): 53–108.

Henrich, J., Heine, S. J., and Norenzayan, A. 2010. "Most people are not WEIRD," *Nature* 466: 29.

Hickson, D. J. 1996. "The ASQ years: Then and now through the eyes of a Euro-Brit," *Administrative Science Quarterly*, 41: 217–228.

Hinings, R. and Greenwood, R. 1982. "ASQ Forum: Disconnects and consequences in organization theory?" *Administrative Science Quarterly* (September 2002) 47: 411–421.

Jones, T. M. 1991. "Ethical decision making by individuals in organizations: An issue-contingent model," *Academy of Management Review* 16: 366–395.

Jonsson, S., Greve, H. R., and Fujiwara-Greve, T. 2009. "Lost without deserving: The spread of legitimacy loss in response to reported deviance," *Administrative Science Quarterly* 54: 195–228.

Kish-Gephart, J. J., Harrison, D. A., and Treviño, L. K. 2010. "Bad apples, bad cases, and bad barrels: Meta-analytic evidence about sources of unethical decisions at work," *Journal of Applied Psychology* 95: 1–31.

McKendall, M. A. and Wagner, J. 1997. "Motive, opportunity, choice, and corporate illegality," *Organization Science* 8: 624–647.

Mishina, Y., Dykes, B. J., Block, E. S., and Pollock, T. G. 2010. "Why 'good' firms do bad things: The effects of high aspirations, high expectations and prominence on the incidence of corporate illegality," *Academy of Management Journal* 53(4): 701–722.

Mohliver, A. C. 2012. "The legitimacy of corrupt practices: Geography of auditors advice and backdating of stock option grants," Paper presented at the Academy of Management Annual Meeting, Boston, MA.

Mullen, E. and Monin, B. 2016. "Consistency versus licensing effects of past moral behavior," *Annual Review of Psychology* 67: 363–385.

Palmer, D. 2006. "Taking stock of the criteria we use to evaluate one another's work: ASQ 50 years out," *Administrative Science Quarterly* 51(4): 535–559.

Palmer, D. 2008. "Extending the process model of collective organizational wrongdoing," *Research in Organizational Behavior* 28: 107–135.

Palmer, D. 2013. *Normal Organizational Wrongdoing: A Critical Analysis of Theories of Misconduct in and by Organizations.* Oxford: Oxford University Press.

Palmer, D. and Yenkey, C. 2015. "Drugs, sweat and gears: An organizational analysis of performance enhancing drug use in the 2010 Tour de France," *Social Forces* 94 (2): 891–922.

Pfeffer, J. and Sutton, R. 2006. *Hard Facts, Dangerous Half-Truths and Total Nonsense: Profiting from Evidence-Based Management.* Cambridge, MA: Harvard Business Review Press.

Porter, L. W. 1996. "Forty years of organization studies: Reflections from a micro perspective," *Administrative Science Quarterly* 41: 262–269.

Pozner, J. 2008. "Stigma and settling up: An integrated approach to the consequences of organizational misconduct for organizational elites," *Journal of Business Ethics* 80(1): 141–150.

Prechel, H. and Morris, T. 2010. "The effects of organizational and political embeddedness on financial malfeasance in the largest U.S. corporations," *American Sociological Review* 75: 331–354.

Simpson, S. S. 1986. "The decomposition of antitrust: Testing a multilevel, longitudinal model of profit-squeeze," *American Sociological Review* 51: 859–975.

Sims, R. R. and Brinkmann, J. 2003. "Enron ethics (Or: Culture matters more than codes)," *Journal of Business Ethics* 45(3): 243–256.

Smith-Crowe, K. and Warren, D. E. 2014. "The emotion-evoked collective corruption model: The role of emotion in the spread of corruption within organizations," *Organization Science* 25: 1154–1171.

Staw, B. M. 2016. "Stumbling toward a social psychology of organizations: Some tales from the past and guidelines for the future," *Review of Organizational Psychology and Organizational Behavior* 3: 1–19.

Staw, B. M. and Szwajkowski, E. 1975. "The scarcity-munificence component of organizational environments and the commission of illegal acts," *Administrative Science Quarterly* 20: 345–354.

Tenbrunsel, A. E. and Smith-Crowe, K. 2008. "Ethical decision making: Where we've been and where we're going," *Academy of Management Annals* 2: 545–607.

Treviño, L. K., den Nieuwenboer, N. A., and Kish-Gephart, J. J. 2014. "(Un) ethical behavior in organizations," *Annual Review of Psychology* 65: 635–660.

Treviño, L. K., Weaver, G. R., and Reynolds, S. J. 2006. "Behavioral ethics in organizations: A review," *Journal of Management* 32(6): 951–990.

Usdiken, B., and Pasadeos, Y. 1995. "Organizational analysis in North America and Europe: A comparison of co-citation networks," *Organization Studies*, 16: 503–526.

Vadera, A. K. and Pratt, M. G. 2013. "Love, hate, ambivalence, or indifference? A conceptual examination of workplace crimes and organizational identification," *Organization Science* 24: 172–188.

Vaughan, D. 1996. *The Challenger Launch Decision: Risky Technology, Culture, and Deviance at NASA*. Chicago: University of Chicago Press.

2 On taking the theoretical substance of outcomes seriously: a meta-conversation

KRISTIN SMITH-CROWE AND TENG ZHANG

As the large number of review articles in recent memory demonstrates, research on behavioral ethics in organizations has exploded (e.g., Bazerman and Gino 2012; Kish-Gephart, Harrison, and Treviño 2010; Tenbrunsel and Smith-Crowe 2008; Treviño, den Nieuwenboer, and Kish-Gephart 2014; Treviño, Weaver, and Reynolds 2006; Weaver, Reynolds, and Brown 2014). Scholars in this area focus on individuals' ethical judgments, decisions, and behaviors, particularly those relevant to organizations.[1] Treviño and colleagues (2014) trace the beginnings of this field to the 1980s and describe the overall endeavor like this: "Most research in the field begins with the premise that ethical behavior in organizations is good and unethical behavior is bad, and that understanding the predictors of each can help organizations produce more of the former and less of the latter" (p. 637). We find this description to be not only apt but also illuminating. It highlights something that those of us working in this area seem to take for granted: our theoretical focus should be on the predictor side of the model.[2] While we struggle to achieve a degree of parsimony out of the kaleidoscope of possibilities on the predictor side of the equation, we tend to keep things simple on the criterion side (i.e., the outcomes we study). There is ethical and unethical. Usually, we focus on predicting unethical outcomes.

We thank Irina Cojuharenco, Ben Crowe, and Don Palmer for excellent comments on previous versions of this chapter.

[1] We use the terms "ethical" and "moral" interchangeably.

[2] We do not take this statement to be a reflection of Treviño et al.'s (2014) view on how things *should* be as they are explicitly describing the field as it exists, rather than offering normative commentary. Also here and elsewhere (e.g., Kish-Gephart et al. 2010; Treviño et al. 2006) they give greater attention to the criterion side of the equation than is the norm.

The cost of relative inattention to theory development on the criterion side is ultimately an impoverishment of theory more generally. We often vaguely refer to "unethical" behavior without acknowledging the potential for conceptual complexity. Such complexity surely holds implications for theorizing on the predictor side. In the long run, we cannot expect our theories to systematically connect predictors with outcomes when we have not specified the nature of the outcomes. Our contention is that, to the end of systematic theorizing, as a field we should take the theoretical substance of outcomes seriously, meaning that we should focus theory development not only on the predictor side of the equation but also on the criterion side.

In order to support our contention, we report the results of a somewhat unconventional literature review. First, we review the outcomes employed by those studying behavioral ethics in organizations. Though there are numerous reviews to date, they are organized around the predictors of unethical outcomes. By focusing on the outcomes, we highlight some limitations of this body of work. Second, we review a series of scholarly conversations about the theoretical substance of morally relevant outcomes. We use the term "conversations" in a nontechnical sense to refer to instances of scholars explicitly writing about this topic. These conversations are drawn largely from literatures outside of the literature on behavioral ethics in organizations, particularly psychology. We present them in the context of a "meta-conversation," or a conversation about the potential fruitfulness of having such conversations within our own field and the forms that they might take. Rather than agreeing or disagreeing with their content, we highlight features of these conversations, connecting them to theoretical advancements. While an overarching theoretical framework of behavioral ethics outcomes in organizations is beyond the scope of this chapter, we hope that reflection upon these examples, which we organize by type, will inspire and otherwise engender similar conversations within our literature. We conclude by suggesting topics for further conversations that are particularly relevant to behavioral ethics in organizations. Importantly, we number among those engaging in this field of research and we mean to include ourselves in the collective "we," making our essay both outwardly and inwardly focused, a reflection on the state of the field and a reflection on our own work.

The outcomes we study

We begin by reporting the results of our review of the outcomes we study in the field of behavioral ethics in organizations. Here our focus is contemporary rather than historical. As such, we limited our review to recently published articles: 2009–2015.[3] Given our focus on organizational research, we also limited our review to six top organizational behavior and management journals publishing empirical work: the *Academy of Management Journal, Administrative Science Quarterly, Organization Science, Organizational Behavior and Human Decision Processes*, the *Journal of Applied Psychology*, and *Personnel Psychology*. We searched each issue of these six journals during the specified time period to identify all behavioral ethics articles – that is, articles in which the outcome variables were individuals' ethical judgments, decisions, or behaviors.[4] Based on this criterion, we identified 201 studies reported within 74 articles[5] published with the following frequencies across journals: 67.1 percent in *Organizational Behavior and Human Decision Processes*, 13.4 percent in the *Journal of Applied Psychology*, 9.5 percent in the *Academy of Management Journal*, 4.5 percent in *Administrative Science Quarterly*, 3.5 percent in *Organization Science*, and 2 percent in *Personnel Psychology*.

The vast majority of the studies were conducted in the laboratory (80 percent), with field (18 percent) and archival (2 percent) studies occurring in smaller numbers. The studies were also largely experimental (73 percent), rather than correlational (24 percent) or other types of designs (i.e., quasi-experimental, qualitative, and exploratory). Most studies entailed student (51 percent) or online (26 percent) samples; 18 percent of the samples consisted of employees, managers, professionals, or military personnel. The remaining samples were drawn from other sources (e.g., individuals at an airport). Consistent with Rest's (1986) four-stage moral decision-making

---

[3] We concluded our search for articles in early November of 2015; thus, our date range is just short of six full years.

[4] Consistent with the behavioral ethics literature, we use the terms "decisions" and "behaviors" largely interchangeably. For instance, the decision to cheat in an experimental task is equivalent to the behavior of cheating.

[5] Consistent with meta-analytic techniques, which focus on effect sizes, here, unless otherwise noted, we focus on studies as the unit of interest rather than articles.

model, we can classify the outcomes of these studies generally as being related to awareness of a moral issue, a moral judgment as to whether something is right or wrong, intention to act based on one's judgment, and the resulting decision or behavior. In the majority of these studies the outcomes were participants' decisions or behaviors (62 percent), with the second most modal type of outcome being judgments (28 percent). Relatively few studies focused on intentions (16 percent) or awareness (1.5 percent). Note that these percentages sum to more than one hundred because in a small portion of studies researchers employed multiple types of outcomes. Also, very few studies (7.5 percent) focus on prosocial outcomes like charitable donations.

Beyond being classifiable in these general terms, the outcomes employed were for the most part not grounded in a conceptual definition of what is unethical. Only twenty of the articles (27 percent) included an explicit definition. In nine of these articles Jones' (1991) definition was cited: "... an *ethical decision* is defined as a decision that is both legal and morally acceptable to the larger community. Conversely, an *unethical decision* is either illegal or morally unacceptable to the larger community" (p. 367). Notably, Jones characterized his definition as being "admittedly imprecise and relativistic" but "adequate for the purposes of [his] article" (p. 367). In ten of the articles the definitions presented were broadly consistent with Jones', including features like "legal," "normative," "consensual," and "universal." In only one article did the presented definition diverge from this pattern, with the authors specifying that altruistic intention is necessary for an action to be moral (Casciaro, Gino, and Kouchaki 2014).

In addition to the absence of an explicit definition in 73 percent of the articles, also striking is the limited variety of outcome variables in terms of moral content. Across studies, 69 percent of the decision and behavioral outcomes were either cheating (44 percent) or lying (25 percent). For example, researchers frequently used the matrix task (Mazar, Amir, and Ariely 2008) to assess cheating and the Gneezy (2005) deception game to assess lying in laboratory studies.[6] In the matrix task, participants are instructed to search for

---

[6] Indeed, we ourselves have used the Gneezy (2005) deception game in our published and ongoing research.

two numbers that add up to ten (e.g., 3.81 and 6.19) in a set of twelve three-digit numbers (i.e., matrix) and to report on a separate sheet the number of matrices they have successfully solved. Since their payment is determined by their self-reported performance, participants can earn more money by cheating or over-reporting the number of matrices they have solved. The deception game is, at least ostensibly, dyadic and entails two payoff options. The participant stands to gain more money from one option (Option A) than the other (Option B), and the reverse is true for the other player who stands to gain more money from Option B compared to Option A. The participant knows what these options are, but the other player does not. The other player must choose between Options A and B, thereby determining how much money each player gets, based on information provided by the participant. The participant has an opportunity (and incentive) to lie to the other player by saying that Option A is better for her (i.e., the other player) than Option B, or to honestly tell the other player that Option B is better for her than Option A. Lying is measured according to which message the participant sends to the other player. Like the matrix task and deception game, the majority of studies (53 percent) were carried out via decontextualized, non-organizational materials.

These results suggest that, as a field, we are not talking much about the theoretical substance of outcomes and the outcomes employed are drawn from a fairly narrow set. We wish to be clear that we consider the research we are reviewing to be a fine body of work. Fundamentally, rather than quality, the issue we raise here is one of scope. The study of individuals' moral judgments, decisions, and behaviors in organizations is a very large topic, of which we seem to study a very narrow slice. We suggest that to the extent that we want to build a body of knowledge about ethics in organizations more generally, we would do well to expand our horizons. A primary obstacle to such an expansion is our limited understanding of the theoretical substance of outcomes. In the next section we engage in a meta-conversation – a conversation about having conversations – in which we describe the existing conversation in our field around the theoretical substance of outcomes and then we describe a number of relevant conversations outside of our field, which we present as examples. These examples serve to illustrate what such conversations might look like in our own field and how productive they can be.

Conversations around the theoretical substance of outcomes

Though we are a field of study essentially aimed at predicting when people will cross the line into immorality and when they will refrain from doing so, we ourselves do not seem to really know where that line is. In the parlance of science, we do not have a generally accepted construct definition of our primary outcome variable: ethicality. To be sure, this is a particularly thorny issue. When faced with the question of how to define ethicality, the familiar refrain justifying retreat is that philosophers and other scholars have wrestled with this question for centuries with no consensus in sight. Thus, we cannot expect to resolve the issue, especially as our expertise is in descriptive research (focusing on what people do) rather than normative theorizing (focusing on what people ought to do). We see the wisdom in this humility. Yet defining one's constructs is fundamental to good descriptive research. It affects the questions we ask, the data we collect, and the inferences we derive from our data. Herein lies the conundrum: when it comes to behavioral ethics research, it is not possible to draw a solid, impermeable line between descriptive and normative ethics, yet how to proceed?

Tenbrunsel and Smith-Crowe (2008) suggested that our field could draw on the work of those who engage in normative theorizing, philosophers and theologians, to help us think about a construct definition. They offered Kant's (1785/1964) respect principle as an example: what is ethical is to treat people always as ends in themselves and never merely as means to ends. That is, this principle provides one conceptualization of ethicality. Palmer (2012) questioned whether this *content approach* to defining ethicality is likely to be fruitful, pointing out that it has yet to produce a consensus on the definition of ethicality. Drawing on sociological traditions, he suggested an alternative particularly meant to capitalize on consensus: what is unethical is what is labeled as such by social control agents, who are those designated to monitor and control unethical behavior. Taking this approach, we can look to a body like the Supreme Court to see what is moral and what is not. His suggestion overlaps with the tack taken by the few researchers who have offered definitions of ethicality in their work, generally stipulating that what is ethical is what is normative and widely accepted. Thus, the *consensus approach* is the dominant definitional approach in the field (among those providing explicit definitions).

While the consensus approach has its appeal, Warren and Smith-Crowe (2008) argued that by focusing exclusively on outcomes that are obviously or intuitively unethical (arguably two pathways to consensus), we miss important ethically relevant experiences of people in organizations, namely the experience of grappling with moral ambiguity – those things that seem to have ethical import, but which are neither obvious nor intuitive. Palmer also noted that some would take issue with the relativistic nature of the consensus approach. Most recently, Moore and Gino (2015) raised the question of whether a precise definition of what is ethical is indeed needed by the field.

One might look at this exchange and conclude that, alas, still no progress has been made as researchers have not been able to rally around a singular definition of what is ethical. We, however, see progress in that we are collectively engaging in a burgeoning conversation about the theoretical substance of our outcome variables, raising questions about how to proceed and engaging in debate about what is ethical. This exercise in itself holds promise and we should carry it further. We take the opportunity here to engage in a meta-conversation, a conversation about having conversations in which we focus on examples of relevant, fruitful conversations around the theoretical substance of morally relevant outcomes. We present these examples not to the end of producing an overarching theoretical framework of moral outcomes but rather to the end of promoting the notion that having these conversations is valuable. Importantly, our purpose is not to take a stance of our own with regard to the specific content of the example conversations; rather it is to highlight the connections between having these conversations and theoretical progress. Given these connections, instead of marking progress by whether or not we have achieved consensus on a singular definition of ethicality (a rather all-or-nothing proposition), perhaps we could better mark progress by the quality of the conversations we are having around the theoretical substance of the outcomes we study. Interestingly and contrary to a convergence on a singular definition, the examples we present in large part are conversations about expanding the notion of ethicality, with scholars arguing that phenomena are misunderstood when ethicality is conceived within overly narrow bounds.

Next, we describe three relevant debates. In each of these cases, scholars took the substance of moral outcomes seriously and in doing so opened up opportunities for questioning assumptions, examining disagreements, and promoting prescriptions. We then provide examples of other ways

of engaging in a conversation around the theoretical substance of outcome variables: mapping the moral domain, reconsidering moral status,
and building theory. These conversations too, we show, have been productive. We organize these examples by the forms they have taken, as we
assume that, in addition to the general point that these conversations have
been theoretically valuable, the forms themselves may be instructive to
anyone wishing to engage in such conversations. We draw these examples
from the psychology and management literatures, though, notably, the
majority of them are from psychology, where such examples are far more
plentiful.

Debates

Questioning assumptions. Of long-standing interest to psychologists
has been human moral development. In this tradition Kohlberg (1963,
1976) advanced his highly influential cognitive-developmental stage
theory of moral development. It has been said that his work and ideas
reflect his experience of being imprisoned by the British in Cyprus after
World War II for his attempts to help Jewish refugees break through the
British blockade on Jewish immigration to Israel (Garz 2009). Notably,
his conception of the moral domain is "deontic," entailing obligations
and rights (Colby et al. 1983); it is often described in terms of justice
and rules. His theory is grounded in the ideas that moral judgments
about right and wrong reflect reasoning, and that one's reasoning shifts
qualitatively across developmental stages. He identifies six successive
stages occurring at three levels: preconventional (characterized by obe-
dience and a self-serving morality), conventional (characterized by
prioritizing duties to close others and society), and postconventional
(characterized by an appreciation of social contracts, individual rights,
and universal principles).

Kohlberg and his colleagues (Colby et al. 1983; Colby and Kohlberg
1987; Kohlberg 1976) developed interview protocols designed to elicit
the reasoning underlying people's moral judgments. For instance, they
devised the now well-known Heinz dilemma, pitting the preservation
of life against upholding the law: Heinz's wife is sick and will die unless
she takes a drug, which they cannot afford, and, thus, she can survive
only if Heinz steals the drug from the druggist. Participants are asked
what Heinz should do (Colby et al.): 77 Should he steal the drug? What
if he doesn't love his wife? What if it's not his wife but a stranger who is

threatened with death? What if it's not his wife, but a pet, whom he loves and is threatened with death? They developed corresponding procedures to score participants' reasoning according to the theoretically specified stages of development. Kohlberg and his colleagues, using such protocols, find evidence supportive of his theory. For instance, Colby et al. (1983) report the results of a twenty-year longitudinal study of fifty-eight boys who began the study at ages ten, thirteen, and sixteen. They proceeded through the stages as specified by the theory, without skipping any steps, and only in very few cases regressing.

Gilligan (1982/1993) questioned the prevailing assumption of what constituted the moral domain, reacting to Kohlberg's theory and research, as well as a tradition of understanding human development using male development as the yardstick (in which she also implicates Freud, Piaget, and Erikson). She quipped that "it all goes back, of course, to Adam and Eve – a story which shows, among other things, that if you make a woman out of a man, you are bound to get into trouble" (p. 6). The trouble she saw was that women and girls were seen as flawed, failed, or underdeveloped. As such, she came to question the validity of the yardstick. She illustrates her point by describing the responses of Amy and Jake, two eleven-year-olds, to the Heinz dilemma; notably, besides age, they are matched for socio-economic status and intelligence. Also notable, they in some ways defy gender stereotypes in that Amy wants to be a scientist and Jake prefers English to Math. They also differ markedly in terms of their moral reasoning.

Jake is confident that Heinz should steal the drug and makes compelling points for his assertion:

> For one thing, a human life is worth more than money, and if the druggist only makes $1,000, he is still going to live, but if Heinz doesn't steal the drug, his wife is going to die. (*Why is life worth more than money?*) Because the druggist can get a thousand dollars later from rich people with cancer, but Heinz can't get his wife again. (*Why not?*) Because people are all different and so you couldn't get Heinz's wife again. (Gilligan 1982/1993: 26)

He also speculates that if Heinz did steal the drug, a judge presiding over the trial, were he arrested, would deem Heinz's actions as "the right thing to do," reasoning that "the laws have mistakes, and you can't go writing up a law for everything that you can imagine" (p. 26). Amy sees the situation quite differently, also making compelling points.

In fact, she rejects the intended dilemma altogether when asked if Heinz should steal the drug: "Well, I don't think so. I think there might be other ways besides stealing it, like if he could borrow the money or make a loan or something, but he really shouldn't steal the drug – but his wife shouldn't die either" (Gilligan 1982/1993: 28). Amy goes on to say:

> If he stole the drug, he might save his wife then, but if he did, he might have to go to jail, and then his wife might get sicker again, and he couldn't get more of the drug, and it might not be good. So, they should really just talk it out and find some other way to make the money. (Gilligan 1982/1993: 28)

Gilligan interprets the difference between Jake and Amy like this:

> Seeing in the dilemma not a math problem with humans [as Jake sees it] but a narrative of relationships that extends over time, Amy envisions the wife's continuing need for her husband and the husband's continuing concern for his wife and seeks to respond to the druggist's need in a way that would sustain rather than sever connection. (p.28)

Gilligan further argues that

> Just as Jake is confident the judge would agree that stealing is the right thing for Heinz to do, so Amy is confident that, "if Heinz and the druggist had talked it out long enough, they could reach something besides stealing." As he considers the law to "have mistakes," so she see this drama as a mistake, believing that "the world should just share things more and then people wouldn't have to steal." (p. 29)

Importantly, using Kohlberg's scheme, Amy is rated as less morally developed than Jake (Gilligan 1982/1993).[7] Gilligan argues that this assessment is unreasonable, that it reflects a value of justice over care: whereas Jake sees "a conflict between life and property that can be resolved by logical deduction, Amy [sees] a fracture of human relationship that must be mended with its own thread" (p. 31). Gilligan contends that an ethic of care is just as valid as an ethic of justice and that Amy's reasoning is therefore just as valid as Jake's. In this way, Gilligan entered into a debate about the theoretical substance of the relevant outcomes: moral judgment and reasoning. She questioned the assumption that these outcomes should be conceptualized exclusively in terms of justice and rules, with relational aspects of morality being devalued.

---

[7] Gilligan (1982/1993) observed that adult women reasoned similarly to Amy when faced with the Heinz dilemma (i.e., they reasoned in relational terms).

Two especially interesting elements of this debate are Gilligan's (1982/1993) academic insider status and the historical context with regard to women's rights. She was trained in the tradition that she came to criticize. She worked with Erikson and Kohlberg at Harvard; she found Kohlberg's arguments to be "powerful" (p. xvii). She taught psychology "in the traditions of Freud and Piaget" (p. xiv). She described suppressing inklings of dissent:

> I remember moments in classes when a woman would ask a question that illuminated with sudden brilliance the foundations of the subject we were discussing. And now, remembering those moments, I also can hear the sounds of my own inner division: my saying to the woman, "That's a good question," and then saying, "but that's not what we are talking about here." (p. xiv)

Gilligan's eventual dissent was predicated on self-awareness, listening to her own voice, which was telling her that she should be listening to other female voices too, even if these voices were pushing against the weight of accepted scholarship stretching back to the previous century. This came during what she described as a "resurgence in the Women's Movement" (p. iv), including the 1973 Supreme Court decision legalizing abortion, when women were struggling to speak up and to be heard. Today, the ethic of care is generally an uncontroversial component of the moral domain. In fact, as we will discuss in a later example, researchers are again criticizing the narrowness of the moral domain, but now the movement is to expand beyond the limitations of justice and care to include other aspects of morality (e.g., Graham et al. 2011). Even so, the taken-for-grantedness of Gilligan's (1982/1993) relational view of morality seems somewhat unlikely upon reflection on the factors surrounding its genesis. One might even read this as a David and Goliath story, the Goliath being both Gilligan herself and her academic discipline; in this light, it suggests the potential fruitfulness of debate even if it is against the odds.

Examining disagreements. Our next example of a debate is more recent but is grounded overtly in Kohlberg's (1963) work. Wading into the debate on whether moral judgment is the product of reason or emotion, Monin, Pizarro, and Beer (2007) argue that it depends on the situation. They trace the current debate in psychology back to eighteenth-century philosophy (Kant versus Hume, advocating for reason and emotion, respectively). In modern times, Kohlberg's view that judgment is a product of reasoning has dominated, though research on bounded rationality, automaticity, and emotion has made way for a different perspective, one in which emotion is primary (e.g., Haidt 2001). Yet sound arguments and compelling data exist on both sides of the debate, making neither easily dismissible. Monin et al. contend that the debate hinges on researchers' conceptualization of moral judgment: "we suggest that these diverging conclusions have arisen because investigators have started with differing understandings of what constitutes moral judgment and, as a result, have designed methods that capture very different phenomena" (p. 101).

They identify two "prototypical situations" – moral dilemmas and moral reactions – and demonstrate their asymmetrical employment (Monin et al. 2007). Those who conceptualize moral judgment as a reasoned process test their hypotheses in the context of moral dilemmas, and those who conceptualize moral judgment as an emotional process test their hypotheses in the context of moral reactions. Kohlberg is well known for confronting his participants with moral dilemmas, whereby satisfaction of one moral principle means the violation of another (e.g., in the Heinz dilemma). Monin et al. point out that not only is there no easy answer to the question of what the actor in these dilemmas should do, thus necessitating reasoning on the part of participants, but also participants would be typically probed by the researcher to explain and elaborate on their reasoning (via 9–12 "standardized probe questions"; Colby et al. 1983: 9), thus further necessitating reason. Hence, the methodology itself, based on a particular conceptualization of moral judgment, seems to inevitably provide evidence of moral judgment as a reason-based process.

In contrast is research on the emotion-based view of moral judgment, particularly Haidt's (2001) social intuitionist model, which holds that moral judgment (almost always) is affective and intuitive and arises suddenly in one's consciousness. In this tradition the methodological approach is to present participants with the shocking transgressions of others and ask them whether the behavior is moral, effectively measuring participants' moral reactions (Monin et al. 2007). Such transgressions include the following: college-aged brother and sister, Mark and Julie, while vacationing in France, have sex using two forms of birth control, enjoy it but decide not to do it again and to keep it as their special secret (Haidt 2001); and a man weekly buys a chicken at the grocery store, takes it home, masturbates with it, cooks it, and then eats it (Haidt, Koller, and Dias 1993). Monin et al. suggest here too that the choice of methodology, derived from the researchers' conceptualization of what constitutes a moral judgment, likely promotes theory-consistent results. Participants faced with these scenarios react immediately and emotionally to behaviors that are likely to provoke disgust and contempt. What is more, the action in the scenario has already taken place, leaving participants with no decision to make, only with an opportunity to react.

In light of their critique, Monin et al. (2007) emphasize two points. First, far from being unfruitful, this research has advanced our collective understanding of moral judgment albeit in a less generalizable way than was perhaps originally intended. That is, Kohlberg and his colleagues' research sheds light on how people reason in the face of moral dilemmas, and Haidt and his colleagues' research sheds light on the affective nature of moral reactions. Furthermore, they argue that there is room for emotion in a reason-based conceptualization of moral judgment: anticipated emotions (e.g., guilt), or even incidental emotions (i.e., those not related to the situation at hand), can influence one's choices, and strong emotions experienced because of the aversive experience of being in a dilemma might lead some to avoid making a choice altogether. They also maintain that there is room for reason in an emotion-based conceptualization of moral judgment: intuitions may be formed, activated, or overridden by reason, and reason may direct one to engage or disengage with emotions depending on their utility or disutility. Second, to the extent that methodological choices represent a broader set of options, our collective understanding of a phenomenon is enhanced. Even moral dilemmas and shocking transgressions, they contend, are a limited set. As such, they advocate for an expansion of the types of situations studied to include, for instance, moral temptation situations, whereby moral judgment is considered from a self-regulation perspective.

Promoting prescription. Our final example of a debate is more formalized than the previous examples: a point–counterpoint exchange in a single journal issue in which one set of scholars presented an argument in an initial article, other scholars commented on this initial article in three subsequent articles, and then the original scholars responded to these comments in a final article. At stake in this debate is prescription: the most effective process for making moral decisions and, hence, the process one should use for making moral decisions. Far from being merely an academic exercise, the consequences are far-reaching. Bazerman and Greene (2010) note the influence of decision science research on what is taught in professional schools, which explicitly focus on improving the effectiveness of students' decision-making skills. They also suggest the promise of this work for informing national policies around things like organ donations. Importantly, the Obama administration seems to agree: "by executive order Mr. Obama directed federal agencies to incorporate behavioral science – insights into how people actually make decisions – into their programs" (Sustein 2015).

Hence, decision science is quite influential, and in their focal article Bennis, Medin, and Bartels (2010a) raise doubts about its core prescription with regard to moral decision-making. They describe the project of decision science like this: the quality of decisions should be judged based on the likelihood of their leading to outcomes consistent with decision-makers' goals, raising the question of which decision-making process is most likely to produce the highest-quality decisions. The dominant answer in the field, they contend, is cost–benefit analysis. Their essential question is whether cost–benefit analysis is the optimal process for all types of decisions, particularly moral decisions. They focus particularly on moral rule adherence as an alternative consideration, noting that it is seen as the product of biased (and, thus, suboptimal) decision-making. To illustrate their point, they refer to the interpretation of participants' decisions with regard to the following scenario:

> As a result of a dam on a river, 20 species of fish are threatened with extinction. By opening the dam a month each year, you can save those species, but 2 species downstream will become extinct because of the changing water level. Would you open the dam? (Ritov and Baron 1999: 87)

The optimal answer derived from the cost–benefit analysis prescription is "yes." Some participants, however, answered "no" because they did not want to cause the extinction of any species. The decisions of these participants are considered "biased." Notably, the rightness of the decision is defined in terms of the decision-making process deemed to be optimal; said differently, the decision science prescription for effective moral decision-making is based on the field's definition of morality. According to Bennis et al. (2010a), if moral rule adherence were to be the prescribed process, then "no" would be considered the right course of action as it is consistent with the rule of "do no harm."

Similar to the argument made by Monin et al. (2007), Bennis et al. (2010a) raise the issue of methodological choices based on theoretical commitments. They criticize what they call "closed world assumptions," essentially arguing that scenarios designed to clearly distinguish an optimal decision from a suboptimal decision (via calculable costs and benefits) necessarily present participants with artificial decision-making situations that do not reflect the complexity of real life.[8] They argue that when people make moral decisions they care about and attend to a variety of features, not only maximizing benefits relative to costs. They also criticize what they see as the false transparency of the "right" answer in these scenarios, arguing largely in bounded rationality terms that real-world cost–benefit analyses are fraught with numerous limitations and do not readily yield right answers. Given their criticisms of cost–benefit analysis, they consider moral rule adherence as an alternative conceptualization of the best decision-making process, particularly drawing on game theory research to argue that groups and individuals are better off when they adhere to moral rules compared to other strategies.

Commenting on Bennis et al.'s (2010a) article, Schwartz (2010) and Tetlock and Mitchell (2010) present largely sympathetic views, posing challenges to a morality defined exclusively in terms of cost–benefit analysis. Schwartz describes practical wisdom (Schwartz and Sharpe 2010): a truly wise person is anchored by moral rules, making "exceptions at just the right times, in just the right ways, for just the right reasons" (Schwartz 2010: 204). Taking it to its extreme end, he characterizes the widespread and routine use of cost–benefit analysis, whereby rule-following occurs only when the benefits outweigh the costs, as socially destabilizing. Tetlock and Mitchell portray real-world decision-makers as pragmatists who are accountable to a variety of audiences, including themselves, to whom they would like to appear both morally principled and cognitively flexible. They argue that decision-making shifts according to the social context, where moral rule adherence is the relevant process in one situation and cost–benefit analysis in another. Tetlock and Mitchell's perspective raises the question of whether the pursuit of a single best decision-making process for moral decision-making is even a sensible endeavor.

---

[8] Gilligan (1982/1993) made a similar point (cf. Schwartz 2010), which is exemplified by the eleven-year-old Amy's attempts to expand the dilemma posed to her so that she could access additional possible solutions beyond Heinz stealing the drug and his wife dying.

In contrast, Bazerman and Greene (2010) take a stand against what they characterize as Bennis et al.'s (2010a) misrepresentation of cost–benefit analysis and subsequent unjustifiable prescriptions for moral decision-making. The foundation of their counter-argument is their contention that Bennis et al. present a "straw man" argument grounded in a version of cost–benefit analysis that relies on a "deprived utility function" (Bazerman and Greene 2010: 209). Essentially, they argue that this portrayal of cost–benefit analysis is overly simplistic in its narrow definition of utility, and that the scholars who advocate for this decision-making approach are talking about a much richer form of cost–benefit analysis that incorporates a variety of considerations, including moral rules. They dispute some of Bennis et al.'s points (that closed-world experiments are not readily generalizable outside the laboratory and that moral rule adherence is a superior decision-making strategy), but embrace others, albeit coming to a different conclusion: "In sum, we agree with most of the challenges to CBA [cost–benefit analysis] that BMB [Bennis, Medin, and Bartels] identify, but we view their critiques as a set of considerations that can contribute to more careful CBAs" (Bazerman and Greene 2010: 211).

In their reply to these commentary articles, Bennis, Medin, and Bartels (2010b) acknowledge points of common ground, particularly that, as decision-making processes, cost–benefit analysis has its advantages and moral rule adherence has its disadvantages and that closed-world assumptions are not exclusive to cost–benefit analysis. They also reaffirm several of their initial points in response to Bazerman and Greene's (2010) counter-arguments. Not surprisingly, the two sets of authors who started from the most distal points of view did not come to perfect agreement through the process of this debate. Yet, both also indicate having benefited from the process. Related, Schwartz (2010) made a point in the context of the closed-world assumptions question that we think is more generalizable. We need to have conversations, not because we can expect the end result to be agreement, but because they can bring clarity and, we think, insights into the phenomena we are studying. In the course of this particular conversation, a number of important issues came to light, including the dominant definition of morality within decision science and the implications for its far-reaching decision-making prescriptions, the relation between cost–benefit analysis and moral rule adherence, and the place of moral flexibility.

Other types of conversations

Mapping the moral domain.   Beyond debates, there are a number of other types of conversations to be had around the theoretical substance of outcome variables. Perhaps the most obvious conversation is one about what constitutes the moral domain. Undaunted by the lack of agreement on the normative question of the line between right and wrong, Haidt and his colleagues' reaction to this state of affairs is to advocate for a conceptualization of morality that embraces diversity (Haidt and Graham 2007; Haidt and Joseph 2004), a moral pluralism (Graham et al. 2012). As they put it, "people disagree about the size and content of the moral domain – that is, about what 'morality' means. Researchers therefore need theories that encompass the true breadth of human morality, and they need measurement tools that can detect a broad array of moral concerns" (Graham et al. 2011: 382). They particularly note that the ethics of justice (Kohlberg 1963) and care (Gilligan 1982/1993) have been the rather exclusive focus of researchers for some decades (Haidt and Graham 2007) and that, while these ethics may largely represent Western, educated liberals (Graham et al. 2011), they do not capture the full spectrum of moral concerns of people more generally. As such, "a major goal of MFT [moral foundations theory] is to expand the range of phenomena studied in moral psychology so that it matches the full range of moral concerns, including those found in non-Western cultures, in religious practices, and among political conservatives" (Graham et al. 2011: 366).

In order to generate a more inclusive mapping of the moral domain, they (Haidt and Graham 2007; Haidt and Joseph 2004) draw on anthropological and evolutionary perspectives, as well as previous efforts to map the moral domain (e.g., Fiske 1992; Schwartz and Bilsky 1990; Schweder et al. 1997). The result of their efforts is moral foundations theory, which indicates five foundations as constituting the moral domain, with the possibility of additional foundations being recognized (Graham et al. 2011): care/harm, fairness/cheating, loyalty/betrayal, authority/subversion, and sanctity/degradation.[9] Put simply, fairness/cheating has to do with issues of justice, rights, and autonomy, while care/harm has to do with compassion and an aversion to others'

---

[9]   Different labels have been used for the foundations over time. To reflect the most updated wording, we took these labels from www.moralfoundations.org.

suffering. Together these comprise the "individualizing" foundations because they prioritize the protection of the individual (Graham, Haidt, and Nosek 2009). The remaining foundations comprise the "binding" foundations because they prioritize the protection of the group above the individual (Graham et al. 2009). Loyalty/betrayal reflects a devotion to the group, while authority/subversion reflects respect for authority. Sanctity/degradation reflects the human capacity for disgust binding groups through a common sense of what is sacred.

Research on moral foundations theory has been generative (see Graham et al. 2012, for a review) not only in terms of research testing the core theory and additional hypotheses derived from the theory (e.g., Cornwell and Higgins 2014; Smith et al. 2014) and research to develop new theory (e.g., Fehr, Yam, and Dang 2015) but also in terms of sparking fundamental debates, such as whether pluralism is the best approach to conceptualizing the moral domain (e.g., Frimer, Tell, and Haidt 2015; Graham 2015; Gray and Keeney 2015a, b; Gray, Schein, and Ward 2014). Notably, moral foundations theory has been applied to the US culture war and the seemingly intractable divide between political liberals and conservatives. Graham et al. (2009) argue that liberalism is grounded in an optimistic view of human nature and a belief in individual liberty whereby individuals are allowed to pursue their potential. This viewpoint privileges the individual, consistent with the individualizing foundations. They argue, conversely, that conservatism is grounded in a pessimistic view of human nature and a belief that individual liberty must be curtailed for the greater good. This viewpoint privileges the group, consistent with the binding foundations. They hypothesize that, while conservatives would tend to care about all five moral foundations to an equivalent extent, liberals would care more about the individualizing foundations than the binding foundations. They report data consistent with this hypothesis.

Building on this work, Day et al. (2014) recently investigated the extent to which framing messages in terms of moral foundations can actually change liberals' and conservatives' political attitudes, either further entrenching an existing attitude or leading to a shift in attitude. They find that framing conservative issues in terms of authority or purity (e.g., "Authorities should not allow people to live off the system" and "Our way of life is sacred, and should not be sacrificed by new environmental policies," p. 1562) leads conservatives to become further entrenched in their existing attitudes, while framing liberal issues in terms of harm or fairness leads liberals to become further entrenched in their existing attitudes. Very interestingly, Day et al. also find that conservatives' attitudes became more liberal when liberal issues are framed in terms of the ingroup (loyalty), authority, or purity foundations. Grounded in an understanding of the conflicting moral systems of conservatives and liberals (and more fundamentally in the project of mapping the moral domain), this work is an important step toward the possibility of these groups gaining common ground, which is of no small significance in an era of political dysfunction to the point of federal government shutdowns.

Reconsidering moral status. Another example of how we can engage in a conversation about the theoretical substance of outcomes is to question the moral status of our well-trod outcome variables. Levine and Schweitzer (2014) challenge the scholarly wisdom and common sense by which deception is classified as immoral and harmful. They point out that prior research confounds deception with selfishness, thus promoting the view that deception is immoral. Instead, they consider deception through the lens of an ethical dilemma: justice versus care.[10] Levine and Schweitzer argue that while principles of justice prescribe rule-following (and hence honesty), principles of care prescribe the protection of others, and at times protecting others may entail dishonesty. They define prosocial lies as "false statements made with the intention of misleading and benefitting a target" (2014: 108). Reasoning that care and the protection of others are more fundamental to morality, with justice and rule-following likely to have evolved as a means to promote care, they predict that when faced with a moral dilemma in which care and justice are in conflict, individuals would likely prioritize care over justice, judging prosocial lies to be morally permissible. They test their hypothesis in a series of laboratory studies based on a modification of Gneezy's (2005) deception game, in which participants judge the morality of others' honesty or dishonesty. They find that participants judge prosocial lying (beneficial to the other party but disadvantageous to the liar, or in some cases not affecting the liar) to be more indicative of moral character than selfish truth-telling (disadvantageous to the other party but beneficial to the truth-teller). This effect holds regardless of whether prosocial lying entailed self-sacrifice or beneficial outcomes.

---

[10] Notably, recognition of this dilemma can be credited to Gilligan (1982/1993), whose work put the ethic of care on a moral par with the ethic of justice.

Levine and Schweitzer (2015) follow this initial work with research on the implications of deception for trust. Again, they challenge conventional thinking, which holds dishonesty to be detrimental to trust. They argue that prior research confounds benevolence with integrity, in that reductions in trust are seen in the wake of behaviors that are both harmful and unethical. Similar to their argument about justice versus care dilemmas, they argue that benevolence and integrity may sometimes conflict such that acting with integrity is harmful to others and that benevolence ultimately influences the extent to which individuals trust one another more so than integrity. They demonstrate support for their hypothesis in a series of laboratory studies entailing economic and trust games. Prosocial lying increases trust in the prosocial liar, both among those lied to directly and those who observed lying to a third party. Consistent with their reasoning, prosocial lying increases trust in another's benevolence but not in another's integrity.

Notably, deception is one of the most common operationalizations of unethicality used in our field. Taking the rare approach of thinking in terms of moral dilemmas, Levine and Schweitzer (2014, 2015) consider complexities of the moral status of deception not well documented in our field. More specifically, by disentangling notions of justice, care, benevolence, and integrity, they are able to offer a more nuanced view of deception. As they put it, "quite possibly, our understanding of deception may simply reflect attitudes towards selfish behavior, rather than deception per se" (Levine and Schweitzer 2014: 108). Not only is their research fruitful in the sense of promoting our understanding of the moral status of deception, but it is also fruitful in the sense that it opens the door to previously unasked questions, like the one addressed in their subsequent article (Levine and Schweitzer 2015): if prosocial liars are seen as moral, then might such behavior also engender trust? Additionally, their work raises questions around the moral status of deception when motivations are mixed (prosocial and selfish) or unclear, when morality is conceived in terms of courage (perhaps prosocial lying is seen as cowardly), and when prosocial lying behavior is habitual (perhaps eroding the liar's credibility over time; Levine and Schweitzer 2014). Without first reconsidering the moral status of deception, these questions are unlikely to have arisen.

Building theory.   Our final example is theory-building substantiated by an approach to defining ethicality. We end with this example purposefully as it is a departure from the others. Whereas they all share a psychological approach and are connected to the earlier work of Kohlberg (1963) and Gilligan (1982/1993), our final example comes from Palmer (2012), who, as we noted previously, advocates a sociological approach to defining what is ethical and what is not. His premise is provocative: wrongdoing is *created* by social control agents who draw the line between right and wrong. For instance, governments act as social control agents when they deem some behaviors as illegal and others as legal. Drawing on examples from the legal domain, he noted that social control agents can create wrongdoing by instituting new rules (e.g., passing new laws) or altering the enforcement of existing rules (e.g., by delaying enforcement of new laws). Palmer gives the example of the Celler–Kefauver Act, passed in 1950, which strengthened earlier anti-trust laws. The passing of this act gave rise to cases in which certain types of organizational acquisitions were legal in 1949, but not in 1950. Further complicating the matter, the Federal Trade Commission (FTC) and Department of Justice (DOJ) largely turned a blind eye to these newly illegal practices until the 1960s, meaning that companies were prosecuted for anti-trust law violations in the 1960s, which went unprosecuted, while being just as illegal, in the 1950s.

Further, Palmer (2012) provides an extensive analysis of social control theory's implications for wrongdoing in organizations, including both why social control agents draw lines where they do and how the lines drawn can increase wrongdoing. In explaining how social control agents influence individuals, he describes instances of first- and second-order wrongdoing. First-order wrongdoing is constituted by a relatively direct path stemming from social control agents. He argues that social control agents can blur the line between right and wrong (e.g., by creating confusing rules and inconsistently reinforcing them), thus leading to individuals inadvertently crossing the line. Referring back to the Celler–Kefauver Act, he notes that the corporate executives in this era complained that they could not pursue acquisitions without fear of inadvertent wrongdoing. The FTC and DOJ blurred the line by enforcing the same law differently. Palmer further argues that social control agents can facilitate individuals crossing the line in an even more direct manner (e.g., through entrapment). He refers to the Archer Daniels Midland scandal, which involved a company executive, who, in his role of FBI informant, participated in price-fixing deals. Second-order wrongdoing is constituted by a relatively indirect path stemming from social control agents. Individuals may engage in wrongdoing in order to cover up previously committed wrongdoing, like the Arthur Andersen executive who was convicted of impeding an investigation because he shredded documents. Or they may engage in wrongdoing in order to facilitate engagement in subsequent wrongdoing. For instance, Lance Armstrong and the US Postal Team were investigated for fraud because they allegedly sold sponsor-donated bikes in order to raise funds to pay for their illicit performance-enhancing drugs.

Moreover, Palmer (2012) considers the influence of incentives on behavior and the ensuing possibilities for how social control agents can influence individuals' identities, potentially fostering what he calls a "deviant identity," such as that exemplified by Walter Pavlo, who defrauded MCI and named a boat purchased with the proceeds "Miss Deeds" (p. 250). To the extent that individuals labeled as "wrongdoers" by social control agents may come to see themselves as deviants, it will be more natural for them to cross the line between right and wrong. The concept of this identity follows from Palmer's analysis of why social control agents draw lines where they do. He argues that it is inherently a political process and that realizing the political nature of where the line is drawn can lead some to the cynical perspective that compliance is a "practical necessity" rather than a "moral imperative." The implication is that those with a deviant identity are likely to engage in unethical behavior when it benefits them and they feel they are unlikely to be caught.

Beyond the particulars of Palmer's (2012) analysis, we want to highlight the fruitfulness of his consideration of the best approach to defining ethicality. His application of social control theory suggests a theoretically grounded path toward a definition of right and wrong, and, even more relevant to our contention that we should take the theoretical substance of outcomes seriously, it led to novel questions and insights about why individuals engage in unethical behavior in organizations. In particular, he engaged with the question of why some actions are considered wrong and others are not. As a field, we have largely ignored this question. In contrast, through his engagement of this question, he develops novel theory, connecting structural and psychological factors that facilitate wrongdoing in organizations.

Summary

Here we have presented a meta-conversation about conversations on the theoretical substance of morally relevant outcome variables. We have detailed six examples of conversations. Our purpose in doing so has been to suggest what such conversations might look like, as well as to provide evidence of their fruitfulness in terms of advancing theory and providing insights. Based on these examples, we might expect that such conversations in the field of behavioral ethics in organizations could positively affect the questions we ask, the data we collect, and the inferences we draw from our data. We hope that our discussion of these rich examples might inspire our colleagues to join in the burgeoning conversation in our field. We conclude by suggesting pathways for further conversation.

Carrying the conversation forward

The conversations we present in the preceding section are all highly relevant to the field of behavioral ethics in organizations, but they are largely not grounded in an organizational context per se. As rich and as useful as decontextualized conversations may be, they are not sufficient for a science of organizations. Rather it is important that we also think and talk about the theoretical substance of outcome variables in the context of organizations. A parallel point has been made by others who have argued that we should attend to the contextual forces that influence moral outcomes (Anteby 2013; Brief and Smith-Crowe in press; Tetlock and Mitchell 2010; Treviño et al. 2014). More broadly, Staw (in press), in reaction to what he describes as the movement of the overall field of organizational behavior toward decontextualized research, calls for phenomenon-driven scholarship. This is to say that we should look to organizations to learn what problems are relevant and we should set about to study those problems (cf. Tushman and O'Reilly 2007). Thinking in terms of phenomenon-driven organizational problem-solving could help us to expand the scope of our field in terms of the outcomes we study, as well as helping us to think through their theoretical substance.

While there are any number of possibilities, we limit ourselves to raising one general topic, though one that is rich enough to sustain numerous conversations: the problem of how and when and why individuals deal with moral ambiguity in organizations (e.g., Sonenshein 2007, 2009; Warren and Smith-Crowe 2008). Though there is some recognition of this problem, more typically we think of morality in organizations as being dichotomous: ethical and unethical. We less often seem to recognize shades of gray. Yet there is work, which is notably phenomenon-driven (Staw in press), demonstrating the reality of moral ambiguity for organizational members. For instance, Manning and Anteby (Chapter 3, this volume) contemplate situations in which social control agents (e.g., organizations) do not draw clear lines of right and wrong for members, leaving them to figure it out for themselves. Drawing on rich examples from a variety of organizational and cross-cultural settings, they detail the types of strategies people employ to justify where they draw the line for themselves. Reinecke and Ansari (2015) too provide rich, cross-cultural examples in describing the highly complex collective sensemaking that goes into the Fairtrade pricing of coffee, rooibos, and cotton, where what is ethical is far from apparent. Without first conceding uncertainty and equivocality, questions of justification strategies and bases for collective understandings of morality are much less apparent.

One can also think about moral ambiguity in terms of dilemmas, whereby one moral principle is pitted against another, leaving the actor with the choice of which principle to violate. Though there is a rich history of studying how people grapple with dilemmas (e.g., Colby et al. 1983; Gilligan 1982/1993), it is rarely pursued today. The work by Levine and Schweitzer (2014, 2015), in which they consider the dilemmas of justice versus care and integrity versus benevolence, is exceptional and, as we noted previously, allowed for an opportunity to reconsider the moral status of one of the most widely used outcome variables (deception) in the field of behavioral ethics in organizations. Flynn and Wiltermuth's (2010) use of moral dilemmas is also a rare exception. They constructed dilemmas based on three "right-right" dilemmas discussed by Kidder (1995): individual versus community (where either an individual or a community must bear a cost), truth versus loyalty (where one must be honest or keep a confidence), and justice versus mercy (where one must choose between delivering a swift punishment and leniency). The ambiguity introduced by these dilemmas afforded them the opportunity to study the extent to which people assume others agree with their moral judgments, finding evidence of a false consensus bias among employees in the marketing department of a large food manufacturing company, MBA students, and executive students. Without introducing ambiguity and the variance it affords, it would seem difficult to study such a phenomenon.

Moreover, one can think about moral ambiguity in the sense of situated morality, whereby people's judgments may change across time and space. Tetlock and Mitchell (2010) raised this issue in response to the debate in decision science over the ideal process for moral decision-making, suggesting that a more illuminating question is why and when do people use different processes for making such decisions. They draw on Tetlock's (2002) social-functionalist metaphors to describe moral decision-makers as "intuitive politicians," who operate in a social environment and must cope with its complex of cues, pressures, and constituencies to whom they are accountable. In the context of the decision science debate, Tetlock and Mitchell characterize the choice between cost–benefit analysis and moral rule adherence as the threat of appearing unprincipled or self-righteous. Consistent with these ideas about the effect of accountability on moral reasoning, Leavitt et al. (2012) found evidence among engineers and army soldiers that their moral judgments shifted according to which of their occupational identities and corresponding relational obligations were cued. Related, Smith-Crowe and Warren (2014) theorized that sanctions from organizational spokespersons can evoke moral emotions (shame, guilt, and embarrassment), which can trigger shifts in moral judgment even if these shifts are away from societal norms. Importantly, the questions raised in these articles stem from a recognition of moral ambiguity.

Conclusion

Here we offer a reflection on the state of the field of behavioral ethics in organizations, albeit from an unusual vantage point: the outcomes we study. Based on a review of the recent literature, we contend that we would do well as a field to focus greater attention on the theoretical substance of our outcome variables. We present, in meta-conversation form, examples of what taking the theoretical substance of our outcomes more seriously might look like and evidence of the potential fruitfulness of doing so. We also suggest a path for carrying the conversation forward that is particularly grounded in an organizational context. We hope that this conversation about having a conversation will engender a useful dialogue for the field.

References

Anteby, M. 2013. *Manufacturing Morals: The Values of Silence in Business School Education*. Chicago: University of Chicago Press.

Bazerman, M. H. and Gino, F. 2012. "Behavioral ethics: Toward a deeper understanding of moral judgment and dishonesty," *Annual Review of Law and Social Science* 8: 85–104.

Bazerman, M. H. and Greene, J. D. 2010. "In favor of clear thinking: Incorporating moral rules into a wise cost–benefit analysis – Commentary on Bennis, Medin, & Bartels," *Perspective on Psychological Science* 5: 209–212.

Bennis, W. M., Medin, D. L., and Bartels, D. M. 2010a. "The costs and benefits of calculation and moral rules," *Perspectives on Psychological Science* 5: 187–202.

Bennis, W. M., Medin, D. L., and Bartels, D. M. 2010b. "Perspectives on the ecology of decision modes: Reply to comments," *Perspectives on Psychological Science* 5: 213–215.

Brief, A. P. and Smith-Crowe, K. in press. "Organizations matter," in A. G. Miller (ed.), *The Social Psychology of Good and Evil* (2nd edn.). New York: Guilford Press.

Casciaro, T., Gino, F., and Kouchaki, M. 2014. "The contaminating effects of building instrumental ties: How networking can make us feel dirty," *Administrative Science Quarterly* 59: 705–735.

Colby, A. and Kohlberg, L. 1987. *The Measurement of Moral Judgment, Vol. 1*. Cambridge, UK: Cambridge University Press.

Colby, A., Kohlberg, L., Gibbs, J., and Lieberman, M. 1983. "A longitudinal study of moral development," *Monographs for the Society for Research in Child Development* 28: 1–96.

Cornwell, J. F. M. and Higgins, E. T. 2014. "Locomotion concerns with moral usefulness: When liberals endorse conservative binding moral foundations," *Journal of Experimental Social Psychology* 50: 109–117.

Day, M. V., Fiske, S. T., Downing, E. L., and Trail, T. E. 2014. "Shifting liberal and conservative attitudes using moral foundations theory," *Personality and Social Psychology Bulletin* 40: 1559–1573.

Fehr, R., Yam, K. C. S., and Dang, C. 2015. "Moralized leadership: The construction and consequences of ethical leader perceptions," *Academy of Management Review* 40: 182–209.

Fiske, A. P. 1992. "Four elementary forms of sociality: Framework for a unified theory of social relations," *Psychological Review* 99: 689–723.

Flynn, F. J. and Wiltermuth, S. S. 2010. "Who is with me? False consensus, brokerage, and ethical decision making in organizations," *Academy of Management Journal* 53: 1074–1089.

Frimer, J. A., Tell, C. E., and Haidt, J. 2015. "Liberals condemn sacrilege too: The harmless desecration of Cerro Torre," *Social Psychological and Personality Science* 6: 878–886.

Garz, D. 2009. *Lawrence Kohlberg – An Introduction*. Opladen & Farmington Hills, MI: Barbara Budrich Publishers.

Gilligan, C. 1993. *In a Different Voice: Psychological Theory and Women's Development*. Cambridge, MA: Harvard University Press (Original work published 1982).

Gneezy, U. 2005. "Deception: The role of consequences," *The American Economic Review* 95: 384–394.

Graham, J. 2015. "Explaining away differences in moral judgment: Comment on Gray and Kenney," *Social Psychological and Personality Science* 6(8): 869–873.

Graham, J., Haidt, J., Koleva, S., Motyl, M., Iyer, R., Wojcik, S., and Ditto, P. H. 2012. "Moral foundations theory: The pragmatic validity of moral pluralism," *Advances in Experimental Social Psychology* 47: 55–130.

Graham, J., Haidt, J., and Nosek, B. A. 2009. "Liberals and conservatives rely on different sets of moral foundations," *Journal of Personality and Social Psychology* 96: 1029–1046.

Graham, J., Nosek, B. A., Haidt, J., Iyer, R., Koleva, S., and Ditto, P. H. 2011. "Mapping the moral domain," *Journal of Personality and Social Psychology* 101: 366–385.

Gray, K. and Keeney, J. E. 2015. "Impure or just weird? Scenario sampling bias raises questions about the foundation of morality," *Social Psychological and Personality Science* 6(8): 859–868.

Gray, K. and Keeney, J. E. 2015. "Disconfirming moral foundations theory in its own terms: Reply to Graham 2015," *Social Psychological and Personality Science* 6(8): 874–877.

Gray, K., Schein, C., and Ward, A. F. 2014. "The myth of harmless wrongs in moral cognition: Automatic dyadic completion from sin to suffering," *Journal of Experimental Psychology: General* 143(4): 1600–1615.

Haidt, J. 2001. "The emotional dog and its rational tail: A social intuitionist approach to moral judgment," *Psychological Review* 108: 814–834.

Haidt, J. and Graham, J. 2007. "When morality opposes justice: Conservatives have moral intuitions that liberals may not recognize," *Social Justice Research* 20(1): 98–116.

Haidt, J. and Joseph, C. 2004. "Intuitive ethics: How innately prepared intuitions generate culturally variable virtues," *Daedalus* 133(4): 55–66.

Haidt, J., Koller, S. H., and Dias, M. G. 1993. "Affect, culture and morality, or is it wrong to eat your dog?" *Journal of Personality and Social Psychology* 65: 613–628.

Jones, T. M. 1991. "Ethical decision making by individuals in organizations: An issue-contingent model," *Academy of Management Review* 16: 366–395.

Kant, I. 1964. *Groundwork of the Metaphysics of Morals* (H. J. Paton, Trans.). New York: Harper & Row (Original work published in 1785).

Kidder, R. M. 1995. *How Good People Make Tough Choices: Resolving the Dilemmas of Ethical Living.* New York: Fireside.

Kish-Gephart, J. J., Harrison, D. A., and Treviño, L. K. 2010. "Bad apples, bad cases, and bad barrels: Meta-analytic evidence about sources of unethical decisions at work," *Journal of Applied Psychology* 95(1): 1–31.

Kohlberg, L. 1963. "Moral development and identification," in H. Stevenson (ed.), *Child Psychology; 62nd Yearbook of the National Society for the Study of Education.* Chicago: University of Chicago Press.

Kohlberg, L. 1976. "Moral stages and moral development: The cognitive-developmental approach," in T. Lickona (ed.), *Moral Development and Behavior: Theory, Research, and Social Issues*: 31–53. New York: Holt, Rinehart and Winston.

Leavitt, K., Reynolds, S. J., Barnes, C. M., Schilpzand, P., and Hannah, S. T. 2012. "Different hats, different obligations: Plural occupational identities and situated moral judgments," *Academy of Management Journal* 55: 1316–1333.

Levine, E. E. and Schweitzer, M. E. 2014. "Are liars ethical? On the tension between benevolence and honesty," *Journal of Experimental Social Psychology* 53: 107–117.

Levine, E. E. and Schweitzer, M. E. 2015. "Prosocial lies: When deception breeds trust," *Organizational Behavior and Human Decision Processes* 126: 88–106.

Mazar, N., Amir, O., and Ariely, D. 2008. "The dishonesty of honest people: A theory of self-concept maintenance," *Journal of Marketing Research* 45(6): 633–644.

Monin, B., Pizarro, D. A., and Beer, J. S. 2007. "Deciding versus reacting: Conceptions of moral judgment and the reason-affect debate," *Review of General Psychology* 11: 99–111.

Moore, C. and Gino, F. 2015. "Approach, ability, aftermath: A psychological process framework of unethical behavior at work," *The Academy of Management Annals* 9: 235–289.

Palmer, D. 2012. *Normal Organizational Wrongdoing: A Critical Analysis of Theories of Misconduct in and by Organizations.* Oxford: Oxford University Press.

Reinecke, J. and Ansari, S. 2015. "What is a 'fair' price? Ethics as sensemaking," *Organization Science* 26(3): 867–888.

Rest, J. R. 1986. *Moral Development: Advances in Research and Theory.* New York: Praeger.

Ritov, I. and Baron, J. 1999. "Protected values and omission bias," *Organizational Behavior and Human Decision Processes* 79: 79–94.

Schwartz, B. 2010. "The limits of cost-benefit calculation: Commentary on Binnis, Medin, & Bartels (2010)," *Perspectives on Psychological Science* 5: 203–205.

Schwartz, B. and Sharpe, K. 2010. *Practical Wisdom: The Right Way to Do the Right Thing.* New York: Riverhead Books.

Schwartz, S. H. and Bilsky, W. 1990. "Toward a theory of the universal content and structure of values: Extensions and cross-cultural replications," *Journal of Personality and Social Psychology* 58: 878–891.

Schweder, R. A., Much, N. C., Mahapatra, M., and Park, L. 1997. "The 'big three' of morality (autonomy, community, and divinity), and the 'big three' explanations of suffering," in A. Brandt and P. Rozin (eds.), *Morality and Health*: 119–169. New York: Routledge.

Smith, I. H., Aquino, K., Koleva, S., and Graham, J. 2014. "The moral ties that bind ... even to outgroups: The interactive effect of moral identity and the binding foundations," *Psychological Science* 25: 1554–1562.

Smith-Crowe, K. and Warren, D. E. 2014. "The emotion-evoked collective corruption model: The role of emotion in the spread of corruption within organizations," *Organization Science* 25: 1154–1171.

Sonenshein, S. 2007. "The role of construction, intuition, and justification in responding to ethical issues at work: The sensemaking-intuition model," *Academy of Management Review* 32: 1022–1040.

Sonenshein, S. 2009. "Emergence of ethical issues during strategic change implementation," *Organization Science* 20: 223–239.

Staw, B. M. in press. "Stumbling toward a social psychology of organizations: Some tales from the past and guidelines for the future," *Review of Organizational Psychology and Organizational Behavior.*

Sustein, C. R. 2015. "Making government logical," *The New York Times*, September 15.

Tenbrunsel, A. E. and Smith-Crowe, K. 2008. "Ethical decision making: Where we've been and where we're going," *Academy of Management Annals* 2: 545–607.

Tetlock, P. E. 2002. "Social-functionalist metaphors for judgment and choice: The intuitive politician, theologian, and prosecutor," *Psychological Review* 109: 451–472.

Tetlock, P. E. and Mitchell, G. 2010. "Situated social identities constrain morally defensible choices: Commentary on Binnis, Medin, C Bartels (2010)," *Perspectives on Psychological Science* 5: 206–208.

Treviño, L. K., den Nieuwenboer, N. A., and Kish-Gephart, J. J. 2014. "(Un) ethical behavior in organizations," *Annual Review of Psychology* 65: 635–660.

Treviño, L. K., Weaver, G. R., and Reynolds, S. J. 2006. "Behavioral Ethics in Organizations: A Review," *Journal of Management* 32(6): 951–990.

Tushman, M. L. and O'Reilly, C. 2007. "Research and relevance: Implications of Pasteur's quadrant for doctoral programs and faculty development," *Academy of Management Journal* 50: 769–774.

Warren, D. E. and Smith-Crowe, K. 2008. "Deciding what's right: The role of external sanctions and embarrassment in shaping moral judgments in the workplace," *Research in Organizational Behavior* 28: 81–105.

Weaver, G., Reynolds, S. J., and Brown, M. E. 2014. "Moral intuition: Connecting current knowledge to future organizational research and practice," *Journal of Management* 40: 100–129.

3 Wrong paths to right: defining morality with or without a clear red line

RYANN MANNING AND MICHEL ANTEBY

The moral terrain of organizational life is often conceived as divided by a clear red line, with rightdoing on one side and wrongdoing on the other. Like highway markings, this line is bright and unambiguous, laid down by social control agents – mostly compliance officers or state officials – to ensure adherence to a specific order and to sanction definitions of right and wrong. Organizational actors may be drawn across the line for reasons of self-enrichment or competitive pressures. They may also find themselves on the wrong side by mistake (Vaughan 1999; Warren and Smith-Crowe 2008), as when they do not recognize what they are doing as having ethical implications (Bazerman and Gino 2012; Tenbrunsel and Smith-Crowe 2008), or when they are lured across the line by social control agents looking to uncover and punish wrongdoing (Palmer 2012). Regardless of the reasons, once organizational actors find themselves on the wrong side of the line, the moral order perspective leaves little doubt that their actions will be labeled as wrongdoing (Greve, Palmer, and Pozner 2010: 56).

This vision of a clear and decisive moral order is at best incomplete, and we know that morality and immorality in organizations – defined as what a community deems right or wrong (Durkheim 1973; Mauss 1967) – are often more equivocal. For example, organizational actors frequently face moral dilemmas in which the right thing to do is unclear because different sets of moral prescriptions or principles conflict, or because their consciously reasoned moral response is contradicted by

We are grateful to Donald Palmer, Royston Greenwood, and Christopher Winship, as well as the participants in Harvard University's Work, Organizations, and Markets seminar and the Academy of Management Annual Meeting in Vancouver for their helpful comments on earlier versions of this chapter.

an emotional reaction about what "feels" wrong (Greene 2014; Walzer 1973; Winston 2015). These examples highlight a more general observation: the location of a line separating right from wrong is not a concrete absolute but something determined through people's interactions and therefore relative, disputed, and dynamic. Indeed, many organizations intentionally avoid establishing an explicit definition of right and wrong, or at least one that is easily identifiable and applies to all members, and instead allow each individual to draw his or her own line. We conceptualize such organizations as "moral pursuits" (Anteby 2013: 130–134), in which rightdoing involves an ongoing pursuit of personal morality and wrongdoing is in the eye of each individual beholder.[1] We distinguish these from moral orders, in which rightdoing and wrongdoing are defined ex ante by social control agents.

Existing organizational literature has focused primarily on why organizations and their members cross the moral line and what managers, regulators, professional associations, and others might do to reduce the likelihood of unethical behavior (Litzky, Eddleston, and Kidder 2006; Martin and Cullen 2006; Tenbrunsel, Smith-Crowe, and Umphress 2003; Vaughan 1999; Weaver, Treviño, and Cochran 1999). Such a research stance implies the existence of a moral order. In this chapter, we take a different stance and ask a different set of questions: How is the line between right and wrong positioned, where is it drawn, by whom, and for whom? How does our (re)conceptualization of the line change our understanding of wrongdoing? These questions precede, analytically, the definition of an act as wrong or unethical, because an actor cannot cross a line that does not exist. They also point to a poorly understood dimension of organizational wrongdoing (that is, the process of drawing a red line) with important implications for management and organizational theory.

We are not the first organizational scholars to examine the process by which social actors delineate right from wrong. Sociologists have long been interested in how classifications of moral versus immoral can vary across social and historical contexts (Hitlin and Vaisey 2013). A few studies in organizational research have looked at how the interests,

---

[1] An organization may also *unintentionally* lack a moral order, or have a weak, ill-defined, or inconsistent moral order. In such cases, some members may engage in moral pursuits, while others just pursue other goals. These unintentional cases do not meet our definition of a moral pursuit, and are not the focus of this chapter.

capabilities, and power of actors affect where the line is drawn, positing that state social control agents usually draw the line where it protects their own interests or those of constituents (Greve et al. 2010; Jackall 2010; Palmer 2012). These prior accounts give us important insight into some of the factors that determine where social control agents draw the line between right and wrong. However, they leave open the question of what strategies less powerful, rank-and-file organizational members may use to justify, for themselves or others, the nature and location of the line – or, in the case of moral pursuits, its absence. We are therefore indebted to the extensive literature on the psychology of moral judgments (e.g., Bazerman and Gino 2012; Greene 2014), but we seek to theorize around a different question: not how individuals decide between right and wrong, but how they explain that decision to themselves and others – that is, the accounts they use to define right and wrong and to justify drawing the line in a particular place.

This chapter makes several contributions to the organizational wrongdoing literature. First, we elaborate on the difference between moral orders and moral pursuits, and explore specifically how wrongdoing is defined in these contrasting contexts. Second, we identify several strategies by which individuals may strive to (re)define right and wrong – and pursue what they consider right – in ways that conflict with the expectations of their organizational setting. We focus on two broad categories of misaligned moral strategies, or what might be labeled "wrong paths to right": when individuals aim for moral pursuit from within a moral order and when they aim for moral order from within a moral pursuit. We suggest that their efforts to pursue right-doing will often entail what other members of their community see as wrongdoing. By exploring cases of actors who are "out-of-sync" with their setting (Warren and Smith-Crowe 2008: 85), we cast light on some of the ways members define and enact right and wrong inside organizations.

Wrongdoing in moral orders versus moral pursuits

Rightdoing and wrongdoing have very different meanings in moral orders and in moral pursuits, as summarized in Table 3.1. In moral orders, the line between right and wrong is drawn by those actors who "exert social control over organizations and organizational partici-pants" and are "responsible for monitoring and controlling wrongful

Table 3.1 *Contrasted views of wrongdoing*

	Definition of right and wrong	What constitutes wrongdoing?
Moral order	Clear line drawn ex ante by powerful social control agents	Crossing the line
		Breaking the rules
	Definition applies across organizational actors	May include behavior perceived as moral in another context
Moral pursuit	Not defined ex ante	Failing to reflect and/or pursue one's own version of morality
	Pursued by all organizational actors according to their own moral perspectives	Aiming to stabilize the moral pursuit by drawing a clear line between right and wrong

behavior" (Palmer 2012: 29, 34). For organizations, the most obvious social control agents are representatives of the state – those responsible for establishing and enforcing laws and regulations – and these actors are the focus of much of the past research on wrongdoing in organizations. Here we define social control agents more broadly to include individuals at all levels, regardless of whether they are officially entrusted with control, who might take it upon themselves to define and enforce a moral order in their setting. This conceptualization is consistent with sociological literature that views all individuals as potential agents of social control, who can and do use a range of strategies – not only punishment, but also scandal, gossip, demands for compensation, or expressions of disapproval – to define and enforce moral standards (Black 1993).

In a moral order, the line that social control agents draw between right and wrong applies, in principle, across organizational actors, though it is likely drawn where the most powerful want it drawn (Anteby 2008; Greve et al. 2010; Jackall 2010; Palmer 2012). The norms that constitute a moral order need not be formally codified and may instead be implied or taken for granted. Neither is it necessary for organizational actors to fully understand or agree with the moral order for it to exist; indeed, there may be considerable confusion or disagreement about the location of the line or the practices that fall on either side (Flynn and Wiltermuth 2010). Regardless of this uncertainty or of the reasons that organizational actors cross the line, their behavior will likely be considered wrong if labeled as such by the relevant social control agents.

Wrongdoing in a moral order is defined by crossing the line and breaking rules written and enforced by control agents. However, those same actions that constitute wrongdoing in one moral order may be considered rightdoing in another order. For instance, British and German lawyers both operate in their respective firms under strict (well-defined) moral orders, but these orders are quite distinct, with British lawyers taught to use the law to serve their clients' interests and German lawyers focused on serving justice in a more neutral way (Smets, Morris, and Greenwood 2012). In other words, the line can be clear and explicit but contingent on its social context. Similarly, some doctors working in poor African countries at the height of the HIV/AIDS epidemic chose to violate laws prohibiting importation of cheap generic AIDS drugs (Heimer 2010). To justify violating the moral order represented by these laws, they invoked two moral principles: to save lives and to confront global inequities. As such, an act that crossed the line into the realm of wrongdoing according to one moral order was justified as rightdoing according to the principles governing the individual's own moral pursuit.

A moral pursuit is characterized by the absence of an ex ante definition of right and wrong. Morality in this context is instead an intentional pursuit involving personal reflection, with each individual drawing her own line based on the moral principles with which she is familiar or on her own sense of right and wrong. Wrongdoing in a moral pursuit is relative, ambiguous, and disputed: what one person considers immoral may be considered righteous by someone else. A moral pursuit is also dynamic, involving a process of reflection and striving, rather than a static categorization of wrongdoing. The Harvard Business School's approach to morality exemplifies such an approach (Anteby 2013). While the School prides itself in aiming for higher business standards, never are these standards made explicit. Instead, an ideology of non-ideology permeates the school's daily operations, and silence pervades on where the red line should be drawn. Another example of a moral pursuit is the Jesuits' early relation to administrative accounting practices (Quattrone 2009, 2015). Balancing books for a Jesuit community amounted to listing on one side all credits received and on the other all debits owed. The goal was not, however, to simply balance the books but to lay bare the situation of a community and reflect on whether these movements of debits and credits lived up to the community's moral aspirations. Put otherwise, accounting was seen as a dynamic practice to uncover what was right or wrong, rather than a rulebook that explicitly told administrators what to do or which accounts to settle.

Given this, how might we conceptualize wrongdoing in a moral pursuit? While prior research tends to see wrongdoing as a deviation from an established order (e.g., violation of a state law or professional code), we posit that "wrongdoing" can also be applied to the processes by which moral orders are negotiated within an organization. We argue that there are at least two distinct categories of behavior that would constitute wrongdoing in such a setting: first, failing to consider, reflect upon, or uphold one's own version of morality; and second, aiming to stabilize the community's view of morality by, for instance, imposing one's views on others. In the first category, an individual fails to live up to her own moral aspirations. As an illustration, a natural grocery's "idealist" employee – one who feels strongly about sustainability – may feel she has failed to live up to her own moral standards if she neglects to ask a customer whether he needs a bag before giving one out (Besharov 2014). The second category may capture behaviors that would be defined as rightdoing in a moral order and by the individual himself but are considered wrong in the context of a pursuit. As an example, consider the recent efforts to promote gender equity at the Harvard Business School, which triggered a debate on female faculty representation (Kantor 2013). Resistance to these efforts may have emerged not because of disagreement over the goal (here, gender equity) but because a majority of organizational members perceived the initiative as an attempt by the organization's leaders to impose their worldview on others. Their resistance, in other words, may have reflected their distaste for being told what is right or wrong.

Relationships between moral orders and moral pursuits

Although a given setting – be it a single organization, a sub-organizational unit, or a supra-organizational field – is likely characterized primarily as either a moral order or a moral pursuit, it is also situated within a broader, complex moral landscape (Fourcade and Healy 2007;

Vaughan 1999).[2] For instance, individuals engaged in a moral pursuit are also embedded in, or at least familiar with, various moral orders – such as religious faith, workplace codes of conduct, or legal regulations – and will often draw upon these orders when engaged in moral deliberation (Sonenshein 2007; Trevino 1986; Winston 2015). Often, moral pursuits are nested explicitly within moral orders, and those orders delineate the boundaries of acceptable behavior, within which there is freedom for a more customized moral pursuit. For instance, an intentionally pluralistic setting may encourage members to pursue their own notions of right and wrong according to their personal or cultural beliefs, as long as such pursuits do not infringe on the rights of others to behave accordingly (Abend 2014).

The existence of multiple moral orders may also require actors to choose between systems or exercise discernment in applying the order appropriately. Orders may operate in parallel, as in systems characterized by legal pluralism, in which multiple distinct legal codes and justice institutions coexist (Heimer 2010). Actions that violate one order may be permissible or even prescribed by another, and organizational actors may select among these orders in deciding which to follow or apply in a given circumstance. Alternatively, moral orders may be nested hierarchically within one another, as when the human resource codes and practices of a given organization operate within and draw upon, but do not exactly replicate, the relevant legal regulations. In such cases, an individual may violate the moral order of her organization without violating the law, but not vice versa, because the organizational order is nested within the legal order. Finally, moral orders may be contested or their lines may be ill-defined and in flux, in which case it may not be clear whether a given act should be considered right or wrong (Anteby 2010; Becker 1973; Chan 2009; Zelizer 1979; Zilber 2002).

The coexistence of moral orders and moral pursuits is even more complicated when the two come into conflict. For instance, an individual operating within a moral order may find that prescriptions set forth by the order (e.g., disregarding ethnicity as an admission criterion) violate

---

[2] We use the term setting to be deliberately neutral about the appropriate level of analysis, because we believe our framework applies across levels. As illustrated by the vignettes introduced later, some organizations may be best understood as a single moral system – be it a moral order or a moral pursuit – while others are better understood as comprising multiple distinct moral orders or pursuits. The same is true at the level of an industry or field.

her own personal sense of right and wrong (e.g., corrective racial justice) and thus contradict what she would strive for in a moral pursuit (e.g., affirmative action policies). This realization can be an emotional one (Haidt 2003; Smith-Crowe and Warren 2014; Turner and Stets 2006; Warren and Smith-Crowe 2008). The experience may cause her to question the legitimacy of the social control agents, and even to disregard the moral order in favor of higher principles (Palmer 2012). An individual operating within a moral pursuit, in turn, may feel discomfort at the level of ambiguity inherent to the pursuit (e.g., selectively endorsing gender equity), or with some of the behaviors of others, or herself, that are deemed moral by others but seem to her to be wrong (e.g., tolerating female under-representation). In either context, the experience of one's moral identity coming into conflict with the organizational setting can be distressing (Stets 2010).

Given the coexistence of multiple moral orders and moral pursuits, the potential for friction between and among them, and the strong emotions this friction can produce, it is not surprising that individuals may strive to (re)define right and wrong in ways that conflict with the expectations of their organizational setting. However, existing literature tells us little about what forms this striving might take, or what strategies organizational members, particularly those with relatively little power, might deploy to distinguish rightdoing from wrongdoing.

In the next section, we focus on two broad categories of misaligned moral strategies, or what might be better labeled "wrong paths to right": first, those involved when individuals aim for moral pursuit from within a moral order, and second, when they aim for moral order from within a moral pursuit. We describe six illustrative cases of moral actions that are "out-of-sync" with the organizational setting (Warren and Smith-Crowe 2008: 85), and in which organizational actors use a range of strategies to (re)define and pursue rightdoing along paths that are likely considered wrong by their respective communities. We derive these examples of misaligned moral action from two sources: some are examples from published scholarship, while in others we draw on previously unpublished empirical data. Because the published studies were originally conducted to investigate other research questions, our interpretation and categorization of those studies should be understood not as conclusive evidence, but as an effort to illustrate concepts, advance theory, and spur future research. By presenting these examples of "wrong paths to right," we hope to inspire other scholars to pay closer attention to the various ways rightdoing and wrongdoing may be delineated within organizations and to make salient the key role played by context (particularly moral order vs. pursuit) in that delineation.

Moral pursuits from within a moral order

Some organizational actors in moral orders might feel uncomfortable with where and how the line between right and wrong is drawn. Those who find themselves too often on the wrong side of a red line might test creative ways to reposition, reconfigure, or blur the line to achieve a more personally gratifying moral outcome – in essence, striving to follow a moral pursuit within the confines of a moral order. These acts of creativity may help the actors successfully pursue what they consider right, but if discovered these are likely to be seen by others in the moral order as acts of defiance or deviance.

By surveying various fields, we identify three main strategies used to strive for moral pursuits within moral orders: *moral hijacking, moral assembling*, and *moral blurring*. These strategies are neither exhaustive nor mutually exclusive. Individuals may, and sometimes do, employ more than one strategy simultaneously or sequentially, and there are likely other strategies beyond these three. That said, we believe these strategies capture the diversity of ways in which organizational actors might engage in misaligned moral behavior in a moral order. Through these misaligned actions, they also seek to change *who* draws the line between right and wrong (from often external control agents to rank-and-file organizational insiders) and *to whom* that line applies (from all or most organizational actors to just the individual herself).

Moral hijacking

We define the first strategy, moral hijacking, as using the viewpoint(s) of external moral order(s) to justify a pursuit that the person doing the hijacking considers morally right but that the moral order in their own setting would define as unacceptable.[3] In this way, moral hijacking

---

[3] Moral hijacking echoes the strategy employed by actors in the US drug courts described by McPherson and Sauder (2013) who are aligned with a given logic but flip and rely on another logic to achieve their goals.

enables actors to reposition the line between right and wrong – not necessarily for everyone in their organization, but for themselves – and to engage in a moral pursuit, charting their own personal moral path. We illustrate and probe deeper into this strategy with a vignette taken from the commerce of human cadavers for medical research and education.

Procuring sufficient cadavers to educate medical students, affiliated health professionals, and practicing physicians can prove problematic because the supply is limited. Moreover, academic researchers and private firms (such as medical device makers or pharmaceutical companies) also need cadavers in their endeavors. Historically, cadavers were obtained by medical schools and then redistributed to faculty members. Increasingly, however, independent ventures have emerged in the United States to become the dominant "brokers" in this field (Anteby 2010; Anteby and Hyman 2008). To secure donations either directly from donors (prior to death) or from family members (after the donor's death), these ventures need to advertise their services and reach out to potential donors and their families.

Medical school procurement programs have long been supervised and often run by clinical anatomists with fairly clear viewpoints on what constitutes right or wrong specimen usage. In many schools, the proper order of usage is explicitly spelled out and specimens go first to physicians in training. In this way, a clear moral order is constructed and reproduced across programs in the United States. By contrast, independent ventures follow their own rules for allocating supply. While the cadavers acquired by medical schools are mainly targeted toward (only) medical education, those acquired by ventures are allocated for multiple uses, generally by for-profit companies (i.e., the torsos are separated from the limbs and each "part" is sent to a different user). The independent ventures use these practices because they allow them to more intensively "exploit" each donation's potential, which is something they consider a moral obligation under the terms of their moral pursuit. However, because these practices might prove off-putting to some donors and their families, the ventures employ moral hijacking to justify their actions.

A review of whole-body donation program descriptions shows that few independent ventures advertise that they dissect a cadaver prior to use, even though they consider this morally right according to their moral pursuit, because it allows them to maximize the utility of donations. Instead, they tend to heavily advertise their goals as being "the advancement of science" – a moral order long promoted by clinical anatomists and attractive to donors and families, but more closely associated with medical schools than with for-profit companies – as a way to justify and legitimize their novel presence in the field and help them secure donations.

By hijacking the moral order established by medical schools, these ventures are able to rely on an established order, subvert it to what they see as an ethical mission to precisely and efficiently match anatomical resources to (multiple) users' needs, and thereby carve out an alternate moral niche within a broader order. The venture leaders do so despite the fact that clinical anatomists, whom they see as guardians of the field's moral order, would strongly object to distributing human remains without giving prior consideration to medical students' training. In other words, moral hijacking allows the ventures to advance a moral pursuit (extensive use of specimens) from within the existing moral order.

Moral assembling

We define the second strategy, moral assembling, as selectively drawing elements from multiple distinct and coexisting moral orders and reassembling them to justify a moral pursuit that the established order in their own setting would deem unacceptable. As such, moral assembling represents an effort to reconfigure the line between right and wrong. Assembling – which is similar to the concept of bricolage (Lévi-Strauss 1966) – resembles hijacking, in that it represents an effort to change who gets to draw the red line. However, it differs from hijacking because when individuals engage in assembling, they not only bring in elements from another order but recombine them with each other and with elements of the existing order. In short, they form something new rather than relying on previously tested justifications. In the vignette below, we provide an illustration of moral assembling that occurred in the West African nation of Sierra Leone, and more specifically in an organization called Timap ("Stand Up") for Justice, hereafter referred to as Timap. This organization provides free justice services through a network of paralegals based in communities around the country (Dale 2009; Maru 2006).

Sierra Leone's justice system is typified by legal pluralism, in which formal justice institutions based on statutes passed in Freetown and British-style common law coexist with customary legal and governance institutions (Manning 2009). Timap trains and encourages its paralegals to engage in a moral pursuit to further the "principles of justice" and of human rights (Maru 2006: 456), while still operating within the prevailing customary and legal moral orders. Paralegals are given considerable discretion not only to decide how best to pursue justice but also to "define what is just" (Dale 2009: 20–21).

In their pursuit of a just outcome, paralegals often navigate strategically the ambiguity created by legal pluralism by "selecting and applying the legal principle most likely to achieve an acceptable outcome" (Dale 2009: 19). For example, Timap paralegals use customary law to negotiate child support payments much higher than the maximum allowed under outdated formal statutes (Maru 2006). In other cases, they use the formal system to develop justifications for opposing practices sanctioned by the customary moral order but that the paralegals consider unjust. Often, as in this example, the paralegals' efforts involve moral assembling.

> In 2006, Timap paralegals received a complaint from a woman whose four-year-old daughter had been taken without her permission to be initiated into one of Sierra Leone's traditional secret societies. The girl had already undergone genital circumcision, a key step in initiation, but her mother wanted Timap's help in securing the girl's release and an exemption from paying the initiation fees usually demanded by the secret society (Maru 2006: 463).
>
> Given cultural prohibitions against non-initiates discussing society matters (Richards, Bah, and Vincent 2004), the paralegals decided to proceed using customary rather than formal justice institutions. To do so, they first approached the local paramount chief, the highest official in the chiefdom governance system (Manning 2009). In their case to the chief, they drew selectively from the customary moral order and argued that the society heads had violated customary law by initiating a young child without her family's permission. Although the chief did not oppose female circumcision and regularly subsidized initiations, he agreed with the paralegals' argument, issued a fine against the society heads, and declared they had acted without his authorization.
>
> Armed with the chief's decision, the paralegals approached the secret society heads. Societies are closely intertwined with the chieftaincy system, but operate according to their own moral order, enforcing their own definition of wrongdoing and sometimes serving as a check on the power of the chiefs (Fanthorpe 2007; Manning 2009). In assembling an argument to convince the society heads to return the girl and forgo the initiation fee they would usually demand from her family, the paralegals blended elements of customary law with their own understanding of the secret society's moral order. For example, their arguments likely cited the fact that societies had traditionally initiated pubescent girls, and only began initiating very young girls in response to the disruption of war

(Fanthorpe 2007). Assembling this element of the secret society's moral order along with aspects of the chief's moral authority, the paralegals successfully argued the family's case.

Here, the Timap paralegals engaged in moral assembling in the context of a specific negotiation, recombining elements of multiple moral orders – those associated with customary law and with a secret society – to justify and achieve an outcome consistent with their own human rights-based moral pursuit. With their actions, they claimed from the traditional control agents (e.g., chiefs) the right to reconfigure the line between right and wrong. The paralegals' strategy in this case may not technically be labeled "wrongdoing" by the respective moral orders, in part because of the paralegals' skill in moral assembling, but the outcome could easily be objected to in each distinct moral order for legitimizing a moral pursuit the orders' representatives did not fully support. More generally, this case shows that by assembling elements from multiple moral orders, individuals can find ways to redraw the line between right and wrong and aim for a moral pursuit within the apparently strict boundaries of moral orders.

Moral blurring

A third strategy to promote a moral pursuit within a moral order is by engaging in moral blurring, which we define as using prohibited practices that mimic authorized ones but are intended to achieve a moral pursuit that the moral order in their setting would define as unacceptable. By mimicking behavior that the moral order considers acceptable, those involved in moral blurring are able to avoid being "caught" deviating from or challenging the moral order. Unlike hijacking and assembling, individuals engaged in moral blurring do not openly assert an alternate morality to justify (re)defining right and wrong, but rather they quietly blur the line in pursuit of what they consider morally right.

For an illustration, we move from communities to health facilities, and specifically to the pediatric wards of two government hospitals in Sierra Leone (Manning 2014). Nurses in these hospitals are trained to operate within a specific moral order, with clearly articulated rules and procedures for how to treat patients and interact with their family members. This moral order is drilled into nurses during training and socialization and is reinforced by cultural objects such as prominent notices posted around the wards extolling professionalism and compassionate care. Despite this prominent, explicit expression of the moral order, it is weakly enforced, in part because supervisors in these extremely resource-constrained hospitals are few in number, rarely spend time on the wards, and (due to inflexible civil service rules) have virtually no power to fire, suspend, or otherwise significantly punish or reward nurses.

As a result, the nurses in these hospitals confront considerable moral ambiguity in their day-to-day practice. Sometimes, when they find that their own sense of right and wrong contradicts the rules laid out by the hospital's moral order, or that the hospital's rules fail to account for reality, they find ways to blur the line and pursue what they consider right. A telling example involves how nurses manage the bodies of young patients who die on the wards.

> Although the vast majority of patients on the pediatric wards suffer from largely preventable and treatable conditions (like malaria and diarrhea), the mortality rates among hospital inpatients are high. In 2012 nearly 13% of children admitted to one of these hospitals did not survive. As a result, nurses regularly presided over the death of their young charges, and handled their dead bodies.[4] The training and protocol for this, which nurses called "last offices," was clear: a medicalized, dispassionate, but also ritualized process for preparing a child's body to be taken away by family members. Nurses first removed any tubes or bandages, then wiped the face clean, and finally wrapped the body in fabric provided by the family, usually the same cotton used to carry the child on arrival. As one nurse said, "When a person dies, you clean them up, you do the last offices, you write, you wrap him, you label him."
>
> Occasionally, however, nurses skipped this process – in clear contravention of the hospital's moral order – and instead sent the child away in a loose fabric wrap or tied to a mother's back, in the same way she would carry a living child. In talking with nurses and observing their interactions with parents, it became clear that this omission, though counter to protocol, was actually intended to help impoverished families. Those traveling by bus or shared taxi would otherwise be charged a premium for transporting a dead

---

[4] This vignette draws on fieldwork conducted by the first author several years prior to the 2014–2015 Ebola Virus Disease outbreak in the region. At the time, infection prevention was likely one rationale underlying the protocol for handling dead bodies, but was not a particularly salient concern for nurses – who regularly touched patients, alive and dead, without wearing protective gloves – or for families and visitors.

body, and might find it difficult to convince drivers to take them on as passengers. By not wrapping the child, the nurses allowed family members to pretend the child was simply asleep. In one case a mother was sent away with her dead child tied to her back and instructed by the staff to "hold your heart until you reach" home and "don't cry out." In a small way, this blurring of the line eased the parents' journey home during a tremendously difficult time.

Nurses who blurred the hospital's rules for how to prepare a body for transport did so because their understanding of their core moral pursuit – providing compassionate care – required that they not put an extra burden on parents after the death of their child. They experienced the hospital's moral order as conflicting with their desired moral pursuit, thereby presenting a moral dilemma, and they found a way to redraw the line for themselves in a new place. In so doing, they blurred the moral order in order to justify what they considered a more just outcome. Their actions, however, would still be technically labeled "wrongdoing" by the representatives of the hospital's moral order.

Moral blurring is not unique to the Sierra Leonean context, or to organizations with poor enforcement of the moral order. One doctor's experience in a top US academic medical center recently launched him into a debate over selectively blurring moral codes. In an opinion piece, the doctor recounted his experience with one patient: "After 2 hours on the telephone trying (and failing) to get her insurance plan to pay for her medication refill, I reached into my pocket and handed the patient $30 so she could fill the prescription." He continued, "It seemed both kinder and more honest than sending her away saying, 'I'm sorry I can't help you'" (Schiff 2013: 1233).

Deciding to pay for his patient's prescription was, for this doctor, an act of generosity and caregiving, consistent both with his personal sense of morality – that is, with his personal moral pursuit – and with his understanding of his profession's core principles. As he pointed out, the code of medical ethics from the American Medical Association calls the practice of medicine "fundamentally a moral activity that arises from the imperative to care for patients and to alleviate suffering" (Schiff 2013: 1233–1234). However, his act was considered a violation by the guardians of his hospital's moral order, and the doctor found himself "being reprimanded for [his] 'unprofessional boundary-crossing behavior'" (Schiff 2013: 1233). Without explicitly saying he would blur the hospital's moral order again, he took issue with where and how the line was drawn and argued that strict adherence to a particular code may violate larger moral principles. As another doctor described it, this revealed a fundamental disagreement among physicians about where to draw the line between right and wrong (Zuger 2013).

The above strategies of moral hijacking, moral assembling, and moral blurring make clear that "wrongdoing" in moral orders can include well-intentioned attempts by organizational actors to destabilize the red line between right and wrong in pursuit of what they consider just. Under such circumstances, wrongdoing can be conceptualized as a "wrong path to right." We next consider strategies employed by individuals who have a similar desire to change or deviate from established norms, but this time in contexts characterized as moral pursuits.

Moral order from within a moral pursuit

Organizational actors in a setting characterized as a moral pursuit may find themselves uncomfortable with the contextual ambiguity inherent to such settings. They may see this ambiguity as moral relativism, the idea that "answers to moral questions ... can be true or false for one particular group, community, society, culture, and even person, yet not true for others" (Abend 2014: 48). They may object to where others draw the moral line and may even feel disgust or contempt for behaviors that others consider moral. In response, they may strive for greater stability and clarity in the definition of right and wrong, seeking to draw a stark red line where none exists. Put otherwise, they may pursue the establishment of a moral order from within a moral pursuit. Other members of their moral pursuit, however, are likely to interpret this imposition of order – though intended to promote rightdoing – as a form of wrongdoing.

We identify three typical strategies for achieving moral orders within moral pursuits: *moral circumscribing, moral spotlighting*, and *moral seceding*. Like the strategies for achieving a moral pursuit within a moral order, these strategies are neither exhaustive nor mutually exclusive, but we believe they capture the many potentially powerful ways that actors can claim agency and authority to define and impose that line on others, despite the fact that this imposition would be seen as wrong by others in that organizational setting.

Moral circumscribing

We label the first strategy for pursuing order in a moral pursuit as moral circumscribing, and define it as imposing limits on the extent of a moral pursuit by specifying what behaviors fall outside the boundary of acceptable behavior. Circumscribing does not eliminate the moral pursuit nor transform a context characterized by moral pursuit into one characterized by order. Rather, it draws a particular kind of moral line: a boundary. Inside this boundary, actors are free to engage in moral pursuits, but behaviors that fall outside will be considered unacceptable. To elaborate, we turn to the ancient but hotly contested moral pursuit of parenting.

Efforts to define the right and wrong sort of parenting are longstanding and widespread, from social workers and judges distinguishing fit from unfit parents (Campion 1995; Wallace and Pruitt 2012) to professional bodies like the American Academy of Pediatrics weighing in on appropriate and inappropriate caregiving practices, to strangers in restaurants or playgrounds openly judging one another's parenting styles. Even though parenting is usually, and perhaps inevitably, a moral pursuit – parents must decide for themselves the right way to rear their children, and their striving for morality is a process that evolves over time – there have long been outside actors who seek to impose limits on that pursuit.

One example of an effort to circumscribe the moral pursuit of parenting can be seen in Heimer and Staffen's study (1995) of a neonatal intensive care unit (NICU), a hospital ward that cares for very sick newborn children. Staff engage in moral circumscribing, bounding what they consider morally right behavior by their patients' parents. As the authors note, "although parents are generally free to raise their children as they see fit, when infants are critically ill the range of behavior that constitutes 'good enough parenting' shrinks, and questions about the quality of care loom larger" (637). The process described next, by which NICU staff delineate the pursuit of good parenting and thereby define bad parenting, has implications for clinical decisions, staff–parent interactions, and even child custody.

A "dominant feature of the social organization of the NICU" is the staff's labeling of parents, and particularly the use of terms such as "'appropriate' or 'inappropriate,' 'good' or 'bad'" (1995: 637). In other words, without recasting the parents' role within a fully settled moral order, nurses and doctors on the NICU impose various constraints on the range of parenting behavior they will consider appropriate. In some cases, these boundaries are explicit and transparent, as with rules that require parents to wear hospital gowns and scrub their hands before entering the unit. In others, they retain significant ambiguity, while nonetheless bounding the range of appropriate behavior. For example, parents are told to "bond" with their infants, but are not given explicit instructions regarding what that bonding should entail. NICU staff nonetheless assess the parents' actions, and whether they are displaying what staff members consider sufficient commitment and connection to their critically ill children.

Parents who fall outside of this circumscribed moral pursuit – e.g., because they are seen to visit the ward too infrequently or do not seem sufficiently engaged in their child's care – may be labeled "inappropriate." In extreme cases, the staff will delay or avoid discharging patients into the care of parents who repeatedly fall outside the boundaries of appropriate behavior, and may even involve law enforcement and child protection officials to pursue termination of parental rights.

Overall, NICU staff engage in moral circumscribing by delimiting the bounds of appropriate parenting and thereby justifying restrictions on the moral pursuit of parenting within the hospital context. Although the imposition of moral order based on the staff members' definition of good and bad parenting likely violates the principles of a moral pursuit – in which parents must engage in a personal and reflective pursuit of how best to raise their children – the NICU staff see this imposition to protect very vulnerable children as a form of rightdoing. This strategy of moral circumscribing exemplifies one type of "wrong path to right" used for achieving moral order within a moral pursuit.

Moral spotlighting

We define the second strategy to promote order within a pursuit, moral spotlighting, as selecting from among the elements of a moral pursuit and imposing a subset of them as necessary for behavior to be considered moral. In contrast to moral circumscribing, which defines which behaviors *do not* fall within the boundaries of acceptable moral pursuit, moral spotlighting defines which behaviors *are required* for a pursuit to be moral. Spotlighting prescribes what must be attended to, rather than ruling out what should not be done.

To better understand the strategy of moral spotlighting, we return to the Sierra Leonean hospitals discussed earlier and examine the nurses' attempts to justify their imposition of order on family members' caregiving on the wards (a moral pursuit). This example also showcases how moral domains can be nested. Here, one workplace harbors both moral orders (hospital rules) and moral pursuits (caregiving).

The moral pursuit involved in caregiving is complex and multifaceted. Caregivers of young children seek to protect them from harm, support their development, and promote their well-being. In a medical setting, the caregiver of a sick child may provide comfort, monitor their condition, learn more about their diagnosis, and advocate for the best possible care, among many other things. In the Sierra Leonean pediatric wards studied by the first author, nurses not only observed and assessed the caregivers of their patients but also intervened to "correct" perceived shortcomings, particularly to enforce certain behaviors they considered necessary for good caregiving in this setting. In so doing, they engaged in spotlighting: selecting from among the many dimensions of caregiving and highlighting one or a few of those dimensions as essential to the moral pursuit. Specifically, they sought to define good and bad caregiving narrowly, focusing on whether caregivers obeyed nurses' instructions (even about seemingly petty issues, such as not dressing children in clothes that nurses considered too fancy) rather than on other dimensions of caregiving (such as advocating for the child's care). Based on this spotlighted definition, good caregiving requires that caregivers follow nurses' instructions without question or complaint, while other aspects of caregiving are seen as irrelevant or even problematic.

One of the most infuriating occurrences for nurses at these hospitals was when caregivers could not be located when the nurses needed them. This frequently happened during medication rounds, which should take place at designated times but in practice were often delayed for various reasons, including bottlenecks at the hospital pharmacy. For family members, particularly those who recently arrived in the hospital and may have received only a cursory introduction (if any) to the rules and rhythms of the ward, these rounds likely seemed utterly unpredictable.

On many occasions, family caregivers were scolded by nurses for not being readily available when their names were called. Their absence was deemed evidence of poor caregiving, because good caregiving had been defined as following the nurses' instructions and remaining available at all times during their child's stay in the hospital. This was true even if their absence resulted from another act of caring for the child: e.g., going outside to feed or bathe them, or to buy clean water or medical supplies from nearby shops. In these hospitals, nurses had distilled the moral pursuit of caregiving to being available and obedient to health workers.

As with the earlier example of moral circumscribing, the nurses engaged in moral spotlighting impose on family members a kind of moral order: a particular definition of what makes for good and bad caregiving in hospital settings within the fuzzier moral pursuit of caregiving. Spotlighting differs from circumscribing because it does not just define which behaviors fall outside the boundary of acceptable behavior but proactively defines which behaviors are required for caregivers to do right. Put otherwise, spotlighting involves defining a necessary condition for morality to exist within a moral pursuit.

Moral seceding

The third and final strategy of moral ordering within a moral pursuit involves either secession or expulsion and is defined as withdrawing from a moral pursuit or expelling others from a moral pursuit to (re)instate a moral order. This strategy amounts to creating sub-populations within a wider group and distinguishing them along degrees of "purity" (Douglas 1966) with respect to a new or espoused line between right and wrong. Members are considered more pure if they adhere closely to the dictates asserted by those who seek to impose order and less pure if they continue to engage in a broader pursuit.

For an example of moral seceding, we look to the Presbyterian Church USA (PCUSA), part of a group of progressive US Christian denominations that are collectively known as the Protestant mainline (Creed, DeJordy, and Lok 2010). Traditionally, the PCUSA was structured as a centralized moral order, in which key moral decisions – such as how to divide right from wrong on issues ranging from theology to the ordination of women – were made at higher levels of the hierarchy and handed down to local churches (Creed et al. 2010). However, in recent decades, the PCUSA's governing bodies and member congregations moved toward becoming more of a moral pursuit, by deciding, for instance, that individual congregations could determine for themselves whether or not to require that members called to PCUSA ministry have literal belief in certain tenets of Christian theology (Longfield 2000; Quirk 1975). A subset of members of the PCUSA saw these changes as sanctioning behaviors that they considered morally wrong; they responded by seceding so they could reassert a moral order elsewhere. In the vignette below, we consider secessions that resulted from the PCUSA's changing stance toward lesbian, gay, bisexual, or transgender (LGBT) members.

> Homosexuality has been a divisive issue in many Christian denominations in the United States, and the PCUSA has been mired since the 1990s in debates over the role of LGBT church members, their possible ordination as ministers, and the PCUSA's stance toward same-sex marriage (Goodstein 2014). Until recently, the denomination's governing constitution, the Book of Order, explicitly prohibited LGBT individuals from being ordained as ministers in the church and banned PCUSA ministers from presiding over same-sex marriages (Moon 2014).
>
> Efforts to overturn these bans in favor of a more permissive moral pursuit – one that would allow individual ministers and congregations to define for themselves what they considered right and wrong regarding LGBT ministers and marriages – finally bore fruit in 2010, when the General Assembly voted to allow local ordaining bodies to choose whether or not to ordain openly gay members as church deacons or ministers (Moon 2014). This shifted the moral question of eligibility for ordination from a top-down moral order to a moral pursuit determined at the local or regional level (Young 2011).
>
> Although church leaders claimed this change "reaffirm[ed]" a "long-held right and responsibility of ordaining bodies" (Young 2011: para. 4), some members found the change unacceptable. Following that decision, between 350 and 428 congregations (out of more than 10,000 nationwide, and including some of the largest) opted to secede from the church rather than accede to what they considered an immoral pursuit (Goodstein 2014; Moon 2014). Many of these formed or joined groups of more conservative former PCUSA members.

By seceding from what they considered to be the organization's increasingly permissive moral pursuit, these more conservative congregations were able to reinstate a moral order and draw a clear red line that justified prohibiting behaviors they considered wrong. Moral secession is not unique to religious contexts, and can occur wherever organizational actors disagree with aspects of a moral pursuit but have few options to impose order except by seceding themselves or expelling others. Other examples of moral secession include employees who choose to exit a firm whose practices they disagree with on moral grounds, rather than exercising voice to change those practices (Withey and Cooper 1989).

In these three different strategies – moral circumscribing, spotlighting, and seceding – we see efforts to stabilize, sharpen, and illuminate a clear red line between right and wrong. This contrasts with the earlier examples of actors destabilizing and dimming red lines by pursuing moral pursuits from within moral orders. In the latter cases, the actors' "wrong paths to right" involve imposing a (re)definition of right and wrong on other organizational members, thereby attempting to disrupt and constrain others' diverse moral pursuits in favor of a singular moral order.

In summary, organizational actors are motivated to employ various strategies to pursue what they believe to be right, but sometimes those strategies are misaligned with their respective settings. In both moral orders and moral pursuits, we see examples of actors seeking to (re) define the line between wrong and right in ways with which others in their setting disagree. These instances cast light on a previously understudied facet of morality in organizational life, thereby illuminating the importance of how wrongdoing is defined – where the line is drawn and by whom – and the resulting variety of wrongdoing in organizations.

Conclusion

Organizational members are also, inevitably, moral actors, and they must often navigate morally ambiguous terrain. In many cases, their own moral intuition or judgment about what constitutes right and wrong will diverge from where the line is drawn by others in their organizational setting. In this chapter, we discussed six ways in which organizational members might seek to (re)define wrongdoing and justify the pursuit of what they consider right but what others in their setting will likely label wrong. These contrasted strategies are summarized in Table 3.2. Three of the strategies involve pursuing moral order from within a context of moral pursuit, while the others involve aiming for moral pursuit in a context of moral order.

The six strategies described here are certainly not the only form of misaligned moral action. Actors may also engage in actions that are misaligned with the definition of right and wrong in their setting because they are uncertain about that definition (Wuthnow 1989) or they simply do not realize that their behavior violates a particular

Table 3.2 *"Wrong paths to right" in moral orders versus moral pursuits*

Moral pursuits from within a moral order		
Moral hijacking Using the viewpoint(s) of external moral order(s) to justify a moral pursuit that the moral order in that setting would define as unacceptable	*Moral assembling* Selectively drawing elements from multiple distinct and coexisting moral orders and reassembling them to justify a moral pursuit that the moral order in that setting would define as unacceptable	*Moral blurring* Using prohibited practices that mimic authorized ones but are intended to achieve a moral pursuit that the moral order in that setting would define as unacceptable
Moral order from within a moral pursuit		
Moral circumscribing Imposing limits on the extent of a moral pursuit by specifying which behaviors fall outside the boundary of acceptable behavior	*Moral spotlighting* Selecting from among the elements of a moral pursuit and imposing a subset of them as necessary for behavior to be considered moral	*Moral seceding* Withdrawing from a moral pursuit or expelling others from the pursuit to (re)instate a moral order

moral order or moral pursuit (Green 2004; Warren and Smith-Crowe 2008). Alternatively, they may engage in behaviors that are considered moral in a broader context (e.g., whistleblowing) but are considered immoral within an organization (e.g., because they obstruct the organization's corrupt practices) (Smith-Crowe and Warren 2014). Actors may also face moral dilemmas in which they must choose between violating a moral order to achieve what is best for the larger society – that is, doing "bad" in order to do "good" – or keeping their hands clean but missing the opportunity to achieve the greater moral good (Griffin 1995; Walzer 1973; Winston 2015). While acknowledging these other types of misaligned moral action, we believe the strategies defined in Table 3.2 are an important understudied aspect of organizational wrongdoing: the process by which individuals within organizations seek to draw and redraw the line between right and wrong in order to justify the pursuit of what they consider morally right but their organizational setting considers morally wrong.

These insights have important implications for management and organizational theory, which has typically focused more on the reasons for unethical behavior in organizations and what might be done to minimize such misconduct and less on how or by whom wrongdoing gets defined. We build on scholarship emphasizing the role of power and interests in determining where social control agents draw the line between right and wrong (Anteby 2013; Greve et al. 2010; Jackall 2010; Palmer 2012) to emphasize the strategies that rank-and-file organizational members use to justify, for themselves or others, the nature and location of the line, and how those strategies vary across contexts (i.e., moral orders vs. pursuits). Future research could also examine how other moral outcomes, like whistleblowing (Miceli, Near, and Dworkin 2013; Morrison 2011), white-collar crime (Braithwaite 1985; Shapiro 1990), and corruption (Lange 2008; Smith-Crowe and Warren 2014), might vary across these contexts.

Obviously, separating moral orders from moral pursuits is not always as easy as we have assumed, and these two ideal types encompass a wide range of organizational forms and occasionally overlap. More research is needed to explore cases in which there is disagreement or confusion – either for scholars or among the organizational members themselves – over whether a given setting is a moral order or moral pursuit. These boundary cases may provide further insight into how organizational actors understand and respond to moral ambiguity and into the implications for their organizations and the broader society.

Moreover, future research is needed to explore the positive and negative implications of misaligned moral action. When nurses blur the lines of a hospital's moral order to justify doing what they consider right, does that undermine the hospital as an organization or does it paradoxically protect it from doing wrong by its patients and staff? When some member churches secede from a denomination that they believe has become an immoral pursuit, what are the implications for the secessionist churches and for those left behind? It may be that organizations benefit from having a balance between members who adhere to the expectations of the particular setting – be it a moral order or moral pursuit – and those who dim or sharpen those expectations through misaligned moral strategies, akin to the beneficial balance brought by rule-benders and rule-enforcers (Canales 2014). In short, an organization may need a few people engaged in moral pursuits to challenge, change, and give flexibility to a moral order, while a few people striving for moral order may provide needed structure and boundaries to a moral pursuit. Future studies could examine the demography of morality within organizations, teasing out the proportion of members who need to follow a moral order or align with a moral pursuit for it to best be sustained; exploring how different members relate to each other; and understanding how these interactions affect outcomes (see, for example, Besharov 2014).

We hope that this chapter will inspire new theoretical and empirical insights into the ways in which organizational members can find themselves on the wrong path to right, and why understanding how lines are drawn and redrawn between right and wrong matters for a deeper grasp of organizational life. Studying how human cadavers in whole-body donation programs are used or intentionally "misused" or how deceased children in hospital wards are handled or purposely "mishandled" illuminates not only how organizational actors in these contexts justify right and wrong but also the various strategies they might employ to ensure that their "wrong paths to right" yield outcomes they consider morally desirable.

References

Abend, G. 2014. *The Moral Background: An Inquiry in the History of Business Ethics*. Princeton: Princeton University Press.

Anteby, M. 2008. *Moral Gray Zones: Side Productions, Identity, and Regulation in an Aeronautic Plant*. Princeton: Princeton University Press.

Anteby, M. 2010. "Markets, morals, and practices of trade: Jurisdictional disputes in the U.S. commerce in cadavers," *Administrative Science Quarterly* 55: 606–638.

Anteby, M. 2013. *Manufacturing Morals: The Values of Silence in Business School Education*. Chicago: University of Chicago Press.

Anteby, M. and Hyman, M. 2008. "Entrepreneurial ventures and whole-body donations: A regional perspective from the United States," *Social Science & Medicine* 68(4): 963–969.

Bazerman, M. H. and Gino, F. 2012. "Behavioral ethics: Toward a deeper understanding of moral judgment and dishonesty," *Annual Review of Law and Social Science* 8(617): 1–44.

Becker, H. S. 1973. "Moral entrepreneurs," in *Outsiders: Studies in the Sociology of Deviance*: 147–164. New York: Free Press.

Besharov, M. L. 2014. "The relational ecology of identification: How organizational identification emerges when individuals hold divergent values," *Academy of Management Journal* 57(5): 1485–1512.

Black, D. 1993. *The Social Structure of Right and Wrong*. San Diego: Academic Press.

Braithwaite, J. 1985. "White collar crime," *Annual Review of Sociology* 11: 1–25.

Campion, M. J. 1995. *Who's Fit to Be a Parent?* New York: Routledge.

Canales, R. 2014. "Weaving straw into gold: Managing organizational tensions between standardization and flexibility in microfinance," *Organization Science* 25(1): 1–28.

Chan, C. S. 2009. "Creating a market in the presence of cultural resistance: The case of life insurance in China," *Theory and Society* 38(3): 271–305.

Creed, W. E. D., DeJordy, R., and Lok, J. 2010. "Being the change: Resolving institutional contradiction through identity work," *Academy of Management Journal* 53(6): 1336–1364.

Dale, P. 2009. "Delivering justice to Sierra Leone's poor: An analysis of the work of Timap for justice," in *Justice for the Poor Research Report*. Washington, DC: The World Bank.

Douglas, M. 1966. *Purity and Danger: An Analysis of Concepts of Pollution and Taboo*. London: Routledge and Kegan Paul.

Durkheim, E. 1973. *Emile Durkheim on Morality and Society*, edited by R. N. Bellah. Chicago: University of Chicago Press.

Fanthorpe, R. 2007. *Sierra Leone: The Influence of the Secret Societies, with Special Reference to Female Genital Mutilation*. Writenet Report. United Nations High Commissioner for Refugees, Status Determination and Protection Information Section (DIPS), Geneva, Switzerland.

Flynn, F. and Wiltermuth, S. 2010. "Who's with me? False consensus, brokerage, and ethical decision making in organizations," *Academy of Management Journal* 53(5): 1074–1089.

Fourcade, M. and Healy, K. 2007. "Moral views of market society," *Annual Review of Sociology* 33: 285–311.

Goodstein, L. 2014. "Presbyterians vote to allow same sex marriages," *The New York Times*, June 20, p. 11a.

Green, S. P. 2004. "Moral ambiguity in white collar criminal law," *Notre Dame Journal of Law, Ethics and Public Policy* 18: 501–521.

Greene, J. D. 2014. "Beyond point-and-shoot morality: Why cognitive (neuro) science matters for ethics," *Ethics* 124(4): 695–726.

Greve, H. R., Palmer, D., and Pozner, J. 2010. "Organizations gone wild: The causes, processes, and consequences of organizational misconduct," *The Academy of Management Annals* 4(1): 53–107.

Griffin, L. 1995. "The lawyer's dirty hands," *Georgetown Journal of Legal Ethics* 8: 219–281.

Haidt, J. 2003. "The moral emotions," in R. J. Davidson, K. R. Scherer, and H. H. Goldsmith (eds.), *Handbook of Affective Sciences*: 852–870. Oxford: Oxford University Press.

Heimer, C. A. 2010. "The unstable alliance of law and morality," in S. Hitlin and S. Vaisey (eds.), *Handbook of the Sociology of Morality*: 179–202. New York: Springer.

Heimer, C. A. and Staffen, L. R. 1995. "Interdependence and reintegrative social control: Labeling and reforming 'inappropriate' parents in neonatal intensive care units," *American Sociological Review* 60(5): 635–654.

Hitlin, S. and Vaisey, S. 2013. "The new sociology of morality." *Annual Review of Sociology* 39(1): 51–68.

Jackall, R. 2010. "Morality in organizations," in S. Hitlin and S. Vaisey (eds.), *Handbook of the Sociology of Morality*: 203–210. New York: Springer.

Kantor, J. 2013. "Harvard Business School case study: Gender equity," *The New York Times*, September 7, p. 1a.

Lange, D. 2008. "A multidimensional conceptualization of organizational corruption control," *Academy of Management Review* 33(3):710–729.

Lévi-Strauss, C. 1966. *The Savage Mind*. Chicago: University of Chicago Press.

Litzky, B. E., Eddleston, K. A., and Kidder, D. L. 2006. "The good, the bad, and the misguided: How managers inadvertently encourage deviant behaviors," *Academy of Management Perspectives* 20(1): 91–103.

Longfield, B. J. 2000. "For church and country: The fundamentalist-modernist conflict in the Presbyterian Church," *Journal of Presbyterian History* 78(1): 35–50.

Manning, R. 2009. "The landscape of local authority in Sierra Leone: How 'traditional' and 'modern' justice systems interact," in *Justice & Development Working Paper Series* 1(1). Washington, DC: The World Bank.

Manning, R. 2014. "A place for emotion: How space structures nurse–parent interactions in West African pediatric wards," *Academy of Management Annual Meeting Proceedings*.

Martin, K. D. and Cullen, J. B. 2006. "Continuities and extensions of ethical climate theory: A meta-analytic review," *Journal of Business Ethics* 69: 175–194.

Maru, V. 2006. "Between law and society: Paralegals and the provision of justice services in Sierra Leone and worldwide," *The Yale Journal of International Law* 31: 427–476.

Mauss, M. 1967. *Manuel d'Éthnographie*. Paris: Editions Payot.

McPherson, C. M. and Sauder, M. 2013. "Logics in action: Managing institutional complexity in a drug court," *Administrative Science Quarterly* 58(2): 165–196.

Miceli, M. P., Near, J. P., and Dworkin, T. M. 2013. *Whistle-Blowing in Organizations*. New York: Routledge: Taylor & Francis Group.

Moon, R. 2014. "PC(USA) permits pastors to perform same-sex marriages, thanks to conservative exodus," *Christianity Today*, June 20. Available from www.christianitytoday.com.

Morrison, E. W. 2011. "Employee voice behavior: Integration and directions for future research," *The Academy of Management Annals* 5(1): 373–412.

Palmer, D. 2012. *Normal Organizational Wrongdoing: A Critical Analysis of Theories of Misconduct in and by Organizations*. Oxford: Oxford University Press.

Quattrone, P. 2009. "Books to be practiced: Memory, the power of the visual, and the success of accounting," *Accounting, Organizations and Society* 34(1): 85–118.

Quattrone, P. 2015. "Governing social orders, unfolding rationality, and Jesuit accounting practices: A procedural approach to institutional logics," *Administrative Science Quarterly* 60(3): 411–445.

Quirk, C. E. 1975. "Origins of the Auburn affirmation," *Journal of Presbyterian History* 53(2): 120–142.

Richards, P., Bah, K., and Vincent, J. 2004. "Social capital and survival: Prospects for community-driven development in post-conflict Sierra Leone," in *Social Development Papers: Community-Driven Development, Conflict Prevention & Reconstruction* 12. Washington, DC: The World Bank.

Schiff, G. D. 2013. "Crossing boundaries – violation or obligation?" *JAMA: The Journal of the American Medical Association* 310(12): 1233–1234.

Shapiro, S. P. 1990. "Collaring the crime, not the criminal: Reconsidering the concept of white-collar crime," *American Sociological Review* 55(3): 346–365.

Smets, M., Morris, T., and Greenwood, R. 2012. "From practice to field: A multilevel model of practice driven institutional change," *Academy of Management Journal* 55(4): 877–904.

Smith-Crowe, K. and Warren, D. E. 2014. "The emotion-evoked collective corruption model: The role of emotion in the spread of corruption within organizations," *Organization Science* 25(4): 1154–1171.

Sonenshein, S. 2007. "The role of construction, intuition, and justification in responding to ethical issues at work: The sensemaking-intuition model," *Academy of Management Review* 32(4): 1022–1040.

Stets, J. E. 2010. "The social psychology of the moral identity," in S. Hitlin and S. Vaisey (eds.), *Handbook of the Sociology of Morality*: 385–409. New York: Springer.

Tenbrunsel, A. E., Smith-Crowe, K., and Umphress, E. E. 2003. "Building houses on rocks: The role of the ethical infrastructure in organizations," *Social Justice Research* 16(3): 285–307.

Tenbrunsel, A. E. and Smith-Crowe, K. 2008. "Ethical decision making: Where we've been and where we're going," *The Academy of Management Annals* 2(1): 545–607.

Trevino, L. K. 1986. "Ethical decision making in organizations: A person-situation interactionist model," *Academy of Management Review* 11(3): 601–617.

Turner, J. H. and Stets, J. E. 2006. "Moral emotions," in J. E. Stets and J. H. Turner (eds.), *Handbook of the Sociology of Emotions*: 544–568. New York: Springer.

Vaughan, D. 1999. "The dark side of organizations: Mistake, misconduct, and disaster," *Annual Review of Sociology* 25: 271–305.

Wallace, J. L. and Pruitt, L. R. 2012. "Judging parents, judging place: Poverty, rurality, and termination of parental rights," *Missouri Law Review* 77(1): 1–54.

Walzer, M. 1973. "Political action: The problem of dirty hands," *Philosophy & Public Affairs* 2(2): 160–180.

Warren, D. E. and Smith-Crowe, K. 2008. "Deciding what's right: The role of external sanctions and embarrassment in shaping moral judgments in the workplace," *Research in Organizational Behavior* 28: 81–105.

Weaver, G. R., Treviño, L. K., and Cochran, P. L. 1999. "Corporate ethics programs as control systems: Influences of executive commitment and environmental factors," *Academy of Management Journal* 42(1): 41–57.

Winston, K. 2015. *Ethics in Public Life: Good Practitioners in a Rising Asia*. New York: Palgrave Macmillan.

Withey, M. J. and Cooper, W. H. 1989. "Predicting exit, voice, loyalty, and neglect," *Administrative Science Quarterly* 34: 521–539.

Wuthnow, R. 1989. *Meaning and Moral Order: Explorations in Cultural Analysis.* Berkeley: University of California Press.

Young, S. 2011. "Presbyterian Church (U.S.A.) approves change in ordination standard," *Presbyterian Church (U.S.A.) News & Announcements,* May 10. Available from www.pcusa.org.

Zelizer, V. A. 1979. *Morals and Markets: The Development of Life Insurance in the United States.* New York: Columbia University Press.

Zilber, T. B. 2002. "Institutionalization as an interplay between actions, meanings, and actors: The case of a rape crisis center in Israel," *Academy of Management Journal* 45(1): 234–254.

Zuger, A. 2013. "When healers get too friendly," *The New York Times,* November 11.

4 From market enablers to market participants: redefining organizational and political-legal arrangements and opportunities for financial wrongdoing, 1930s–2000

HARLAND PRECHEL AND DADAO HOU

It is widely accepted that the spread of high-risk financial instruments and financial wrongdoing contributed to failures in the US home mortgage market, the 2008 financial crisis, and upheaval in the global economy. Initially, corporate leaders, government officials, and some researchers attributed the crisis to individuals and suggested that individual characteristics such as greed and self-interest explain these events. Clearly, the perpetrators of financial wrongdoing are individuals with self-interests. However, the focus on individual characteristics does not answer an important question: Why was financial wrongdoing so widespread in financial markets at this point in history?

Current research shows that corporate wrongdoing occurs in response to cognitive assumptions (Gabbioneta, Prakash, and Greenwood 2014), risk-taking norms (Abolafia 2010), and is normal and undetectable in complex structures where bounded rationality impedes social actors from grasping the implications of their decisions (Palmer 2013; Palmer and Maher 2010). Others maintain that Congress and the Executive Branch facilitated the emergence of financial markets and risky financial instruments (Campbell 2010; Krippner 2011; Lavelle 2013), and the federal government "pulled the banks into the … secondary mortgage market" and trusted that banks understood what they were doing (Fligstein and Goldstein 2010: 31, 63–64). Still others show that whereas the multilayer-subsidiary form created opportunities, pressure to

The authors thank Royston Greenwood, Donald Palmer, and Kristen Smith-Crowe for their constructive comment on the previous versions of this paper.

increase shareholder value created incentives for managers to engage in financial wrongdoing (Prechel and Morris 2010).

Although these studies advance our understanding of corporate wrongdoing, little research exists on how interrelated parts of the social structure were changed in ways that created opportunities for social actors to engage in wrongdoing in the first place. We suggest that this lacuna in the literature exists because of the increased specialization and division within the social and organizational sciences and the narrow focus on a single dimension of the social structure. To fill this gap in the literature, we elaborate Sutherland's (1949) conception of differential social structure and focus on the following questions. How were the organizational and political-legal arrangements transformed in ways that created opportunities for social actors to engage in financial wrongdoing? How did the emergent organizational and political-legal arrangements interact to create opportunities for financial wrongdoing?

To answer these questions, we employ a historical analysis over a sufficiently long time period (1930s–2000) to examine how corporate power and state power were exercised to transform organizational and political-legal arrangements to structure the home mortgage market in ways that created opportunities for financial wrongdoing to occur. *Financial wrongdoing* is defined as (1) acts that violate a law or the intent of a law established by government agencies responsible for ensuring the integrity of the financial system and (2) acts that violate the public's understanding of the business code of conduct that consumers and investors use when making financial decisions (Prechel 2016; Prechel and Morris 2010).

Theoretical framework: organizational political economy

Organizational political economy theorizes the state, which is the principal social control agent in society, as an organization that is influenced by other organizations in its environment, and analyzes the interaction between potential corporate wrongdoers and the state, which is charged with controlling them. The state is a complex organization that is affected by its own agendas (e.g., maintaining economic stability) and structures that include separate large "supra-units" (i.e., Executive, Legislative, and Judicial branches) and subunits (e.g., Treasury) and its resource-dependent relations with organizations and political coalitions that emerge inside and outside the state (Prechel 1990). Dependence on resources controlled by other organizations creates uncertainty and loss of autonomy, both of which threaten organizations' capacity to survive (Pfeffer and Salancik 1978). Although corporations and markets are always culturally and politically embedded in modern society (Polanyi 1944), when the state controls resources that limit corporations' capacity to realize their goals corporations mobilize politically to redefine corporate–state relations in ways that give them access to critical resources (e.g., markets). Because political embeddedness and disembeddedness are historically contingent, these concepts are best understood as ideal types that are located on two ends of a single continuum. Thus, the empirical form of political embeddedness is a variable whose location on this continuum is affected by historically specific corporate–state arrangements (Prechel 2003: 314).

The organizational complexity of the modern state provides corporations with multiple venues to overcome their resource dependence. If corporations fail to achieve their agenda in one dimension of the state (e.g., Congress), then they refocus their efforts on other parts of the state (e.g., Treasury Department) that have control over related resources. However, resource dependence is a two-way relationship; the state is dependent, in part, on revenues from corporate taxes because it has no independent means to raise revenues. Therefore, the state implements policies that facilitate economic growth in order to raise revenues to fulfill its goals and preserve its legitimacy (O'Connor 1973). The balance between corporate power and state power is also dependent on the capacity of social actors to advance their economic interests politically. Organizations are a primary basis of collective action and constitute the primary means to exercise power in modern society (Offe and Wiesenthal 1980: 76–80; Prechel 1990, 2000; Roy 1997; Walker and Rea 2014). Organizations provide mechanisms to forge political alliances with other organizations when their economic interests coincide. In this respect, organizations are tools for shaping the world. However, access to organizations is not equally distributed in society. Organizations are largely the tools of elites; "the power of the rich lies not in their ability to buy goods and services, but in their capacity to control the ends toward which the vast resources of corporations are directed" (Perrow 1986: 12).

Throughout most of the twentieth century the political embeddedness of banks and financial organizations limited their behavior to
enablers of the market; they supplied capital to other economic
sectors that produced commodities. By the 1990s, changes in political embeddedness transformed these corporations to market participants that produced commodities in their own right (e.g.,
mortgage-backed securities). The primary concern here is with the
social structural changes that allowed corporations to become market participants· and engage in financial wrongdoing. To examine
this issue, we employ Weber's conception of multicausality where
economic, legal, organizational, political, and cultural forces constitute the broad social structural categories that influence social
action (Kalberg 1994; Weber 1978). We focus on how changes in
organizational and political-legal arrangements resulted in a *turning
point*: a shift that redirects a historical process that makes certain
actions viable (Abbott 1997). In particular, we examine how corporations were decoupled from the state in ways that created structural holes and opportunities for managers to engage in financial
wrongdoing.

The concept of structural holes was developed to show how entrepreneurial managers obtain resource benefits to advance their careers
by legitimately exploiting information (e.g., a producer negotiating
with a supplier). When *structural holes* exist, which are separations
between nonredundant contacts (Burt 1992), social actors have autonomy (i.e., lack of constraint) that translates into social capital and the
opportunity to benefit from the relationship. The capacity to identify
and act on information entails *human capital* (e.g., knowledge and
skills), but *social capital* (e.g., relationships with other social actors)
is of primary importance because managers establish networks to
bridge structural holes to gain benefits (Burt 1992: 8; Corra and
Willer 2002; Granovetter 1973). The analysis here extends the definition of structural holes to include managerial behavior that *illegiti-
mately* exploits information to gain resources and benefits.
The illegitimate exploitation of information includes violating the
intent of, for example, an accounting rule or understood practice
such that corporate balance sheets are inflated or risk is concealed
(Prechel and Morris 2010). Because dimensions of the social structure
are intertwined, structural holes are created when one part of the social
structure is changed without a concomitant change in another part that

ensures third-party oversight. This condition permits social actors to bridge structural holes and engage in financial wrongdoing.

The analysis focuses on how changes in corporate–state relations decoupled corporations from the state agencies responsible to ensure the stability of the financial system. Decoupling takes place when (1) changes occur in organizational arrangements without concomitant changes in political-legal arrangements and (2) changes in political-legal arrangements occur without concomitant changes in organizational arrangements. Decoupling creates gaps between means and ends (Antonio 1979; Bromley and Powell 2012; Weber 1978). In this case, the means, which entail the day-to-day organizational decisions and practices of management, are decoupled from the state, which is the principal social control agent in society and whose substantive ends include safeguarding society from catastrophic financial crises.

Historical contextualization

In the nineteenth century, the US state was small and had little authority to intervene in economic activity because the federalist structure granted subnational states authority over economic activity that occurred inside their borders. However, the authority over economic activity by the federal government expanded with the increase in interstate commerce in the early twentieth century, the inability of subnational states to resolve the periodic recessions in the 1920s, and the prolonged Great Depression in the 1930s. In response to the deepening economic crises, the federal government took an active role embedding markets and corporations in political-legal arrangements in ways that were designed to reinvigorate economic growth and stability. Government policies, laws, and subsequent structures defined banks as enablers of the market whose primary function was to provide capital to businesses and homeowners. The federal government also attempted to curtail bankruptcies in smaller state banks that disrupted capital to local markets. Toward this end, Congress passed the 1927 McFadden Act to prohibit national banks from branching into state bank markets unless permitted by state law. Because most states did not permit branch banking, the McFadden Act prohibited national banks from operating in state markets. Oversight of this market was an extension of the federalist structure; state-chartered banks were regulated by the state where they were incorporated, national bank holding companies and their subsidiaries were regulated by the Federal Reserve Bank, and other national banks were controlled by the Office of the Comptroller of Currency, which is organized within the Treasury Department.

Congress also passed the Banking Act of 1933 to enable banks to provide capital to struggling communities and businesses. This law established three interrelated mechanisms to stabilize banks. First, to limit competition and the potential for bankruptcy, the Banking Act gave the Federal Reserve Bank the authority to set limits on bank interest rates. Second, to encourage bank deposits, Congress established the Federal Deposit Insurance Corporation (FDIC) to insure bank deposits. Third, the Glass–Steagall component of this law separated commercial from investment banking. Forced to give up deposits, investment banks lost their primary source of capital and power (Mintz and Schwartz 1985; Mizruchi 1982).

Although state managers (i.e., elected and appointed government officials) in the Roosevelt Administration attempted to limit mergers between banks and non-banks, these efforts did not succeed until Congress passed the Bank Holding Company Act in 1956 (Congressional Quarterly Almanac 1999). This legislation created barriers to mergers between banks and non-banks (e.g., insurance companies). The Douglas Amendment to the 1956 legislation further limited bank powers by tightening restrictions on out-of-state banking established by the 1927 McFadden Act.

The following identifies three policy periods that redefined these corporate–state relations in ways that transformed banks and other organizations from market enablers to market participants and then decoupled them from government oversight, thereby creating structural holes and opportunities for managers to engage in financial wrongdoing.

Policy period I: creating the secondary home mortgage market to overcome economic crises, 1930s–1970

Already weakened by corporate bankruptcies that followed the 1929 stock market crash, real-estate values were further eroded by the Great Depression. Because state banks held a substantial number of home mortgages, the prolonged economic downturn devalued their assets, which weakened these banks. By 1933, state banks' failures became widespread, which left many parts of the country without mortgage lending institutions (CQ Weekly 1989a). To restore bank assets and increase the flow of capital into the housing market, the federal government enacted three interrelated policies. First, the Homeowners Loan Act of 1933 created federally chartered savings and loan associations (S&Ls) to refinance home mortgages. Second, Congress passed the National Housing Act of 1934 to create the Federal Housing Administration (FHA) to insure mortgages, thereby limiting risk to S&Ls that financed home mortgages (McCoy and Renuart 2008). Third, Congress amended the National Housing Act to create a new government agency, the Federal National Mortgage Association, which became known as Fannie Mae, under the Department of Housing and Urban Development (HUD). Fannie Mae was authorized to acquire home mortgages from banks, thereby increasing the flow of capital and enabling banks to sell more mortgages. This legislation included government guarantees to cover losses in Fannie Mae and authorized the Treasury Department to provide low interest financing to purchase FHA-insured mortgages.

Concerned that the economy would spiral downward into a recession at the end of World War II, the federal government passed the Serviceman's Readjustment Act of 1944. This legislation further increased the role of banks as enablers of the housing market by authorizing the Veterans Administration (VA) to insure home mortgages. This legislation also extended Fannie Mae's authority to purchase VA-insured mortgages.

Fiscal crisis and expanding the secondary home mortgage market

Fannie Mae remained the only participant in the secondary mortgage market until the 1960s when President Johnson proposed the Great Society programs, which included expanding home ownership to low-income families. However, budget deficits associated with other Great Society programs and the escalating cost of the Vietnam War stretched the state's fiscal capacity. To overcome this obstacle, with support from organizations representing home builders, real estate, mortgage bankers, labor unions (e.g., AFL-CIO, United Automobile Workers), insurance companies, and local and state government associations (CQ Almanac 1968), Congress passed the Housing and Urban

Development Act of 1968. This legislation ended Fannie Mae's thirty-year monopoly in the secondary mortgage market by splitting the old Fannie Mae into the new Fannie Mae and creating the Government National Mortgage Association (Ginnie Mae). Organized under HUD, Ginnie Mae continued to carry out Fannie Mae's original mandate to increase liquidity in the secondary mortgage market by buying government-insured mortgages.

To reduce the fiscal burden of the state, this legislation also transformed Fannie Mae from a government agency into a *government-sponsored enterprise* (GSE): a publicly traded company with government support. The new Fannie Mae was authorized to raise capital by issuing securities and use this capital to purchase more home mortgages (CQ Weekly 1998). This law also extended Fannie Mae's authority to purchase insured mortgages from the Farmers Home Administration (FmHA). Throughout this period, Fannie Mae continued to have access to low-interest-rate credit from the Treasury Department (CQ Weekly 1989c). After the government withdrew its guarantee on mortgages, Fannie Mae itself guaranteed the principal and interest on the mortgages it acquired from banks. Most important, transforming Fannie Mae from a state agency into a GSE made it a government off-balance-sheet entity, which decoupled it from Congressional budgetary oversight. These organizational and political-legal arrangements created structural holes, which provided managers at Fannie Mae with the autonomy to purchase mortgages from bank managers that were sold to homeowners with less capacity to repay (i.e., subprime). The increased risk to potential homeowners did not go unnoticed. With support from consumer organizations, William Proxmire (D-WI) introduced legislation that resulted in the Truth in Lending Act of 1968 (TILA). This legislation required lenders to disclose the terms of loans, including all fees and interests. The increased transparency allowed consumers to compare the cost of loans, thereby reducing abusive practices (McCoy and Renuart 2008) by lenders who benefited from selling a greater volume of home mortgage that charged higher interest rates.

In response to slow economic growth during the 1969–1970 recession, the housing sector was again identified as a means to stimulate economic growth. However, political coalitions inside and outside the state disagreed on the specific mechanisms to accomplish this goal. Much of the debate focused on whether to further extend Fannie

Mae's property rights to acquire conventional mortgages (i.e., those not insured by government agencies). In contrast to Federal Reserve administrators, who argued that the absence of government-underwriting protection of conventional mortgages would erode Congressional support for low- and middle-income credit programs (CQ Almanac 1970), the Secretary of HUD supported this policy. In addition, a political coalition outside the state consisting of the banking, housing, real estate, and the insurance sectors – all of which would benefit from Fannie Mae's increased capacity to acquire home mortgages – lobbied for this legislation. Organizations in this political coalition included the Federal Home Loan Bank Board, National Association of Home Builders, National Association of Real Estate Boards, Home Manufacturing Association, American Bankers Association, United States Savings and Loan League, and the Life Insurance Association of America (CQ Almanac 1970). In response to pressure from this political coalition, Congress passed the Emergency Home Finance Act of 1970 authorizing Fannie Mae to purchase conventional mortgages (CQ Almanac 1970).

This legislation also created another GSE, Federal Home Loan Mortgage Corporation, commonly known as Freddie Mac. Like Fannie Mae, Freddie Mac was authorized to purchase conventional mortgages and hold them in its portfolio. Oversight for Freddie Mac was given to the Federal Home Loan Bank Board, which was also responsible to oversee S&Ls. Freddie Mac's charter also includes the right to pool mortgages into bonds and sell securities in them (CQ Weekly 1989a, 1998). These *mortgage-backed securities* (MBSs) are derivative contracts whose value is derived from an underlying commodity (i.e., home mortgages). Freddie Mac purchased home mortgages from banks, pooled them to create bonds, and issued securities in the bonds that were sold to investors. The cash flow from MBSs is derived from the principal and interest payments of homeowners. Investors in these financial instruments included large institutional investors such as pension funds and insurance companies (CQ Almanac 2003; CQ Weekly 1993). In response to a cash flow crisis in the housing market during the back-to-back recession in the early 1980s, Congress extended Fannie Mae's property rights to create MBSs (CQ Weekly 1989a). Extending the property rights of GSEs substantially increased their capacity to increase liquidity in the home mortgage market. However, in the absence of concomitant change in government (i.e., third-party) oversight, these arrangements created more structural holes and opportunities for financial wrongdoing.

To summarize, three critical changes occurred in organizational and political-legal arrangements during this policy period (1930s–1970) that contributed to a turning point in corporate–state relations. First, Fannie Mae was transformed from a government agency that enabled the market to a GSE that participated in financial markets (e.g., creating MBSs and selling securities in them). Freddie Mac was also created as a GSE and allocated similar property rights. As GSEs, Fannie Mae and Freddie Mac were the Executive Branch's' off-balance sheet entities, which decoupled them from Congressional oversight. Newly created structural holes provided managers at Fannie and Freddie with the autonomy to lower their MBSs underwriting standards, which they did in 2006 and 2007 just when the housing market bubble grew. This untimely decision exposed Fannie and Freddie to additional risk. Second, organizing oversight of Fannie and Freddie under HUD increased regulatory complexity in this economic sector, which was already regulated by a complex of subnational and federal state agencies. Third, the federal government withdrew its guarantee of principal and interest payments on MBSs in the event that homeowners default. However, third-party rating agencies (e.g., Moody's Investor Services) assumed an implicit government guarantee and exercised autonomy by giving Fannie and Freddie high securities ratings on MBSs. These securities were sold to investors, many of whom continued to assume that they were backed by government guarantees.

Policy period II: economic constraints, political conflict, and expanding financial markets, 1970–1991

After Congress extended GSEs' right to issue MBSs, banks realized the capital accumulation opportunities in this lucrative market and mobilized politically to gain access to it. Throughout the middle decades of the twentieth century, banks were a low-profit and low-risk economic sector. However, national banks perceived economic downturns in the 1970s and early 1980s, globalization of the economy, and the loss of competitiveness of the dominant manufacturing sector as a political opportunity. These events coincided with legislation that legalized Political Action Committees (PACs), which gave corporations and their managers the right to make contributions to election campaigns that, in turn, gave corporations access to state managers and more opportunities to present their economic agendas (Clawson, Neustadtl, and Scott 1993).

Led by the Business Roundtable, business leaders maintained that revitalization of the economy was dependent on stimulating the housing sector and modernizing the manufacturing sector. However, banks were unable to attract enough capital to meet borrowing demand (Garten 1991; Morris 2005). Banks argued that providing the capital necessary to stimulate economic growth required redefining banking laws. State banks, S&Ls, financial services firms, and insurance firms all joined national banks and argued for expanded property rights as the means to achieve this end. However, political divisions emerged within these sectors, because extending the property rights of one economic sector encroached on markets controlled by other sectors. These differences can be summarized in the following way.

The financial services industry, which included investment banks and approximately 650 money market mutual funds, wanted to expand into traditional bank markets. The Investment Company Institute and the Securities Investment Association represent their political interests.

The insurance industry wanted to access financial markets. Extending this property right required dismantling the 1956 Bank Holding Company Act, which prohibited bank and non-bank mergers. This economic sector was represented by the American Council of Life.

National banks had two central objectives. First, they wanted to access local mortgage markets, which meant competing with state banks, credit unions, and S&Ls. National banks maintained they could better serve potential homeowners in local markets because they could draw on national pools of capital and distribute it to regions where capital shortages existed. Second, national banks wanted to dismantle the Glass–Steagall Act so they could expand into the securities markets (Reinicke 1995); instead of selling home mortgages to Fannie Mae and Freddie Mac, national banks wanted to package mortgages they held into MBSs, sell securities in them, and collect the profits themselves. Although the American Bankers Association represented 13,000 banks of various sizes, it tended to advance the interests of large national banks.

State banks, S&Ls, and credit unions argued that eliminating the Glass–Steagall Act would permit consolidation of national (commercial) banks with investment banks and give them an unfair advantage in most markets. These smaller banks also wanted to preserve their market niche as primary providers of home mortgage loans. However, the ability of S&Ls to meet demand in the home mortgage market was hampered by interest rate ceilings and high inflation in the 1970s. These conditions encouraged customers to move their deposits to organizations that offered money market funds and other accounts that paid higher interests rates (McLean and Norcea 2010: 5). The 7,000 small banks were represented by the Independent Bankers Association of America (CQ Weekly 1984b).

Creating the subprime mortgage market: dismantling bank interest rate ceilings and creating adjustable-rate mortgages

After business and political elites agreed that overcoming the protracted recession in the 1970s depended on increasing liquidity in financial markets, national banks identified banking laws as the primary obstacle to economy recovery. State banks joined this political coalition, arguing that state usury laws created obstacles to economic growth because they limited interest rates and other charges that undermined their ability to compete for deposits and supply capital to local markets. In response, with support from the Carter Administration, Congress passed the Depository Institutions Deregulation and Monetary Control Act of 1980. Title V of this legislation eliminated state interest ceilings on deposits and home mortgages. This legislation also permitted state banks, S&Ls, credit unions and small investment companies to charge interest on loans 1 percent above the Federal Reserve discount rate. Eliminating state usury laws paved the way for adjustable-rate mortgages where interest rates varied and qualification for a loan was often determined by the lower initial interest rate. Because borrowers might not be able to meet the higher payments when interest rates increased, many of these mortgages were classified as subprime.

Banks also lobbied to weaken TILA by removing credit disclosure requirements. Despite opposition from consumer organizations and House Banking Consumer Affairs Subcommittee Chairman Frank Annunzio (D-IL), Congress eliminated the requirement for banks to provide an itemized disclosure statement (e.g., interest rate hikes). Now, homeowners had to request disclosure statements describing the details of their loans (CQ Almanac 1980). By making it legal not to inform customers of the financial obligations specified in their home mortgages, this law partially decoupled banks from regulatory agencies and provided bank managers with more autonomy and opportunity for financial wrongdoing.

At the same time, the nation was confronted with a new economic phenomenon, *stagflation*: sluggish economic growth and high inflation. As long as inflation persisted, economic growth was curtailed because businesses were unwilling to invest in new production facilities when these assets would rapidly decline in value. Federal Reserve Chairman Paul Volcker's strategy to control inflation raised the prime interest rate, which reached a record high of over 20 percent in June 1981. High interest rates dramatically increased the cost of new construction, which brought the housing and construction industries to a standstill. In response, the National Association of Home Builders, and the AFL-CIO's Building that Construction Trades Department formed a political coalition that pressured President Reagan and Congress to enact policies to stimulate growth in the housing market. These historical conditions legitimated Reagan's neoliberal agenda to permit banks to enter securities, real estate, and insurance markets. Although substantial support for Reagan's proposal existed in the Senate, little support existed in the House because it entailed dismantling the Glass–Steagall Act and the Bank Holding Company Act, which would adversely affect small banks that existed in virtually every district represented in the House of Representatives.

As the number of bankruptcies escalated, the bank lobby increased its pressure on Congress. Senate Banking Committee Chairman Jake Garn (R-UT), who supported Reagan's agenda, and House Banking Chairman Fernand St. Germain (D-RI) proposed legislation to resolve this crisis. An early version of their legislation permitted banks to enter financial markets by underwriting revenue bonds and offering Money Market Mutual Fund accounts. However, state banks opposed this legislation, arguing that it would give large banks an unfair advantage over banks competing for deposits in local markets. Investment banks and securities firms also opposed allowing banks to enter the bond market. One of the most vocal critics of the bill was Senator Al D'Amato (D-NY), who represented a state where many of the nation's large investment banks and securities firms were located.

To mediate this conflict, Congress modified the bill to only permit banks to offer Money Market Deposit accounts. The securities industry

agreed to this change because, unlike the Money Market Mutual
Funds, these accounts did not allow commercial banks to compete
directly with investment banks. The bill also appeased small banks by
allowing them to expand their lending activities. Under certain conditions, the bill also permitted banks to merge with thrifts. Most
important, the final version of the Garn–St. Germain Act permitted
state banks to sell adjustable-rate mortgages (CQ Weekly 1984d).
Together with the weakened disclosure requirements under the revised
TILA, adjustable-rate mortgages created more opportunities for lenders to sell higher-profit mortgages to consumers who may not be able
to meet their payments after interest rates increased.

Banks received national media attention in 1984 when bank failures
broke the post-Depression era record and one of the largest regional
banks, Continental Illinois National Bank and Trust of Chicago, failed
to meet its capital adequacy requirements. Although Continental Trust
was a state bank, it received a $4.5 billion federal government bailout
because the Reagan Administration feared that allowing it to fail would
result in a run on the bank's $41 billion in assets (CQ Weekly 1985a,
1985b). This decision represents the first major instances of the informal "too big to fail" policy. It also increased political conflict between
large and small banks. Small banks argued that this bailout represented
the creation of a two-class bank system where small banks would be
permitted to fail and large banks would be bailed out by the federal
government (CQ Almanac 1984b).

Non-bank banks: corporate diversification into financial markets

Despite objections from small banks, Reagan continued to pursue his
neoliberal agenda and appointed executives from the private sector to
key government agencies, including Donald Regan, former chairman of
investment bank Merrill Lynch, as Secretary of the Treasury. He also
appointed C. Todd Conover, a banking and management consultant,
as Comptroller of the Currency, which is responsible for regulating
4,800 national banks and approving applications for bank charters,
branch offices, mergers, and new services (e.g., discount brokerages).

As political momentum for bank reform increased in the Executive
Branch, more corporations viewed financial markets as lucrative profit-
making opportunities and lobbied for access to them (CQ Weekly

1984b). However, diversification into financial markets required that corporations circumvent the primary purpose of the Bank Holding Company Act: to separate bank from non-bank financial activities. A major breakthrough in this political stalemate occurred when corporations identified a loophole in how the Bank Holding Company Act defined banks: organizations that offered commercial loans and demand deposits (e.g., savings and checking accounts). Corporations argued that if a firm engages in only one of these activities, it is not a bank and is not subject to federal bank laws (CQ Weekly 1984b).

To exploit this loophole, several large corporations in retail, real estate, insurance, and investment banking applied for bank charters. Despite continued opposition from national banks, the Comptroller of the Currency granted these charters. Taking advantage of the loophole was typically done by creating legally independent subsidiary corporations. To illustrate, Sears, Roebuck and Co. created subsidiaries that provided a range of financial products, including credit cards, insurance, money market accounts, bank transactions using automated teller machines, and buying and selling real estate, stocks, and bonds (CQ Almanac 1984b).

Banks' political response to the loophole

After corporations obtained the right to enter financial markets, national banks attempted to access these markets by exploiting the same loophole in the Bank Holding Company Act. Although the dual subnational state and federal regulatory structure made entering financial markets more complicated for banks, national banks exploited financially weak states to circumvent federal law. Eager to attract business during this protracted economic downturn, subnational states were receptive to cooperating with national banks. South Dakota, which had liberal interstate banking laws, was the first state to create a non-bank loophole permitting banks to create *non-bank subsidiaries*: firms owned by national bank-holding companies that offer non-bank products and services such as insurance, equities, and investment services. The "South Dakota loophole" was named after two 1983 subnational state banking laws. The first law authorized bank-holding companies located out-of-state to acquire South Dakota banks and incorporate them as subsidiaries or create subsidiary banks with a South Dakota charter. The second law gave South Dakota banks

, authority to own insurance firms that operated out-of-state. Together, these laws allowed national banks to diversify into non-bank markets. Eager to generate revenues, the "South Dakota Loophole" initiated a "race to the bottom." Soon, other subnational states passed laws that provided national banks with the right to enter markets not permitted under federal law (CQ Weekly 1984b).

After the Comptroller of the Currency approved national bank applications to open non-bank subsidiaries, political conflict escalated when the insurance industry intensified its lobby effort to protect its markets. Insurance companies were supported by Federal Reserve Chairman Paul Volcker, who maintained that the actions of national banks were blatant attempts to circumvent federal law and refused to approve these bank charters. In response, banks and financial firms filed lawsuits against the Federal Reserve in the US Circuit Court of Appeals and in the Supreme Court (CQ Weekly 1984b). Both courts ruled that the Federal Reserve's actions were illegal, which paved the way for more subnational states to follow the South Dakota model.

In response to the expansion of national banks into local markets, several state banks and state bank regulators argued that these arrangements allowed national banks to siphon capital away from communities and invest it in more lucrative national and global markets. To block national banks from entering state markets, some states refused to grant state charters to national banks and developed pacts with other states to permit branch banking across state lines (CQ Weekly 1984g). Although Maine and Alaska were the only states that allowed state banks to open interstate branches prior to 1984 (CQ Weekly 1984b), state banks in New England, the West, and the Southeast formed pacts to engage in interstate banking.

In response to this political strategy by subnational states, national banks renewed their political strategy at the federal level, where they maintained that these organizational and political-legal arrangements gave unfair advantages to financial firms and insurance companies by permitting them to enter bank markets. National banks argued that "levelling the playing field" required dismantling the Glass–Steagall Act and the Bank Holding Company Act (CQ Weekly 1984c). Senators Al D'Amato (R-NY) and Daniel Patrick Moynihan (D-NY), whose home state was the corporate headquarters of several large national banks, argued that the current arrangements unfairly allowed state banks to form regional agreements and open out-of-state branches while refusing state charters for national banks, which restricted them from entering local markets (CQ Weekly 1984e, 1984f). Although disagreements continued to exist among the insurance companies, securities firms, and small banks, they unified politically on this issue and maintained that dismantling the Glass–Steagall and the Bank Holding Company Acts would result in a few giant banks with control over banking, financial, and insurance markets.

Despite opposition in Congress, neoliberals in the Reagan Administration continued to assert their agenda to dismantle the Glass–Steagall Act. As the Administration became increasingly impatient with resistance in Congress, it threatened to grant more charters to financial firms to engage in banking activities and allow national banks to open out-of-state non-bank subsidiaries. These Executive Branch threats raised concerns among some members of Congress and Federal Reserve Chairman Paul Volcker, who argued that doing nothing would create two banking systems, with one removed from federal regulatory control, thereby increasing risk that would result in a financial crisis. Volcker stated:

> I can well visualize the day, if we don't act and all the states go their own way and all the loopholes are exploited, that in a few years, we'll be back here and we will have a great crisis. (CQ Almanac 1984b)

Expanding the MBSs market: creating more risks and opportunities for financial wrongdoing

After a protracted debate, members of Congress withdrew their bill to overhaul the bank and financial sectors. However, the Reagan Administration was not deterred and supported investment banks' effort to gain access to the MBSs market. Although the Executive Branch presented the narrower Secondary Mortgage Market Enhancement Act of 1984 as a benefit to the public by stimulating the housing industry, the primary author of the bill was a trader for the investment bank Salomon Brothers, Lewis Ranieri. This legislation removed many restrictions on MBSs (CQ Almanac 1984a), thereby permitting banks and financial firms to participate in this market (CQ Weekly 1984c, 1984h, 1984i; Gotham 2006: 260). This pivotal legislation "sanctioned the *securitization* of mortgages on the secondary market" (Smith 2012: 224) and affirmed a June court ruling that permitted banks to acquire a subsidiary to broker securities, which partially achieved their goal to participate in the MBSs market (CQ Almanac 1984a; CQ Weekly 1984i, 1985b, 2005). It also decoupled some financial firms from government oversight by exempting issuers of MBSs from registering with the Securities and Exchange Commission (SEC) (CQ Weekly 1984a, 1984e).

By decoupling financial firms from the SEC, which is the agency with primary responsibility for financial oversight, this provision created more structural holes that gave managers unprecedented autonomy in issuing MBSs. These financial managers exercised their autonomy by placing MBSs on off-balance-sheet entities. Although managers in the manufacturing sector placed physical assets (e.g., steel mills, computers) in off-balance-sheet entities (Prechel 2016), placing derivative contracts off-balance-sheet introduces a much higher degree of risk and violates the intent of the general accounting rule governing these entities. Most important, home mortgages are not passive assets and, therefore, do not meet the traditional criteria for off-balance-sheet treatment. Instead, home mortgages are affected by a long chain of decision-makers, which makes it impossible to understand or predict the risk associated with them. This chain of decision-makers begins with real-estate brokers who under the revised TILA are not obligated to inform clients of the repayment conditions in adjustable-rate mortgages. Also, assuming that houses would continue to increase in value, some middle- and upper-middle-class homeowners knowingly made decisions to purchase homes that they could not afford with the intention of selling them at a profit before interest rates increased on their adjustable-rate mortgages (Financial Crisis Inquiry Commission 2011).

Risk in financial markets was also increased by a change in the arrangements between firms and rating agencies. From the time when John Moody created the securities rating system until the 1970s, investors paid securities rating agencies. However, beginning in the 1970s, issuers of securities paid securities rating agencies (Lavelle 2013: 181). This interorganizational arrangement created conflicts of interest and incentives for corporations to terminate contracts with the rating agency that gave them low securities ratings. Soon, rating agencies enabled corporations to participate in financial markets by sanctioning MBSs, many of which were derived from high-risk subprime loans. As the subprime mortgage market expanded, information asymmetry in these interorganizational arrangements provided banks and financial firms with the capacity to pass more high-risk securities onto investors.

As the manufacturing sector continued to weaken, this political coalition pressured Congress to enact legislation to increase its capacity to raise capital. In response, Congress included a provision in the Tax Reform Act of 1986 (TRA86) that eliminated the New Deal tax on capital transfers from subsidiaries to parent companies. Soon, corporations began to restructure their divisions, which are part of the same legal entity as the central office, as subsidiaries and issue stock in them; parent companies can sell up to 50 percent of a subsidiary's stock and retain ownership control over it. This multilayer-subsidiary form has a parent-holding company at the top of the organizational hierarchy that operates as a financial management company over its legally independent subsidiaries (Prechel 2000: 209–210), which provides an organizational structure for non-banks such as Sears to create subsidiaries and diversify into financial markets. Additionally, this legislation eliminated the need to report capital transfers among subsidiaries and parent companies to the Internal Revenue Service (IRS). By decoupling corporations from this third-party oversight agency, these organizational and political-legal arrangements created structural holes and opportunities for managers to transfer capital among corporate entities in ways that bolstered their balance sheets.

The TRA86 also facilitated securitization by creating the Real Estate Investment Mortgage Conduit (REMIC). Although investment banks were the primary beneficiaries of this new financial instrument, commercial banks and S&Ls also used REMICs to shift the risk of their fixed-rate mortgages, which lose value if interest rates increase, to MBSs (Johnson and Kwak 2010: 73). REMICs, as a means to financialize the mortgage market, were preceded by Real Estate Investment Trusts (REITs), which were created in the 1960s to increase the flow of capital into commercial real estate. Structured like mutual funds, which provide investors with opportunities to invest in income-producing assets, REITs became popular with investors and rapidly expanded because they must pay 90 percent of their taxable income as dividends. REITs soon expanded outside the US and became one of the primary mechanism to spread MBSs to global markets (Gotham 2006).

By increasing corporations' access to equity markets, the TRA86 reduced manufacturing corporations' dependence on bank loans while increasing profits for investment banks who underwrote securities issued by subsidiary corporations. In response, banks renewed their political efforts and continued to argue that these organizational and political-legal arrangements unfairly favored non-banks. By the late 1980s, their long-term lobby efforts resulted in several political successes. One important victory occurred in 1987 when Reagan replaced Paul Volcker with Alan Greenspan to head the Federal Reserve. In the first year of his appointment, Greenspan, who was deeply committed to neoliberal ideology, abrogated the provision in the Glass–Steagall Act that prohibited bank affiliates from underwriting asset-backed securities (Prechel 2000: 213). A year later, in 1988, when banks were making little progress in Congress, Greenspan interpreted Glass–Steagall in a way that allowed bank-holding companies to create non-bank subsidiary corporations to underwrite and sell securities (CQ Weekly 1989b). Permitting banks and non-banks to engage in securitization created new risk and opportunities for financial wrongdoing. However, Greenspan and other neoliberals repeatedly stated the risks in this market were well understood and did not threaten the stability of the economy.

Resolving the S&L crisis and more inroads into interstate banking

With little success in Congress, national banks shifted their political strategy and launched an extensive media campaign to convince the public that current regulations undermined the ability of US banks to compete with foreign banks, which threatened long-term economic growth. As the S&L crisis dragged on, the national bank lobby argued that S&Ls were inherently unstable. Banks maintained that their access to national pools of capital gave them the capacity to bring stability to local markets. In response, Treasury Secretary Nicholas Brady proposed allowing banks to enter financial services and insurance markets. However, the insurance lobby mobilized against encroachment into its market and was joined by consumer organizations who continued to argue that bank consolidation would create more risks and costs to consumers. A "Main Street Coalition" quickly emerged consisting of small banks, farmers, small-business owners, and consumer groups to oppose national banks (CQ Almanac 1991). Together with the insurance industry lobby, this coalition convinced Congress to prohibit banks from entering insurance markets (CQ Weekly 1994b). In response, Congress passed the Federal Deposit Insurance Corporation Improvement Act of 1991. Although narrower in scope than national banks' initial proposal, it made S&Ls takeover candidates, which achieved the long-term agenda of national banks to gain access to the home mortgage market.

To summarize, the second policy period (1970–1991) further decoupled banks and financial firms from government oversight in ways that created opportunities for financial wrongdoing. Unlike the first policy period when most of the changes occurred among political-legal arrangements, *both* organizational and political-legal arrangements changed in the second policy period. There are three critical components of the emergent organizational and political-legal arrangements. First, among the most important change was a little-known provision in the TRA86, which made subsidiaries viable throughout corporate America. Now, non-bank corporations could enter the home mortgage market through legally independent subsidiary corporations. To illustrate, soon after this legislation was enacted, General Electric's subsidiary GE Capital became one of the largest participants in the home mortgage market. Second, although bank-holding companies could organize their operations as subsidiary under the Banking Act of 1933, they were not permitted to acquire S&Ls and state banks. When this legislation was overturned, bank-holding companies began to acquire these smaller financial institutions, which gave them access to the home mortgage market. Together these political-legal arrangements increased organizational size and complexity, with various subsidiary corporations operating in different financial markets. Third, changes in organizational arrangements occurred without concomitant changes in oversight agencies. These new organizational and political-legal arrangements had two important outcomes. On the one hand, they created a patchwork of national and subnational state agencies responsible to oversee various legally independent subsidiaries organized under a single parent company. On the other, in the absence of changes in oversight that paralleled these new organizational arrangements, no third-party state agencies had the authority or responsibility to assess the financial integrity of the entire conglomerate. Together these organizational and political-legal arrangements created multiple structural holes that provided managers with the autonomy to engage in financial wrongdoing, which included shifting high-risk MBSs into off-balance-sheet entities that were originally intended to hold passive assets.

Policy period III: more contested terrain and creation of the Finance, Insurance, and Real Estate sector, 1990s

Despite court rulings and Executive Branch decisions that forced a reluctant Congress to enact legislation providing banks with greater access to financial markets, many members of Congress continued to express concern over "systemic risk" and "too big to fail." Uneasy about Congressional opposition to these political-legal arrangements, banks continued their media campaign and appealed to neoliberal advocates in the Executive Branch, asserting that government interference undermined market efficiencies. Two historical conditions strengthened banks' political strategy. First, despite massive tax breaks and protectionist policies (Prechel 1990, 2000), it became clear that the manufacturing sector would not return to its dominant position in the global economy. Second, financial markets, especially derivatives markets, were considered a new growth area in the global economy. In response to these historical contingencies, banks and financial organizations formed a political coalition to pressure state managers to enact interstate banking laws to gain greater access to financial markets. This agenda received support in Congress because it coincided with the government's agenda to facilitate economic growth.

Although President Clinton was not interested in bank policy, he opposed permitting national banks to engage in interstate banking. However, in 1993, Clinton appointed Robert Rubin, a former co-chairman of Goldman Sachs, to head his newly created National Economic Council, which provides economic policy advice to the president. In 1995, Rubin was appointed Secretary of the Treasury, where he could directly affect the political embeddedness of the banking and financial sectors. Like Greenspan, Rubin endorsed neoliberal market efficiency assumptions and became one of the most vocal advocates for expanding bank property rights. Greenspan and Rubin also argued that expanding the secondary mortgage market would facilitate economic growth. With strong allies in the Executive Branch, national banks pursued their agenda in Congress. The bank lobby maintained that eliminating restrictions on bank mergers would encourage financially stronger banks to acquire weaker banks, thereby creating stability and efficiency in the banking system as a whole (Morris 2005). National banks also opposed two other components of the political-legal arrangement designed to stabilize financial markets. On the one hand, they argued that regulations requiring capitalization of subsidiaries engaged in interstate banking drained capital away from investment in productive economic activity. On the other hand, banks argued that the federalist state structure, which provides states with the right to regulate bank subsidiaries located in their state, was complex and costly because banks were required to report to several different agencies. Both arguments appealed to neoliberals, who argued that markets provided adequate information to decision-makers and government regulations undermined market efficiency. Although consumer organizations and small banks continued to oppose further consolidation in the banking industry, their efforts were dwarfed by the well-financed national bank lobby, which developed widespread support in Congress for interstate branch banking (CQ Almanac 1994).

The long-standing political conflicts among economic sectors over non-bank activities were resolved in 1994 when two key parts of the proposed legislation were dropped. First, Senator Christopher Dodd (D-CT) withdrew his provision that restricted banks from selling insurance (CQ Weekly 1994a). This compromise satisfied national banks that objected to political-legal arrangements permitting insurance companies to enter bank markets but restricted banks from entering insurance markets. Second, the restriction against creating new branch banks across state lines was dropped. This provision signified the defeat of smaller state banks; now smaller state banks would be acquired by larger national banks or forced to compete with them. The final version of the legislation reaffirmed the federalist state structure, which authorized subnational states to decide whether national banks could open branch banks in their state. If passed, this law would achieve banks' long-term agenda of expanding geographically without setting up independent capitalized subsidiary corporations.

Although Clinton continued to oppose this legislation, he needed Congressional approval to fulfil his campaign promise to create one hundred community development banks. To obtain support for his social agenda, Clinton compromised by supporting the provision that permitted national banks to merge with or acquire out-of-state S&Ls and organize them as branches instead of capitalized subsidiaries (CQ

Weekly 1994a, 1994c). The subsequent Riegle-Neal Interstate Banking and Branching Efficiency Act of 1994 created two mechanisms for banks to expand into new markets. First, in 1995, national bank-holding companies could acquire banks in any state. Second, in 1997, national banks were permitted to convert their state subsidiaries into branches.

This legislation dramatically reduced the cost for national banks to enter financial markets, which made more capital available to pursue their consolidation strategies. National banks took advantage of these political-legal arrangements and created giant bank conglomerates with organizational entities in many locations selling many financial products. These complex organizational structures restricted information flows and increased the problem of bounded rationality. Information flows in this complex structure were hampered because national banks may have multiple subsidiaries with an unknown number of off-balance-sheet entities containing multiple MBSs and other financial instruments. Within these organizational and political-legal arrangements, traders had the autonomy to create MBSs and place them in off-balance-sheet entities. Moreover, if traders lose money in these complex organizations, unless the parent company has adequate oversight mechanisms, they have the autonomy to continue trading to cover their losses before they are discovered. In some cases, such as the 2012 $6 billon loss at JPMorgan, traders continue to take risks and mount even greater losses.

The Private Securities Litigation Reform Act of 1995 and the Gramm–Leach–Bliley Financial Services Modernization Act of 1999

In a related policy arena, corporations mobilized politically to further weaken consumers' and investors' rights by making it more difficult to bring class-action lawsuits against managers and related occupations for engaging or collaborating in financial wrongdoing. Their first major legal victory occurred in 1991 when the Supreme Court ruled that shareholders must bring legal actions within one year of discovering a violation and not more than three years following a potential fraud. Then, in 1994, a Supreme Court ruling limited the capacity of investors to hold lawyers liable for giving advice that aided and abetted white-collar crime (US Congress 1994). In addition, a political coalition led

by the financial services industry maintained that securities and racketeering laws permitted unwarranted and meritless securities fraud
litigation and pressured Congress to protect managers, lawyers, and
financial advisors from "frivolous" investor lawsuits (US Congress
1991, 1994). The Republican-controlled Congress passed this legislation, but it was vetoed by Clinton. However, Congress overrode
Clinton's veto. This law, the Private Securities Litigation Reform Act,
further decoupled corporations from government oversight agencies by
substantially weakened shareholder and consumer protections in the
Securities Exchange Act of 1933, the Glass–Steagall Act, the Securities
Exchange Act of 1934, and the Racketeering Influence and Corrupt
Organizations Act of 1970. The corporate–state relations made it more
difficult to use securities laws to bring lawsuits against management,
accountants, lawyers, and consultants who made speculative statements about corporate finances (CQ Weekly 1995), which created
more opportunities for these social actors to misrepresent banks' financial strength.

After two decades of incremental changes by the Courts, Congress,
and the Executive Branch, the federal government no longer enforced
key provisions in the Glass–Steagall Act and the Bank Holding
Company Act. However, the banks were concerned that a new
Executive Branch could reverse these decisions. Knowing that they
had support from key members of Congress and the Executive
Branch, in April 1998, Citibank and Travelers insurance initiated
a merger to create Citigroup. Then, Travelers acquired the investment
bank Salomon Brothers. If successful, the $70 billion combination
would form the largest banking, financial services, and insurance conglomerate in the world (Lipin 1998).

The Citibank–Travelers proposed merger coincided with a political
strategy by neoliberal advocates inside the federal government to lega-
lize mergers among financial, insurance, and real estate (i.e., FIRE)
corporations. This effort was led by Senator Phil Gramm (R-TX),
Chair of the powerful Senate Financial Services Committee, and
Secretary of the Treasury Robert Rubin. Both stressed the importance
of expanding bank access to capital markets to increase
US competitiveness in global financial markets. After resolving disagreements on oversight, Congress passed the Gramm–Leach–Bliley
Act in November 1999 (CQ Almanac 1999). In addition to permitting
consolidation of these economic sectors, this legislation allowed the

largest one hundred US banks to create subsidiaries to engage in securities underwriting, if the parent company met predetermined debt rating requirements. The Gramm–Leach–Bliley Act was the outcome of a twenty-nine-year political strategy (1970–1999) by national banks to gain access to financial and insurance markets, which included the lucrative home mortgage market. In the end, extensive changes in corporate property rights allowed most corporations to provide multiple financial services, including home mortgages, securities underwriting, insurance underwriting, advising on mergers and acquisitions, stock analyses, and investment advice.

Although consumer organizations lobbied to preserve insurance industry oversight by states, which they perceived as more consumer oriented, the bill shifted partial oversight to federal regulators (CQ Almanac 1999). This legislation also transferred regulatory power from the Federal Reserve over non-bank banks and other entities to the SEC because some foreign governments required SEC oversight. These changes contributed to the patchwork of oversight agencies to monitor banks, financial firms, and FIRE conglomerates. To illustrate, although the Federal Reserve retained regulatory control over federally insured national banks, it did have the authority to impose capital adequacy requirements on bank subsidiaries and affiliates. Authority over capital adequacy was allocated to their functional regulator, which was typically the SEC or the subnational state where these corporations and their subsidiaries were located. Further, no single agency had authority to ensure that all parts of the regulatory system fit into a coherent oversight mechanism. Moreover, underfunded since the 1980s when the Reagan Administration cut its budget, the SEC did not have the resources to oversee these large and complex corporate structures. The absence of adequate third-party oversight created opportunities for financial wrongdoing. By 2003, SEC investigations revealed that "inappropriate influence" by investment bankers created conflicts for research analysts in JPMorgan's investment banking subsidiary, JPMorgan Securities Inc. (Securities and Exchange Commission 2003). Similar violations of securities rules and laws occurred in Bear Stearns, Salomon Brothers, Goldman Sachs, Merrill Lynch, Lehman Brothers, and Morgan Stanley. In short, despite claims by corporate executives and lobbyists asserting that management would eliminate potential conflicts of interests by creating internal firewalls if corporations were permitted to engage in multiple financial activities, in the absence of adequate third-party oversight, management bridged structural holes and engaged in financial wrongdoing.

Political coalitions creating more opportunities for wrongdoing: over-the-counter derivatives trading

Like banks, New Dealers tightly regulated the energy sector because capitalist growth and development was dependent on this vital resource. However, similar to banks, the energy industry argued for decades that the regulatory structure undermined market efficiency, restricted innovation, and undermined its capacity to meet the nation's growing energy needs. In the late 1990s, when Congress was due to reauthorize the Commodity Exchange Act of 1936, the energy industry viewed this as an opportunity to advance their agenda to develop a natural gas derivative market. The energy sector was joined by the FIRE sector, which argued that cumbersome regulations undermined their capacity to compete with foreign banks in the global derivative market.

The energy and FIRE coalition launched a well-financed lobby campaign to allow derivatives to be traded on unregulated exchanges (e.g., inside the corporation). However, they failed to obtain the necessary votes to pass the proposed legislation because oversight agencies and members of Congress continued to express concern over risk in derivatives markets. After several unsuccessful attempts to pass this legislation, Senator Gramm (R-TX) and the Republican leaders in the House attached the Commodity Futures Modernization Act of 2000 to the 11,000 page Consolidated Appropriations Act for FY2001. This omnibus budget bill was passed with virtually no discussion of the attached derivatives trading legislation and President Clinton signed it into law on December 21, 2000.

A crucial provision of the Commodity Futures Modernization Act exempted many high-risk derivative trades from regulatory oversight by permitting energy and FIRE-sector corporations to create over-the-counter derivatives trading exchanges (e.g., inside the firm) (US Congress 2002: 3; US Senate 1999). Although banks were previously permitted to trade certain over-the-counter derivatives (e.g., foreign exchange rates), this legislation greatly expanded energy and FIRE-sector firms' capacity to create new financial instruments, including MBSs. By removing these transactions from public scrutiny and government oversight, this legislation created more structural holes that increased information asymmetry and managers' autonomy to engage in financial wrongdoing.

Crisis in the FIRE sector

The MBSs market grew at a rapid pace after bank conglomerates, investment banks, and financial services firms became participants in this market. Moreover, the percentage of home-loan originations by Fannie and Freddie dropped from approximately 50 percent in 2002 to 30 percent in 2005. This market growth occurred, in part, because these corporations had the human capital to carve MBSs into tranches with different risk levels that appealed to investors with different risk tolerance (Johnson and Kwak 2010: 124). They also had the social capital – via their access to a large network of investors – to sell these securities. Although the risk of securities in different tranches varied, rating agencies continue to assume that the value of the underlying commodities (i.e., home mortgages) would continue to increase like they did in the past and gave MBSs high ratings. These securities were sold to investors throughout the global economy, including other banks, corporations, mutual funds, pension funds, governments, municipalities, school districts, and individuals. Moreover, because MBSs created steady income streams, most FIRE-sector firms kept some MBSs and placed them off-balance-sheet. Prior to the emergence of these organizational arrangements, banks' balance sheets were not particularly transparent. However, because interest rates on mortgages did not vary substantially over time and defaults were relatively predictable, banks' loan balances were considered adequate representations of their financial strength. In contrast, derivatives can "dramatically gain or lose value in seconds, which diminish the reliability of balance sheets as measures of corporations' financial stability" (Steinherr 2000: 203).

To summarize, the third policy period represents a continuation of the neoliberal historical trajectory, which created more structural holes and opportunities for managers to engage in financial wrongdoing. Although the 2000 Enron crisis exposed the false assumptions of market fundamentalism that "inefficiencies of markets are relatively small and the inefficiencies of governments are relatively large" (Stiglitz 2002: 219), the 2008 financial crisis was caused by the same false assumption. Like natural gas derivatives that were placed in off-balance-sheet entities (Prechel 2003), MBSs lost value because of the decline in value of the underlying commodity (e.g., houses) they were derived from. Although MBSs began to lose value in 2007, structural holes in the new organizational and political-legal arrangements created opportunities for FIRE-sector firms to hide their losses. By the summer of 2008, GSEs and FIRE-sector corporations were no longer able to cover their losses. Fannie Mae and Freddie Mac, which were the federal government's off-balance-sheet entities, were backed by an implicit government guarantee that became explicit on September 7, 2008, when the government bailed them out.

However, FIRE conglomerates and other firms did not have a government guarantee. When Lehman Brothers failed, it set off a panic because no one knew the extent of "toxic assets" on FIRE-sector off-balance-sheet entities. Within days trust disappeared, banks and other corporations would not loan capital to one another, and credit markets came to a standstill, which resulted in the 2008 financial meltdown (Financial Crisis Inquiry Commission 2011). The crisis quickly spread from the FIRE sector to other economic sectors with financial services subsidiaries that included giant retail and manufacturing corporations such as Ford, General Electric, General Motors, and Sears.

Conclusion

Whereas government policies to facilitate capitalist growth and development between the 1930s and 1960s created a secondary home mortgage market, incremental changes in corporate–state relations between 1970 and 2000 transformed banks from market enablers to participants in the secondary mortgage market and other financial markets. This transformation was the outcome of a long-term political strategy by corporate managers who used the organizational resources under their control to access financial markets. These changes decoupled corporations from government oversight, which shifted banks, financial firms, and financial subsidiaries in manufacturing and retail firms toward the politically disembedded end of the embedded–disembedded continuum. These new organizational and political-legal arrangements created structural holes and opportunities for financial wrongdoing.

During the early stages of this process, corporations aligned their capital accumulation agenda with a supportive Reagan Administration that embraced neoliberalism and pressured Congress to enact policies to re-regulate financial markets. Once policies were enacted and the state structures were established to implement them, corporate lobbyists used existing legislation and state structures to legitimate future policy initiatives to advance their agendas. To illustrate, after the laws were changed to permit national banks to create non-bank subsidiaries, they argued that these political-legal arrangements undermined efficiency. Using this argument, national banks pursued a long-term lobby effort to pressure the Executive Branch and Congress to transform their subsidiaries into branch banks, which are not capitalized and are lightly regulated.

As the mortgage market expanded, financial managers used their human capital to create MBSs and off-balance-sheet entities and place MBSs in these entities. Then, managers used their social capital to market securities. In a separate policy arena, corporations successfully lobbied to weaken the truth in lending laws by removing credit disclosure requirements to mortgage holders and securities laws holding managers and professional responsible for providing misleading information to investors. The costs for engaging in wrongdoing were substantially diminished when corporate elites succeeded in convincing Congress and the Courts to enact laws that limited the capacity of investors to hold financial managers and professionals liable for giving advice that aided and abetted financial wrongdoing. Together, these organizational and political-legal arrangements increased risk in this market and contributed to the rapid expansion of MBSs. However, little information existed on the financial integrity of these financial instruments. When Lehman Brothers failed in 2008, it set off a panic because no one knew the extent of toxic MBSs assets on FIRE-sector off-balance-sheet entities.

It is noteworthy that UK Prime Minister Margaret Thatcher and other British elites were equally committed to neoliberalism as Reagan and US elites. Despite this similarity, the UK did not endorse market fundamentalism to the same degree as the US.[1] Several differences between the US and the UK explain why risk and financial wrongdoing were more widespread in the US. First, since the 1930s, the US government enacted legislation and created

---

[1] However, in some areas, the UK provided more property rights to financial organizations than the US In these cases, US parent companies established subsidiaries in the UK to exploit those opportunities.

state structures to facilitate the flow of capital into the housing sector as a means to stimulate economic growth. As a result, the secondary mortgage market expanded at a faster rate in the US than in other countries. As this market expanded, GSEs became the political target of bank-holding companies, which viewed the secondary mortgage market as a lucrative capital accumulation opportunity. The organizational and political-legal arrangements that provided corporations with access to this lucrative market also decoupled firms from government oversight, thereby creating structural holes in the form of off-balance-sheet entities that created widespread opportunities for financial wrongdoing.

Second, the sheer complexity of US corporate–state relations created opportunities for financial wrongdoing. This complexity has its roots in the origins and subsequent history of the US federalist state structure that resulted in two distinct banking systems. When capital accumulation was constrained in the 1970s, economic conflict emerged among these banking sectors over access to financial markets that was manifested as political conflict. As banks restructured and gained access to more markets, their structural complexity increased. In the absence of concomitant change in the political-legal arrangements responsible to oversee them, banks and financial firms became decoupled from government oversight, creating structural holes that provided managers with autonomy to engage in financial wrongdoing.

A third unique characteristic of US corporate–state relations is the amount of resources that corporate elites are permitted to spend on politics. After the corporate lobby succeeded in changing the campaign finance laws in the 1970s, elites used the organizational resources at their disposal to shape corporate–state relations in ways that advanced their capital-accumulation agendas. To illustrate, during the Clinton Administration, when several major financial reforms were enacted, the financial sector spent more money on campaign contributions than any other economic sector. By the late twentieth century, corporate–state relations were reconfigured in ways that achieved banks' long-term agenda to transform themselves from market enablers to participants in financial markets. This transformation permitted firms to engage in behavior that violated laws or the intent of laws established by government agencies responsible for ensuring the integrity of the financial system, or the public's understanding of the business code of conduct that consumers and investors use when making financial decisions.

References

Abbott, A. 1997. "On the concept of turning point," *Comparative and Historical Research* 16: 85–106.

Abolafia, M. 2010. "The institutional embeddedness of market failure," *Research in the Sociology of Organizations* 30B: 177–200.

Antonio, R. 1979. "The contradiction of domination and production in bureaucracy," *American Sociological Review* 44: 895–912.

Bromley P. and Powell, W. W. 2012. "From smoke and mirrors to walking the talk: Decoupling in the contemporary world," *The Academy of Management Annals* 6: 1–48.

Burt, R. 1992. *Structural Holes*. Cambridge, MA: Harvard University Press.

Campbell, J. 2010. "Neoliberalism in crisis," *Research in the Sociology of Organizations* 30B: 65–101.

Clawson, D., Neustadtl, A., and Scott, D. 1993. *Money Talks*. New York: Basic Books.

Congressional Quarterly Almanac. 1968. "Housing bill provides home-buying, riot, other aid," in *CQ Almanac 1968*: 313–335. Washington, DC: Congressional Quarterly.

Congressional Quarterly Almanac. 1970. "Congress clears emergency home finance act of 1970," in *CQ Almanac 1970*: 277–287. Washington, DC: Congressional Quarterly.

Congressional Quarterly Almanac. 1980. "Truth in lending," in *CQ Almanac 1980*: 236–237. Washington, DC: Congressional Quarterly.

Congressional Quarterly Almanac 1984a. "Mortgage bill cleared," in *CQ Almanac 1984*: 170. Washington, DC: Congressional Quarterly.

Congressional Quarterly Almanac 1984b. "Standoff blocks banking deregulation bill," in *CQ Almanac 1984*: 271–276. Washington, DC: Congressional Quarterly.

Congressional Quarterly Almanac. 1991. "Congress clears slimmed-down banking bill," in *CQ Almanac 1991*: 75–97. Washington, DC: Congressional Quarterly.

Congressional Quarterly Almanac. 1994. "Banking law undergoes revision," in *CQ Almanac 1994*: 93–100. Washington, DC: Congressional Quarterly.

Congressional Quarterly Almanac. 1999. "Overhaul enacted of rules governing the financial services industry," in *CQ Almanac 1999*: 3–31. Washington, DC: Congressional Quarterly.

Congressional Quarterly Almanac. 2003. "Mortgage regulation bill stuck," in *CQ Almanac 2003*: 4–8. Washington, DC: Congressional Quarterly.

Congressional Quarterly Weekly. 1984a. "Summary of major issues facing congress in 1984: Housing/community development," *CQ Weekly*, January 21.

Congressional Quarterly Weekly. 1984b. "Banking bill may emerge: Interstate forays by big banks revive interest in legislation," *CQ Weekly*, May 5.

Congressional Quarterly Weekly. 1984c. "Loopholes closed but deregulation differs," *CQ Weekly*, June 30.

Congressional Quarterly Weekly. 1984d. "Potential 'payment shock' ahead? Built-in mortgage rate hikes prompt new review of ARMs," *CQ Weekly*, August 4.

Congressional Quarterly Weekly. 1984e. "Mortgage backed securities bill approved," *CQ Weekly*, August 4.

Congressional Quarterly Weekly. 1984f. "Senate endorses further bank deregulation," *CQ Weekly*, September 15.

Congressional Quarterly Weekly. 1984g. "St Germain jettisons bank deregulation bills," *CQ Weekly*, September 22.

Congressional Quarterly Weekly. 1984h. "Secondary mortgage bill cleared," *CQ Weekly*, September 29.

Congressional Quarterly Weekly. 1984i. "Summary of major 1984 congressional action: Housing/development," *CQ Weekly*, October 20.

Congressional Quarterly Weekly. 1985a. "Chairman's views remain divided," *CQ Weekly*, February 2.

Congressional Quarterly Weekly. 1985b. "Deregulation debate clouded: Bank scandals prompt review to reassure investors, public," *CQ Weekly*, April 20.

Congressional Quarterly Weekly. 1989a. "A history of the thrift industry," *CQ Weekly*, February 18.

Congressional Quarterly Weekly. 1989b. "Banking: Next on agenda? Glass–Steagall," *CQ Weekly*, May 27.

Congressional Quarterly Weekly. 1989c. "GSEs: Risky but handy," *CQ Weekly*, October 4.

Congressional Quarterly Weekly. 1993. "How a secondary market works," *CQ Weekly*, May 1.

Congressional Quarterly Weekly. 1994a. "Banking: Bill on interstate branching sails though senate panel," *CQ Weekly*, February 26.

Congressional Quarterly Weekly. 1994b. "Banking: Senate votes to topple barriers, OKs interstate branching," *CQ Weekly*, April 30.

Congressional Quarterly Weekly. 1994c. "Banking: Conferees iron out final knots, combine two major bills," *CQ Weekly*, July 30.

Congressional Quarterly Weekly. 1995. "Banking: Provisions of bank bill," *CQ Weekly*, June 24.

Congressional Quarterly Weekly. 1998. "Mandates and money," *CQ Weekly*, June 13.

Congressional Quarterly Weekly. 2005. "Mortgage giants' assets setting off hill alarms," *CQ Weekly*, August 15.

Corra, M. and Willer, D. 2002. "The gatekeepers," *Sociological Theory* 22: 180–207.

Financial Crisis Inquiry Commission. 2011. *The Financial Crisis Inquiry Report*. New York: Public Affairs.

Fligstein, N. and Goldstein, A. 2010. "The anatomy of the market securitization crisis," *Research in the Sociology of Organizations* 30A: 29–70.

Gabbioneta, C., Prakash, R., and Greenwood, R. 2014. "Sustained corporate corruption and processes of institutional ascription within professional networks," *Journal of Professions and Organizations* 1: 16–32.

Garten, H. A. 1991. *Why Bank Regulation Failed*. New York: Quorum Books.

Gotham, K. 2006. "The secondary circuit of capital reconsidered," *American Journal of Sociology* 112: 231–275.

Granovetter, M. 1973. "The strength of weak ties," *American Journal of Sociology* 78: 1360–1380.

Johnson, S. and Kwak, J. 2010. *13 Bankers*. New York: Pantheon Books.

Kalberg, S. 1994. *Max Weber's Comparative–Historical Sociology*. Chicago, IL: University of Chicago Press.

Krippner, G. 2011. *Capitalizing on Crisis*. Cambridge, MA: Harvard University Press.

Lavelle, K. C. 2013. *Money and Banks in the American Political System*. New York: Cambridge University Press.

Lipin, S. 1998. "One-two punch: NationsBank to merge with BankAmerica, and that's not all," *Wall Street Journal*, April 13.

McCoy, P. A. and Renuart, E. 2008. "The legal infrastructure of subprime and nontraditional home mortgages," in N. P. Restinas and E. S. Belsky (eds.), *Borrowing to Live: Consumer and Mortgage Credit Revisited*: 110–137. Cambridge, MA: Brookings Institution Press and Harvard University Joint Center for Housing Studies.

McLean, B. and Nocera, J. 2010. *All the Devils Are Here*. New York: Portfolio/ Penguin.

Mintz, B. and Schwartz, M. 1985. *The Structure of Power in American Business*. Chicago: University of Chicago Press.

Mizruchi, M. 1982. *The American Corporate Network, 1904–1974.* Beverly Hills, CA: Sage Publications.

Morris, T. 2005. "Banks in crisis," in H. Prechel (ed.), *Research in Political Sociology: Politics and the Corporation, Vol. 14:* 151–181. Oxford: Elsevier.

O'Connor, J. 1973. *Fiscal Crisis of the State.* New York: St. Martin's Press.

Offe, C. and Wiesenthal, H. 1980. "Two logics of collective action," *Political Power and Social Theory* 1: 67–115.

Palmer, D. 2013. *Normal Organizational Wrongdoing.* Oxford: Oxford University Press.

Palmer, D. and Maher, M. 2010. "The mortgage meltdown as a normal accident," *Research in the Sociology of Organizations* 30A: 219–256.

Perrow, C. 1986. *Complex Organizations: A Critical Essay.* New York: Random House.

Pfeffer, J. and Salancik, G. R. 1978. *The External Control of Organizations: A Resource Dependence Perspective.* New York: Harper and Row.

Polanyi, K. 1944. *The Great Transformation.* Boston, MA: Beacon Press.

Prechel, H. 1990. "Steel and the State: Industry Politics and Business Policy Formation, 1940–1989," *American Sociological Review* 55: 648–668.

Prechel, H. 2000. *Big Business and the State.* Albany, NY: State University of New York Press.

Prechel, H. 2003. "Historical contingency theory, policy paradigm shifts, and corporate malfeasance at the turn of the 21st century," in B. Dobratz, L. Waldner, and T. Buzzell (eds.), *Political Sociology for the 21st Century: Research in Political Sociology, Vol. 12:* 311–340. Oxford: Elsevier.

Prechel, H. 2016. "Organizational political economy of white-collar crime," in S. Van Slyke, M. Benson, and F Cullen (eds.), *The Oxford Handbook of White-Collar Crime.* Oxford: Oxford University Press.

Prechel, H. and Morris, T. 2010. "The effects of organizational and political embeddedness on financial malfeasance in the largest U.S. corporations," *American Sociological Review* 75: 331–354.

Reinicke, W. H. 1995. *Banking, Politics and Global Finance.* Washington, DC: The Brookings Institute.

Roy, W. 1997. *Socializing Capital.* Princeton: Princeton University Press.

Securities and Exchange Commission. 2003. *Securities and Exchange Commission v. J.P. Morgan Securities Inc., 03 CV 2939 (WHP) (S.D.N.Y.).* Washington, DC: Securities and Exchange Commission.

Available from www.sec.gov/litigation/litreleases/lr18114.htm [Accessed: August 5, 2015].

Smith, H. 2012. *Who Stole the American Dream?* New York: Random House.

Steinherr, A. 2000. *Derivatives: The Wild Beast of Finance.* New York: John Wiley & Sons.

Stiglitz, J. 2002. *Globalization and Its Discontent.* New York: W.W. Norton & Company.

Sutherland, E. 1949. *White Collar Crime.* New York: Dryden.

US Congress. 1991. "Hearing: Securities investors legal rights," Committee on Energy and Commerce, House, November 21.

US Congress. 1994. "Hearing: Abandonment of the private right of action for aiding and abetting securities fraud/staff report on private securities litigation," Committee on Banking, Housing, and Urban Affairs, Senate, May 12.

US Congress. 2002. "How lax regulation and inadequate oversight contributed to the Enron collapse," House of Representatives, Minority Staff, Committee on Government Reform, 107th Congress, February 7.

US Senate. 1999. *The Financial Services and Modernization Act of 1999. Committee on Banking, Housing, and Urban Affairs. 106th Congress.* Washington, DC: Government Printing Office.

Walker, E. and Rea, C. 2014. "The political mobilization of firms and industries," *Annual Review of Sociology* 40: 281–304.

Weber, M. 1978. *Economy and Society.* Berkeley, CA: University of California Press.

Appendix

Abbreviations

AFL-CIO	American Federation of Labor and Congress of Industrial Organizations
CQ	Congressional Quarterly
FDIC	Federal Deposit Insurance Corporation
FDICIA	Federal Deposit Insurance Corporation Improvement Act
FmHA	Farmers Home Administration
FHA	Federal Housing Administration
FIRE	Finance, Insurance, and Real Estate
GSE	Government-Sponsored Enterprise
HUD	Department of Housing and Urban Development

MBSs	Mortgage-Backed Securities
REIT	Real Estate Investment Trust
REMIC	Real Estate Mortgage Investment Conduit
S&L	Savings and Loan association
SEC	Securities and Exchange Commission
TILA	Truth in Lending Act of 1968
TRA86	Tax Reform Act of 1986
VA	Veterans Administration

5 | Wrongdoing and market development: an examination of the distinct roles of trust and distrust

CHRISTOPHER B. YENKEY

Research on organizational wrongdoing has grown considerably in recent years. The focus of most recent work on wrongdoing is on better understanding the causes of organizational malfeasance and detecting its occurrence. This focus is understandable, as organization theorists are primarily interested in influences on organizational behavior that incentivize corrupt practices (for a review, see Greve, Palmer, and Pozner 2010), and a core interest of accounting scholars is the detection of corrupt practices such that stakeholders can more easily identify and punish deviant behavior (e.g., Cecchini et al. 2010; Corona and Randhawa 2010).

In this chapter, I explore an understudied aspect of organizational wrongdoing: victims' reactions to it. Specifically, I am interested in the effects of organizational wrongdoing on market participation and thus market development. Market forms of exchange in contemporary societies are underpinned by trust, but given that wrongdoing is a common feature of economic and social life (Palmer 2012), we need a better understanding of whether, to what extent, and why malfeasance affects the actors' willingness to continue to participate in a market after being a victim of malfeasance. Earlier work from multiple disciplines has demonstrated negative effects of wrongdoing for the firms that commit it (Baucus and Baucus 1997; Palmrose, Richardson, and Scholz 2004; Sharkey 2014), the markets in which they are situated (Mauro 1995; Wei 2000), and the states that appear inadequate for protecting against it (Easterly, Ritzen, and Woolcock 2006; La Porta et al. 1997; Zak and Knack 2001). I follow these latter lines of work by addressing the effects of misconduct in emerging markets, but I depart from their macro-level measurement of outcomes to theorize about variation in individual-level reactions. Building market institutions in developing countries depends upon actors' willingness to participate, and much earlier work has highlighted the central role of trust in fostering participation (Woolcock 1998; Zak and Knack 2001; Zucker 1986). But we also know that trust-damaging fraud and corruption are especially common features in developing contexts; thus, studying the effects of misconduct on individuals' continued participation in developing markets provides a valuable way to expand theory linking trust to market participation and development.

My approach has the advantage of offering a more nuanced set of reasons why distrust should be linked to lower market participation, including some individual-level reasons why distrust arising from organizational misconduct might *not* reduce market participation. Drawing primarily from organization theory and social psychology, with secondary references to criminology and behavioral finance, I outline seven testable propositions about why and to what extent exposure to trust-damaging wrongdoing might affect market participation. These propositions begin by arguing that individual-level variation in reactions to wrongdoing is a function of fraud being interpreted as an instrumental rather than a normative violation (P1). Recognizing that fraud is an instrumental concern of market participation provides an opening to consider ways that individuals may vary in their calculations of the costs and benefits of continued participation as a function of their social similarity with the perpetrator (P2 and P3), similarities between the offending organization and others in the market (P4), the mix of foreign versus domestic participants in a market (P5 and P6), and the ways that misconduct triggers performance strain among victims (P7 and P8).

In order to theorize about more individual-level ways that misconduct affects market participation, it is necessary to theoretically distinguish between the positive effects of trust and the negative effects of distrust. Broadly, I take the view that the causal effects of distrust are not simply the negative of those of trust; instead, distrust operates according to a unique set of mechanisms that moderates actors' reactions to experiencing wrongdoing, distinguishable from those of trust. I argue that trust is a normative construct that operates in a generalized setting, while distrust is an instrumental construct that operates when actors are exposed to a specific act of wrongdoing. Trust is a more passive organizing principle, at work when actions and performance are unobservable (McEvily, Perrone, and Zaheer 2003), while distrust is a more active state triggered by observable deviant acts (Hardin 2007; Sitkin and Roth 1993), which forces a recalculation of expected outcomes of some action in a market. The reasons why generalized trust and specific distrust affect actors' willingness to participate in a market differ according to these mechanisms, and furthermore, there are a number of mechanisms that moderate actors' expressions of distrust such that distrust might often fail to deter future exchange. In the presence of concrete instances of deviant actions, affected actors are forced to make sense of and form reactions to the negative event, a process that creates an opening for social and environmental attributes to moderate, positively or negatively, their experience with malfeasance.

It is important to specify what I mean by reaction. Certainly, being a victim of organizational misconduct demonstrates that a morally offensive act has been committed common and understandable reactions include outrage and moral indignation. But this is a cognitive reaction, and I am primarily interested in the material reaction in the form of future decisions about market participation. It can be the case that victimization triggers significant moral outrage without triggering significant changes in material economic behavior. Take reactions to the 2008 financial crisis as a clear example: Fed Chairman Ben Bernanke (2008) cited the investing public's dramatic loss of trust in financial markets resulting from perceptions of mismanagement, speculation, and opportunism among Wall Street financial engineers; yet despite the fact that the value of Americans' retirement savings was significantly impacted, there was no appreciable movement away from the use of 401(k)s and related financial instruments. Outrage, moral indignation, and outright screaming and shouting were common, but de-investing in the same financial products was not. This is what I mean by reaction: it is the material actions taken or not taken rather than the rhetoric that arises.

The US investor is not alone in separating her moral outrage from her material economic behavior, and in this chapter I will focus on mechanisms governing distrust in the context of developing markets. We know that market institutions are underpinned by trust and that trust is low in most developing markets due to weak institutional regimes and high rates of malfeasance. Developing markets offer an understudied context for organization theorists interested in malfeasance and an opportunity to both build organization theory on reactions to misconduct and demonstrate the value of organization theory for explaining market development in weak institutional environments beyond the basic the notion that prices are lower and risk premia are higher. Broadly, I will argue that mechanisms governing social relations are central in moderating actors' reactions to experiencing corruption and fraud. Because developing countries are especially reliant on informal social institutions in the absence of strong formal institutions for governing economic exchange (Greif 1994; Landa 1995; Zucker 1986), the implications of this argument are likely stronger in developing countries than in developed countries. That does not mean that social relations are not important in organizing economic action in developed markets, but just that social structure is likely to be activated more as a source of trust than as a source of direct information access in environments where formal institutional protections are weaker. Thus, a secondary goal of this chapter is to stimulate additional attention of organization theorists on understanding both the similarities and differences in wrongdoing in developed and developing markets.

Generalized trust versus specific distrust: separating normative from instrumental claims

Normative trust and market participation

Markets are the central institutions of capitalism, and there is interdisciplinary agreement that trust is necessary for market exchange in the presence of information asymmetries, incomplete contracts, principal–agent problems, and other sources of uncertainty (Arrow 1972; for a review, see Beckert 2006). Trust is the primary organizing principle when actions and performance are unobservable (McEvily et al. 2003). Trust is required when the terms of a contract are uncertain and when the actions of a transaction partner cannot be verified ex ante (Burt 2005: 93). Trust allows us to conserve cognitive resources (Uzzi 1997) and save on transaction costs by avoiding the price of monitoring and enforcement (Ensminger 1996; Landa 1995). It facilitates market participation because actors organize according to normative expectations: we collectively agree that cheating is wrong, and when we agree on this norm, it delivers a material benefit of more efficient exchange. Trust is the lubricant that smooths exchange relationships (Hardin 2007), less so by providing a clearer calculation of gains from exchange, than by creating a shared understanding of acceptable behavior. While there is undoubtedly an instrumental dimension to trust (see Hardin's encapsulated interest theory, 2004), most conceptions of trust begin with a normative understanding of fairness between transaction partners (Granovetter 1985) that subsequently produces economic benefits, rather than economic benefits being the source itself.

Large literatures in sociology, economics, development, and finance point to the role of trust in fostering market participation and thus market development. National levels of trust indicate the presence or absence of a range of social, political, and economic institutions that foster investment and subsequent growth (Fukuyama 1995; Putnam 1993; Woolcock 1998; Zak and Knack 2001). Trust at the group level fosters information and resource sharing, which in turn supports the growth of small enterprise (Aldrich and Waldinger 1990; Portes and Jensen 1989; Portes and Sensenbrenner 1993). Trust is linked to higher rates of financial market development (Guiso, Sapienza, and Zingales 2004), specifically by way of facilitating greater investor participation in countries with higher levels of reported trust (Georgarakos and Pasini 2011; Guiso, Sapienza, and Zingales 2008).

Most of this earlier work on trust and market development is characterized by two common elements that support the view that the normative dimension of trust supports market participation and thus economic development. First, trust is measured as generalized trust at a national level. Several studies make use of survey data from the World Values Survey that measure national levels of "faith in most people," which provides an analytical framework for cross-national comparisons of trust as adherence with social norms (Georgarakos and Pasini 2011; Guiso et al. 2008; Knack and Keefer 1997). Behavioral measures of trust that indirectly measure normative orientation are also used, such as rates of electoral participation and blood donation (Guiso et al. 2004).

A second common element in this literature is that trust and distrust are assumed to be each other's negative, such that lower values of observed indicators of trust are considered measures of distrust. In addition to distrust being measured as the lack of generalized trust, a respondent's indication that she cannot trust most people, other generalized, normative indicators of an absence of trust include beliefs about the persistence of corruption in a country (Lambsdorff, Taube, and Schramm 2004), which is tied to a lack of formal institutional safeguards (Fosu, Bates, and Hoeffler 2006; Glaeser et al. 2004; La Porta et al. 1997; Portes 2006). Thus, these studies consider the effects of trust and distrust as the presence or absence of generalized expectations of norm adherence in a given context.

In contrast to these measures of "generalized distrust," acts of wrongdoing committed by a particular perpetrator affecting a particular victim trigger specific individual-level sense-making and decision-making as a function of the relationship between the two. Victims of the wrongdoing want specific knowledge of who committed the offense, why, and what implications it has for the larger set of other transaction relationships they are involved in. Details or attributions of this newly distrusted relationship are both distinguishable from the loss of generalized trust and also specific to the two parties in the relationship. In the next section, I outline how specific acts of wrongdoing that generate distrust are distinguishable from acts of generalized distrust, which then provides my starting point for seven theoretical propositions about how actors make sense of and react to specific deviant acts.

Separating normative from instrumental distrust

Wrongdoing has a highly normative element to it, stemming from the primary belief that cheating and related abuses of power are morally offensive. A growing literature links social norms to the prevalence of corruption. For example, Fisman and Miguel (2007) find that diplomats from countries with higher levels of corruption enact that corrupt culture while on assignment abroad, as measured by the number of parking violations they are cited for in New York City. Corrupt behavior is more likely to occur in countries where social norms are more tolerant of it (Gatti, Paternostro, and Rigolini 2003), and arguments are made that changing social norms by educating the youth of corrupt countries is a key step in the fight against corruption (Hauk and Saez-Marti 2002). Palmer (2012) provides a comprehensive review of the normative, cultural perspective on organizational wrongdoing, summarizing it as "a theoretical perspective that views organizations as communities, and organizational participants as normative appropriateness assessors" (p. 66). The cultural content of organizations includes the norms, values, and beliefs of actors as defined by their social context. Thus, the extant literature on the normative, cultural causes of organizational wrongdoing is in line with the literature on the cultural, normative aspects of corruption in developing countries.

Of course, fraud and corruption are not just normative. Exposure to normative violations is closely linked to material, instrumental harms. What I want to do next is suggest that victims distinguish the normative from the instrumental elements of corruption and fraud. Doing so puts us in a position to consider variation in how actors respond to instrumental expressions of distrust. Consider an example from the 2005 Afrobarometer survey, in which 51,000 respondents from 34 African countries answer a range of questions regarding corruption, trust in government officials, and material difficulties faced in daily life. The normalcy of wrongdoing in the form of corruption is clear: 84 percent of Afrobarometer respondents believe that their president or prime minister is involved in corruption, and 89 percent believe their member of parliament has corrupt dealings. Consistent with a normative view of trust, 74 percent of respondents report mild to strong distrust of their president and 82 percent report mild to strong distrust of their parliament. Furthermore, Afrobarometer respondents also perceive weak regulation against corrupt practices, reporting that government officials who commit such crimes are three times less likely to be punished than private citizens. But when asked to identify the most pressing problem facing their country, less than 4 percent of respondents name corruption. In contrast, one-third of respondents report that economic issues like unemployment, wages, and management of the economy are the most pressing issues, while another 23 percent cite poverty and security of food and water as the most pressing problems. The link between corruption and underdevelopment is clear, but the point I wish to make here is that when asked to prioritize what problems are more pressing, respondents point to instrumental rather than normative concerns. Even when actors lose trust in others as a result of normative violations, priority is given to addressing instrumental outcomes of those normative violations. Rather than prioritizing the end of these moral violations which cause material detriment, respondents call for ending the material harms themselves. Granovetter (1985) argued that trust arose from normative expectations of positive behavior within inter-personal relationships, and that these norms then carried over into economic life. The Afrobarometer data show a decoupling between the normative and instrumental when looking at the process in the reverse: normative violations trigger condemnation and reports of distrust, but material reactions do not follow the same path. Are the reactions of Africans to state-level corruption qualitatively different than Americans' reticence to give up mutual funds following the distrustful acts of the financial crisis? This chapter focuses on the former, but future work should find fertile research grounds for investigating the latter.

This normative versus instrumental perspective has roots in the academic literature, as scholars have noted two distinguishable components to trust that help highlight the difference between these perspectives: trust is both competence to complete a job and willingness to complete it as agreed (Cook, Hardin, and Levi 2007; McEvily et al. 2003). These two components illustrate the conflict experienced by market actors when trying to decide how to react to a fraud: I can simultaneously believe that a market opportunity or a transaction partner is *capable* of producing positive outcomes (i.e., profits), and I separately assess how much I trust the partner's *willingness* to deliver that outcome as a function of her fraudulent actions. In the instrumental context of a market exchange, one can calculate separately the expected gains from participation and the probability that such gains will be made available.

This is one of the key findings in my recent work on investor recruitment into Kenya's emerging stock market: potential investors understand levels of profits earned on prior investments by their earlier-adopting peers located nearby, but potential investors who belong to ethnic groups that are rivals to those who control the market's governance regime do not trust that they can receive fair treatment in the market (Yenkey 2015). Kenyan investors can simultaneously believe the market is competent or capable of delivering a positive return, but that unfair treatment at the hands of distrusted ethnic rivals will interfere with their ability to realize that return. Here, the social norms of inter-ethnic conflict reduce the value of the instrumental signal of profits earned by proximate peers. As a result, potential Kenyan investors actually become less likely to invest in shares when distrusted ethnic rivals earn greater profits in the market.

This example gives us another way to tie back in with the academic literature. Sitkin and Roth (1993) provided a typology separating trust and distrust. The critical dimension is the extent to which the violation was specific to the local context or generalizable as a disregard for social norms and values. In the former, trust is reduced, but in the latter, distrust is engendered. Sitkin and Roth's typology is useful for my purposes here, but I would explicitly note that they have identified a normative distrust. That is, actors react negatively to their transaction partners (whether individuals, organizations, states, or markets) when their assumptions about agreed upon norms of fair treatment are violated. This normative violation alters their expectations of future interactions, calling into question the desirability of keeping them as a transaction partner. There is almost certainly an instrumental, material component to this, but it is important to note that such concerns are only indirect at this point. The direct violation has been to the group's agreed-upon norms for fair conduct, which conjures indirect thoughts about the impact on future costs and benefits of transacting. As my example of ethnic rivals in Kenya again illustrates, it is not possible to calculate the actual expected losses of investing in a market governed by ethnic rivals. Instead, the mismatch of normative expectations produces a broad, negative reaction that reduces the probability of the material act of market participation. In this scenario, potential investors operate in an environment with lower generalized trust resulting from lower expectations of fair treatment from ethnic rivals.

Beyond violations of normative values, much wrongdoing is experienced as a more specific form of victimization. Workers whose retirement savings were invested with Enron, for example, can easily quantify their losses and specifically identity the corrupt actors responsible. Nigerian or Tanzanian entrepreneurs who try to register their firms encounter specific corrupt bureaucrats who demand specific bribes to process their forms. Americans who believe the 2008 financial crisis was triggered by opportunism by Wall Street financial engineers can see the decline in their portfolio values. In these cases, the generalized, normative aspects of wrongdoing transform into or are secondary to what now is experienced as a more direct cost–benefit analysis made possible by the actor's direct exposure to the corrupt actor to which she attributes blame for the fraudulent event. In these circumstances, do we think the normative or instrumental violations will have a greater impact? Do defrauded investors in any context avoid future investing out of moral outrage at a normative violation or because that violation suggests greater risk of future material losses? Put another way, do we think that fraud victims will avoid future investing if the moral component of the violation is strong but they believe that the material benefit of future investing could also be high? In this case, which is stronger: norms or outcomes?

If we took the normatively oriented literature on generalized trust and market participation to a logical end, it would predict that markets are severely and systematically harmed in the aftermath of such corrupt events. But history tells us this does not happen as often as the generalized trust perspective would suggest. When one's cost of enforcing a norm violation exceeds the material benefits of doing so, it is in our material interest to deemphasize the norm violation. Seen from this perspective, we can see theoretical similarity between our vulnerable Nigerian entrepreneur and the victims of Bernie Madoff's pyramid scheme: they both can calculate their cost of exposure to the corruption or fraud, but both can also calculate the expected benefits of engaging with it *again*, either by registering their firm or by taking investment advice from another socially similar peer, regardless of their moral outrage at being forced into such a decision.

As stated by McEvily et al. (2003), trust is an organizing principle during times of stability, while breaches of trust force a reconsideration of that organizing structure. That reconsidering can focus on either the normative or the instrumental aspect of the wrongdoing event. My argument here is not that one is of higher magnitude than the other. Instead, I follow Sitkin and Roth's typology to argue that normative violations will consistently lead to lower willingness to participate in a market, while instrumental violations trigger a cost–benefit analysis in which the negative effect can be moderated either positively or negatively depending on the perspective of the victim relative to the perpetrator. I recognize that a similar line of reasoning may be possible for moderators of normative violations, but focusing on variation in individual-level reactions in instrumental violations provides a cleaner starting point for a new line of theorizing about the effects of organizational misconduct.

P1: Wrongdoing perceived as a normative violation has a consistently negative aggregate effect on market participation. The effect of wrongdoing perceived as an instrumental violation will vary according to how actors calculate the costs of the violation.

Social context as a moderator of instrumental distrust

My next task is to review earlier work from several literatures to provide a framework for thinking about how social context between victims and perpetrators of wrongdoing might moderate the negative effects of fraud and corruption. In the context of market participation, these moderators more often than not attenuate the negative effects of wrongdoing such that fraud and corruption might not dissuade continued participation. Cook et al. (2007) call this cooperation without trust, and my task in this section is to outline testable propositions about how social context alters instrumental assessments of trust violations. A great number of social conditions could be expected to moderate reactions to instrumental distrust, but I will limit my discussion to three: social similarity between victims and perpetrators, pathways for the transmission of stigma from the perpetrator to other parts of the market, and the relative performance of fraud victims.

Competing predictions of the effect of social proximity between victims and perpetrators

In this section, I review work from criminology, social psychology, and social network theory that provides competing predictions about how victims of wrongdoing will react to fraud and corruption as a function of their social proximity to the perpetrator.

Criminologists have given more attention to the role of social proximity in moderating victim reactions than other social science disciplines, although it is noteworthy that most of this work is in the context of reactions to violent crime or crimes of aggression between intimates. Of particular interest for our study of investor reactions to fraud and corruption is the finding that victims who are socially closer to their perpetrators are less likely to report their victimization and less likely to seek damages than socially distant victims (Black 2010; Davis and Henderson 2003; Felson, Messner, and Hoskin 1999). Underreporting of victimization at the hands of socially similar fraudsters could reduce the negative effects of wrongdoing in two ways: by reducing the likelihood of victims themselves reacting to the event and by reducing the likelihood those victims will spread the negative information about the malfeasance to others in the market. Other work in criminology suggests this underreporting by socially similar victims will be compounded in socially homogeneous settings, as victims are increasingly likely to feel that their victimization questions the legitimacy of their membership within the group (Goudriaan, Wittebrood, and Nieuwbeerta 2006).

Social psychology offers predictions that both contradict and support this perspective from criminology. The core tenet of social identity theory is that trust is higher within a social group than between groups (Tajfel 1974). When this assumed trust is violated, we would expect one of two outcomes. First, in-group members might feel particularly taken advantage of and react more negatively because of the greater disparity between expected and realized behavior. Second, in-group victims might recognize a wider set of benefits of group membership that social outsiders do not have, thus attenuating their felt level of victimization because of remaining beliefs about benefits available from other group members. A great deal of work in social psychology around this first possibility contradicts the criminological argument that social ties with a perpetrator should reduce reactions to victimization from wrongdoing. Foddy, Platow, and Yamagishi (2009) find that trustworthy behavior is particularly expected by members of a social in-group. Buchan, Croson, and Dawes (2002) show that social proximity is directly related to expectations of trustworthy behavior in reciprocity games. Even more specific to the developing contexts studied here, trust in group members underlies the formation of ethnically homogeneous middlemen groups (Greif 1994; Landa 1995) which facilitate exchange in high-risk environments. Tropp et al. (2006) argue that victims who belong to a local minority have lower-felt victimization as a result of not expecting fair treatment initially. Cohen and Steele (2002) similarly argue that trust is less likely to form between members of opposing social groups, providing less of a basis for negative feelings of victimization in a wrongdoing event. In short, social outsiders feel less victimization precisely because they expected less trust initially.

In contrast, scholars studying what has come to be referred to as the "dark side" of social capital suggest reasons why shared group membership between a victim and her perpetrator might reduce the negativity of the victim's reactions. Research in this area is more in agreement with the criminological perspective above, although caused by different mechanisms. Working from the starting point that social actors have less objective assessments of the exchange performance of socially similar transaction partners (Lawler 1992), Sorenson and Waguespack (2006) demonstrate that repeated exchange between partners results in biased assessment of the performance of that relationship and therefore the likelihood of continuing in underperforming transaction relationships. Sgourev and Zuckerman (2011) come to a similar conclusion, based on the formation of affective relations within a transaction relationship.

In the context of a developing market, affective attachment with deviant transaction partners can occur in two ways. First, relational embedding resulting from a history of legitimate trades may lead a victim to discount the fraudulent behavior if it has not been detected before. If actors make use of their social networks to choose transaction partners (DiMaggio and Louch 1998), then repeat exchange is more likely among partners already socially proximate to each other. Second, it is likely that victims who are socially similar to the perpetrator also consider the benefits of group membership when accounting for the harm inflicted by the fraud. Hall (1988) argues that group membership is a key determinant of individual survival, and Lawler (1992) points to shared group membership as a key driver of individuals' sense of social control. Conflict theorists have long demonstrated that group-level associations are of paramount importance to feelings of security in diverse settings characterized by intergroup frictions (Allport 1958; Rydgren, Sofi, and Hällsten 2013). Together, these arguments suggest that victims of fraud and corruption are more likely to discount their individual losses when they result from wrongdoing enacted by a member of their own social group.

Theory and evidence from criminology, social psychology, and social network theory offer competing but compelling predictions of the moderating role of social similarity between victims and perpetrators on reactions to fraud. Criminology research and some work in social psychology predict muted reactions to fraud when victims are socially similar to the perpetrator, a result driven by several possible mechanisms, including reticence to publicly report the misconduct, reticence to inflict harm on the group by punishing the deviant member, or bias in assessing the harm inflicted by the fraud. In contrast, social identity theory predicts that victims who are socially similar to the perpetrator will experience especially acute feelings of loss and victimization precisely because the perpetrator has violated strongly held norms of in-group trustworthy behavior.

Variation in individual-level reactions to fraud by in- versus out-group members is likely when there are clearly identified, salient social groups within a market. Examples are not difficult to conjure. The military dominated Egypt's publicly traded firms prior to the

Arab Spring (Tadros 2012). White South Africans hold a two-to-one majority over black South Africans on the Johannesburg Stock Exchange's (JSE) Board of Directors, while upper-caste Brahmins have an even larger majority on the Board of India's National Stock Exchange (INSE). American voters have widely adopted social identities as belonging to red versus blue state voting blocks, and socioeconomic divides in developed countries have been recently highlighted by the Occupy Wall Street movement. Religion can also easily trigger salient social identities in the marketplace: do you think that Jewish victims who shared a religious identity with Bernie Madoff reacted differently than Madoff's non-Jewish victims? The direction of these reactions is an open question for future research, and it is even possible that some forms of social relations exacerbate negative reactions while others attenuate them.

P2a: Victims will react more negatively to wrongdoing committed by socially similar perpetrators.

P2b: Victims will react less negatively to wrongdoing committed by socially similar perpetrators.

These two competing propositions are of broad theoretical interest to organizational scholars of wrongdoing because they link social relations to reactions to organizational misconduct. They are also relevant to my focus on market development because of the additional potential they represent for altering the composition of an investing population. Recent research in an experimental setting shows that social diversity is healthy for market performance because socially diverse markets avert market failures. Levine et al. (2014) present evidence from laboratory studies showing that socially homogeneous trading populations assume that the prices paid by homophilous other traders are legitimate, leading to the formation of price bubbles due to excessive willingness to continue to escalate the price. In contrast, socially diverse traders actively question each other's trades, resulting in more efficient and less bubble-prone pricing. This study is important because it points to market-level benefits of diverse inputs improving pricing mechanisms, as organization theorists have demonstrated at the organizational level relating to innovation and firm and team performance.

Put into the context of fraud, corruption, and developing markets, this perspective suggests that if victims of fraud and corruption react less negatively when it is committed by socially similar perpetrators, then the composition of the investing population itself will become not only more socially homogeneous, but also increasingly tolerant of fraud and corruption. In this scenario, wrongdoing would have a doubly negative impact on the market by first cheating investors and then filtering out those socially diverse investors who are more attentive to governance issues. If this is the case, then each event of fraud and corruption paradoxically makes future events of fraud and corruption more likely by weeding out those investors intolerant of it. This pattern could potentially explain the paradoxical pattern of high corruption and repeat market participation in developing markets: members of the market's in-group are willing to continue to participate which helps sustain the market's survival, but their reduced sensitivity to in-group malfeasance also fosters future wrongdoing.

Two of my own papers on investor recruitment and fraud in Kenya's Nairobi Securities Exchange (NSE) illustrate this point. Kenya's emerging market is governed by members of Kenya's Kikuyu ethnic group. The Kikuyu are Kenya's largest ethnic group at approximately 22 percent of the national population, but critically, they constitute the majority of executive management positions at the NSE and seats on the Boards of Directors of the NSE and the state regulatory agency. In research on investor recruitment in Kenya discussed above (Yenkey 2015), I showed the difficulty in recruiting investors from ethnic groups who are rivals to the Kikuyu into the national market. In a follow-up paper, I study the victimization of Kenyan investors in a large-scale stockbroker fraud, where the largest stockbroker in the market defrauded more than one-quarter of its 100,000 clients. I find that the corrupt broker exploited the assumed trust, the social capital, embedded in ethnic ties: across more than a dozen subsamples, coethnic victims are always more likely to be victimized by the corrupt broker. However, in another analysis I find that these defrauded in-group investors are also more likely than rival group investors to continue to participate in the market. Together, these three analyses tell a compelling story of the role of trust and distrust in market participation: distrust inhibits recruiting diverse social groups into the market; corrupt agents exploit the assumed trust of in-group members when committing fraud; but nonetheless, out-group investors react more negatively to the fraud and are more likely to exit the market. Proposition 3 contrasts the difficulty in recruiting a diverse population of investors with the relative ease of losing their trust after a fraud. If this is the case, then the larger negative effect of a fraud is that it filters out some of the productive social diversity in the investing population, which then lowers disincentives for future misconduct.

P3: Wrongdoing will reduce the diversity of participation in a developing market, making future episodes of wrongdoing more likely.

Stigma's multiple pathways for spreading distrust

Organization theory provides another framework for thinking about how wrongdoing is likely to affect market participation. A growing literature on organizational stigma studies how actors attribute the negative actions of one organization to independent, uninvolved organizations (Devers et al. 2009) by way of their similarity to the deviant organization. The mechanism through which this happens is generalizability, where individuals identify attributes shared by the deviant organization and non-deviant organizations and use those similarities to attribute probabilities of deviant behavior by the non-deviant organization. In doing so, they stereotype other similar organizations according to the negative behavior of the lone deviant.

Stigma by association is a particularly important pathway through which instrumental distrust from fraud and corruption in market settings might spread because of the likelihood that deviant organizations that are caught will be expelled from the market. We understand that distrustful, fraudulent activity often has a positive short-term payoff for the fraudster but a long-term negative payoff via loss of all future business. While this is true, such fraudsters are often expelled from the market, so fraud victims have to decide whether to trust other, similar organizations that remain in the market. That is, victims are often prohibited from punishing the corrupt organization; its expulsion from that market means that their market-related decision-making revolves around how to react to other organizations that remain in the market after the scandal. Organizations available as focal points can include the market's governance regime or other intermediaries that might need to be retained in order to continue to access the market. To the extent that any of these other organizations are seen as similar to the deviant organization, we would expect a negative reaction to the wrongdoing event that spreads well beyond the actual corrupt organization that committed it.

Organizational stigma by association bred from stereotyping makes it particularly hard to control the diffusion of the negative effects of a corrupt episode due to the multiple pathways that victims might identify. Similarities in terms of social identities (Tajfel and Turner 1986) or professional categories (Hannan, Pólos, and Carroll 2007) can serve as such pathways for the contagion of a fraud. The former is exemplified by Pontikes, Negro, and Rao (2010), who found that stigmatization from being labelled a communist, a salient social identity at the time, traveled across professional boundaries. Studies of corrupt practices by auditing firms (Jensen 2006) and mutual fund providers (Jonsson, Greve, and Fujiwara-Greve 2009) show that potential customers and investors avoid otherwise innocent organizations when they share professional identities with known deviant organizations. Institutional economists argue that investors attribute blame for fraud and corruption to weak governance regimes as incapable protectors of property rights, an implicit form of stigmatization of a state incapable of controlling malfeasance.

The literature on organizational stigma thus suggests that even expelling a corrupt organization from a market might not reverse the distrust triggered by the wrongdoing if other organizational parts of the market (i.e. the governance regime or other organizations serving the market) are seen as socially or professionally similar to the deviant organization. The same set of examples used in Proposition 2 can be applied here: fraud-exposed investors may generalize their experience with a corrupt white or black South African agent to other agents in that racial group and to the majority-white governance regime of the JSE; in India, misconduct by a corrupt Brahmin agent may have stronger implications for the continued legitimacy of a Brahmin-governed market than misconduct by a member of another caste.

The extent to which stigma by association diffuses across types of organizations in a developing market is also an open question deserving greater study. Multiple pathways exist through which a stigma might travel upwards and delegitimize a market. In a study of the detrimental effects of being labeled a communist in post-World War II Hollywood, Pontikes et al. (2010) find that stigma by association can travel across professional categories; in contrast, Jonsson et al's. (2009) study of wrongdoing by a Swedish mutual fund provider diffused to other mutual funds but not to the ratings agencies that evaluated them. These studies suggest that the diffusion of stigma by association is affected either by the context in which malfeasance occurs or variations in ease of generalizability across professional categories. Such variations are critically important in building theory around stigma by association and the extent to which it is detrimental to market development.

P4: Wrongdoing by a particular corrupt organization in the market will have greater negative effects on market development the greater the similarity between it and the other organizations that comprise the market.

So far, my discussion of the effect of organizational stigma has treated investors who react to wrongdoing as a single population. We know, however, that foreign investors often have a disproportionate influence in many emerging markets. For example, foreigners owned 52 percent of total investments in emerging markets in 2013, a trend significantly stimulated by the global spread of market liberalization policies in the 1990s and 2000s (Coppejans and Domowitz 2000). High rates of foreign ownership demonstrate a common feature of many emerging markets where investors who are less embedded in the local social environment are disproportionately influential in market performance. This has potential implications for the diffusion of organizational stigma by association: if stereotyping is more prevalent among actors who are less embedded in the local social context, then it is likely that the actions of a single corrupt actor are more likely to result in faster, farther diffusion of the stigma. If this is the case, then we would expect that equally corrupt acts might have greater negative implications for performance in markets with a higher portion of foreign investors. However, it may be that foreigners by virtue of their greater social distance from the local context are less likely to stereotype at all, relying more on the best available calculations of expected returns rather than heuristics based on social identity to resolve uncertainties. A middle ground between these two would predict that foreign investors would behave with high variance in a manner that might resemble fickleness: these outsiders are relatively easily scared out of the market by misconduct, but their memories are short and changes in market performance quickly bring them back. This latter prediction need not be explicitly about the same foreign investors. It may be the case that existing foreign investors who experience malfeasance quickly exit the market, but their low levels of connectivity with other foreign investors, such as those from different countries, lowers levels of communication about the deviance and therefore a return to positive performance quickly attracts new foreign investors. These scenarios alternatively describe fickle foreigners and/or a revolving door of foreign investors, and both are empirically testable given sufficient data.

P5: Foreign investors are more likely than domestic investors to transmit the organizational stigma of an act of wrongdoing.

P6: Wrongdoing will result in higher volatility in markets with higher rates of foreign ownership.

Performance strain and the paradox of distrust

The last aspect of social context as a moderator of fraud and corruption that I want to discuss is performance strain, the felt difference between actual and aspirational levels of outcomes. Actors can experience strain as a result of underperformance relative to competitors (Staw and Szwajkowski 1975) or their own performance trajectories (Simpson 1986). To date, performance strain has been used by organization theorists as a way to predict organizational wrongdoing (Greve 2003), but it is also applicable to thinking about how investors might react to corruption and fraud. Although it violates conventional wisdom on the negative effects of fraud, it seems theoretically plausible to consider that defrauded investors may experience a form of performance strain that stimulates them to reinvest in order to make up the losses with increasingly risky investments. This outcome is entirely consistent with psychological work on prospect theory (Kahneman and Tversky 1979), which predicts increasing risk tolerance when performance is negative. This "gamblers fallacy" argument has been demonstrated with investment activity by behavioral finance scholars, who find that investors are more willing to hold shares that are declining in price (Odean 1998). Performance strain would be expected to be felt by investors who lose larger portions of available capital and who have fewer alternative opportunities for profit-making. In earlier work using the Kenyan stock market, I show that domestic investors are disproportionately drawn from lower-income brackets in a pattern that suggests share ownership resembles lottery participation (Yenkey 2015).

Together, this suggests that smaller retail investors who lack alternative investment outlets will be more likely to continue to invest after experiencing a fraud as a high-risk strategy for making up losses. If this is the case, then a longer-term implication of corrupt acts for an emerging market would be the institutionalization of an image of the domestic market as a high-risk, lottery-style financial practice.

P7: Lower-wealth and/or opportunity-constrained victims of wrongdoing are more likely to continue to participate after an episode of wrongdoing than victims with higher wealth and greater alternative investment opportunities.

P8: Repeated wrongdoing events will result in domestic market participation shifting increasingly toward lower-wealth and/or opportunity-constrained participants.

Conclusion

My goal in this chapter has been less about making predictions about what is true in fraud-affected markets and more about stimulating broader attention to the potential consequences of organizational wrongdoing, particularly in the context of markets situated in weak institutional environments. I began by arguing that distrust arising from instrumental concerns can be thought of separately from that of the normative concerns of trust. I then proposed a range of ways in which instrumental concerns might produce significant variation in reactions by victims as a function of different aspects of the social environment in which those decisions are made by victims and their social relations to their perpetrator. In doing so, I have called attention to intersecting theoretical work from sociology, social psychology, economics, development, finance, and criminology that speaks to issues of importance to researchers of organizational wrongdoing, while also demonstrating the value of organization theory for deepening our understanding of market development at a global level.

The balance of these moderators is toward the attenuation of the effects of wrongdoing, and if so, future empirical work should show that the actual short-term effects of fraud and corruption are less than conventional wisdom predicts. Many market participants get cheated at some point, but most if not all of us find a way to rationalize that experience and find a reason to get back into the game. An interesting implication of this perspective is that it contradicts not only conventional wisdom on the effects of fraud but also the perceived wisdom that bad news is stronger than good news (Baumeister et al. 2001). In the market context, seeking gain is a primary driver, so that bad news is assessed relative to potential for gain. Perhaps, in other social settings, where cohesion and acceptance are the goals, avoidance of harm is the primary driver. If so, this perspective could explain why fraud and corruption are such regular, normal events (Palmer 2012): motivations for market gains create a replenishing supply of potential victims by way of providing a set of decision-making criteria biased toward overcoming negative stimuli. On the other hand, if my predictions are true, then the negative effects of fraud and corruption on market development, and economic development more broadly, are likely underestimated. The more insidious implication of the predictions made here is that wrongdoing filters out participants that value higher standards of market governance, suggesting an endogenous process where current wrongdoing makes future wrongdoing more rather than less likely.

This raises a key question that has not yet been addressed: how can policy-makers and market organizations restore participants' trust in a market without incentivizing future wrongdoing? That is, if we understand why individuals are likely to react negatively to a fraud, then organization theory can be of use to policy-makers and market operators in strategically managing the aftermath of wrongdoing. Doing so, however, creates a paradox: if theory is used more to explain why actors respond to fraud than to understand what causes fraud in the first place, then we risk creating knowledge that could perpetuate wrongdoing in a manner similar to that outlined just above. Within market institutions, it is important to remember that distrust serves a positive function when it is well directed (Hardin 2007), and a certain amount of distrust is particularly called for in the developing contexts studied here that are characterized by weak institutional protections for participants.

How do policy-makers in developing contexts manage the stigma of fraud-related distrust in order to get new investors into the market and existing investors to continue? Institutional economists focusing on the negative effects of weak formal institutions suggest an obvious recommendation: strengthen institutional protections. But beyond the obvious difficulty of affecting formal institutional change in such settings, organization theorists demonstrated more than twenty years ago that legal remedies alone would likely be ineffective in resolving distrust (Sitkin and Roth 1993). Beyond the observation that additional legal mandates are unlikely to be effective at constraining malfeasance or be seen as legitimate by investors in weak institutional environments, there is evidence that the practice of adopting additional formal regulations can paradoxically increase the distance between would-be trustors and trustees by reinforcing recognition of the source of the contestation. A critical issue not dealt with in this chapter is how to detect and deter malfeasance while at the same time reassuring market participants that one incident of organizational misconduct should not delegitimize the market as a whole. This paradox starts to take on all the trappings of a public goods dilemma, where a more developed market benefits national development but is only possible if more members of the public make themselves vulnerable to the high levels of malfeasance that characterize developing markets. Clearly, there is more work to be done to provide a comprehensive organizational theory of market development capable of offering policy recommendations.

It is my hope that this chapter can stimulate further work on the consequences of wrongdoing, perhaps with the additional benefit that individual reactions to wrongdoing may come to be understood as a reflexive cause of it as well. Doing so would create a unique opportunity for organization theory to better inform policy and practice in markets situated in weak institutional environments.

References

Aldrich, H. E. and Waldinger, R. 1990. "Ethnicity and entrepreneurship," *Annual Review of Sociology* 16: 111–135.

Allport, G. W. 1958. *The Nature of Prejudice. Abridged* (1st edn.). Garden City, NY: Doubleday.

Arrow, K. J. 1972. "Gifts and exchanges," *Philosophy & Public Affairs* 1(4): 343–362.

Baucus, M. S. and Baucus, D. A. 1997. "Paying the piper: An empirical examination of longer-term financial consequences of illegal corporate behavior," *Academy of Management Journal* 40(1): 129–151.

Baumeister, R. F., Bratslavsky, E., Finkenauer, C., and Vohs, K. D. 2001. "Bad is stronger than good," *Review of General Psychology* 5(4): 323–370.

Beckert, J. 2006. "Trust and markets," in R. Bachmann and A. Zaheer (eds.), *Handbook of Trust Research*: 318–331. Cheltenham: Edward Elgar Publishing Ltd.

Bernanke, B. S. 2008. "Stabilizing the financial markets and the economy," Presented at the Economic Club of New York, October 15. www .federalreserve.gov/newsevents/speech/bernanke20081015a.htm.

Black, D. 2010. *The Behavior of Law.* (Special edn). New York, NY: Springer-Verlag.

Buchan, N. R., Croson, R. T. A., and Dawes, R. M. 2002. "Swift neighbors and persistent strangers: A cross-cultural investigation of trust and reciprocity in social exchange," *American Journal of Sociology* 108(1): 168–206.

Burt, R. S. 2005. *Brokerage and Closure: An Introduction to Social Capital.* Oxford: Oxford University Press.

Cecchini, M., Aytug, H., Koehler, G. J., and Pathak, P. 2010. "Detecting management fraud in public companies," *Management Science* 56(7): 1146–1160.

Cohen, G. and Steele, C. 2002. "A barrier of mistrust: How negative stereotypes affect cross-race mentoring," in J. Aronson (ed.), *Improving Academic Achievement: Impact of Psychological Factors on Education*: 303–327. San Diego, CA: Academic Press.

Cook, K. S., Hardin, R., and Levi, M. 2007. *Cooperation Without Trust? Russell Sage Foundation Series on Trust, IX*. New York: Russell Sage Foundation Publications.

Coppejans, M. and Domowitz, I. 2000. "The impact of foreign equity ownership on emerging market share price volatility," *International Finance* 3(1): 95–122.

Corona, C. and Randhawa, R. S. 2010. "The auditor's slippery slope: An analysis of reputational incentives," *Management Science* 56(6): 924–937.

Davis, R. C. and Henderson, N. J. 2003. "Willingness to report crimes: The role of ethnic group membership and community efficacy," *Crime & Delinquency* 49(4): 564–580.

Devers, C. E., Dewett, T., Mishina, Y., and Belsito, C. A. 2009. "A general theory of organizational stigma," *Organization Science* 20(1): 154–171.

DiMaggio, P. and Louch, H. 1998. "Socially embedded consumer transactions: For what kinds of purchases do people most often use networks?" *American Sociological Review* 63(5): 619–637.

Easterly, W., Ritzen, J., and Woolcock, M. 2006. "Social cohesion, institutions, and growth," *Economics & Politics* 18(2): 103–120.

Ensminger, J. 1996. *Making a Market: The Institutional Transformation of an African Society*. Cambridge: Cambridge University Press.

Felson, R. B., Messner, S. F., and Hoskin, A. 1999. "The victim-offender relationship and calling the police in assaults," *Criminology* 37(4): 931–948.

Fisman, R. and Miguel, E. 2007. "Corruption, norms, and legal enforcement: Evidence from diplomatic parking tickets," *Journal of Political Economy* 115(6): 1020–1048.

Foddy, M., Platow, M., and Yamagishi, T. 2009. "Group-based trust in strangers: The role of stereotypes and expectations," *Psychological Science* 20(4): 419–422.

Fosu, A., Bates, R., and Hoeffler, A. 2006. "Institutions, governance and economic development in Africa: An overview," *Journal of African Economies* 15: 1–9.

Fukuyama, F. 1995. *Trust: The Social Virtues and the Creation of Prosperity*. New York, NY: Free Press.

Gatti, R., Paternostro, S., and Rigolini, J. 2003. "Individual attitudes toward corruption: Do social effects matter?" World Bank Policy Research Paper 3122.

Georgarakos, D. and Pasini, G. 2011. "Trust, sociability, and stock market participation," *Review of Finance* 15(4): 693–725.

Glaeser, E. L., La Porta, R., Lopez-De-Silanes, F., and Shleifer, A. 2004. "Do institutions cause growth?" *Journal of Economic Growth* 9(3): 271–303.

Goudriaan, H., Wittebrood, K., and Nieuwbeerta, P. 2006. "Neighborhood characteristics and reporting crime: Effects of social cohesion, confidence in police effectiveness and socio-economic disadvantage," *The British Journal of Criminology* 46(4): 719–742.

Granovetter, M. 1985. "Economic action and social structure: The problem of embeddedness," *American Journal of Sociology* 91(3): 481–510.

Greif, A. 1994. "Cultural beliefs and the organization of society: A historical and theoretical reflection on collectivist and individualist societies," *Journal of Political Economy* 102(5): 912–950.

Greve, H. R. 2003. *Organizational Learning from Performance Feedback: A Behavioral Perspective on Innovation and Change*. Cambridge: Cambridge University Press.

Greve, H. R., Palmer, D., and Pozner, J.-E. 2010. "Organizations gone wild: The causes, processes, and consequences of organizational misconduct," *The Academy of Management Annals* 4(1): 53–107.

Guiso, L., Sapienza, P., and Zingales, L. 2004. "The role of social capital in financial development," *The American Economic Review* 94(3): 526–556.

Guiso, L., Sapienza, P., and Zingales, L. 2008. "Trusting the stock market," *The Journal of Finance* 63(6): 2557–2600.

Hall, J. R. 1988. "Social organization and pathways of commitment: Types of communal groups, rational choice theory, and the Kanter thesis," *American Sociological Review* 53(5): 679.

Hannan, M. T., Pólos, L., and Carroll, G. R. 2007. *Logics of Organization Theory: Audiences, Codes, and Ecologies.* Princeton, NJ: Princeton University Press.

Hardin, R. 2004. *Trust and Trustworthiness.* New York: Russell Sage Foundation Publications.

Hardin, R. 2007. "Distrust," in K. S. Cook, R. Hardin, and M. Levi (eds.), *Cooperation Without Trust?*: 60–82. New York: Russell Sage Foundation Publications.

Hauk, E. and Saez-Marti, M. 2002. "On the cultural transmission of corruption," *Journal of Economic Theory* 107(2): 311–335.

Jensen, M. 2006. "Should we stay or should we go? Accountability, status anxiety, and client defections," *Administrative Science Quarterly* 51(1): 97–128.

Jonsson, S., Greve, H. R., and Fujiwara-Greve, T. 2009. "Undeserved loss: The spread of legitimacy loss to innocent organizations in response to reported corporate deviance," *Administrative Science Quarterly* 54(2): 195–228.

Kahneman, D. and Tversky, A. 1979. "Prospect theory: An analysis of decision under risk," *Econometrica* 47(2): 263–291.

Knack, S. and Keefer, P. 1997. "Does social capital have an economic payoff? A cross-country investigation," *The Quarterly Journal of Economics* 112 (4): 1251–1288.

Lambsdorff, J. G., Taube, M., and Schramm, M. (eds.). 2004. *The New Institutional Economics of Corruption.* London. New York: Routledge.

Landa, J. 1995. *Trust, Ethnicity, and Identity: Beyond the New Institutional Economics of Ethnic Trading Networks, Contract Law, and Gift-Exchange.* Ann Arbor: University of Michigan Press.

La Porta, R., Lopez-De-Silanes, F., Shleifer, A., and Vishny, R. W. 1997. "Legal determinants of external finance," *The Journal of Finance* 52(3): 1131–1150.

Lawler, E. J. 1992. "Affective attachments to nested groups: A choice-process theory," *American Sociological Review* 57(3): 327–339.

Levine, S. S., Apfelbaum, E. P., Bernard, M., Bartelt, V. L., Zajac, E. J., and Stark, D. 2014. "Ethnic diversity deflates price bubbles," *Proceedings of the National Academy of Sciences* 111(52): 18524–18529.

Mauro, P. 1995. "Corruption and growth," *The Quarterly Journal of Economics* 110(3): 681–712.

McEvily, B., Perrone, V., and Zaheer, A. 2003. "Trust as an organizing principle," *Organization Science* 14(1): 91–103.

Odean, Te. 1998. "Are investors reluctant to realize their losses?" *The Journal of Finance* 53(5): 1775–1798.

Palmer, D. 2012. *Normal Organizational Wrongdoing: A Critical Analysis of Theories of Misconduct in and by Organizations*. New York: Oxford University Press.

Palmrose, Z.-V., Richardson, V. J., and Scholz, S. 2004. "Determinants of market reactions to restatement announcements," *Journal of Accounting and Economics* 37(1): 59–89.

Pontikes, E., Negro, G., and Rao, H. 2010. "Stained red: A study of stigma by association to blacklisted artists during the 'Red Scare' in Hollywood, 1945 to 1960," *American Sociological Review* 75(3): 456–478.

Portes, A. 2006. "Institutions and development: A conceptual reanalysis," *Population and Development Review* 32(2): 233–262.

Portes, A. and Jensen, L. 1989. "The enclave and the entrants: Patterns of ethnic enterprise in Miami before and after Mariel," *American Sociological Review* 54(6): 929–949.

Portes, A. and Sensenbrenner, J. 1993. "Embeddedness and immigration: Notes on the social determinants of economic action," *The American Journal of Sociology* 98(6): 1320–1350.

Putnam, R. D. 1993. *Making Democracy Work: Civic Traditions in Modern Italy*. Princeton, NJ: Princeton University Press.

Rydgren, J., Sofi, D., and Hällsten, M. 2013. "Interethnic friendship, trust, and tolerance: Findings from two north Iraqi cities," *American Journal of Sociology* 118(6): 1650–1694.

Sgourev, S. V. and Zuckerman, E. W. 2011. "Breaking up is hard to do: Irrational inconsistency in commitment to an industry peer network," *Rationality and Society* 23(1): 3–34.

Sharkey, A. J. 2014. "Categories and organizational status: The role of industry status in the response to organizational deviance," *American Journal of Sociology* 119(5): 1380–1433.

Simpson, S. S. 1986. "The decomposition of antitrust: Testing a multi-level, longitudinal model of profit-squeeze," *American Sociological Review* 51(6): 859–875.

Sitkin, S. B. and Roth, N. L. 1993. "Explaining the limited effectiveness of legalistic 'remedies' for trust/distrust," *Organization Science* 4(3): 367–392.

Sorenson, O. and Waguespack, D. M. 2006. "Social structure and exchange: Self-confirming dynamics in Hollywood," *Administrative Science Quarterly* 51(4): 560–589.

Staw, B. M. and Szwajkowski, E. 1975. "The scarcity-munificence component of organizational environments and the commission of illegal acts," *Administrative Science Quarterly* 20(3): 345–354.

Tadros, S. 2012. "Egypt military's economic empire," *Aljazeera.com.* February 15. www.aljazeera.com/indepth/features/2012/02/201221519 5912519142.html.

Tajfel, H. 1974. "Social identity and intergroup behavior," *Social Science Information* 13(2): 65–93.

Tajfel, H. and Turner, J. C. 1986. "The social identity theory of intergroup behavior," in W. G Austin and S. Worchel (eds.), *The Social Psychology of Intergroup Relations*: 7–24. Chicago: Nelson Hall.

Tropp, L. R., Stout, A. M., Boatswain, C., Wright, S. C., and Pettigrew, T. F. 2006. "Trust and acceptance in response to references to group membership: Minority and majority perspectives on cross-group interactions," *Journal of Applied Social Psychology* 36(3): 769–794.

Uzzi, B. 1997. "Social structure and competition in interfirm networks: The paradox of embeddedness," *Administrative Science Quarterly* 42(1): 35–67.

Wei, S.-J. 2000. "How taxing is corruption on international investors?" *The Review of Economics and Statistics* 82(1): 1–11.

Woolcock, M. 1998. "Social capital and economic development: Toward a theoretical synthesis and policy framework," *Theory and Society* 27(2): 151–208.

Yenkey, C. B. 2015. "Mobilizing a market: Ethnic segmentation and investor recruitment into the Nairobi Securities Exchange," *Administrative Science Quarterly* 60(4): 561–595.

Zak, P. J. and Knack, S. 2001. "Trust and growth," *The Economic Journal* 111(470): 295–321.

Zucker, L. G. 1986. "Production of trust: Institutional sources of economic structure, 1840–1920," *Research in Organizational Behavior* 8: 53–111.

6 Bad apples, bad barrels and bad cellars: a "boundaries" perspective on professional misconduct

DANIEL MUZIO, JAMES FAULCONBRIDGE,
CLAUDIA GABBIONETA, AND ROYSTON
GREENWOOD

Parmalat – formerly one of the largest dairy companies in the world – went bankrupt on December 24, 2003, leaving behind a "hole" of 14 billion euros, a sum almost twice the company's 2002 sales turnover. Subsequent investigations revealed that the company's financial accounts had consistently and deliberately been falsified for each of the thirteen years that Parmalat was listed on the Milan Stock Exchange. During those years, professionals – who are supposed to act as gatekeepers (Coffee 2005, 2006) – did not (or, in some cases, decided not to) see what was going on. Deloitte – which was auditing the company's group accounts – did not raise any concerns until October 2003 when they issued a disclaimer on the company's accounts, as they could not determine the amount of a fund held by a subsidiary. Standard and Poor's constantly rated the company at the investment grade and even improved its outlook only a few months before the company defaulted. Securities analysts, similarly, remained positive on Parmalat's shares until the company was already on the verge of bankruptcy; only a few days before the fraud was detected, fifty-seven of sixty-six of their equity research reports recommended buying or holding the company's shares.

Enron's story, one of the biggest scandals in American history, is not much different, although it took place in the supposedly more developed US stock market. As in the Parmalat story, professionals did not effectively perform their ascribed roles. Arthur Andersen, the company's auditors, consistently approved Enron's accounts without raising any concerns and failed to inform "the company's audit committee about both the accounting policies in use at Enron and the unusual transactions the company had conducted" (Batson Report 2003: 40–41). Management consultancies such as McKinsey, which advised Enron, endorsed its strategic repositioning and praised its "asset light" strategy (Kipping, Kirkpatrick, and Muzio 2006). Not until four days before bankruptcy was declared on December 2, 2001, did rating agencies lower their ratings of the company to below the mark of a safe investment. As late as October in the same year, fifteen securities analysts rated Enron a "buy" and twelve of them recommended it as a "strong buy." Even as late as November 8, when Enron disclosed that nearly five years of earnings would have to be recalculated, eleven of fifteen analysts continued to recommend buying the stock. Only three analysts issued "holds" and one a "strong sell" – even though (admittedly in retrospect) Howard Schilit, an independent analyst, dismissively concluded that "for any analyst to say there were no warning signs in the public filings, they could not have been reading the same public filings as I did" (*Forbes* Report 2003).

The above stories reveal how elite professions and professional service firms are implicated in some of the world's most prominent examples of corporate corruption. Moreover, there is no apparent slackening of the trend: "If accounting scandals no longer dominate headlines as they did when Enron and WorldCom imploded in 2001–02, that is not because they have vanished but because they have become routine" (*The Economist* 2014: 24). Yet the professions have historically justified their influence and privileges with reference to their "gate-keeping" responsibilities (Coffee 2005, 2006), their commitment to social trusteeship (Brint 1994) and the importance of their fiduciary role (Thornton, Jones, and Kury 2005). There is, in other words, a "regulative bargain" (Cooper et al. 1988: 8; Freidson 2001) whereby the state grants the professions a monopoly and self-regulation in exchange for the commitment to maintain ethical standards and use their expertise to serve the public interest (MacDonald 1995).

Instances of wrongdoing by any occupation or organization are cause for concern, but those practised by professions such as law and accountancy are especially worrisome, for two reasons. First, the organizational form of the professional service firm is designed to ensure professional competence and integrity – so its apparent failure requires understanding. Second, and more profoundly, the professions are integral parts of the institutional system of checks and balances which should prevent corporate corruption of the sort practised by Parmalat and Enron. As such, the professions play a critical role in the financial markets because "capitalism cannot function without trust" (*The New York Times* 2012). However, as the episodes of corporate corruption reported above unequivocally indicate, they are, at best, failing in this gate-keeping role or, at worst, they are actively involved in the very forms of misconduct that they are responsible for overseeing. Instead of being lauded exemplars of ethically driven professional conduct, "major accountancy firms have become the unacceptable face of capitalism ... Scratch the surface of any financial scandal or a tax dodge and the invisible hand of major accountancy firms is highly evident" (Mitchell and Sikka 2011: 8).

In this chapter, we analyse the institutional conditions that increase the likelihood of professional misconduct. We seek to address the following questions. To what extent are professionals involved in corporate corruption? Under what circumstances do professions tend to aid rather than police misconduct? What is the relationship between professional misconduct and the institutional context in which professions operate? We define professional misconduct broadly as any behaviours, legal or illegal, that contravene normative expectations and professional codes of conduct. Under this definition, law firms advising their clients on how to shelter their income from taxation, and accounting firms turning a blind eye to their clients' accounts, are instances of professional misconduct. In both cases, professionals violate the professional norms that supposedly regulate their behaviour.

We begin by reviewing three perspectives on professional ethics: the *functionalist perspective* that ties professionalism to the public interest, the *conflict perspective* that focuses on the self-interested practices behind professional claims and the *ecological perspective* that ties misconduct to the changing relationships and boundaries between multiple stakeholders. We then frame and elaborate our analysis against this latter perspective by connecting professional misconduct to the tensions, risks and conflicts generated by key institutional boundaries which are increasingly fragmenting professional practice. These shifting and complex boundaries, we propose, are generating a range of blind spots, opportunities and temptations that are contributing to the incidence – and increased risk – of professional misconduct. We conclude by suggesting a programme for future research.

Professions and ethics

The notion that professional occupations are distinguished from regular businesses and trades by their superior moral fibre is well established in the foundational writings in the sociology of the professions (Carr-Saunders and Wilson 1933; Durkheim 1957; Parsons 1954). For these founding fathers, professions were defined by "an admirable sense of responsibility" and "a pride in service given rather than by interest in opportunity for personal profit" (Carr-Saunders and Wilson 1933: 471). As a result, professions were seen as civilizing forces that could act as "stabilising elements in society" and "centres of resistance to crude forces which threaten steady and peaceful evolution" (Carr-Saunders and Wilson 1933: 497). For Durkheim (1957), the civic sense of the professions was a part of a system of moral restraints that could address the anomie of modernity, and for Carr-Saundera and Wilson (1933), the established professions were even a bastion against the barbarities of Nazism and Stalinism.

In short, for these and other functionalist writers, the professions have a normative value that comes from the role they exercise for the benefit of society, and from the superior ethics, altruism and civic conscience of their members. Similar assumptions, albeit with less hagiographic undertones, characterize the ultimately flawed taxonomic project of trait theorists (e.g., Barber 1963; Greenwood 1957; Millerson 1964), which sought to analytically distinguish professions from other occupations based on their key empirical attributes. Professional ethics based upon a public interest orientation were one of the few traits shared by most checklists.

In these functionalist and trait-based perspectives, professional misconduct is a misnomer that runs counter to the very idea of professionalism. Accordingly, this literature does not directly deal with the issue, but if it could offer an explanation it would probably be in line with the "bad apple" hypothesis (Kisch-Gephart, Harrison, and Treviño 2010), whereby misconduct results from the behaviour of rogue individuals acting against the standards and norms of their profession.

From the 1970s, an alternative and increasingly dominant perspective – conflict theory (Freidson 1970; Johnson 1972; Larson 1977; MacDonald

1995) – began to offer a different take on this issue. For these writers, professionalism is a "peculiar type of occupational control rather than an expression of the inherent nature of particular occupations" (Johnson 1972: 45). Crucially, it is a form of control that empowers producers vis-à-vis consumers by entrusting professionals with "occupational dominance" (Freidson 1970) over the performance of their own work, including its means, ends and the terms and conditions under which it is performed (Freidson 1970). These outcomes are the result of a conscious and systematic political project aimed at translating "a scarce set of cultural and technical resources into a secure and institutionalised system of social and financial rewards" (Larson 1977: xvii).

Professional ethics to these writers are seen as rhetoric that legitimates the privileges of monopoly, self-regulation and higher levels of income. Not only do professions *not* have a special moral commitment, but they also engage in self-serving behaviours. Professional misconduct, in this sense, is consistent with a "bad barrel" hypothesis (Kisch-Gephart et al. 2010) as it reflects the way that professions are designed as social systems, that is, how they are structured to prioritize their own interests over the public good. As George Bernard Shaw put it, the professions are designed to act as conspiracies against the laity (Shaw 2004).

Both the conflict and functional perspectives view misconduct (or, in the latter case, the lack of it) as an inherent and defining feature of professionalism. As such they provide an essentially static account of misconduct and give little attention to how change within and between professional occupations may contribute to its occurrence or form. Particularly important – and so far relatively ignored – are changes to the institutions of the professions – such as training and qualification regimes (Freidson 1994, 2001), ethical codes and disciplinary mechanisms (Brint 1994; Dinovitzer, Gunz, and Gunz 2015; Greenwood 2007; Reynolds 2000), or forms of governance (Greenwood and Empson 2003; Lipartito and Miranti 1998; von Nordenflycht 2014) – which, though designed to support professional standards and constrain the possibility of misconduct, are increasingly becoming undermined. In this context, in our opinion, a more unfolding, dynamic approach to professional misconduct is needed – *an ecological perspective* – in which misconduct is connected to shifting political and economic contexts that are disrupting the traditional institutional arrangements of the professions and eroding their ability to support and regulate appropriate professional behaviour.

Theoretically, the key idea and our starting point is provided by Abbott's notion of professional "ecologies" (1988, 2005) which, through its emphasis on professional competition, offers a dynamic view of changing relationships within and between professional occupations. According to this perspective, professions exist as parts of an interlinked system where they compete against each other to control specific tasks (Halpern 1992). These tasks are organized as jurisdictions over which professions advance more or less exclusive claims. However, because jurisdictions confer material advantages, the claiming and retention of jurisdictional boundaries are inevitably a contested process in which professions advance competing claims in front of key audiences such as the state, the public and the employing organization (e.g., Albrecht and Levy 1982; Begun and Lippincott 1987; Goode 1960, 1969; Halpern 1992; Kronus 1976).

In later work, Abbott (2005; for a similar if less developed argument, see Burrage, Jaraush, and Siegrist 1990) portrays the systems of professions as part of a broader "linked ecology" with adjacent institutions such as the state and the universities, reflecting the fact that the professionalization projects of specific occupations are constrained, supported and generally affected by the moves of social actors adjacent to them and with whom they regularly interact (Muzio, Brock, and Suddaby 2013; Suddaby and Muzio 2015; Suddaby and Viale 2011). As Abbott (2005: 247) observes, "[n]ot only does a jurisdictional tactic like licensing have to succeed in the system of professions, it also has to succeed in the ecology of the state, for quite other reasons."

Abbott's focus on professional ecologies emphasizes the particular importance of "boundaries" that delineate and regulate professional jurisdictions by separating rival interests and the claims of different stakeholders. Based on his work, we identify different types of boundaries which are typically in play within professional ecologies: "jurisdictional" (boundaries between different occupational domains), "geo-political" (between different national realms) and "ecological" (between stakeholders such as practitioners, clients and employers). Importantly, professional ecologies and their boundaries are inherently unstable because of endogenous struggles within the system of the professions itself and exogenous developments in adjacent fields. The redrawing of existing boundaries allows groups to colonize new jurisdictions, exploit new opportunities, avoid regulatory constraints and diminish existing obligations. Professional ecologies, in this sense, are in constant evolution, especially "on the fringes" where different sectional claims and interests are more likely to come into conflict. Indeed, Abbott contrasts relatively stable professional heartlands with the chaotic and disrupted lives along the frontiers. In his words, "boundaries are zones of action because they are zones of conflict" (Abbott 1995: 857).

In this context, professional misconduct arises from the re-drawing of jurisdictional, geo-political and ecological boundaries within and between professional ecologies. In particular, changing boundaries may undermine existing oversight regimes, fuel conflicts of interest, create regulatory blind-spots and generate opportunities for unorthodox, illegitimate and even illegal forms of behaviour. Regulatory, demographic and technological change, in other words, can undermine existing professional and regulatory institutions and disrupt established jurisdictions and their associated organizational forms and work practices (Brock, Powell, and Hinings 1999; Leicht and Fennell 1997). In this context, professional misconduct is consistent with a new "bad cellar" hypothesis, as it arises from the relationships and boundaries between different stakeholders (barrels) in a broader ecological system (cellar). In the rest of this chapter we elaborate how the three sets of boundaries here identified can contribute to professional misconduct.

Changing professional boundaries and misconduct

Jurisdictional boundaries

Jurisdictional boundaries are one of the key elements of the "system of the professions" (Abbott 1988). They identify different professional domains and assign them specific tasks, competences and obligations (Abbott 1988; Freidson 1984, 1994). By doing so, they create an order within the system of professions that, although dynamic and constantly changing, allows it to function in a rather effective way and to survive over time (Albrecht and Levy 1982; Begun and Lippincott 1987; Goode 1960, 1969; Halpern 1992; Kronus 1976). Jurisdictional boundaries, however, may also create opportunities for professional misconduct. We see two main ways by which this can happen.

First, professional misconduct can be the consequence of professionals and professional service firms crossing over different professional jurisdictions. For example, conflicts of interest may arise when audit firms offer their clients non-audit services. When this happens, as highlighted by Levitt (2000), firms may use the audit "as a springboard to more lucrative consulting services" by providing only a cursory audit in the hope that doing so will enhance their relationships with a client. Or, firms may compromise the exercise of professional scepticism when evaluating financial statements in favour of primarily commercial interests. According to the US Securities and Exchange Commission, audit firms that offer both audit and consultancy services may eventually "impair investor confidence in auditor independence and lead to declining confidence in public capital markets" (SEC 2000). Similarly, a conflict of interest may arise when law firms provide consulting in addition to legal services (Rosen 2002), or when securities analysts, who are supposed to produce independent assessments of a company's stock, succumb to the pressures exerted by their employer to issue "more favourable" recommendations (Barber, Lehavy, and Trueman 2007; Dugar and Nathan 1995; Hayward and Boeker 1998; Lin and McNichols 1998; Michaely and Womack 1999; O'Brien, McNichols, and Hsiou-Wei 2005).

The idea that professional misconduct can be the consequence of crossing jurisdictional boundaries is well established (Sikka and Willmott 1995). Much less attention, however, has been paid to a second way by which jurisdictional boundaries may lead to professional misconduct. Reliance upon (rather than the crossing of) jurisdictional boundaries creates the risk of misconduct arising from "institutional ascription" (Gabbioneta et al. 2013; Gabbioneta, Prakash, and Greenwood 2014).

Gabbioneta et al. (2013) emphasize that most instances of corporate corruption involve *several* professional firms. Accounting, law, consultancy, investment firms and rating agencies are often implicated at the same time, confirming Palmer's (2012: 36) suggestion that "most wrongful courses of action require at least the tacit cooperation of others and thus are at least nominally collective". For this reason, attention should be given to the *network* of gatekeepers rather than to dyadic relationships such as those between auditors and clients. It is in this context that Gabbioneta et al. (2013) introduce the idea of institutional ascription. They propose that several conditions – the jurisdictional division of labour among professionals, the over-specialization of professional work (Leicht and Fennel 1997) and the increasing volumes of activity with which professionals and professional service firms have to cope (Braun 2000) – may push professionals to uncritically and unduly rely on the work performed by other professionals and/or professional service firms. It is this passive acceptance of the work of others that opens up the way for misconduct.

The most obvious example of this pattern of behaviour is the heavy reliance upon the reports of auditors. In the Parmalat case, professional reliance was clearly evident, first in the relationships between two accounting firms and later in the relationships between accounting firms, analysts and rating agencies. Gabbioneta et al. (2014) show how Deloitte's "unconditional opinion" on the company's group accounts relied on Grant Thornton's audit of several of Parmalat's subsidiaries, including Bonlat, the group's "garbage can." Similarly, Arnold and Sikka (2001: 483) point out how, in the case of the Bank of Credit and Commerce International (BCCI), the "appointment of two auditors limited the scope of each auditor authority and facilitated BCCI's financial manipulation."

Once audit reports are available they are often uncritically accepted by other professions – even those that are supposed and claim to exercise independent scrutiny and judgement – because "a green light from an auditor means that a company's accounting practices have passed muster" (*New York Times* April 13, 2008; in Sikka 2009). Credit rating agencies, for example, often base their ratings on financial statements that they assume have been appropriately checked. The Public Prosecutor in the Parmalat case was especially critical of rating agencies because they "did not develop a true analysis of the company's financial statements," even though doing so would have shown that these statements "were abundantly false" (Public Prosecutor, Parma). Similarly, the US Senate Committee investigating the role of rating agencies in the Enron case decried their behaviour because they "did not perform a thorough analysis of Enron's public filings; did not pay appropriate attention to allegations of financial fraud; and repeatedly took company officials at their word, without asking probing, specific questions – despite indications that the company had misled the rating agencies in the past" (Senate Governmental Affairs Committee 2002: 108).

The chain of reliance on other professionals in the above stories also implicates securities analysts, who formulated their investment recommendations using financial data that they presumed had been diligently audited *and* had been appropriately examined by the credit rating agencies. This reliance occurred despite the proclamation of analysts that they "exercise independent professional judgment when conducting investment analysis, making investment recommendations, taking investment actions, and engaging in other professional activities" (CFA 2013). As reported in the *New York Times* (2001), one analyst "persisted in recommending the (Enron) stock" because he did not "think accountants and auditors would have allowed total shenanigans." Or, as another securities analyst candidly admitted, "we actually do something similar to an act of faith … if we know that those who have more information than we do have already expressed a positive opinion, to some extent we raise our hands … and consider the financial situation as given … we do not question … [issues] on which rating agencies have already given their opinion" (Gabbioneta et al. 2014).

Coming full circle, audit firms frequently rely on the work of law firms. When asked why Arthur Andersen did not report on Enron's suspicious accounting practices, Nancy Temple – in-house attorney for Arthur Andersen – answered that it was "because Vincent & Elkins had said there was no problem and that no further action would be necessary." Marco Verde – one of the auditors working for Parmalat – testified that he had agreed with the company on the value of a certain transaction because the law firm assisting the company had not raised any concerns about it (Court of Milan 2008).

Institutional ascription can arise from several motivations and perceptions. Observers may misunderstand the basis of others' jurisdictions and attribute a process of diligence and detailed scrutiny that those professions would not claim. Or, it could arise from professional failure – as when an auditor fails to detect a wrongdoing within a client's organization. Or, it could stem from the inappropriate actions of a professional (as in the Parmalat case). Whatever the initial cause, however, the central thrust of the institutional ascription thesis is that any weakness diffuses and infects a professional network and has an amplifying effect – as more and more professions sign off, the less likely that wrongdoing will be inspected and exposed.

Paradoxically, therefore, the existence of jurisdictional boundaries may either decrease or increase the possibility of professional misconduct. It may decrease it by preventing the emergence of conflicts of interests that would arise from professional service firms crossing jurisdictional boundaries. Yet, boundaries may increase the risk of professional misconduct, because of the processes of mutual ascriptions of professional diligence that take place among professionals. Both possibilities – boundary crossing and boundary respect – it is worth noting, increase not only the risk of professional misconduct but also the chances that corruption by clients will occur and remain undetected.

Geo-political boundaries

While not at the centre of Abbott's analysis (but see Krause 1996; MacDonald 1995; Burrage and Torstendahl 1990), professional ecologies and their regulatory regimes have historically existed within national (or in some cases regional) contexts. Differences in qualification frameworks and codes of practice mean that expectation and definitions of professional conduct vary across geo-political boundaries. In a globalizing world, however, professional work is increasingly conducted across these boundaries, and as such geo-political boundaries are an increasingly significant risk factor in professional misconduct (see Faulconbridge and Muzio 2012).

The crossing of geo-political boundaries is reflected in the rise of the large multinational professional service firm which is increasingly replacing the national partnership as the key organizational arrangement for elite professional activity (see Cooper et al. 1996; Faulconbridge and Muzio 2008). The largest multinational law firm Baker and McKenzie has offices in excess of 40 countries and employs over 10,000 lawyers. The "Big Four" accountancy firms are some of the most globalized organizations in the world. PricewaterhouseCoopers, the largest, has offices in over 150 countries and almost 200,000 employees (Empson et al. 2015). The transnational scope of these organizations creates three new risks and opportunities for professional misconduct.

First, as they cross geo-political boundaries, professionals may face uncertainty over the nature and source of their obligations – Nagel's (2007) dilemma of double deontology. Historically, professionals derived their normative obligations from the specific geo-political jurisdictions in which they were based (Krause 1996). However, as Etherington and Lee (2007: 96–97) sharply illustrate, in an era of frequent boundary crossing, "we might not be too surprised to find an Australian lawyer working in the Brussels office of a New York law firm on a contract for a Japanese client with a German counterpart, which is governed by English common law, but in which disputes are to be referred to the International Chamber of Commerce's International Court of Arbitration in Paris." The result is an ethical conundrum for professionals and clients caught between national jurisdictions and their respective deontological rules. Nicolson and Webb (1999) suggest that such situations of double (or perhaps multiple) deontology lead to systematic uncertainties and unintentional misconduct as professionals struggle to understand and reconcile the demands of competing jurisdictions.

A good example of double deontology relates to Swiss banks and their US clients (see Broom and Bandel 2014). To prevent money laundering and tax evasion, in 2010 US authorities demanded that Swiss banks with branches in the US reveal details of accounts held in Switzerland by US nationals. This immediately left Swiss professionals in a situation of double deontology. Complying with the disclosure request would violate Swiss privacy laws, but not doing so would violate US laws. The Swiss Secretariat released a statement in 2012 noting that "the implementation of these provisions is generating high costs and legal uncertainty worldwide" (quoted in Novack 2012). Ultimately, a special agreement had to be reached that allowed Swiss privacy laws to be broken. This involved Swiss professionals gaining consent from clients to break Swiss laws. A related but slightly different example is provided by Smets, Morris and Greenwood (2012) who found that German and UK lawyers working in the same firm initially found it difficult to collaborate on cross-border transactions because differences in their respective deontological codes made certain actions illegal in one jurisdiction while legal in the other. Again workarounds were needed, or what Smets et al. (2012) refer to as "situated improvising." Both examples raise questions about the malleability of rules and standards and, as we demonstrate below, the potential to enable wrongdoing through forms of arbitrage.

A similar form of risk relates to the trend towards off-shoring (see Daly and Silver 2006; Sako 2015). In such scenarios, double deontology is again a problem because it is not typically evident which set of ethical standards should apply. Should it be those of the offshore jurisdiction in which the work is completed, or those of the jurisdiction of the professional service firm off-shoring the work? Or should it be those of the jurisdiction where the client is located? Such uncertainty led the UK Financial Reporting Council to question whether the off-shore activities of accountancy firms are sufficiently managed to ensure adherence to ethical standards (Crump 2013).

A second risk concerns more intentional misconduct. Off-shoring provides corporations with opportunities to escape the reach of national regulations and regulators – as illustrated by the case of off-shore financial centres. These are not a new phenomenon (see, for example, Roberts 1994) and have significant financial implications – Sikka and Hampton (2005: 327) estimate that in 2001 they cost the US government $311 billion in tax revenues. Importantly for our purpose, off-shore centres could not operate without the support of professionals, especially accountants and lawyers and those holding new forms of expertise, such as asset and wealth managers (see Harrington 2015; Wójcik 2013). As Palan, Murphy and Chavagneux (2010: 13) observe, it is no coincidence that accountants from the Big Four are found in nearly all off-shore financial centres and that their client base in these jurisdictions is almost exclusively comprised of corporations seeking to minimize their tax liabilities. Indeed, following the collapse of WorldCom, a US Senate Permanent Subcommittee on Investigations revealed that the Big Four accountancy firms had developed multiple tax "products" designed to exploit differences across national jurisdictions and had done so without apparent regard for their broader professional and fiduciary obligations (Sikka and Hampton 2005: 333). Similarly, in the UK, KPMG developed a tax-avoidance scheme which used Jersey as an offshore centre in order to reduce sales tax liability, a practice since deemed illegal throughout the EU (Sikka and Hampton 2005: 337). In Australia, lawyers enabled the movement of the entire James Hardie company off-shore to the Netherlands in order to minimize potential liabilities arising from the company's asbestos-based products (Le Mire 2007). A national outcry forced the Australian Federal government to step in to top-up the compensation fund available to plaintiffs. In these situations the behaviour of professionals may not necessarily involve illegal actions, but their advice can be construed as a form of normative misconduct. As Urry (2014: 44) notes, "even George Osborne, the Conservative Chancellor of the Exchequer in the UK, describes 'aggressive tax avoidance' as 'morally repugnant'."

The wider issue relates to the responsibility that professionals hold in the use and impact of their advice. In many instances, professional advice which is legally sound enables and supports wrongdoing by their clients, implicating professionals in the transgression of normative standards. After the demise of Lehman Brothers it became clear that the Repo 105 instrument used to remove liabilities from its balance sheet and the ultimate cause of the firm's collapse was adopted as a result of a legal opinion provided by the London office of Linklaters. This opinion stated that under English law Lehman's treatment of Repo 105's instrument was legal. However, Lehman had previously been advised that under US law such a use of a Repo 105 instrument would not be permitted. Professionals at Lehman's had exploited their firm's ability to cross geo-political boundaries to seek a favourable professional opinion elsewhere, in order to circumvent its own national regulations. Moreover, lawyers at Linklaters failed to consider how technically sound legal advice might be exploited and have unintended implications – something perfectly feasible given Linklaters' activities as a global law firm in New York City. As Kershaw and Moorhead (2013: 51) note, the question arises: "Whether the lawyer giving the true sale opinion perceived, or ought to have perceived, that providing the opinion was likely to give rise to a real risk of accounting or securities breaches. Or, to echo Lord Nicholl's words set forth above in relation to dishonest assistance, if they were not so aware, had they deliberately closed their eyes and ears to this risk?"

Similar questions exist with regard to the role of professional services firms in facilitating tax avoidance. Burger, Mayer and Bowal (2007: 49) note that clients are often "advised in 'comfort or opinion letters' issued by law firms to the effect that the tax shelters are 'perfectly legal'," despite the fact that by exploiting an off-shore jurisdiction the client is breaking laws in another country in which they operate. Geo-political boundary crossing, then, raises not only new deontological uncertainties but generates situations in which professionals can become implicated in corporate wrongdoing.

The third risk associated with the crossing of geo-political boundaries is the lobbying of national governments for regulatory changes that increase the possibility of misconduct. As Flood (2011: 510) emphasizes: "the size and scope of global law firms has made them difficult to encompass within a single regulatory jurisdiction" and "put them beyond the reach of effective national regulation" (for an accounting example, see Greenwood and Suddaby 2006). Moreover, their scale gives them the ability to pressure national governments for favourable regulatory treatment.

A clear example was the threat by the Big Four accountancy firms to relocate to Jersey if the British government failed to introduce "limited liability partnerships" (Mitchell et al. 2002). The Big Four engaged two law firms in London (Slaughter & May and Simmons & Simmons) and one in Jersey (Mourant du Feu & Jeune) to introduce limited liability partnerships in Jersey. They then used the threat of relocation to successfully lobby for similar legal arrangements to be introduced in the UK. The motivation for introducing this new organizational form was to limit liability in cases involving professional negligence. In effect, the ability to move across national boundaries was used to undermine the concept of joint and several liability that has traditionally been portrayed as a fundamental mechanism for reducing the risk of professional misconduct (Greenwood and Empson 2003; Briscoe and Von Nordenflycht 2014).

The size and significance of global professional services firms gives them not only leverage over national regulators but also influence over the design of international regulatory arrangements. As Flood points out, "global capitalism has been predicated on the rule of law ... *and among its chief architects* are the large international law firms" (2011: 511, emphasis added). In performing this role, firms accomplish two things. First, as Suddaby, Cooper and Greenwood (2007: 334 – see also, Arnold 2005; Faulconbridge and Muzio 2012) note, "the historical regulatory bargain between professional associations and nation states is being superseded by a new compact between conglomerate professional firms and transnational trade organizations." This new compact uses the growing size and the power of global professional service firms, in alliance with international organizations such as the WTO, to support deregulatory agendas and develop globally integrated markets for professional expertise. Five US law firms, for example, formed the backbone of the legal division of the Council of Service Industries which lobbied hard for the de-regulation of professional services markets as part of the WTO's GATS agreement (Terry 2001).

Second, the legitimacy and effectiveness of *national* regulatory frameworks are being constantly undermined. The global law firm, for example, has managed "to sideline the inconvenience of conflict of interest rules while continuing to pay lip service to them" (Flood 2011: 508–509). Caramanis (2002: 400) describes how in the 1990s the then

"Big Five" accounting firms "co-ordinated or at least initiated" a series of reforms to the Greek audit profession, which made it easier for them to employ foreign accountants in Greece. This made the Greek accountancy profession "gravely concerned as these measures (the new qualification exams [especially]) could call into question its [the Greek profession's] standing and reputation" (quoted in Caramanis 2002: 400). Similarly, residency requirements in Canada that "protect(ed) consumers from malpractice by making disciplinary control more practicable and by facilitating the ability of injured parties to sue for negligence" were undermined by WTO free trade regimes (Arnold 2005: 313).

Ecological boundaries: clients, investors and employers

A series of "ecological" boundaries separate and regulate professional relationships with clients, employers and, increasingly, financial investors (Abbott 1988, 2005; Burrage et al. 1990). These boundaries establish professional duties by specifying the rights and obligations of different parties – such as the duty to avoid conflicts of interest or to ensure client confidentiality (Dinovitzer et al. 2015). They are also designed to limit the possibility that professionals may be unduly influenced such that they fail to observe their own deontological obligations. Three boundaries are especially noteworthy: between professionals and their clients; between professionals and the organizations in which they work; and, third, those between professional firms and investors.

Boundaries between professionals and clients
It used to be thought that clients are less knowledgeable and organized than their professional advisors and therefore less able to define and ensure that their interests are appropriately addressed (Johnson 1972). Yet, in the corporate world at least, clients are becoming increasingly sophisticated (Sturdy 1997). Furthermore, they are increasingly taking a more short-term and transactional approach to professional relationships, constantly reviewing their suppliers (Broschak 2015). The outcome is client capture: "companies tend to select auditors who will provide a clean opinion as cheaply and quickly as possible. Similarly, accountants who discover irregularities may be better off asking management to make minor adjustments, rather than blowing

the whistle on a mis-statement that could embroil their firm in costly litigation" (*The Economist*, December 13, 2014). In this context, auditors have become "dozy watchdogs" (*The Economist* 2014: 25). As a result, boundaries originally designed to protect clients acquire a new significance in protecting professionals themselves (Heinz 1982).

"Client capture" (Dinovitzer, Gunz, and Gunz 2014; Gabbioneta et al. 2014; Gunz and Gunz 2008; Leicht and Fennel 2001) refers to situations where advice is tailored to the commercial interests of clients and weakens the professional's fiduciary obligations to the broader public. In other words, the interests of clients are prioritized to the point where the "social trusteeship" (Brint 1994) responsibilities of professionals are compromised. Although capture may occur over relatively mundane issues (Dinovitzer et al. 2014), it particularly matters where it affects the "gatekeeping" role of the professions – such as their commitment to the administration of justice or to the accuracy of financial statements.

The implications of client capture are starkly illustrated by the involvement of the professions in corporate wrongdoings such as those committed by Enron, WorldCom, Tyco and Parmalat. In each case, a professional firm was deflected from behaving "professionally" either by explicit pressure from the client or by the implicit fear of losing the client. In the case of Enron, "[Arthur] Andersen team members routinely succumbed to demands for certification from Enron management," spectacularly failing in their obligations towards third parties, especially investors (Macey and Sale 2003: 1179). In the legal profession, to give one example, Australian large law firm Clayton Utz was complicit in the strategy of its client British American Tobacco to destroy documentation so as to minimize litigation risks (Cameron 2002; Parker 2004).

Rating agencies have been similarly criticized for their lack of independence. As Crotty (2009: 566) observes, "ratings agencies are paid by the investment banks whose products they rate. Their profits therefore depend on whether they keep these banks happy … If one agency gave realistic assessments of the high risk associated with these securities while others did not, that firm would see its profit plummet. Thus, it made sense for investment banks to shop their securities around, looking for the agency that would give them the highest ratings and it made sense for agencies to provide excessively optimistic ratings." Such a view is echoed by Partnoy (2009: 432), who argues that "credit-rating agencies ... sell not information, but keys that unlock the financial markets" and that, as a consequence, issuers have strong incentives to look for the agency that would give them the highest possible rating.

A growing literature seeks to identify the circumstances that increase the likelihood of client capture – or at least the risk of its occurrence. For Sharma (1997), who uses the term client control, it is most likely to occur in situations where clients have alternative providers, where professionals make significant investments in a particular client relationship and where there is a high degree of dependency upon a particular client. Macey and Sale (2003) refer to the size of the client, the dependency of the firm upon revenues from a particular client and the weakening of collective accountability implied by the limited liability partnership format. Klimentchenko (2009) and Sikka (2009), referring to the relationship between auditing and consulting, stress the impact of "cross selling" and how this can compromise fiduciary services.

Several factors are supposed to reduce the risk of client capture. Since the Sarbanes–Oxley reforms of 2002, the extent of consulting that can be provided to an audit client has been constrained. Similarly, many countries worldwide have introduced mandatory audit rotation every three to five years. But the evidence to date is that these factors are, at best, only partially effective in reducing the risk of client capture (e.g., Abbott, Parker, and Peters 2004; Blouin, Grein, and Roundtree 2007; Cullinan 2004; DeFond and Francis 2005; Myers, Myers, and Omer 2003; Ribstein 2003).

Boundaries between professionals and employers. A particularly important ecological boundary, and, again, one that is changing and that has potential significance for the possibility of misconduct, is that between the individual and the employing organization. The relationship between professionals and bureaucratic organizations has long been a concern in the literature and was, initially, considered to be an area of tension because of the (assumed) inherent conflict between professional and bureaucratic contexts. It was supposed that professionals would find it difficult to sustain their professional commitment (e.g., Goode 1957). However, "this line of reasoning has not been supported by empirical research. Professionals have actually adapted well to work in large organizations" (Suddaby and Viale 2011: 423). Moreover, as noted above, professionals have developed a particular governance form – the "professional partnership" – which is intended to underpin and reinforce professional values.

However, as members of professions have moved from being primarily self-employed or employed in modest-sized firms to become employees of increasingly large firms, the boundary between the professional as a member of a profession and as an organizational employee has assumed high significance (Ackroyd and Muzio 2007; Larson 1977; MacDonald 1995). It has long been recognized that organizational size can undermine – at least to some extent – the traditional autonomy and discretion provided by collegial professionalism and can raise the risk of ethical challenges (Brock et al. 1999; Cooper et al. 1996; Greenwood and Hinings 1993).

The reason why this particular boundary has worrying consequences is twofold. Larger firms can unwittingly distance their professionals from the cultural and normative influence of the broader professional community. Thus, for example, large English law firms have largely opted out from national vocational training processes and in conjunction with commercial providers like BPP University developed their own in-house training programmes (Faulconbridge and Muzio 2012; Malhotra, Morris, and Hinings 2006). Through these programmes, trainees are socialized into the organization's systems, practices and values. This distancing process is further facilitated by the development of increasingly sophisticated identity management techniques designed to control and align individual subjectivities with organizational priorities (Anderson-Gough, Grey, and Robson 1999, 2000; Cooper and Robson 2006; Covaleski et al. 1998; Grey 1998). Thus, through "the use of a bundle of increasingly sophisticated HR practices such as selective recruitment, in-house training, performance appraisal and mentoring these firms mould their recruits" to fit in with *their* values and priorities (Flood 2011: 510).

The second way by which size and organizational status might compromise professional norms is that professionals within a large and prestigious firm are more susceptible to the gentle and often implicit expectations to do things in a particular way. A firm's prestige provides a form of "structural assurance" that its way of doing things is appropriate (Grey 2003; Wilson et al. 2008; Smets et al. 2012). Structural assurance, in other words, "is especially apposite in professional settings because it lowers professional concerns that organizational practices and expectations are appropriate, even though they may run counter to institutionalized norms of conduct" (Smets et al. 2012: 897). Crucially, this tends to facilitate misconduct as professionals in prestigious firms assume that their objectives are "safe and fair" (Wilson et al. 2008: 989). Importantly, structural assurance applies not only to employees but to other stakeholders, such as other organizations in broader networks of expertise, and to regulators, who are likely to exercise less scrutiny to large firms (Grey 2003; Smets et al. 2012).

Boundaries with investors. Finally, a recent and still developing boundary that may represent an increasingly important source of ethical tensions and dilemmas resides between professionals and outside investors. Traditionally, professionals have been organized as sole practitioners or as part of "partnerships," which merge ownership with managerial control (Empson and Chapman 2006; Greenwood, Hinings, and Brown 1990; Greenwood and Empson 2003; Maister 1993; Briscoe and Von Nordenflycht 2014). As such, partners are jointly and severally liable for each other's liabilities, a pattern of responsibility intended to ensure the quality and integrity of professional work. Joint liability, in other words, at least in theory, should motivate professionals to monitor each other and therefore safeguard the interests of clients and the broader public.

A distinctive feature of the partnership format – at least until recently – has been the prohibition of external investors. There was to be no internal "representatives" (i.e., proponents) of the commercial "logic" (Pache and Santos 2010). Instead, the professional logic was to be ubiquitous and thus nurtured and protected. Yet over the last few decades (Faulconbridge and Muzio 2009; Greenwood and Empson 2003; Briscoe and Von Nordenflycht 2014) an increasing number of professional service firms, especially management consultants and investment banks (Briscoe and Von Nordenflycht 2014), have restructured themselves as publicly listed corporations – moving away from and potentially undermining the motivation and value of peer control. This shift has been proposed as a major reason why, for example, investment banks became more commercially oriented (Santoro and Strauss 2013).

Some occupations, notably management consulting, adopted the professional partnership form because it gave them symbolic legitimacy. It made them appear professional because that was the format associated with the established professions – especially law and accounting for whom the partnership format was mandatory (McKenna 2006). Recently, however, some jurisdictions – such as

New South Wales in Australia, and England and Wales – have allowed external investment in and ownership of law firms. Two Australian law firms have listed on the stock exchange and expanded through high-profile acquisitions in the UK (Dowell 2012; Gannage-Stewart 2014; Briscoe and Von Nordenflycht 2014). The UK law firm Gateley was floated on the London Stock Exchange on June 8, 2015 (Manning 2015), soon to be followed by the larger firm Irwin Mitchell (*The Lawyer* 2015). The move to allow external shareholders is significant because they represent another key stakeholder within professional ecologies and, as such, provide another set of relationships and tensions that have to be managed by professional firms and their professional associations. As indicated by the quote below, which is taken from the prospectus of Slater & Gordon, for a publicly listed law firm securing a return on investments potentially clashes with fiduciary obligations towards other stakeholders:

> Lawyers have a primary duty to the courts and a secondary duty to their clients. These duties – including the attendant responsibilities such as client confidentiality and the rules relating to legal professional privilege – are paramount given the nature of the company's business as an incorporated legal practice. There could be circumstances in which the lawyers of Slater & Gordon are required to act in accordance with these duties and contrary to other corporate responsibilities and against the interests of Shareholders and the short-term profitability of the company (Slater and Gordon 2007).

The fear, hinted in the quote and articulated elsewhere is that the duty to investors to maximize returns on their investment may compromise standards (Markle 2014; Parker 2004; Rayne 2014). Firms may come under pressure to maximize billing from existing clients through aggressive cross-selling, or to compromise quality in order to boost their profitability. In effect, the breaching of this boundary may reinforce the client capture dynamics described above. It is, however, too early to know how these changes in the ownership boundaries will play out, but not all observers are pessimistic. Some have argued that outside investors could *reduce* the incidence of misconduct by imposing higher regulatory standards and tightening internal controls (Fortney and Gordon 2013; Parker 2004; Parker et al. 2008; Parker, Gordon, and Mark 2010). Nevertheless, the growing role of investors as an important stakeholder in professional ecologies and the conflicts of interest that this additional complexity may generate represent an important new source of tensions and, potentially, of misconduct.

Conclusions and future research agenda

Our chapter supports the view that professional misconduct arises from the transformation of professional institutions rather than being inherent in the nature of the professions themselves. Our analysis places particular emphasis on changing relational patterns within broader professional ecologies. At the heart of our argument is the importance of boundaries with professional ecologies, as these demark distinct remits, roles and responsibilities and regulate the competing claims of different stakeholders. We have identified jurisdictional, geo-political and ecological boundaries, reviewed changes to them that are destabilizing professional ecologies, and linked these shifts in, and pressures upon, boundaries to professional misconduct.

We have proposed that, in some cases, boundaries may simply be too weak. Clients and employers may too easily override the deontological obligations and fiduciary duties of individual professionals. Similarly, within multi-disciplinary firms, boundaries between different profes-sional groups may be too thin and porous to provide an effective barrier against conflicts of interest and opportunistic behaviour. In this most obvious of scenarios, boundaries simply fail in their objective to sepa-rate distinct remits, interests and stakeholders. However, in some situations the opposite problem arises: boundaries may be too strong. Boundaries can provide barriers that deprive professionals of the full picture and cloud their professional judgment. They can create blind spots and lead to processes of collective myopia. In other situations, boundaries create uncertainties or dilemmas where existing regulatory and normative orders are weakened if not suspended. In a globalized professional services market, the gaze and reach of national regulators are increasingly compromised. The result is a liminal place character-ized by ambiguity and increased opportunities for questionable experi-mentation and entrepreneurial behaviours. Indeed, our analysis suggests how professional firms may actively exploit the gaps and inconsistencies between national boundaries on behalf of themselves and their clients. Thus on the basis of our conceptual framework, we suggest a "bad cellar" hypothesis that ties misconduct to the contested and shifting boundaries between different actors in broader ecological

systems. While the "bad apple" and "bad barrel" hypotheses emphasized the role of rogue individuals and flawed organizational designs,
we invite researchers to broaden their focus to consider how misconduct may arise at the next level of analysis, that is, on the boundaries
between actors within linked ecologies.

Future research agenda

Our conceptual framework calls for a programme of empirical work to
measure, elaborate and confirm (or modify) the arguments developed
here. This is particularly true with regard to the relationship between
boundaries and professional misconduct. For instance, to what extent
are recent regulatory changes and developments with professional
ecologies reducing the scope for professional misconduct? Obvious
examples include legislation introduced in the wake of Enron and
Parmalat, such as the Sarbanes–Oxley Act in the US, which sought to
re-regulate the relationship between professionals and their advisors
and reinforce jurisdictional boundaries by re-asserting the separation
of auditing from consulting. On the other hand, legislation such as the
Legal Services Act (2007) in England and Wales introduces new stakeholders (i.e., investors) within professional ecologies and potentially
creates new sources of tensions that have to be managed. These may
lead to increased opportunities for misconduct or help to bring in more
comprehensive ethical infrastructures which help to manage such risks.
In this context, it is very important to ask, how are recent regulatory
reforms affecting professional ecologies? What is their impact on professional misconduct? How can new regulatory risks be appropriately
managed? Related to this, there needs to be a further debate on where
professional regulation is best located. Historically, professional occupations have admitted and regulated individual practitioners.
However, following the rise of the large professional services firm,
the emphasis has somewhat shifted towards entity regulation (Flood
2011). Perhaps, on the basis of the analysis developed here, professional regulation should also take a more ecological view and focus on
the boundaries between different actors and jurisdictions

Connected to this point, we need to better understand what factors
are likely to weaken and compromise existing boundaries. For
instance, is capture more likely to occur within stable long-term relationships, where there may be a high degree of proximity between

clients and their advisors, or in transactional relationships, where professionals are under pressure to retain increasingly mobile clients? Is the presence of outside investors going to exercise new pressures towards misconduct or will they bring enhanced regulatory regimes which may reduce these risks?

We also need more research on the relationship between national regulatory frameworks and the new transnational regimes which are emerging, around agreements such as GATS, the EU and NAFTA. While professional practice is increasingly global and requires a global oversight, it has historically been regulated at the national level. Although inevitable, the re-scaling of regulation from the national to the transnational level may undermine existing arrangements and leave behind a series of "black-holes" where professional practice can escape proper oversight (Faulconbridge and Muzio 2012). As such, more research needs to be focused on the relationship between established national and developing transnational regimes and its likely impact on the potential for professional misconduct. Which regulatory powers and competences are best left at the national level and which at the transnational level? What is required to ensure an adequate dialogue and coordination between different regulatory levels? What is the best way to regulate global professional services firms?

Finally, more research is required in other than Anglo-Saxon contexts. There are significant national variations not only in how professional ecologies are structured (Burrage and Torstendhal 1990; Faulconbridge and Muzio 2007) but also in corporate wrongdoing patterns. Yet these differences have not been adequately explored. We need to understand how professional ecologies in continental societies, which are more closely structured around the state and characterized by stronger jurisdictional boundaries and tighter levels of regulation (Paterson, Fink, and Ongus 2003), shape professional patterns of misconduct. Coffee (2006), for example, makes a distinction between continental models, where cases of corruption often involve strong block-holders (like Tanzi at Parmalat) transferring resources from the company to themselves, and Anglo-Saxon contexts, where fragmented shareholding is associated with wrongdoing by managers who engage in earnings manipulation in order to inflate the value of their variable remuneration. Given these differences in context and the form of wrongdoing with which they are most associated, what is their link with professional misconduct? There is much we still need to know.

References

Abbott, A. 1988. *The System of Professions: An Essay on the Division of Expert Labor*. University of Chicago Press.

Abbott, A. 1995. "Boundaries of social work or social work of boundaries?" *Social Service Review* 69: 545–562.

Abbott, A. 2005. "Linked ecologies: States and universities as environments for professions," *Sociological Theory* 23: 245–274.

Abbott, L., Parker, S., and Peters, J. 2004. "Audit committee characteristics and restatements," *Auditing: A Journal of Practice and Theory* 23(1): 69–87.

Ackroyd, S. and Muzio, D. 2007. "The reconstructed professional firm explaining change in English legal practices," *Organization Studies* 48: 1–19.

Albrecht, G. L. and Levy, J. A. 1982. "The professionalization of osteopathy: Adaptation in the medical marketplace," *Research in the Sociology of Health Care* 2: 161–206.

Anderson-Gough, F., Grey, C., and Robson, K. 1999. "Making up accountants: the organisational and professional socialisation of trainee chartered accounts," in R. Roslender (ed.), *Accounting and Business Research*, 29: 259–260. Aldershot: Gower Ashgate.

Anderson-Gough, F., Grey, C., and Robson, K. 2000. "In the name of the client: The service ethic in two international accounting firms," *Human Relations* 53: 1151–1174.

Arnold, P. J. 2005. "Disciplining domestic regulation: The World Trade Organization and the market for professional services," *Accounting, Organizations and Society* 30: 299–330.

Arnold, P. J. and Sikka, P. 2001. "Globalization and the state–profession relationship: The case the Bank of Credit and Commerce International," *Accounting, Organizations and Society* 26: 475–499.

Barber, B. 1963. "Some problems in the sociology of the professions," *Daedalus* 92: 669–688.

Barber, B. M., Lehavy, R., and Trueman, B. 2007. "Comparing the stock recommendation performance of investment banks and independent research firms," *Journal of Financial Economics* 85: 490–517.

Batson Report. 2003. *The final report of Neal Batson, Court-appointed examiner, in re: ENRON CORP., et al., debtors*. United States Bankruptcy Court, Southern District of New York.

Begun, J. W. and Lippincott, R. C. 1987. "The origins and resolution of interoccupational conflict," *Work and Occupations* 14: 368–386.

Blouin, J., Grein, B., and Roundtree, B. 2007. "An analysis of forced auditor change: The case of former Arthur Andersen clients," *The Accounting Review* 82: 621–650.

Braun, R. L. 2000. "The effect of time pressure on auditor attention to qualitative aspects of misstatements indicative of potential fraudulent financial reporting," *Accounting, Organizations and Society* 25: 243–259.

Brint, S. G. 1994. *In an Age of Experts: The Changing Role of Professionals in Politics and Public Life.* Princeton University Press.

Briscoe, F. and Von Nordenflycht, A. 2014. "Which path to power? Workplace networks and the relative effectiveness of inheritance and rainmaking strategies for professional partners," *Journal of Professions and Organization* 1(1): 33–48.

Brock, D., Powell, M., and Hinings, C. R. 1999. *Restructuring the Professional Organization: Accounting, Healthcare and Law.* London and New York: Routledge.

Broom, G. and Bandel, C. 2014. "Swiss banks send U.S. client data before cascade of accords," Bloomberg Business, July 31.

Broschak, J. 2015. "Client Relationships in Professional Service Firms," in L. Empson, D. Muzio, J. Broschak, and B. Hinings (eds.), *The Handbook of Professional Services Firms*: 304–326. Oxford University Press.

Burger, E. S., Mayer, D., and Bowal, P. 2007. "KPMG and abusive tax shelters: Key ethical implications for legal and accounting professionals," *Journal of Legal Profession* 31: 43–74.

Burrage, M., Jaraush, K., and Siegrist, H. 1990. "An actor based framework for the study of professionalism," in M. Burrage and R. Torstendahl (eds.), *The Professions in Theory and History*: 202–226. London: Rutledge.

Burrage, M. and Torstendahl, R. 1990. *Professions in Theory and History.* London: Sage.

Cameron, C. 2002. "Hired guns and smoking guns: McCabe v British American Tobacco Australia Ltd," *University of New South Wales Law Journal* 25: 768–773.

Caramanis, C. V. 2002. "The interplay between professional groups, the state and supranational agents: Pax Americana in the age of 'globalisation,'" *Accounting, Organizations and Society* 27: 379–408.

Carr-Saunders, A. M., and Wilson, P. A. 1933. *The Professions.* Oxford: Clarendon Press.

CFA. 2013. *Code of Ethics and Standards of Professional Conduct.*

Coffee, J. C. 2005. "A Theory of Corporate Scandals: Why the U.S. and Europe Differ." Columbia Law and Economics Working Paper No. 274.

Coffee, J. C. 2006. *Gatekeepers: The Professions and Corporate Governance.* Oxford University Press.

Cooper, D., Hinings, C. R., Greenwood, R., and Brown, J. L. 1996. "Sedimentation and transformation in organizational change: The case of Canadian law firms," *Organization Studies* 17: 623–647.

Cooper, D., Lowe, A., Puxty, A., Robson, K., and Willmott, H. 1988. *Regulating the UK Accountancy Profession: Episodes in the Relation Between the Profession and the State.* Paper presented at the Economic and Social Research Council Conference on Corporatism at the Policy Studies Institute, London, January.

Cooper, D. L. and Robson, K. 2006. "Accounting, professions and regulation: Locating the sites of professionalization," *Accounting, Organizations and Society* 31: 415–444.

Court of Milan. 2008. I Section Criminal Law. Sentence. N. 10465/04 R.G. n.r. N. 12473/04 + 7436/08 +9538/05 R.G. Trib.

Covaleski, M. A., Dirsmith, M. L., Heian, J. B., and Samuel, S. 1998. "The calculated and the avowed: Techniques of discipline and struggles over identity in Big Six public accounting firms," *Administrative Science Quarterly* 43: 293–327.

Crotty, J. 2009. "Structural causes of the global financial crisis: A critical assessment of the 'new financial architecture,'" *Cambridge Journal of Economics* 33: 563–580.

Crump, R. 2013. "FRC warns auditors over ethical failings," *Accountancy Age.* May 29.

Cullinan, C. 2004. "Enron as a symptom of audit process breakdown: Can the Sarbanes-Oxley Act cure the disease?," *Critical Perspectives in Accounting* 15: 853–864.

Daly, M. C. and Silver, C. 2006. "Flattening the world of legal services: The ethical and liability minefields of offshoring legal and law-related services," *Georgetown Journal of International Law* 38: 401–447.

DeFond, M. L. and Francis, J. R. 2005. "Audit research after Sarbanes-Oxley," *Auditing: A Journal of Practice & Theory* 25: 5–30.

Dinovitzer, R., Gunz, H., and Gunz, S. 2014. "Unpacking client capture: Evidence from corporate law firms," *Journal of Professions and Organization* 1: 99–117.

Dinovitzer, R., Gunz, H., and Gunz, S. 2015. "Professional ethics: Origins, applications and developments," in L. Empson, D. Muzio, J. Broschak, and B. Hinings (eds.), *The Handbook of Professional Services Firms*: 113–134. Oxford University Press.

Dowell, K. 2012. "Russell Jones & Walker acquired by listed Aussie firm Slater & Gordon," *The Lawyer*. Available from: www.thelawyer.com/analysis/the-lawyer-management/abs-news-and-analysis/russell-jones-and-walker-acquired-by-listed-aussie-firm-slater-and-gordon/1011140.article [Acessed: January 30, 2012].

Dugar, A. and Nathan, S. 1995. "The effect of investment banking relationships on financial analysts' earnings forecasts and investment recommendations," *Contemporary Accounting Research* 12: 131–160.

Durkheim, E. 1957. *Professional Ethics and Civic Morals*. London: Routledge and Kegan Paul.

Empson, L. and Chapman, C. 2006. "Partnership versus corporation: Implications of alternative forms of governance in professional service firms," *Research in the Sociology of Organizations* 24: 139–170.

Empson, L., Muzio, D., Broschak, J., and Hinings, B. 2015. "Introduction," in L. Empson, D. Muzio, J. Broschak, and B. Hinings (eds.), *The Handbook of Professional Services Firms*: 1–22. Oxford University Press.

Etherington, L. and Lee, R. 2007. "Ethical codes and cultural context: Ensuring legal ethics in the global law firm," *Indiana Journal of Global Legal Studies* 14: 95–118.

Faulconbridge, J. R. and Muzio, D. 2007. "Re-inserting the professional in the study of PSFs," *Global Networks* 7: 249–270.

Faulconbridge, J. R. and Muzio, D. 2008. "Organizational professionalism in globalizing law firms," *Work, Employment & Society* 22: 7–25.

Faulconbridge, J. R. and Muzio, D. 2009. "The financialization of large law firms: Situated discourses and practices of organization," *The Journal of Economic Geography* 9: 641–661.

Faulconbridge, J. R. and Muzio, D. 2012. "The rescaling of the professions: towards a transnational sociology of the professions," *International Sociology* 27: 109–125.

Flood, J. 2011. "The re-landscaping of the legal profession: Large law firms and professional re-regulation," *Current Sociology* 59: 507–529.

Forbes Report. 2003. *Final report of Neal Batson, court-appointed examiner*. Chapter 11, Case No. 01–16034 (AJG). Jointly Administered.

Fortney, S. and Gordon, T. 2013. "Adopting law firm management system to survive and thrive: A study of the Australian approach to management-based regulation," *University of St. Thomas Law Journal* 10: 152.

Freidson, E. 1970. *Profession of Medicine: A Study of the Sociology of Applied Knowledge.* New York: Dodd, Mead & Co.

Freidson, E. 1984. "The changing nature of professional control," *Annual Review of Sociology* 10: 1–20.

Freidson, E. 1994. *Professionalism Reborn: Theory, Prophecy, and Policy.* University of Chicago Press.

Freidson, E. 2001. *Professionalism: The Third Logic.* University of Chicago Press.

Gabbioneta, C., Greenwood, R., Mazzola, P., and Minoja, M. 2013. "The influence of the institutional context on corporate illegality," *Accounting, Organizations and Society* 38: 484–504.

Gabbioneta, C., Prakash, R., and Greenwood, R. 2014. "Sustained corporate corruption and processes of institutional ascription within professional networks," *Journal of Professions and Organization* 1: 16–32.

Gannagé-Stewart, H. 2014. "Slater & Gordon completes Pannone takeover." *The Lawyer.* Available from: www.thelawyer.com/analysis/the-lawyer-management/merger-watch/slater-and-gordon-completes-pannone-takeover/3016466.article [Accessed: February 17, 2015].

Grey, C. 1998. "On being a professional in a Big Six firm," *Accounting, Organizations and Society* 23: 569–587.

Grey, C. 2003. "The real world of Enron's auditors," *Organization* 10: 572–576.

Goode, W. J. 1957. "Community within a community: The professions," *American Sociological Review* 22: 194–200.

Goode, W. J. 1960. "The profession: reports and opinion," *American Sociological Review* 25: 902–965.

Goode, W. J. 1969. "The theoretical limits of professionalization," in A. Etzioni (ed.), *The Semi-Professions and Their Organization*: 266–313. New York: Free Press.

Greenwood, E. 1957. "Attributes of a profession," *Social Work* 2: 45–55.

Greenwood, R. 2007. "Your ethics," in L. Empson (ed.), *Managing the Modern Law Firm*: 186–195. Oxford University Press.

Greenwood, R. and Empson, L. 2003. "The professional partnership: Relic or exemplary form of governance?," *Organization Studies* 24: 909–933.

Greenwood, R. and Hinings, C. R. 1993. "Understanding strategic change: The contribution of archetypes," *Academy of Management Journal* 36: 1052–1081.

Greenwood, R., Hinings, C. R., and Brown, J. 1990. "'P2-form' strategic management: Corporate practices in professional partnerships," *Academy of Management Journal* 33: 725–755.

Greenwood, R. and Suddaby, R. 2006. "Institutional entrepreneurship in mature fields: The big five accounting firms," *Academy of Management Journal* 49: 27–48.

Gunz, H. P. and Gunz, S. P. 2008. "Client capture and the professional service firm," *American Business Law Journal* 45: 685–721.

Halpern, S. A. 1992. "Dynamics of professional control: Internal coalitions and crossprofessional boundaries," *American Journal of Sociology* 97: 994–1021.

Harrington, B. 2015. "Going global: professionals and the micro-foundations of institutional change," *Journal of Professions and Organization* 2(2): 103–121.

Hayward, M. L. A. and Boeker, W. 1998. "Power and conflicts of interest in professional firms: Evidence from investment banking," *Administrative Science Quarterly* 43: 1–22.

Heinz, J. P. 1982. "The power of lawyers," *Georgia Law Review* 17: 891–911.

Johnson, T. J. 1972. *Professions and Power*. London: Macmillan.

Kershaw, D. and Moorhead, R. 2013. "Consequential responsibility for client wrongs: Lehman Brothers and the regulation of the legal profession," *The Modern Law Review* 76: 26–61.

Kipping, M., Kirkpatrick, I., and Muzio, G. D. 2006. "Overly controlled or out of control? Management consultants and the new corporate professionalism," in John., C. (ed.), *Production Values: Futures for Professionalism*: 153–168. DEMOS: London.

Kish-Gephart J. J., Harrison D. A., and Treviño, L. K. 2010. "Bad apples, bad cases, and bad barrels: Meta-analytic evidence about sources of unethical decisions at work," *Journal of Applied Psychology* 95: 1–31.

Klimentchenko, D. A. 2009. "Myth of auditor independence," *University of Illinois Law Review*: 1275–1299.

Krause, E. A. 1996. *Death of the Guilds*. New Haven, CT: Yale University Press.

Kronus, C. L. 1976. "The evolution of occupational power an historical study of task boundaries between physicians and pharmacists," *Work and Occupations* 3: 3–37.

Larson, M. S. 1977. *The Rise of Professionalism: A Sociological Analysis*. The University of California Press.

Leicht, K. T. and Fennell, M. L. 1997. "The changing organizational context of professional work," *Annual Review of Sociology* 23: 215–231.

Leicht, K. and Fennell, M. 2001. *Professional Work: A Sociological Approach*. Oxford: Blackwell.

Le Mire, S. 2007. "The case study: James Hardie and its implications for the teaching of ethics," in B. Naylor and R. Hyams (eds.), *Innovation in Clinical Legal Education: Educating Lawyers for the Future*: 237–241. Melbourne: Cambridge University Press.

Levitt, A. 2000. *Renewing the Covenant with Investors*. New York University. Centre for Law and Business. May 10th, 2000.

Lin, H. W. and McNichols, M. F. 1998. "Underwriting relationships, analysts' earnings forecasts and investment recommendations," *Journal of Accounting and Economics* 25: 101–127.

Lipartito, K. J. and Miranti, P. J. 1998. "Professions and organizations in twentieth-century America," *Social Science Quarterly* 79: 301–320.

MacDonald, K. M. 1995. *The Sociology of the Professions*. London: Sage.

Macey, J. R. and Sale, H. A. 2003. "Observations on the role of commodification, independence, and governance in the accounting industry," *Villanova Law Review* 48: 1167–1187.

Maister, D. H. 1993. *Managing the Professional Service Firm*. New York: The Free Press.

Malhotra, N., Morris, T., and Hinings, C. B. 2006. "Variation in organizational form among professional service organizations," *Research in the Sociology of Organizations* 24: 171–202.

Manning, J. 2015. "Gateley IPO: demand high as firm raises £30 m from first legal IPO," *The Lawyer*. Available from: www.thelawyer.com/gateley-ipo-demand-high-as-firm-raises-30m-from-first-legal-ipo/3035946.article [Acessed: June 8, 2015].

Markle, T. 2014. "A call to partners with outside capital. The non-lawyer investment approach must be updated," *Arizona State Law Journal* 45: 1251.

McKenna, C. D. 2006. *The World's Newest Profession: Management Consulting in the Twentieth Century*. New York: Cambridge University Press.

Michaely, R. and Womack, K. L. 1999. "Conflict of interest and the credibility of underwriter analyst recommendations," *Review of Financial Studies* 12: 653–86.

Millerson, G. 1964. *The Qualifying Associations: A Study in Professionalization*. London: Routledge & Kegan Paul.

Mitchell, A. and Sikka, P. 2011. *The Pin-stripe Mafia: How Accounting Firms Destroy Societies*. Basildon, UK: Association for Accountancy & Business Affairs.

Mitchell, A., Sikka, P., Christensen, J., Morris, P., and Filling, P. 2002. *No Accounting for Tax Havens*. Basildon, UK: Association for Accountancy & Business Affairs.

Muzio, D., Brock, D. M., and Suddaby, R. 2013. "Professions and institutional change: Towards an institutionalist sociology of the professions," *Journal of Management Studies* 50: 699–721.

Myers, J., Myers, L., and Omer, T. 2003. "Exploring the term of the auditor-client relationship and the quality of earnings," *The Accounting Review* 78(3): 779–799.

Nagel, M. T. 2007. "Double deontology and the CCBE: Harmonizing the double trouble in Europe," *Washington University Global Studies Law Review* 6: 455–481.

Nicolson, D. and Webb, J. S. 1999. *Professional Legal Ethics: Critical Interrogations*. Oxford University Press.

Novack, J. 2012. "Latest U.S.-Swiss deal makes clear: No hiding cash in big Swiss banks," *Forbes*, June 21.

O'Brien, P. C., McNichols, M. F., and Hsiou-Wei, L. 2005. "Analyst impartiality and investment banking relationships," *Journal of Accounting Research* 43: 623–650.

Pache, A. and Santos, F. 2010. "When worlds collide: The internal dynamics of organizational responses to conflicting institutional demands," *Academy of Management Review* 35: 455–476.

Palan, R., Murphy, R., and Chavagneux, C. 2010. *Tax Havens: How Globalization Really Works*. Ithaca, NY: Cornell University Press.

Palmer, D. 2012. *Normal Organizational Wrongdoing: A Critical Analysis of Theories of Misconduct in and by Organizations*. Oxford University Press.

Parker, C. E. 2004. "Law firms incorporated: How incorporation could and should make firms more ethically responsible," *University of Queensland Law Journal* 25: 347.

Parker, C. E., Evans, A. H., Haller, L. R., Le Mire, S., and Mortensen, R. G. 2008. "The ethical infrastructure of legal practice in large law firms: Values, policy and behaviour," *The University of New South Wales Law Journal* 31: 158–188.

Parker, C. E., Gordon, T., and Mark, S. 2010. "Regulating law firms ethics management: An empirical assessment of an innovation in regulation of the legal profession in New South Wales," *Journal of Law and Society* 37: 466–500.

Parsons, T. 1954. *Professional and Social Structure. In Essays in Sociological Theory*. Glencoe, IL: Free Press.

Partnoy, F. 2009. Legal Studies Research Paper Series Research Paper No. 09–014 Rethinking Regulation of Credit Rating Agencies: An Institutional Investor Perspective.

Paterson, I., Fink, M., and Ongus, A. 2003. "Economic impact of regulation in the field of liberal professions in different Member States," Research Report Institute for Advanced Studies, Vienna – Study for the European Commission, DG Competition – Available from www.google.co.uk/url? sa=t&rct=j&q=&esrc=s&source=web&cd=2&ved=0CC8QFjAB&url= http%3A%2F%2Fec.europa.eu%2Fcompetition%2Fsectors%2Fprofes sional_services%2Fstudies%2Fexecutive_en.pdf&ei=7oDWU9chiNjsBq yngIAP&usg=AFQjCNHHYE3m9ubt7lKuzX6IGYq5nKpIxg&bvm=bv .71778758,d.ZGU [Acessed July 28, 2014].

Public Prosecutor Parma. 2010. Notice of termination of preliminary investigations, art. 415/bis, Italy's Code of Criminal procedure (CPP).

Rayne, R. 2014. "Do U.S. firms need external equity investments to remain competitive?," *Texas International Law Journal* 49: 559.

Reynolds, M. A. 2000. "Professionalism, ethical codes and the internal auditor: A moral argument," *Journal of Business Ethics* 2492: 115–124.

Ribstein, L. E. 2003. "Bubble laws," *Houston Law Review* 40: 77–97.

Roberts, S. 1994. "Fictitious capital, fictitious spaces: The geography of offshore financial flows," in S. Corbridge, N. Thrift, and R. Martin (eds.), *Money, Power and Space*: 91–115. Oxford: Blackwell.

Rosen, R. 2002. "'We're all consultants now': How change in client organizational strategies influences change in the organization of corporate legal services," *Arizona Law Review* 22: 637–684.

Sako, M. 2015. "Outsourcing and offshoring of professional services," in L. Muzio, D. Muzio, J. Broschak, and B. Hinings (eds.), *The Handbook of Professional Services Firms*: 327–347. Oxford University Press.

Santoro, M. A. and Strauss, R. J. 2013. *Wall Street Values. Business Ethics and the Global Financial Crisis*. Cambridge University Press.

SEC, Securities and Exchange Commission. 2000. *Final rule: Revision of the Commission's auditor independence requirements*, November 21, 2000.

Senate Governmental Affairs Committee. 2002. *Rating the raters: Enron and the credit rating agencies*. Hearing before the Senate Governmental Affairs Committee, 107th Cong., S. Hrg. 107–471 (March 20, 2002) at 65–66, 122.

Sharma, A. 1997. "Professional as agent: Knowledge asymmetry in agency exchange," *Academy of Management Review* 22: 758–98.

Shaw, G. B. 2004. *The Doctor's Dilemma*. Sioux Falls: NuVisions Publications.

Sikka, P. 2009. "Financial crisis and the silence of the auditors," *Accounting, Organizations and Society* 34: 868–873.

Sikka, P. and Hampton, M. P. 2005. "The role of accountancy firms in tax avoidance: Some evidence and issues," *Accounting Forum* 29: 325–343.

Sikka, P. and Willmott, H. 1995. "'The power of "independence': Defending and extending the jurisdiction of accounting in the United Kingdom," *Accounting, Organizations and Society* 20: 547–581.

Slater & Gordon. 2007. "Prospectus". Available from www.slatergordon.com .au/docs/prospectus/Prospectus.pdf [Accessed: April 23, 2008].

Smets, M., Morris, T., and Greenwood, R. 2012. "From practice to field: A multilevel model of practice-driven institutional change," *Academy of Management Journal* 55: 877–904.

Suddaby, R., Cooper, D. J., and Greenwood, R. 2007. "Transnational regulation of professional services: Governance dynamics of field level organizational change," *Accounting Organizations and Society* 32: 333–362.

Suddaby, R., and Muzio, D. 2015. "Theoretical perspective on the professions," in L. Empson, D. Muzio, J. Broschack, and B. Hinings (eds.), *The Oxford Handbook of Professional Services Firms*: 25–47. Oxford University Press.

Suddaby, R. and Viale, T. 2011. "Professionals and field-level change: Institutional work and the professional project," *Current Sociology* 59: 423–41.

Sturdy, A. 1997. "The consultancy process – an insecure business?," *Journal of Management Studies* 34: 389–413.

Terry, L. S. 2001. "'GATS' Applicability to transnational lawyering and its potential impact on US state regulation of lawyers," *Vanderbilt Journal of Transnational Law* 34: 989–1096.

The Economist. 2014. *The dozy watchdogs.* December 13: 24–26.

The Lawyer. 2015. *Making history: Irwin Mitchell appoints brokers as it eyes 2015 float.* Available from: www.thelawyer.com/news/lawyer-news-daily /making-history-irwin-mitchell-appoints-brokers-as-it-eyes-2015-float/ 3030662.article [Acessed: January 22, 2015].

The New York Times. 2001. *Enron tries to dismiss finance doubts.* October 24.

The New York Times. 2012. *The spreading scourge of corporate corruption.* October 7.

Thornton, P., Jones, C., and Kury, K. 2005. "Institutional logics and institutional change: Transformation in accounting, architecture, and publishing," in C. Jones and P. Thornton (eds.), *Research in the Sociology of Organizations*: 125–170. London: JAI.

Urry, J. 2014. *Offshoring.* London: Polity Press.

von Nordenflycht, A. 2014. "Does the emergence of publicly traded professional service firms undermine the theory of the professional partnership? A cross-industry historical analysis." *Journal of Professions and Organization* 1(2): 137–160.

Wilson, J. M., Boyer O'Leary, M., Metiu, A., and Jett, Q. R. 2008. "Perceived proximity in virtual work: Explaining the paradox of far-but-close," *Organization Studies* 29: 979–1002.

Wójcik, D. 2013. "Where governance fails: Advanced business services and the offshore world," *Progress in Human Geography* 37: 330.

7 | S/he blinded me with science: the sociology of scientific misconduct

JAMES N. BARON, MARISSA D. KING, AND
OLAV SORENSON

Recent years have witnessed increasing attention to misconduct and fraud in academic scholarship, particularly in scientific research. As shown in Figure 7.1, retraction rates among publications in scientific journals have increased astronomically – roughly ten-fold since 2000 (Steen, Casadevall, and Fang 2013; Van Noorden 2011).

That trend seems both stunning and perplexing if one considers the typical narrative provided to explain these events: Some individual scientist, succumbing to avarice, insecurity, or incompetence, whether knowingly or unwittingly, publishes erroneous findings. His peers nevertheless discover this deviance and ensure its correction. In essence, errant research, whether intentional or not, comes from a set of "bad apples." But given the slow rate at which turnover occurs in the population of scientists, this explanation would appear to have little purchase in explaining the dramatic rise in retractions over the past decade. Other putative causes – such as the increased competition for scarce funding and positions and improvements in the ability to detect errors and fraud – have also changed far more gradually and slowly than the rate of retractions. Therefore, they would appear incomplete, at best, as explanations for this trend.

However, this trend *does* closely resemble the rate at which the popular press has called attention to misconduct and fraud in another setting: the corporate world. Figure 7.2 documents that trend, with a pattern and magnitude of increase strongly resembling Figure 7.1, save for two anomalous years: 1996 (fallout from the price-fixing

The authors gratefully acknowledge generous research support from the Yale School of Management, especially through its Initiative on Leadership and Organization. Donald Palmer offered invaluable comments on an earlier version of this chapter.

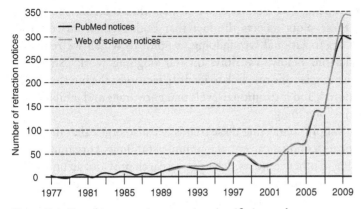

Figure 7.1 Trend in retraction rates in scientific journals
Source: Van Noorden (2011: 36)

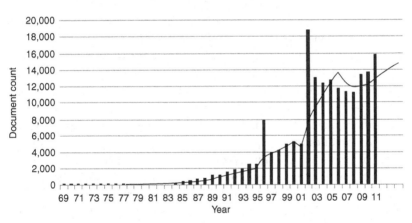

Figure 7.2 Trend in media mentions of organizational wrongdoing with five-year moving average
(see fn. 1 for details)

scandal involving Archer Daniels Midland) and 2002 (notable for the collapse of Enron and Andersen).[1]

---

[1] Figure 7.2 reports results from a search on August 14, 2014, of all publications tracked by Dow Jones' FACTIVA Online database, using the following query: *mention of the word* (company OR companies OR corporation OR corporations OR corporate OR business OR businesses OR organizational OR organization OR organizations OR firm OR firms) *within three words of a mention of the term* (corrupt OR corruption OR crime OR criminal OR fraud OR fraudulent OR unethical OR wrongdoing OR misconduct OR misbehavior).

Far from being a coincidence, we suspect that the correspondence between these plots reflects the fact that both stem from common causes of organizational wrongdoing, a point to which we return in our conclusion. Below, we draw on our ongoing work examining misconduct in scientific research to identify factors at the interpersonal, organizational, and institutional levels that encourage and inhibit organizational wrongdoing.

Beyond simply connecting these trends, we also argue that the study of scientific misconduct can enrich our understanding of organizational wrongdoing in other contexts. Scientific research provides an unusually fruitful domain within which to broaden and deepen this understanding for at least two reasons. First, relative to the corporate world and many voluntary associations, academic science takes place within relatively "weak" organizations, with highly autonomous and mobile actors. Documenting the embeddedness of academic science (and scientific misconduct) within its social and organizational contexts should therefore provide something of a *lower bound* on the extent and consequences of such embeddedness in other settings. Second, academic publications offer the equivalent of a fossil record through which one can infer the probable occurrence of misconduct over time and across settings. Recently developed statistical techniques, for example, allow one to estimate the probabilities that particular investigators have engaged in questionable practices, such as "p-hacking" and use of the "file drawer" – which misrepresent the nature of empirical relationships through selective reporting – even when no questions have been raised about the quality or validity of their articles (Benford 1938; Goldfarb and King 2013; Ioandidis and Trikalinos 2007; Simonsohn, Nelson, and Simmons 2014). By contrast, studies of scientific misconduct that have relied only on retractions suffer from the same obvious limitation as studies of corporate wrongdoing that have analyzed earnings restatements and other irregularities: selection on the dependent variable – they only include instances that have already been discovered as erroneous or fraudulent.

Whereas unintentional errors have generally been considered random or the result of incompetence, the dominant approach to scientific fraud has portrayed it as a rational calculation, balancing the benefits of publication against the probability and costs of detection. In our view, such rational cost–benefit perspectives give inadequate weight to the context (in our case, academic science) within which action is embedded.

Varieties of scientific wrongdoing

The trend in retractions documented in Figure 7.1 subsumes a wide variety of types of scientific misconduct. We define scientific misconduct as behavior that violates professional or institutional norms and standards governing scientific inquiry. Scientific inquiry, in turn, includes both the planning and execution of scientific projects, as well as their dissemination. Misconduct can occur not simply in a given scientific investigation but also in the communications and claims of credit associated with its findings (Meyers 2012).

We find it useful to distinguish between two dimensions of scientific conduct: cognizance and agency. Cognizance captures whether individuals involved understand their misconduct. Agency captures the proactivity involved: the degree to which misconduct reflects the *commission* of specific acts versus the *failure* to engage in some specific actions. Combining the two dimensions yields the typology shown in Table 7.1. We include negligence, error, and incompetence under the rubric of scientific wrongdoing because, like fraud and plagiarism, they contravene the norms and standards of scientific inquiry (even if by accident), serving thereby to erode trust in the scientific enterprise.

Characterizing specific instances of misconduct along the dimensions of cognizance and agency can prove difficult, even with detailed information about an episode and its context. Furthermore, wrongdoing can evolve over time, so that behavior that began as unintentional becomes deliberate.[2] For instance, a poorly designed or ineptly executed study might (unwittingly) produce a pattern of (bogus) results in which the investigator becomes invested, to the point that, even after learning of the mistakes, he or she continues to represent the findings or the methods as legitimate.

Table 7.1 *A typology of scientific misconduct*

	Commission	Omission
Intentional	Fraud, Plagiarism	Negligence
Unintentional	Error (or Incompetence)	Incompetence

[2] We thank Donald Palmer for bringing this point to our attention.

Case studies: not-so-great moments from the annals of science

To motivate our discussion and illustrate the importance of some contextual factors in scientific wrongdoing, we first summarize three prominent cases of scientific misconduct, which vary markedly in the strength of incentives for fraud and the probability of the protagonists being detected.

Suspicious social psychology: Diederik A. Stapel (weak incentives, low probability of detection)

Diederik Stapel had been seen as a future star even from his early days of graduate study in psychology at the University of Amsterdam. He had developed a reputation for being a talented experimentalist who almost always got his results. Following the completion of his dissertation in 1997, his fame and fortune grew rapidly as he published nearly ten papers per year in prominent journals. Only three years after beginning his academic career at Tilburg University, he received a full professorship at the University of Groningen. Six years later, he returned to Tilburg as the head of a research institute and, in short order, became the dean of the social and behavioral science faculty.

In 2011, it all came crashing down on Stapel. Three graduate students alerted the Rector to irregularities in Stapel's research practices and findings (Levalt, Drenth, and Noort 2012). Those allegations led to the formation of three commissions – one each at Tilberg University, the University of Groningen, and the University of Amsterdam – that investigated nearly every one of his published papers and every dissertation that he had supervised. When the investigators delivered their verdicts, they declared that sixty-two of his publications reported fraudulent research (Levalt et al. 2012), resulting in fifty-four retractions to date. The extent of his deception and misconduct seems all the more striking given that the rewards appear weak relative to the risks, at least once Stapel had achieved prominence.

Stapel's frauds generally took one of two forms (Levalt et al. 2012). Sometimes he would claim to have data from an earlier set of experiments that could answer important questions raised by another scholar. In other cases, together with coauthors, Stapel would plan a set of clever and careful experiments to examine the next logical, incremental step in some line of research, often to the point of writing up all of the experimental materials (e.g., survey instruments). Stapel would then volunteer to run these experiments himself, supposedly drawing on contacts at schools across the Netherlands. But in either version of the fraud, instead of actually conducting the experiments, he would simply fabricate a dataset on his computer, which he would then pass on to a graduate student or a coauthor for analysis.

Although the commissions investigating the fraud concluded that no one beyond Stapel himself could be held accountable for these crimes, they also noted that a number of factors contributed to the long time that it took for his deception to be discovered. By claiming absolute and sole control over the process of collecting and entering the data, Stapel provided himself the opportunity to fabricate the data without accomplices. He also maintained control over those post-docs and graduate students working with him by being unusually friendly but simultaneously threatening anyone who questioned him. His stellar reputation also helped to protect him against earlier allegations when some suggested that his results seemed too good to be true.

But blame also resides in the culture of the departments in which he worked and, indeed, in the entire field of social psychology (Levalt et al. 2012). Despite the fact that many of his papers included statistical issues that should have raised red flags – if not about the veracity of the data at least about the quality of the analysis – numerous colleagues and dozens of editors and peer reviewers failed to notice these problems as they authorized promotions and accepted papers for publication.

The commissions attributed these issues to a culture of sloppy science where even those not engaged in fraud would nonetheless see no issues with questionable practices: failing to report the results or even the existence of some experimental conditions; removing subjects without reporting either the reason for their removal or the fact that they had been removed; merging cases from more than one experiment; measuring multiple potential dependent variables but only reporting those that yielded significant results; and so on. In such a culture, where much "research" offered little more than an exercise in confirmation bias, the fabrication of the data itself may have seemed a small step to Stapel.

Phony physics: Jan Hendrik Schön (strong incentives, low probability of detection)

It was arguable that the scientific misconduct was Schön's alone, and not an indictment of Bell Labs. But it was difficult to believe such an incident could have occurred years before. "What does the Schön scandal mean?" an interviewer from the *New York Times* asked a young physicist named Paul Ginsparg. "The demise of Bell Labs by becoming corporate," Ginsparg replied.

(Gertner 2012: 337)

In late 2002, the revelation that Jan Hendrik Schön, of the renowned Bell Labs, had fabricated numerous seminal findings in condensed matter physics and nanotechnology shook the physics community. After completing a lackluster dissertation at the University of Konstanz in 1997, Schön moved to Bell Labs and began publishing pioneering results at an astounding rate. Schön claimed to have created an organic superconductor, an electrically driven organic laser, and a single-molecule transistor that outperformed silicon-based devices while being orders of magnitude smaller. Simply put, if Schön's findings stood, they could have laid the foundation for a new era in computing and electronics. Based on these discoveries and others, Schön averaged a publication every eight days between 2000 and 2001 (Agin 2007); in that period, Schön and his coauthors published seven papers in *Nature*, nine in *Science*, and five in *Physical Review*. All of these papers, however, ended up being retracted after an investigation found that they contained fabricated and duplicated figures, as well as results inconsistent with accepted physics.

Suspicion of Schön's fraud surfaced in the summer of 2001 (Reich 2009). Numerous groups found it impossible to replicate his results. Moreover, no one, including his own coauthors, had ever witnessed any of the experiments Schön reported. Then, in October of that year, a chi-square test revealed that a figure in one of his papers reported a distribution unrealistically similar to a Gaussian. But Schön's detractors remained largely at bay because the materials he supposedly worked with had been notorious for their sample-specific properties, and the methods he claimed to have used would have been difficult to master. Although the mounting concerns led to informal questioning at Bell Labs, a formal investigation did not begin until coworkers serendipitously discovered that two papers – one published in *Science*, a second in *Nature* – contained the exact same figure, even though they supposedly analyzed two very different materials (see Reich 2009 for a detailed account).

The external investigative committee convened by Bell Labs found Schön guilty of scientific misconduct in sixteen cases and his conduct "troubling" in six of the remaining eight cases investigated (Beasley et al. 2002). In their report, the committee concluded that Schön alone bore responsibility for the fraudulent findings; none of his more than twenty coauthors appeared guilty. According to Dr. Malcom Beasley, who headed the committee, "He committed scientific fraud ... Nobody else did" (quoted in Chang 2002). Typical of historical accounts of scientific misconduct, Schön has been portrayed as a lone, rogue perpetrator – a bad apple.

Institutional changes at Bell Labs may nevertheless have allowed fraudulent behavior – which historically would have been detected quickly – to go unnoticed. Henrik Schön had been the first case of fraud discovered at Bell Labs. When asked whether duplicity similar to that committed by Schön would have been possible in the past, a former Bell Labs chemist remarked, "I honestly don't believe it would have ... As soon as we tried to release [our own ground-breaking findings] for publication, we had a director and two department heads coming down and demanding to see this experiment work" (Haddon in Chang 2002). For much of the twentieth century, Bell Labs held the distinction of being the most innovative research institution in the world: "This was a company that literally dumped technology on our country. I don't think we'll see an organization with that kind of record ever again" (Michael Riordan in Gertner 2012). During this period, Bell Labs maintained a strict internal review system. Prior to publication, scientists would circulate an internal memorandum describing their findings. Managers had to approve these memoranda, which they would typically subject to peer review by Bell scientists outside the department of origin, before they would allow authors to submit their research to journals. But when the breakup of AT&T led to Bell Labs being transferred to Lucent Technologies, oversight began to weaken. Subsequent to the revelations of Schön's fraud, managers admitted that the system had fallen into disuse in the 1990s, perhaps as a response to the pressures associated with the parent company's poor financial performance (Reich 2009). But Bell Labs' reputation for research integrity persisted; Schön's affiliation with it may therefore have helped protect him from earlier scrutiny.

Faux fusion: Martin Fleischmann and B. Stanley Pons (strong incentives, high probability of detection)

On March 23, 1989, Martin Fleischmann and B. Stanley Pons of the University of Utah announced the sustained production of "cold fusion," using the most rudimentary of materials and equipment. Over the next year, millions of dollars and countless person-hours went toward assessing their claim. Aside from a few persistent believers, the scientific community soon concluded that the research had been flawed, sloppy, rushed, and inadequately reviewed prior to the announcement.

At a critical point, Fleischmann and Pons learned of seemingly related work being done at nearby Brigham Young University. Pressured by University of Utah officials and patent attorneys, the researchers became secretive and hastily convened a press conference to announce their discovery, seeking to secure subsequent intellectual property rights. But the work had not been thoroughly vetted. Fleischmann and Pons' research cut across scientific boundaries, including electrochemistry, nuclear physics, materials science and metallurgy, and radiation measurement (Close 1990: 105). With such expertise absent from their team, this lack of review, combined with the frenetic rush to get "results," led to numerous errors and oversights.

The chemists' announcement made for a fascinating and exciting story line, promising a future in which the power of the Sun could be harnessed inexpensively and safely. Overnight, Fleischmann and Pons literally became household names, with cold fusion stories gracing the covers of *Newsweek, Time,* and *Business Week.* The media *wanted* the claims to be true, and Fleischmann and Pons *wanted* the media to want the claims to be true, fueling the cold fusion fire. Compelling conspiracy theories, such as the oil companies and military establishment being behind the naysayers, helped to dismiss the detractors.

Certain features of the organization and division of labor seem to have exacerbated the shortcomings of the science. In 1988 alone, Fleischman and Pons collaborated on sixteen papers, and Pons' name appeared on another twenty publications, *all unrelated to test-tube fusion* (Close 1990: 74). But Fleischmann, a British citizen, spent much of his time consulting to a major atomic energy laboratory in England; Pons, meanwhile, chaired Utah's chemistry department. Neither of them seems to have had much bandwidth to oversee research. Indeed, responsibility for carrying out the experiments fell mainly to an inexperienced graduate student and to a radiation safety officer (RSO) at the University of Utah, who "was used to measuring … [radiation] … in rather different circumstances and with different instruments" (Close 1990: 280–281). Interviewed by the *New York Times* months after completing the measurements, the RSO said, "the cold-fusion researchers used the data 'any way they liked' without consulting [me]" (Broad 1991: 30); months later, he added that he had found the measuring instrument used to be faulty.

Status considerations also shaped early reactions to the announcement. Fleischmann's pre-eminence led some initially to give him the benefit of the doubt. One British fusion expert stated, "it is hard to see how a competent electrochemist could be mistaken on this scale" (Close 1990: 236). Investigators reporting replications at BYU, Texas A&M, and other institutions expressed glee at having (at least momentarily) outflanked America's East and West Coast scientific elite (Close 1990: 244). Under pressure from the White House, the Department of Energy urgently convened a meeting of the directors of its major research laboratories, the "collective Goliath whom David, in the guise of the [Utah] chemists, seemed to have felled" (Close 1990: 143). Fleishmann and Pons' reported discoveries not only threatened the existing status hierarchy and funding priorities within energy research but also called into question the prevailing "big science" model for funding research, which supported premier institutions with large staffs, massive physical plants, and cutting-edge technology.

Locally, institutional rivalry and resource competition also clearly came into play. With only the most preliminary of findings in hand, University of Utah leaders decided to pursue public announcement, even at substantial cost and reputational risk. The University, for example, secretly gave a $500,000 grant to the off-campus National Cold Fusion Institute established by the Utah legislature, falsely representing the transfer as an anonymous gift from an outside donor. After documenting that no fusion had occurred, a Utah physics professor, asked by the University to do measurements in Pons' lab, received a letter from an attorney representing Pons, demanding that he retract a manuscript reporting his negative findings. Some of the funds paid to this attorney came from the University's own Office of Technology Transfer. Amid these revelations and facing a loss of faculty confidence, Utah President Chase Peterson resigned.

Beyond bad apples and good cops: the social organization of scientific wrongdoing

These vignettes underscore several important points. First, the anecdotes vary in terms of agency and cognizance – for example, more intentional errors of commission in the case of Stapel versus more (probably) unintentional errors of omission in the case of Fleischmann and Pons. As elaborated below, *intentional* and *unintentional* errors, in particular, likely differ in their determinants as well as their consequences, meaning that researchers should distinguish between them in examining organizational wrongdoing.

Second, they highlight the limitations of prevailing accounts of misconduct. As noted by Palmer (2012), one approach has characterized these events as the consequence of "bad apples" – the moral or intellectual shortcomings of the individuals involved, or perhaps the ethical inferiority of the culture of an entire organization. Another common approach grossly oversimplifies the phenomenon as rational responses to incentives, policing, and sanctions. In this narrative, most of us have the potential for misconduct; it just depends on the potential costs and benefits that each actor faces. In a two-by-two table with strong versus weak incentives on one axis and high versus low probability of detection on the other, one would expect fraud primarily in the quadrant with strong incentives and a low probability of being caught. The cases above, however, do not fit neatly into either of these narratives (note that we have roughly assigned these cases to their risk-reward quadrants). Diederick Stapel, for example, would appear to have had little to gain from his fraud; Martin Fleischmann and Stanley Pons, meanwhile, had little hope of going undetected.

Third, some similar interpersonal, organizational, and institutional factors appear to underlie these three episodes. Incentives, monitoring, and sanctions do not operate in a vacuum; rather, they interact with and are shaped by features of the interpersonal, organizational, and institutional contexts (Greve, Palmer, and Pozner 2010). Inspired by these three cases, we draw on economic and organizational sociology to identify four sets of contextual influences likely to influence the dynamics of wrongdoing: *network embeddedness; organizational design, demography, and the division of labor; institutional fields; and status processes.* Below we discuss how, when, and where each of these factors might influence scientific misconduct, and we conclude by pointing to commonalities with respect to the four sets of factors in science and commerce.

Network embeddedness

Social structures importantly shape the propensity for intentional misconduct by restricting the transmission of information. Simmel (1906) brought early attention to this issue, arguing that secrets could only remain safe in dyads. But subsequent theory and empirical research has expanded these ideas beyond the dyad. Granovetter (1985: 490), for example, noted, "The embeddedness argument stresses instead the role of concrete personal relations and structures (or 'networks') of such relations in generating trust and discouraging malfeasance." In essence, both Granovetter and Simmel argue that denser levels of connectedness dissuade individuals from engaging in aberrant behavior because their peers quickly become aware of it and sanction them.

What network structures then would allow conspiracies and fraud to occur? Networks with a high degree of centralization – think of a star (or hub-and-spoke) structure, with sparse and asymmetric communication, moving information from the center outward. These structures prevent knowledge of illicit activities from diffusing widely into the community, compartmentalizing awareness of wrongdoing and preventing defection by raising fears of becoming the fall guy. Baker and Faulkner (1993) found just such patterns of interaction among the organizations involved in price-fixing scandals. And Aven (2012) calls attention to parallel patterns among the employees at Enron involved in the creation and maintenance of that firm's illegal accounting entities.

We might expect similar patterns of communication and connection among teams of scientists to enable intentional misconduct. More precisely, scientists occupying boundary-spanning positions, sitting between otherwise unconnected sets of collaborators, would appear to have the greatest capacity for engaging in fraud. One would expect this capacity to become most pronounced in situations in which the boundary spanner also holds higher status than most of his collaborators (Brass, Butterfield, and Skaggs 1998). Those two conditions, in essence, allow the individual at the center to control flows of information and therefore quickly to squelch questioning of dubious practices. Stapel appears to have been just such an example, both in structure and in relative status: for instance, compared to his legitimate publications, a higher proportion of his fraudulent articles had been co-authored with junior and/or female colleagues.[3] The other two cases exhibit some similarities, with the protagonists interacting primarily alone or in dyads, rather than promoting multilateral exchange among all other members of their teams.

Another interesting manner in which network structures might shape misconduct, particularly intentional misconduct, emerges from their role in transmitting and enforcing norms. Since Sutherland (1947), scholars have argued that individuals learn criminal and delinquent behavior in intimate groups. The timing, frequency, and intensity of exposure to norms supporting misconduct shape an individual's propensity to engage in such behavior. Thus, the extent to which scientists consider various forms of behavior illegitimate may depend both on their training – the practices they observe in their advisors or mentors – and on their peers. Both have been shown to be important in determining who engages in deviant behavior. Stuart and Ding (2006), for example, found that the commercial activities of advisors, mentors, and senior members of departments significantly influenced the commercial behavior of scientists – whether they would license their inventions, whether they would sit on advisory boards, and whether they would found their own companies. Although such activity now seems normal, only a couple of decades ago most in academia would have considered it deviant. Along similar lines, Pierce and Snyder (2008) reported a strong tendency for individuals to follow the ethical norms of their organizations and colleagues; when employees moved from an automotive smog testing facility with average pass rates to one with suspiciously high rates, the frequency with which those same individuals passed vehicles subsequently rose dramatically.

Organizational design, demography, and division of labor

The organizations literature has also frequently called attention to the ways in which organizational design, operating routines, and the division of labor can lead to unintended errors. Consider, for example, Perrow's (1984) study of Three Mile Island, which ascribed the meltdown to "normal accidents" – almost inevitable events given the

---

[3] Based on our analysis of the information provided in Levalt et al. (2012).

complexity of the system, the degree of interdependence among its subsystems, and the limited understanding of these connections among those involved in operating the system. Vaughan (1997) points to similar problems that led to the demise of the space shuttle Challenger. Organizations can solve complex problems efficiently by dividing problems and production into simpler pieces that individuals or subgroups of people can perform more effectively. But doing so does not come without cost. Responsibility for the end product can become diffuse and the potential for miscommunication rife. One therefore often witnesses problems "falling between the cracks" (i.e., between domains of responsibility) and people believing that someone else has taken (or will take) care of it.

In the cross-section, one would expect these errors to emerge from larger, more complex, and more dispersed research teams. Individuals on the team not only bear distinct responsibilities but also, to the extent that they do not overlap in their abilities and training, may not even have the *capacity* to screen for and correct potential errors made by their colleagues. We observe this in the case of Schön. Because his research crossed many different domains within physics, each requiring specialized technical skill, his team and outsiders had limited ability to replicate his work, allowing his fraud to go undetected far longer than it otherwise might have.

Consistent with the trend in Figure 7.1, we also expect that these coordination challenges have become more pronounced over time. Jones (2009) described the problems associated with the "burden of knowledge" in innovation, both in science and in industry. As the community accumulates knowledge, any research project must incorporate more and more information to produce ideas at the frontier. Indeed, the current stock of knowledge in most fields appears to have exceeded the ability of any individual to learn it. As a consequence, scientific research increasingly occurs in teams, with differentiated expertise and an extended division of labor. These teams, moreover, have grown ever larger as the role of each member has necessarily become increasingly narrow (Wuchty, Jones, and Uzzi 2007).

Beyond the simple size of the team, its demography might also influence the probability of scientific misconduct. Interestingly, here, the predictions would appear to run in opposite directions for witting versus unwitting wrongdoing. Diversity – of expertise or along demographic, geographic, or linguistic dimensions – should generally increase the difficulty of coordination and consequently also the probability of errors. By contrast, sorting on similarity may facilitate the formation of teams in which all of the members feel comfortable engaging in fraud. Whereas a diverse team might keep in check someone prone to pursuing questionable research practices, a group of likeminded scientists could fall prey to believing such behaviors normal and thus that nothing should preclude them from participating in them. We would therefore expect the odds of unintentional errors to rise, but the probability of intentional malfeasance to fall with team heterogeneity.

Another interesting structural dimension of scientific inquiry concerns an analog of the organizational boundary. Studies in petrochemicals, aircraft maintenance, and other settings have raised serious questions about the relationship between the outsourcing of maintenance and subsequent safety or accident records (e.g., Kochan et al. 2006). A common refrain from such studies has been that outsourcing erodes internal understanding of the outsourced activities and results in poor communication between the employees of the primary firm and those of the contractor. Although outsourcing per se has generally not been prevalent in science, it seems another natural response to the burden of knowledge noted above. In some cases, teams may choose to pay for expertise, such as specialized statistical advice, rather than including the source as a coauthor. One sees this choice at work increasingly in clinical trials, where clinics and contract research organizations receive contracts to provide a certain number of subjects (Bodenheimer 2001). Not only does such outsourcing increase the odds of unintentional errors due to miscommunication, but it may also raise the probability of fraud to the extent that it reduces the ability of the primary investigators to monitor and ensure the quality of the inputs from their subcontractors.

Institutional field

Organizational scholars have documented quite convincingly how an organization's institutional context shapes its structures, processes, routines, and outcomes. Just as some neighborhoods are more dangerous than others, institutional fields likely vary in their propensities to produce errors and outright fraud.

Scientists typically operate simultaneously within multiple institutions – laboratories, departments, universities, scientific societies, and fields and disciplines. One dimension on which these institutions vary is the intensity of competition for resources and status. Competition should increase the rate of both intentional and unintentional wrongdoing. Resource scarcity may mean that scholars cannot afford to use sufficiently large samples or to replicate their own results before attempting to publish them, thereby reducing the probability of internal error detection. Moreover, the race for priority, to publish first, may lead even well-funded teams to go forward with results before they have been properly vetted, as occurred in the cold fusion case. But competition can also promote intentional wrongdoing to the extent that it creates a culture of results and publications "at any cost." Growing fields, with an abundance of resources, therefore, should witness fewer problems than declining ones, where scientists may have begun fretting about finding funding.

Uncertainty over the availability of resources can arise not only from competition but also from changes in the political environment (e.g., Pfeffer and Salancik 1978). This uncertainty typically leads actors to engage in defensive maneuvers designed to solidify their positions in a rapidly changing landscape. In the context of scientific research, changes in political administrations and agency directorships may represent such occasions, due to shifting priorities in the federal funding of research and to changing budgets and administrative rules regarding research grants. Individuals threatened by such institutional changes may cut corners to strengthen their position amidst increasing competition and/or diminished resources, leading to an increase in intentional misconduct. Or, threatened researchers might attempt to shift fields, funders, and journals, in the pursuit of "hotter" or less rigorous arenas, potentially then leading to an increase in *unintended* errors.

Fields vary not only in the incentives to engage in wrongdoing but also in their ability to detect it. For example, we expect to see dubious science occurring more frequently in those fields that have the weakest gatekeeping and monitoring institutions. The more rigorous and involved the review processes to obtain funding and to achieve publication, the less likely research with intentional or unintentional errors is to receive support and publicity. Of course, such review processes have their own costs and associated risks (Meyer 2012), including the possibility that they motivate scientists to migrate toward less rigorous fields and journals.

One might also expect the propensity for errors and malfeasance to vary as fields and disciplines mature. Studies of competitive environments across many sectors suggest a pattern of increasing legitimation when fields or industries emerge, with an accumulating critical mass enhancing the prospects for most actors (Carroll and Hannan 2000). As industries mature, however, competitive forces come to the fore, with each entrant in an already crowded field pulling resources away from those already there. The returns to policing others also decline as fields mature and research shifts toward increasingly incremental results (Lacetera and Zirulia 2011). Given the increasing difficulty of innovating in and contributing to established fields, combined with the lower incentives of peers to monitor incremental research, one might expect errors and fraud in a field to increase over time.

But other forces act in the opposite direction as areas of study mature. Norms, standards, and values emerge over time as the scientific community develops a shared understanding of problems and accepts certain approaches to addressing them. Without these norms and agreed-upon practices, peers likely find it difficult to detect scientific wrongdoing, inadvertent or otherwise, in nascent fields compared to mature ones. Consistent with this idea, in the case of Diederich Stapel, his fraudulent work appeared primarily in the newly emerging fields of moods and of embodied cognition, not in his contributions (often with eminent coauthors) to the more established psychology subfields of stereotyping and power and status.

Status processes

Status processes undoubtedly interact with these factors in a variety of ways. One way concerns the allocation of attention. The community pays disproportionate attention to the opinions of and the research done by those of high status (Merton 1968; Simcoe and Waguespack 2011). One might therefore expect articles authored by high-status scientists to receive a higher level of scrutiny and attempted replication. Conditional on having produced problematic research, one would expect the scientific community to uncover with greater probability both the accidental errors of high-status individuals and any research manipulation or fraud in which they might have engaged. Given that the community holds them in such high esteem, moreover, both errors of omission and commission by high-status investigators might result in more severe punishments when discovered. Baker and Faulkner (1993), for instance, reported that juries more commonly found higher-status actors guilty in price-fixing scandals and judges punished them with more severe fines and sentences. Having discovered misconduct, the community might therefore sanction high-status scientists more strongly. Consistent with these ideas, Furman and his colleagues (2012) reported that the author(s) of a scientific article being associated with a premier research university was the strongest predictor of the future retraction of that publication. And, indeed, we saw this pattern illustrated poignantly in the case of Diederik Stapel.

But might status also influence the probability of producing problematic research? At first blush, one might expect it to decrease it. Recognizing themselves as being subject to greater scrutiny and potentially as having more to lose, both in terms of their positions and in terms of punishment, high-status scientists should exert extra care in the reporting of their results (as one saw during the halcyon days of Bell Labs) and consider the cost of fraud simply too high relative to any potential gains.

Even without this extra effort, one might still expect high-status scientists to produce fewer unintended errors. Consider the relationship between status and quality. Audiences often view status as a proxy for quality and, indeed, achieving high status generally requires producing at least some high-quality output (Gould 2002; Merton 1968; Podolny 1993). High-status scientists have therefore typically achieved this prominence, at least in part, by producing better-than-average research (Merton 1968). If status remains tightly connected to quality even once high status has been achieved, then one would simply expect fewer errors from high-status scientists. Status, however, has a strong tendency to become decoupled from quality, particularly in contexts where people find that quality difficult to assess. As Merton (1968: 2) noted, "eminent scientists get disproportionately great credit for their contributions to science while relatively unknown scientists tend to get disproportionately little credit for comparable contributions." To the extent that such decoupling occurs, one might find few differences in the error rates between those of higher versus lower status.

Status processes also influence other aspects of research production. Merton (1968) coined the term *the Matthew Effect* – named after the passage in the Gospel of St. Matthew about the rich getting richer – to refer to the disproportionate rewards and resources received by high-status scientists. Those of high status accrue more and larger grants and attract larger numbers of students, for example. High-status individuals in modern science, therefore, run larger organizations, with more postdocs, more graduate students, and more researchers. They also tend to collaborate at higher rates (Moody 2004). As we noted above, this expanded scale, diversity, and division of labor increase the odds of unintentional errors for a variety of reasons. On this dimension, one might therefore expect the laboratories of high-status scientists to produce errors at a higher rate than those of lower status peers, particularly as these scientists progress in their careers and manage larger and larger operations.

Another strand of literature, meanwhile, suggests that those of high (and low) status might engage in intentional misconduct more frequently than those of intermediate status. The organizational literature on middle-status conformity argues that adherence to community norms should operate most intensely in the middle of the status distribution (e.g., Phillips and Zuckerman 2001). Those of high status, believing themselves less likely to be punished for deviance (Jin et al. 2013), flout convention. Those of low status, meanwhile, have little to lose by risking deviance and therefore do not bother to conform. In the middle of the status hierarchy, individuals perceive themselves both as having a lot to lose and a high probability of being punished, therefore refraining from behavior that might threaten their positions. This theory would then point to an inverted-U relationship between the status of scientists and their rates of intentional misconduct.

Another likely effect of status processes on wrongdoing in science relates to our previous discussion of institutional fields. Fields and sectors vary a great deal, both cross-sectionally and over time, in the permeability and visibility of their status hierarchies. Similarly, they vary in the frequency and accuracy of the ongoing assessments of key stakeholders. We would expect status structures to be less permeable in fields characterized by: slow and small changes in content and methodology; longer cycle times for developing, implementing, and publishing results; higher barriers to entry; longer-term funding cycles; and less frequent formal assessments by external evaluators (e.g., the magazines that rate hospitals and business schools on an annual basis). Under such circumstances, wrongdoers find that it is more difficult or time-consuming to appropriate the benefits of their deceit in the form of greater rewards. In other words, one potential consequence of the increasing frequency and prominence of ranking exercises within fields and sectors may be to increase behaviors, including forms of wrong-doing, that would enhance the status of a given individual, team, or organization.

Summary and conclusions

Prior research within organizational theory leads to several clear – but sometimes competing – hypotheses about factors that are likely to increase the rates of scientific misconduct. Table 7.2 briefly summarizes our predictions about how the prevalence of witting and unwitting wrongdoing vary as a function of network embeddedness, organizational design and division of labor, institutional factors, and status processes. Adjudicating between these propositions will provide evidence as to the mechanisms and processes underlying unintentional versus intentional scientific errors.

We have now reached a point where we can return to the similarity noted at the outset of this chapter between two graphs: one (Figure 7.1) showing trends in detected scientific misconduct; the other (Figure 7.2) showing trends over the same time frame in media references to corporate wrongdoing. A substantial body of research has been devoted to understanding the increased prevalence of corporate wrongdoing. Increased complexity (Boisot et al. 2011; Jelinek 2013; Weinschenk 2012), resource scarcity, intensified competition, an emphasis on meeting performance expectations (Kaplan 2010), and perverse managerial incentives (*Economist* 2009) have all been blamed for contributing to corporate fraud. Moral "credentialing" (Monin and Miller 2001) – the idea that professing responsibility in one domain might lead actors to feel authorized to act less morally in another – has also been suggested as an unintended consequence of Sarbanes–Oxley and other regulations (*Megan's Law Journal* 2012). Others suggest that a paucity of inside ownership, long-standing organizational or professional tenure, inadequate internal controls, and an unquestioning culture of trust combine to create a toxic cocktail that undermines organizational barriers to wrongdoing (e.g., Finotti 2011; Weinschenk 2012).

All of these processes have analogs in the world of science. In the cold fusion case, for instance, we see increases in the scale, number, scope,

Table 7.2 *Hypothesized determinants of intentional and unintentional errors in scientific inquiry*

	Intentional errors	Unintentional errors
Network embeddedness	Higher in hub and spoke-shaped networks, by higher-status boundary spanners	
	Evidence over time of assortative mating by error rates (through mentorship and collaborator relationships)	Evidence over time of assortative mating by error rates (through mentorship and collaborator relationships)
Organizational design, demography, and division of labor	Possible increase with complexity, hierarchy, and division of labor	Increase with complexity, hierarchy, and division of labor
	Possible increase with "outsourcing" of key . facets of research process	Increase with "outsourcing" of key facets of research process
		Increase with diffusion of PI effort across multiple projects and/or roles
	Decrease with scope and quality of internal review processes at sponsoring institution	Decrease with scope and quality of internal review processes at sponsoring institution
	Decrease with team diversity	Increase with team diversity (demographic, functional, geographic, etc.)
Institutional field	Higher in established, mature, declining, resource-poor fields; possible U-shaped relationship (with greater incidence in fields that are new/hot or old/maturing)	Decrease with maturity and competitiveness of research field

Table 7.2 (*cont.*)

	Intentional errors	Unintentional errors
	Higher in fields with permeable status hierarchies	
	Lower in fields with rigorous, lengthy journal review processes	Lower in fields with rigorous, lengthy journal review processes
	Higher during periods of economic or political upheaval affecting the research field	Higher in "hot" fields with many new entrants
	Lower on projects with corporate funding (more cautious vetting given financial stakes)	Higher on projects with corporate funding
Status processes	U-shaped relationship (middle-status conformity)	Inverse relationship (status as proxy for quality); net of experience and training, positive relationship due to competing demands of multiple responsibilities among those with high status
	Increase with status inequality on research team	
	Increase with proximity to promotion and research-funding decisions	Possible increase with proximity to promotion and research-funding decisions

complexity, skill diversity, and geographic scope of the projects under management within investigators' portfolios. In the Schön case, we see heightened performance expectations, including from corporate sponsors, along with an erosion of internal controls, possibly driven by increased cost pressures. In the Stapel case, we see hierarchical control supplanting norms of collegiality and shared responsibility. We also find it intriguing that the network structures observed in these cases mirror those that distinguished between corrupt and non-corrupt projects at Enron (Aven 2012). Academic researchers have also begun to face increasing human subjects and clinical trials requirements, conflicts of interests, and other ethical mine fields, which may have fostered moral credentialing effects similar to those that observers of corporate wrongdoing attribute to Sarbanes–Oxley. More generally, numerous scholars have noted that higher education and academic science have become increasingly "corporatized" (e.g., Soley 1995; Bok 2004; Mills 2012), implying that academic science has become increasingly similar to big business along many of the dimensions claimed to have heightened corporate wrongdoing.

Indeed, by virtue of these similarities, we believe that studies of wrongdoing in the scientific setting hold the promise of forwarding our understanding of intentional and unintentional misconduct in the broader organizational world. As noted above, insofar as scientific collaborations represent relatively "weak" organizations, documenting the importance of social structure to wrongdoing in science should provide a lower bound on the importance of similar processes in other organizational settings.

In developing hypotheses about likely correlates of scientific wrongdoing, we have found numerous parallels between *known* cases of corporate and scientific wrongdoing. To develop a true understanding of what increases the likelihood of corporate or scientific wrongdoing, however, we must move beyond examining only cases where deliberate misconduct has occurred and been detected. Here, the study of wrongdoing in science has an unusually attractive feature. The public and digitized nature of the outputs of contemporary scientific research makes detecting errors and fraud considerably more feasible than is the case for most organizational behavior. Academic scientists almost inevitably leave a wider trail of publicly available forensic evidence than do corporate actors, enabling outsiders to assess the veracity of the scholarship. Furthermore, a variety of methodological tools allows one to assess the likelihood of misconduct *even in situations where it has not (yet) been identified or alleged,* thereby circumventing the selection bias that perennially plagues research on organizational wrongdoing. Hence, we believe that studying wrongdoing in academic science – and building increasing bridges between the sociology of science and organizational and economic sociology – will greatly enhance our understanding of the social structure of intentional and unintentional wrongdoing within contemporary workplaces.

References

Agin, D. 2007. *Junk Science: An Overdue Indictment of Government, Industry, and Faith Groups that Twist Science for Their Own Gain*. New York: Macmillan.

Aven, B. 2012. "The effects of corruption on organizational networks and individual behavior," Carnegie Mellon University Tepper School of Business, Paper 1399. Available from http://repository.cmu.edu/tepper/1399.

Baker, W. E. and Faulkner, R. R. 1993. "The social organization of conspiracy: Illegal networks in the heavy electrical equipment industry," *American Sociological Review* 58: 837–860.

Beasley, M., Datta, S., Kogelnik, H., Kroemer, H., and Monroe, D. 2002. *Report of the Investigation Committee on the Possibility of Scientific Misconduct in the Work of Hendrik Schön and Coauthors*. Bell Laboratories.

Benford, F. 1938. "The law of anomalous numbers," *Proceedings of the American Philosophical Society* 78: 551–572.

Bodenheimer, T. 2001. "Uneasy alliance: Clinical investigators and the pharmaceutical industry," *New England Journal of Medicine* 342: 1539–1544.

Boisot, M., Nordberg, M., Yami, S., and Nicquevert, B. (eds.). 2011. *Collisions and Collaboration: The Organization of Learning in the ATLAS Experiment at the LHC*. Oxford: Oxford University Press.

Bok, D. 2004. *Universities in the Marketplace: The Commercialization of Higher Education*. Princeton University Press.

Brass, D. J., Butterfield, K. D., and Skaggs, B. C. 1998. "Relationships and unethical behavior: A social network perspective," *Academy of Management Review* 23: 14–31.

Broad, W. J. 1991. "Cold-fusion claim is faulted on ethics as well as science," *New York Times*, March 17, pp. A1, A30.

Carroll, G. R. and Hannan, M. T. 2000. *The Demography of Organizations and Industries*. Princeton University Press.

Chang, K. 2002. "Panel says Bell Labs scientist faked discoveries in physics," *New York Times*, September 26, pp. A1, A20.

Close, F. 1990. *Too Hot to Handle: The Story of the Race for Cold Fusion*. London: W. H. Allen.

Economist. 2009. "Corporate crime is on the rise: The rot spreads," November 19. Available from www.economist.com/node/14931615? zid=300&ah=e7b9370e170850b88ef129fa625b13c4.

Finotti, M. C. 2011. "New study shows corporate fraud has increased with fewer internal controls," *Jacksonville Business Journal*, October 14. Available from www.bizjournals.com/jacksonville/print-edition/2011/10 /14/new-study-shows-corporate-fraud-has.html?page=2.

Furman, J., Jensen, K., and Murray, F. 2012. "Governing knowledge in the scientific community: Exploring the role of retractions in biomedicine," *Research Policy* 41: 276–290.

Gertner, J. 2012. *The Idea Factory: Bell Labs and the Great Age of American Innovation.* New York: The Penguin Press.

Goldfarb, B. and King, A. 2013. "Scientific apophenia in strategic management research," Unpublished manuscript, University of Maryland.

Gould, R. V. 2002. "The origins of status hierarchies: A formal theory and empirical test," *American Journal of Sociology* 107: 1143–1178.

Granovetter, M. S. 1985. "Economic action and social structure: The problem of embeddedness," *American Journal of Sociology* 91: 481–510.

Greve, H. R., Palmer, D., and Pozner, J. 2010. "Organizations gone wild: The causes, processes, and consequences of organizational misconduct," *Academy of Management Annals* 4: 53–107.

Ioannidis, J. P. A. and Trikalinos, T. A. 2007. "An exploratory test for an excess of significant findings," *Clinical Trials* 4: 245–253.

Jelinek, M. 2013. "What big science teaches about collaboration, complexity, and innovation," Center for Innovation Management Studies, North Carolina State University. Available from http://cims.ncsu.edu/what-big-science-teaches-about-collaboration-complexity-and-innovation/ [Accessed: August 13, 2014].

Jin, G. Z., Jones, B., Lu, S., and Uzzi, B. 2013. "The reverse Matthew effect: Catastrophe and consequence in scientific teams," NBER Working Paper #19489.

Jones, B. F. 2009. "The burden of knowledge and the 'death of the Renaissance man': Is innovation getting harder?," *Review of Economic Studies* 76: 283–317.

Kaplan, J. A. 2010. "Why corporate fraud is on the rise," *Forbes*, June 10. Available from www.forbes.com/2010/06/10/corporate-fraud-executive-compensation-personal-finance-risk-list-2-10-kaplan.html.

Kochan, T. A., Smith, M., Wells, J. C., and Rebitzer, J. B. 2006. "Human resource strategies and contingent workers: The case of safety and health in the petrochemical industry," *Human Resource Management* 33: 55–77.

Lacetera, N. and Zirulia, L. 2011. "The economics of scientific misconduct," *Journal of Law, Economics, and Organization* 27: 563–603.

Levelt, W. J. M., Drenth, P., and Noort, E. (Eds.). 2012. *Flawed Science: The Fraudulent Research Practices of Social Psychologist Diederik Stapel.* Tilburg: Commissioned by the Tilburg University, University of Amsterdam and the University of Groningen.

Megan's Law Journal. 2012. "The potential causes and solutions of corporate crime," November 12. Available from http://meganslawjournal.com/201 2/11/20/the-potential-causes-and-solutions-of-corporate-crime/.

Merton, R. K. 1968. "The Matthew effect in science," *Science* 159: 56–63.

Meyer, M. A. 2012. *Prize Fight: The Race and the Rivalry to be the First in Science.* New York: Palgrave Macmillan.

Mills, N. 2012. "The corporatization of higher education," *Dissent* 59(Fall): 6–9.

Monin, B. and Miller, D. 2001. "Moral credentials and the expression of prejudice," *Journal of Personality and Social Psychology* 81(July): 33–43.

Moody, J. 2004. "The structure of a social science collaboration network: Disciplinary cohesion from 1963–1999," *American Sociological Review* 69: 213–238.

Palmer, D. A. 2012. *Normal Organizational Wrongdoing: A Critical Analysis of Misconduct in and by Organizations.* Oxford: Oxford University Press.

Perrow, C. 1984. *Normal Accidents: Living with High Risk Technologies.* New York: Basic Books.

Pfeffer, J. and Salancik, G. R. 1978. *The External Control of Organizations: A Resource Dependence Perspective.* New York: Harper & Row.

Phillips, D. J. and Zuckerman, E. W. 2001. "Middle-status conformity: Theoretical restatement and empirical demonstration in two markets," *American Journal of Sociology* 107: 379–429.

Pierce, L. and Snyder, J. 2008. "Ethical spillovers in firms: Evidence from vehicle emissions testing," *Management Science* 54: 1891–1903.

Podolny, J. M. 1993. "A status-based model of market competition," *American Journal of Sociology* 98: 829–872.

Reich, E. 2009. *Plastic Fantastic: How the Biggest Fraud in Physics Shook the Scientific World.* New York: Palgrave Macmillan.

Simcoe, T. and Waguespack, D. M. 2011. "Status, quality and attention: What's in a (missing) name?," *Management Science* 57:274–290.

Simmel, G. 1906. "The sociology of secrecy and of secret societies," *American Journal of Sociology* 11: 441–498.

Simonsohn, U., Nelson, L. D., and Simmons, J. P. 2014. "P-curve: A key to the file-drawer," *Journal of Experimental Psychology: General* 143: 534–537.

Soley, L. C. 1995. *Leasing the Ivory Tower: The Corporate Takeover of Academia*. Cambridge, MA: South End Press.

Steen, R. G., Casadevall, A., and Fang, F. C. 2013. "Why has the number of scientific retractions increased?," *PLoS One* 8(7): e68397. Published online Jul 8, 2013. doi:10.1371/journal.pone.0068397 PMCID: PMC3704583.

Stuart, T. and Ding, W. W. 2006. "When do scientists become entrepreneurs? The social structural antecedents of commercial activity in the academic life sciences," *American Journal of Sociology* 112: 97–144.

Sutherland, E. 1947. *Principles of Criminology* (4th edn.). Philadelphia: Lippincott.

Van Noorden, R. 2011. *"Science Publishing: The Problem with Retractions,"* Published online October 5, 2011 | *Nature* 478: 26–8.| doi:10.1038/478026a.

Vaughan, D. 1997. *The Challenger Launch Decision: Risky Technology, Culture, and Deviance at NASA*. Chicago: University of Chicago Press.

Weinschenk, M. 2012. "The rise of corporate criminals and how to protect yourself," *Wall Street Daily*, August 13. Available from www.wallstreetdaily.com/2012/08/13/the-rise-of-corporate-criminals-and-how-to-protect-yourself/.

Wuchty, S., Jones, B. F., and Uzzi, B. 2007. "The increasing dominance of teams in production of knowledge," *Science* 316: 1036–1039.

8 | Social networks and organizational wrongdoing in context

DONALD PALMER AND CELIA MOORE

This chapter critically reviews extant social network theory and research on misconduct in and by organizations, focusing primarily on the individual level of analysis and considering the role that social networks play in the initiation, diffusion, effectiveness, and demise of wrongdoing. We conclude that a more comprehensive understanding of the role of social networks in wrongdoing in and by organizations hinges on four contextual factors: (1) the predispositions of the actors involved, (2) the nature of the wrongdoing in question, (3) the institutional environment in which the wrongdoing is perpetrated, and (4) the temporal dynamics through which the wrongdoing unfolds. We also conclude that a more nuanced understanding of the role of social networks in organizational wrongdoing requires greater attention to the quality and type of relationship that a given social tie represents, more extensive utilization of qualitative research methods, learning from emerging social network theory and research in other disciplines, particularly criminology, and further incorporation of the organizational level of analysis.

Introduction

Theory and research on social networks has a long tradition in sociology, social psychology, and anthropology and an increasing presence in organizational studies. In this chapter, we critically review the embryonic but growing body of social network theory and research on misconduct in and by organizations. We structure our review around the three main areas of prior research: the role of social networks in the initiation, evolution, and consequences of wrongdoing. We use Brass, Butterfield, and Skaggs' (1998) seminal theoretical analysis of the role

We are grateful to Kristin Smith-Crowe and Christopher Yenkey for their helpful comments on earlier versions of this chapter.

203

that social networks play in unethical behavior as the starting point for our review, which reaffirms, extends, and in some cases suggests modifications to their arguments. We tap a range of empirical studies on social networks and organizational misconduct, most importantly a series of investigations by Baker, Faulkner, and associates (Baker and Faulkner 1993, 2003, 2004; Faulkner and Cheney 2014; Faulkner et al. 2003) to flesh out our discussion. We conclude that a comprehensive understanding of the role of social networks in wrongdoing in and by organizations hinges on several contextual factors that social network analyses sometimes overlook in the drive to use the patterns of relationships among wrongdoers and their victims as the dominant explanatory device. We end by suggesting several lines of inquiry that social network analysts might explore in connection with organizational wrongdoing in the future.

One can conceptualize wrongdoing narrowly, to include only behaviors that violate a society's laws, or broadly, to include any behavior considered deviant from the standpoint of social norms and ethical principles. We conceptualize wrongdoing broadly, including behaviors ranging from the unethical to the illegal, so as to allow consideration of the full range of management theory and research on topics related to misconduct. This conception of wrongdoing does not eliminate ambiguity, as classifying behavior as unethical or even illegal is contingent on an audience's judgment. Judging a behavior as unethical depends on the subjective assessments of researchers and perhaps their subjects. Judging a behavior as illegal depends on the actions of formally established social control agents (e.g., law enforcement officers, government prosecutors, etc.). However, for the purposes of this chapter, we take researchers' definitions of behavior as either unethical or illegal for granted.

The nature of wrongdoing in and by organizations

One can also conceive of organizations narrowly, to include only formally organized private-sector businesses, or broadly, to include any informally organized group of mutually interacting individuals. Here we focus on business organizations, because this is the principal interest of management scholars. But in the conclusion we point to recent research on the role social networks play in the misconduct within other kinds of organizations, including drug distribution rings, organized crime families, and terrorist groups.

Finally, one can distinguish between two ideal types of organizational wrongdoing. Some wrongdoing is perpetrated by individuals to advance their parochial interests at the expense of the organizations with which they are affiliated (sometimes referred to as occupational or white-collar wrongdoing). Other wrongdoing is perpetrated by individuals to advance the interests of the organizations to which they are affiliated (sometimes referred to as organizational or corporate misconduct) (Clinard and Quinney 1973; Finney and Lesieur 1982). When social network researchers study prototypical occupational misconduct, they tend to focus on individuals and interpersonal relations. When they study prototypical organizational misconduct, they focus on organizations and interorganizational relationships. The ideal types of occupational and organizational misconduct, though, are often difficult to distinguish in concrete cases of wrongdoing, which frequently benefit both organizational participants and their organizations. In this chapter we focus on individuals and interpersonal relations, regardless of the apparent beneficiaries and victims of the misconduct they perpetrate, because these relations are the focus of most social network analyses of misconduct in and by organizations. And for simplicity, we refer to the misconduct they perpetrate as organizational wrongdoing. In the conclusion we briefly consider the smaller body of social network analyses that focuses on organizations and inter-organizational relationships.

Types of social network analysis

Social network analysis focuses on the structure of relations among actors, how the structures arise, and how an actor's position in those structures shapes their outlook and behavior (Everton 2012). As such, it contrasts with modes of analysis that focus on the attributes of actors, ascribed (e.g., race and gender) and acquired (e.g., education:), as independent and dependent variables. Social network analysis is guided by both methodological and theoretical concerns. And while there is general agreement on the nature of network methods, which consist of well-accepted measures that describe network ties and structure (e.g., centrality, density, tie strength) and increasingly sophisticated mathematical algorithms that calculate these conceptually based measures (e.g., clique detection methods and block models), there is divergence on the nature of network theory.

Some researchers strive to develop new social network theory; others strive to tease out the network implications of existing social theory. Burt's theory of structural holes (1992), which has its roots in the fundamental insights of Simmel (1950), represents the former theoretical enterprise. Papachristos's (2013) analysis of street crime, which operationalizes existing criminological theory on differential association, represents the latter. More fundamentally, some believe that social networks provide the micro foundations of social structure, while others understand networks as one type of social structure embedded in more encompassing structures such as market systems. Everton's (2012) analysis of terrorist networks, which derives its inspiration from Granovetter's (1973) classic work on labor markets, represents the former point of view. Orru, Biggart, and Hamilton's (1996) analysis of three Asian economies represents the latter. The research on organizational wrongdoing that we consider in this chapter exhibits a relentless focus on social relationships among actors, the use of widely accepted sophisticated network measures and statistical algorithms to capture these relationships, and the full diversity of orientations to theorizing them.

The initiation of wrongdoing

Scholars have explored how social networks influence the initiation of wrongdoing at two levels of analysis: how individuals initiate misconduct and how misconduct emerges in groups.

Individual misconduct

Brass and associates' (1998) theoretical analysis of social networks and unethical behavior focuses primarily on how individuals' social network relationships influence the initiation of misconduct. They argue that social ties both offer actors opportunities to engage in unethical behavior vis-à-vis their tie partners and constrain actors' pursuits of such behavior. They then draw on this argument to develop seven formal propositions about the association between an individual's network ties and his/her propensity to embark on unethical behavior.

Brass and associates contend that three aspects of social ties create opportunities to engage in unethical behavior toward others. First, opportunities for a focal actor to behave unethically toward his/her tie partners increase when the actor's relationships with them become *asymmetrical* (i.e., when a focal actor perceives the relationship to be weaker than the tie partner perceives it to be). When ties are asymmetrical, the focal actor is less encumbered by the empathy and psychological proximity s/he might otherwise feel for his/her tie partner, who is then less likely to closely monitor the focal actor's behavior. Second, opportunities for a focal actor to behave unethically toward his/her tie partners also increase when the actor's relationships with them become *status imbalanced* (i.e., when the focal actor has power over his/her tie partners). When ties are status imbalanced, the focal actor is able to impose his/her unethical will on his/her tie partners. Finally, opportunities for a focal actor to victimize his/her tie partners also grow when the actor's local network contains numerous *structural holes*. When a focal actor's network contains structural holes, s/he is subject to less scrutiny by his/her tie partners and is less fearful of reputation loss if scrutinized and "busted" (because his/her tie partners do not exchange information about the focal actor's behavior with each other).

In addition, Brass and colleagues maintain that four aspects of social ties constrain an individual's proclivity to engage in unethical behavior toward others. Constraints on a focal actor's proclivity to behave unethically toward his/her tie partners increase when the actor's relationships with them are *strong* (i.e., when they are characterized by frequent and intense interaction) and multiplex (i.e., when they facilitate many different types of relationships). When ties are strong and multiplex, a focal actor is more empathetic and psychologically close to his/her tie partners and has more to lose if they treat their tie partners unethically and are discovered. Consistent with this proposition, the inhibiting effects that social ties can have on an actor's proclivity to engage in unethical behavior vis-à-vis a tie partner also grow as the focal actor's *centrality* in their global network grows and the *density* of his/her global network increases. Central actors embedded in dense networks are subject to greater scrutiny and increased reputation loss if scrutinized and found to have behaved unethically.

On the basis of these arguments, Brass and associates develop propositions that have three important features. First, the propositions pertain to the magnitude of the enabling or inhibiting effects that social ties can have in regard to unethical behavior. Second, they stipulate that the magnitude of the enabling or inhibiting effects that social ties can have regarding unethical behavior depends on an individual's general propensity to engage in such behavior. Third, they assume that an individual's general propensity to engage in unethical behavior is a function of individual factors (e.g., moral development), organizational factors (e.g., incentive systems and culture), and issue-related factors (e.g., the seriousness of the potential ethical breach). For example, Brass and associates' first proposition states that "the effects of the constraints of strong relationships on unethical behavior will increase as the constraints of characteristics of individuals, organizations, and issues decrease and vice versa."

Brass and associates' propositions do not lead to hypotheses that are easy to test. First, they specify that social ties affect *opportunities* or *constraints* to engage in unethical behavior toward tied others, which are not directly observable. Second, they specify that the impact of social network ties on opportunities and constraints hinges on an individual's multidimensional general disposition to engage in unethical behavior, which means that the hypotheses derived from their propositions specify complex interaction effects that are difficult to estimate. As a result, direct tests of most of Brass and colleagues' propositions are absent from the literature. Nonetheless, their theoretical arguments are extremely important because, as will be shown below, they inform much extant social network research on the initiation, evolution, and consequences of organizational misconduct.

Group misconduct

Much wrongdoing in organizations is collective in nature, involving multiple interacting individuals in pursuit of a common malevolent objective. Brass and associates also consider how wrongdoing of this sort might arise. They contend that as organizations grow in size, informal groups consisting of similar interacting organizational participants emerge. As the strength and density of the ties among group members increase, the likelihood that groups will treat other similar emergent groups unethically also increases. Brass and associates maintain that in-group and out-group biases underpin this tendency. Though their proposition hasn't been tested directly, recent work in social psychology attests to the role that in-group/out-group bias plays in unethical behavior. In a series of experiments, Waytz and Epley (2012) documented how merely thinking about the social connections one has with others increases one's likelihood of dehumanizing others. They argue that when one feels that one's need to be connected to others is met, one can more easily treat outsiders harshly. Their findings support the notion that in-group biases – activated through thinking about one's social connections – may increase the likelihood that group members will behave unethically toward out-group members.

Brass and colleagues' proposition about the ethical dangers of cohesive (tightly connected) groups echoes Janis' work on "groupthink" (1983). Janis maintained that cohesive groups, strongly and densely connected by definition, lead members to see themselves as morally superior and outsiders as morally inferior, and, as a result, deserving of harsh treatment. Further, he argued that these tendencies were particularly likely to manifest in contexts where group members perceived themselves to be under attack by a common enemy. Consistent with this formulation, Gerald Mars documented how subgroups of hotel employees (1973) and dock workers (1974) organized as subgroups to pilfer from their organizations. Similarly, Raven (1974) argued that the Nixon administration's insular inner circle stressed the need to hit hard against all enemies of the administration, which contributed to the relaxation of moral restraints that characterized the Watergate scandal.

The evolution of wrongdoing

Scholars have also explored two ways in which social networks influence the evolution of organizational wrongdoing: via the entrapment of new victims and the recruitment of additional perpetrators.

The extension of wrongdoing to increasing numbers of victims

Several studies examine the extent to which the owners and managers of fraudulent business (hereafter, "principals") extend their illegitimate activities to increasing numbers of victims. Brass and associates' (1998) propositions about the initiation of misconduct imply that the principals of illegitimate businesses will make less use of their strong ties to potential victims when expanding the scope of their illegitimate activities, because strong ties are associated with affective bonds that inhibit people from taking advantage of tie partners. Their propositions also imply that the principals of illegitimate businesses will make less extensive use of their victims' social ties when recruiting additional victims, because expanding in this way tends to result in dense networks of duped victims, which increase the likelihood that the suspicions that arise among victims of fraudulent enterprises will diffuse quickly and amplify, increasing the likelihood that the enterprise's fraudulent character will be unearthed and broadcast.

Baker and Faulkner analyzed the extension of wrongdoing to an increasing number of victims in connection with a fraudulent oil and gas exploration investment scheme (2003, 2004). Fountain Oil and Gas began as a legitimate company, but its principals progressively engaged in two related frauds: they misrepresented the firm's success to investors and obscured investors' losses by transferring funds from some investors' accounts to others. Contrary to the implications of Brass and associates' arguments, Baker and Faulkner found that Fountain's principals expanded their firm's reach through their direct contacts and through their existing investors' ties at roughly the same rate as the principals of legitimate enterprises have been shown to do (see Dimaggio and Louch 1998). They also found that Fountain's principals actively encouraged their investors to refer their friends to the firm, although their investors tended to resist such entreaties.

Baker and Faulkner attribute these unanticipated results to two characteristics of the misconduct in question. First, Fountain's misconduct was an intermediate fraud, in which the principals began their efforts as a legitimate enterprise and only later redirected their efforts in an illegitimate direction. Thus, the way Fountain recruited investors followed a pattern typical of legitimate enterprises. The authors speculate that their results might look different had they studied a preplanned fraud such as a classic Ponzi scheme. Second, the misconduct at Fountain involved recruiting individuals to take advantage of presumably limited investment opportunities, a feature of both classic and evolved Ponzi schemes, such as the one orchestrated by Bernie Madoff (Henriques 2011). Thus, Fountain's investors were disinclined to cave in to the company's (apparently self-defeating) entreaties to recruit new investors. The more new investors recruited to Fountain, the fewer investment opportunities would remain for current investors.

Another study analyzing the extension of fraud to increasing numbers of victims appears to contradict both the implications of Brass and colleagues' arguments and Baker and Faulkner's results. Nash, Bouchard, and Malm (2013) investigated the ERON Mortgage Corporation fraud, in which investors were recruited for bogus investment opportunities and paid off with prior investors' outlays. They found that ERON's principles recruited victims from their strong tie networks and actively stimulated the spread of the fraud through their initial victims' family and friends, generating the fraud's exponential growth, typical of legitimate innovations' patterns of diffusion. Perhaps ERON's principals were able to grow their illegitimate business through strong ties, contrary to the implications of Brass and associates' argument about strong ties, because ERON's victims were more strongly tied to the firm's principals than the firm's principals were to them. If so, this would dovetail with Granovetter's implicit observation that strong ties enhance opportunities for malfeasance *when they are asymmetrical* (1985: 491). Perhaps ERON's principals were able to spread their fraud at an exponential rate through the victim's family and friends, whereas Fountain's principals were not, because ERON's victims did not think the investment opportunities of which they were availing themselves were limited in nature.

The diffusion of wrongdoing to increasing numbers of perpetrators

Brass et al. (1998) consider two ways in which network relationships can shape the spread of unethical behavior to increasing numbers of perpetrators. First, they maintain that unethical behavior tends to spread from those already engaged in unethical behavior to others with whom the unethical actor is tied, especially when the tie is strong. The mechanism they contend underpins this "cohesion" effect is social influence, the tendency of actors who interact directly, frequently, and empathetically to develop similar attitudes and behaviors. A raft of psychological studies suggest that being directly tied to others engaged in unethical behavior increases a person's propensity to engage in unethical behavior (Gino, Ayal, and Ariely 2009; Gino, Gu, and Zhong 2009; Robinson, Wang, and Kiewitz 2014; Zey-Ferrell and Ferrell 1982; Zey-Ferrell, Weaver, and Ferrell 1979)

Brass and associates' cohesion argument follows the lead of Edwin Sutherland's classic differential association theory of white-collar crime (1949/1983). But it makes incomplete use of Sutherland's theory, which holds that direct ties with white-collar criminals also transmit motives, techniques (including techniques of neutralizing guilt), and resources for engaging in crime (Ashforth and Anand 2003; Caravita et al. 2014; Sykes and Matza 1957). Moreover, Brass and associates' argument fails to take into account learning theorists' argument that organizational participants who are tied to others engaged in wrong-doing receive information about the costs and benefits of engaging in wrongdoing (Manz and Sims 1981; O'Fallon and Butterfield 2012). These additional mechanisms set in motion by ties to deviant others imply more complex empirical associations between network position on the one hand and the propensity to engage in wrongdoing on the other. Specifically, insofar as ties can transmit information about the costs of engaging in wrongdoing and insofar as information can be transmitted through indirect as well as direct ties, they imply that both direct and indirect ties to deviant peers can suppress the likelihood of engaging in wrongdoing.

Palmer and Yenkey's (2015) analysis of the use of banned performance-enhancing drugs (PEDs) in professional cycling indicates that this learning mechanism was at work in advance of the 2010 Tour de France. They show that competitors who had direct and indirect ties (operationalized as common team memberships) to peers who had known prior involvement with PEDs and received *no* sanctions for their involvements were *more* likely to have used PEDs in advance of the 2010 Tour. But competitors who had direct and indirect ties to peers who had known prior involvement with PEDs and received *severe* sanctions for their involvements were *less* likely to have used PEDs in advance of the Tour. Palmer and Yenkey's analysis also suggests that the institutional context in which the wrongdoing is situated can mod-erate the impact of other mechanisms of diffusion. They found little evidence that ties to peers who had known prior involvement with PEDs, undifferentiated by sanction, influenced rider PED use in advance of the 2010 Tour. They speculate that this reflects the fact that almost all of the riders competing in the 2010 Tour de France (the sport's penultimate race) had been active in the professional ranks in the early years of the new decade (2000–2008) and that PED use was pervasive in that period. Thus, all riders competing in the 2010 Tour were likely well acquainted with the logic and techniques of PED use at this time, irrespective of their teammates' known prior involvement with PEDs.

Second, Brass and associates maintain that unethical behavior spreads from unethical actors to other actors that maintain the same types of relationships as the unethical actor. The mechanism underpinning this "structural equivalence" relationship is social comparison. They contend that actors who maintain similar relationships with others tend to look to one another to determine how to think and behave. To the best of our knowledge, no one has examined how structural equivalence influences the diffusion of misconduct, perhaps because it is difficult to distinguish structural equivalence-based mimicry from role pressures.

Stuart and Moore's (2015) study of the enforcer role in professional ice hockey illustrates how mimicry based on structural equivalence and role pressures might be confounded in the spread of misconduct. It is common for professional hockey teams to allocate one player, known as the enforcer, to a role dedicated to breaking the rules that govern acceptable physical contact between competitors. Stuart and Moore found that teams with a designated enforcer suffer performance declines when he is injured. In fact, team performance is more negatively affected when an enforcer is injured than when other players are injured, suggesting that this dedicated rule-breaking role is valuable to teams, and its value is one reason why the role has diffused throughout hockey. This argument is consistent with Pinto, Leana, and Pil (2008), who argue that role equivalence can be a mechanism for the diffusion of corruption in that, when it becomes apparent that a corrupt role (such as an enforcer in a hockey team, or a sales agent offering kickbacks) is valuable, similar organizations will adopt the practice, so as not to lose out on the competitive advantage it brings.

The consequences of wrongdoing

Finally, scholars have examined how social networks impact three consequences of wrongdoing: perpetrators' payoffs, victims' exposure to harm, and perpetrators' susceptibility to detection and punishment.

Perpetrators' payoffs

Brass and associates' (1998) theoretical analysis of how individuals' social ties influence their propensity to engage in misconduct has implications for the study of individuals' capacity to reap benefits from the wrongdoing they perpetrate. If ties create opportunities to engage in misconduct as well as impose constraints on wrongdoing, then ties should also influence wrongdoers' capacity to reap benefits from their misconduct. To the best of our knowledge, only one study has attempted to explore this line of inquiry. Jancsics (2015) analyzed the illegal transfer of resources via brokers from private citizens to state- and private-sector organizations in Hungary. His analysis suggests that brokers who know the greatest number of willing agents and in-need clients are in the best position to sustain a profitable corrupt brokerage business, as they are in the best position to develop and maintain a steady stream of successful corrupt transactions.

The bulk of research on the payoffs of wrongdoing, though, focuses on collective wrongdoing; in particular, misconduct that takes the form of conspiracies in which multiple actors intentionally orchestrate their behavior to accomplish an illegitimate objective. For example, Ahern (2015) has studied insider-trading rings in which persons with access to private information pertaining to a firm's likely future stock price share that information with others who buy or sell the firm's stock to reap illegal profits. Using data from the Securities and Exchange Commission (SEC) and Department of Justice (DOJ) to identify the players in 183 insider-trading networks, he found that insider traders share strong social connections – 23 percent of the sample are family members, 74 percent met before college, and 19 percent met during college – suggesting that individuals share potentially profitable insider tips to close others. He also found that insiders earn returns of 35 per- cent over 21 days, an average of $1.3 million average per tip. Traders farther from the original source earn lower percentage returns, but higher dollar gains, due to larger investments.

Most research on the payoffs of collective wrongdoing focuses on the tradeoff between the secrecy and efficacy benefits of different types of ties and network structures. This work tends to assume that the need for secrecy limits and even dominates the need for efficacy in the construction of conspiracies (Baccara and Bar-Isaac 2008; Baker and Faulkner 1993; Lehman and Ramanujam 2009; Morselli, Giguère, and Petit 2007). Brass and associates (1998) theorize that conspiracies will "leak" less information to those who seek to control them when they are small, sparsely connected, and composed of weak ties. For this reason, they predict that the organizers of conspiracies will typically recruit only the minimum number of co-conspirators necessary to achieve the conspirators' goals and, importantly, will recruit co- conspirators to whom they are only weakly tied and who have no relationships with existing co-conspirators. This prediction contrasts with their argument about the way in which wrongdoing diffuses between perpetrators operating in parallel (as opposed to in tandem), which they contend diffuses via strong ties.

Aven's (2015) study of corrupt networks at Enron tests Brass and associates' predictions about the strength and density of social ties linking conspiratorial wrongdoers. She analyzed email communications between Enron employees involved in six projects, three of which were legal endeavors and three of which were corrupt. She found that the employees involved in the corrupt projects tended to engage in less frequent and fewer reciprocal communications with their co-conspirators during the initial phase of the projects. However, reciprocal communication and local network density increased over the life of the conspiracies, presumably because conspirators came to trust that their co-conspirators would not defect and rat them out. If her findings generalize, they suggest that co-conspirators' subjectively perceived need to employ secrecy protecting network structures declines over the life course of a conspiracy.

Although conspiracies must organize with secrecy in mind, they also must take into account efficacy considerations. Baker and Faulkner (1993) explored this tension in their study of corruption in the heavy electrical equipment industry in the 1950s, which involved the rigging of bids for turbines, switchgear, and transformers sold to state and municipal governments in the US. They theorized that secrecy considerations would dictate that the conspiracies would be organized in a sparsely connected and decentralized fashion, but efficacy considerations would dictate that they be organized according to variable task requirements. In Baker and Faulkner's assessment, the bid rigging of switchgear and transformer contracts was relatively straightforward, which small group research suggests would be most efficiently accomplished in a sparsely connected and centralized fashion. However, in their judgment, the bid rigging of turbine contracts was more complex, which small group research suggests would be most efficiently accomplished in a densely connected and decentralized fashion. Baker and Faulkner found that the switchgear and transformer conspiracies were relatively sparsely connected and *de*centralized, which suggested that secrecy imperatives dominated efficacy considerations in these conspiracies. However, the turbines conspiracy was densely connected and *centralized*, which suggested that efficacy imperatives tempered secrecy considerations in this conspiracy. That is, the relative importance of secrecy and efficacy imperatives was contingent on the complexity of the conspiracy in question. Further, they concluded from supplemental qualitative analysis that this intermediate result reflected the turbine conspirators' need to resolve numerous conflicts in secret, which required extensive communication between the conspiracy's leaders and the multitude of rank-and-file co-conspirators.

In a follow-up study that focused solely on the turbines conspiracy, Faulkner and associates (2003) examined the relationship between conspiracy structure and efficacy more directly. In this study, they theorized and found that the conspiracy generated the most collusive (above market) prices for transformers in fiscal quarters when co-conspirators engaged in more continuous interactions (i.e., were densely connected via strong ties). Yet the relationship between the continuity of interaction among co-conspirators and the efficacy of the conspiracy was complex. Up to moderate levels of interaction continuity, conflict among co-conspirators decreased. But beyond moderate levels of interaction continuity, conflict intensified, because (the authors presume) the opportunities for conflict multiplied, leading to contradictory effects. On one hand, conflict dampened rates of interaction, undermining the conspiracy's efficacy. On the other hand, conflict increased direct involvement from high-level corporate officials, which increased the conspiracy's efficacy. Qualitative analysis of detailed descriptions of bi-weekly co-conspirator meetings suggests the conspiracy followed a cyclical pattern. Meetings were called, co-conspirator ties became dense and strong, and the conspiracy produced intended results. After a time, though, the continuity of interaction among co-conspirators and/or exogenous shocks (such as co-conspirator defections and market downturns) generated conflicts that eroded continuity of interaction and conspiracy efficacy. These problems precipitated the involvement of high-level corporate officials, who then got the conspiracy back on track.

Taken together, Aven's study of illegitimate deals at Enron (2015) and Baker, Faulkner, and associates' two studies of bid rigging in the heavy electrical equipment industry (Baker and Faulkner 1993; Faulkner et al. 2003) suggest that the heterogeneity of co-conspirator interests and thus the level of co-conspirator conflict influence which social network structures will be most efficacious for conspiracies. In the conspiracies studied by Aven, all of the conspirators were employees of Enron and thus had common organizational interests.

In the conspiracies studied by Baker and Faulkner, the conspirators represented different firms and thus had divergent interests. The commonality of interests in the former case gave rise to sparsely connected conspiracy networks, whereas the divergence of interests (and resultant conflicts) in the later case made centralized and densely connected networks more effective.

Victims' exposure to harm

Brass and associates' (1998) analysis of how individuals' social ties influence their propensity to engage in misconduct also has implications for the study of potential victims' exposure to harm. Most obviously, their argument that strong ties constrain potential wrongdoers from treating their tie partners unethically implies that persons who maintain strong ties to persons engaged in misconduct will be insulated from victimization.

Baker and Faulkner's (2003) study of the Fountain Oil and Gas intermediate fraud explored the potentially insulating effect that strong ties to the firm's principals might have on the likelihood that investors were victimized, as measured by investors' total loss of their outlay. They found that investors who had strong ties to the company's principals simultaneously benefited and suffered from their relationships to the principals, relative to investors who maintained only arm's-length ties to the company's principals. Having strong ties to Fountain's principals reduced the likelihood that investors lost all of their money, even controlling for the extent to which investors conducted due diligence in connection with their investments, presumably because Fountain's principals felt empathy for their strong tie partners or because they feared the reputational damage that might result from victimizing them. But having strong ties to Fountain's principals reduced the likelihood that investors conducted due diligence, presumably because strong tie investors trusted the principals. And failure to conduct due diligence increased the probability that investors lost their entire outlay.

Coupled with Baker and Faulkner's findings about how Fountain's principals recruited investors, this suggests that the principals recruited investors from their strong tie network, and as the firm's legitimate enterprise evolved into a criminal one, they took advantage of the fact that these strong tie investors were less inclined to conduct due diligence on their investments. In a sense, Fountain's principals were of "two minds" in their pursuit of fraud. Thus, the effect of strong ties on the likelihood of victimization was complex. In fact, Baker and Faulkner found qualitative evidence that demands for high returns voiced by investors with whom Fountain's principals were strongly tied might have been one of the forces compelling the principles to move funds from weakly tied investors' better performing wells to the strongly tied investors' underperforming wells.

Several studies of pre-planned frauds contradict more thoroughly Brass and associates' (1998) implicit contention that strong ties to wrongdoers insulate individuals from victimization. Anecdotal evidence on classic Ponzi schemes suggests that the first victims of such schemes tend to be members of the initiator's family (Lowry 1988), professional community (Iowa Securities Bureau 2001), or ethnic community (Kirby and Hanna 1994). Nash and colleagues' analysis of the ERON Mortgage Corporation fraud suggests the same (2013). This is consistent with the results of research on the *expansion* of pre-planned frauds as well as Granovettor's (1985) observation that strong ties may create enhanced opportunity for malfeasance when they are asymmetrical (i.e., when the Ponzi schemer or mature intermediate fraudster is less attached to his/her victims than vice versa).

Perpetrators' susceptibility to detection and punishment

Brass and associates (1998) also offer arguments related to the detection and punishment of wrongdoers involved in conspiratorial misconduct, contending that if a conspiracy is uncovered, the most central conspirators will be at greatest risk of being fingered and punished. Baker and Faulkner (1993) tested this prediction in their study of price-fixing in the heavy electrical equipment industry. They found that occupying a central position in a conspiracy was associated with increased risk of being fingered and punished, but only in the case of the turbines conspiracy, which was organized in a centralized and densely connected fashion. Thus, the impact of centrality on risk of detection and punishment depended on the structure of the network in which a perpetrator was embedded. Further, Baker and Faulkner found that even in the turbines case, centrality only increased a perpetrator's risk of indictment, conviction, and punishment when it was characterized by "degree centrality" (the number of ties individuals have to others in the network). Individuals' "betweenness centrality" (the number of ties an individual has to actors who are not tied to each other), one measure of brokerage, was not predictive of punishment.

Faulkner and Cheney (2014) offer the opposite argument in their analysis of the Watergate conspiracy. They proposed that persons who occupied brokerage positions in that conspiracy enjoyed privileged status during the illicit enterprise, but were subject to greater risk of conviction and punishment once their illicit activities were brought to light. Consistent with this prediction, they found that individuals were more likely to be testified against, to be found guilty, and to be sentenced to long prison sentences if they were tied both to the tightly connected core of the conspiracy (President Nixon and his inner circle) and to the multiple tightly connected cabals that carried out the core's illicit objectives (e.g., the group known as the "plumbers" that installed the illegal wiretap in the Democratic National Committee's headquarters), compared to those occupying other positions in the conspiracy's network. They speculated that serving as a broker increased conspirators' risk of detection and prosecution in the Watergate conspiracy because they were engaged in a political as opposed to an economic conspiracy.

Finally, there is a growing body of research that explores how social network position influences the extent to which actors *associated* with wrongdoers are punished for that tie, an effect known as "stigma by association." Both Pozner (2008, and Pozner & Harris (Chapter 14)) and Wurthmann (2014) have found that the directors of corporations discovered to have engaged in misconduct are penalized in the market for corporate board appointments, losing more and obtaining fewer board positions in the years following the detected fraud. However, directors' social networks provide a buffer that can mitigate these penalties. Pozner (2008) demonstrates that this penalty is diminished in the case of high-status directors, where status is measured partly by a director's centrality in the corporate interlock network, and Wurthmann (2014) shows that this penalty is mitigated for directors with upper-class origins and presumably upper-class social network connections.

Paths forward

Taking greater account of context

Our review of existing network theory and research on organizational wrongdoing indicates that the role social networks play in the initiation, evolution, and consequences of wrongdoing depends on contextual factors, in a way that has not been acknowledged by prior theorizing and empirical research. We discuss four primary contextual factors surfaced by our review below.

Individual propensities to engage in misconduct. Arguably, the most important contextual factor that moderates how social network ties and structure influence misconduct is the extent to which potential wrongdoers are predisposed to engage in misconduct. Most of Brass and associates' (1998) propositions are based on the assumption that an individual's social ties do not directly influence his/her propensity to treat his/her tie partners unethically. Rather, they stipulate that an individual's social ties only influence his/her propensity to treat his/her tie partners unethically when s/he has a general inclination to engage in unethical behavior, which itself is a function of individual factors (e.g., moral development), organizational factors (e.g., organizational culture), and issue-related factors (e.g., moral intensity). We agree with the general thrust of Brass and associates' propositions, but think the relationship between potential wrongdoers' predisposition to treat others unethically, their social network ties, and their propensity to engage in misconduct toward their tie partners might be even more complex than Brass and associates theorize.

First, theory suggests that the opportunity to engage in a behavior and reap the rewards that flow from it influences one's motivation to engage in the behavior (Nadler and Lawler 1977). Thus, any aspect of a person's social network position that might create opportunities for him/her to engage in misconduct should increase the person's propensity to treat his/her tie partners unethically. As an example, research indicates that actors who possess power and exert influence over others become predisposed to treating these others unethically (Keltner, Gruenfeld, and Anderson 2003). Thus, the degree to which a focal actor's social ties to others are status (power) unbalanced should also increase his/her propensity (not just his/her opportunities) to treat his/her tie partners unethically. Similarly, the extent to which a focal actor occupies a brokerage position should increase his/her propensity (again, not just his/her opportunities) to treat his/her tie partners unethically, because brokers tend to have power over their tie partners.

Second, logic suggests that individuals' predispositions to engage in misconduct will influence the network ties they develop. Brass and associates' propositions pertain to the tendency of organizational participants to behave unethically toward people to whom they are *already* tied. But their arguments can be extended logically to situations in which the predisposition to engage in wrongdoing *precedes* the formation of social ties. Specifically, Brass and associates imply that individuals predisposed to treat others unethically may create social ties and social tie configurations with others that create opportunities for and relax constraints against unethical behavior toward others. Thus, fraudsters seeking to take advantage of investors will strive to create asymmetrical and status-imbalanced relationships with their intended marks.

The nature of the wrongdoing.   Another contextual factor moderating the role that social networks play in misconduct is the nature of the wrongdoing in question. The importance of this contextual factor has remained largely hidden in extant research, because most studies focus on one type of wrongdoing. For example, our review suggests that the effectiveness of different types of network structures and the consequences of different network positions for individuals in conspiracies vary between "intermediate fraud," such as the Fountain Oil and Gas fraud, and pre-planned wrongdoing, such as the ERON Mortgage Corporation fraud. Similarly, our review suggests that the network structure of misconduct varies depending on whether misconduct is contained in a single organization, as was the case at Enron, or spans multiple organizations, as was the case with the bid-rigging conspiracy in the heavy electrical equipment industry.

We suggest that the nature of misconduct in which perpetrators are engaged might be differentiated in a more refined fashion. For example, not all intermediate frauds are alike. While all begin with actors pursuing legitimate business opportunities, some result in actors pursuing piecemeal illegitimate behaviors (the case of Fountain Oil and Gas) and others result in actors pursuing comprehensively illegitimate business models (the case of evolved Ponzi schemes). Further, we think the nature of misconduct might be differentiated along other dimensions. For example, in the case of large organizations, misconduct may be contained in relatively delimited parts of the firm (the case of insider-trading conspiracies) or may permeate the entire organization (such as "boiler room" stock brokerages). We suspect the role that social networks play in the initiation, evolution, and consequences of misconduct will vary across these additional types of organizational wrongdoing as well.

The institutional context. The institutional context in which misconduct is embedded also moderates the role that social networks play in misconduct. Our review indicates that institutional contexts vary across organizational fields in ways that influence the relationships between social networks and misconduct. For example, Baker, Faulkner, and associates' several studies on organizational conspiracies suggest that the effect of a co-conspirators' network location on his/her risk of detection and punishment varies depending on whether the conspiracy unfolds in a political as opposed to an economic environment. Additionally, our review suggests that institutional contexts vary within organizational fields over time in ways that influence the relationships between social networks and misconduct. For example, Palmer and Yenkey's study of PED use in professional cycling suggests that the impact of differential association on a rider's propensity to use PEDs was relatively limited in the latter part of the twentieth century when PED use was normative and thus ubiquitous, but it might become important in the current period when PED use is increasingly counter-normative and more constrained.

We think other dimensions along which institutional contexts vary might also have a profound impact on the role that social networks play in the initiation, evolution, and consequences of organizational misconduct. Most obviously, institutional contexts vary significantly across geopolitical space. Comparative economic sociologists have demonstrated that nations differ with regard to the role social networks play in economic behavior (Orru et al. 1996). It is thus likely that the relationship between social networks and misconduct also varies across national environments. For example, nations have unique legal and cultural environments; these differences likely play into the noticeable differences in the levels of misconduct they exhibit (Fisman and Miguel 2007).

Temporal dynamics. Finally, temporal dynamics also moderate the role that social networks play in misconduct. For example, in the illegitimate Enron deals studied by Aven (2015), the ties among conspirators became increasingly reciprocal and dense over time, reflecting the increased trust and thus ease of coordination among participants. Further, evidence of the network structure of the turbines bid-rigging conspiracy studied by Faulkner et al. (2003) reveals that temporal dynamics can be non-monotonic. In that conspiracy, the density of interaction among co-conspirators oscillated between sparse and dense connections, depending on the level of conflict among conspiracy participants that itself was partly a function of exogenous factors.

We suspect that more comprehensive attempts to study the moderating role of temporal dynamics will have to take into account one or more of the other three contextual factors surfaced by our review. For example, temporal dynamics likely vary across types of misconduct. This is evident in Baker and Faulkner's analysis of the Fountain Oil and Gas intermediate fraud. They found that when Fountain's principals were growing their legitimate business, they tapped their strong tie network for investors, presumably because they believed that persons with whom they maintained strong ties were more likely to support their business. But when Fountain's principals began to engage in illegitimate practices, they protected those with whom they had strong ties, presumably because they had affective bonds with those investors or feared the disapproval and perhaps reputation loss that might follow harming them. Clearly contextual factors can have multifarious and interrelated effects on the relationships between social networks and misconduct. Researchers might do well to explore these effects in greater depth and breadth in the future.

Other avenues for exploration

Adopting a more fine-grained conceptualization of tie type.   Social network theorists and researchers tend to focus on the distinction between two broad classes of ties; strong ties (typified by frequent and reciprocal relationships) and weak ties (typified by infrequent nonreciprocal relationships). While this basic distinction is useful, it does not tap the wide range of relationships that social ties can facilitate. We think that a more fine-grained approach to characterizing the types of ties between perpetrators, co-conspirators, and victims might lead to a more comprehensive and in some instances different understanding of the role social networks play in the initiation, evolution, and consequences of organizational misconduct. For example, Jancsics' (2015) qualitative study of low-level corruption in Hungary identified several types of brokerage, defined by whether the broker was an insider or outsider to the organization granting the illegitimate service in the corrupt exchange, whether the benefits received by the broker were social or financial, and whether the broker merely introduced the agent and the client or actually managed the transaction. The richness he captured by analyzing the fine-grained quality of ties adds richness to our understanding of how social networks facilitate wrongdoing.

Even more fundamentally, all of the social network theorists and researchers reviewed here implicitly assume that social ties and the networks they compose are objective realities. But there is much anecdotal evidence that people embarking on unethical behavior often work to create impressions about the relationships they maintain, in an attempt to benefit from the enabling effects that social ties can generate. For example, Barry Minkow attracted investors for his non-existent building restoration business by cultivating the impression that he was linked to his investors in a reciprocal strong relationship, when in fact he was linked to them in an asymmetrical one in which they felt emotionally close to him but he felt little affection for them (Domanick 1991). This work suggests that researchers need to pay attention not only to the existence of ties between actors, but also to the perceptions of ties from both actors' and their tie partners' perspectives.

Embracing a wider range of data and methods. Social network methodologists have developed an impressive array of sophisticated mathematical techniques to analyze important features of social networks (e.g., density and centralization) and network locations (e.g., centrality and brokerage). But, the mathematical algorithms currently available to analyze social networks have so far failed to capture the richness of the social ties linking co-conspirators to one another and with their victims (e.g., the extent to which ties are multiplex and symmetrical). This leaves network methodologists with more work to do. Further, researchers have demonstrated considerable creativity in extracting social network information from archival data, using email logs (Aven 2015), court records, and SEC documents (Ahern 2015), as well as congressional testimony (Baker and Faulkner 1993). But when it comes to mining archival data sources for network relationships, the surface has only been scratched. Other potential archival data sources, such as social network websites like LinkedIn, await investigation.

With this said, even the most sophisticated and creative quantitative empirical analyses of social networks have limitations. Many of the fine-grained features of social networks considered above remain outside the purview of quantitative empirical social network research. Thus, we believe researchers who seek a deep understanding of the role that social networks play in the initiation, evolution, and consequences of organizational misconduct would do well to make greater use of qualitative methods. Indeed, some of the most interesting insights provided by Baker, Faulkner, and associates are derived from supplemental post hoc qualitative analyses of their data (Baker and Faulkner 1993, 2003, 2004; Faulkner and Cheney 2014; Faulkner et al. 2003). In addition, some of the most novel insights about how wrongdoing is initiated and spreads within and across organizations comes from qualitative analyses of wrongdoing, including Maclean's study of churning in the life insurance industry (2001), Mars' ethnographies of employee pilferage (1973, 1974), and Neu and colleagues' analysis of the scandal surrounding the Canadian government's Sponsorship program (2013).

Drawing on work conducted by criminologists. A new wave of criminologists is embracing social network theory and methodologies to develop an enhanced understanding of a range of non-organizational crimes. We think this "networked criminology" (Kappen et al. 2010; Papachristos 2009, 2011; Papachristos, Braga, and Hureau 2012; Papachristos, Hureau, and Braga 2013; Papachritos, Meares, and Fagan 2012) speaks to several of the topics we considered and issues we raised in our review and might be mined by future researchers on the topic.

Papachristos, Braga, and Hureau's (Papachristos et al. 2012, 2013) analysis of gun violence in an urban community examines how a person's social ties can influence his/her exposure to harm from wrongdoing. These authors use co-arrest records to identify a social network of individuals who were known gang members or who had encounters with law enforcement in a neighborhood of Boston in 2008. They show that a person's proximity to prior gunshot victims within this network increased his/her risk of being shot by a handgun; each network association removed from a gunshot victim reduced the odds of gunshot victimization by 25 percent.

Several studies of non-organizational crime suggest how the limits that secrecy imperatives impose on a conspiracy's size, noted by Brass and associates, can be relaxed. Morselli and Roy (2008) found that the large stolen vehicle exportation rings they examined were managed by small groups of criminals linked via brokers, as small groups allow for the structural flexibility necessary for wrongdoing to persist, while brokers provide avenues to flexibly adapt to changed circumstances. Likewise, Natarajan (2006) found that a large heroin distribution network was constituted by small groups of individuals loosely linked by brokers, because this structure provided the secrecy and flexible coordination benefits of small size, while at the same time allowing for the expansion of the enterprise and its illicit payoffs. Perrow (2007) argues that terrorist groups employ much the same type of structure for similar reasons.

Morselli et al.'s (2007) comparative analysis of the 9/11 terrorist conspiracy and a Montreal drug dealing network explores how misconduct type and temporal dynamics can jointly shape how conspiracies manage the secrecy/efficiency tradeoff. They show that the length of time between initiating and fulfilling plans to act, which they refer to as "time-to-task," influences the manner in which conspiracies manage the tradeoff between efficiency and secrecy as they enact their wrongdoing. When conspiracies enjoy long "time-to-task" intervals, as is the case with terrorist networks, they can afford to organize as sparse and decentralized networks. Such networks do not allow for extensive and efficient communication, but they do reduce the chance that individual members will be detected (because the more a group's members communicate, the more opportunities social control agents have to detect a group's members in action). In addition, individual members will be less likely to compromise the group's integrity in sparse and decentralized networks, because, if a member is detected, there are no leaders to "give up." However, when conspiracies face short "time-to-task" intervals, as is the case in drug dealing conspiracies, they must organize in dense and centralized networks. Such networks leave the conspiracy at heightened risk of detection and, if detected, increased risk of compromise, but allow for higher levels and more efficient communication necessary to get the group's work done.

Morselli's (2010) analysis of a drug distribution enterprise organized by the Hell's Angel's motorcycle gang underscores the importance of differentiating between types of centrality when analyzing perpetrators' risk of being punished. He found that actors with high degree centrality were more likely to be arrested, while individuals with high betweenness centrality were less so. At least in this context, it was how many implicated parties one knew, and not how many co-conspirators one indirectly connected to each other (i.e., the extent to which one served as a broker) that led to an increased risk of punishment.

Finally, Campana and Varese's (2013) analysis of wiretapped phone conversations between members of two organized crime groups indicates the benefits of a more fine-grained approach to dimensionalizing social ties. They argue that in order for two Mafiosi to work together, each must trust that the other will follow through on their promise to engage in behaviors crucial for the conspiracy *and* not defect from the conspiracy and rat out their co-conspirator. Further, they contend that strong ties most credibly insure these "commitments," because they subject tie partners to greater constraint with respect to the shirking of obligations and recourse to defection. Consistent with this assertion, they found that ties linking mafia co-conspirators tended to be overlaid with kinship relationships and to entail the exchange of information about violence perpetrated. They argue that by working with kin, tie partners can both enjoy greater trust in their co-conspirators and count on common third parties (other family members) to monitor and control their co-conspirators. By sharing information about violence perpetrated, tie partners become hostage to each other and thus have a stake in keeping their criminal involvements secret from outsiders.

The overwhelming majority of wrongdoing in and by organizations does not involve physical violence. But much wrongdoing in and by organizations entails the perpetration of acts that, if exposed, place the perpetrators at risk of sanction. Thus, one would expect that ties that entail the sharing of such information would increase the effectiveness of the conspiracies. It is noteworthy that Campana and Varese's arguments and results, which make use of fine-grained distinctions between types of ties, contradict Brass and associate's contention that conspirators will tend to enact weak ties with their co-conspirators in order to reduce the likelihood that their joint activities will leak information that will be detected by social control agents.

Exploring the organizational level of analysis. We have restricted our attention to social network research on misconduct that focuses on individuals, either acting alone or in conjunction with others as members of conspiracies. We have not focused on social network research that focuses on organizations, which in many cases can be considered actors with their own interests and capacities. There is some social network research on misconduct that adopts the organizational level of analysis, but it remains in embryonic form. The few studies that take this approach primarily focus on the diffusion of misconduct between organizations and translate Brass and associates' argument about how misconduct spreads among individuals to the organizational level of analysis.

For example, Westphal and Zajac (2001) examined the diffusion of the announcement but incomplete fulfillment of stock buy-back programs, which can be considered an act of deception. Consistent with the cohesion version of Brass and associates' arguments about the diffusion of misconduct, they find that firms are more likely to engage in this practice when they are linked via interlocking directorates to other firms that have previously done so, suggesting that this unethical behavior diffused through corporate directors' social networks. Similarly, Mohliver (2012) examined the diffusion of stock option backdating, a process that was originally considered deceptive and later was labeled illegal. Consistent with the structural equivalence version of Brass and associates' arguments about the diffusion of misconduct, he found that firms more frequently backdated stock options when other clients of their local accounting office, a crucial intermediary, backdated as well. Braithwaite's (2005) qualitative analysis of the proliferation of legally questionable tax shelters in the US and Australia helps explain why intermediaries may become diffusers of misconduct. He found that clients' demand for legally questionable tax shelters compel accounting firms to develop this expertise, in the process creating a market for questionable tax consultancy.

There is one social network analysis of misconduct at the organizational level that focuses on the consequences of misconduct. It examines the impact that misconduct has on an organization's interorganizational relationships. Sullivan, Haunschild, and Page (2007) explored the effect that a corporation's unethical and illegal acts had on its position in the network of interlocking directorates. They found that firms discovered to have engaged in misconduct experienced a decline in the average reputation of the firms to which they were interlocked. They also found that interlock partners who disassociated from the wrongdoer were on average more respected than the interlock partners who remained. This suggests that firms lose high-quality interlock partners in the wake of misconduct, presumably because the revelation of their misconduct undercuts their legitimacy. Sullivan and associates also found that corporations that engaged in misconduct experienced a decline in local network closure (although not in the average network prominence of their interlock partners). This suggests that firms that engaged in misconduct replaced lost interlock partners with new interlock partners who were socially distant from current partners, presumably because their local network was disenchanted with them. In addition, firms that engaged in misconduct experienced a decline in the average size and profitability of the firms to which they were interlocked, but that the departing interlock partners were no larger and more profitable than those who remained. They suggest that being an interlock partner with a firm exposed for engaging in wrongdoing can damage a firm economically. If they are correct, it suggests that stigma by association can have concrete economic consequences for organizations.

Conclusion

Brass and associates' seminal theoretical analysis of social networks and unethical behavior offered an important theoretical advancement in our understanding of the role that social networks play in misconduct within organizations. A growing number of empirical analyses, most importantly those conducted by Baker, Faulkner, and associates, validate, extend, and in some cases call into question Brass and associates' path-breaking ideas.

Our review of work in this area indicates that the role that social networks play in the initiation, evolution, and consequences of organizational wrongdoing depends on four contextual factors: potential wrongdoers' predispositions, the institutional context, temporal dynamics, and the type of wrongdoing perpetrated. Clearly, much work remains to be done. We considered the four factors moderating the impact of social networks on misconduct on a case-by-case basis. Researchers might benefit from a more systematic understanding of how these factors jointly affect the relationships between social networks and the initiation, evolution, and consequences of wrongdoing. We think that theoretical advances along these lines are most likely to emerge from interdisciplinary thinking, applying insights from research on terrorist networks (Raab and Milward 2003), drug distribution networks (Morselli 2010; Natarajan 2006), urban street gangs (Papachristos 2009; Papachristos et al. 2013; Papachritos, Meares et al. 2012), organized criminal syndicates (Campana and Varese 2013; Varese 2013), and political conspiracies (Faulkner and Cheney 2014; Neu et al. 2013) as well as traditional business contexts.

Wrongdoing is seldom undertaken in isolation. Even apparently independent perpetrators are located within networks of other relationships and are socially tied to victims, colleagues with whom they might be colluding, and others from whom they need to hide their activity. The social structures within which we are embedded play an important and to-date underexplored role in the likelihood that individuals, groups, or organizations will engage in wrongdoing, how that wrongdoing will spread, and what the consequences of wrongdoing will be. We hope this chapter provides a worthwhile overview of the existing research on the topic and can help inspire future work in this vein.

References

Ahern, K. R. 2015. "Information networks: Evidence from illegal insider trading tips," Working paper, Marshall School of Business, University of Southern California.

Ashforth, B. E. and Anand, V. 2003. "The normalization of corruption in organizations," *Research in Organizational Behavior* 25: 1–52.

Aven, B. L. 2015. "The paradox of corrupt networks: An analysis of organizational crime at Enron," *Organization Science* 26: 980–996.

Baccara, M. and Bar-Isaac, H. 2008. "How to organize crime," *Review of Economic Studies* 75: 1039–1067.

Baker, W. E. and Faulkner, R. R. 1993. "The social organization of conspiracy: Illegal networks in the heavy electrical equipment industry," *American Sociological Review* 58: 837–860.

Baker, W. E. and Faulkner, R. R. 2003. "Diffusion of fraud: Intermediate economic crime and investor dynamics," *Criminology* 41: 1173–1206.

Baker, W. E. and Faulkner, R. R. 2004. "Social networks and loss of capital," *Social Networks* 26: 91–111.

Braithwaite, J. 2005. *Markets in Vice, Markets in Virtue.* New York: Oxford University Press.

Brass, D. J., Butterfield, K. D., and Skaggs, B. C. 1998. "Relationships and unethical behavior: A social network perspective," *Academy of Management Review* 23: 14–31.

Burt, R. S. 1992. *Structural Holes: The Social Structure of Competition*. Cambridge: Harvard University Press.

Campana, P. and Varese, F. 2013. "Cooperation in criminal organizations: Kinship and violence as credible commitments," *Rationality and Society* 25: 263–289.

Caravita, S. C., Sijtsema, J. J., Rambaran, J. A., and Gini, G. 2014. "Peer influences on moral disengagement in late childhood and early adolescence," *Journal of Youth and Adolescence* 43: 193–207.

Clinard, M. B. and Quinney, R. 1973. *Criminal Behavior Systems: A Typology*. New York: Holt, Rinehart and Winston.

DiMaggio, P. and Louch, H. 1998. "Socially embedded consumer transactions: For what kinds of purchases do people most often use networks?" American Sociological Review 63: 619–637.

Domanick, J. 1991. *Faking It in America: Barry Minkow and the Great ZZZZ Best Scam*. New York: Knightsbridge Publishing Company.

Everton, S. F. 2012. *Disrupting Dark Networks*. New York: Cambridge University Press.

Faulkner, R. R. and Cheney, E. R. 2014. "Breakdown of brokerage: Crisis and collapse in the Watergate conspiracy," in Carlo Morselli (ed.), *Crime and Networks*: 263–284. New York: Routledge.

Faulkner, R. R., Cheney, E. R., Fisher, G. A., and Baker, W. E. 2003. "Crime by committee: Conspirators and company men in the illegal electrical industry cartel, 1954–1959," *Criminology* 41: 511–554.

Finney, H. C. and Lesieur, H. R. 1982. "A contingency theory of organizational crime," in S. B. Bacharach (ed.), *Research in the Sociology of Organizations*: 255–299. Greenwich, CT: JAI Press.

Fisman, R. and Miguel, E. 2007. "Corruption, norms, and legal enforcement: Evidence from diplomatic parking tickets," *Journal of Political Economy* 115: 1020–1048.

Gino, F., Ayal, S., and Ariely, D. 2009. "Contagion and differentiation in unethical behavior: The effect of one bad apple on the barrel," *Psychological Science* 20: 393–398.

Gino, F., Gu, J., and Zhong, C.-B. 2009. "Contagion or restitution? When bad apples can motivate ethical behavior," *Journal of Experimental Social Psychology* 45: 1299–1302.

Granovetter, M. 1985. "Economic action and social structure: The problem of embeddedness," *American Journal of Sociology* 91: 481–510.

Granovetter, M. S. 1973. "The strength of weak ties," *American Journal of Sociology* 78: 1360–1380.

Henriques, D. B. 2011. *The Wizard of Lies: Bernie Madoff and the Death of Trust*. New York: Henry Holt.

Iowa Securities Bureau. 2001. "Affinity Fraud." Iowa Insurance Division. Available from www.iid.state.ia.us/division/securities/InvestorEd/.

Jancsics, D. 2015. "'A friend gave me a phone number' – Brokerage in low-level corruption,"*International Journal of Law, Crime and Justice* 43: 68–87.

Janis, I. L. 1983. *Groupthink: Psychological Studies of Policy Decisions and Fiascoes*. Boston: Houghton Mifflin.

Kappen, J., Papachristos, A., Faulkner, R., and Cheney, E. 2010. "In the Den: The evolution of illegal networks," Working paper, Isenberg School of Management, University of Massachusetts, Amherst.

Keltner, D., Gruenfeld, D. H., and Anderson, C. 2003. "Power, approach, and inhibition," *Psychological Review* 110: 265–284.

Kirby, J. A. and Hanna, J. 1994. "Broker beckons clients, restauranteurs prime targets," *Chicago Tribune*, June 19.

Lehman, D. W. and Ramanujam, R. 2009. "Selectivity in organizational rule violations," *Academy of Management Review* 34: 643–657.

Lowry, T. 1998. "Broker's pyramid falls on friends, neighbors," *USA Today*, October 21.

MacLean, T. 2001. "Thick as thieves: A socially embedded model of rule breaking in organizations," *Business and Society* 40: 167–196.

Manz, C. C. and Sims, H. P. 1981. "Vicarious learning: The influence of modeling on organizational behavior," *Academy of Management Review* 6: 105–113.

Mars, G. 1973. "Hotel pilferage: A case study in occupational theft," in Malcolm Warner (ed.), *The Sociology of the Workplace: An Interdisciplinary Approach:* 200–210. London: George Allen and Unwin.

Mars, G. 1974. "Dock pilferage: A case study in occupational theft," in P. Rock and M. McIntosh (eds.), *Deviance and Social Control:* 209–228. London: Tavistock Institute.

Mohliver, A. C. 2012. "The legitimacy of corrupt practices: Geography of auditors advice and backdating of stock option grants," Paper presented at the Academy of Management Annual Meeting, Boston.

Morselli, C. 2010. "Assessing vulnerable and strategic positions in a criminal network," *Journal of Contemporary Criminal Justice* 26: 382–392.

Morselli, C., Giguère, C., and Petit, K. 2007. "The efficiency/security trade-off in criminal networks," *Social Networks* 29: 143–153.

Morselli, C. and Roy, J. 2008. "Brokerage qualifications in ringing operations," *Criminology* 46: 71–98.

Nadler, D. A. and Lawler, E. E. 1977. "Motivation: A diagnostic approach," in J. R. Hackman, Edward E. Lawler, and Lyman W. Porter (eds.), *Perspectives on Behavior in Organizations*: 26–38. New York: McGraw-Hill.

Nash, R., Bouchard, M., and Malm, A. 2013. "Investing in people: The role of social networks in the diffusion of a large scale fraud," *Social Networks* 35: 686–698.

Natarajan, M. 2006. "Understanding the structure of a large heroin distribution network: A quantitative analysis of qualitative data," *Journal of Quantitative Criminology* 22: 171–192.

Neu, D., Everett, J., Rahaman, A. S., and Martinez, D. 2013. "Accounting and networks of corruption," *Accounting, Organizations and Society* 38: 505–524.

O'Fallon, M. J. and Butterfield, K. D. 2012. "The influence of unethical peer behavior on observers' unethical behavior: A social cognitive perspective," *Journal of Business Ethics* 109: 117–131.

Orru, M., Biggart, N. W., and Hamilton, G. G. (eds.). 1996. *Economic Organization of East Asian Capitalism*. Thousand Oaks, CA: Sage.

Palmer, D. and Yenkey, C. 2015. "Drugs, sweat and gears: An organizational analysis of performance enhancing drug use in the 2010 Tour de France," *Social Forces* 94(2): 891–922.

Papachristos, A., Braga, A., and Hureau, D. 2012. "Social networks and the risk of gunshot injury," *Journal of Urban Health* 89: 992–1003.

Papachristos, A. V. 2009. "Murder by structure: Dominance relations and the social structure of gang homicide," *American Journal of Sociology* 115: 74–128.

Papachristos, A. V. 2011. "The coming of a networked criminology," in J. MacDonald (ed.), *Measuring Crime and Criminality*: 101–140. New Brunswick, NJ: Transaction Publishers.

Papachristos, A. V., Hureau, D. M., and Braga, A. A. 2013. "The corner and the crew: The influence of geography and social networks on gang violence," *American Sociological Review* 78: 417–447.

Papachristos, A. V., Meares, T. L., and Fagan, J. 2012. "Why do criminals obey the law? The influence of legitimacy and social networks on active gun offenders," *Journal of Criminal Law & Criminology* 102: 397.

Perrow, C. 2007. *The Next Catastrophe: Reducing Our Vulnerabilities to Natural, Industrial, and Terrorist Disasters*. Princeton: Princeton University Press.

Pinto, J., Leana, C. R., and Pil, F. K. 2008. "Corrupt organizations of organizations of corrupt individuals? Two types of organization-level corruption," *Academy of Management Review* 33: 685–709.

Pozner, J. E. 2008. "Stigma and settling up: An integrated approach to the consequences of organizational misconduct for organizational elites," *Journal of Business Ethics* 80: 141–150.

Raab, J. R. and Milward, H. B. 2003. "Dark networks as problems," *Journal of Public Administration Research and Theory* 13: 413–439.

Raven, B. H. 1974. "The Nixon group," *Journal of Social Issues* 30: 297–320.

Robinson, S. L., Wang, W., and Kiewitz, C. 2014. "Coworkers behaving badly: The impact of coworker deviant behavior upon individual employees," *Organizational Psychology and Organizational Behavior* 1: 123–143.

Simmel, G. 1950. *The Sociology of Georg Simmel*. New York: Free Press.

Stuart, C. and Moore, C. 2015. "Shady characters: The implications of illicit organizational roles for resilient team performance," Working paper, The Johns Hopkins Carey Business School.

Sullivan, B. N., Haunschild, P., and Page, K. 2007. "Organizations non gratae? The impact of unethical corporate acts on interorganizational networks," *Organization Science* 18: 55–70.

Sutherland, E. H. 1949/1983. *White Collar Crime: The Uncut Version*. New Haven: Yale University Press.

Sykes, G. M. and Matza, D. 1957. "Techniques of neutralization: A theory of delinquency," *American Sociological Review* 22: 664–670.

Varese, F. 2013. "The structure and the content of criminal connections: The Russian mafia in Italy," *European Sociological Review* 29: 899–909.

Waytz, A. and Epley, N. 2012. "Social connection enables dehumanization," *Journal of Experimental Social Psychology* 48: 70–76.

Westphal, J. D. and Zajac, E. J. 2001. "Decoupling policy from practice: The case of stock repurchase programs," *Administrative Science Quarterly* 46: 202–228.

Wurthmann, K. A. 2014. "Service on a stigmatized board, social capital, and change in number of directorships," *Journal of Management Studies* 51: 814–841.

Zey-Ferrell, M. and Ferrell, O. C. 1982. "Role-set configuration and opportunity as predictors of unethical behavior in organizations," *Human Relations* 35: 587–604.

Zey-Ferrell, M., Weaver, K. M., and Ferrell, O. C. 1979. "Predicting unethical behavior among marketing practitioners," *Human Relations* 32: 557–569.

9 | Falling stars: celebrity, infamy, and the fall from (and return to) grace

TIMOTHY G. POLLOCK, YURI MISHINA, AND YEONJI SEO

Celebrity firms are firms that attract a high level of public attention and generate positive affective[1] responses from stakeholder audiences (Rindova, Pollock, and Hayward 2006). Recent research has explored how and why firms become celebrities (Rindova et al. 2006; Zavyalova and Pfarrer 2015) and how celebrity creates value for firms (Pfarrer, Pollock, and Rindova 2010). Celebrity firms are more likely to have unexpectedly high performance – and gain additional benefits when they do so – while suffering fewer penalties when their performance is lower than expected (Pfarrer et al. 2010).

Rindova and colleagues have also argued that firms can engender "infamy," which results from generating a high level of public attention and negative affective responses from stakeholder audiences. Central to both celebrity and infamy is that firms must engage in "deviant" or non-conforming behaviors. When viewed positively, these behaviors create a "rebel" celebrity persona attractive to at least some stakeholders; however, if the non-conforming behaviors are viewed negatively they can lead to an "outlaw" persona that at a minimum results in a loss of celebrity and possibly increases infamy.

Although researchers have begun to explore the causes and consequences of firm celebrity, little research (for a recent exception, see

---

[1] The original definition uses the word "emotion" rather than "affect." However, throughout this paper we use the term affect because affect is defined as "'goodness' or 'badness' (1) experienced as a feeling state (with or without consciousness) and (2) demarcating a positive or negative quality of a specific stimulus" (Finucane, Peters, and Slovic 2003: 328). We prefer this term because as Finucane and colleagues note, like emotion and mood, affect can vary in valence and intensity, but unlike these other constructs, it can be subtle and does not require elaborate appraisal properties, and it directly (rather than indirectly) affects motivation.

Zavyalova and Pfarrer [2015]) has considered how firms become infamous. Building on Rindova and colleagues (2006), Zavyalova and Pfarrer (2015) argued that celebrity occurs through audience members' identification with a firm's values and beliefs as presented in media-created narratives, and that infamy results from dis-identification with the organization's values and beliefs. Because firms face a plethora of stakeholder audiences with differing priorities and values, they further argued that the same firm can possess both celebrity and infamy simultaneously, as the same set of organizational values and beliefs can be the cause for identification with the firm by one stakeholder audience and dis-identification by another. Consequently, firms can lose celebrity in their quest to maintain it by eventually engaging in behaviors or revealing information that is inconsistent with audience members' bases for identification.

Fundamental to the process of becoming infamous is the belief by a stakeholder group or groups that the firm is engaging in deviant behaviors that they consider wrongdoing. That is, in their judgment the firm is violating some norms or understandings of appropriate behaviors that are strongly held by the stakeholder group, and that provoke these "social control agents" (Black 1993; Greve, Palmer, and Posner 2010; Palmer 2012) to take actions that reduce or completely eliminate the social approval enjoyed by the celebrity firm, replacing the "social approval" asset (Pfarrer et al. 2010) celebrity with a "social disapproval" liability – infamy.

We build on the celebrity (Pfarrer et al. 2010; Rindova et al. 2006; Zavyalova and Pfarrer 2015) and wrongdoing (Greve et al. 2010; Palmer 2012; Treviño, den Nieuwenboer, and Kish-Gephart 2014; Vaughan 1999) literatures to develop a more complex understanding of the dynamics of celebrity, infamy, and wrongdoing. Specifically, we examine how celebrity and infamy influence a firm's activities and how those activities might be assessed by multiple audiences. We do not consider the more common case of how a firm loses its celebrity; instead, we focus on how celebrities become infamous. In doing so we develop an expanded typology of celebrity and infamy, considering "clear" and "mixed" forms of each construct, explore how and why firms may move from celebrity to infamy, and identify actions they can take to recover from their "fall from grace." In doing so, we contribute to both the wrongdoing and celebrity literatures.

We extend the wrongdoing literature by emphasizing that wrongdoing is constructed by social control agents, that there are a wider variety of social control agents than the wrongdoing literature has typically considered, and that a wider variety of behaviors can be considered wrongdoing than has been considered previously. We thus recognize that a firm's wrongdoing can be contested, and that different stakeholders can have different perceptions of the same behaviors. Another important consideration that has received limited attention in the wrongdoing literature is whether and how firms recover from their wrongdoing. We consider how these "fallen stars" can find their way back to their former celebrity, highlighting that what is considered wrongdoing is also dynamic, and that wrongdoing can be determined and sanctioned even in the absence of a centralized authority.

We contribute to the literature on celebrity and infamy by dimensionalizing the multiple audiences that celebrities address, considering how the audience configuration influences the type of celebrity and/or infamy a firm possesses, and exploring not only how and why a firm may become infamous by changing its behaviors, but also how it may end up becoming infamous by not changing its behaviors at all. We also develop a more comprehensive understanding of the complex dynamics of celebrity creation and loss.

What is wrongdoing?

Before discussing different types of celebrity and infamy and how they come about, it is first important to define wrongdoing. Wrongdoing has been defined in a variety of ways, often by applying narrow criteria to characterize a negative behavior. For example, corporate illegality or corporate crimes include actions committed by one or more individuals that violate legal norms in order to benefit a firm (McKendall and Wagner 1997; Mishina et al. 2010). However, constructs such as wrongdoing, misconduct, unethical behavior, corruption, and deviance also encompass behaviors that breach broader criteria; they include not just violating laws but also violating ethical and social principles (Ashforth and Anand 2003; Greve et al. 2010; Heckert and Heckert 2002; Palmer 2012; Treviño et al. 2014; Vaughan 1999).

Palmer (2012) identified these three normative categories – the law, ethical principles, and social responsibility doctrines – as the general criteria used to judge a behavior as right or wrong. The law is the most formal category, where law enforcement professionals such as federal and state government agencies and judicial systems evaluate whether organizations run afoul of written guidelines or prohibitions. The sanctions for violating the law are often severe, and can include seizure of property, paying fines and compensation, and incarceration.

Ethical principles include both written and unwritten guidelines and prohibitions that are monitored and policed by self-organized governing bodies (e.g., National Collegiate Athletic Association, American Medical Association [AMA], Food and Drug Administration, state bar associations, and organized religions) and more informally by community members who have a tacit understanding of what the community's norms are and when they are being violated. While they can be less severe than legal sanctions, failing to conform to professional societies' codes of ethics could result in official sanctions such as loss of licensure or membership.

Social responsibility doctrines involve the most informal unwritten guidelines and prohibitions, and include actions that are believed to damage society in a material way. For instance, organizations that mainly use non-renewable energy sources, or that produce tobacco or alcohol could be viewed as socially irresponsible since they undermine future generations by depleting resources or threatening human health. Although these standards are the most informal they can still result in significant sanctions, from public criticism or humiliation to expulsion from a social group or community.

While these three general categories can be used to evaluate wrongdoing in the abstract, it is often difficult to apply them to specific behaviors. This limitation can be overcome by taking a sociological approach to defining wrongdoing that involves understanding the law, ethics, and social responsibility as they are used in society (Palmer 2012; Vaughan 1999). Heckert and Heckert (2002: 452–453) called this approach "reactivist" or "subjectivist" because "the reactions and values of a social group seem crucial" in identifying a behavior as deviant or as an act of wrongdoing. This approach is distinguished from an "exegetical" approach that analyzes works in philosophy and theology to derive an "objective," universal definition of wrongdoing that all researchers can embrace (Tenbrunsel and Smith-Crowe 2008). The exegetical approach can benefit scholars by providing a definition that is temporally and spatially invariant; however, as a practical matter it is difficult to achieve a single, widely accepted definition applicable in all cases.

We adopt the sociological or reactivist perspective and define wrongdoing as any behavior that social control agents judge transgresses the legal, ethical, and/or socially responsible line that separates right from wrong (Greve et al. 2010; Palmer 2012). By defining wrongdoing as the behavior that social control agents demarcate as acceptable and unacceptable, we take a social constructionist or a relativistic approach and assume that social dynamics determine what is right and wrong in a particular time and place (Greve et al. 2010; Heckert and Heckert 2002; Palmer 2012).

Our approach is also congruent with Black's (1993) approach to social control. He defined social control as including "any process by which people define and respond to deviant behavior" (Black 1993: 4). Black embraced expanding the definition of wrongdoing beyond violating the law to include anything that people express grievances about that activates social control. Any form of punishment, from incarceration to forced compensation, humiliation, gossip, or even a scowl, can be a means of social control by a particular social group if it influences perceptions of what is thought of as right or wrong. Thus, Black also argued that definitions of wrongdoing are relativistic and socially constructed by the actors and the context. Along with viewing wrongdoing as a dynamic phenomenon, this approach implicitly recognizes that social control agents, by sanctioning particular behaviors, are also responsible for creating wrongdoing (Palmer 2012).

The sociology of deviance literature (e.g., Erickson 1962; Kitsuse 1962) takes a similar approach. Kitsuse stated, for example, that "[f]orms of behavior per se do not differentiate deviants from non-deviants; it is the responses of the conventional and conforming members of the society who identify and interpret behavior as deviant which sociologically transform persons into deviants" (1962: 253), and that "the critical feature of the deviant-defining process is not the behavior of individuals who are defined as deviants, but rather the interpretations others make of their behaviors, whatever those behaviors may be" (1962: 255). Thus, in defining wrongdoing and understanding how it can lead celebrities to become infamous, it is important to understand in whose eyes a behavior may be considered wrongdoing.

Multiple stakeholder audiences and the assessment of wrongdoing

As noted above, social control agents play a crucial role in determining wrongdoing. Palmer and colleagues (Greve et al. 2010; Palmer 2012) identified a social control agent as an actor who represents a collectivity that can impose sanctions on the collectivity's behalf. Social control agents include various entities that differ in the formality of their constitution, the breadth of their jurisdiction, and the severity of the punishments that they can administer. For instance, governmental bodies are social control agents that can apply severe sanctions to organizations through judicial and regulatory proceedings. Although they possess less formality and may not be able to levy as severe punishments, associations that set professional standards, like the AMA or state bar associations, also qualify as social control agents. The norms they enforce can take the form of explicitly stated regulations and rules of conduct, or they can be more informally recognized. Either way, their norm violations are socially reinforced through negative reactions, sanctioning, and/or excommunication from the group.

However, even collectives with no formal authority (i.e., the media, collectives of which the organization is not a member, or collectives that are not identifiable as a formal group but have a collective identity, such as liberals, conservatives, environmentalists, or the "twitterati") can act as social control agents. In this sense, "[w]henever and wherever people express grievances against their fellows" (Black 1993: 4) through various mechanisms and attempt to bring changes to what they think is wrong (Black 1993) they are acting as social control agents and can be a powerful entity in deciding wrongdoing. For example, social protest groups often act collectively to sanction organizations they believe are engaging in wrongdoing. Occupy Wall Street and other offshoot "occupy" groups (e.g., the "occupy" protests in Hong Kong over free and fair elections) offer recent examples. A study of the British MP expense scandal (Graffin et al. 2013) offers another example, showing how the media were more likely to target high-status actors than low-status actors for sanctioning following similar acts of wrongdoing.

Zavyalova and Pfarrer (2015) noted that organizations have multiple stakeholder audiences, and a firm can be a celebrity with one audience and be infamous with another audience. Further, although the media controls the flow of information about a firm (Carroll and McCombs 2003; Graffin et al. 2013; Pollock and Rindova 2003), Zavyalova and Pfarrer noted that the same information – and even the same information provided by the same media outlet – can be interpreted by and reacted to positively or negatively by different stakeholder audiences who have different values and beliefs. Thus, in order to understand the effect of wrongdoing on celebrity and infamy, like Black (1993) we expand the definition of social control agents to include the collective reactions of stakeholder groups or audiences. That is, even if the actions an organization takes do not violate any formal laws, regulations, or association by-laws, organizations can still be convicted in the "court of public opinion" (Rindova et al. 2006; Zavyalova and Pfarrer 2015). We further argue that these reactions can be from society at large (Bundy and Pfarrer 2015; Graffin et al. 2013), or from a vocal sub-group with a shared identity (Zavyalova and Pfarrer 2015). We call these latter groups "constituencies" and differentiate them from "society," which encompasses more widely-held beliefs and norms agreed on by the larger social collective (i.e., that generally have widely held "concurrence" among most individuals and groups within a social collective [Bundy and Pfarrer 2015]).[2] However, we argue that society can also engage in the same kinds of collective actions as a constituency, and both can have more formal means of sanctioning they can employ, depending on who the constituency is.

A particularly important social control agent for celebrity firms is the constituency (or set of constituencies) that has conferred celebrity on the organization via their high level of attention and positive affective responses (Rindova et al. 2006). Because the firm's celebrity is dependent on continuing to attract their attention and positive affect, the top management team of the celebrity firm may be particularly sensitive to how they are viewed by this constituency. At the same time, this constituency may have values and beliefs that are at odds with broader societal values. Even if their values are not at odds with larger societal values, the constituency may place greater or lesser weight on certain actions or values than the broader public.

---

[2] This does not mean that society is merely the sum of its constituencies. Rather, as Bundy and Pfarrer (2015: 349) noted, "While an organization with higher or lower levels of social approval can have defectors, the concurring perception among most evaluators will be consistent." Thus a constituency within the society can disagree in their assessment with society at large.

In this regard celebrity organizations walk a slippery slope, as their actions could be viewed as acceptable or unacceptable depending on the group. Warren (2003) also acknowledged that wrongdoing can be defined by considering reference group norms, and that "hyper-norms" which are widely held can be seen as global standards. We argue that in order to understand why celebrity firms might engage in wrongdoing and become infamous, and to identify the type of celebrity and/or infamy we are talking about, the reactions of multiple social control agents have to be considered together. In developing our theory we argue that society and constituents represent two different sets of social control agents and that the amount of alignment between their values and beliefs determines the kind of celebrity and/or infamy a firm experiences.

Types of celebrity and infamy

Figure 9.1 is the figure Rindova et al. (2006) used to describe different kinds of deviance – behaviors that under- and over-conform to existing norms. They discussed these behaviors with respect to a single

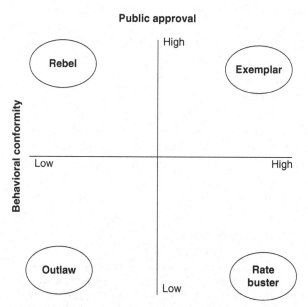

Figure 9.1 The Rindova et al. (2006) typology of deviant behaviors

audience's norms and focused on whether the behavior was viewed positively or negatively. Rebels are celebrities who engage in under-conforming behaviors that are viewed positively. These behaviors may include engaging in fewer or none of the behaviors that are viewed negatively by stakeholders, but that are nonetheless considered "normal" (e.g., Southwest not charging a checked-bag fee, which has become an industry norm), and/or engaging in behaviors that are not considered the norm (e.g., Uber's policy of drivers and passengers rating each other). Exemplars, on the other hand, are celebrities that over-conform to existing norms and engage in expected behaviors at a higher than typical level (e.g., Apple's focus on simplicity and quality in design). They further argued that these behaviors could be taken to extremes such that they become negatively viewed, leading to two types of infamy: rebels could become "outlaws" and "exemplars" could become "rate busters." They also noted that the norms line could shift, such that behaviors that were once considered over- or under-conforming become the "new normal," in which case celebrity would be lost, but the firm would not become infamous.

Implicit in Rindova and colleagues' (2006) discussion is that there can be more than one audience, although they did not elaborate on this point. Zavyalova and Pfarrer (2015) acknowledged the existence of multiple audiences with different values and beliefs in developing their argument that the *same* behaviors can lead to both celebrity and infamy if they lead some stakeholder audiences to identify and others to dis-identify with the organization. However, they were not specific about who these stakeholder audiences were. Firms may be celebrities in the eyes of society at large, but there may also be a sub-segment or sub-segments of the broader society that hold different values or expectations, which is why under-conforming to societal values results in "rebel" celebrities – while they are *under*-conforming to societal norms, they are *over*-conforming to the norms and values of the constituency. Viewed from this perspective, then, celebrity only arises from over-conforming to norms, and infamy only arises from under-conforming to norms in ways defined as wrongdoing. The key is recognizing whose norms they are over- or under-conforming to.

We argue that in order to understand how and why celebrities engage in wrongdoing and how it leads to different types of infamy, two sets of norms have to be considered: (1) the norms of the constituents among whom the organization is a celebrity, and (2) broader

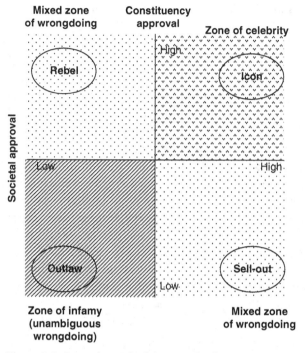

Figure 9.2 A typology of celebrity and infamy

societal norms.[3] Figure 9.2 illustrates this alternative model. The vertical axis represents the norms of the constituents among whom the organization is a celebrity. The firm's personification of the constituents' values and beliefs, and thus their identification with and/or level of positive or negative affective resonance with the firm, can range from low (i.e., completely incongruent) to high (i.e., completely congruent). Low congruence would lead the constituency to view the organization's behavior as wrongdoing. The midpoint can be thought of as a situation where the firm's behaviors are congruent with the norms of the constituents and society, but not at a level that will generate either positive or negative affect. The horizontal axis represents the norms of society more generally and can similarly range

---

[3] We focus on these two sets of norms in order to provide a simple and parsimonious way to discuss this issue. However, the same model can be used to compare the norms from any two sets of constituencies that a celebrity firm may face by substituting the other constituency's norms in place of societal norms.

from low to high. The farther a firm's behaviors lie away from the intersection of constituent and societal norms and toward an end-point for each group, the stronger that group's affective response to that firm will be. If they move toward the high end, the response will be positive and increase celebrity with that audience; if they move toward the low end, the response will be negative and increase their infamy.

Thus, we are explicitly considering two different sets of norms and beliefs. Further, as Figure 9.2 shows, it is possible that the norms of the constituency and society may be congruent, or they may be in conflict. Thus our celebrity/infamy typology overlaps with those presented by Rindova and colleagues (2006) and Zavyalova and Pfarrer (2015), but also differs from each.

We argue that celebrity and infamy can be "clear" or "mixed." "Icons" are clear celebrities in that they are more universally approved of; they appeal to the values and beliefs of society and the constituents granting them celebrity. This may be because they over-conform to societal values and beliefs that are more highly valued by the constituency than other groups, or because there is no specific sub-group and they are more universally approved of within the broader society.[4] For example, Apple has long been a celebrity with specific constituencies that appreciated their products' elegance and ease-of-use. However, since the introduction of the iPod Apple has become widely hailed for its attractive, innovative, high-quality, and easy to use products that function on both Apple and Microsoft platforms, and a wide range of individuals line up to purchase each new version of its phones, tablets, and music players.

Conversely, "outlaws" are a clear form of infamy. They display low conformity to both constituent and societal norms and generate negative affective responses from both groups who treat their behaviors as wrongdoing. The low-cost airline Ryanair is an example of an outlaw. Ryanair is a no-frills airline that charges additional fees for just about everything, such that there have been persistent rumors they may begin to charge fees for using the lavatory. Indeed, they have taken cost-cutting to such an extreme that they have been named the world's least

---

[4] Of course, different societies can hold different values, so an organization could be universally loved in one society and reviled in another. However, to avoid infinite regression, we bound our theory within the confines of a single society and its constituent sub-groups.

favorite airline on sites such as TripAdvisor for many years in a row (Daily Mail Online 2008). Ryanair generates negative affective responses not only from frequent air travelers but also from the general public.

However, as there are multiple stakeholders that hold different sets of norms and beliefs, firms may be viewed as a celebrity by one group and as infamous by another. We call these firms "mixed" because they possess both celebrity and infamy. "Rebels" have low conformity to societal norms but high conformity to constituent norms. This is the mixed form Zavyalova and Pfarrer (2015) specifically focused on. For example, AirBnB is a celebrity among those who consider themselves members of the "sharing" economy but is infamous among government regulators and the hospitality industry, who believe those renting rooms in their homes through the service are violating health, safety, and tax regulations on hoteliers (Disser 2015).

Another mixed form is when the firm has low conformity to constituent norms but high conformity to societal norms. Actors in this category usually conformed highly to a constituent group's norms at one time, but now engage in behaviors and/or reveal identity-relevant information that society views favourably but that the constituency considers wrongdoing. We label these celebrity firms "sell-outs," because they traded what is often a more intense level of celebrity with the smaller constituency for a broader but perhaps more weakly held celebrity among a larger audience. Sell-outs may migrate from either the rebel or icon zones, but they probably are most often rebels who go "mainstream" and take actions that violate the constituencies' norms of conduct.

An example of a firm that moved from rebel to sell-out is Starbucks. In its early days Starbucks tapped into the ethos of small, independent coffee houses serving high-quality coffee and coffee-based drinks such as lattes and cappuccinos – a passionate sub-culture within the US at the time. Starbucks became a celebrity among this constituency for "elevating the coffee experience" in the US by using higher-quality coffee, darker roasts, and baristas who hand-pulled espresso shots and crafted various coffee drinks (Schultz and Yang 1997). However, as it became bigger and more popular with the mass market, its early constituents began to see Starbucks as another large, generic chain like McDonalds and developed negative perceptions of the firm's activities, criticizing Starbucks's coffee-buying practices, de-skilling of baristas, increasingly generic and undistinguished décor, and "a store on every corner" business model, even as Starbucks has become more popular with the general public and substantially changed Americans' perceptions of what "good" coffee is.

Google is an example of a firm that moved from icon to sell-out. Google has long been the dominant search tool on the Internet and generates positive affect among the population at large. However, it also had special popularity among a constituency that was concerned with technology company over-reach due to its stated dictum "Don't be evil." As Google grew, this group became concerned that Google was no longer living up to this credo, and felt betrayed when Google acquiesced to requests from the Chinese government to censor certain websites in Chinese citizens' search results (Halliday 2013). Thus, Google went from being an icon to a sell-out, as its celebrity with the constituency turned to infamy, even though its celebrity with society was generally unaffected.

Based on these arguments we therefore propose:

Proposition 1a: *Firms with high (low) conformity to both constituent and societal norms exhibit pure forms of celebrity (infamy) and become icons (outlaws).*

Proposition 1b: *Firms with high conformity to constituent or societal norms but low conformity to the other audience's norms exhibit mixed forms of celebrity and infamy and become either rebels or sell-outs.*

Prior theorizing and empirical research also suggests that celebrity tends to be more fleeting than other social approval assets (Pfarrer et al. 2010; Rindova et al. 2006; Zavyalova and Pfarrer 2015). Zavyalova and Pfarrer (2015) argued that this is because of the asymmetric influence that positive and negative information have on perceptions (Haack, Pfarrer, and Scherer 2014; Rozin and Royzman 2001); whereas new positive information has diminishing marginal benefits, the effects of new negative information tends to accumulate without diminishing. Along with Rindova and colleagues (2006), they also argued that changes in stakeholder audiences' affective responses can result from celebrities taking different actions and/or engaging in more extreme versions of actions that led to their celebrity. Moving from one category to another can happen either because the firm's behaviors change and they violate existing norms or because either society's or constituents' norms change, but the celebrity's behavior does not change along with the changing norms and values. The question becomes, why do they do it?

Falling from grace: moving from celebrity to infamy

Behavioral changes

One way that celebrities become infamous is by changing the behaviors that led to their celebrity, leading the constituency and/or society to deem their behaviors wrongdoing. These changes can either be (1) engaging in more extreme versions of the behaviors that led to their celebrity (Adler and Adler 1989; Rindova et al. 2006); or (2) engaging in different behaviors. In either case, these behaviors violate the norms and expectations of their constituency and/or society and create negative affect among their audience (Heckert and Heckert 2002; Pfarrer et al. 2010; Rindova et al. 2006; Zavyalova and Pfarrer 2015).

Engaging in more extreme actions is most likely to occur when organizational members internalize the values underlying the firm's celebrity and try to live up to what they feel is expected of them (e.g., Adler and Adler 1989; Heckert and Heckert 2002; Rindova et al. 2006). In order to maintain or enhance their celebrity, firms may extrapolate from the behaviors that earned them celebrity in the first place, taking a "more is better" approach that leads to non-conforming actions which are increasingly incongruent with societal norms, and are potentially inconsistent with constituents' norms (Heckert and Heckert 2002). Celebrity firms feel increased pressure to engage in more extreme behaviors of the same type because they believe it is necessary to continue stimulating the same affective response from their audience. Continually generating strong positive affective responses is difficult to do over time because the firm's past actions begin to seem less radical and more commonplace; thus, the positive incremental benefits of its actions begin to diminish (Rozin and Royzman 2001; Zavyalova and Pfarrer 2015). At the extreme, this could result in crossing the boundary between legal and illegal behavior in an effort to continue stimulating positive affective responses (Mishina et al. 2010).

Engaging in different behaviors considered wrongdoing also often results from the celebrity firm and its leaders becoming hubristic and taking the positive affect generated by the firm's celebrity as a signal that they have carte blanche to behave in ways that they feel is consistent with the celebrity persona of the firm (e.g., Hayward and Hambrick 1997; Li and Tang 2010). In doing so, they engage in behaviors that cross ethical boundaries or violate expectations of social responsibility or propriety (Treviño et al. 2014).

Adler and Adler (1989) argued that both types of behaviors can result when celebrity creates a new type of identity, which they called the "gloried self." They argued that the media creates and the public adopts and reinforces "public" personas for celebrities that are different from and less complex than their "private" personas, and that this creates a period of alienation and conflict within celebrities that is resolved by revising their self-conception to be more in line with their public persona. They argued, "Characteristically, the gloried self is a greedy self, seeking to ascend in importance and to cast aside other self-dimensions as it grows. It is an intoxicating and riveting self, which overpowers other aspects of the individual and seeks increasing reinforcement to fuel its growth" (Adler and Adler 1989: 300). They also noted that embracing the gloried self results in self-diminishment, or the restriction of personal characteristics considered other than those related to their glory; a reduction in the capacity to consider the potential future consequences of actions; and a lack of self-reflectiveness that can lead to detachment from their former selves. The need for self-aggrandizement and continued social approval, the entitlement that accompanies the gloried self, and the inability to consider other issues or future consequences thus motivate behaviors that can lead to infamy.[5]

Figure 9.3 illustrates the different directions that a celebrity can fall. If a celebrity firm engages in behaviors that are not congruent with constituent norms but that are not specifically in conflict with them, they may merely lose their celebrity with respect to that constituency. More problematic, however, is if their actions are considered wrongdoing that specifically violates constituents' norms. Icons and rebels can

---

[5] A similar process has been identified in the sociology of deviance literature: in an act of self-fulfilling prophecy, individuals labeled deviants internalize the label as part of their identity and begin engaging in behaviors consistent with the label. This is referred to as "secondary deviance" (e.g., Gibbs and Erickson 1975).

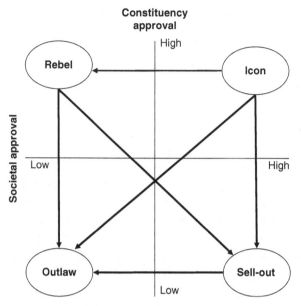

Figure 9.3 Directions celebrities fall

become sell-outs if they violate constituents' norms but their behaviors are congruent with the norms of society at large; for example, when Starbucks grew into a large restaurant chain and the uniqueness of its stores began to suffer, even as it became more popular with the masses. These kinds of behavioral changes result in a perceived loss of the authenticity or edginess that initially appealed to the constituent group while making them more palatable and accessible to a broader audience.

For example, when bands like Green Day, the Offspring, or Blink 182 moved from traditional punk to pop punk, their former core punk rock audiences turned their backs on them. Similarly, when corporations with strong social responsibility credentials adopt practices or make statements associated with more conventional companies (e.g., conducting layoffs for the first time, adopting less than green practices due to scale and cost considerations), or change their products to have more mass appeal (e.g., increasing the sweetness of food products or reducing product quality in order to lower the product's cost and price), their core constituency may see these behaviors as wrongdoing that violates their norms and principles even as the firm increases its celebrity, more generally.

A recent example of this latter shift is Timberland. As a recent article in the *Washington Post* (Halzack 2015) noted, "Here in the United States it [Timberland] had become something of a hip-hop brand as rappers name-checked 'Timbs' in countless songs ... Still more customers perceived Timberland as gear for the rugged outdoorsman, the kind of guy who hikes in the woods for days with nothing but his backpack and his Eagle Scout skills." Thus, Timberland has been a celebrity with two very different constituencies – the urban hip-hop community and serious outdoor enthusiasts. The article goes on to discuss how Timberland has reconceived its product lines and advertising to broaden the brand's appeal and focus instead on the "outdoor lifestyler," whom they describe as an urban dweller with a more casual interest in the outdoors, and who is more interested in style than the technical capabilities of the apparel. While this shift is calculated to broaden Timberland's appeal with the general market, it is likely to result in a deterioration of their appeal with their traditional constituencies, neither of whom would want to be associated with the newly targeted demographic group.

Alternatively, firms can become rebels if they take actions that make them infamous with their current constituency or society, but increase their celebrity with a new constituency. For example, although Chick-Fil-A was not previously a celebrity or infamous, by making public statements opposing gay marriage it increased its celebrity among religious conservatives, who flocked to their stores in support when protesters called for a boycott. These same actions also increased its infamy with the general public, as gay marriage is becoming increasingly accepted by mainstream America and intolerance of gay marriage is increasingly viewed negatively (O'Connor 2014).

Further, icons, rebels, and sell-outs can all become outlaws if they violate both their constituents' and society's norms. By now classic examples are firms such as Enron and Worldcom, who engaged in fraud and other illegal actions in order to maintain their otherwise unsustainable financial performance (Mishina et al. 2010). Those firms that already mix celebrity and infamy – rebels and sell-outs – are especially susceptible to becoming outlaws, as they are already infamous with either a constituency or society. Rebels display behaviors that are congruent with constituent norms and incongruent with societal norms. Thus, they are particularly liable to become outlaws if they take their behaviors to extremes in order to continue maintaining their celebrity with the constituency (Mishina et al. 2010).

For example, many forms of risky financial trading are an integral part of how financial capitalism generates high returns. Nonetheless, such "financial edgework" (Knorr-Cetina and Bruegger 2002; Wexler 2010) is generally viewed negatively by society, even as it is valorized within the financial community of traders. Risky investments made by star traders of financial institutions like Barings Bank and Société Générale show how a rebel can become an outlaw. In the case of Nick Leeson and Jerome Kerviel, risk-taking was encouraged as long as it generated profits for their firm. Although their excessive risk-taking initially yielded high returns, it became more and more reckless and they took actions to cover up for their mounting losses, eventually causing their employer to file for bankruptcy (Brown 2005; Gilligan 2011).

Sell-outs generate celebrity with society at large and infamy with one or more constituencies, and are susceptible to becoming outlaws if they take actions that violate society's norms. For example, organic brands such as Kashi, Odwalla, Stonyfield, and Naked Juice were all known for small-scale, environmentally friendly production that emphasized the use of organic ingredients and sustainable manufacturing practices in their production. Once they were acquired by large conventional food companies these firms became infamous to many in the organic industry, who saw them as greedy sell-outs that traded their social consciousness for profits. They also viewed such acquisitions as attempts by food conglomerates to water down organic standards and quality while seeking to reap larger profits from the organic label and image (Howard 2009). As *Forbes* (Hoffman 2013) noted, "It's very common that when an organic food brand is acquired, that the new parent corporation reduces its commitment to organic ingredients and seeks out cheaper substitutes." In the eyes of broader society, though, the increased visibility and popularity of organic brands facilitated by the large firms' marketing, public relations, and distribution efforts could increase their celebrity with the general populace. However, this increased attention also makes any violations of organic norms more visible, and risks alienating the buying public (Pfarrer et al. 2010).

For example, Silk Soymilk started to use conventional instead of organic soybeans after it was acquired by Dean Foods, and PepsiCo was sued for using phrases like "All Natural" in marketing Naked Juice when the product contained genetically modified organisms (GMOs).

Moreover, these firms use their profits from the sales of organic brands to support legislation that could harm society in general; for instance, by opposing Proposition 37 in California, which required firms to label GMO foods (Hoffman 2013).

However, although all types of celebrities can become more infamous, it will likely be more difficult for icons to become outlaws than rebels or sell-outs. This is because they have to engage in actions that are incongruent with both their constituency and society at large. Such actions will have to be of significant magnitude, and thus are relatively rare. Rebels and sell-outs, on the other hand, are already infamous with either society or a constituency. Thus, they may be more likely to fall from celebrity to infamy, particularly since additional information that leads to celebrity has a decreasing effect, while negative information that increases infamy is cumulative (Rozin and Roysman 2001; Zavyalova and Pfarrer 2015), making it increasingly figural and likely to stand out, and garnering more attention. It is also possible that the infamy creates an "interpretive frame" (Pfarrer et al. 2010) that affects how information that would normally enhance celebrity is interpreted.

Proposition 2a: *Celebrities are more likely to become infamous if they engage in different actions and/or more extreme versions of the actions that generated their celebrity.*

Proposition 2b: *Rebels and sell-outs, who already possess infamy with either society or a constituency are more likely to become outlaws than icons, who would have to lose celebrity and gain infamy with both society and their constituencies. Icons are thus more likely to become rebels or sell-outs than outlaws.*

Normative changes

Celebrities may also fall not because they change their behavior in any significant way, but because constituents and/or society's norms and expectations change while the celebrity's behavior does not (Heckert and Heckert 2002). This can again take two forms: (1) What was once seen as under- or over-conforming to norms changes; and (2) Congruence between constituents' and societal norms increases or decreases. Constituent and societal norms are not static and unchanging; rather, they can shift and evolve over time (e.g., Earle, Spicer, and

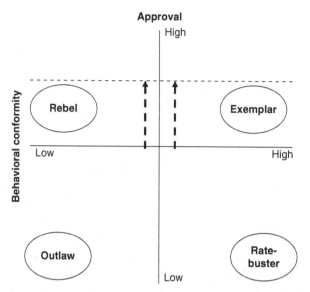

Figure 9.4 How stakeholders' perceptions of deviance change

Peter 2010). Thus, behaviors that are approved of and that generate positive affective responses at one point in time may generate negative affective responses at a different point in time (Heckert and Heckert 2002).

For example, both literature (e.g., the works of Ernest Hemingway) and Hollywood films (e.g., James Bond films) of the twentieth century often portrayed conspicuous womanizing and copious consumption of alcohol as desirable traits that symbolized masculinity. More recently, however, these traits have begun to be viewed more negatively, or at least in a less positive light than before (e.g., Bilmes 2014; Lotz 2014). Similarly, whereas the pursuit of profit without concern for other stakeholders was valorized through much of the 1980s and 1990s, it is now viewed more negatively, particularly by millennials who prefer that companies also provide social and environmental benefits (Sharp 2014).

Figure 9.4 illustrates the first circumstance with respect to a single stakeholder audience. As you will recall, Figure 9.1 illustrates that a celebrity is an actor that either over-conforms to a given group's norms or under-conforms to other norms in a way that generates positive affective responses with the focal audience. These processes

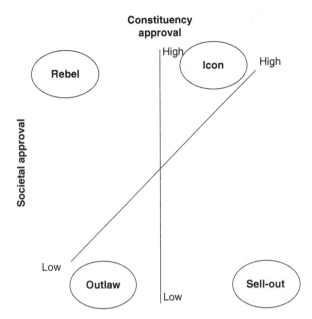

Figure 9.5 Less congruence

can be simultaneous; that is, a constituency or sub-group may approve if their norms are over-conformed to but societal norms with which they disagree are under-conformed to, and society may approve if their norms are over-conformed to and the sub-group's norms are under-conformed to. Figure 9.4 illustrates a shift in the intersection between over/under-conforming behaviors and approval. Behaviors that previously led an actor to be a rebel now make it an outlaw and/or behaviors that led a celebrity to be an exemplar now make it a rate-buster.

Figures 9.5 and 9.6 illustrate the second kind of normative shift. Here, the norms of society and the constituency become more or less similar to each other, as reflected by the rotation in the X-axis. As Figure 9.5 illustrates, if there is less congruence the range of behaviors they both agree and disagree on becomes small, thus compressing the range of behaviors that make an actor an icon or an outlaw and increasing the range of behaviors that make firms both celebrated and infamous – that is, make them either a rebel or a sell-out. In other words, there is less consensus about what is considered wrongdoing,

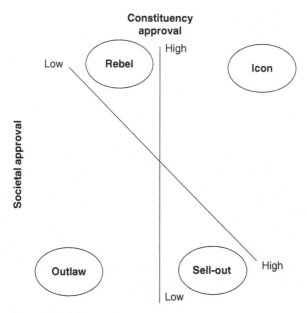

Figure 9.6 More congruence

and deviations from the constituent's or society's orthodoxy are not tolerated. Conversely, as Figure 9.6 illustrates, if there is more congruence, then the constituency's and society's norms are largely aligned; hence, celebrities are more likely to be icons and infamous firms are more likely to be outlaws since there is more consensus on what is considered wrongdoing, and thus behaviors are more likely to meet or violate both groups' norms and expectations. The range of behaviors that are approved of by both society and the constituency grows, and the range of behaviors disapproved of by one or the other shrinks – thus shrinking the zones for rebels and sell-outs.

Sociologists have provided examples of when a constituency's norms became more similar to those of society at large. Adut (2005), for example, examined the case of Oscar Wilde and found that although Victorian society viewed homosexuality as repulsive, Oscar Wilde's sexual orientation was an open secret that was initially tolerated among the elites of the day. Once scandals regarding his sexuality broke publicly, however, the elites who had tolerated or even protected him had to act in a punitive manner to protect their own reputations and the sanctity of the existing status structures.

Similarly, Fine (1997) examined how the Fatty Arbuckle case precipitated a scandal that led the norms of Hollywood and broader society to grow a little closer together. Fatty Arbuckle, one of the most popular comedians of the 1920s and 1930s, was accused of rape and murder when a young model and actress died after attending a party he hosted. Although prohibition had recently been enacted, the party was "generously lubricated with bootleg whiskey and gin," and during the party one of the attendees "became ill, started to scream, and tore off her clothing," eventually dying from "complications of a ruptured bladder from peritonitis" a few days later (Fine 1997: 300). Although many in Hollywood initially supported Arbuckle and he was acquitted of the charges, the Hollywood elite (i.e., the Motion Picture Producers and Distributors Association) took symbolic social control efforts against previously tolerated activities (e.g., parties, "loose" morals) in order to protect itself from attack by the broader public, who viewed Hollywood as a hotbed of sin synonymous with moral decay.

In both the Oscar Wilde and Fatty Arbuckle cases, a constituency's norms were in conflict with broader societal norms, but there was no move to resolve the conflict until the constituency's existing institutional structures were threatened by society at large due to negative attention and the efforts of moral entrepreneurs. In order to counter the threat, the elites in each constituency acted as social control agents, shifting the constituency's norms to more closely align with broader societal norms – or they at least made symbolic concessions to make it seem that way (Adut 2005; Fine 1997).

For corporations, crisis events have led industry norms to change in ways that make them more similar to societal norms. For example, following the toxic chemical spill from a Union Carbide facility in Bhopal, India, that killed thousands of people, chemical companies were eager to create a self-regulatory institution that would prevent such accidents in the future (Barnett and King 2008). The Responsible Care program was launched and adopted by many chemical associations, who made association membership conditional on adopting the program (American Chemistry Council 2013). The chemical industry's norms regarding prioritizing worker safety and the prevention of hazardous chemical releases over cost-cutting changed and became closer to societal norms.

Changes can also occur as a result of sustained activism, rather than a precipitating event. For example, the Sustainable Slopes Program was launched by the National Ski Areas Association (NSAA) in 2000 as a response to increasing scrutiny from environmentalists. The program led 75 percent of US ski resorts to adopt Sustainable Slope Principles promoting compliance with twenty-one aspects of environmental management (e.g., construction of slopes, water usage for snowmaking, conserving fish and wildlife, etc.) (NSAA 2014; Rivera and de Leon 2004). By becoming more environmentally conscious in their operations, the ski industry's norms changed to accommodate social norms that opposed landscape destruction, deforestation, and damaging wildlife habitats.

Alternatively, the social movement literature suggests that broader societal norms may become more similar to those of a particular constituency if the constituency is successful in its efforts to change societal norms. For example, Haines (1984) examined major black movement organizations between 1952 and 1970 and identified a positive radical "flank" effect, where the presence of radical black activist organizations convinced societal elites of the need to pacify the African-American population. This resulted in support for more moderate groups whose aims and methods seemed more reasonable in comparison, thereby moving societal norms closer to those of black movement organizations in general. More recently, the rapid changes in societal attitudes toward same-sex marriage (Briscoe and Safford 2008) and the medical use of marijuana (Dickinson 2015) illustrate how societal values and beliefs can change to align more with those of vocal subgroups that were previously seen as outside societal norms.

Proposition 3a: *Normative changes that lead to less congruence between constituents' and society's norms increase the likelihood that firms will possess mixed forms (rebel and sell-out) of celebrity and infamy.*

Proposition 3b: *Normative changes that lead to a greater congruence between constituents' and societal norms increase the likelihood that firms will possess pure forms of celebrity (icon) and infamy (outlaw).*

Redemption, or the "Behind the Music effect"

In the 1990s and early 2000s the US music television channel VH1 ran a popular show called "Behind the Music" that profiled different rock bands. These episodes followed a predictable arc that roughly mirrored

Freytag's pyramid (1863[1900]) articulating the structure of a drama: inciting moment and exposition (the band members meet), rising action (they perform early gigs and achieve success and celebrity), complication and climax (the band reaches the peak of its fame, but bad behaviors, jealously, and other stressors also reach their peak), reversal (band members fight, quit, or have drug overdoses), falling action (the band breaks up, or nearly breaks up as their celebrity fades), and denouement (sometimes the band members go their separate ways, but sometimes they overcome their challenges and mount a comeback, even if they never achieve their prior level of celebrity).

This pattern of positive and negative behaviors accompanied by the rise and fall of a band's celebrity was so ubiquitous that it has been dubbed by some the "Behind the Music effect" as shorthand for describing other types of actors who experience similar rises and falls. The Behind the Music effect can also be used to describe the arc of celebrity firms that become infamous. The question becomes, what happens in the denouement, and how can some firms that go from celebrity to infamy regain at least some of their celebrity?

We have detailed some of the reasons why a rebel may become an outlaw or a sell-out, how a sell-out can become an outlaw, and how an icon can become a rebel, sell-out, or outlaw. As Zavyalova and Pfarrer (2015) discussed, it is easier to lose celebrity and become infamous than it is to move from infamy to celebrity. We believe that shifts in norms and/or changes in behavior are necessary conditions for moving from one of the mixed forms of celebrity to another. But, because negative information tends to have stronger and more persistent effects than positive information (e.g., Baumeister et al. 2001; Rozin and Royzman 2001), particularly when audiences are making judgments about a target's values and beliefs (e.g., Birnbaum 1972, 1973; Skowronski and Carlston, 1987; Mishina, Block, and Mannor 2012), these factors alone may not be sufficient to redeem an outlaw, or change from one of the mixed forms into an icon. In this regard, the work that Fine and his colleagues (Bromberg and Fine 2002; Fine 1999) have done at the individual level on problematic, or "difficult," reputations may provide some insight.

In looking at figures such as the folk singer Pete Seeger, whose reputation shifted from vilified communist to national hero during his lifetime (Bromberg and Fine 2002), and abolitionist John Brown, who has been recast as a civil war hero even though he attacked the federal government (Fine 1999), Fine and colleagues suggested that in order to purify a once-tainted reputation a new narrative must be advanced, and this narrative must ultimately become reified as the "true" account about the subject. They also suggested that this may require changes in beliefs and value systems; redefinition of actions, events, and/or meanings; allies to advance the new narrative; and a lack of powerful critics or enemies (e.g., Fine 1999; Bromberg and Fine 2002). From the standpoint of an outlaw, this implies that in addition to the potential change in norms (such that the firm's behaviors would generate positive rather than negative affective responses from constituencies), and/or changes in behavior to those that are highly congruent with those of constituencies, three additional factors are necessary.

First, the firm's previously objectionable activities need to be recast in a more positive light (Bromberg and Fine 2002; Fine 1999). If the norms have changed so that those activities are now acceptable, or even desirable, then this step could potentially be skipped. If not, then this step will entail redefining what the firm did, why the firm took the actions, and otherwise providing accounts and justifications that lead the prior actions to now be viewed as reasonable and acceptable (e.g., Scott and Lyman 1969; Blumstein et al. 1974; Elsbach 1994; Massey, Freeman, and Zelditch 1997).

Second, the firm requires allies to advance the more positive narrative (Bromberg and Fine 2002; Fine 1999). Since the media plays a large part in the construction of firm celebrity (Carroll and McCombs 2003; Rindova et al. 2006; Zavyalova and Pfarrer 2015), it stands to reason that their assistance may be required in order to advance the new narrative and have it accepted as reality by audiences (e.g., Gamson et al. 1992). Additionally, unless at least one powerful constituency accepts this new narrative and reacts positively, the focal firm is unlikely to regain celebrity. There is no guarantee, however, that it will be the same constituency with whom the firm had celebrity before its fall.

Finally, Fine and colleagues (Bromberg and Fine 2002; Fine 1999) suggested that the presence of powerful critics or enemies could derail the new narrative and make it difficult or impossible to rehabilitate a problematic reputation. Since constituencies who disidentify with the firm (and thus to whom the firm is infamous) have a vested interest in maintaining an outlaw's infamy (Elsbach and Bhattacharya 2001; see also Zavyalova and Pfarrer 2015), the firm needs to either eliminate the infamy vis-à-vis this constituency and/or hope that the constituency lacks sufficient power to act as a social control agent and continue enforcing sanctions that reinforce their infamy. For the former to occur, either changing norms and/or redefinition of actions, events, and meanings will help weaken or erase the infamy, but it is not clear what the focal firm would necessarily be able to do to ensure the latter (i.e., weaken the power of those reinforcing the firm's infamy). Some options may include actively attempting to discredit those trying to discredit them, and encouraging the media not to legitimate their claims by covering and reporting them, or by giving them equal weight in their articles and stories when they do cover them. Thus, we propose:

Proposition 4: *To regain celebrity, a firm that has fallen from grace should (1) redefine its activities so they are now viewed positively, (2) find and seek the support of powerful allies who can advance a new narrative about the firm, and (3) co-opt or otherwise neutralize critics or other social control agents reinforcing the firm's infamy.*

Discussion and implications for research

In this chapter we have examined the dynamic interplay among celebrity, infamy, and wrongdoing by discussing the nature of different audiences and developing a typology of different forms of celebrity and infamy, exploring how and why a celebrity firm may engage in wrongdoing, how that wrongdoing may increase a firm's infamy and/or diminish its celebrity, and how an infamous firm may be able to reform itself and regain lost celebrity. In doing so, we make several contributions to the literature on celebrity and wrongdoing.

First, we provide a more comprehensive understanding of the complex dynamics of celebrity creation and loss and develop a greater theoretical understanding of infamy – a social construct based on assessments of wrongdoing that has received limited attention. By considering the constituency to whom the firm is a celebrity or infamous, as well as society in general, we further dimensionalize the multiple audiences that create celebrities and infamous firms, highlighting that celebrity arises from over-conforming to a particular constituency's and/or society's values and beliefs, while infamy arises from under-conforming to the constituency's and/or society's values and beliefs.

This perspective allowed us to derive an expanded typology of different celebrity/infamy combinations that accommodates both mixed and clear forms of celebrity and infamy. It also allows us to consider the differential susceptibility firms may have to losing their celebrity and becoming infamous. For example, because an icon has celebrity with both its core constituency and broader society, it is likely to be in a better position than a rebel who must rely on staying in the good graces of its constituency (since it has infamy with broader society) or a sell-out which may have celebrity with society in general but is infamous with respect to its (former) core constituency. We also theorize about how and why a firm may engage in wrongdoing by changing its behaviors or because the norms of the constituency and/or society change even if it does not change its behaviors. We then consider what would be required for these "fallen" stars to find their way back to their former celebrity.

Second, we contribute to the literature on wrongdoing by highlighting that what is considered wrongdoing is dynamic, and that wrongdoing can be determined and sanctioned even in the absence of a centralized authority. We discussed both the evolving nature of what behaviors are considered wrongdoing, as well as how those definitions may be audience-specific. Consequently what is considered wrongdoing by one audience may be celebrated by another audience. This can create problems for firms as they have to carefully consider their behaviors and navigate a potentially treacherous set of contrasting (and often conflicting) values and beliefs that their multiple audiences may hold. At the same time, we suggest that the focus should specifically be on who the social control agents are, since they are the ones who have the ability to impose sanctions upon the organization. In contributing to these literatures, our theorizing suggests several implications for future research.

First, it suggests that rather than focusing on celebrity in the abstract, greater insight may be gained regarding the role of firm celebrity and infamy if we consider exactly what type of celebrity or infamy a firm has (i.e., icon, rebel, sell-out, outlaw) and who the constituency(ies) are (e.g., industry association, activist group, customer group) granting the celebrity and/or infamy. By doing so, researchers will be able to identify the differential pressures that the firm may face, as well as the types of rewards that they may enjoy. Relatedly, it may be possible to trace the different types of paths that firms may take in their journey as they gain and lose celebrity and infamy.

Second, our theorizing suggests that celebrity may indeed be a mixed blessing; although it may bring some tangible benefits (Pfarrer et al. 2010), it can also induce firms to behave in problematic ways because its members feel pressure to live up to these heightened expectations (e.g., Adler and Adler 1989; Heckert and Heckert 2002; Rindova et al. 2006). Indeed, even if the firm does not alter its actions, it may still face problems as celebrity may heighten the expectations of the firm's constituencies (Zavyalova and Pfarrer 2015) and norms shift over time (Earle et al. 2010). Future research could continue to explore the double-edged nature of celebrity, the costs of infamy, and how firms can manage or influence these normative shifts.

Finally, an additional direction for future research would be to examine the relationship between infamy and other social evaluation constructs. The relationship between infamy and stigma might be particularly interesting to examine, especially since they both include a negative affective component, they both arise from being defined as deviant, and both infamous and stigmatized firms are likely to be viewed as symbols of the types of behaviors that are considered unacceptable by particular audiences (e.g., Erickson 1962).

At the same time, we do not believe the two constructs are equivalent. Devers and colleagues (2009), for example, stated that stigma and celebrity differ along a number of dimensions. Even though celebrity and infamy are likely to be distinct from one another in the same manner as positive and negative affect (Watson and Tellegen 1999) or identification and dis-identification (Elsbach and Bhattacharya 2001; Zavyalova and Pfarrer 2015), infamy and celebrity are similar enough that infamy is also likely to differ from stigma in terms of its theoretical basis, social basis, and whether or not it is individuating (e.g., Devers et al. 2009). In particular, whereas stigma paints firms as being an undifferentiated member of a devalued category (Devers et al. 2009), infamy tends to set a firm apart from others based on the degree of prominence and negative affect that constituents feel (Zavyalova and Pfarrer 2015). To the extent that future research can elaborate on the "dark side" of social approval and distinguish among different forms of negative social approval, our theoretical understanding of social approval assets and liabilities will be enhanced.

One possibility is that, over time, infamous firms may shift from being viewed as unique entities and instead begin to be viewed as merely an exemplar that embodies a set of undesirable behaviors and characteristics of a larger group. If so, this may further clarify the manner in which a new stigmatized category might arise (cf., Devers et al. 2009). Another possibility is to consider whether stigma and infamy are specific to different types of constituencies or audiences. Although both lead to negative perceptions, stigma is de-individuating (i.e., class distinctions override individual differences within the group, and all firms in the group are viewed negatively), whereas celebrity and infamy are individuating (i.e., they enhance individual distinctiveness within a group). Thus, one constituency may view the focal firm as being a member of a stigmatized category in which all firms are negatively viewed, while a different constituency may merely view the individual firm as infamous, while viewing the broader category of firms more neutrally, or even positively. Since the stigmatizing constituency may not even notice or pay attention to the idiosyncratic actions or characteristics of individual firms, the processes necessary for destigmatization may be very different than those used to eliminate infamy, where individual firm actions receive more attention. Such linkages only represent a couple of the many possible relationships that celebrity and infamy may have with stigma, and we encourage scholars to explore these various dynamics.

References

Adler, P. and Adler, P. 1989. "The gloried self: The aggrandizement and the construction of self," *Social Psychological Quarterly* 52: 299–310.

Adut, A. 2005. "A theory of scandal: 'Victorians, homosexuality, and the fall of Oscar Wilde'," *American Journal of Sociology* 111(1): 213–248.

American Chemistry Council. 2013. "Responsible care: Milestones and achievements," *American Chemistry Council*. Available from www .responsiblecare.americanchemistry.com/Home-Page-Content/Responsib le-Care-Timeline.pdf [Accessed: May 13, 2015].

Ashforth, B. E. and Anand, V. 2003. "The normalization of corruption in organizations," *Research in Organizational Behavior* 25: 1–52.

Barnett, M. L. and King, A. A. 2008. "Good fences make good neighbors: A longitudinal analysis of an industry self-regulatory institution," *Academy of Management Journal* 51(6): 1150–1170.

Baumeister, R. F., Bratslavsky, E., Finkenauer, C., and Vohs, K. D. 2001. "Bad is stronger than good," *Review of General Psychology* 5(4): 323–370.

Bilmes, A. 2014. "Jon Hamm is not the man you think he is," *Esquire* April 15. Available from www.esquire.co.uk/culture/features/6124/jon-hamm-exclusive-esquire-interview [Accessed: January 13, 2015].

Birnbaum, M. H. 1972. "Morality judgments: Tests of an averaging model," *Journal of Experimental Psychology* 93(1): 35–42.

Birnbaum, M. H. 1973. "Morality judgments: Test of an averaging model with differential weights," *Journal of Experimental Psychology* 99(3): 395–399.

Black, D. 1993. *The Social Structure of Right and Wrong*. Bingley, UK: Emerald.

Blumstein, P. W., Carssow, K. G., Hall, J., Hawkins, B., Hoffman, R., Ishem, E., Maurer, C. P., Spens, D., Taylor, J., and Zimmerman, D. L. 1974. "The honoring of accounts," *American Sociological Review* 39: 551–566.

Briscoe, F. and Safford, S. 2008. "The Nixon-in China effect: Activism, imitation and the institutionalization of contentious practices," *Administrative Science Quarterly* 53(3): 460–491.

Bromberg, M. and Fine, G. A. 2002. "Resurrecting the red: Pete Seeger and the purification of difficult reputations," *Social Forces* 80(4): 1135–1155.

Brown, A. D. 2005. "Making sense of the collapse of Barings Bank," *Human Relations* 58: 1579–1604.

Bundy, J. and Pfarrer, M. D. 2015. "A burden of responsibility: The role of social approval at the onset of a crisis," *Academy of Management Review* 40(3): 345–369.

Carroll, C. E. and McCombs, M. 2003. "Agenda setting effects of business news on the public's images and opinions about major corporations," *Corporate Reputation Review* 6: 36–46.

Daily Mail. 2008. "Ryanair 'least favourite airline,'" *Daily Mail Online*, October 16. Available from www.dailymail.co.uk/travel/article-615875/Ryanair-favourite-airline.html [Accessed: January 7, 2015].

Devers, C. E., Dewett, T., Mishina, Y., and Belsito, C. A. 2009. "A general theory of organizational stigma," *Organization Science* 20(1): 154–171.

Dickinson, T. 2015. "The war on drugs is burning out," *Rolling Stone*, January 8. Available from www.rollingstone.com/politics/news/the-war-on-drugs-is-burning-out-20150108 [Accessed: January 15, 2015].

Disser, N. 2015. "AirBnB supporters and haters rally in advance of city council meeting," *Brooklyn Magazine*, January 20. Available from www.bkmag .com/2015/01/20/airbnb-supporters-and-haters-demonstrate-ahead-of-ci ty-council-hearing [Accessed: January, 24, 2015].

Earle, J. S., Spicer, A., and Peter, K. S. 2010. "The normalization of deviant organizational practices: Wage arrears in Russia, 1991–98," *Academy of Management Journal* 53(2): 218–237.

Elsbach, K. D. 1994. "Managing organizational legitimacy in the California cattle industry: The construction and effectiveness of verbal accounts," *Administrative Science Quarterly* 39(1): 57–88.

Elsbach, K. D. and Bhattacharya, C. B. 2001. "Defining who you are by what you're not: Organizational disidentification and the National Rifle Association," *Organization Science* 12(4): 393–413.

Erickson, K. T. 1962. "Notes on the sociology of deviance," *Social Problems* 9: 307–314.

Fine, G. A. 1997. "Scandal, social conditions, and the creation of public attention: Fatty Arbuckle and the 'problem of Hollywood,'" *Social Problems* 44(3): 297–323.

Fine, G. A. 1999. "John Brown's body: Elites, heroic embodiment, and the legitimation of political violence," *Social Problems* 46(2): 225–249.

Finucane, M. L., Peters, E., and Slovic, P. 2003. "Judgment and decision making: The dance of affect and reason," in S. L. Schneider and J. Shanteau (eds.), *Emerging Perspectives on Judgment and Decision Research*: 327–364. Cambridge University Press.

Freytag, G. 1863[1900]. *Technique of the Drama: An Exposition of Dramatic Composition and Art* (E. J. MacEwan, Trans.). Chicago, IL: Scott, Foresman and Co.

Gamson, W., Croteau, D., Hoynes, W., and Sasson, T. 1992. "Media images and the social construction of reality," *Annual Review of Sociology* 18: 373–393.

Gibbs, J. P. and Erickson, M. L. 1975. "Major developments in the sociological study of deviance," *Annual Review of Sociology* 1: 21–42.

Gilligan, G. 2011. "Jérôme Kerviel the 'rogue trader' of Société Générale: Bad luck, bad apple, bad tree or bad orchard?" *Company Lawyer* 32: 355–362.

Graffin, S. D., Bundy, J., Porac, J. F., Wade, J. B., and Quinn, D. P. 2013. "Falls from grace and the hazards of high status: The 2009 British MP expense scandal and its impact on parlimentary elites," *Administrative Science Quarterly* 58(3): 313–345.

Greve, H. R., Palmer, D., and Pozner, J. E. 2010. "Organizations gone wild: The causes, processes, and consequences of organizational misconduct," *Academy of Management Annals*, 4: 53–107.

Haack, P., Pfarrer, M. D., and Scherer, A. G. 2014. "Legitimacy-as-feeling: How affect leads to vertical legitimacy spillovers in transnational governance," *Journal of Management Studies* 51(4): 634–666.

Haines, H. H. 1984. "Black radicalization and the funding of civil rights: 1957–1970," *Social Problems* 32(1): 31–43.

Halliday, J. 2013. "Google's dropped anti-censorship warning marks quiet defeat in China," *The Guardian*, January 7. Available from www .theguardian.com/technology/2013/jan/04/google-defeat-china-censor ship-battle [Accessed: January 13, 2014].

Halzack, S. 2015. "How Timberland used data to reboot its brand," *Washington Post*, January 4, Available from www.washingtonpost.com /news/business/wp/2015/01/02/how-timberland-used-customer-data-to-r eboot-its-brand [Accessed: January 13, 2015].

Hayward M. L. A. and Hambrick, D. C. 1997. "Explaining the premiums paid for large acquisitions: Evidence of CEO hubris," *Administrative Science Quarterly* 42(1): 103–127.

Heckert, A. and Heckert, D. 2002. "A new typology of deviance: Integrating normative and reactivist definitions of deviance," *Deviant Behavior: An Interdisciplinary Journal* 23: 449–479.

Hoffman, B. 2013. "Who owns organic brands and why you should care," *Forbes*, May 25. Available from www.forbes.com/sites/bethhoffman/20 13/05/25/who-owns-organic-brands-and-why-you-should-care [Accessed: January 9, 2015].

Howard, P. 2009. "Consolidation in the North American organic food processing sector, 1997 to 2007," *International Journal of Sociology of Agriculture and Food* 16(1): 13–30.

Kitsuse, J. I. 1962. "Societal reaction to deviant behavior: Problems of theory and method," *Social Problems* 9: 247–256.

Knorr-Cetina, K. and Bruegger, U. 2002. "Global microstructures: The virtual societies of financial markets," *American Journal of Sociology* 107: 905–950.

Li, J. and Tang, Y. 2010. "CEO hubris and firm risk taking in China: The moderating role of managerial discretion," *Academy of Management Journal* 53(1): 45–68.

Lotz, A. D. 2014. "Don Draper's sad manhood: What makes 'Mad Men' different from 'Breaking Bad', 'Sopranos'," *Salon*, April 12. Available from www.salon.com/2014/04/11/don_drapers_sad_manhood_what_ makes_mad_men_different_from_breaking_bad_sopranos [Accessed: January 13, 2015].

Massey, K., Freeman, S., and Zelditch, M. 1997. "Status, power, and accounts," *Social Psychology Quarterly* 60(3): 238–251.

McKendall, M. A. and Wagner, J. A. III. 1997. "Motive, opportunity, choice, and corporate illegality," *Organization Science* 8: 624–647.

Mishina, Y., Block, E. S., and Mannor, M. J. 2012. "The path dependence of organizational reputation: How social judgment influences assessments of capability and character," *Strategic Management Journal* 33(5): 459–477.

Mishina, Y., Dykes, B. J., Block, E. S., and Pollock, T. G. 2010. "Why 'good' firms do bad things: The effects of high aspirations, high expectations and prominence on the incidence of corporate illegality," *Academy of Management Journal* 53(4): 701–722.

NSAA, 2014. "NSAA sustainable slopes annual report 2014," *NSAA.* Available from www.nsaa.org/media/210657/SSAR_2014.pdf [Accessed: May 12, 2015].

O'Connor, C. 2014. "Chick-Fil-A CEO Cathy: Gay marriage still wrong, but I'll shut up about it now and sell chicken," *Forbes*, March 19. Available from www.forbes.com/sites/clareoconnor/2014/03/19/chick-fil-a-ceo-cathy-gay-marriage-still-wrong-but-ill-shut-up-about-it-and-sell-chicken [Accessed: January 12, 2015].

Palmer, D. 2012. *Normal Organizational Wrongdoing: A Critical Analysis of Theories of Misconduct in and by Organizations.* Oxford University Press.

Pfarrer, M. D., Pollock, T. G., and Rindova, V. P. 2010. "A tale of two assets: The effects of firm reputation and celebrity on earnings surprises and investors' reactions," *Academy of Management Journal* 53(5): 1131–1152.

Pollock, T. G. and Rindova, V. P. 2003. "Media legitimation effects in the market for initial public offerings," *Academy of Management Journal* 46 (5): 631–642.

Rindova, V. P., Pollock, T. G., and Hayward, M. L. A. 2006. "Celebrity firms: The social construction of market popularity," *Academy of Management Review* 31(1): 50–71.

Rivera, J. and De Leon, P. 2004. "Is greener whiter? Voluntary environmental performance of western ski areas," *Policy Studies Journal* 32(3): 417–437.

Rozin, P. and Royzman, E. B. 2001. "Negativity bias, negativity dominance, and contagion," *Personality and Social Psychology Review* 5(4): 296–320.

Schultz, H. and Yang, D. J. 1997. *Pour Your Heart Into It: How Starbucks Built a Company, One Cup at a Time.* New York: Hyperion.

Scott, M. B. and Lyman, S. M. 1969. "Accounts," *American Sociological Review* 33(1): 46–62.

Sharp, K. 2014. "Millennials' bold new business plan: Corporations with a conscience," *Salon*, January 20. Available from www.salon.com/2014/02/09/millennials_bold_new_business_plan_corporations_with_a_conscience [Accessed: January 9, 2015].

Skowronski, J. J. and Carlston, D. E. 1987. "Social judgment and social memory: The role of cue diagnosticity in negativity, positivity, and extremity biases," *Journal of Personality and Social Psychology* 52(4): 689–699.

Tenbrunsel, A. E. and Smith-Crowe, K. 2008. "Ethical decision making: Where we've been and where we're going," *Academy of Management Annals* 2(1): 545–607.

Treviño, L. K. den Nieuwenboer, N. A., and Kish-Gephart, J. J. 2014. "(Un) Ethical behavior in organizations," *Annual Review of Psychology* 65: 635–660.

Vaughan, D. 1999. "The dark side of organizations: Mistake, misconduct, and disaster," *Annual Review of Sociology* 25: 271–305.

Warren, D. E. 2003. "Constructive and destructive deviance in organizations," *Academy of Management Review* 28(4): 622–632.

Watson, D. and Tellegen, A. 1999. "Issues in the dimensional structure of affect – Effects of descriptors, measurement error, and response formats: Comment on Russell and Carroll," *Psychological Bulletin* 125(5): 601–610.

Wexler, M. N. 2010. "Financial edgework and the persistence of rogue traders," *Business and Society Review* 115: 1–25.

Zavyalova, A. and Pfarrer, M. D. 2015. "Celebrity or infamy? The consequences of revealing an organization's identity," Working Paper, Rice University.

10 | Compensation and employee misconduct: the inseparability of productive and counterproductive behavior in firms

IAN LARKIN AND LAMAR PIERCE

Incentive systems play a fundamental role in organizations. Financial compensation represents the largest single cost for the average company (Gerhart, Rynes, and Fulmer 2009), and compensation is intimately tied to firm strategy and performance (Larkin, Pierce, and Gino 2012; Nickerson and Zenger 2008). Well-designed compensation systems allow firms to direct employee effort toward productive activities that improve firm performance and survival. Just as importantly, compensation systems can play a key role in attracting and retaining the right types of employees based on heterogeneous ability, motivation levels, and social connections. Although financial and other extrinsic incentives built into compensation systems are powerful tools for improving productivity, they also carry substantial risks. Compensation systems can generate perverse economic incentives as well as psychological and social responses that motivate a wide class of counterproductive behaviors ranging from lack of cooperation to explicitly illegal misconduct.

This chapter focuses on illuminating the holistic implications of multiple classes of compensation systems for employee behavior. We focus on non-executive employees for several reasons. First, an extensive literature in finance, strategy, and management covers executive compensation. Second, the key issues in executive compensation, such as motivating the appropriate level of risk and minimizing high-level corporate fraud, are quite different from the tradeoffs managers face when motivating non-executive employees (Larkin et al. 2012). Finally, the pay of top executives typically accounts for only a few percentage points of total firm compensation costs (Whittlesey 2006).

Incentive systems are fundamentally about motivating employee behavior (Hall 2000). In this chapter, we focus on both productive behaviors and counterproductive misconduct that are motivated by compensation systems. Productive behaviors are defined as those that contribute to the performance and ultimate success of the firm (as measured by profitability for most for-profit firms, but that can include other metrics). Misconduct includes several types of behaviors that are counterproductive to the firm: actions that are explicitly illegal, actions that violate formal organizational rules, actions that may not violate rules but are against the spirit of the rules, and actions that are counter-normative. Fundamentally, employees engage in misconduct because they believe it will increase their utility or happiness; misconduct can generate higher extrinsic rewards, such as pay, promotion, or status, and can also increase psychological well-being.

Our primary arguments are threefold. First, we hold that the effect of compensation on the two classes of behavior – productivity and misconduct – tends to go in the same direction. That is, systems that increase productive behavior usually also increase misconduct even, at times, by the exact same employee. Second, we argue that managers and academics often make a fundamental mistake when implementing and studying compensation, in that both groups have a tendency to focus only on a single class of behavior. An incentive system that promotes a high level of productive effort might be heralded as a success because the costs of misconduct are ignored. Conversely, systems that lead to some level of misconduct are often criticized as sub-optimal, even without a careful examination of the productive actions motivated by the system. Taken together, these two points lead to our third argument: In almost any optimal incentive system, the level of misconduct is almost never zero. Put another way, the optimal compensation system will almost always foster some level of illegal, unethical, or other counterproductive behavior.

This is consistent with the idea that organizational misconduct is a normal and inevitable byproduct of necessary and important structural elements of the firm (Palmer 2012). In our view, these insights mean that academic research and managerial practice need to consider the holistic cost–benefit calculus of a given compensation system. This realization means that a compensation system which maximizes productivity often will carry unacceptable levels of misconduct, while a compensation system that minimizes misconduct will often lead to low productivity by employees.

Classes of compensation systems

Compensation schemes differ in the immediacy of the link between performance and compensation and whether performance is measured at an individual level or at a team or group level. Only about one-third of employees in the United States are paid via a system which links pay to immediate performance measures such as job productivity (Lemieux, MacLeod, and Parent 2007). While two-thirds of employees are paid via a *flat wage*, meaning their monthly paycheck does not depend on performance, most of these employees are compensated in the long term for performance via annual salary increases, often coupled with promotions to higher-paying and/or higher-visibility jobs. These systems are often termed as *scaled wages* (Larkin et al. 2012). Employees paid via scaled wages are more likely to have their performance measured via subjective rather than objective performance measures, and the criteria determining wage increases are often not directly related to an employee's performance per se (Hall 2000). For example, length of tenure at a firm and the level of seniority compared to peers are common factors determining an employee's compensation in a scaled wage system. We consider promotion-based reward systems based on competition for advancement as a separate scheme from *scaled wages*, since the former is a type of *tournament* that relies on performance, not simply tenure or seniority.

The term *pay-for-performance* is commonly used to refer to systems where pay is based at least partly on short-term performance (Prendergast 1999). *Individual pay-for-performance* tightly links compensation to individual job performance such as productivity on a job task. *Team-based pay-for-performance* links compensation to the performance of a larger group of individuals who are typically organized in a team, group, functional area, or business unit. The size of teams varies widely. In fact, stock options and other equity-based compensation, which are used for approximately 20 percent of US employees (most often as part of a retirement plan [Hall 2000]), effectively set the size of the team as the entire firm.

The key challenge in pay-for-performance schemes revolves around whether job performance is completely observable to the manager and firm (Baker 2000; Lazear 1979). Performance at some job tasks is inherently difficult to measure at the individual level in a way that is objective and perceived to be fair by workers simply because of production technology (Nickerson and Zenger 2008). Although production technologies that cleanly identify individual performance, such as the isolation of individual tasks, may facilitate the implementation of individual pay-for-performance, they may be grossly inefficient compared with more collaborative team-based production. Such team-based tasks may make individual pay-for-performance schemes intractable and may encourage team-based pay-for-performance systems that allow for performance observability at higher levels.

It is common for employees to have several different classes of compensation within a single plan. For example, salespeople often receive a flat, guaranteed wage; are paid commissions based on individual sales; are paid commissions based on their contribution to team-based sales; are paid stock options as part of their retirement plans; and are rewarded overtime via increases in their base pay and promotions to more senior sales positions (Dartnell 2009). The combination of compensation classes can allow firms to address employee risk aversion, create group and firm identity, and tailor specific compensation components to multiple tasks, some of which involve cooperation and some of which are individually separable.

Performance measurement for each compensation plan type can be organized around either cardinal or ordinal metrics (Baker 1992). Tournament-based compensation links rewards to individual or team performance relative to others (Lazear and Rosen 1981). In a tournament-based scheme involving promotions, for example, there are more employees vying for promotion than the number of available promotion slots. This means that the promotion reward must be allocated via consideration of relative performance, at least to some extent. In contrast, absolute performance-based systems tie pay to a cardinal scale, independent of relative performance.

It is important to emphasize that compensation encapsulates more than just monetary pay (Hall 2000). To reward strong performance, firms use non-monetary rewards, such as job awards, titles, and promotions not tied to increased pay, as well as non-monetary perks, such as a desirable workspace, flexible job hours, and autonomy in job design.

Compensation and employee actions: mechanisms and positive effects

Compensation systems are designed to influence the actions of employees. At their best, compensation systems motivate productive actions in line with the mission of the organization. However, compensation systems often cause employees to act in unexpected and/or unintended ways that detract from this mission, which we broadly define as misconduct that can range from shirking to explicit illegality. One major employee action heavily influenced by compensation is the decision to join, remain with, or leave an organization. Many scholars believe these decisions, which are referred to as *sorting*, play the largest role in determining the efficacy of a compensation system (Lazear and Oyer 2012). All other employee actions are typically referred to as *effort* (Prendergast 1999).

Effort vs. shirking

The most direct mechanism by which compensation influences employee action is around the choice of overall effort level while on the job (Prendergast 1999). Economic behavioral models typically assume that in the absence of compensation, employees prefer to shirk rather than work, such that individuals will reach a point where no additional effort is being exerted, despite potential rewards. Specifically, employees exert effort only to the point at which the marginal reward for increased effort equals the marginal cost of the effort. Importantly, this means that *any* compensation plan involves employees not working "as hard as possible" because, at each person's true effort limit, marginal effort is infinitely costly (e.g., death). Since employees have heterogeneous costs of effort and intrinsic motivation, this limit varies across individuals. Under a given compensation plan, the limit may be at 30 percent effort for one employee, while at 99 percent effort for another. This heterogeneity highlights the importance of compensation's sorting mechanism mentioned before. Designing a compensation system that attracts the 99 percent effort individual is far more important than one that improves the 30 percent individual's effort by 10 percent.

Although not universally accepted in the social sciences, every large-sample empirical study of pay-for-performance in actual

firms, for example, in settings such as automobile windshield instal-
lation (Lazear 2000), agriculture (Bandiera, Rasul, and Barankay
2005), enterprise software (Larkin 2014), tree planting (Paarsch and
Shearer 2000), long-distance trucking (Burks et al. 2009), professional services (Hitt et al. 2001), has shown that higher compensation increases average job effort (Prendergast 1999). Consequently,
the incentives provided by compensation tied to performance generally achieve some degree of increase in productive behavior via
increased effort, although this increased effort does not necessarily
make such schemes optimal.

Pay-for-performance at the individual level results in the greatest
increase in individual effort, since gains from such effort are internalized by the individual. *Ceteris paribus*, team-based pay-for-
performance produces lower levels of direct effort because the gains
from such effort must be shared across multiple individuals
(Prendergast 1999). This sharing of rewards leads to the classic free-
rider problem, or shirking, where each individual reduces effort and
relies on the contributions of teammates. Typically, the free-rider problem increases with team size due to reduced incentives and observability by managers (Holmstrom 1982).

The effort implications of tournament-based pay structures, whether
through short-term pay-for-performance or through longer-term promotion systems, are more complex than those of cardinal systems
(Lazear and Rosen 1981). Since tournament structures reward individuals' performance relative to others, effort will be primarily driven by
the likelihood of "winning" by outperforming others. Although this
competition can powerfully drive effort through both rational incentive
response and competitive drive, it can also dramatically reduce effort
under several circumstances. First, workers with strong preferences
against competition may reduce effort to avoid intense rivalry
(Niederle and Vesterlund 2007). Second, if workers perceive the probability of successfully outcompeting others to be very low, they may
produce minimal effort (Boudreau, Lacetera, and Lakhani 2011;
Carpenter, Matthews, and Schirm 2010) – a serious concern in organizations of diverse worker ability where stars are likely to win any
tournament. Unless the tournament structure sufficiently rewards those
who finish well relative to other non-stars, the returns from effort are
effectively zero. These problems with tournament-based systems highlight the importance of understanding the distribution of abilities

within the firm and how those often subtly change the incentives for each worker type to exert effort.

Sorting, attraction, and selection

Perhaps even more important is how compensation motivates individuals to join, stay, or leave the firm (Lazear 2000; Zenger 1994). In a world with heterogeneous pay structures across firms, individuals tend to join those that reward them best. Although pay *levels* considerably influence this decision, so too will compensation structure. Scaled wages attract lower-ability and risk-averse workers who fear low performance-based pay. In contrast, individual pay-for-performance attracts the highest-ability workers because of their superior earning potential. Stars will avoid team-based pay-for-performance for fear of sharing the rewards of their contributions with weaker teammates. Consequently, firms using individual-based systems tend to attract more skilled and higher-effort employees, while lower-ability and lower-effort workers prefer team-based systems, where they can free-ride on better teammates. This dynamic was shown by Lazear (2000) when unproductive technicians sorted away from Safelite after the company moved to a pay-for-performance structure. Tournament settings also tend to attract higher-skill employees (Iranzo, Fabiano, and Tosetti 2008). We note that pay does not purely determine sorting. Hamilton, Nickerson, and Owan (2003) found that some high-ability workers simply prefer team-based pay, while Niederle and Vesterlund (2007) found lower preferences for tournaments among women. Larkin and Leider (2012) explain how individual-based pay attracts overconfident people.

The relative importance of effort provision versus sorting depends on the heterogeneity of employee skill within the industry (Lazear and Rosen 1981). In industries with heterogeneous employee ability, such as enterprise software sales (Larkin 2014), financial services, and law (Hitt et al. 2001), compensation systems focus on attracting star workers and sorting out low-ability workers.

Cooperation

Organizations fundamentally exist to coordinate resources, including the actions of employees; and, the incentives built into compensation systems can dramatically alter cooperative behavior (Fehr and Gächter 2002). Individual pay-for-performance systems, for example, reward individuals for their own productivity, without consideration of the outcomes of others. Consequently, such systems tend to encourage low levels of cooperation or helping unless such behavior directly results in improved performance for the helping individual (Chan, Li, and Pierce 2014a, 2014b; Fehr and Gächter 2002). In contrast, team-based pay-for-performance not only emphasizes but also explicitly incentivizes cooperative behavior (DeMatteo, Eby, and Sundstrom 1998; Itoh 1991; Kandel and Lazear 1992), yielding superior firm performance when cooperation and learning are critical to the production technology (Chan et al. 2014a, 2014b; Nickerson and Zenger 2008).

The effect of scale-based pay on cooperation depends on whether promotions are based on tenure and/or experience or are the result of tournament-based competition. Tournament-based compensation systems produce extremely low levels of cooperation and helping behavior because a worker's pay increases not only with their own improved productivity but also with the poor performance of their peers.

Competition

Compensation systems can induce competition if the system rewards some employees while at the same time excluding others, which can directly increase effort when employees must split a fixed reward and that effort increases the share of the reward (Nalebuff and Stiglitz 1983). At the extreme, if only one person will receive the entire reward, as in a promotion tournament, increased competition may lower the probability a given employee will gain the reward at a given level of effort, possibly spurring an increased level of effort to compensate. The mechanism of healthy competition and its inducement of maximal effort is why labor economists so often believe that tournament-based compensation practices are optimal (Holmstrom 1982; Lazear and Rosen 1981).

Competition can also increase effort via psychological mechanisms absent from the "rational" reward versus cost of effort calculus. Scholars from social psychology have explored the impact of competition on employee performance for nearly a century (e.g., Whittemore 1924), with many studies suggesting that some people are motivated to perform better when competing with others, even absent a reward. For example, schoolchildren have been shown to run faster when running next to another student (Gneezy and Rustchini 2004). Research in sports settings also finds that teams play harder against established rivals (Kilduff, Elfenbein, and Staw 2010) and when slightly behind halfway through the game (Berger and Pope 2011). Competition with peers has been shown to increase effort in non-reward settings such as online gaming (Liu et al. 2013) and Linux software coding (Hertel, Niedner, and Herrmann 2003). The simple observability of peer productivity can increase effort through social comparison processes (Blanes, Vidal, and Nossol 2011; Mas and Moretti 2009).

Fairness

A recent but burgeoning literature demonstrates that compensation systems that are viewed as fair by employees induce higher effort (Fehr, Schmidt, and Klein 2007). "Fairness" is a broad term that encompasses no fewer than twelve separate ideals (Vaughan-Whitehead 2010) from legal system requirements on compensation, such as minimum wage levels, to the degree of wage competition at the market level, to social concerns such as the wage providing an adequate standard of living.

Employee perceptions of compensation system fairness are typically established via comparisons to reference points (Fehr, Hart, and Zehnder 2011). The most common reference point used by employees is the pay of similar employees, either in the same company or in other companies (Brown et al. 2008; Card et al. 2012; Carrell and Dittrich 1978), although other reference points such as prior income (Bewley 1998) or minimum wage (Falk, Fehr, and Zehnder 2006) are also important. The use of social comparisons to assess the fairness of compensation means that, unlike the standard utility model of economics, employees not only analyze their own effort and reward tradeoffs when deciding how much effort to exert but also consider the effort-reward tradeoff of others (Akerlof and Yellen 1990). A wide range of experimental and correlative studies using archival data suggests a positive relationship between wage equity and effort, meaning employees work harder in situations where others are paid similarly (Fehr and Gächter 2000).

Compensation and employee actions: negative effects

Through the same five mechanisms discussed above (effort, sorting, cooperation, competition, and fairness) compensation systems can also generate a host of negative employee actions, which we term "misconduct." In fact, logical consideration of the five mechanisms indicates that they are often mutually contradictory within a given compensation system. For example, using an individual pay-for-performance system inevitably causes heterogeneity in pay due to differences in employee skill and/or heterogeneity in the cost of employee effort. Indeed, these sources of heterogeneity are one of the fundamental reasons many scholars espouse the use of pay-for-performance in compensation. However, the heterogeneous compensation that results in these systems, by definition, reduces perceived fairness of the system. Tournament-based pay provides another example of the tradeoffs across mechanisms when determining employee reaction to compensation. The competition inherent in tournament-based systems in many cases can increase effort, but the fact that there is such a large difference in employee outcomes in tournaments (that is, one employee is promoted while the rest are not) fundamentally reduces perceived fairness.

In the quest to increase employee productivity via the compensation system, firms often unintentionally incentivize pernicious behavior that destroys value. These negative behaviors can occur across employees, with a given compensation system promoting positive behavior in some employees and negative behavior in others; however, because of the contradictions inherent in any compensation plan, it is often the case that a given compensation system induces both productive behavior and misconduct by the same employee. For example, an employee may work harder in a given system, but also game the system in a way that is costly to the employer in order to increase pay even more. Compensation, then, acts as a double-edged sword (Jensen 2001), incentivizing both productivity and misconduct in the same employee.

Demotivation from crowding out

One key benefit of pay-for-performance systems is that they engender increased effort on desired tasks. However, in some cases, the use of financial compensation may actually reduce effort provision on desired tasks, largely through employee demotivation due to psychological mechanisms. As noted previously, pay-for-performance incontrovertibly reduces employee shirking. Nevertheless, pay-for-performance can reduce employee effort by affecting baseline motivation for the job.

The most well-known mechanism by which pay-for-performance can reduce motivation and therefore effort is through the crowding out of intrinsic motivation (Deci, Koestner, and Ryan 1999). In crowding out theory, the introduction of a financial reward not only increases extrinsic motivation toward a task but also reduces intrinsic motivation coming from love of the job, a sense of duty toward or shared purpose with the employer, and other non-extrinsic factors. This is consistent with insufficient justification theory (Staw 1974), which argues that extrinsic and internal motivation are substitutes because individuals flexibly seek sufficient justification for prior decisions or behavior. Many scholars and practitioners mistakenly believe that crowding-out theory predicts that financial incentives reduce employee performance. In reality, crowding-out theory recognizes that financial incentives increase extrinsic motivation while reducing intrinsic motivation, leading to an ambiguous prediction of the effect on effort (Frey and Jegen 2001). If the increased extrinsic motivation is smaller than the decreased intrinsic motivation, employees will work less hard despite higher pay. This partially explains why field evidence on crowding out is so rare (Gubler, Larkin, and Pierce 2016). Identifying it requires either the combination of a weak extrinsic motivation increase and strong intrinsic motivation decreases, or else the observation of decreased productivity after the extrinsic reward is removed.

Most experimental studies of crowding out rely on measuring task performance in three periods: pre-reward introduction, the reward period, and the period after which the reward is removed. The typical study compares pre-reward task performance with performance after the reward was introduced and then removed (Esteves-Sorenson, Pohl, and Freitas 2013). These studies almost unanimously find lower performance in the period after removal compared to before introduction (Deci et al. 1999). However, in most experiments, performance in the intermediate phase, when financial rewards were paid to subjects, is actually higher than that in the pre-reward phase (Esteves-Sorenson et al. 2013). It is even more difficult to cleanly identify crowding out using real-world data because it is rare to have exogenous introductions then removals of rewards. In fact, most empirical studies of financial rewards are not suggestive of crowding out (Prendergast

1999). Nevertheless, one recent field study suggests that crowding out did occur after a reward was introduced for a previously uncompensated task; previously highly punctual employees became eight times more likely than a control group of workers to show up late after an industrial laundry plant introduced a highly visible award for punctuality (Gubler et al. 2016).

Demotivation and cheating from unfairness

Financial rewards can also reduce employee effort due to perceived unfairness or inequity in the system. Recent research has demonstrated that employee job satisfaction and reported workplace morale markedly decline when employees learn they earn less than their peers (Card et al. 2012) or that the company's CEO is paid more than their peers (Cornelissen, Himmler, and Koenig 2011). In the Card et al. (2012) study, a random group of University of California employees were told that peer salaries were publicly available via a website, leading 80 percent of these employees to access the website. Employees paid below the median for their occupational category reported a 5.2 percent reduction in job satisfaction, and a self-reported 20 percent increase in likelihood of looking for a new job. A study of mergers in Korea found a much higher likelihood of voluntary employee departure postmerger when employees were paid significantly less than similar employees of the newly merged firm (Kwon and Milgrom 2007).

Employee overconfidence exacerbates the problem of perceived inequity. Many employees feel they have higher skills or better performance than they actually do, and attribute lower-than-expected measured performance to biases in the system (de la Rosa 2011). In tandem, overconfidence and social comparisons mean that employees with below-average skill may react to pay-for-performance systems by reducing effort because of perceived unfairness (Larkin et al. 2012), a result also suggested by Card et al. (2012).

Multitasking and gaming

Until now, we have focused on the effect of compensation on the task being compensated. However, in reality, job functions are usually complex and involve a large number of related tasks. Especially in job settings where it is easier to measure performance on individual tasks rather than holistic performance across these tasks, pay-for-performance is often focused only on a subset of the tasks important to an organization. Multitasking theory (Holmstrom and Milgrom 1991) holds that employees will over direct effort toward compensated tasks at the expense of non-compensated tasks. Because tasks are interdependent, this can cause overall employee performance to fall.

The negative effects of multitasking can represent a simple, non-strategic response by employees to the firm's incentive system. Employees may not even be aware that their misplaced emphasis on compensated tasks is hurting overall performance (Kerr 1975). Firms may find it difficult to adequately measure performance on every important task and may choose to reward the most easily measured or highly observable task (Lado and Wilson 1994).

In many cases involving multitasking problems, employees strategically "game" the system in order to maximize their own pay. Incentive system gaming refers to deliberate manipulation of an employee's task performance in a way that increases their pay in a way that is clearly outside the spirit of the incentive system, even if the action is within the system's rules (Frank and Obloj 2014; Larkin 2014; Obloj and Sengul 2012; Oyer 1998). For example, an employee may strategically delay the completion of a task so that the task is credited in a job period where pay is higher. Larkin (2014) shows that enterprise software salespeople strategically accelerate and delay deals in order to maximize their commissions and offer lower prices to customers to incentivize their cooperation. This research estimates that this deliberate "timing gaming" costs 5 percent to 8 percent of overall firm revenue.

For employees with multiple important tasks, the multitasking problem becomes even more complex to solve because rewarding any one task inherently causes negative spillovers to all other tasks. When a firm decides to base worker pay on performance of a specific task, they inherently devalue all other tasks in the minds of employees, who will in turn reallocate effort away from those tasks.

Fraud and theft

Compensation systems that reward performance on a specific dimension may motivate productive behavior on that dimension, but may also motivate workers to fraudulently increase the *appearance* of performance on the dimension. If the rewarded dimension is perfectly observable and measurable, then such fraud is of little concern. But if it is possible for workers to increase their pay by faking performance, then a number of counterproductive outcomes can ensue.

Workers may directly misreport performance, either by self-reporting higher productivity or by falsifying productivity data. In pay-for-performance systems, lying produces a direct financial payoff and may be rational if the probability of and punishment associated with detection are low (Gneezy 2005; Gneezy, Rockenbach, and Serra-Garcia 2013). The incentives for overreporting performance may be further accelerated when the pay system has a tournament element, because of increased competition and the expectation of others cheating (Schwieren and Weichselbaumer 2010). Many employees will honestly report performance even under such conditions because of their own preferences for honesty; but, a substantial portion of the population is indeed willing to cheat (Mazar and Ariely 2006). This motivation to inflate performance will be accelerated for those low-ability (or low-effort) workers who earn low amounts under pay-for-performance systems, partly because they may view the unequal wages as being unfair or inequitable, which may invoke feelings of envy.

In a series of laboratory settings, Gino and Pierce (2009a, 2010a, 2010b) demonstrated that even randomly generated pay inequity can motivate dishonest performance reporting. Furthermore, they showed that this inequity need not be directly associated with the liar. Their work suggests that workers may help one another by misreporting performance to address perceptions of pay inequity, even when that dishonesty is personally financially costly. This is consistent with earlier work by Greenberg (1990, 1993) as well as a broader line of laboratory research showing that individuals justify dishonest acts based on their financial and utility benefits to others (Erat and Gneezy 2012; Gneezy 2005; Wiltermuth 2011; Wiltermuth, Bennett, and Pierce 2013). This work suggests that although team-based pay-for-performance may reduce issues of inequity and reduce incentives to overreport performance (Larkin et al. 2012), it may also help individual workers justify their dishonesty. Indeed, recent work by Conrads et al. (2013) found that teams are more likely to cheat than individuals.

In a set of laboratory experiments, John, Loewenstein, and Rick (2014) demonstrated that the inequity associated with wage comparison may dominate incentives. Under piece-rate pay systems, workers had stronger financial incentives to inflate their self-reported performance when the rates were highest. Nevertheless, they found that those with lower piece-rates were more likely to inflate performance when able to observe others who earned higher rates. The study demonstrates that this effect is about social comparison process and not about decreasing marginal utility of money. The implication is that heterogeneity in performance-based pay rates creates psychological motivators to cheat the employer. Related work by Gill, Prowse, and Vlassopoulos (2013) shows that perceived inequity from bonuses can work in the same way, motivating increased cheating among those whose pay is disproportionately low compared to their contribution. An important finding in their study is that the best workers are most likely to cheat because they are the ones most likely to be wronged by a system where pay is not perfectly tuned to performance.

The second result is that workers, in devoting effort to generating and hiding fraud, will divert effort from other important tasks. This type of fraudulent multitasking generates spillovers to other tasks from the dishonesty of the compensated task. In recent work by Pierce, Snow, and McAfee (2015), restaurants using a pay-for-performance system experienced improved sales when theft was reduced through improved monitoring. This is consistent with workers shifting effort from theft to sales, and more broadly with compensation systems being critical conduits through which any type of misconduct might also impact other tasks.

Third, fraudulent performance reporting may expose the firm to extensive financial and legal liabilities (Baucus and Baucus 1997; Smith-Crowe et al. 2015). Overbilled clients of consulting or law firms could cancel large contracts because of the overreporting of one employee. Manipulation of financial return reporting could lead to investor lawsuits. Government contractors with inaccurate billing or performance claims could invalidate the company's qualification to bid for future contracts, and thus effectively end the firm.

Finally, fraudulent performance reporting by one worker can undermine the motivation of other workers who are either unable or unwilling to engage in the fraud. Those unwilling to report may view the fraudulent worker as unfairly achieving additional pay under the system, but rather than report the individual, may either reduce effort or leave the firm.

Although fraudulently reporting higher performance is an important type of misconduct stemming from pay-for-performance systems, it is not the only type of fraud motivated by such compensation schemes. Workers may accurately achieve certain performance levels, but may cross ethical and legal boundaries to achieve them. One of the clearest examples of this occurred during the housing market bubble of 2005 to 2008, when real estate agents, mortgage brokers, and investment bankers were all primarily paid based on performance. Each of these groups had the ability to manipulate performance metrics by misrepresenting some aspect of a transaction in order to facilitate a sale (Ben-David 2011; Mian and Sufi 2009). Real estate agents could misrepresent the condition of a house, bringing in inspectors and appraisers who would overlook shortcomings and exaggerate positive attributes. Mortgage brokers, also paid on commission, could overstate borrower creditworthiness or income or offer mortgages to borrowers who did not truly understand the terms. Investment bankers, operating on high-powered bonuses, could knowingly package high-risk mortgages (often originated in-house) into securities for sale to unsuspecting third parties.

The likelihood that individuals will cross ethical or legal boundaries is further accelerated under compensation systems that are inherently tournament-based (Stowe and Gilpatric 2010). The sports world provides many excellent examples, where the compensation tied to winning or ranking is inherently based on relative performance. Palmer and Yenkey (2015) and Gould and Kaplan (2011) detail the use of performance-enhancing drugs in cycling and baseball. The tournament structure, particularly in cycling, generates widespread illegal drug usage because one's perception that others are gaining an advantage by breaking rules increases the motivation to break rules oneself.

In addition, compensation systems may cause spillover effects to other types of misconduct such as theft. As noted earlier, one key detrimental mechanism born from compensation systems is perceptions of inequity, unfairness, and related envy (Larkin et al. 2012). In a set of famous studies from social psychology, Greenberg (1990, 1993) showed that employees who received pay cuts that they perceived to be unfair were more likely to engage in theft. In the field, a pay cut at one plant resulted in increased inventory theft (Greenberg 1990), while in the lab, participants who were paid less than promised were more likely to steal cash (Greenberg 1993). Chen and Sandino (2012) found evidence that the psychological costs of pay comparisons may extend beyond locational boundaries in multi-unit firms. Studying convenience stores, they found store-level theft to be correlated with pay level relative to other stores. Pierce et al. (2015), who find theft reduction from monitoring in restaurants to be correlated with productivity gains, also present fairness concerns as a possible motivator, but are unable to provide substantial evidence to support this mechanism.

Lack of cooperation

Recent research has shown that the use of ranking systems may reduce cooperative behavior and lead to excessive competition (Garcia and Tor 2007; Garcia, Tor, and Gonzalez 2006). This competition is often detrimental because it can lead to noncooperative, value-destroying behavior. For example, Garcia et al. (2006) introduced a number of scenarios to experimental subjects, such as being at risk of exclusion from the list of Fortune 500 corporations, for example, a corporation currently ranked #500 or #501, versus a control condition where there was no risk of exclusion, for example, companies with a rank of #350 or #351. These papers indicate that experimental subjects are more likely to behave competitively, and in so doing reduce the amount of value created, when reaching to achieve a meaningful standard.

One explicit example comes from the different compensation systems studied by Chan and Pierce (2014a, 2014b) among cosmetics salespeople in a Chinese department store. In that setting, some counters employed individual commissions, while others used team-based commissions. The differences in both productive and counterproductive behavior were striking. In individual-based counters, star salespeople focus most of their effort on stealing customers from their own teammates, forcing those teammates to compete through price reductions. This internal competition was in lieu of the coordinated effort and specialization necessary to compete with adjacent counters, who benefited from the internal poaching of customers. Even more costly, stars at individual-based counters put no effort into teaching new salespeople, permanently impeding their sales ability growth. In contrast, team-based counters showed better cooperation, better teaching, and more successful cross-firm competition.

Competition has been shown to produce negative emotions such as disappointment, frustration, and anger both when an employee's expectations are higher than actual achievement (McGraw, Mellers, and Tetlock 2005) and when competition occurs between employees where at least one employee feels threatened by another's status or control over resources (Fiske et al. 2002).

Negative sorting

There are several ways in which pay-for-performance systems can lead to negative sorting, defined as the attraction and retention of undesirable employees, or the failure to retain desirable employees. Negative sorting commonly occurs because pay-for-performance systems can affect the culture of an organization, and employees have heterogeneous preferences around an organization's cultural traits. For example, laboratory experimental research has demonstrated that peer effects play a strong role in predicting unethical behavior; employees often learn about the methods of unethical behavior, as well as the organizational acceptability of this behavior, by observing peers (Jones and Kavanagh 1996). In a field study of automotive emissions testers, where fraudulent manipulation of testing results is fairly common, Pierce and Snyder (2015) show that these peer effects also lead to clustering of unethical employees within certain firms. These results suggest that employees prone to engage in unethical behavior will learn about it from their more experienced colleagues, while those who find such behavior unacceptable will choose to leave a firm with unethical employees. Similarly, Hoffman and Morgan (2015) found that prosocial individuals naturally self-select out of industries with higher levels of "cutthroat" competition. If attracting and retaining ethical employees is important to an organization, either for its own sake or because it is correlated with other positive employee traits, the fact that pay-for-performance often leads to fraud will in turn lead to negative sorting of ethical employees.

Negative sorting can also play out on dimensions other than employee ethics. For example, employees are heterogeneous regarding their preferences for competition. Significant research has suggested that, for many tasks, a higher percentage of women tend to avoid individually competitive environments (Niederle and Vesterlund 2007). Tournament-based pay-for-performance schemes are inherently competitive and may therefore lead to a negative sorting of women. The effects of this negative sorting on workplace diversity can be pernicious; indeed, some scholars hold that the relative paucity of senior female executives is as much due to negative sorting as it is to outright discrimination (Eagly and Carli 2007). Furthermore, if men and women have distinctly different moral preferences or ethical standards, as a body of experimental research suggests (Tenbrunsel and Smith-Crowe 2008), any compensation system that encourages misconduct may increase voluntary attrition of female workers and hinder diversity in workforce recruitment.

Negative sorting can also occur if competitors use pay-for-performance schemes to poach "superstar" employees from competitors. Research has demonstrated that star employees are rarely as successful at their new firms as their old ones (Groysberg 2012; Groysberg, Nanda, and Nohria 2004), likely because superstars rely, more than anticipated, on organizational support.

Sabotage

Although choosing not to cooperate when expected is passive misconduct, even more costly behavior occurs when workers actively act to sabotage the work of others. This most commonly occurs under a tournament-based compensation system, where workers benefit not only from their own success but also from others' failures (Charness, Masclet, and Villeval 2013; Lazear 1989). For a worker who can easily undermine their peers' productivity, it may be rational for them to expend effort on sabotaging coworkers rather than attempting to improve their own behavior. Such sabotage may involve actively reducing the objective performance of the coworker, but it may also involve politically undermining them in a longer-term promotion- or bonus-based tournament either through rumors or true revelations of undesirable behavior. Even when short-term compensation is relatively flat, the tournament incentives embedded in promotions can motivate widespread sabotage (Drago and Garvey 1998).

Although sabotage is most likely to occur under a tournament-based system because of incentives, workers under other systems may also sabotage if they feel a system is producing unfair outcomes (Fehr and Gachter 2000; Rabin 1993). Any system that produces pay disparity can potentially produce perceived inequity and the associated emotion of envy (Larkin et al. 2012; Nickerson and Zenger 2008). Individual pay-for-performance, for example, can generate feelings of inequity and envy if workers cannot agree that the performance on the rewarded dimension is accurately measured. Ambrose, Seabright, and Schminke (2002) detail a large organizational behavior literature on how feelings of injustice, which are closely related to inequity, can generate sabotage and aggression on multiple dimensions. Given the saliency of compensation as a job attribute, any compensation system deemed unjust, either because of its pay levels or distribution across employees, can motivate sabotage.

Although compensation systems with wide pay dispersion are most likely to engender feelings of inequity or injustice that lead to sabotage, recent work by Bose, Pal, and Sappington (2010) explains that sabotage can also result from the equal pay policies in scaled wages. Since inequity is a function of the ratio of rewards to contributions, if the rewards are equal for all workers but contributions are not, misconduct, such as sabotage, can occur. This further highlights why jobs with wide arrays of ability typically use pay-for-performance. Similarly, though team-based compensation typically removes localized sabotage, both through the motivation to cooperate and the incentive to monitor peers, it can generate sabotage *across* teams (Gürtler 2008).

Excessive risk-taking

Another class of misconduct that can be influenced by compensation systems is excessive risk-taking, where individual employees risk substantial losses or liabilities for the firm to attempt to achieve financial rewards for themselves. Excessive risk-taking by employees can include reducing product safety to cut costs (e.g., food contamination), reducing environmental safety precautions (e.g., BP Deep Water Horizon), or excessively risky lending or financial instruments (e.g., Countrywide). Explicitly illegal or forbidden misconduct can also be classified as risk-taking in and of itself, since it involves a probability of detection and punishment, particularly when such misconduct creates legal liability for the individual or firm. In each case, individuals are likely to dramatically increase risk-taking when the compensation system strongly rewards successes in ways that cannot be counterbalanced by failures.

The underlying source of this excessive risk-taking is the asymmetry in the potential gains and losses to the individual built into the compensation system. This asymmetry is inherent in any system with high-powered incentives from pay-for-performance for several reasons. First, even though compensation can increase significantly with positive outcomes, it is typically guaranteed at a minimum level. Even high-powered commission-based pay, as is typical in sales, almost always includes a base salary that insures risk-averse workers against uncontrollable outside economic factors. Although guaranteed base pay helps smooth incomes and attract workers, it also can encourage excessive risk-taking because it insures workers against the financial downside of major mistakes such as losing a large sales contract.

The second reason is that workers are typically protected from being held liable by their employers for such financial losses except in cases of extreme malfeasance. As employees take larger risks, the upside increases while the downside has a floor at termination. Even if employees fear that their behavior might hurt their reputation, they frequently need not. Firms are typically reluctant to publicly reveal large losses or misconduct by employees for fear of its effect on their own reputation.

Potential for misconduct leading to excessive risk is particularly high in a tournament-based system for three additional reasons. First, the financial or promotion-based reward for finishing first is typically much better than a second-place prize, thereby creating strong non-linear incentives to take risks when performance is near a - competitor. Second, such tournament structures can lead to a "race to the bottom," where competing individuals (or teams or firms) iteratively increase their risk-taking and rule-breaking to outperform one another (Bennett et al. 2013; Snyder 2010). Bothner, Kang, and Stuart (2007) provide evidence of such risk-taking among close competitors in a tournament-based system in NASCAR. Competitive cycling, where widespread drug usage made a competitive finish without doping nearly impossible, presents another clear example (Palmer 2012; Palmer and Yenkey 2015). Third, tournament-based systems create the potential for loss-aversion mechanisms to motivate leaders to take extreme risks to avoid losing their position (Kern and Chugh 2009).

Finally, it is worth noting that this excessive risk-taking under pay-for-performance schemes is accelerated by overconfidence bias. Because individuals commonly overestimate their own ability (Zenger 1992), they miscalculate their ability to successfully achieve high performance-based pay (Larkin and Leider 2012). This problem is particularly severe in tournament-based systems such as promotion, since excessive risk-taking by overconfident employees will often yield a few successful decisions (and a lot of failures), purely by chance. This can lead to problems where overconfident individuals, who take excessive risks (either financial or ethical), end up being promoted to higher levels of management (Goel and Thakor 2008) and then, in turn, attract and hire other overconfident individuals (Van den Steen 2005).

From individual- to organization-level effects

Thus far, we have considered the effects of compensation systems on employee productivity and misconduct. One clear implication from a careful read of the literature is that the optimal level of employee misconduct is greater than zero. Compensation systems that tend to spur greater misconduct also tend to lead to factors that increase productivity via higher employee effort and the attraction and retention of higher-ability workers.

One additional factor that managers must consider when designing compensation systems is the potential for misconduct by one employee to spill over to other employees. Misconduct by a small number of employees has the potential to induce other employees to engage in misconduct and can lead to widespread organizational misconduct that can quickly swamp any productivity gains from the original compensation system. Any highly performing organization will have some level of misconduct, but organizations that are rife with misconduct will never perform at an optimal level. It is, therefore, critical to review the processes by which individual misconduct can spur broader organizational-level misconduct by spillovers to other employees.

First, misconduct by even small numbers of employees can begin to shift organizational culture toward one where misconduct is accepted or even celebrated. The most direct shift in culture happens through employee learning. New workers may adopt the misconduct patterns of coworkers (Pierce and Snyder 2008) either by learning the culture (Roy 1952) or by observing specific peer behaviors (Gino, Ayal, and Ariely 2009). This learning may be accelerated if the focal employee is in a leadership position (supervisor or manager) (Brown, Treviño, and Harrison 2005). Each of these learning processes will not only impart the means of misconduct, but also downplay the moral judgment of it, leading to a normalization of corruption (Ashforth and Anand 2003).

Surprisingly, the slower these practices disseminate, the less likely it is that employees will recognize them as unethical (Gino and Bazerman 2009).

Second, the problem of peer learning of the methods of misconduct is exacerbated when top employees are both highly skilled and highly prone to engage in misconduct. Learning the skills needed to be a top employee is often very difficult, but learning how to game the system, cheat employers or customers, or engage in other types of misconduct is relatively easier. When compensation systems lead to disproportionately higher rewards for top performers, average performers may fixate on the misconduct carried out by top performers and downplay top performers' effort and skills (Larkin 2011). This can lead to a widespread view by employees that the most effective method by which to be recognized and rewarded as a top employee is to engage in misconduct (Larkin 2011).

Third, feedback loops from the results of misconduct may in turn generate more misconduct. In team-based compensation, one worker shirking their responsibility inherently incentivizes others to do so as well. Similarly, in a tournament-based setting, the explicit misconduct of one employee may force others to compete through misconduct. Again, professional sports provide an illuminating example. Performance-enhancing drug use was endemic in baseball and cycling throughout the 1980s, 1990s, and 2000s, and the most common rationales athletes gave for taking the drugs were that, "everyone else is using them," and "I could not compete if I didn't follow along" (Green et al. 2001).

Fourth, misconduct by a few employees may also lead to "negative sorting," where employees who refuse to engage in misconduct choose to completely depart from a firm where peers engage in this misconduct (Pierce and Snyder 2015). Again, "negative sorting" is exacerbated when the rewards to top employees are disproportionate. In almost any compensation scheme, an employee willing to engage in misconduct will earn higher rewards than an employee with the exact same skill level and effort provision. Given the strong peer effects and fairness concerns that govern employee perception of job satisfaction, ethical high performers are more likely to seek out jobs where misconduct is minimal.

Finally, compensation systems can also signal the types of behaviors that are valued by the firm, thereby setting culture across a multitude of behaviors that are not formally measured or compensated (Brown et al. 2005). Individual pay-for-performance, for example, signals the primacy of solo productivity and individuality and the secondary importance of cooperation and group identity. In contrast, team-based pay can signal the value of cooperation and coordination, which in turn can change behavior across many job tasks that are not explicitly compensated. Tournament-based systems, which emphasize relative performance, can frame coworkers as the enemy and generate excessive competition and lack of coordination even on tasks where this is explicitly destructive. The use of employee forced ranking systems at firms such as Microsoft and Enron, for example, have been widely blamed for hurting team culture and motivating multiple classes of misconduct (Ackman 2002; Eichenwald 2012). The broader organizational impact of compensation on one job task is analogous to what Gubler et al. (2016) refer to as "motivational spillovers," where formally rewarding one task can reduce internal motivation for a host of others. This may occur because an employee feels it is unfair for the firm to reward a certain task over others.

Conclusion

Compensation systems represent one of the most important tools for firms to improve employee performance through sorting and motivation. Yet, compensation systems also produce counterproductive behaviors that range from legal but costly behavior, such as shirking or lack of cooperation, to explicitly unethical and illegal behaviors, such as fraud, theft, and sabotage. In this sense, compensation systems represent a strong example of what Palmer (2012) refers to as "normal organizational wrongdoing." Misconduct is an inevitable byproduct of structures, roles, and abilities in the organization necessary to achieve goals and objectives. The challenge for managers is balancing the productivity rewards and misconduct costs that come from each compensation system. For example, individual pay-for-performance may attract star workers and motivate improved effort, but does the lost cooperation and potential sabotage and fraud overwhelm the benefits?

The key recognition for managers is that a compensation policy intended to improve productivity is also likely to generate misconduct.

Similarly, a compensation policy intended to reduce misconduct is likely to reduce productivity. This recognition allows managers to begin to evaluate the net benefit of a policy change, rather than being surprised by unexpected costs after the change has been implemented.

One of the key shortcomings in the literature on employee compensation is the shortage of papers that simultaneously measure both the productivity and misconduct implications of compensation policy. Although a substantial body of work does so for more minor types of misconduct, such as gaming (Frank and Obloj 2014; Larkin 2014), lack of cooperation (Chan and Pierce 2014a), and free-riding (Hamilton et al. 2003), there is a dearth of fieldwork jointly estimating productivity and misconduct that explicitly violates organizational or legal rules. Pierce et al.'s (2015) study of restaurant theft represents a rare example. The shortage of such work is understandable, given that it would require both variation in compensation system (cross-sectionally or across time) and detailed productivity and misconduct data.

Despite these challenges, we believe it is of paramount importance for scholars to focus on settings where they can jointly estimate the impact of compensation on productivity and misconduct. Sports settings provide some potential for this (e.g., Palmer and Yenkey 2015), presuming that one is observing an unbiased sample of misconduct and not just those who are caught. Notwithstanding, changes to compensation systems are relatively rare. Real estate or sales settings, where one can measure both sales and fraud, and where there is cross-sectional variation in pay across firms, might also provide potential.

Finally, we note that a host of additional psychological factors (see Moore and Gino [2015] for deeper discussion) may arise from compensation systems that, in turn, influence both misconduct and productivity. Although we have touched on a select set of emotional responses (e.g., envy), others have been widely shown to emerge as a function of compensation. A growing literature shows how the love of money can influence several classes of misconduct (Gino and Pierce 2009b; Tang and Chiu 2003; Vohs, Mead, and Goode 2006). Similarly, if pay-for-performance compensation systems use nonlinear schemes that involve quotas or accelerators, then they may evoke misconduct that has been associated with goals (Ordóñez et al. 2009). Furthermore, a much broader literature on how incidental emotions can influence unrelated ethical decision-making (Andrade and Ariely 2009; Yip and Schweitzer 2015) implies that employee emotional responses to compensation (of which there are many) may produce a myriad of types of misconduct. Anxiety and stress are thought to increase unethical behavior (Fast and Chen 2009; Kouchaki and Desai 2015), which implies that the pay uncertainty of pay-for-performance, particularly in tournament settings, may systematically increase misconduct across the firm. The universe of psychological responses to compensation and their implications for misconduct is an important subject far beyond the limits of this chapter.

References

Ackman, D. 2002. "Pay madness at Enron," *Forbes.com*. Available from www .forbes.com/2002/03/22/0322enronpay.html.

Akerlof, G. and Yellen, J. 1990. "The fair wage-effort hypothesis and unemployment," *Quarterly Journal of Economics* 105(2): 255–283.

Ambrose, M., Seabright, M., and Schminke, M. 2002. "Sabotage in the workplace: The role of organizational injustice," *Organizational Behavior and Human Decision Processes* 89(1): 947–965.

Andrade, E. and Ariely, D. 2009. "The enduring impact of transient emotions on decision making," *Organizational Behavior and Human Decision Processes* 109(1): 1–8.

Ashforth, B. and Anand, V. 2003. "The normalization of corruption in organizations," *Research in Organizational Behavior* 25: 1–52.

Baker, G. 1992. "Incentive contracts and performance measurement," *Journal of Political Economy* 100(3): 598–614.

Baker, G. 2000. "The use of performance measures in incentive contracting," *American Economic Review* 90(2): 415–420.

Bandiera, O., Rasul, I., and Barankay, I. 2005. "Social preferences and the response to incentives: Evidence from personnel data," with Rasul, I. and Barankay, I, *Quarterly Journal of Economics* 120(3): 917–962.

Baucus, M. and Baucus, D. 1997. "Paying the piper: An empirical examination of longer-term financial consequences of illegal corporate behavior," *Academy of Management Journal* 40(1): 129–151.

Ben-David, I. 2011. "Financial constraints and inflated home prices during the real estate boom," *American Economic Journal: Applied Economics* 3(3): 55–87.

Bennett, V., Pierce, L., Snyder, J., and Toffel, M. 2013. "Customer-driven misconduct: How competition corrupts business practices," *Management Science* 59(8): 1725–1742.

Berger, J. and Pope, D. 2011. "Can losing lead to winning?" *Management Science* 57(5): 817–827.

Bewley, T. F. 1998. "Why not cut pay?" *European Economic Review* 42(3–5): 459–490.

Blanes, I., Vidal, J., and Nossol, M. 2011. "Tournaments without prizes: Evidence from personnel records," *Management Science* 57: 1721–1736.

Bose, A., Pal, D., and Sappington, D. E. 2010. "Equal pay for unequal work: Limiting sabotage in teams," *Journal of Economics and Management Strategy* 19(1): 25–53.

Bothner, M., Kang, J., and Stuart, T. 2007. "Competitive crowding and risk taking in a tournament: Evidence from NASCAR racing," *Administrative Science Quarterly* 52(2): 208–247.

Boudreau, K. J., Lacetera, N., and Lakhani, K. R. 2011. "Incentives and problem uncertainty in innovation contests: An empirical analysis," *Management Science* 57(5): 843–863.

Brown, G., Gardner, J., Oswald, A., and Qian, J. 2008. "Does wage rank affect employees' well-being?," *Industrial Relations* 47(3): 355–389.

Brown, M., Treviño, L., and Harrison, D. 2005. "Ethical leadership: A social learning perspective for construct development and testing," *Organizational Behavior and Human Decision Processes* 97(2): 117–134.

Burks, S., Carpenter, J., Goette, L., and Rustichini, A. 2009. "Cognitive skills affect economic preferences, strategic behavior, and job attachment," *Proceedings of the National Academy of Sciences* 106(19): 7745–7750.

Card, D., Mas, A., Moretti, E., and Saez, E. 2012. "Inequality at work: The effect of peer salaries on job satisfaction," *American Economic Review* 102(6): 2981–3003.

Carpenter, J., Matthews, P., and Schirm, J. 2010. "Tournaments and office politics: Evidence from a real effort experiment," *American Economic Review* 100(1): 504–517.

Carrell, M. and Dittrich, J. 1978. "Equity theory: The recent literature, methodological considerations, and new directions," *The Academy of Management Review* 3(2): 202–210.

Chan, T., Li, J., and Pierce, L. 2014a. "Compensation and peer effects in competing sales teams," *Management Science* 60(8): 1965–1984.

Chan, T., Li, J., and Pierce, L. 2014b. "Learning from peers: Knowledge transfer and sales force productivity growth," *Marketing Science* 33(4): 463–484.

Charness, G., Masclet, D., and Villeval, M. 2013. "The dark side of competition for status," *Management Science* 60(1): 38–55.

Chen, C. X. and Sandino, T. 2012. "Can wages buy honesty? The relationship between relative wages and employee theft," *Journal of Accounting Research* 50(4): 967–1000.

Conrads, J., Irlenbusch, B., Rilke, R., and Walkowitz, G. 2013. "Lying and team incentives," *Journal of Economic Psychology* 34: 1–7.

Cornelissen, T., Himmler, O., and Koenig, T. 2011. "Perceived unfairness in CEO compensation and work morale," *Economics Letters* 110(1): 45–48.

Dartnell Corporation. 2009. *Dartnell's 30th Sales Force Compensation Survey*. Chicago: The Dartnell Corporation.

de la Rosa, L. 2011. "Overconfidence and moral hazard," *Games and Economic Behavior* 73(2): 429–451.

Deci, E., Koestner, R., and Ryan, R. 1999. "A meta-analytic review of experiments examining the effects of extrinsic rewards on intrinsic motivation," *Psychological Bulletin* 125: 627–668.

DeMatteo, J., Eby, L., and Sundstrom, E. 1998. "Team-based rewards: Current empirical evidence and directions for future research," *Research in Organizational Behavior* 20: 141–183.

Drago, R. and Garvey, G. T. 1998. "Incentives for helping on the job: Theory and evidence," *Journal of Labor Economics* 16(1): 1–25.

Eagly, A. H. and Carli, L. L. 2007. "Women and the labyrinth of leadership," *Harvard Business Review* 85(9): 62.

Eichenwald, K. 2012. "Microsoft's lost decade," *Vanity Fair* 54(August): 108.

Erat, S. and Gneezy, U. 2012. "White lies," *Management Science* 58(4): 723–733.

Esteves-Sorenson, C., Pohl, V., and Freitas, E. 2013. "*Efficiency* wages *and* its mechanisms: Empirical evidence," Working Paper, Yale University.

Falk, A., Fehr, E., and Zehnder, C. 2006. "Fairness perceptions and reservation wages: The behavioral effects of minimum wage laws," *Quarterly Journal of Economics* 121(4): 1347–1381.

Fast, N. J. and Chen, S. 2009. "When the boss feels inadequate power, incompetence, and aggression," *Psychological Science* 20(11): 1406–1413.

Fehr, E. and Gächter, S. 2000. "Fairness and retaliation: The economics of reciprocity," *Journal of Economic Perspectives* 14(2): 159–181.

Fehr, E. and Gächter, S. 2002. "Altruistic punishment in humans," *Nature* 415: 137–140.

Fehr, E., Hart, O., and Zehnder, C. 2011. "Contracts as reference points – Experimental evidence," *American Economic Review* 101(2): 493–525.

Fehr, E., Schmidt, K., and Klein, A. 2007. "Fairness and contract design," *Econometrica* 75: 121–154.

Fiske, S., Cuddy, A., Glick, P., and Xu, J. 2002. "A model of (often mixed) stereotype content: Competence and warmth respectively follow from status and competition," *Journal of Personality and Social Psychology* 82(6): 878–902.

Frank, D. H. and Obloj, T. 2014. "Firm-specific human capital, organizational incentives, and agency costs: Evidence from retail banking," *Strategic Management Journal* 35(9): 1279–1301.

Frey, B. and Jegen, R. 2001. "Motivational crowding theory," *Journal of Economic Surveys* 15(5): 589–611.

Garcia, S. M. and Tor, A. 2007. "Rankings, standards, and competition: Task vs. scale comparisons," *Organizational Behavior and Human Decision Processes* 102: 95–108.

Garcia, S. M., Tor, A., and Gonzalez, R. D. 2006. "Ranks and rivals: A theory of competition," *Pers. Social Psychology Bulletin* 32(7): 970–982.

Gerhart, B., Rynes, S., and Fulmer, I. 2009. "Pay and performance: Individuals, groups, and executives," *Academy of Management Annals* 3(1): 251–315.

Gill, D., Prowse, V., and Vlassopoulos, M. 2013. "Cheating in the workplace: An experimental study of the impact of bonuses and productivity," *Journal of Economic Behavior & Organization* 96(C): 120–134.

Gino, F., Ayal, S., and Ariely, D. 2009. "Contagion and differentiation in unethical behavior the effect of one bad apple on the barrel," *Psychological Science* 20(3): 393–398.

Gino, F. and Bazerman, M. 2009. "When misconduct goes unnoticed: The acceptability of gradual erosion in others' unethical behavior," *Journal of Experimental Social Psychology* 45(4): 708–719.

Gino, F. and Pierce, L. 2009a. "Dishonesty in the name of equity," *Psychological Science* 20: 1153–1160.

Gino, F. and Pierce, L. 2009b. "The abundance effect: Unethical behavior in the presence of wealth," *Organizational Behavior and Human Decision Processes* 109(2): 142–155.

Gino, F. and Pierce, L. 2010a. "Robin Hood under the hood: Wealth-based discrimination in illicit customer help," *Organ Science* 21(6): 1176–1194.

Gino, F. and Pierce, L. 2010b. "Lying to level the playing field: Why people may dishonestly help or hurt others to create equity," *Journal of Business Ethics* 95(1): 89–103.

Gneezy, U. 2005. "Step-level reasoning and bidding in auctions," *Management Science* 51(11): 1633–1642.

Gneezy, U., Rockenbach, B., and Serra-Garcia, M. 2013. "Measuring lying aversion," *Journal of Economic Behavior & Organization* 93: 293–300.

Gneezy, U. and Rustichini, A. 2004. "Gender and competition at a young age," *American Economic Review Papers & Proceedings* 94(2): 377–381.

Goel, A. and Thakor, A. 2008. "Overconfidence, CEO selection, and corporate governance," *The Journal of Finance* 63(6): 2737–2784.

Gould, E. and Kaplan, T. 2011. "Learning unethical practices from a co-worker: The peer effect of Jose Canseco," *Labour Economics* 18(3): 338–348.

Green, G. A., Uryasz, F. D., Petr, T. A., and Bray, C. D. 2001. "NCAA study of substance use and abuse habits of college student-athletes," *Clinical Journal of Sport Medicine* 11(1): 51–56.

Greenberg, J. 1990. "Employee theft as a reaction to underpayment inequity: The hidden cost of pay cuts," *Journal of Applied Psychology* 75: 561–568.

Greenberg, J. 1993. "Stealing in the name of justice: Informational and interpersonal moderators of theft reactions to underpayment inequity," *Organizational Behavior and Human Decision Processes* 54(1): 81–103.

Groysberg, B. 2012. *Chasing Stars: The Myth of Talent and the Portability of Performance*. Princeton: Princeton University Press.

Groysberg, B., Nanda, A., and Nohria, N. 2004. "The risky business of hiring stars," *Harvard Business Review* 82(5): 92–101.

Gubler, T., Larkin, I., and Pierce, L. 2016. "Motivational spillovers from awards: Crowding out in a multitasking environment," *Organization Science*. Forthcoming.

Gürtler, O. 2008. "On sabotage in collective tournaments," *Journal of Mathematical Economics* 44(3): 383–393.

Hall, B. 2000. "Incentives and controllability: A note and exercise," Harvard Business School Background Note 801–334.

Hamilton, B., Nickerson, J., and Owan, H. 2003. "Team incentives and worker heterogeneity: An empirical analysis of the impact of teams on productivity and participation," *Journal of Political Economy* 111(3): 465–497.

Hertel, G., Niedner, S., and Herrmann, S. 2003. "Motivation of software developers in open source projects: An Internet-based survey of contributors to the Linux kernel," *Research Policy* 32: 1159–1177.

Hitt, M. A., Bierman, L., Shimizu, K., and Kochhar, R. 2001. "Direct and moderating effects of human capital on strategy and performance in professional service firms: A resource-based perspective," *Academy of Management Journal* 44: 13–28.

Hoffman, M. and Morgan, J. 2015. "Who's naughty? Who's nice? Experiments on whether pro-social workers are selected out of cutthroat business environments," *Journal of Economic Behavior & Organization* 109: 173–187.

Holmstrom, B. 1982. "Moral hazard in teams," *The Bell Journal of Economics* 13(2): 324–340.

Holmstrom, B. and Milgrom, P. 1991. "Multitask principal-agent analyses: Incentive contracts, asset ownership, and job design," *Journal of Law, Economics, & Organization* 7: 24–52.

Iranzo, S., Fabiano, S., and Tosetti, E. 2008. "Skill dispersion and firm productivity: An analysis with employer-employee matched data," *Journal of Labor Economics* 26(2): 247–285.

Itoh, H. 1991. "Incentives to help in multi-agent situations," *Econometrica: Journal of the Econometric Society* 59(3): 611–636.

Jensen, M. 2001. "Corporate budgeting is broken, let's fix it," *Harvard Business Review* 79(10): 94–101.

John, L., Loewenstein, G., and Rick, S. 2014. "Cheating more for less: Upward social comparisons motivate the poorly compensated to cheat," *Organizational Behavior and Human Decision Processes* 123(2): 101–109.

Jones, G. and Kavanagh, M. 1996. "An experimental examination of the effects of individual and situational factors on unethical behavioral intentions in the workplace," *Journal of Business Ethics* 15(5): 511–523.

Kandel, E. and Lazear, E. 1992. "Peer pressure and partnerships," *Journal of Political Economy* 100(4): 801–817.

Kern, M. and Chugh, D. 2009. "Bounded ethicality the perils of loss framing," *Psychological Science* 20(3): 378–384.

Kerr, S. 1975. "On the folly of rewarding A, while hoping for B," *Academy of Management Journal* 18(4): 769–783.

Kilduff, G., Elfenbein, H., and Staw, B. 2010. "The psychology of rivalry: A relationally dependent analysis of competition," *Academy of Management Journal* 53: 943–969.

Kouchaki, M. and Desai, S. 2015. "Anxious, threatened, and also unethical: How anxiety makes individuals feel threatened and commit unethical acts," *Journal of Applied Psychology* 100(2): 360.

Kwon, I. and Milgrom, E. 2007. "Status, relative pay, and wage growth: Evidence from M&A," Discussion Papers 07-026, Stanford Institute for Economic Policy Research.

Lado, A. A. and Wilson, M. C. 1994. "Human resource systems and sustained competitive advantage: A competency-based perspective," *Academy of Management Review* 19(4): 699–727.

Larkin, I. 2011. "Paying $30,000 for a gold star: An empirical investigation into the value of peer recognition to software salespeople," Working paper, Harvard Business School.

Larkin, I. 2014. "The cost of high-powered incentives: Employee gaming in enterprise software sales," *Journal of Labor Economics* 32(2): 199–227.

Larkin, I. and Leider, S. 2012. "Incentive schemes, sorting and behavioral biases of employees: Experimental evidence," *American Economic Journal: Microeconomics* 4(2): 184–214.

Larkin, I., Pierce, L., and Gino, F. 2012. "The psychological costs of pay-for-performance: Implications for the strategic compensation of employees," *Strategic Management Journal* 33: 1194–1214.

Lazear, E. 1979. "Why is there mandatory retirement?," *The Journal of Political Economy* 87(6): 1261–1284.

Lazear, E. P. 1989. "Pay equality and industrial politics," *Journal of Political Economy* 97(3): 561–580.

Lazear, E. 2000. "Performance pay and productivity," *American Economic Review* 90(5): 1346–1361.

Lazear, E. and Oyer, P. 2012. "Personnel economics," in Robert Gibbons and John Roberts (eds.), *The Handbook of Organizational Economics*. Princeton: Princeton University Press.

Lazear, E. and Rosen, S. 1981. "Rank-order tournaments as optimum labor contracts," *Journal of Political Economy* 89(5): 841–864.

Lemieux, T., MacLeod, W., and Parent, D. 2007. "Performance pay and wage inequality," *The Quarterly Journal of Economics* 124(1):1–49.

Liu, D., Li, X., and Santhanam, R. 2013. "Digital Games and Beyond: What Happens When Players Compete," *Mis Quarterly* 37(1): 111–124.

Mas, A. and Moretti, E. 2009. "Peers at work," *American Economic Review* 99: 112–145.

Mazar, N. and Ariely, D. 2006. "Dishonesty in everyday life and its policy implications," *Journal of Public Policy and Marketing* 25(1): 117–126.

McGraw, P., Mellers, B. A., and Tetlock, P. E. 2005. "Expectations and emotions of Olympic athletes," *Journal of Experimental Social Psychology* 41(4): 438–446.

Mian, A. and Sufi, A. 2009. The consequences of mortgage credit expansion: Evidence from the US mortgage default crisis. *The Quarterly Journal of Economics* 124(4): 1449–1496.

Moore, C. and Gino, F. 2015. "Approach, ability, aftermath: A psychological process framework of unethical behavior at work," *The Academy of Management Annals* 9(1): 235–289.

Nalebuff, B. and Stiglitz, J. 1983. "Prizes and incentives: Towards a general theory of compensation and competition," *The Bell Journal of Economics* 14(1): 21–43.

Nickerson, J. and Zenger, T. 2008. "Envy, comparison costs, and the economic theory of the firm," *Strategic Management Journal* 29: 1429–1449.

Niederle, M. and Vesterlund, L. 2007. "Do women shy away from competition? Do men compete too much?," *The Quarterly Journal of Economics* 122(3): 1067–1101.

Obloj, T. and Sengul, M. 2012. Incentive life-cycles learning and the division of value in firms. *Administrative Science Quarterly* 57(2): 305–347.

Ordóñez, L., Schweitzer, M., Galinsky, A., and Bazerman, M. 2009. "Goals gone wild: The systematic side effects of overprescribing goal setting," *The Academy of Management Perspectives* 23(1): 6–16.

Oyer, P. 1998. "Fiscal year ends and nonlinear incentive contracts: The effect on business seasonality," *Quarterly Journal of Economics* 113(1): 149–185.

Paarsch, H. J. and Shearer, B. 2000. "Piece rates, fixed wages, and incentive effects: Statistical evidence from payroll records," *International Economic Review* 41(1): 59–62.

Palmer, D. 2012. *Normal Organizational Wrongdoing: A Critical Analysis of Theories of Misconduct in and by Organizations.* Oxford: Oxford University Press.

Palmer, D. and Yenkey, C. B. 2015. "Drugs, sweat, and gears: An organizational analysis of performance-enhancing drug use in the 2010 Tour de France," *Social Forces* 94(2): 891–922.

Pierce, L., Snow, D., and McAfee, A. 2015. "Cleaning house: The impact of information technology on employee corruption and productivity," *Management Science* 61(10): 2299–2319.

Pierce, L. and Snyder, J. 2008. "Ethical spillovers in firms: Evidence from vehicle emissions testing," *Management Science* 54(11): 1891–1903.

Pierce, L. and Snyder, J. 2015. "Unethical demand and employee turnover," *Journal of Business Ethics* 131(4): 853–869.

Prendergast, C. 1999. "The provision of incentives in firms," *Journal of Economic Literature* 37: 7–63.

Rabin, M. 1993. "Incorporating fairness into game theory and economics," *The American Economic Review* 83(5): 1281–1302.

Roy, D. 1952. "Quota restriction and goldbricking in a machine shop," *American Journal of Sociology* 57: 427–442.

Schwieren, C. and Weichselbaumer, D. 2010. "Does competition enhance performance or cheating? A laboratory experiment," *Journal of Economic Psychology* 31(3): 241–253.

Smith-Crowe, K., Tenbrunsel, A. E., Chan-Serafin, S., Brief, A. P., Umphress, E. E., and Joseph, J. 2015. "The ethics 'fix': When formal systems make a difference,"*Journal of Business Ethics* 131(4): 791–801.

Snyder, J. 2010. "Gaming the liver transplant market," *Journal of Law, Economics, & Organization* 26(3): 546–568.

Staw, B. M. 1974. "Attitudinal and behavioral consequences of changing a major organizational reward: A natural field experiment," *Journal of Personality and Social Psychology* 29(6): 742.

Stowe, C. J. and Gilpatric, S. M. 2010. "Cheating and enforcement in asymmetric rank-order tournaments," *Southern Economic Journal* 77 (1): 1–14.

Tang, T. L. P. and Chiu, R. K. 2003. "Income, money ethic, pay satisfaction, commitment, and unethical behavior: Is the love of money the root of evil for Hong Kong employees?," *Journal of Business Ethics* 46(1): 13–30.

Tenbrunsel, A. E. and Smith-Crowe, K. 2008. "13 ethical decision making: Where we've been and where we're going," *The Academy of Management Annals* 2(1): 545–607.

Van den Steen, E. 2005. "Organizational beliefs and managerial vision," *Journal of Law, Economics, and Organization* 21(1): 256–283.

Vaughan-Whitehead, D. 2010. *Fair Wages – Strengthening Corporate Social Responsibility*. Cheltenham: Edward Elgar Publishing.

Vohs, K. D., Mead, N. L., and Goode, M. R. 2006. "The psychological consequences of money," *Science* 314(5802): 1154–1156.

Whittemore, I. C. 1924. "The influence of competition on performance: An experimental study," *The Journal of Abnormal Psychology and Social Psychology* 19(3): 236.

Whittlesey, F. 2006. "The great overpaid CEO debate," *CNET News*, June 1.

Wiltermuth, S. S. 2011. "Cheating more when the spoils are split," *Organizational Behavior and Human Decision Processes* 115(2): 157–168.

Wiltermuth, S. S., Bennett, V., and Pierce, L. 2013. "Doing as they would do: How the perceived ethical preferences of third-party beneficiaries impact ethical decision-making," *Organizational Behavior and Human Decision Processes* 122: 280–290.

Yip, J. A. and Schweitzer, M. 2015. "Mad and misleading: Incidental anger promotes deception," Available at SSRN 2478692.

Zenger, T. 1992. "Why do employers only reward extreme performance? Examining the relationships among performance, pay, and turnover," *Administrative Science Quarterly* 37(2): 198–219.

Zenger, T. 1994. "Explaining organizational diseconomies of scale in R&D: Agency problems and the allocation of engineering talent, ideas, and effort by firm size," *Management Science* 40(6): 708–729.

11 | Beware of organizational saints: how a moral self-concept may foster immoral behavior

BLAKE E. ASHFORTH AND DONALD LANGE

The road to hell is paved with good intentions.

– an often-heard proverb

Organizational sinners – be they "bad apple" individuals or "bad barrel" organizations (Kish-Gephart, Harrison, and Treviño 2010; Treviño and Youngblood 1990) – are hugely problematic for society, exploiting our faith in actors to do the right thing, to respect norms, and to play not only by the letter of the rules but also by the spirit of ethics. However, as devastating as the actions of bad apples and bad barrels are, the silver lining is that society tends to condemn such actors and that, once identified, they can be rooted out.

But what about "organizational saints," the purported good apples and good barrels that society lauds? To be sure, research on such individual-level constructs as moral development and moral identity (Rest 1986; Shao, Aquino, and Freeman 2008) and on such organizational-level constructs as ethical infrastructure and corporate social responsibility (Aguinis and Glavas 2012; Tenbrunsel and Smith-Crowe 2008) suggests that good actors do tend to do good things. Unfortunately, there are also disturbing hints that a moral self-concept[1] – an actor's self-perception of being ethical – can sometimes paradoxically foster *immoral* behavior. For current purposes, we are defining immoral behavior simply as self-interested behavior that intentionally or unintentionally harms others (e.g., causes them pain and

We thank Rachel Balven, Don Palmer, and Kristin Smith-Crowe for their very helpful comments on earlier drafts of this chapter.
[1] We actually prefer the term "moral identity," as identity is often applied to actors at various levels of analysis. However, we opted for "moral self-concept" to avoid confusion with the burgeoning literature on individuals' "moral identity" (see Shao et al. [2008] for a review).

suffering, is unfair to them, treats them with disrespect; Haidt and Bjorklund 2008) in a way that generally would be considered unjustified and inappropriate by third-party observers.

As examples of how a moral self-concept might foster immoral behavior, research suggests that actors are adept at licensing themselves to engage in bad behaviors to the extent they see themselves as generally good (Klotz and Bolino 2013; Merritt, Effron, and Monin 2010), and that a strongly held set of moral convictions may lead actors to pursue preferred ends via means that are considered by others to be harmful (e.g., "tree-spiking," a practice meant to discourage logging and save old-growth forests, but which presents real danger to loggers, has been attributed to the organization Earth First!; Elsbach and Sutton 1992). What is implied by these and other examples that we will draw on here is that a moral self-concept may have a dark side, that "morality is a double-edged sword" (Skitka and Morgan 2009: 370).

Clearly, then, it's important to investigate how a moral self-concept can go awry – how it can facilitate and justify behavior that is widely considered to be unethical. We discuss five related processes through which this moral inversion may occur for individuals and organizations alike. In short, a moral self-concept may: (1) foster an absolutist stance that in turn induces immoral behavior; (2) spur burnout, entailing mistreatment of others; (3) license less moral behavior; (4) foster mindlessness and subsequent moral drift; and (5) trigger efforts to protect and reinforce the self-concept that led to counterintentional effects. *Our fundamental argument is not that a moral self-concept is undesirable, but rather that it is quite fallible, and the more extreme and dominating the moral component of an actor's self-concept, the more potentially problematic it becomes.*

Before we begin, a note on terminology. A set of related constructs has emerged bearing on how actors form, regard, and express their moral predispositions and beliefs. At the individual level, these include moral identity (e.g., Aquino and Reed 2002; Blasi 1984), moral character (e.g., Cohen and Morse 2014), moral foundations (e.g., Graham et al. 2013), moral attentiveness (e.g., Reynolds 2008), moral beliefs or convictions (e.g., Peterson 2003; Skitka 2010), moral certainty (e.g., Shaw, Quezada, and Zárate 2011), moral development (e.g., Kohlberg 1969), and moral integrity or hypocrisy (e.g., Batson et al. 1999; Tomlinson, Lewicki, and Ash 2014). At the organizational level, these constructs include ethical identity (e.g., Berrone, Surroca, and

Tribó 2007), ethical infrastructure (e.g., Tenbrunsel and Smith-Crowe 2008), ethical culture (e.g., Kaptein 2008), ethical climate (e.g., Mayer, Kuenzi, and Greenbaum 2009), corporate social responsibility (e.g., Horrigan 2010), and organizational virtuousness (e.g., Cameron and Winn 2012). We use the term "moral self-concept" as an umbrella to encompass the aspects of these constructs that pertain to how an actor sees itself, recognizing that the notion of "self" is not usually applied to collectives (cf. King, Felin, and Whetten 2010). Whether viewed as a trait/organizational attribute (something an actor has) or a state (something an actor is currently experiencing), a moral self-concept can be primed or made salient by situational cues such as framing a decision in terms of ethics and reminding an actor of prior ethical behaviors, and thereby have a greater impact on the actor's behavior (e.g., Aquino and Freeman 2009; Butterfield, Treviño, and Weaver 2000; Mazar, Amir, and Ariely 2008).

How might a moral self-concept foster immoral behaviors?

For each of the ways in which a moral self-concept may ironically foster immoral behaviors, we discuss both the individual and organizational levels of analysis, using the term "actor" where a particular argument applies to both. Except where noted, we contend that all five processes apply in roughly similar fashion to both levels of analysis; that is, each process can emerge at either level (or both levels) and potentially spread to the other level. How does spreading occur? Kozlowski and Klein (2000: 55) state that a "phenomenon is emergent when it originates in the cognition, affect, behaviors, or other characteristics of individuals, is amplified by their interactions, and manifests as a higher-level, collective phenomenon." Conversely, a phenomenon can originate in the mission, identity, structure, culture, or climate of the organization – including the machinations of top managers on behalf of the organiza-tion – and cascade down or suffuse to the individual level (e.g., Preuss 2010). As with any schema, knowledge (or at least the belief) that moral self-concepts and convictions are shared by others tends to validate and reinforce those qualities for the members of a collective (Flynn and Wiltermuth 2010; Moore and Gino 2013). Thus, at the individual level, members may readily and even unreflectively interna-lize the proffered morals of the collective, and at the collective level, actors may be emboldened by social validation to strongly assert their presumed moral authority.

Because each of the five processes can originate anywhere in the organization and infect multiple levels, no organization is immune to these processes. Indeed, we argue that it is precisely those individuals and organizations that most strongly believe in their own inherent morality that are most susceptible to each of the five processes.

A *moral self-concept may foster an absolutist stance that in turn induces immoral behavior*

[I]dealism has produced the highest body counts of all the roots of evil.

– Baumeister and Vohs (2004: 93)

Actors with a strong moral self-concept are likely to hold steadfast moral beliefs and interpret issues through a moral frame. Those moral beliefs and the resulting moral frame tend to be experienced as objective truths or "absolute standards" of right or wrong that transcend context (van Zomeren, Postmes, and Spears 2012: 55), whereas non-moral beliefs tend to be experienced as relativistic and dependent on the context (Skitka, Bauman, and Sargis 2005). Relative to non-moral beliefs, moral beliefs seem more self-evident to their holder (e.g., defrauding customers is inherently wrong) and are more motivating and self-justifying, more likely to be associated with strong emotions, and more likely to be seen as non-negotiable (Effron and Miller 2012; Skitka, Bauman, and Mullen 2008; Turiel 1998). As Skitka (2010: 267) put it: "To support alternatives to what is 'right,' 'moral,' and 'good' is to be absolutely 'wrong,' 'immoral,' if not evil." Indeed, even entertaining thoughts of compromising one's strongly held moral beliefs is apt to make one feel morally dirty (e.g., Tetlock et al. 2000).

The sense that moral issues are absolute can lead to quixotic stands on principle that may undermine larger moral considerations. Often, complex decisions involve ethical tradeoffs between particular morals, as in a boss–subordinate relationship where the value of impartiality in the business relationship conflicts with the value of partiality in the friendship (Bridge and Baxter 1992). Absolutism may render one unwilling or unable to appreciate the need for considering the larger moral picture.

Absolutism can also foster a lack of compassion or concern for fairness regarding actors on the other side of a perceived moral issue. When moral convictions are violated or even threatened, individuals may experience strong feelings of anger toward the source of the threat (e.g., van Zomeren and Lodewijkx 2005). For example, in a series of experiments, Wright, Cullum, and Schwab (2008) found that believing an issue to be moral fostered intolerance of those espousing discrepant views, and the emotional intensity behind that belief magnified the intolerance. An absolutist stance may thus foster malign discrimination against the intolerable other.

Importantly, because moral beliefs are predicated on a seemingly objective moral code with strong "ought" prescriptions, individuals may be willing to defy group consensus, established norms, organizational rules and procedures, and the dictates of managers if those beliefs are perceived to be threatened (e.g., Hornsey et al. 2003; Mullen and Nadler 2008). Indeed, "strong moral convictions are associated with accepting any means to achieve preferred ends" (Skitka 2010: 278), suggesting the possibility of disregarding the harm caused to others in order to secure moral ends. To be sure, such defiance may serve as a form of positive deviance (e.g., whistle-blowing) – meaning behavior that ultimately enables the organization to remedy dysfunctional and perhaps unethical practices (Spreitzer and Sonenshein 2004). However, because the individual is acting on the basis of his or her own moral convictions, the defiance instead may constitute *negative* deviance, upending order that reasonable observers would regard as morally sound. For example, a manager may harass or fire a subordinate because he disagrees on moral grounds with that person's lifestyle, religion, or sexual orientation.

Just as a moral self-concept may foster intolerance at the individual level, so it may foster intergroup conflict at the collective level. We noted that believing that a moral self-concept is shared tends to validate and reinforce that self-concept. Thus, collectives may be even more inclined to interpret given issues as implicating morals and be even less tolerant of dissent on moral issues. In short, identity-fueled antipathy may well be magnified at the collective level, tipping functional intergroup conflict into harmful misconduct (cf. group polarization; Isenberg 1986). Ashforth and Reingen's (2014) study of an organic food co-op suggests how this might transpire. Core members endorsed the value set of equality, social justice, and peace as guiding principles more strongly than the value set of competition, profit, and success, but both sets were accorded some importance. However, one informal group, dubbed the "idealists" by the researchers, favored the first value set more than did a second informal group, dubbed the "pragmatists," who favored the second value set more than did the idealists. In short, the groups differed only in the emphasis that they gave the two sets. And yet this difference in emphasis caused even minor issues to be interpreted through a moralistic frame, such as whether product placement was a means of increasing sales or an "antagonistic" (p. 489) manipulation of customers.

Once issues were interpreted as moral, they became flashpoints for very bruising and divisive political battles. Members of both groups were routinely upset by the vehemence of the arguments, a vehemence seemingly at odds with the very notion of a "co-op." However, the idealists saw themselves as upholding the moral self-concept of the co-op and, therefore, as occupying the moral high ground. Compared to the pragmatists, the idealists were more likely to describe themselves as "'aggressive,' 'outspoken,' or 'passionate'" (p. 495) in how they advanced their views. Not surprisingly, this self-righteousness greatly perturbed the pragmatists who, after all, also viewed equality, social justice, and peace as the central values of the co-op. After a meeting featuring sharp exchanges between idealists and pragmatists, a pragmatist lamented "being yelled at in a morally superior tone." Another pragmatist complained that idealist members "feel it is they who hold everyone else to ethical practices" (p. 495).

The irony was that both value sets were essential to the long-term welfare of the co-op, and yet the pragmatists were made to feel that their concerns with operational matters such as balanced budgets and employee dress bordered on the immoral. It's not hard to see how the disrespect may have bullied some pragmatists into submission, threatening not only their personal well-being but also that of the co-op.

The perils of self-righteousness. Taking an absolutist stance can easily cause an actor to be seen as claiming moral superiority over less-absolutist actors (Kreps and Monin 2011). Indeed, terms like "self-righteous," "sanctimonious," "holier-than-thou," and "puritanical" are typically used in a derogatory manner, suggesting that observers do not appreciate the implication that they are morally inferior to someone who, perhaps smugly, espouses high moral standards. In the real world, continuously upholding an absolutist moral stance can be difficult or impossible, and inevitably invites scrutiny from critics. As the literature on schadenfreude suggests (Smith 2013), when self-righteous actors unsurprisingly fall short of their espoused ideals, others may take delight in recognizing and publicizing those failures. For instance, given Google's well-known motto of "Don't be evil," many observers have gleefully pointed out various failings of the company (e.g., Foskett 2010).

Further, the literature on self-affirmation theory indicates that actors may respond to attributions of hypocrisy by attempting to reaffirm their moral self-concept, essentially doubling down on the behaviors that led to perceptions of self-righteousness (Sherman and Cohen 2006). The notion of reaction formation is instructive regarding how the resulting tension between one's moral self-concept and temptation may result in self-sabotage in the form of immoral behavior (Baumeister, Dale, and Sommer 1998). When one feels a temptation that is contrary to one's moral self-concept, one may seek to bolster that self-concept so as to suppress the temptation. However, the increased tension may ultimately prove overwhelming such that one gives in; and, like the release of a coiled spring, the expression of that temptation may be dramatic. The fall of televangelist Jimmy Swaggart provides an archetypal example. Swaggart was caught patronizing prostitutes. Wright (1993) argues that the relentless need to publicly uphold the role of moral standard-bearer proved too much for Swaggart. The ongoing suppression of his sexual desires ultimately prompted their exaggerated expression. Wright implies that Swaggart acted as if he *wanted* to be caught so as to end the vicious circle of suppression-compulsion. In short, attributions of hypocrisy, by inducing actors to redouble their commitment to high-minded morals, may ultimately prove self-fulfilling.

The occurrence of sacralization and thus absolutism. Harrison, Ashforth, and Corley (2009) describe the sacralization process through which organizational identities are rendered sacred. Individuals seek meaning in their various social domains, including work. Organizations oblige by providing meaning, as reflected in their central, distinctive, and more or less enduring identities. Finally, the institutional context, such as regulators and educational institutions, legitimates that meaning. An organizational identity that may have begun as an opportunistic and instrumental means of fulfilling a mission comes to define – at a visceral level – the organization and its members. Indeed, the very means through which the identity is fulfilled – strategy, procedures, norms, and so on – may become sacralized by association (Selznick 1957). Means become ends in themselves, the convenient becomes essential, and the instrumental becomes expressive; "*is*, in short, becomes *ought*" (Ashforth and Vaidyanath 2002: 365, their emphasis). In other words, identities and the means through which they are enacted are seen in terms of good and right rather than efficient and effective. Similarly, individuals come to regard their core, distinctive, and more or less enduring qualities as important precisely because they are self-defining. Thus, the goals and behavioral routines that signify those qualities also tend to become moral ends in themselves – proxies for the identity itself. The result is a set of qualities that are rendered sacred and thus inviolable.

What this means is that sacralization creates many more opportunities for moral absolutism to occur, along with the immoral behaviors chronicled above. This is perhaps most evident in the phenomenon of willful ignorance, where individuals or collectives choose not to accept (or be exposed to) overwhelming evidence that is contrary to their fundamental belief systems (cf. Ehrich and Irwin 2005). An example is Holocaust deniers, who ignore clear and compelling evidence of the Holocaust in order to maintain their particular worldview (Lipstadt 1993). We argue that it is because their worldview has been rendered sacred – and thus moralized – that Holocaust deniers are so vehement in ignoring the evidence. In short, data and change that threaten a sacralized identity may be resisted, even if resistance entails immoral action.

In sum, a moral self-concept may increase the likelihood that a given issue is perceived through a moral lens, encouraging an absolutist stance. Such a stance may in turn foster quixotic stands on principle that may undermine larger moral considerations, intolerance and harm toward actors holding different views, a willingness to engage in immoral means to reach moral ends, self-sabotage via immoral behavior, and resistance to anything that threatens a sacralized identity – even if that resistance entails immoral behavior.

A moral self-concept may foster burnout, entailing mistreatment of others

Even if an actor is not absolutist about a given set of morals, attempting to honor a moral self-concept may foster burnout, meaning the combined state of being exhausted, having a distant attitude toward the tasks at hand and individuals involved (cynicism), and having degraded efficacy in performing those tasks (Maslach, Schaufeli, and Leiter 2001). Bandura (1999: 206) wrote that, "Most everyone is virtuous at the abstract level." However, inevitable and ongoing pressures – including role conflicts, role overload, resource constraints, time squeezes, and peer pressure – can impede an actor's ability to align behavior with moral values. The messy reality of struggling with these ongoing pressures puts virtue to the test.

Pooler (2011), for example, describes the moral challenges faced by pastors. Communities, congregations, and pastors themselves have high expectations of pastoral rectitude and competence. Pastors, who are only human, often struggle to live up to their lofty occupational identity. Moreover, like those in many helping professions (Siebert and Siebert 2007), pastors tend to have difficulty seeking help as they are expected to have the internal resources to transcend the obstacles that cause "lesser" individuals to seek help. Denying their own need for help, they may redouble their efforts in order to fulfill their duties, doing more of the same behavior that proved debilitating in the first place. Indeed, the burnout literature suggests that it is precisely those actors who most identify with the implied moral code of their role – those with strong moral self-concepts – that are most at risk (Maslach 1982); they become exhausted by constantly attempting to fulfill the high-minded image they have of themselves.

Relatedly, research on doctors in the military (Howe 1986), salespeople working in unethical climates (Eichenwald 1995), and ethical companies doing business in nations with high corruption (Donaldson and Dunfee 1999), documents the difficulty that actors have honoring their moral self-concepts in contexts that do not value those self-concepts as highly. Further, exercising moral self-control consumes psychological and social resources (Muraven, Tice, and Baumeister 1998), which may deplete an actor's ability to withstand situational demands and even the actor's own temptations. The gulf, then, between the moral aspirations embodied in a moral self-concept and the demands and constraints of the context in which the actor operates (aggravated by the actor's own darker desires) may foster exhaustion.

A sense of exhaustion has been found to cause or reinforce the other two aspects of burnout, namely cynicism and degraded efficacy (e.g., Toppinen-Tanner, Kalimo, and Mutanen 2002). At the individual level, exhaustion may thus be associated with such dubious behaviors as treating others as if they were interchangeable numbers rather than people and cutting ethical corners (Maslach 1982; Swider and Zimmerman 2010). A police officer stated:

> When you first get on the job ... you look for ways to help. But then you grow weary. After a few years, when you see an old lady with a flat tire, you turn your head the other way when you ride by, and hope you don't get caught. (Rachlin 1991: 300)

While exhaustion has seldom been studied at the collective level (see Rumbles and Rees [2013] for one exception), "organizational exhaustion" likely exists as both an aggregation of individuals' exhaustion (due to common demands, perhaps magnified by emotional contagion) and as the exhaustion of the collective itself. Organizational analogs to the individual-level dubious behaviors include an institutionalized disregard for clients and taking ethical shortcuts, such as the widespread neglect of patients at Veterans Affairs facilities (e.g., Dooley 2014).

In sum, a moral self-concept predisposes an actor to exhaustion because it entails a moral code that may be difficult to uphold in the face of role conflicts, role overload, resource constraints, and so on. In turn, exhaustion has been found to foster cynicism toward tasks and others and decreased efficacy. The upshot is that actors may come to act in immoral ways toward precisely those tasks and other individuals that they once took pride in serving well.

A *moral self-concept may license less moral behavior*

Research on moral licensing indicates that individuals seek to balance their moral self-concept with the costs of maintaining that self-concept (Sachdeva, Iliev, and Medin 2009). Moral behavior, after all, often entails self-sacrifice. Thus, when individuals view themselves and are viewed by others as relatively moral, they tend to reduce their moral behavior, and conversely, when they view themselves and are viewed by others as less moral, they tend to increase their moral behavior. As Zhong et al. (2010: 329) put it, "Individuals can tell themselves (and others), 'Although I've just chosen the self-interested action, I was very ethical previously, so I am not a horrible person.'" Or, more succinctly, "being good frees us to be bad" (Merritt et al. 2010: 344; see Klotz and Bolino [2013] for an application to organizations). For example,

Sachdeva et al. (2009) had individuals write a brief story about themselves that included a set of positive (e.g., caring, generous), neutral (e.g., book, keys), or negative words (e.g., disloyal, greedy). Participants were later asked to role play being a plant manager. Participants primed to think of themselves positively decided to emit more pollution (in order to save money) than participants in the neutral condition. Participants primed to think of themselves negatively chose to emit less pollution. In short, prosocial self-attributions provide a moral license (Monin and Miller 2001) to behave less morally, and antisocial attributions motivate moral cleansing by behaving more morally, at least until the scale is back in balance.[2]

A similar logic has been used to explain employee theft and deviance (i.e., "metaphor of the ledger," Hollinger [1991]; see also Pillutla's [2011] compensatory model of ethical behavior). For example, the most common rationalization offered by hospital nurses for their theft of supplies was that the goods were a "fringe benefit" that had presumably been earned (Dabney 1995: 320).

Distressingly, research suggests that simply imagining doing good (Khan and Dhar 2006), imagining *not* doing bad (Miller and Effron 2010), or expressing prosocial intentions (Tanner and Carlson 2009) may license more hedonistic behavior. In other words, hypothetical thoughts of being good – even if unanchored to reality – may provide a license for less moral behavior. Similarly, the good deeds of others with whom one identifies (e.g., fellow group members; Kouchaki 2011) also appear to let one off the moral hook. Thus, the good deeds of one's peers, subunit, or organization may license one's bad deeds, suggesting a cross-level effect. All of these studies underscore the ease with which a patina of morality can seduce individuals into doing bad. Further, even acts ostensibly intended to forestall bad behavior may actually have the effect of licensing it. In an experimental study, Cain, Loewenstein, and Moore (2005) found that disclosure of a conflict of interest led to advice that was *more* biased than when the conflict was

[2] Scholars disagree on whether moral licensing is better understood as moral credentialing, where one's moral self-concept remains intact ("Because I'm a good person this behavior can't really be that bad and does not reflect who I am"), or moral crediting, where good and bad behavior are analogous to deposits and withdrawals from a bank account ("Because I have done good I have earned the right to do bad"; see Merritt et al. 2010). We see these explanations as complementary – "two independent routes to licensing" (Miller and Effron 2010: 128) – rather than competing.

not disclosed. The authors argued that disclosure allowed advisors to feel that they had properly warned their clients, giving them the moral license to then provide biased advice. Finally, consistent with self-affirmation theory, doing bad in one social domain or against one particular actor may be psychologically redressed by compensatory behavior in another domain or for another actor (Zhong, Liljenquist, and Cain 2009). For example, the threat to one's moral self-concept caused by stealing goods from one's employer may be countered by donating time to a volunteer cause. Note, however, that the latter behavior in no way repairs the damage caused to one's employer.

Because collectives, like individuals, can be said to have moral self-concepts, moral licensing is also likely to apply at the collective level. However, we are aware of only one relevant study; in support of the licensing thesis, Ormiston and Wong (2013) found that corporate social responsibility during a two-year span predicted corporate social *irresponsibility* during the subsequent two-year span. Moreover, the researchers found evidence of a cross-level effect. Specifically, the licensing effect was stronger for organizations with CEOs high on "moral identity symbolization" (Aquino and Reed 2002), that is, CEOs whose behavior reflects their moral self-concept. Ormiston and Wong argue that such CEOs are more cognizant of their moral reputation and thus know when they can afford to indulge in less moral behavior.

Although research on moral licensing provides compelling evidence that previous moral behavior can lead to less moral behavior, that is, a *compensatory* effect, countervailing research on moral identity suggests that such an identity predicts *more* moral behavior, that is, a *consistency* effect (see a review by Shao et al. 2008). Why the difference? Our take is that the stronger and more salient one's moral self-concept – that is, the more central it is to one's sense of self and the more relevant it's seen to be in a given situation – the less likely one is to engage in licensing *if* the behavior will jeopardize one's moral self-concept (whether in one's own eyes or in others'; cf. Pillutla 2011). In other words, individuals are more protective of a strong and salient moral self-concept, predisposing them to consistency. As Miller and Effron (2010: 130) put it, "individuals who place a high value on morality ... may not allow themselves to deviate much from the straight and narrow path."

This is good news. However, there is a very important proviso to consider. Actors have a well-documented facility for rationalizing away behavior that threatens their moral self-concept (e.g., Bandura 1999; Moore et al. 2012; Tenbrunsel and Messick 2004). Examples of common rationalizations in organizational contexts include denial of responsibility (e.g., "management ordered us to do it"), denial of injury (e.g., "no one was harmed very much"), denial of victim (e.g., "they had it coming to them"), and appeal to higher loyalties (e.g., a police officer lying in court to convict someone she believes is guilty; Ashforth and Anand 2003; Robinson and Kraatz 1998). The result is that "corrupt [actors] tend not to view themselves as corrupt" (Ashforth and Anand 2003: 15). Such rationalizations weaken the consistency effect, enabling actors to deviate somewhat from even central and salient moral self-concepts.

In sum, good behavior may provide a moral license for actors to subsequently indulge in bad behavior. However, licensing may only occur if the bad behavior is experienced by the actor as *not* reflecting poorly on a strong and salient moral self-concept. That said, actors tend to be quite facile at rationalizing away behavior that threatens a moral self-concept, enabling them to engage in behaviors that a reasonable outsider would regard as immoral.

A moral self-concept may foster mindlessness and subsequent moral drift

Scholars have argued that moral awareness is a necessary antecedent of moral decisions and actions (e.g., Butterfield et al. 2000; Jones 1991; Rest 1986). Because a moral self-concept sensitizes an actor to moral issues, it's likely to be associated with moral awareness. However, given that individuals tend to see themselves as more ethical than others (Tenbrunsel 1998), they are likely to assume that they are basically "a good person." This assumption feeds a "goodness heuristic" where they seem to conclude: "Because I'm a good person, I can trust myself to do the right thing." It seems likely that this heuristic will be particularly pronounced for actors with a strong moral self-concept. The goodness heuristic inoculates individuals against reflecting very deeply on the ethical implications of their decisions and actions. Further, the presumption of goodness facilitates rationalizations for any troubling thoughts that may break through.

Additionally, moral awareness may become less frequent the more an individual enacts a particular role. Roles are associated with recurring actions, problems, and decisions, such that cognitive and behavioral scripts tend to develop that reduce the need to think deeply about those issues (Ashforth and Fried 1988; Martin, Kish-Gephart, and Detert 2014). The resulting "mindlessness" tends to dim awareness on all fronts, including moral awareness (Ashforth and Anand 2003; Martin et al. 2014; Palmer 2012). Mindlessness is facilitated in contexts that obscure moral cues, such as when one's peers do not raise moral red flags, and the potential harm to others is not large, obvious, immediate, or probable, or is concentrated in only a few actors (Jones 1991).

Absent ongoing moral reflection, individuals tend to gravitate to decisions and actions that favor their self-interests (Murnighan, Cantelon, and Elyashiv 2001). The result may be "moral drift" (cf. Moore and Gino 2013; Sabini and Silver 1978), where an erstwhile ethically oriented individual gradually shifts to more ethically questionable decisions and actions. Our key point is that believing oneself to be morally sound may liberate one to drift from the moral set-point. Much like a hiker who, confident in her sense of direction, fails to consult her compass, it is easy to gradually drift away from one's moral "true north" without actively realizing it (cf. Moore and Gino 2013; Palmer 2012). For instance, Magdalene (2012: 23) describes "seemingly unimportant decisions" that gradually led an otherwise ethical financial planner down a slippery slope of increasingly unethical behavior. The first such decision occurred when a friend said that someone she knew might become the state treasurer for Oklahoma and, if so, that she'd become a bond trader under the treasurer and could direct business his way: would he be interested? When he assented, she said she would expect a share of his commissions. "I suggested she first get her friend elected to office, and then we'd talk ... not a big commitment to anything on my end, right?" (p. 29). Although he knew kickbacks were illegal, "My emotional mind said why not, you haven't done anything yet." With that "baby step" (p. 29), the slide began. Each subsequent decision was seemingly unimportant because the financial planner, buoyed by rationalizations, failed to actively process how the decision pushed him further off an ethical course (see also Welsh et al. 2015).

It seems likely that mindlessness and moral drift may also occur within collectives, including the organization. Janis's (1982: 174) model of groupthink includes an "unquestioned belief in the group's inherent morality," where groups develop a reflexive and usually tacit assumption of their inherent goodness. In organizational settings, signals of morality such as a formal code of ethics and ethical training may lull organizational members into assuming the ends they pursue, and the means through which they pursue them, are inherently moral. The "unquestioned" nature of the assumption reduces moral awareness, allowing moral issues to be recast as simply business, legal, or technical issues. Ford's infamous decision regarding the Pinto provides an example (Gioia 1992). Ford marketed the Pinto even after determining that it had a design flaw that greatly increased the likelihood that the vehicle would burst into flames in a relatively slow-speed rear-end collision. At the time, decisions-makers within Ford treated the problem as a business calculation and not as a moral problem. Absent moral awareness, it becomes relatively easy for moral drift to occur.

Further, akin to the moral licensing argument, Godfrey (2005: 778) argues that an organization's "moral capital can provide shareholders with 'insurance-like' protection." To the extent that an organization's ethical infrastructure and/or prior moral behavior have earned it a positive reputation and goodwill, external stakeholders may be inclined to give the organization the benefit of the doubt (Harrison et al. 2009; cf. Coombs and Holladay 2006). Similarly, organizational members who identify with their organization and its ethical infrastructure are inclined, at least initially, to believe in the inherent goodness of the organization and thus adduce rationalizations in the face of immoral behavior (Martin et al. 2014). Accordingly, if an organization begins to drift from its moral moorings, external and internal stakeholders alike may be slow to notice and react, thereby abetting the drift.

In sum, while moral awareness is a necessary antecedent of moral actions, actors' assumptions of their own inherent goodness tend to dim such awareness and facilitate rationalizations for any troubling thoughts that may occur. Also, repeated role enactments tend to further dim moral awareness. Absent moral awareness, actors may drift toward self-interested actions, recasting moral issues as business, legal, or technical issues. Finally, this moral drift may be enabled by the willingness of stakeholders to believe in the actor's inherent goodness.

Efforts to protect and reinforce a moral self-concept may lead to counterintentional effects

Individuals or organizations that wish to protect and reinforce a moral self-concept – that aspire to specific moral standards and a high level of ethical behavior – will seek to control themselves. Individuals will try to control their thoughts and actions, and organizations will try to control processes and outcomes. At the individual level, Wegner (1994) describes mental control as involving two processes – an intentional operating process that searches the mind for evidence of the desired state (e.g., eating properly in accordance with a weight-loss diet) and a monitoring process that searches for evidence of failure (e.g., cravings for fattening food not on the diet). The operating process often dominates, leading to control as intended. But at times, and especially under conditions of stress or high cognitive load, the search for failure entailed by monitoring can dominate and actually prompt failure by bringing counterintentional thoughts into consciousness. Mental control, therefore, can involve *ironic processes*, meaning that the very attempts to exercise control may work against the effectiveness of the control (Wegner 1994). For example, it may be difficult to fall asleep if one starts thinking and worrying about not sleeping.

Ironic processes may undermine attempts to be a good person. In particular, researchers have demonstrated that the desire to control one's own prejudice can lead to counterintentional effects (Macrae et al. 1994, 1996). As one strives not to act according to negative stereotypes (based on, e.g., racial categories, nationality, religion, sexual orientation, gender), one works to "marshall appropriate thoughts and quell inappropriate ones repeatedly in daily life" (Wegner 1994: 46). By priming the unwanted thoughts, the monitoring process can make those thoughts especially accessible in the mind, reinforcing unwanted prejudicial attitudes (cf. Monteith, Spicer, and Tooman 1998). Wegner (1994: 34) states that, "According to this idea, the ironies of mental life are not just happenstance examples of the frailty of human endeavors but rather are logically entailed by the nature of mental control."

We draw a rough analogy between the ironic processes of mental control and organizational control efforts. An organization that aspires to be morally good in processes and outcomes will attempt to implement controls that ensure those ends. Our central argument is that inherent in those approaches – both social/cultural and administrative (Lange 2008) – that organizations use to maintain high moral standards are processes that work against the success of those approaches. The ironies of organizational efforts to protect and reinforce a collective moral self-concept are not just due to the faulty or clumsy implementation of those efforts, but rather are entailed by their very nature.

To consider how organizational controls on bad behavior might sow the seeds of their own ineffectiveness, we note that those controls are based on certain assumptions (Dukerich, Lange, and Huber 2005). These assumptions may contain internal contradictions, or they may conflict with the assumptions underlying other controls that the organization is relying on concurrently. Following are some of the assumptions that underlie controls that organizations use to maintain high moral standards (Dukerich et al. 2005).

Individuals will play within the rules. Controls that attempt to reduce employee autonomy to engage in bad behavior must implicitly or explicitly define the rules of acceptable behavior, and it's assumed that organizational members will adhere to those rules. It could also be thought by members, though, that a highly defined system of rules implicitly condones unethical behavior that is not officially proscribed or that is not subject to detection (cf. Anteby 2013). A related assumption is that not all people play within the rules, and that for those people, a clear understanding of the rules effectively establishes the roadmap for bad behavior.

Individuals will infer and internalize the values underlying the organizational rules and reinforcement systems. Bad behavior by and within the organization might effectively be stemmed if organizational members are vigilant about monitoring their surroundings and behaviors for unethical processes and outcomes. Such vigilance could result if individuals extrapolate from the organizational rules and from the reward and punishment systems the values that underlie those control systems, and then adopt a commitment to pursue those values. An alternative assumption is that, given a set of rules and reward and punishment systems, individuals will learn how to achieve their outcomes within those systems, but that the efforts to adhere to rules, receive rewards, and avoid punishments will in fact divert individuals' attention from understanding and adopting the values underlying those control systems. As Martin et al. (2014: 310) put it:

> When individuals believe they work in a strong ethical environment, they may be less likely to "decide" what is ethical in a conscious manner and instead rely on organizational norms, assuming that the bounds of

ethicality have already been decided (Tenbrunsel et al. [Tenbrunsel, Smith-Crowe, and Umphress], 2003) and that the organization's procedures and formal systems are sufficient checks against unethical behavior.

Further, as Merton (1968) observed, organizations that maintain a strict focus on following established rules lead employees to view the rules as ends in themselves. Thus, codifying morality may induce individuals to attend to the letter of the rules as the arbiter of right and wrong rather than internalize the spirit of the rules (the implied values underlying the rules). For example, in a series of prisoner's dilemma experiments, participants experiencing weak sanctions cooperated less than participants experiencing *no* sanctions. The very existence of sanctions implicitly encouraged participants to think in terms not of ethical principles but of a cost–benefit trade-off – to consider simply whether the risk of the weak punishment is worth the reward from not cooperating (Tenbrunsel and Messick 1999).

Individuals who understand and adopt the values underlying organizational control systems will watch out for bad behavior in the organization. An alternative assumption is that, even if individuals have internalized organizational values, organizational security and monitoring systems can cause individuals to be lax about the monitoring of others simply because they assume that those systems make it difficult for others to misbehave. Individuals may recognize that certain others might be prone to unethical or illegal behavior and assume that the control systems have eliminated relevant opportunities. So, individuals may not be concerned that the bank vault is left open, for example, because they assume that any fellow employee attempting to steal will most certainly be caught. Interestingly, lax monitoring of others could also result if individuals operate under the strong assumption that no other members are in fact willing to engage in illegal or unethical behavior. Organizational social control systems that aim for high convergence between individual and organizational values can foster that strong assumption. Thus, even if the bank vault door were left wide open, the strongly socialized employee might assume that "it's inconceivable that anyone here would ever steal from the organization," and therefore deem it unnecessary to watch others for signs of bad behavior.

Individuals will not resent the organization's attempts to control them or, even if there is some resentment, it will not be manifested in bad behavior. An alternative assumption is that some individuals will resent and react conversely to organizational attempts to restrict their autonomy or to manipulate their behavior through reward and punishment systems or other social processes. Organizational attempts to control individual behavior may result in distrust and retaliation, or in "reactance," whereby even an individual predisposed to act consistently with organizational expectations acts contrarily in an attempt to preserve autonomy and express attitudinal freedom (Brehm and Brehm 1981; Nail, Van Leeuwen, and Powell 1996; Ouchi 1979). Further, and quite apart from individuals' affective responses to reward and punishment systems, individuals respond to incentive systems in complex ways that are not easily anticipated by the designers of those systems. Unintended consequences are perhaps the rule rather than the exception, given organizational incentive systems. For instance, stock-based incentives for CEOs, designed to align the CEO's interests with those of the shareholders, may have the unintended effect of promoting CEO misconduct such as earnings manipulation (Zhang et al. 2008).

In sum, the notion of ironic processes suggests that, at the individual level, one's attempts to control one's unethical thoughts and actions may paradoxically prime those thoughts, and sometimes undermine the effectiveness of the control. At the organizational level, attempts to control unethical behavior may actually exacerbate it by: (1) implicitly condoning behavior that is not officially proscribed or detectable; (2) diverting attention from ethical values to rules, rewards, and punishments (and therefore how to game the system); (3) encouraging individuals to assume that others will behave ethically, reducing their own vigilance; and (4) encouraging resentment and reactance against the constraints on their autonomy.

Bringing it all together

Research indicates that good actors tend to do good things (e.g., Aguinis and Glavas 2012; Shao et al. 2008). However, we have argued here that, "organizational saints" nonetheless bear scrutiny, as it is precisely their high-minded moral self-concepts that may lead them to behave immorally. As summarized in Table 11.1, we described five overlapping processes through which a moral self-concept may foster immoral behavior – processes that can emerge at the individual or organizational level of analysis and spread to the other. The result is a system where individuals and the organizational context within

Table 11.1 *How a moral self-concept may foster immoral behaviors*

A moral self-concept may foster an absolutist stance that in turn induces immoral behavior	A moral self-concept entails beliefs that may be held as absolute standards or "objective truths" that are non-negotiable. Thus, a moral self-concept may lead to: • quixotic stands on principle that undermine larger moral considerations • intolerance and harm toward actors holding divergent views • a willingness to engage in immoral means to obtain moral ends • self-sabotage via immoral behavior • resistance to whatever threatens a sacralized identity even if it entails immoral behavior
A moral self-concept may foster burnout, entailing mistreatment of others	The high standards implied by a moral self-concept can conflict with real-world pressures. Thus, a moral self-concept: • predisposes one to burnout because of the difficulty of maintaining an uncompromising moral code in the face of such pressures as role conflicts, role overload, and peer pressure 　• burnout entails cynical behavior toward the task and others and decreased efficacy for doing good
A moral self-concept may license less moral behavior	A moral self-concept may be difficult to fulfill and maintain, seeming to entail considerable self-sacrifice. Thus, a moral self-concept: • may promote a license for less desirable behavior, as actors seek to balance their moral self-concept with the costs of maintaining it 　• however, this is less likely if such behavior is perceived to jeopardize a strong and salient moral self-concept 　• that said, actors are facile at rationalizing away behavior that threatens their moral self-concept

Table 11.1 (*cont.*)

A moral self-concept may foster mindlessness and subsequent moral drift	Moral awareness is a necessary antecedent of moral action. However: • actors tend to see themselves as more ethical than others, such that they assume their actions are inherently moral; a moral self-concept can contribute to that assumption • the resulting goodness heuristic lessens moral awareness • with repeated role enactment, moral awareness further dims • absent moral awareness, actors may drift toward self-interested actions, and moral issues can be easily and unwittingly recast as business, legal, or technical issues • moral drift may be enabled by others' belief in the actor's inherent goodness
Efforts to protect and reinforce a moral self-concept may lead to counterintentional effects	Actors wishing to protect and reinforce a moral self-concept will seek to control their own behavior. However: • the control systems themselves – whether they be cognitive control functions or organizational social/culture and administrative approaches to maintain high moral standards – can involve processes that work against the effectiveness of those controls • the act of monitoring one's own thoughts and behavior for signs of immorality may prime unwanted immoral thoughts and reinforce unwanted, immoral attitudes • at the organizational level, assumptions that underpin efforts to control bad behavior may contain internal contradictions, or they may conflict with the assumptions underlying other controls that the organization is relying on concurrently. Those contradictions and conflicts may lead to the belief that bad behavior is being controlled, when it is not

which they are embedded may mutually reinforce immoral behavior, even while the relevant actors laud the morality of that system.

The overarching theme to the five processes is, we believe, the perils of *identity extremism and exclusivity*. Identity, for good reason, is conceived in organizational studies to be a positive force (Albert and Whetten 1985; Riketta 2005; Roberts and Dutton 2009). An identity provides a situated definition of self for the individual ("This is who I am") and organization ("This is who we are"), which in turn helps provide security, purpose, and direction. However, when an identity far is taken by the actor to be an end in itself (extremism) and is so central to the definition of self that it dominates or renders other identities far less salient (exclusivity), it can set in motion processes that ultimately undermine its own efficacy and legitimacy. This is because each actor is essentially "a parliament of selves" (Weick 1995: 18, quoting George Herbert Mead), that is, a complex being with multiple identities, each of which adds diversity and nuance to how that actor views and acts in the world. No single identity – including a moral self-concept – can provide the multiple perspectives, richness, and internal debates that are the hallmark of the "practical wisdom" (Schwartz and Sharpe 2006: 377) that is needed to effectively engage a complex, dynamic, and ambiguous world. For example, a soldier's moral self-concept may urge him/her to be caring and forgiving toward a poorly performing platoon member, whereas the identity of the platoon may instead urge him/her to display tough love. Absent the practical wisdom borne of diverse identities, one's moral self-concept may insist on a solution in a particular context that only makes matters worse.

A moral self-concept is particularly susceptible to extremism and exclusivity precisely because it provides overarching principles for engagement during turbulent times where ambiguity, change, and moral relativism are common. As such, it can function like a powerful beacon, overriding other lights and blinding the actor (cf. organizational orthodoxy; Hogg 2007). But it is exactly in turbulent times that practical wisdom is most needed. The upshot of an extreme and exclusive moral self-concept, then, is the set of dynamics we have discussed: an absolutist stance that fosters immoral behavior, burnout entailing mistreatment of others, the licensing of immoral means, moral drift because one's goodness is taken for granted, and ironic self-defeating processes.

Paradoxically, people seem to intuitively grasp the dangers of a pronounced moral self-concept. That's why, as noted, terms such as "self-righteous," "sanctimonious," "holier-than-thou," "puritanical," and "extremist" are viewed as pejorative. We hold up organizational saints as role models of rectitude, even as we are wary of what that rectitude may bring.

In closing, our fundamental argument is decidedly *not* that a moral self-concept is undesirable. As we noted at the outset, research indicates that individuals and organizations that view themselves as essentially good do tend to honor that identity by doing good things. Our argument is that a moral self-concept, like any identity, is inherently myopic in that it necessarily has a bounded purview. The stronger and more exclusive the actor's moral self-concept, the more susceptible is the actor to the various dynamics summarized in Table 11.1. Ironically, it is precisely because of the self-perception of goodness that a moral self-concept predisposes the actor to overreach in the self-justifying name of morality.

References

Aguinis, H. and Glavas, A. 2012. "What we know and don't know about corporate social responsibility: A review and research agenda," *Journal of Management* 38: 932–968.

Albert, S. and Whetten, D. A. 1985. "Organizational identity," *Research in Organizational Behavior* 7: 263–295.

Anteby, M. 2013. *Manufacturing Morals: The Values of Silence in Business School Education.* Chicago: University of Chicago Press.

Aquino, K. and Freeman, D. 2009. "Moral identity in business situations: A social-cognitive framework for understanding moral functioning," in D. Narvaez and D. K. Lapsley (eds.), *Personality, Identity, and Character: Explorations in Moral Psychology*: 375–395. Cambridge, UK: Cambridge University Press.

Aquino, K. and Reed, A., II. 2002. "The self-importance of moral identity," *Journal of Personality and Social Psychology* 83: 1423–1440.

Ashforth, B. E. and Anand, V. 2003. "The normalization of corruption in organizations," *Research in Organizational Behavior* 25: 1–52.

Ashforth, B. E. and Fried, Y. 1988. "The mindlessness of organizational behaviors," *Human Relations* 41: 305–329.

Ashforth, B. E. and Reingen, P. H. 2014. "Functions of dysfunction: Managing the dynamics of an organizational duality in a natural food cooperative," *Administrative Science Quarterly* 59: 474–516.

Ashforth, B. E. and Vaidyanath, D. 2002. "Work organizations as secular religions," *Journal of Management Inquiry* 11: 359–370.

Bandura, A. 1999. "Moral disengagement in the perpetration of inhumanities," *Personality and Social Psychology Review* 3: 193–209.

Batson, C. D., Thompson, E. R., Seuferling, G., Whitney, H., and Strongman, J. A. 1999. "Moral hypocrisy: Appearing moral to oneself without being so," *Journal of Personality and Social Psychology* 77: 525–537.

Baumeister, R. F., Dale, K., and Sommer, K. L. 1998. "Freudian defense mechanisms and empirical findings in modern social psychology: Reaction formation, projection, displacement, undoing, isolation, sublimation, and denial," *Journal of Personality* 66: 1081–1124.

Baumeister, R. F. and Vohs, K. D. 2004. "Four roots of evil," in A. G. Miller (ed.), *The Social Psychology of Good and Evil*: 85–101. New York: Guilford Press.

Berrone, P., Surroca, J., and Tribó, J. A. 2007. "Corporate ethical identity as a determinant of firm performance: A test of the mediating role of stakeholder satisfaction," *Journal of Business Ethics* 76: 35–53.

Blasi, A. 1984. "Moral identity: Its role in moral functioning," in W. M. Kurtines and J. L. Gewirtz (eds.), *Morality, Moral Behavior, and Moral Development*: 128–139. New York: Wiley.

Brehm, S. S. and Brehm, J. W. 1981. *Psychological Reactance: A Theory of Freedom and Control*. New York: Academic Press.

Bridge, K. and Baxter, L. A. 1992. "Blended relationships: Friends as work associates," *Western Journal of Communication* 56: 200–225.

Butterfield, K. D., Treviño, L. K., and Weaver, G. R. 2000. "Moral awareness in business organizations: Influences of issue-related and social context factors," *Human Relations* 53: 981–1018.

Cain, D. M., Loewenstein, G., and Moore, D. A. 2005. "The dirt on coming clean: Perverse effects of disclosing conflicts of interest," *Journal of Legal Studies* 34: 1–25.

Cameron, K. and Winn, B. 2012. "Virtuousness in organizations," in K. S. Cameron and G. M. Spreitzer (eds.), *The Oxford Handbook of Positive Organizational Scholarship*: 231–243. Oxford, UK: Oxford University Press.

Cohen, T. R. and Morse, L. 2014. "Moral character: What it is and what it does," *Research in Organizational Behavior* 34: 43–61.

Coombs, W. T. and Holladay, S. J. 2006. "Unpacking the halo effect: Reputation and crisis management," *Journal of Communication Management* 10: 123–137.

Dabney, D. 1995. "Neutralization and deviance in the workplace: Theft of supplies and medicines by hospital nurses," *Deviant Behavior* 16: 313–331.

Donaldson, T. and Dunfee, T. W. 1999. "When ethics travel: The promise and peril of global business ethics," *California Management Review* 41(4): 45–63.

Dooley, E. 2014. "Veterans Affairs scandal: What you need to know," *abcnews. com*. May 29. Available from http://abcnews.go.com/Politics/veterans-adminstration-scandal/story?id=23914029 [Accessed: July 27, 2015].

Dukerich, J. M., Lange, D. A., and Huber, G. P. 2005. *Ironic Processes in Organizational Corruption Control*. Paper presented at the Ethics and the Corporate Environment symposium at the National Academy of Management Meetings, Honolulu, HI.

Effron, D. A. and Miller, D. T. 2012. "How the moralization of issues grants social legitimacy to act on one's attitudes," *Personality and Social Psychology Bulletin* 38: 690–701.

Ehrich, K. R. and Irwin, J. R. 2005. "Willful ignorance in the request for product attribute information," *Journal of Marketing Research* 42: 266–277.

Eichenwald, K. 1995. *Serpent on the Rock*. New York: HarperBusiness.

Elsbach, K. D. and Sutton, R. I. 1992. "Acquiring organizational legitimacy through illegitimate actions: A marriage of institutional and impression management theories," *Academy of Management Journal* 35: 699–738.

Flynn, F. J. and Wiltermuth, S. S. 2010. "Who's with me? False consensus, brokerage, and ethical decision making in organizations," *Academy of Management Journal* 53: 1074–1089.

Foskett, S. 2010. "Google's evil buzz is building," *siliconANGLE*. February 17. Available from http://siliconangle.com/blog/2010/02/17/googles-evil-buzz-is-building/ [Accessed: January 6, 2015].

Gioia, D. A. 1992. "Pinto fires and personal ethics: A script analysis of missed opportunities," *Journal of Business Ethics* 11: 379–389.

Godfrey, P. C. 2005. "The relationship between corporate philanthropy and shareholder wealth: A risk management perspective," *Academy of Management Review* 30: 777–798.

Graham, J., Haidt, J., Koleva, S., Motyl, M., Iyer, R., Wojcik, S. P., and Ditto, P. H. 2013. "Moral foundations theory: The pragmatic validity of moral pluralism," *Advances in Experimental Social Psychology* 47: 55–130.

Haidt, J. and Bjorklund, F. 2008. "Social intuitionists answer six questions about morality," in W. Sinnott-Armstrong (ed.), *Moral Psychology*, *vol. 2: The Cognitive Science of Morality: Intuition and Diversity*: 181–217. Cambridge, MA: MIT Press.

Harrison, S. H., Ashforth, B. E., and Corley, K. G. 2009. "Organizational sacralization and sacrilege," *Research in Organizational Behavior* 29: 225–254.

Hogg, M. A. 2007. "Organizational orthodoxy and corporate autocrats: Some nasty consequences of organizational identification in uncertain times," in C. A. Bartel, S. L. Blader, and A. Wrzesniewski (eds.), *Identity and the Modern Organization*: 35–59. Mahwah, NJ: Erlbaum.

Hollinger, R. C. 1991. "Neutralizing in the workplace: An empirical analysis of property theft and production deviance," *Deviant Behavior* 12: 169–202.

Hornsey, M. J., Majkut, L., Terry, D. J., and McKimmie, B. M. 2003. "On being loud and proud: Non-conformity and counter-conformity to group norms," *British Journal of Social Psychology* 42: 319–335.

Horrigan, B. 2010. *Corporate Social Responsibility in the 21st Century: Debates, Models and Practices across Government, Law and Business*. Chelthenham, UK: Edward Elgar.

Howe, E. G. 1986. "Ethical issues regarding mixed agency of military physicians," *Social Science and Medicine* 23: 803–815.

Isenberg, D. J. 1986. "Group polarization: A critical review and meta-analysis," *Journal of Personality and Social Psychology* 50: 1141–1151.

Janis, I. L. 1982. *Groupthink: Psychological Studies of Policy Decisions and Fiascoes* (2nd edn). Boston: Houghton Mifflin.

Jones, T. M. 1991. "Ethical decision making by individuals in organizations: An issue-contingent model," *Academy of Management Review* 16: 366–395.

Kaptein, M. 2008. "Developing and testing a measure for the ethical culture of organizations: The corporate ethical virtues model," *Journal of Organizational Behavior* 29: 923–947.

Khan, U. and Dhar, R. 2006. "Licensing effect in consumer choice," *Journal of Marketing Research* 43: 259–266.

King, B. G., Felin, T., and Whetten, D. A. 2010. "Finding the organization in organizational theory: A meta-theory of the organization as a social actor," *Organization Science* 21: 290–305.

Kish-Gephart, J. J., Harrison, D. A., and Treviño, L. K. 2010. "Bad apples, bad cases, and bad barrels: Meta-analytic evidence about sources of unethical decisions at work," *Journal of Applied Psychology* 95: 1–31.

Klotz, A. C. and Bolino, M. C. 2013. "Citizenship and counterproductive work behavior: A moral licensing view," *Academy of Management Review* 38: 292–306.

Kohlberg, L. 1969. "Stage and sequence: The cognitive developmental approach to socialization," in D. A. Goslin (ed.), *Handbook of Socialization Theory and Research*: 347–480. Chicago: Rand McNally.

Kouchaki, M. 2011. "Vicarious moral licensing: The influence of others' past moral actions on moral behavior," *Journal of Personality and Social Psychology* 101: 702–715.

Kozlowski, S. W. J. and Klein, K. J. 2000. "A multilevel approach to theory and research in organizations: Contextual, temporal, and emergent processes," in K. J. Klein and S. W. J. Kozlowski (eds.), *Multilevel Theory, Research, and Methods in Organizations: Foundations, Extensions, and New Directions*: 3–90. San Francisco: Jossey-Bass.

Kreps, T. A. and Monin, B. 2011. "'Doing well by doing good'? Ambivalent moral framing in organizations," *Research in Organizational Behavior* 31: 99–123.

Lange, D. 2008. "A multidimensional conceptualization of organizational corruption control," *Academy of Management Review* 33: 710–729.

Lipstadt, D. 1993. *Denying the Holocaust: The Growing Assault on Truth and Memory*. New York: Simon and Schuster.

Macrae, C. N., Bodenhausen, G. V., Milne, A. B., and Jetten, J. 1994. "Out of mind but back in sight: Stereotypes on the rebound," *Journal of Personality and Social Psychology* 67: 808–817.

Macrae, C. N., Bodenhausen, G. V., Milne, A. B., and Wheeler, V. 1996. "On resisting the temptation for simplification: Counterintentional effects of stereotype suppression on social memory," *Social Cognition* 14: 1–20.

Magdalene, J. M. 2012. *Seduced by Success: 8 Critical Thinking Errors that Cause Smart People To Do Dumb Things*. Carlsbad, CA: Inspirational Publishing.

Martin, S. R., Kish-Gephart, J. J., and Detert, J. R. 2014. "Blind forces: Ethical infrastructures and moral disengagement in organizations," *Organizational Psychology Review* 4: 295–325.

Maslach, C. 1982. *Burnout: The Cost of Caring*. Englewood Cliffs, NJ: Prentice-Hall.

Maslach, C., Schaufeli, W. B., and Leiter, M. P. 2001. "Job burnout," *Annual Review of Psychology* 52: 397–422.

Mayer, D. M., Kuenzi, M., and Greenbaum, R. L. 2009. "Making ethical climate a mainstream management topic: A review, critique, and prescription for the empirical research on ethical climate," in D. De Cremer (ed.), *Psychological Perspectives on Ethical Behavior and Decision Making*: 181–213. Charlotte, NC: Information Age.

Mazar, N., Amir, O., and Ariely, D. 2008. "The dishonesty of honest people: A theory of self-concept maintenance," *Journal of Marketing Research* 45: 633–644.

Merritt, A. C., Effron, D. A., and Monin, B. 2010. "Moral self-licensing: When being good frees us to be bad," *Social and Personality Psychology Compass* 4: 344–357.

Merton, R. K. 1968. *Social Theory and Social Structure* (rev. edn). New York: Free Press.

Miller, D. T. and Effron, D. A. 2010. "Psychological license: When it is needed and how it functions," *Advances in Experimental Social Psychology* 43: 115–155.

Monin, B. and Miller, D. T. 2001. "Moral credentials and the expression of prejudice," *Journal of Personality and Social Psychology* 81: 33–43.

Monteith, M. J., Spicer, C. V., and Tooman, G. D. 1998. "Consequences of stereotype suppression: Stereotypes on AND not on the rebound," *Journal of Experimental Social Psychology* 34: 355–377.

Moore, C., Detert, J. R., Treviño, L. K., Baker, V. L., and Mayer, D. M. 2012. "Why employees do bad things: Moral disengagement and unethical organizational behavior," *Personnel Psychology* 65: 1–48.

Moore, C. and Gino, F. 2013. "Ethically adrift: How others pull our moral compass from true North, and how we can fix it," *Research in Organizational Behavior* 33: 53–77.

Mullen, E. and Nadler, J. 2008. "Moral spillovers: The effect of moral violations on deviant behavior," *Journal of Experimental Social Psychology* 44: 1239–1245.

Muraven, M., Tice, D. M., and Baumeister, R. F. 1998. "Self-control as a limited resource: Regulatory depletion patterns," *Journal of Personality and Social Psychology* 74: 774–789.

Murnighan, J. K., Cantelon, D. A., and Elyashiv, T. 2001. "Bounded personal ethics and the tap dance of real estate agency," *Advances in Qualitative Organization Research* 3: 1–40.

Nail, P. R., Van Leeuwen, M. D., and Powell, A. B. 1996. "The effectance versus the self-presentational view of reactance: Are importance ratings influenced by anticipated surveillance?," *Journal of Social Behavior and Personality* 11: 573–584.

Ormiston, M. E. and Wong, E. M. 2013. "License to ill: The effects of corporate social responsibility and CEO moral identity on corporate social irresponsibility," *Personnel Psychology* 66: 861–893.

Ouchi, W. G. 1979. "A conceptual framework for the design of organizational control mechanisms," *Management Science* 25: 833–848.

Palmer, D. 2012. *Normal Organizational Wrongdoing: A Critical Analysis of Theories of Misconduct in and by Organizations.* Oxford, UK: Oxford University Press.

Peterson, D. K. 2003. "The relationship between ethical pressure, relativistic moral beliefs and organizational commitment," *Journal of Managerial Psychology* 18: 557–572.

Pillutla, M. M. 2011. "When good people do wrong: Morality, social identity, and ethical behavior," in D. De Cremer, R. van Dick, and J. K. Murnighan (eds.), *Social Psychology and Organizations*: 353–369. New York: Routledge.

Pooler, D. K. 2011. "Pastors and congregations at risk: Insights from role identity theory," *Pastoral Psychology* 60: 705–712.

Preuss, L. 2010. "Codes of conduct in organisational context: From cascade to lattice-work of codes," *Journal of Business Ethics* 94: 471–487.

Rachlin, H. 1991. *The Making of a Cop.* New York: Pocket Books.

Rest, J. R. 1986. *Moral Development: Advances in Research and Theory.* New York: Praeger.

Reynolds, S. J. 2008. "Moral attentiveness: Who pays attention to the moral aspects of life?," *Journal of Applied Psychology* 93: 1027–1041.

Riketta, M. 2005. "Organizational identification: A meta-analysis," *Journal of Vocational Behavior* 66: 358–384.

Roberts, L. M. and Dutton, J. E. (eds.). 2009. *Exploring Positive Identities and Organizations: Building a Theoretical and Research Foundation.* New York: Routledge.

Robinson, S. L. and Kraatz, M. S. 1998. "Constructing the reality of normative behavior: The use of neutralization strategies by organizational deviants," in R. W. Griffin, A. O'Leary-Kelly, and J. M. Collins (eds.), *Dysfunctional Behavior in Organizations, vol. 1: Violent and Deviant Behavior*: 203–220. Stamford, CT: JAI Press.

Rumbles, S. and Rees, G. 2013. "Continuous changes, organizational burnout and the implications for HRD," *Industrial and Commercial Training* 45: 236–242.

Sabini, J. P. and Silver, M. 1978. "Moral reproach and moral action," *Journal for the Theory of Social Behaviour* 8: 103–123.

Sachdeva, S., Iliev, R., and Medin, D. L. 2009. "Sinning saints and saintly sinners: The paradox of moral self-regulation," *Psychological Science* 20: 523–528.

Schwartz, B. and Sharpe, K. E. 2006. "Practical wisdom: Aristotle meets positive psychology," *Journal of Happiness Studies* 7: 377–395.

Selznick, P. 1957. *Leadership in Administration: A Sociological Interpretation.* Berkeley, CA: University of California Press.

Shao, R., Aquino, K., and Freeman, D. 2008. "Beyond moral reasoning: A review of moral identity research and its implications for business ethics," *Business Ethics Quarterly* 18: 513–540.

Shaw, M., Quezada, S. A., and Zárate, M. A. 2011. "Violence with a conscience: Religiosity and moral certainty as predictors of support for violent warfare," *Psychology of Violence* 1: 275–286.

Sherman, D. K. and Cohen, G. L. 2006. "The psychology of self-defense: Self-affirmation theory," *Advances in Experimental Social Psychology* 38: 183–242.

Siebert, D. C. and Siebert, C. F. 2007. "Help seeking among helping professionals: A role identity perspective," *American Journal of Orthopsychiatry* 77: 49–55.

Skitka, L. J. 2010. "The psychology of moral conviction," *Social and Personality Psychology Compass* 4: 267–281.

Skitka, L. J., Bauman, C. W., and Mullen, E. 2008. "Morality and justice: An expanded theoretical perspective and empirical review," *Advances in Group Processes* 25: 1–27.

Skitka, L. J., Bauman, C. W., and Sargis, E. G. 2005. "Moral conviction: Another contributor to attitude strength or something more?," *Journal of Personality and Social Psychology* 88: 895–917.

Skitka, L. J. and Morgan, G. S. 2009. "The double-edged sword of a moral state of mind," in D. Narvaez and D. K. Lapsley (eds.), *Personality, Identity, and Character: Explorations in Moral Psychology*: 355–374. Cambridge, UK: Cambridge University Press.

Smith, R. H. 2013. *The Joy of Pain: Schadenfreude and the Dark Side of Human Nature.* New York: Oxford University Press.

Spreitzer, G. M. and Sonenshein, S. 2004. "Toward the construct definition of positive deviance," *American Behavioral Scientist* 47: 828–847.

Swider, B. W. and Zimmerman, R. D. 2010. "Born to burnout: A meta-analytic path model of personality, job burnout, and work outcomes," *Journal of Vocational Behavior* 76: 487–506.

Tanner, R. J. and Carlson, K. A. 2009. "Unrealistically optimistic consumers: A selective hypothesis testing account for optimism in predictions of future behavior," *Journal of Consumer Research* 35: 810–822.

Tenbrunsel, A. E. 1998. "Misrepresentation and expectations of misrepresentation in an ethical dilemma: The role of incentives and temptation," *Academy of Management Journal* 41: 330–339.

Tenbrunsel, A. E. and Messick, D. M. 1999. "Sanctioning systems, decision frames, and cooperation," *Administrative Science Quarterly* 44: 684–707.

Tenbrunsel, A. E. and Messick, D. M. 2004. "Ethical fading: The role of self-deception in unethical behavior," *Social Justice Research* 17: 223–236.

Tenbrunsel, A. E. and Smith-Crowe, K. 2008. "Ethical decision making: Where we've been and where we're going," *Academy of Management Annals* 2: 545–607.

Tenbrunsel, A. E., Smith-Crowe, K., and Umphress, E. E. 2003. "Building houses on rocks: The role of the ethical infrastructure in organizations," *Social Justice Research* 16: 285–307.

Tetlock, P. E., Kristel, O. V., Elson, S. B., Green, M. C., and Lerner, J. S. 2000. "The psychology of the unthinkable: Taboo trade-offs, forbidden base rates, and heretical counterfactuals," *Journal of Personality and Social Psychology* 78: 853–870.

Tomlinson, E. C., Lewicki, R. J., and Ash, S. R. 2014. "Disentangling the moral integrity construct: Values congruence as a moderator of the behavioral integrity–citizenship relationship," *Group & Organization Management* 39: 720–743.

Toppinen-Tanner, S., Kalimo, R., and Mutanen, P. 2002. "The process of burnout in white-collar and blue-collar jobs: Eight-year prospective study of exhaustion," *Journal of Organizational Behavior* 23: 555–570.

Treviño, L. K., and Youngblood, S. A. 1990. "Bad apples in bad barrels: A causal analysis of ethical decision-making behavior," *Journal of Applied Psychology* 75: 378–385.

Turiel, E. 1998. "The development of morality," in N. Eisenberg (ed.), *Handbook of Child Psychology, vol. 3: Social, Emotional, and Personality Development*, 5th edn: 863–932. New York:Wiley.

van Zomeren, M. and Lodewijkx, H. F. M. 2005. "Motivated responses to 'senseless' violence: Explaining emotional and behavioural responses through person and position identification," *European Journal of Social Psychology* 35: 755–766.

van Zomeren, M., Postmes, T., and Spears, R. 2012. "On conviction's collective consequences: Integrating moral conviction with the social identity model of collective action," *British Journal of Social Psychology* 51: 52–71.

Wegner, D. M. 1994. "Ironic processes of mental control," *Psychological Review* 101: 34–52.

Weick, K. E. 1995. *Sensemaking in Organizations.* Thousand Oaks, CA: Sage.

Welsh, D. T., Ordóñez, L. D., Snyder, D. G., and Christian, M. S. 2015. "The slippery slope: How small ethical transgressions pave the way for larger future transgressions," *Journal of Applied Psychology* 100: 114–127.

Wright, J. C., Cullum, J., and Schwab, N. 2008. "The cognitive and affective dimensions of moral conviction: Implications for attitudinal and behavioral measures of interpersonal tolerance," *Personality and Social Psychology Bulletin* 34: 1461–1476.

Wright, L. 1993. *Saints and Sinners: Walker Railey, Jimmy Swaggart, Madalyn Murray O'Hair, Anton LaVey, Will Campbell, Matthew Fox.* New York: Alfred A. Knopf.

Zhang, X., Bartol, K. M., Smith, K. G., Pfarrer, M. D., and Khanin, D. M. 2008. "CEOs on the edge: Earnings manipulation and stock-based incentive misalignment," *Academy of Management Journal* 51: 241–258.

Zhong, C.-B., Ku, G., Lount, R. B., and Murnighan, J. K. 2010. "Compensatory ethics," *Journal of Business Ethics* 92: 323–239.

Zhong, C.-B., Liljenquist, K. A., and Cain, D. M. 2009. "Moral self-regulation: Licensing and compensation," in D. De Cremer (ed.), *Psychological Perspectives on Ethical Behavior and Decision Making:* 75–89. Charlotte, NC: Information Age.

12 | "Is it me? Or is it me?" The role of coactivated multiple identities and identifications in promoting or discouraging workplace crimes

ABHIJEET K. VADERA AND MICHAEL G. PRATT

While corporate crime is unfortunately not a new phenomenon, high-profile abuses in the last decade have led to a renewed urgency in understanding the precursors of wrongdoing in organizations. In this vein, academic research has recently begun to adopt an identity perspective, especially from social identity theory,[1] to explore the antecedents of ethical misconduct in organizations. Apart from looking at one's moral identity (see Ashforth and Lange, this volume), recent research suggests that organizational identification (i.e., viewing one's role in the organization as self-defining) will influence a person's propensity to engage in workplace crimes (May, Chang, and Shao 2015; Umphress, Bingham, and Mitchell 2010; Vadera and Pratt 2013). Common to these social identity-based perspectives on wrongdoing is a focus on a single identity or identification (e.g., moral identity or organizational identification). However, scholars have long understood that in addition to social identities, any given individual may have a multitude of role identities – tied to various internalized roles he or she plays in society (e.g., parent, accountant, soccer player) – which may be brought to bear in a given social situation (Burke 2003; Stryker and Serpe 1994). In organizational studies, research further suggests that individuals do bring to and express these different identities (e.g., religious, kinship) at work (Ashforth and Pratt 2003; Creed, DeJordy,

Each author contributed equally to this chapter. We wish to thank Lakshmi Ramarajan, Kristin Smith-Crowe, and Don Palmer for their feedback on earlier drafts of this chapter.
[1] Social identity theory differentiates personal – individually held, or idiosyncratic – identities, from ones based on social membership. For the sake of parsimony, we do not discuss other idiosyncratic identities.

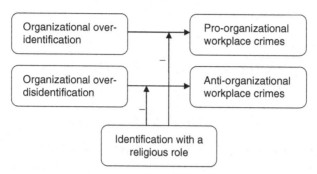

Figure 12.1 Our proposed framework

and Lok 2010; Fitzsimmons 2013; Kreiner, Hollensbe, and Sheep 2006; Pratt and Rafaeli 1997; Ramarajan and Reid 2013). There have even been recent and urgent calls in the popular press for organizations to allow people to bring more of their "whole self" (the self is comprised of multiple identities) to work (e.g., backwest.com/life-back-west-may-2012-bring-your-whole-self/). But how might these multiple identities and identifications influence decisions about whether or not to engage in workplace crimes?

In this chapter, we build off research that ties organizational attachments to workplace crime by articulating how the activation of non-organizational role identities may function in conjunction with organizational identification to influence a person's propensity to commit workplace crimes. We argue that the activation of multiple identities (or identification with multiple social groups and roles) and identity content (i.e., the type of social group or role activated) play a role in either mitigating or strengthening the relationship between someone's identification with the organization and his/her propensity to engage in illegal or unethical behaviors at work. In particular, we examine how organizational identification may interact with internalized role identities in the following domains: religious, professional, and kinship (e.g., child or family). As we discuss below, these internalized role identities may be either triggered by something in the workplace context (e.g., the display of the Hippocratic Oath as a trigger for professional role identities in physicians) or may be chronically salient (e.g., a devoutly religious person may always act in accordance to his or her religious roles). Our major arguments are summarized in Figures 12.1–12.3.

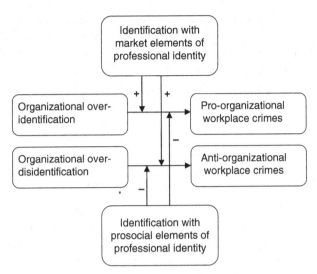

Figure 12.2 Our proposed framework (contd.)

Figure 12.3 Our proposed framework (contd.)

Our chapter is organized as follows. We begin by reviewing our own work on organizational identification and workplace crimes, as well as related work, to argue for a relationship between organizational identification and the propensity for workplace crime. We then discuss research on multiple identities, both in general and in relation to wrongdoing in organizations. Next, we build our framework (see Figures 12.1–12.3) to argue how the co-activation of organizational identification and an internalized role identity influences an individual's propensity to engage in workplace crimes. We conclude with a detailed discussion of the theoretical and managerial implications of our proposed framework and propose several arenas for future research.

Organizational identification and workplace crimes

Workplace crimes are broadly defined as "illegal, illegitimate, or immoral actions deliberately committed by employees in the workplace" (Vadera and Pratt 2013: 173). Our review of extant research revealed that unethical behaviors can be categorized into three key types of workplace crimes: pro-organizational, anti-organizational, and nonaligned (Vadera and Pratt 2013). Each of these crime types are based on the perpetrator's intentions, not on the actual outcome of her or his behaviors. Pro-organizational workplace crimes are carried out with the intention of benefiting the organization, such as dumping toxic waste into a river or other body of water so that the organization can save money. Anti-organizational workplace crimes are enacted with the intent to benefit oneself and harm the organization; such crimes may include embezzlement, other forms of workplace theft, or engaging in antisocial behaviors at the workplace. Nonaligned workplace crimes are those crimes that benefit the perpetrator without any intentional effect on the organization; to illustrate, someone may accept bribes or engage in insider trading to benefit himself or herself, with little thought to how such actions may influence his or her employer.

Our work further posits the degree and valence of one's identification with the organization, which is a "feeling of oneness" (Ashforth and Mael 1989) that occurs as one's organization becomes self-referential (Dutton, Dukerich, and Harquail 1994; Pratt 1998), as being critical to understanding which of these types of crime someone might be predisposed to conduct. Our logic can be distilled in the following way. Individuals who over-identify with the organization – whereby a significant portion of their identity is completely wrapped up in the organization – are most likely to engage in pro-organizational (versus anti-organizational or nonaligned) workplace crimes when such an opportunity arises. If a large part of "who I am" is dependent on my organizational membership (or role) via over-identification, then I will work to protect my identity by protecting the organization at any cost, even if it means engaging in illegal activities. Thus, an engineer at Ford where "Quality is Job One" might cover up reports about car defects – such as the Pinto's vulnerable gas tank (Birsch and Fielder 1994; Gioia 1992). Conversely, if I over-disidentify with the organization, then there is a strong and active separation between my identity and the identity of the organization, and I engage in self-enhancement through dissociation with the organization. When this occurs, I am more likely to protect my identity by engaging in actions that work against the organization, that is, anti-organizational workplace crimes. To illustrate, a bank teller who hated his organization often cashed noticeably forged checks and skipped work on days with predictably high customer volume (Sprouse 1992). Note, in both cases, the organization plays a large part in a person's self-construal, but when someone over-disidentifies with the organization, he or she is more prone to engage in crimes that hurt the organization than protect it.

Sometimes, identification with the organization does not reflect such neat and clean boundaries about "who I am" and "who I am not" in relation to the organization, but reflects a condition whereby some aspects of the organization are self-referential in a positive way (this is "who I am"), while others are self-referential in a negative way (this is "who I am not"). To illustrate, I may see Walmart as self-defining, but view its focus on the environment as reflecting "who I am" and how the company treats employees (e.g., low wages) as reflecting "who I am not." In this situation, we argue that individuals will be pulled in different directions and will look to the actions of organizational agents (e.g., leaders) to resolve their ambivalence. More specifically, drawing on theories of ambivalence amplification (Katz and Glass 1979), we argue that an ambivalently identified individual observing positive behaviors by organizational agents will lead to over-identification and ultimately to pro-organizational crime whereas negative behaviors will lead to over-disidentification and eventually toward anti-organizational workplace crimes (Vadera and Pratt 2013). Finally, when one neither identifies nor disidentifies with the organization, one likely experiences indifference toward the organization. In these situations, an individual's propensity to engage in workplace crimes will largely depend on individual differences (e.g., degree of self-centeredness).

At the heart of our theorizing is that only high, and potentially pathological, degrees of identification should predispose individuals to commit workplace crimes. Thus, when an individual views the organization as largely reflecting "who I am" or "who I am not," the propensity to commit pro-organizational and anti-organizational workplace crime respectively is more likely to occur. There is some empirical research that supports our assertions, especially regarding clearer cases when the organization clearly stands for "who I am" (i.e., organizational identification) or "who I am not" (i.e., organizational disidentification). But surprisingly, this research does not posit such high or pathological degrees of salience.

For instance, Effelsberg, Solga, and Gurt (2014) found that organizational identification mediated the effects of transformational leadership on pro-organizational workplace crimes. That is, they argue that employees with transformational leaders are more willing to engage in unethical behaviors for the benefit of their organization. They find that this relationship occurs because these leaders foster organizational identification in their employees. Umphress and colleagues (2010) also showed in two field studies that as identification with the organization increased, at least among some individuals,[2] individuals were more likely to engage in pro-organizational workplace crimes. By contrast, Becker and Tausch (2014) found that individuals who disidentified with the group engaged in negative ingroup-directed intentions (such as active and passive harm) akin to anti-organizational workplace crimes. Given the empirical support to date, our current models focus on just two types of identification from our pre-existing research: over-identification and over-disidentification. However, we also hold open the possibility that perhaps simply identification and disidentification may evoke similar dynamics.

By our own admission, we see our own research in this area as merely a first step. This research – like most research of its kind – does not explore the fact that individuals (a) identify with multiple social groups; (b) have multiple role identities which are central to an

---

[2] It is important to note that in this study, it was only highly identified individuals who also held strong positive reciprocity beliefs who engaged in pro-organizational workplace crimes: they were willing to engage in crimes in order to "pay back" the organization.

individual's self-concept; and (c) that at a given point in time, these different identifications and identities may influence behavior (McCall and Simmons 1978). We draw on social identity theory (Tajfel and Turner 1979) and identity theory (Stryker 1987; Stryker and Burke 2000; Stryker and Serpe 1994) to propose how different types of work (professional) and nonwork (religious, kinship) identities are likely to moderate the organizational identification–workplace crimes relationship.

Multiple role identities, organizational identification, and workplace crimes

Because we are enriching our previous arguments by adding role identities (from identity theory) to our theorizing about organizational identification (from social identity theory), it is important to delineate what each adds to our theorizing. As noted, in social identity theory, identification occurs when some collectivity (e.g., group or organization) of which one is a member becomes self-defining. That is, once an individual's membership in that collectivity becomes self-referential, we say that (s)he has developed a social identity around that membership. By contrast, the basis for identities in identity theory is roles. When an individual internalizes the meanings associated with his/her role, it becomes a role identity. Because social identity and role identity use different terms to mean similar things, we attempt to use terminology that bridges the two. For example, we will often talk about identification or disidentification with various work-related and nonwork-related roles, which will be equivalent to a role identity (Burke 1989).[3] Moreover, following Burke (1989), we will sometimes use identities and identifications synonymously, given that a role or membership with which one identifies results in a role or social identity respectively. Put another way, when we use "identifications" in this chapter, it refers to an outcome or a "noun" and not a "verb" or the process of identifying (see Pratt 2000 for more on the latter).

In both perspectives, identities influence behavior to the degree that they are "activated" or made salient (Ashforth and Mael 1989; Pratt

---

[3] While we did not find common usage of "role identification," Burke (1989: 160) does use the term "sex role identification," which he then equates with "gender identity" (and ultimately uses the latter). This suggests that role identity as a shorthand for role identification is appropriate.

2001; Stryker 1987; Stryker and Burke 2000; Stryker and Serpe 1994). In social identity theory, activation is often contextually driven – thus, when I am at the office, an organizationally relevant identity is likely to be activated. In identity theory, more than in social identity theory, there is explicit discussion that individuals have multiple identities that are arranged in a relatively stable salience hierarchy (Stryker and Serpe 1994). While the salient or activated identity (or identities) may be contextually triggered, certain role identities may also be chronically salient or always accessible (Burke and Stets 2009).

Recent work from both perspectives, however, emphasizes that multiple identities or, as we will argue, multiple identifications may be coactivated at the same time. The logic of coactivation is based on research on associative networks and builds on the premise that multiple knowledge nodes (in our case, identities) can be activated simultaneously (Pratt and Corley 2007; Rothbard and Ramarajan 2009). To illustrate, for a lone female lawyer in a meeting with male engineers, both a gender and professional identity may be coactivated; similarly, a devout Christian may activate both a religious and an organizationally relevant identity while at work.

Our discussion below merges insights from these two theories. In particular, from identity theory we draw on roles as a fundamental source for identification (i.e., as role identities), and the notion that some role identifications may be salient (i.e., for chronically salient roles) even when contextual conditions are not ideal for triggering them. From social identity theory we draw on membership, especially organizational membership, as a prime source for identification; and from the expanded model of identification (Elsbach 1999; Pratt 2000), we suggest that the nature of this identification can be positive or negative (i.e., disidentification).

Why multiple identities and identifications matter

Why do we believe that multiple identities/identifications will influence workplace crime at all? We base our belief on a review of research that suggests that, whether coactivated or activated one at a time, individuals who have and can deploy multiple identities/identifications behave differently and experience different outcomes (both positive and negative) than those who do not. To illustrate, in identity theory, several studies have adopted the notion of multiple identities and explored its relation to stress, well-being, and self-esteem. Thoits (1983), for example, examined how multiple role identities can influence individual stress and well-being. She found an inverted-U relationship between the number of identities a person possesses and psychological distress. Specifically, the greater the number of identities (e.g., parent, spouse, friend, and church member) individuals possessed, up to a point, the lower the experience of psychological distress; over an optimal number, however, overload occurred and stress increased.

Drawing on social identity theory, researchers have suggested that groups comprised of individuals who can hold (i.e., identify with) both a subordinate identity and a superordinate identity are more likely to have harmonious relationships. For example, Gaertner and colleagues (Gaertner and Dovidio 2000; Gaertner et al. 1993) proposed the Common Ingroup Identity Model, which suggests that factors that induce members of two groups to conceive of themselves as members of a common ingroup as well as members of different subgroups of that common identity (i.e., hold a "dual identity" in which both the subgroup and superordinate identities are salient) were likely to reduce inter-group bias and conflict as well as increase inter-group harmony. Houlette et al. (2004) found support for this theory by assessing its use in a Green Circle Program involving 830 first- and second-grade children. This program was designed to utilize a common ingroup identity to widen the children's circles of inclusion to include people who were different from themselves (based on race, sex, and weight). Houlette et al. (2004) found that the program led the children to be more inclusive in selecting their most preferred playmate.

While the aforementioned studies have occurred largely in psychology and sociology, the notion of multiple identities has also been integral to organizational theorizing. However, rather than focusing primarily on individual costs and benefits, they also look at how multiple identities influence how members see their workplace and enact their jobs. For example, the notion of multiple identities was central to Pratt and Rafaeli's (1997) qualitative study of a rehabilitation unit of a large hospital. Here, they examined how nurses wrestled with the abstract and complex question "who are we as nurses of this unit?" by discussing the question "what should we wear?" On the one hand, wearing street clothes affirmed elements of the unit's rehabilitation philosophy; but these clothes were not viewed as promoting professional equality with physicians. Scrubs, by contrast, reflected nurses as being more equal to doctors, but violated the unit's philosophy that attempted to decrease differences between patients and nurses. Thus, both "unit" and "professional" identities were in play when debating their dress code. Moreover, a nurse's particular combination of unit and professional identities influenced not only what (s)he wore but also how (s)he treated patients.

More recently, Ramarajan and Reid (2013) argued that organizational practices, along with personal preferences, play a critical role in how members view and enact both work and nonwork identities. In particular, organizations and individuals exert pressures to either include (integrate) or exclude (segregate or compartmentalize) nonwork identities while at work. Building on numerous studies in organizational behavior, these authors argue that whether these pressures align or misalign will impact not only how identity is expressed at work but also an individual's well-being, their perceived autonomy, and their productivity. This research, therefore, not only supports the notion that multiple identities can be deployed at work but also that organizational practices may influence this deployment.

Why multiple identities and identifications matter for workplace crime

Taken as a whole, research has suggested that multiple identities may play a critical role in key areas for individuals, such as how stressed they feel, how they think about themselves and others in their organizations, and ultimately how they act and perform. However, research in this area has largely – but not completely – ignored the issue of how multiple identities/identifications may influence whether and how someone engages in illegal or unethical behaviors in organizations. We argue that co-activation of different combinations of work and nonwork identifications (with memberships or roles) may occur in work contexts, and may also, in some circumstances, attenuate or exacerbate the harmful relationships between organizational (dis-) identification and workplace crimes.

While explicit treatment of the relationship between an individual's multiple identities/identifications and workplace crimes are scant, there are a few who tackle this issue. To illustrate, Leavitt and colleagues (2012: 1316) suggest that by focusing on how a unitary, decontextualized moral identity influences moral judgments, researchers have overlooked that occupational identities (which they view as "implicitly held and dynamically activated knowledge structures") are also infused with moral content. They argue that a given occupational identity may be characterized as having either universal or particularistic motives. For the former, moral principles are predicted to be applied indiscriminately (e.g., firefighters should treat everyone the same), while for the latter, they are thought to be hypothesized to a specific group (e.g., lawyers privilege their clients over others). They further argue that individuals may have multiple occupational identities at work (e.g., engineer-manager, physician-HMO administrator) and that these identities may have different motives. Among other things, they were interested in figuring out how individuals with multiple occupational identities behaved ethically at work; in particular, which motives "won out" if there were potentially more than one. They find that cues in the context may determine behavior. Specifically, when occupational identities with universalistic motives are primed, individuals are more likely to act in a morally principled way, whereas when identities with particularistic motives are primed, they are more flexible in their moral judgments.

Pillutla (2011), by contrast, provided a slightly different perspective and suggested that "morality is jointly determined by the importance of morality to the self-concept and by the social identity that is the most important contributor to the self-concept" (p. 362). In other words, while an activated moral identity is important, morality is also a part of one's self-concept derived from various social roles that individuals play. Since morality is a function of both a holistic sense of self, which is relatively constant, and the contents of one's most important identity, it is the latter that is likely to differentiate moral behavior. Pillutla (2011) suggests, for instance, that if an individual identifies with his or her role as a parent more than his or her role as an employee, then morality in the domain of parenthood should have greater influence on his or her moral judgments compared to his or her notions of morality in the domain of employment when both identifications are co-activated.

Taken together, these articles point to the importance of activated roles that are not tied exclusively to a particular organization. Leavitt and colleagues (2012), for example, suggest that occupational identities may influence moral behavior (cf., Pratt and Dutton 2000). In particular, they argue that some occupational identities may be infused with moral content. Pillutla, by contrast, suggests that identification to nonwork roles, such as one's parental role, is also critical in determining one's morality. We extend this work by exploring how these types of identities may interact with organizational identification when examining a specific type of ethical behavior: propensity to engage in workplace crime.

Interplay of coactivated organizational with professional and nonwork identifications on propensity to commit workplace crime

To summarize our arguments to this point, we argue that over-identification or over-disidentification will likely influence one's propensity to engage in certain types of workplace crimes. This is our "main effect" in Figures 12.1–12.3. We further suggest that even though one's (dis-)identification with the organization may likely be salient at work, other identities may be salient as well (i.e., multiple identifications may be coactivated). Given that these other identifications (e.g., with religious roles) may evoke moral behavior, this coactivation will influence the impact of organizational over-(dis-)identification on the propensity to engage in workplace crimes. However, as we argue below, the influence of multiple identifications may not always be straightforward. To begin to disentangle the complex nature of this coactivation dynamic, we will use the coactivation of religious, professional, or kinship identifications – along with organizational identification – to illustrate different ways in which the interplay of identities and identifications may influence someone's predilections toward engaging in criminal behavior in the workplace.

Religious identity, organizational identification, and workplace crimes

Our basic argument about how other identities/identifications work with organizational identification is relatively straightforward. We argue that any identification which makes morality salient for individuals is likely to diminish the effects of over-identification and over-disidentification on workplace crimes. We base our predictions on recent work in behavioral ethics which suggests that drawing people's attention to moral standards reduces unethical behaviors

(Mazar, Amir, and Ariely 2008; Shu, Gino, and Bazerman 2011). For example, Mazar and colleagues (2008) found that participants who were asked to recall the Ten Commandments or to sign an honor code statement (which simply stated "I understand that this short survey falls under MIT's [Yale's] honor system") did not cheat even when they were given the opportunity to financially gain from this action. By contrast, individuals who had not been reminded of the Ten Commandments or who were not asked to sign the honor code statement cheated substantially. In a similar vein, Shu and colleagues (2011) found that students who read and signed an academic honor code before the task (compared to those who did not) reported lower levels of dishonesty. These scholars contended that increasing moral salience by having participants read and sign an honor code significantly reduced unethical behavior. Drawing on the work of Gino and Desai (2012), the relationship between these codes or artifacts and ethical behavior may occur because the former triggers memories within an individual (e.g., I remember hearing about the Ten Commandments when sitting in the synagogue), which activates associated concepts such as moral purity within an individual, which ultimately lead to ethical behavior.

Further extrapolating from this work, we argue that as one's identification with a religious role (or salience of a religious identity) increases, at least in most cases, one's propensity to behave morally also increases.[4] Providing some support to our assertion, there is evidence to suggest that religiosity has a causal connection to a host of positive behaviors including moral behaviors, self-control, and helpfulness (Galen 2012). In this stream of research, religiosity is discussed as a set of moral ideals and promoting the idea that one's actions are being evaluated and monitored by supernatural agents (Galen 2012; McCullough and Willoughby 2009). It is through this coactivation of moral ideals and the salience of evaluation by supernatural agents that religiosity (or we would argue, religious identity) priming is suggested to increase awareness of prosocial behavioral norms and hence prosocial behaviors. For instance, Baumeister, Bauer, and Lloyd (2010) have argued that "religion can play an important role in promoting good self-control by activating and

---

[4] One can, of course, imagine times when people have behaved immorally under the guise of religion. We address this possibility in our discussion section.

keeping salient important values and ideals" (p. 76). The evocation via religiosity or religious identity of these prosocial norms and "important values and ideals," especially the values of friendliness and cooperativeness, has been found by others. Morgan (1983) showed that interviewers rated religious interviewees as being more friendly and cooperative than the nonreligious. Ellison (1992) explored the relationship between religiosity and interpersonal friendliness and cooperation using data from the 1979 to 1980 National Survey of Black Americans (NSBA). Results indicated that respondents for whom religion served as an important source of moral guidance were viewed as friendlier, more interested in participating in the survey, and more open than those for whom this aspect of religion was less salient. And in a more recent meta-analysis across ninety-three studies and 11,653 participants, Shariff and colleagues (2016) showed that different types of religious priming had robust effects across a variety of outcomes, including prosocial behaviors. As is common with priming studies (Ferguson and Bargh 2004), the priming did not reliably affect those without schemas related to the primes, that is, nonreligious participants.

We draw on this scholarly work to propose the moderating effects of identification with a religious role. As we have argued, over-identification with the organization is likely to make one's self-construal too wrapped up in the organization such that the uniqueness of the individual is lost and the individual may engage in workplace crimes in order to benefit the organization (Vadera and Pratt 2013). By contrast, over-disidentification with the organization stems from one's strong, negative feelings toward the organization (cf., Dukerich, Kramer, and McLean Parks 1998; Pratt 2000) and the individual with this identity may engage in workplace crimes which harm the organization (Vadera and Pratt 2013). The above research suggests that as religious identities are activated, immoral behavior – including any pro- or anti-organizational crime – is likely to decrease. Therefore, when one's identification with one's religious role becomes "coactivated" with (dis-)identification with one's organization, the negative effects of over-identification and over-disidentification are likely to diminish. For individuals who strongly identify with a religious role, related concepts of morality, moral purity, moral standards, and so on are likely to be activated, which in turn is likely to motivate these individuals to engage in moral behaviors and not engage in workplace crimes.[5] Hence, we propose:

Proposition 1: *Identification with a religious role moderates the effects of over-(dis-)identification with the organization on workplace crimes such that as the identification with a religious role increases, the effects of over-(dis-)identification with the organization on workplace crimes weaken.*

Professional identity, organizational identification, and workplace crimes

Another identity which may influence the relationship between organizational identification and workplace crimes, albeit in a slightly different way, is professional identity. While there is some debate over what distinguishes professions from other occupations, professionals often have deep, abstract knowledge in a particular area, often acquired through a lengthy socialization process and certified by a professional association (Abbott 1988). Historically, professions have been associated with an ethic that goes beyond self-interest. As Sullivan (2004: 5) has noted, "A profession is by definition 'in business' for the common good as well as for the good of its members, or it is not a profession." Thus, to the degree that individuals identify with those elements of a professional identity associated with "promoting the common good" (i.e., the prosocial elements), this moral standard should limit the degree to which individuals engage in either pro- or anti-organizational workplace crimes. This parallels our arguments about religious identities: identification with prosocial facets of an identity is likely to influence behavior in a more ethical way:

---

[5] There is some research on moral licensing which suggests that when individuals engage in or recall engaging in a moral act, it gives them the license to engage in unethical acts in the future. This theory would therefore suggest that those who identify with a religious role are more likely to engage in workplace crimes because they would feel that they now have the license to do so. However, this theory holds only when one recalls prior moral actions and not moral traits (Conway and Peetz 2012). When one recalls moral traits, one is likely to engage in consistent behaviors, that is, act morally. Our arguments are in line with this perspective since we suggest that as identification with a religious role (or with the prosocial elements of professional identity (Proposition 2a) or with a child role (Proposition 3)) is tied not only to behaviors but to one's identity, it should be more akin to the evocation of moral *traits* rather than just prior actions.

Proposition 2a: *Identification with the prosocial elements of a professional identity moderates the effects of over-(dis-)identification with the organization on workplace crimes such that as the identification with the prosocial elements increases, the effects of over-(dis-) identification with the organization on workplace crimes weaken.*

However, research also suggests that market forces that promote more individualistic values can threaten or even overshadow these prosocial elements of a professional identity (Sullivan 2004; Turco 2012). To the degree that market forces overwhelm these more prosocial ones, Lepisto, Crosina, and Pratt (2015) argue that value displacement can occur. Concern for making a profit for one's organization or one's self, combined with over-identification or over-disidentification with the organization respectively, may exacerbate tendencies to engage in crimes that benefit either one's organization (for over-identifiers) or one's self at the expense of one's organization (for over-disidentifiers):

Proposition 2b: *Identification with the market elements of a professional identity moderates the effects of over-(dis-)identification with the organization on workplace crimes such that as the identification with the market-related elements become salient, the effects of over-(dis-)identification with the organization on workplace crimes strengthen.*

We might further expect that professionals in for-profit organizations characterized by an intense competition for resources may be more amenable to identifying with this facet of their professional identity than the prosocial one.

The issue of identification with an element of a professional identity, in relation with organizational identification, suggests that it is not simply the identification with another workplace role that may influence the over-(dis-)identification–crime relationship. It also suggests that each role itself may have different facets, and that depending on which facet one identifies with, behaviors can change. Thus professionals who identify with their role as "providers to the common good" (e.g., doctors in nonprofit nongovernmental organizations who are arguably solely accountable for their patients) may act differently than professionals who identify with the market-driven facets of their professional identity (e.g., doctors in for-profit enterprises are arguably more accountable to their superiors, partners, and in some cases stockholders). In some ways, our arguments mirror those of Leavitt and colleagues' (2012) work. However, we pose two key differences. First, rather than particularistic versus universal morals which regulate the scope of who someone helps, other professional values such as prosocial versus market may influence whether ethical behavior is engaged in at all. Second, we argue that all professionals, not just those whose jobs involve multiple occupational identities (e.g., physician-manager), may have to deal with more than one source of moral pressure.

Kinship identities, organizational identification, and workplace crimes

We use the term "kinship" identity to refer to any identity based on a familial role. Here we contrast two aspects of kinship roles: child and family. A "child" identity is based on one's role as a child and is likely to be activated when one thinks of one's own childhood or when one is primed with children's toys and artifacts. For instance, when one is in a candy store, toy store, or an amusement park, or when one hears a particular song or story from one's childhood, one may be primed of one's own childhood and one's child identity may thus be activated.

Drawing on research on memory and moral psychology, Gino and Desai (2012) proposed that childhood memories elicit moral purity (which is a psychological state of feeling morally clean and innocent) which in turn leads to greater prosocial behaviors. Children are commonly perceived to be innocent, pure, moral, and selfless (James, Jenks, and Prout 1998; Woodrow 1999). In fact, extensive research in developmental psychology shows that children are kind and fair (Hamlin, Wynn, and Bloom 2007). Children comfort people in distress by caressing them or offering them a bottle or toy (Zahn-Waxler, Radke-Yarrow, and King 1979), help those in need by reaching over and assisting them (Warneken et al. 2007), and when they are treated kindly, they try to reward that behavior (Hamlin et al. 2007). Building on this scholarly work, Gino and Desai (2012) found across five experiments that recalling childhood memories was positively related to (a) helping the experimenter with a supplementary task; (b) the amount of money donated to a good cause; and (c) punishment of others' ethically questionable actions. Gino and Desai argued that when people are asked to recall their experiences as children, the concept of childhood is explicitly or implicitly activated by association, which then triggers the concept of moral purity. Once the psychological state of moral purity is activated, individuals are likely to act in ways which are consistent with a pure and morally clean self-concept, that is, ethically. In another study, Desai and Gino (2012) adopted the same theoretical arguments and found that when participants in an experiment were in a room with children's toys or engaged in children's activities, they lied less often and were more generous than the control group.

We extend this argument further to propose that when individuals identify with being child-like or with their past role as a child, it is likely to elicit moral purity in the same way as recalling childhood memories or presence of children's toys does. Moral purity in turn would minimize the effects of organizational identification on workplace crimes. To elaborate, when they identify with their past role as a child, individuals are reminded of children. This reminder would make these individuals feel morally clean and innocent. When moral purity is activated, individuals will have a desire to remain morally clean since their moral self-concept is likely to be salient. These individuals are less likely to fall prey to the temptations of their over-identification or over-disidentification to engage in workplace crimes. Hence we argue that:

Proposition 3: *Identification with one's role as a child moderates the effects of over-(dis-)identification with the organization on workplace crimes such that as the identification with the role as a child increases, the effects of over-(dis-)identification with the organization on workplace crimes weaken.*

However, we further suggest that not all child-related cues will activate a child identity. Specifically, we argue that cues regarding *one's own children* (or possibly even children from one's broader family such as nieces, nephews, or grandchildren) will trigger a family identity. A family identity may also be primed in other ways. For example, when one is reminded of one's spouse, siblings, or other close relatives via photographs or while watching a movie, one's family identity may be activated. Individuals who identify with their familial role(s) and who identify with the organization may think of themselves as both a member of the organization and a member of their families. As a result of this co-activation, individuals may consider their ties to both identities when considering pro-organizational crimes, thus setting up a conflict: While such crimes may help their organizations, it might signal that they are more loyal to his/her organization than to his/her family. Thus, we would expect that individuals with both identifications co-activated will be less likely to engage in pro-organizational crimes when compared to someone who only over-identifies with the organization. Hence we propose that:

Proposition 4a: *Identification with a familial role moderates the effects of over-identification with the organization on workplace crimes such that as identification with the familial role increases, the effects of over-identification with the organization on pro-organizational workplace crimes weaken.*

We would expect a very different pattern, however, for individuals who over-disidentify with the organization. Here, because there are fewer competing loyalties, individuals who strongly identify with their familial role are more likely to engage in anti-organizational workplace crimes, especially those crimes that lead to significant gains for the perpetrator when the opportunity presents itself. Over-disidentification with the organization will motivate individuals to distance themselves from their organizations, while a strong identification with the familial role will encourage them to engage in acts which benefit their families. Individuals who over-disidentify with their organizations, but strongly identify with their familial roles, are thus likely to engage in crimes which harm the organization and can benefit the family because this will signal where their loyalties lie. For instance, these individuals are likely to engage in crimes such as embezzlement to harm the organization because the proceeds can benefit their families with the extra "income." By contrast, the propensity to commit anti-organizational crimes such as vandalism that would make the perpetrator feel good, but would not likely benefit his or her family, may not be affected. Therefore, we make the following prediction:

Proposition 4b: *Identification with a familial role moderates the effects of over-disidentification with the organization on workplace crimes such that as identification with the familial role increases, the effects of over-disidentification with the organization on anti-organizational workplace crimes strengthen. This effect should be strongest for anti-organizational crimes that can benefit the perpetrator and by extension, his or her family.*

Discussion

Extant research has argued that how people view themselves in terms of their organizations (i.e., if they over-identify or over-disidentify with the organization) affects their propensity to engage in workplace crimes. In this chapter, we build on research which suggests that people bring and deploy other work (e.g., professional) and nonwork (e.g., kinship, religious) identities in the workplace to explore how coactivation of multiple social and role identifications may affect engagement in workplace crimes. At a very basic level, our framework suggests that identification with any identity which evokes morality (e.g., religious, prosocial facet of professional, child), when coactivated with organizational over-(dis-)identification, is likely to lessen the propensity to engage in both pro-organizational and anti-organizational workplace crimes. However, our discussion of identification with professional and kinship roles, in particular, suggests that even this straightforward argument may fail to capture some of the intricacies of the relationship between coactivated multiple identifications and unethical behavior in organizations. Toward this end, we suggest that identities themselves may have different facets, which may be salient at different times. In addition, beyond issues of morality, the competing loyalties evoked with family identities may also influence the relationship between organizational (dis-)identification and workplace crimes. Below we discuss three areas for future research that we believe follow from our arguments.

Avenues for future research

Examine a broader range of identities and identifications in organizations. While researchers are increasingly looking at identification with groups or roles as facilitators or inhibitors of workplace crimes and unethical behaviors more generally, research in this area still suffers from limitations of looking at a small number of identities. With regard to the subset of identities examined, we have argued that most of the work has centered on organizational identification and moral identity, although interesting research has been done on religious (e.g., Hardy et al. 2012), occupational/professional (e.g., Leavitt et al. 2012) and child identities (e.g., Moshman 2005). While this is a promising start, research may want to expand this list even further.

For example, to understand why morality varies across individuals with different political views, Haidt and colleagues (Graham et al. 2009; Haidt and Graham 2007) developed the Moral Foundations Theory, which proposes six foundations of morality: care/harm, fairness/cheating, loyalty/betrayal, authority/subversion, sanctity/degradation, and liberty/oppression. They found that political liberals create morality by relying primarily on care/harm, fairness/cheating, and liberty/oppression, while conservatives rely on all six foundations. This suggests several, and sometimes competing, predictions. On the one hand, because loyalty/betrayal is a foundation used by political conservatives, those who over-identify with their organizations may be even more prone to engage in pro-organizational crimes. Political liberals who over-disidentify with their organizations may not draw on this loyalty base and thus may be even more likely to engage in anti-organizational crimes. On the other hand, by drawing upon more moral bases, political conservatives may have at their disposal more rationales to not engage in, as well as more rationales to engage in, workplace crimes. Thus, future research may explore whether political identity (or identification with a political ideology) influences either the amount or type of corporate crimes committed.

Continue to explore the complexities of coactivated identities and identifications. Building from the prior recommendations, we also suggest that research should look at the dynamics of multiple identities and identifications, particularly coactivated identities and identifications. As we have noted, conflicts can occur between identities (e.g., family vs. organizational), and different role identities can also have diverse and competing facets within them (e.g., common good versus market values in professionals). Future work may want to examine these dynamics more closely. For example, librarians are charged both with safeguarding knowledge and being activate participants in making sure knowledge is available to others (Pratt and Dutton 2000). Different conditions may make different facets of these identities salient at different times, which in turn may influence how these identities interact with organizational over-(dis-)identification in influencing propensity to engage in different types of workplace crimes. While we used professional identities to illustrate this point, such facets may also exist in religious and kinship identities. For example, at times, one's religious identity may suggest "love one another" while at other times it may suggest "denounce heretics." Thus, there may be times when evoking a religious identity may exacerbate workplace crimes, especially if organizational elites are from a negatively perceived religious "outgroup."

These arguments about facets of identity further suggest that researchers exploring multiple identity dynamics in workplace crimes need to pay close attention to context. For example, we suggested that a for-profit organization might trigger a market logic while a nonprofit may trigger a more prosocial logic in professionals. Similarly, pictures of one's self as a kid may trigger a very different response than pictures of one's own kids. The former may signal purity while the latter may signal protectiveness and may lead to the evocation of competing loyalties and possibly very different types of behaviors. Thus, contextual cues may not only trigger a particular type of identity (e.g., professional or religious) but they may also signal which facet of an identity is triggered (e.g., prosocial or market).

In exploring contextual triggers, research may also want to explore the effectiveness of these triggers over time. We have proposed that by increasing identification with a religious role or with one's past role as a child, we may be able to reduce the negative consequences of over-identification or over-disidentification with the organization. One way to increase identification with these roles is by priming individuals with certain artifacts (e.g., religious mottos) and workplace initiatives and thus activating their moral standards and values – factors which will discourage these individuals from engaging in wrongdoing in their organizations. However, repeated exposure to the same artifacts may reduce their effectiveness over time (Bornstein 1989). So future research should: (a) explore which artifacts as well as which organizational initiatives and policies potentially increase identification to these roles; (b) understand how long the effects of these stimuli last; and (c) investigate if and how changing these stimuli over time is likely to increase or decrease the effects of over-identification and over-disidentification with the organization on workplace crimes. Put differently, future research needs to explore ways in which identities and identification to roles (or groups) that propel moral behaviors are activated, and the long-term and short-term effects of these triggers.

Finally, our arguments in this chapter also point to the temporal elements of identities. Identification with some roles such as that of a child may point to who one was in the past, but identification with other roles may direct one to who he or she wants to be in the future (e.g., a PhD student identifying with the role of an academic may view himself or herself as the kind of professor he or she wants to be in the future). This temporality of identities is likely to affect the organizational identification–workplace crimes relationship. Compared to identities which point to the past, those that point to the future may be more likely to induce people to be more positive and optimistic (Wilson and Gilbert 2003). Individuals who identify with future-oriented roles are thus likely to underestimate the effects of external factors on their reactions to events in the future and overestimate their engagement in moral behaviors. They are also likely to view themselves as being moral because they want to hold positive views of themselves (Mazar et al. 2008). Therefore, identification with future-oriented roles may moderate the effects of over-(dis-)identification with the organization on workplace crimes such that as the identification with a future-oriented role increases, the effects of over-(dis-)identification with the organization on workplace crimes may weaken.

Move beyond workplace crime to include other ethical decisions. A third way our framework can be extended is by investigating how the interplay between and among different identities/identifications influences how individuals respond to "right versus right" ethical dilemmas (Kidder 1995). In this chapter, we have exclusively focused on right versus wrong decisions (e.g., engaging in workplace crime or not), but Kidder has proposed four forms of right versus right ethical dilemmas: individual versus community in which one needs to determine if an individual's needs possibly surpass the needs of the community; justice versus mercy, which is about the conflict between fairness and equal treatment on one hand and compassion and understanding of special circumstances on the other; truth versus loyalty, which relates to being honest versus expressing allegiance to an individual, a group, or a set of ideas; and short term versus long term, which deals with the requirements of the present against the need for a safe future. Future research should focus on how multiple identities/identifications affect individuals' decisions when faced with these right versus right dilemmas. For instance, individuals who over-identify with their organizations and who strongly identify with a religious role may find it difficult to resolve justice versus mercy dilemmas, such as someone who violates a company's dress code for wearing a religiously prescribed head covering. The over-identification with the organization may influence the individual to punish, but strong identification with a religious role may inspire the individual to make an exception. Future research should therefore extend our framework to include right versus right ethical dilemmas and explore ways in which these dilemmas can be resolved.

Practical implications

Our framework has several practical implications and we highlight some of them below. In particular, our research suggests that to the degree that "bringing your whole self to work" involves accepting one's identification with religious, professional, and kinship roles, individuals in the workplace may – at least in some circumstances – engage in less workplace crime. But the devil is in the details, and organizations have to be cognizant about which identities, and which facets of these identities, are likely to attenuate as opposed to exacerbate the relationship between organizational identification and engaging in criminal behavior at work. Moreover, there are ethical issues involved with the management of these identities. Below are four general suggestions for organizations to consider:

Personalization of space may lead to unintended consequences. Beyond issues of identity and control that accompany personalization of space in organizations (see Elsbach and Pratt 2008), organizations may want to carefully consider the potential ethical outcomes of allowing certain photos, pictures, and other visible symbols to adorn the office place. For example, in 2012, U.S. News and World Report published an article listing eight items which one might want to keep out of the workplace (Harper 2012). One of these items was "your child's artwork." We contend that this is a complex issue. While we agree that this may trigger protectiveness via a familial role, the co-activation of this role may decrease pro-organizational crime for over-identifiers, but increase the propensity to commit some types of crimes by over-disidentifiers.[6] Adding to this complexity, displaying

---

[6] A recent study by Gallup (2013) showed that among the employed population in 142 countries worldwide, almost 24 percent of the individuals surveyed were "actively disengaged" (and 63 percent were "not engaged") in the workplace. While being actively disengaged may not necessarily mean that individuals strongly disidentify with their organizations, it does highlight the fact that many employed individuals in today's organizations are highly dissatisfied by their work and their organizations. To the degree that such dissatisfaction leads to the formation of over-disidentification with the organization, these individuals may be more likely to engage in workplace crimes which harm the organization if

other children's artifacts – while looking similar to familial artifacts – may lead to a very different result: they may consciously or subconsciously make an employee experience a state of feeling morally clean and innocent. This feeling of moral purity will then defend against temptations which may arise in the workplace to engage in workplace crimes.

Allowing respectful expression of religion in the workplace may minimize wrongdoing in organizations. In the United States, Title VII of the Civil Rights Act of 1964 prohibits employers, including private-sector, state, and local government employers, from discriminating in employment based on race, color, religion, sex, or national origin. With respect to religion, Title VII prohibits, among other things, denial of reasonable accommodation for sincerely held religious practices, unless the accommodation would cause an undue hardship for the employer. Despite this law, there are several reported instances in which expression of religion in the workplace has been denied by organizations in the United States. To illustrate, an NBC news report affirmed that an employee at a ski resort in Colorado was told not to play Christian music while on duty; a doctor interviewing for a job in Dallas was informed that she would not be allowed to wear her hijab (a traditional Muslim head scarf); and Home Depot fired an employee in Florida for wearing a button on his work apron that mentioned God (Tahmincioglu 2009). It is perhaps not surprising that reports suggest that religious discrimination rose more than 50 percent between 1996 and 2006 (Liberman 2007).

There may be several reasons for the organizations' reluctance to allow an expression of religious beliefs in the workplace (e.g., to ensure that employees and customers are not made uncomfortable); however, based on the framework proposed in the chapter, we recommend that by allowing respectful expression of religion in the workplace, leaders and managers may minimize occurrences of workplace crimes since existing research suggests that religious artifacts are likely to make morality salient for individuals. As a result, they may be less likely to engage in wrongdoing in the workplace – irrespective of whether they view the organization as reflecting who they are or who they aren't.

provided with the opportunity. Increasing identification with a familial role – through photographs and artifacts which remind these individuals of the importance of their families – may provide these individuals with additional motivation to engage in these negative behaviors.

Remind professionals of their "institutional roots." Professions began as "institutionalized vocations" (Sullivan 2004: 15) whose purpose was to better society as a whole. While this purpose may be becoming eroded via market forces, it may behoove organizations to attempt to recapture the original purpose of professions. Displays of a profession's code of ethics, testimonials from people who benefit from a professional's selfless actions, or even displaying artifacts harkening to earlier times of professionals (e.g., a stethoscope) might help trigger the prosocial facets of a professional identity. A similar effect could also result from allowing professionals the opportunities to take service sabbaticals or to engage in pro-bono work on behalf of the organization. For example, after the Haiti earthquake in 2010, doctors from the University of Miami Miller School of Medicine staffed and ran a field hospital in Port-au-Prince. One of the doctors who joined this initiative just days after the earthquake later said, "It was just absolutely a profoundly moving experience – sort of getting back the joy of practicing and healing" (npr.org/templates/story/story.php?storyId=123385139), which makes salient and reenergizes the prosocial elements of the professional identity. The net result could be that professionals who view their companies as self-defining (either in terms of "who they are" or "who they are not") may have less of an inclination to engage in either pro-organizational or anti-organizational crime when given the opportunity.

The ethics and legality of managing moral behavior via identity. Perhaps ironically, another managerial issue is the ethics, and perhaps legality, of managing moral behavior via identity. For example, role identity theory suggests that some identities (e.g., religious) may be chronically salient for individuals, that is, individuals may chronically identify with some roles irrespective of the context. If our arguments about the moderating effect of identification with a religious role hold true, does this mean it would be prudent for organizations to select individuals with a chronically salient religious identity because these individuals are less likely to engage in pro- or anti-organizational workplace crimes even if they over-identify or over-disidentify with the organization? Some privately held organizations appear to follow this logic – if not by hiring religious employees, then by espousing religious beliefs at work (see Ashforth and Pratt 2003). However, could such a practice also lead to narrowness in how organizational members function or see the world, as would be expected by an "attraction-selection-attrition" model (Schneider 1987)? Moreover, would hiring upon such grounds be legal in publicly held firms or government organizations?

In addition, we have drawn upon research on priming (Ferguson and Bargh 2004) and argued that organizational artifacts and practices can activate morally infused work and nonwork identities. However, the effects of such primes work outside of conscious awareness (see Pratt and Crosina 2016 for review). Is it ethical for organizations to set up primes that may work nonconsciously? What obligation do organizations have for letting employees know about their attempts to reduce workplace crime in this way? Taken together, while the salience of some work and nonwork identifications may have complex effects on the propensity of employees to commit pro- or anti-organizational crimes, several issues remain regarding the degree to which these dynamics can and should be managed by organizations.

Conclusion

Recent research has argued that when people over-identify or over-disidentify with their organizations, they are more prone to commit workplace crimes. However, people bring and deploy other work (e.g., professional) and nonwork (e.g., religious, kinship) identities in the workplace that may inhibit or strengthen these impulses. Our research suggests that the coactivation of identifications with these roles may set in motion some complex dynamics, which may leave the identity carriers wondering, "Is it me? Or is it me?" when considering their willingness to commit crimes in the workplace.

References

Abbott, A. 1988. *The System of Professions: An Essay on the Division of Labor.* Chicago: University of Chicago.

Ashforth, B. E. and Mael, F. A. 1989. "Social identity theory and the organization," *Academy of Management Review* 14: 20–39.

Ashforth, B. E. and Pratt, M. G. 2003. "Institutionalized spirituality: An oxymoron," in R. A. Giacalone and C. L. Jurkiewicz (eds.), *Handbook of Workplace Spirituality and Organizational Performance*: 93–107. Armonk, NY: M.E. Sharpe.

Baumeister, R. F., Bauer, I. M., and Lloyd, S. A. 2010. "Choice, free will, and religion," *Psychology of Religion and Spirituality* 2(2): 67–82.

Becker, J. C. and Tausch, N. 2014. "When group memberships are negative: The concept, measurement, and behavioral implications of psychological disidentification," *Self and Identity* 13(3): 294–321.

Birsch, D. and Fielder, J. H. 1994. *The Ford Pinto Case: A Study in Applied Ethics, Business, and Technology*. Albany, NY: State University of New York Press.

Bornstein, R. F. 1989. "Exposure and affect: Overview and meta-analysis of research, 1968–1987," *Psychological Bulletin* 106(2): 265–289.

Burke, K. 1989. "Gender identity, sex, and school performance," *Social Psychology Quarterly* 52(2): 159–169.

Burke, K. 2003. "Relationships among multiple identities," in P. J. Burke, T. J. Owens, R. T. Serpe, and P. A. Thoits (eds.), *Advances in Identity Theory and Research*: 195–214. New York: Kluwer Academic/ Plenum Publishers.

Burke, P. J. and Stets, J. E. 2009. *Identity Theory*. New York: Oxford University Press.

Conway, P. and Peetz, J. 2012. "When does feeling moral actually make you a better person? Conceptual abstraction moderates whether past moral deeds motivate consistency or compensatory behavior," *Personality and Social Psychology Bulletin* 38(7): 907–919.

Creed, W. D., DeJordy, R., and Lok, J. 2010. "Being the change: Resolving institutional contradiction through identity work," *Academy of Management Journal* 53(6): 1336–1364.

Desai, S. and Gino, F. 2012. "The return to innocence: Nursery rhymes, soft toys, and everyday morality," *Unpublished manuscript*.

Dukerich, J. M., Kramer, R., and McLean Parks, J. 1998. "The dark side of organizational identification," in D. A. Whetten and P. C. Godfrey (eds.), *Identity in Organizations: Building Theory Through Conversations*: 245–256. Thousand Oaks, CA: Sage.

Dutton, J. E., Dukerich, J. M., and Harquail, C. 1994. "Organizational images and member identification," *Administrative Science Quarterly* 39: 239–263.

Effelsberg, D., Solga, M., and Gurt, J. 2014. "Transformational leadership and follower's unethical behavior for the benefit of the company: A two-study investigation," *Journal of Business Ethics* 120(1): 81–93.

Ellison, C. G. 1992. "Are religious people nice people? Evidence from the national survey of black Americans," *Social Forces* 71(2): 411–430.

Elsbach, K. D. 1999. "An expanded model of identification," *Research in Organizational Behavior* 21: 163–200.

Elsbach, K. D. and Pratt, M. G. 2008. "The physical environment in organizations," *The Academy of Management Annals* 1(1): 181–224.

Ferguson M. J. and Bargh J. A. 2004. "Liking is for doing: The effects of goal pursuit on automatic evaluation," *Journal of Personality and Social Psychology* 87: 557–572.

Fitzsimmons, S. 2013. "Multicultural employees: A framework for understanding how they contribute to organizations," *Academy of Management Review* 38(4): 525–549.

Gaertner, S. L. and Dovidio, J. F. 2000. *Reducing Intergroup Bias: The Common Ingroup Identity*. Philadelphia, PA: The Psychology Press.

Gaertner, S. L., Dovidio, J. F., Anastasio, P. A., Bachman, B. A., and Rust, M. C. 1993. "The common ingroup identity model: Recategorization and the reduction of intergroup bias," in W. Stroebe and M. Hewstone (eds.), *European Review of Social Psychology*, vol. 4: 1–26. New York: John Wiley and Sons.

Galen, L. W. 2012. "Does religious belief promote prosociality? A critical examination," *Psychological Bulletin* 138(5): 876–906.

Gallup, 2013. *State of the Global Workplace*. Washington, DC: Gallup, Inc.

Gino, F. and Desai, S. D. 2012. "Memory lane and morality: How childhood memories promote prosocial behavior," *Journal of Personality and Social Psychology* 102(4): 743–758.

Gioia, D. A. 1992. "Pinto fires and personal ethics: A script analysis of missed opportunities," *Journal of Business Ethics* 11(5–6): 379–389.

Graham, J., Haidt, J., and Nosek, B. A. 2009. "Liberals and conservatives rely on different sets of moral foundations," *Journal of Personality and Social Psychology* 96(5): 1029–1046.

Haidt, J. and Graham, J. 2007. "When morality opposes justice: Conservatives have moral intuitions that liberals may not recognize," *Social Justice Research* 20(1): 98–116.

Hamlin, J. K., Wynn, K., and Bloom, P. 2007. "Social evaluation by preverbal infants," *Nature* 450: 557–560.

Hardy, S. A., Walker, L. J., Rackham, D. D., and Olsen, J. A. 2012. "Religiosity and adolescent empathy and aggression: The mediating role of moral identity," *Psychology of Religion and Spirituality* 4(3): 237–248.

Harper, J. 2012. "8 Tasteless items to remove from your desk," *U.S. News and World Report*.

Houlette, M. A., Gaertner, S. L., Johnson, K. M., Banker, B. S., and Riek, B. M. 2004. "Developing a more inclusive social identity: An elementary school intervention," *Journal of Social Issues* 60(1): 35–55.

James, A., Jenks, C., and Prout, A. 1998. *Theorizing Childhood*. Oxford, England: Blackwell.

Katz, I. and Glass, D. C. 1979. "An ambivalence-amplification theory of behavior toward the stigmatized," in S. Worchel and W. G. Austin (eds.), *Psychology of Intergroup Relations*: 103–117. Chicago: Nelson-Hall.

Kidder, R. M. 1995. *How Good People Make Tough Choices*. New York: William Morrow.

Kreiner, G. E., Hollensbe, E. C., and Sheep, M. L. 2006. "Where is the 'me' among the 'we'? Identity work and the search for optimal balance," *Academy of Management Journal* 49(5): 1031–1057.

Leavitt, K., Reynolds, S., Barnes, C., Schilpzand, P., and Hannah, S. 2012. "Different hats, different obligations: Plural occupational identities and situated moral judgments," *Academy of Management Journal* 55(6): 1316–1333.

Lepisto, D. A., Crosina, E., and Pratt, M. G. 2015. "Identity work within and beyond the professions: Toward a theoretical integration and extension," in A. Desilva and M. Aparicio (eds.), *International Handbook about Professional Identities*: 11–37. Rosemead, CA: Scientific and Academic Publishing.

Liberman, V. 2007. "What happens when an employee's freedom of religion crosses paths with a company's interests?" *The Conference Board Review* September/October: 42–48.

May, D. R., Chang, Y. K., and Shao, R. 2015. "Does ethical membership matter? Moral identification and its organizational implications," *Journal of Applied Psychology* 100(3): 681–694.

Mazar, N., Amir, O., and Ariely, D. 2008. "The dishonesty of honest people: A theory of self-concept maintenance," *Journal of Marketing Research* 45(6): 633–644.

McCall, G. J. and Simmons, J. T. 1978. *Identities and Interaction*. New York: Free Press.

McCullough, M. E. and Willoughby, B. L. 2009. "Religion, self-regulation, and self-control: Associations, explanations, and implications," *Psychological Bulletin* 135(1): 69–93.

Morgan, S. P. 1983. "A research note on religion and morality: Are religious people nice people?" *Social Forces* 61: 683–692.

Moshman, D. 2005. *Adolescent Psychological Development: Rationality, Morality, and Identity.* Mahwah, NJ: Lawrence Erlbaum Associates, Inc.

Pillutla, M. M. 2011. "When good people do wrong: Morality, social identity, and ethical behavior," in D. De Cremer, R. van Dick, and J. K. Murnighan (eds.), *Social Psychology and Organizations (Series in Organization and Management)*: 353–369. New York, NY: Taylor and Francis Group.

Pratt, M. and Dutton, J. 2000. "Owning up or opting out: The conditions for issue ownership in organizations," in N. M. Ashkanasy, C. Hartel, and W. Zerbe (eds.), *Emotions in the Workplace: Research, Theory, and Practice*: 103–129. Westport, CT: Quorum Books.

Pratt, M. G. 1998. "To be or not to be: Central questions in organizational identification," in D. Whetten and P. Godfrey (eds.), *Identity in Organizations: Developing Theory Through Conversations*: 171–207. Thousand Oaks, CA: Sage.

Pratt, M. G. 2000. "The good, the bad, and the ambivalent: Managing identification among Amway distributors," *Administrative Science Quarterly* 45: 456–493.

Pratt, M. G. 2001. "Social identity dynamics in modern organizations: An organizational psychology/organizational behavior perspective," in M. Hogg and D. J. Terry (eds.), *Social Identity Processes in Organizational Contexts*: 13–30. Philadelphia, PA: Psychology Press.

Pratt, M. G. and Corley, K. G. 2007. "Managing multiple organizational identities: On identity ambiguity, identity conflict, and members' reactions," in C. Bartel, S. Blader, and A. Wrzesniewski (eds.), *Identity and the Modern Organization*: 99–118. Mahwah, NJ: Lawrence Erlbaum Associates, Inc.

Pratt, M. G., and Rafaeli, A. 1997. "Organizational dress as a symbol of multilayered social identities," *Academy of Management Journal* 40(4): 862–898.

Pratt, M. G. and Crosina, L. 2016. "The nonconscious at work," *Annual Review of Organizational Psychology and Organizational Behavior* 3: 321–347.

Ramarajan, L. and Reid, E. 2013. "Shattering the myth of separate worlds: Negotiating non-work identities at work," *Academy of Management Review* 38(4): 621–644.

Rothbard, N. P. and Ramarajan, L. 2009. "Checking your identities at the door? Positive relationships between nonwork and work identities," in L. M. Roberts and J. E. Dutton (eds.), *Exploring Positive Identities and Organizations: Building a Theoretical and Research Foundation*: 125–148. New York: Psychology Press.

Schneider, B. 1987. "The people make the place," *Personnel Psychology* 40(3): 437–453.

Shariff, A. F., Willard, A. K., Andersen, T., and Norenzayan, A. 2016. "Religious priming: A meta-analysis with a focus on prosociality," *Personality and Social Psychology Review* 20(1): 27–48.

Shu, L. L., Gino, F., and Bazerman, M. H. 2011. "Dishonest deed, clear conscience: When cheating leads to moral disengagement and motivated forgetting," *Personality and Social Psychology Bulletin* 37 (3): 330–349.

Sprouse, M. 1992. *Sabotage in the American Workplace: Anecdotes of Dissatisfaction, Mischief, and Revenge*. San Francisco: Pressure Drop Press.

Stryker, S. 1987. "Identity theory: Developments and extensions," in K. Yardley and T. Honess (eds.), *Self and Identity: Psychological Perspectives*: 89–103. New York: Wiley.

Stryker, S. and Burke, P. J. 2000. "The past, present, and future of an identity theory," *Social Psychology Quarterly* 63(4): 284–297.

Stryker, S. and Serpe, R. T. 1994. "Identity salience and psychological centrality," *Social Psychology Quarterly* 57: 16–35.

Sullivan, W. M. 2004. "Can professionalism still be a viable ethic?" *The Good Society* 13(1): 15–20.

Tahmincioglu, E. 2009. "Religious expression often frowned on at work: Bias claims on the rise; fitting into company culture also important," *nbcnews.com*.

Tajfel, H. and Turner, J. C. 1979. "An integrative theory of intergroup conflict," in W. G. Austin and S. Worchel (eds.), *The Social Psychology of Group Relations*: 33–47. Monterey, CA: Brooks-Cole.

Thoits, P. 1983. "Multiple identities and psychological well-being: A reformulation and test of the social isolation hypothesis," *American Sociological Review* 48: 174–187.

Turco, C. 2012. "Difficult decoupling: Employee resistance to the commercialization of personal settings1," *American Journal of Sociology* 118(2): 380–419.

Umphress, E. E., Bingham, J., and Mitchell, M. C. 2010. "Unethical behavior in the name of the company: The moderating effect of organizational identification and positive reciprocity beliefs on unethical pro-organizational behavior," *Journal of Applied Psychology* 95(4): 769–780.

Vadera, A. K. and Pratt, M. G. 2013. "Love, hate, ambivalence, or indifference? A conceptual examination of workplace crimes and organizational identification," *Organization Science* 24: 172–188.

Warneken, F., Hare, B., Melis, A. P., Hanus, D., and Tomasello, M. 2007. "Spontaneous altruism by chimpanzees and young children," *PLoS Biology* 5: 1414–1420.

Wilson, T. D. and Gilbert, D. 2003. "Affective forecasting," *Advances in Experimental Social Psychology* 35: 345–411.

Woodrow, C. 1999. "Revisiting images of the child in early childhood education: Reflections and considerations," *Australian Journal of Early Childhood* 24: 7–12.

Zahn-Waxler, C., Radke-Yarrow, M., and King, R. A. 1979. "Child rearing and children's prosocial initiations towards victims of distress," *Child Development* 50: 319–330.

13 Consequences of organizational misconduct: too much and too little punishment

HENRICH R. GREVE AND DAPHNE TEH

Misconduct, malfeasance, and corruption are all terms that describe behaviors that are against common norms and in many cases also illegal. Misconduct can be defined as "behavior in or by an organization that a social control agent judges to transgress a line separating right from wrong" (Greve, Palmer, and Pozner 2010: 56). The definition includes a social control agent, an actor with a mandate to label actions as misconduct and punish them. Accordingly, societal reactions against organizations that engage in misconduct are expected from the state and possibly also from other actors such as exchange partners, professional organizations, individual consumers, or workers. This expectation is so strong that one might wonder whether analysis of misconduct punishment is too obvious to even pursue. Are any surprises possible? In fact, research so far has uncovered a few surprises that suggest a strong need to examine the phenomenon further. First, the extent of punishment varies widely and includes cases of non-punishment. Second, the actors who do the punishment vary and include actors who should be indifferent as they are not harmed by the wrongdoing. Third, the range of organizations that get punished is broad and, as a result of stigmatization, includes organizations that did not engage in the original misconduct. Because punishment can be unrelated to misconduct, we often use the term "punished organization" rather than wrongdoer.

These surprises will remain just that – surprises – until we reach a richer understanding of the consequences of misconduct based on theory and evidence. We are some distance away from this goal, and so

We are grateful to Royston Greenwood and Don Palmer for editorial comments that helped clarify and sharpen the reasoning the aim of this chapter is not to provide answers, but instead to give a map of the task ahead and a description of the early evidence. For convenience, we divide the treatment into discussions of (1) why social control agents punish, (2) how social control agents punish, (3) who are punished by social control agents, and (4) how organizations react to punishments. These issues are interrelated but still best discussed separately. We focus on punishment by actors other than the state to avoid overlap with the criminal justice literature.

To understand the consequences of misconduct, four factors with obvious effects are the nature of the misconduct, the organization responsible for it, the actors observing and reacting to it, and the conditions of the environment of these actors. Each of these has characteristics with effects on the consequences that can be developed theoretically and, in a few cases, have been documented empirically. The natural lens for an organizational scholar is to examine the relation between the organization responsible and the actors observing and reacting, as this theoretical lens is the same as the organization and environment lens that guides much organizational theory at the macro-level. We adopt this lens in this chapter, and thus concentrate on the responsible organization and reacting actors. Misconduct characteristics are less central to the scope of organization theory and will largely be ignored, except to the extent that they are consequential for the organization/environment interaction.

Reactions to misconduct intuitively fall under the category of power use, as punishment is seen as a way to enforce adherence to behavioral norms or legal rules. However, the power use lens is far from the only productive approach to examining reactions to misconduct (Coleman 1988; Creed et al. 2014). Reactions to misconduct are based on a judgment that when an organization engages in misconduct, that is relevant to the focal actor, there is reason for reacting. These are all cognitions held by the focal actor, suggesting that a strong contributor to the theory is how such cognitions are formed. Finally, what an organization experiences as a punitive behavior may not be punishment, but rather a protective reaction by actors who are concerned about the potential damage to themselves from future misconduct. This assessment of potential threat is a third component of the theory. Arguments relevant to these concerns are found in agency theory, institutional theory, power theory, and social identity theory, and we will introduce each theoretical perspective. These theories have not been equally utilized in research so far, so in our review we do not give them equal treatment.

In the following, the main theories are discussed as mechanisms driving motives for punishment. The theories are central also in the discussion of the scope of punishment and the choice of organizations to punish. Some behaviors directed against the organization are not necessarily conceptualized as punishment, but rather are results of other cognitive processes such as reassessment of its legitimacy or caution in transacting with it. They end up being punishment in the sense of having harmful effects on the organization associated with misconduct. Because of these harmful effects, which tend to be recognized by the targeted organization, research on punishment of misconduct also includes consideration of how it responds to the punishment. Finally, punishment occurs in an institutional context that affects both the targeted organization and those reacting to it; thus the effects of this context also matter. The structure of the theory of misconduct reactions is depicted in Figure 13.1, which also shows the key portions of the argument made here. In the figure, each box has the main theoretical elements discussed. The double-headed arrows indicate key relations in the theory, while the thick unidirectional arrows show causal links posited in the theory.

Motives for punishment

A theoretical understanding of how organizations are punished for misconduct needs to start with a theory for the motives for punishment. These motives become mechanisms in the theory that predicts the next steps and are essential for understanding the scope of punishment, attraction of punishment to specific organizations, and organizational responses to punishment. The issue of motives for punishment becomes especially important because research on misconduct has drawn from different theories, explicitly and implicitly, and as a result there are some discrepancies in the explanations of punishment that need to be reconciled in future research.

The following explanations for punishment are prominent currently. First, agency theory sees punishment as a way to discipline actors to meet contractual obligations. Second, institutional theory sees punishment as a consequence of others reacting to loss of legitimacy by an actor who has engaged in misconduct. Third, power theory sees

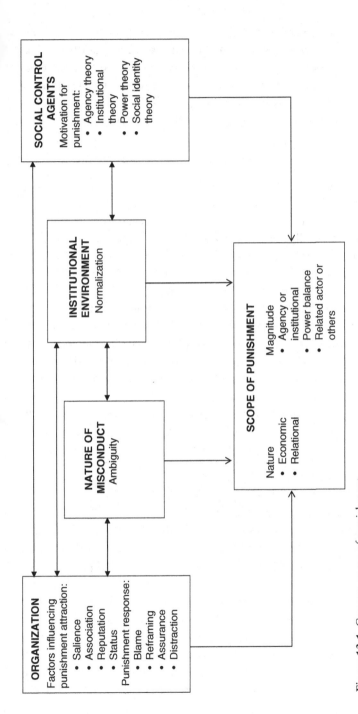

Figure 13.1 Consequences of punishment

punishment as a way to enforce compliance of demands placed on organizations. Fourth, social identity theory sees punishment as a protective action to dissociate from actors associated with misconduct. There are overlaps in explanations and predictions among these theoretical perspectives, but each offers a sufficiently distinct view of misconduct reactions to be treated as a separate theory.

Agency theory

Agency theory seeks to find ways that rational actors with a conflict of interest can collaborate, in the form of one actor (the agent) doing a task for another (the principal). The key assumption is that the principal cannot fully observe whether the agent is completely working in the principal's favor, so there has to be a reward system that works even with concealable information (Holmstrom 1979). The theory is usually phrased in terms of creating incentives that will spur the agent to make effort rather than be lazy, but the same framework can be applied to misconduct. The reason is that the lack of effort rewards the agent and hurts the principal, which is economically the same as misconduct that transfers resources from the principal to the agent. Similarly, the theory applies equally well to individuals and organizations as principals and agents, as it only assumes rational actors (Sappington 1991). The general conclusion from agency theory is that misconduct needs to be punished disproportionately hard because of the difficulty of detecting that it has occurred, which creates a need to set up a tradeoff between the potential for undetected misconduct and the harshness of actual punishment. This closely parallels treatments in the prevention of crime (Nagin 1998). Agency theory offers significantly more detail than this general conclusion, however, because there are multiple ways in which the agent can have information advantages over the principal and multiple task features, each of which leads to a different system for detecting misconduct and punishing it (Lambert 2001).

Agency theory is important to consider for punishment of misconduct because it offers a simple explanation based on economic interest and rationality. It also offers clear predictions on how the strength of punishment depends on the cost of misconduct and the probability that it will be detected by the principal. Empirical realities may be different from these assumptions because punishments can have other motives than economic interest, and actors may be boundedly rational or rule following (March 1994). Actor responses to misconduct may be motivated by non-economic reasons. In addition, agency theory faces challenges being applied at the collective level due to challenges defining who should be the principal and the agent. As demonstrated by studies on shareholder activism and boycotts (Davis and Thompson 1994, Davis et al. 2008), organizations are accountable to a variety of stakeholders who could be potential principals. Similarly, it is arguable if the "agent" being apprehended should be the guilty organization or the individual who enacted the wrongdoing. Nonetheless, irrespective of the actors' motivation, utilizing agency theory as a baseline is useful for investigating alternative mechanisms influencing the nature of punishment. In particular, when examining the quantity of punishment, the agency theoretical view is a useful baseline for comparison.

Institutional theory

Institutional theory takes the legitimacy of organizations and their actions as a central issue and predicts conformity to prescribed actions as the usual organizational response (DiMaggio and Powell 1983; Meyer and Rowan 1977). In this perspective, revelations of misconduct lead to loss of legitimacy for the responsible organization (Koh, Qian, and Wang 2013). This in turn can create a situation in which a focal organization becomes toxic to other organizations because association with it suggests acceptance of actions (misconduct) that are proscribed and condemned (Jensen 2006; Jonsson, Greve, and Fujiwara-Greve 2009). This prediction has distinct conditions and important differences from that of agency theory. One key condition in institutional theory is that association with an organization implies acceptance of its actions, including anti-normative ones such as misconduct. A second condition is that the association between actors is actually observable by others.

Multiple differences with agency theory follow. First, agency theory punishments are viewed as incentive devices that prevent misconduct and that can – if successful – allow future transactions even if misconduct has occurred. The avoidance reaction in institutional theory is not intended to prevent misconduct, though such prevention can be a consequence. Its purpose is to prevent the consequences of misconduct from spilling over to the organization that does the avoidance.

Interestingly, this can lead to punishment of organizations in situations in which no damage to the punisher has occurred, because it is the risk of spillover rather than own loss that triggers the avoidance. Indeed, the institutional perspective predicts dilemmas in which an exchange relation beneficial to both organizations may be considered for termination because one party of the exchange is worried that (harmless to it) misconduct by the other party can reduce its own legitimacy.

Second, closely related to the first, the precision of punishment is reduced. Agency theory requires punishment to be directed toward the organization guilty of misconduct and not other organizations, as far as possible. The main imprecision allowed in agency theory is that signals of misconduct may be incorrect, but still have to be punished. Institutional theory is about preventing the spread of legitimacy loss, which can cause the avoidance reaction to spread further than the organization found guilty of misconduct. Cognitions such as categorical judgments can lead the avoidance reaction to follow branches of the same organization (Jensen 2006), different organizations with the same name or industry (Greve, Kim and Teh 2016; Jonsson et al. 2009), and entire industries (Sharkey 2014).

Third, the strength of punishment is different in agency theory and institutional theory. Agency theory requires disproportionate punishment in order for incentives to be effective when there is some risk of non-detection. Institutional theory calls for avoidance by organizations in the environment of the guilty organization rather than punishment of the guilty organization, so the proportionality of the punishment becomes an outcome of how many other organizations will avoid it, and for how long. It is thus not associated with the agency theoretical variables of cost and likelihood of detection. Examination of variables that determine the proportionality, such as status or prominence (Jonsson et al. 2009; Sharkey 2014), becomes an important part of the research agenda, and research examining these variables sometimes uses other theoretical labels such as status theory (Sharkey 2014).

Power theory

Abstaining from misconduct can be seen as a demand that organizations place on each other, which corresponds to how power theory such as resource dependence theory sees organizations as interacting through placing demands and complying with demands, but not necessarily fully (Pfeffer and Salancik 1978). A key element of resource dependence theory is the identification of exchange partners as the most likely sources of demands and punishment. This is consistent with how agency theory sees punishments as ways of upholding contractual relations, but is broader because the roles implied by a principal–agent relationship is not present. Instead, a key element is considerations of which party of the relationship is more dependent on the other through the importance of the resource and the scarcity of suppliers. Resource dependence theory is more flexible than agency theory in the punishment predictions, as there is no requirement of disproportionality. It is less flexible than institutional theory because it emphasizes resource dependence as a source of demands and potential punishment. In addition, unlike institutional theory, the punished organizations in resource dependency theory tend to be organizations that engaged in misconduct. Punishment of organizations that appear similar to the guilty firm as a result of categorical judgments and spillover is more consistent with institutional theory. A key part of resource dependence theory is that dependence is reciprocal, which can cause punishments to vary depending on how dependent the potential punishing organization is on the organization associated with misconduct. The other theories do not make this prediction.

Social identity theory

There is little research that clearly takes a social identity theory stance, but it seems relevant to some of the work that takes place, and it is also a potential future research direction. Social identity theory focuses on the cognitive creation of social groupings and favorability judgments that differ between actors defined as members of the same group (the in-group) and another group (the out-group) (Tajfel and Turner 1979; Tajfel and Turner 1986). It contains theory of in-group bias, which argues that judgments of status and trustworthiness are more favorable for members of the same group, even in the absence of direct knowledge of such members. Although this theory in its static form does not provide direct predictions on punishment for misconduct, a small alteration is sufficient to make it productive. If we assume that individuals will seek to define group boundaries so that actors who have conducted misconduct become part of an out-group, then they will treat such actors as less trustworthy and desirable exchange partners.

Thus, individuals will protect themselves by halting exchange with guilty actors. The assumption is reasonable because accepting actors who have done misconduct as part of one's own group creates an unfavorable association and is likely avoided. Indeed, institutional theory could be argued to invoke self-protection, like social identity theory. Nonetheless, these theories remain different from each other regarding their predictions on spillover to organizations similar to the organization that engaged in misconduct.

Scope of punishment

Much research is now available to assess the punishment after misconduct. This has happened largely because different researchers have focused on different forms of punishment, both as a result of pursuing different theoretical questions and because of contextual differences. The result is a body of research that suggests that a very broad range of punishment actions are available as reactions to firm misconduct. While this broad perspective on punishment actions is beneficial, each research project focuses on one punishment action, which limits our ability to see whether more than one mechanism is occurring. In the following, we describe key dimensions of the scope of punishment and note that research has been unevenly distributed across them. We also discuss how the nature of punishment and predicted magnitude of the punishment differs depending on the theoretical perspective. These factors are listed in the "Scope of Punishment" box in Figure 13.1.

Economic punishment

There is a rich research tradition on economic penalties associated with agency theory and empirical economics, and the main conclusions can be summarized quickly. There are direct penalties in the form of reduced or withdrawn exchange from customers when the misconduct takes the form of customer fraud, consistent with agency theory predictions (Alexander 2008). Similarly, government reactions to misconduct are in the form of direct penalties, as agency theory would predict (Karpoff, Lee, and Vendrzyk 1999).

However, a key feature of the research on economic penalties has been the focus on punishment through stock market reactions. Such punishment does not hit the firm directly (it reduces firm value, but does not directly imply reduced sales or fines), but it is taken as a reflection of the multi-faceted economic punishments that a firm is expected to experience following misconduct. The findings are in some cases compared with known customer withdrawals and found consistent (Alexander 2008). In other cases it yields interesting subsidiary findings, such as when firms dealing with the government experience lower penalties from fraud when they have power over the government as a result of having exchange relations that are important to regulators (Karpoff et al. 1999), a finding that supports power theory better than agency theory.

These findings do raise a dilemma for the theory, however, because of how they relate to its predictions. They are clearly not direct evidence of agency theory predictions because agency theory punishment is by the principal, not by third parties such as investors. An attribution to principal punishment is possible, but it is weakened by the potential for other accounts of punishment such as institutional theory or power theory, as these would produce similar stock market effects. Second, the property of punishment central to agency theory is disproportionality, which is difficult to show because the dependent variable is owner wealth rather than firm revenue or profits. Owner wealth is different because it also involves considerations of whether misconduct reveals new information about future firm behaviors, and thus is broader than the punishment for the current misconduct event. Overall, this implies that it is unclear if the punishment results from the audiences' reaction to the act of misconduct, or their assessment of the guilty organization.

Clearer evidence on economic punishment requires a focus away from stock market values. It also calls for a work that can compare the agency theory prediction of disproportionality with the power theory prediction of power balance affecting punishment strength or institutional or social identity theory predictions that economic punishments are caused by dissociation from the punished actor rather than attempts to discipline the punished actor.

Relational punishment

An important theme in research based on institutional theory is that misconduct causes other organizations to terminate their relations with the responsible organization. Thus loss of clients was a prominent result of the involvement of Arthur Andersen in the Enron case.

It was seen as a result of clients seeking to avoid status loss and potential need to account for their continued association with the now tainted accounting firm (Jensen 2006). The legitimacy loss from the insurance firm Skandia led to a questioning of legitimacy of other firms in the same corporation, including the mutual funds subsidiary, and spread to mutual funds subsidiaries of other insurance firms or other large organizations such as pension funds, leading to customer exits (Jonsson et al. 2009). Sullivan, Haunschild, and Page (2007) found that misconduct by a firm led to a reduction in the reputation and profitability of firms that had board interlocks with it, leading to board exits from more prominent firms and entries by less prominent directors.

The studies above examined uncoordinated relational punishments, but relational punishments can also be exacted through organized protest demonstrations and boycotts. Protests and boycotts have been used as mechanisms to mobilize social change with respect to the civil rights movement for women and African Americans (McAdam, McCarthy, and Zald 1996; Ramirez, Soysal, and Shanahan 1997). Such protests are not specifically against misconduct as defined by social control agents, but are attempts to move the line between right and wrong so that organizations will change their behavior. Protests and boycotts also manifest themselves when organizations violate audiences' standards on appropriate treatment of features such as the natural environment (Bartley 2003), foreign employees (Bartley and Child 2011), and product quality (Campbell 2007; Rao 1998).

As recently illustrated during the 2011 Anti-Wall Street movement, protestors publicly shamed the Financial Sector as a result of the industry's loss of legitimacy from behaviors labeled as violations of fair practice, such as the treatment of low-income mortgage holders. Thus, protests and boycotts are collective action mechanisms that dissatisfied individuals can use to give voice to their grievances, punish guilty organizations, and influence them to change their perceived problematic practices (King and Pearce 2010; King and Soule 2007).

The findings on relational punishment are usually predicted from institutional theory, sometimes with a social movement component. Relational punishment would also be expected from social identity theory, but would in that case be more strongly guided by the social relation between the organization associated with misconduct and the punishing organization than institutional research has examined so far.

From a social identity theory perspective, punishment is more likely when the organization associated with misconduct can be labeled as categorically different from the organization conducting punishment, leading to a dyadic view of punishment that has not been exploited well so far.

Boundary issues

The division of penalties into economic and relational is sound on the surface, and so is the association of each of them with one theory, because each type of research reflects closely the concerns of the theory underlying the predictions. Closer analysis reveals a potential problem with this interpretation. The economic punishment that has been measured directly and that indirectly leads to reductions in the market value of the firm is a result of transaction partners terminating their transactions with the firm responsible for misconduct. The relational punishment that has been measured is, with few exceptions (King and Soule 2007; Sullivan et al. 2007), break-offs of transactions and hence also economic penalties. The focus on different types of penalties in the research is thus smaller in reality than in the rhetoric.

Distinction between motives for punishment is better done through examination of whether the disproportionality holds, as agency theory requires for incentives to be effective, whether punishment follows power differentials, as power theory would predict, and whether there is imprecision in the target of punishment, as institutional theory would suggest based on the legitimacy argument. Indeed, the theories also have social identity theory as a contender, as classification of an actor engaged in misconduct as an outsider (possibly along with similar ones) and break-off of exchange relations would also be predicted from social identity theory. Further theoretical analysis and empirical adjudication is likely to become an important research arena.

Attracting punishment

An important feature of the research on punishment for misconduct is emphasis on which organizations attract punishment, and how much punishment each attracts. This research documents social mechanisms closely related with the cognitive branch of institutional theory (Scott 2001). These findings consistently challenge agency theory by showing cognitive rather than economic punishment patterns. Some of them are problematic for resource dependence theory because they show punishment patterns that go beyond exchange relations, while other findings support resource dependence theory well. They are compatible with social identity theory because many findings can be explained by social groupings, but distinctive predictions from social identity theory have not been made. We order our discussion following the process from discovery to actual punishment. Thus, the salience of an organization aids discovery of misconduct, ambiguity complicates assessment of the misconduct, its reputation and associations the judgments made, and its status and power influence the reactions made in response. These organizational and environmental features affect the extent to which social control agents will react to it and are listed in the "Organization" box in Figure 13.1.

Salience

It is trivially true that misconduct becomes more available to observers when the focal organization is more salient: they can more easily become aware of events associated with it. Other mechanisms also influence the effect of salience, however, and magnify this effect. Salience can make an actor a particularly valuable target for social control agents who want to set an example, and thus it leads to attraction of punishment. This mechanism has been shown for scandals involving individuals (Adut 2005; Graffin et al. 2013). Salience has also been theorized to attract media attention, which in turn shapes the knowledge and evaluation of misconduct (Yu, Sengul, and Lester 2008). Surprisingly, there is a lack of evidence on organizational responses to punishment at different salience levels (but see Yiu, Xu, and Wan 2014).

Salience can also be used strategically. Studies on the cultural organization of a market have shown that the most powerful organizations tend to be targeted by boycotts and protests, as doing so is the most efficient for social movements. These firms are often salient as well because the power is related to characteristics such as size and market presence. The most powerful and salient firms in market have the greatest capacity to influence activities along their production value chain (Bartley and Child 2011; Schurman 2004). Thus, targeting the most salient and powerful firms allows social movement organizations to incur the most change. This targeting of powerful organizations is an action that matches institutional theory much better than power theory.

A number of studies have shown that organizational size, measured in different ways, causes greater punishment than one would see in smaller and less salient firms. This is partly a result of sheer size, partly a result of large firms having more stakeholders to manage due to their broader scope of transactions (Rindova, Pollock, and Hayward 2006). Consistent with this idea, Pierce and Toffel (2013) find that misconduct was less likely in firms that had branded goods and multiple locations, suggesting that such firms were aware of the greater vulnerability to misconduct punishment caused by their size or brand salience. Direct evidence is also available, as large mutual fund management firms were more strongly affected by the misconduct shown in one of their peer firms than small ones, suggesting that size affects spillover of punishment from a guilty firm to innocent firms (Jonsson et al. 2009). The same spillover effect has been shown for firms in the stock market after revelations of accounting irregularities (Paruchuri and Misangyi 2015).

Ambiguity

Theoretically there are clear arguments that bounded rationality means that ambiguity leads to higher variation in evaluations and in some cases weaker responses (March 1978). This is because ambiguity is a situation in which means–ends relations are unknown and desired means are unclear as well. Thus, ambiguity weakens claims of legitimacy for social control agents that seek to define specific actions as misconduct and punish them. Awareness of weak legitimacy on the part of the social control agent is likely to lead to restraint accusation and punishment in ambiguous situations. For example, work on security analysts has shown that organizations are not easily labeled as engaging in misconduct if they perform tasks that are ambiguous in nature, or simply complex (Hirsch and Pozner 2005). Thus the ambiguity of the misconduct affects the likelihood of social control agents taking action to punish potential misconduct.

Another source of ambiguity is that the information reaching potential social control agents does not have a clear interpretation. For example, information that a firm is engaged in genetic engineering of food crops may imply misconduct if a social movement interprets biotech as problematic, but could otherwise be perceived neutrally (Weber, Rao, and Thomas 2009). An important proposition that can be derived from the role of interpretation is that media coverage significantly affects judgments of misconduct, and this proposition has been shown to hold empirically (Carberry and King 2012; Graffin et al. 2013). It is noteworthy that the role of ambiguity in making evaluations more variable is based on fundamental ideas of individual bounded rationality that are found in multiple theories. Nonetheless, examining media content as a source of resolved ambiguity is most consistent with the cognitive branch of institutional theory. There is currently very little work on the ambiguity and its resolution as a source of variation in punishment strength.

Association

Although it is unsurprising that organizations caught for misconduct may incur various forms of punishment, innocent organizations that are associated with a guilty organization may also get punished if external stakeholders assume that they are liable for violating established standards of conduct. Such assumptions result from categorical judgments in which an organization is seen not only as an independent actor but also as a representative of its category that can act as a predictor of the behaviors or other organizations in the category. The key question then becomes what organizational characteristics are used to make categorical judgments. Evidence so far shows that individuals exert categorical judgments based on dimensions such as geography (Diestre and Rajagopalan 2014), production inputs (Diestre and Rajagopalan 2014), board interlocks (Kang 2008), organizational form (Jonsson et al. 2009), industry (Sharkey 2014), and nationality (Hiatt and Park 2012). Thus, innocent organizations may attract relational punishment, greater regulatory or media scrutiny, or reputational spillovers when external stakeholders categorize them and assume that they are at risk of behaving in a socially undesirable manner.

Beyond attracting punishment, categorical judgments can influence the magnitude of punishment innocent organizations may face. To illustrate, studies on the liability of foreignness demonstrate that foreign companies face higher levels of distrust (Mezias 2002; Miller and Parkhe 2002) which could cause them to face greater penalties. For example, European companies producing genetically modified products have a harder time gaining approval in the United States due to the stigma from food scares in the past (Hiatt and Park 2012). Along this line of reasoning, organizations that are difficult to categorize for reasons such as diversification may face reduced punishment, as when diversified arms manufacturers face less disapproval than specialist arms manufacturers (Vergne 2012).

The theoretical foundation of such categorization-based work is usually institutional theory, but some work has argued from a pure cognitive perspective, and social identity theory is also a possible foundation for this research. Clear distinctions between these theoretical perspectives would be difficult to make based on the research so far, which has not gone into detail on the punisher motivation or potential differences in punishment patterns based on the underlying theory.

Reputation

We define reputation as a generalized expectation of the future behaviors of a firm based on communication or recall of its past behaviors (Deephouse and Suchman 2008). Although reputations can contain highly specific expectations of how a firm behaves (e.g., innovative, price leader), they also can be summed up as an assessment of reliability and quality that allows labeling of a firm as having a good or bad reputation. A good organizational reputation is important for evaluating new information about an organization. It has positive effects, via disbelief in negative information, or negative effects through strong disappointment when facing disconfirming information (Bartley and Child 2011; Rhee and Haunschild 2006). There is evidence outside the domain of misconduct for such effects, as Rhee and Haunschild (2006) found that automobile recalls were more negative for firms with a good reputation. Thus, in their data the disappointment effect was stronger. Similarly, Bartley and Child (2011) found that organizations that infused their brands with meanings of being socially responsible were more likely to attract protests and sanctions from social movement organizations. Interestingly, firms still show interest in building reputations (Potoski and Prakash 2005), suggesting a belief in a good reputation as a shield against the damage from adverse information such as lawsuits (Koh et al. 2013). Alternatively, and perhaps more naturally, firms seek to build reputations after negative information has been released in order to control the damage (McDonnell and King 2013). These studies suggest interesting connections between reputation and misconduct punishment, but it is important to keep in mind that none of them are specifically about misconduct: all concern other forms of negative information about the firm. There is a clear need for more evidence on how firm reputation affects punishment of misconduct.

Status

We define status as a ranked perception of a firm's standing relative to other firms, where the ranking criteria are along some broad dimension of valuation such as overall quality (Podolny 1993). This makes status different from reputation because it is less specific in its relation to organizations' behaviors, and it is more specific in providing an ordered ranking of firms. Because organizational status is a position in a ranked order with some firms seen as better than others, misconduct can be either supportive or contradictory of the status order depending on whether it occurs in a low- or high-status organization. This in turn has significant effects on the punishment of misconduct. Status theory and empirical work have a similar tension as reputation research: High status can shield an organization against negative information, based on the judgment that the prior status is more credible than the new information, but high status can alternatively lead to a stronger reaction, based on the judgment that the new information is credible and highly inconsistent with the status. This tension is likely to be the focus of research in the future and has already been addressed in some work.

The argument that organizations with high status can be buffered from punishment has been made by Sharkey (2014) at the level of industry status (so categories of organizations) and empirically supported for financial market reactions to accounting restatements. She showed that higher-status industries were subject to weaker punishment by investors when their firms were caught in financial statement misconduct. Contrary to this finding, Jonsson et al. (2009) found that high-status firms were more harshly punished through customer withdrawal when they were linked with a managerial misconduct scandal. A third perspective is offered by the finding that punishment has a greater deterrence effect when high-status firms are targeted, suggesting that a state may selectively punish high-status firms to use them as examples for deterrence (Yiu et al. 2014). These studies are so different in the type of misconduct, span of judgment (e.g., organization versus industry), and audience that it is difficult to pin down the source of the different findings. The contrast between the two views of how status could affect misconduct punishment is clear, and parallels that of reputation, so further work to explore such effects would clearly be valuable.

Power

There is also some research that explicitly examines the effects of power on punishment, with a directly relevant finding being the weakening of state punishment when a guilty firm is an important supplier (Karpoff et al. 1999). It is surprising that so little work has sought to document such effects, especially in punishment from non-state actors, who also are likely to take into account power relations and have a weaker norm for fairness in punishment than the state does. An indicator of such effects is the low ability of professional associations to control the largest accounting firms in a dispute over legal standards for work contracts (Suddaby and Greenwood 2005).

It is likely that more complex patterns of power relations also matter, such as network embeddedness and exchange of personal favors and career support (Westphal and Zajac 1995). Such relations have been shown to weaken firm governance by investors and board members (e.g., Westphal and Khanna 2003; Westphal and Bednar 2008), but has not been fully utilized for examining the consequences of misconduct. An indicator that power relations have effects is the documented organizational use of retaliation against employees or auditors who report misconduct (Martin and Combs 2011; Rehg et al. 2008). Although these are useful findings with respect to the organizational efforts to reduce sources of criticism, there seems to be significant potential for examining how the external power through exchanges and network structures can be used to reduce the reporting of organizational misconduct. As an example of the type of relation that could be investigated, CEOs appear to give supportive statements about each other (Westphal et al. 2012), a relation that might extend to support also in the case of misconduct, though this has not been investigated. Such research could be approached both from a resource dependence and an institutional perspective and would seek to trace sources of support or acquiescence following misconduct discovery.

Organizational responses to punishment

A key element of research on misconduct punishment is that organizations that are exposed to such punishment will respond to it. These responses are part of how the organization seeks to control the consequences of the misconduct association and minimize damage and are displayed in the "Organization" box in Figure 13.1. The details on how the organization responds depend on the theory, and it is worth considering these differences.

In agency theory, the assumption is that organizations respond to the existence of incentives and hence to the potential for disproportionate punishment when getting caught. They do this in advance of the actual punishment. However, agency theory models do not predict that misconduct will be extinguished, but rather that each combination of rewards to the principal and agent, task structure, and information characteristics will lead to some combination of activities with less misconduct than in the absence of incentives, but more than the ideal situation of full information (Lambert 2001). Under this theoretical structure, guilty actors are stochastically discovered, and punishment is an expected outcome for agents engaging in misconduct that they think will most likely not be discovered. Both principal and agent understand that punishment is necessary in this situation in order to maintain the incentives, but that it will not change behaviors in the future because these were already adapted to the incentive structure that included the potential for punishment. Thus, punishment happens but does not change subsequent behaviors.[1]

Theories invoking bounded rationality have a different view on the effects of punishment. First, they do not assume anticipation to the same extent as full rationality does. Second, punishment is seen as affecting both the organization caught doing misconduct and other organizations or individuals who may engage in punishment. On the punished organization side, punishment could lead to the discovery

---

[1] It follows that treatments of individual crime does not correspond to agency theory assumptions, because a central law enforcement assumption is that punishment can reduce the potential for new crimes by the same individual.

that actions seen as misconduct may be detected and punished. Also, punishment may lead organizations to discover and address factors that cause misconduct. Outside the organization, it could lead to alertness in the form of damaged reputation and trust, reduced status, and out-group classification. Each of these factors can drive the organization toward more avoidance of misconduct detection (and possibly also avoidance of misconduct), because it is monitored more carefully and has better knowledge of misconduct punishment. This conclusion is conditional on the misconduct punishment being sufficiently strong to actually act as a deterrent. Weaker than expected punishment could drive the organization toward less avoidance, though the discovery could still make others more alert. The actions taken by organizations to reduce punishment impact, prevent further discovery, or reduce future punishment can be categorized as blame, reframing, assurance, and distraction. The theoretical foundation of such studies have varied, and there is currently clear potential for closer analysis of how each theory on misconduct can predict organizational actions to reduce punishment. The empirical research on each mechanism is also quite sparse now, indicating a need for more work.

Blame

An easy-to-follow route for limiting current and future punishment is for the guilty organization to deflect blame for the misconduct to other actors. A broad range of potential scapegoats are available and may include internal as well as external stakeholders, such as auditors (Hennes, Leone, and Miller 2014). Nonetheless, in many cases of misconduct the responsibility is so clearly internal to the organization that the main option is to use employees within or below the top management team as scapegoats (Pozner 2008). For serious misconduct, replacement of the CEO is chosen, and the board decision-making turns to the issue of how to choose a successor that clearly signals that the firm seeks reform (Gomulya and Boeker 2014). Social movement organizations that engaged in illegal and controversial activities to advance their causes have capitalized on the resulting increase in media attention by decoupling the organizational structure from the individuals who engaged in those activities. Thus, these organizations protected their legitimacy using claims of innocence and blaming the individuals who engaged in those activities (Elsbach and Sutton 1992;

Schlenker 1980).While some guilty organizations acknowledge engaging in misconduct or controversial activities to address stakeholder concerns (Elsbach 1994), others may not accept blame for the misconduct and engage in defensive responses (Elsbach and Sutton 1992; Elsbach, Sutton, and Principe 1998; Marcus and Goodman 1991; Oliver 1991). Such behavior could be motivated by misconduct being normalized in the focal organization's environment. Thus, the focal organization may deny allegations of misconduct as it may not perceive its actions as violating any standards in the first place and may assume that it will not get punished because everyone else is doing the same activity. Organizations guilty of violating social standards may also blame other organizations. For example, Exxon, the Coast Guard, and the Governor of Alaska all blamed each other for slowing down the clean-up efforts after the Exxon Valdez oil spill (Peak 1990).

Reframing

The organizational use of language to influence internal identity and external evaluations has been a fruitful research topic, both for organizations facing controversy as a result of controversial actions or disappointing performance and for organizations making major changes (Elsbach and Kramer 1996; Fiss and Zajac 2006). An interesting extension of this research is that organizations can seek to frame events so that even actions that are broadly seen as damaging can be given a justification relative to selected stakeholders. A good example is work demonstrating that the anti-takeover device poison pill, which reduces the potential for windfall stockholder gain and thus should be (and usually was) seen negatively, in fact was assessed positively by stockholders when framed as a way to capture value gains (Rhee and Fiss 2014). Whether framing can be used to obtain such a complete reversal of reactions to misconduct is an unexplored issue, but it would not be a radical step beyond current evidence of stock market reactions that run contrary to actual interests.

Assurance

A more powerful approach to reassuring the environment that the organization will abstain from misconduct is membership in institutions engaged in self-regulation and monitoring of members. Such reassurance methods are in use among organizations that degrade the natural environment and have been shown to reduce the misconduct incidence even among members that are under strong governmental surveillance (Potoski and Prakash 2005). In some cases, assurance is thus not mere window dressing, but an actual commitment (Short and Toffel 2010). Nonetheless, it is not well established that actual commitment is required for assurance to reduce the magnitude of punishments. In addition, assurance has been found to give greater general confidence that the organizations do not commit misconduct in the future (Barnett and King 2008; Potoski and Prakash 2005), though some work has found that the increased confidence is limited to members of the institution rather than distributed to other organizations that do not join (Barnett and King 2008). Thus, this has bearing on predictions by institutional theory as it suggests that providing assurance may be a means to limit punishment spillover. Similarly, this may reduce punishment as a result of social identity theory due to the lower likelihood of categorizing innocent organizations negatively.

Distraction

Organizations also engage in actions that appear to draw attention away from the misconduct. Different motives could drive this behavior. One is that bounded rationality places limits on the information that individuals can process and react to, so in principle any kind of information could make reactions to misconduct weaker. There is no direct evidence on this mechanism, but it would be consistent with how organizations use "noise" announcements around the time of CEO changes to avoid strong (and possibly negative) stock market reactions to the new CEO announcement (Graffin, Carpenter, and Boivie 2011). The mechanism that is more prominent in the theory and selection of empirical contexts is counterbalancing by announcing good deeds. The idea is that audiences will be more forgiving of organizational misconduct if the organization has engaged in good deeds in an unrelated domain of action.

This theoretical claim is similar to the proposed effect of reputation and status: While a high position on a good-deeds ranking could be a form of insurance, it is also possible that it sets up a high standard of behavior that will lead to stronger disappointments when it is not upheld. Evidence so far offers stronger support for organizations engaging in good deeds before or after misconduct revelations than for these good deeds having beneficial effects.

The use of good deeds in the form of prosocial acts (corporate social responsibility) as a way to build up reputation has been well documented (Godfrey, Merrill, and Hansen 2009; Koh et al. 2013). There is also evidence that these actions can reduce the impact of government legal actions against the firm on its stock value (Godfrey et al. 2009), as well as on interfirm legal disputes (Koh et al. 2013). While these studies examine the use of good deeds before problems occur, there is also some evidence of firms responding to charges of wrongdoing in the form of social movement boycotts (McDonnell and King 2013). While boycotts are different from misconduct punishment, the reaction pattern is similar, and the firms also showed a reduction in responsiveness after investing in making prosocial claims, suggesting that they believed in an insurance effect from past prosocial claims.

Institutional conditions and punishment

Perhaps most closely related to institutional theory are a set of considerations centered on the environment of an organization and the misconduct that has been revealed. These considerations take into account the bounded rationality of audiences along with the importance of symbolic considerations in evaluating and reacting to misconduct. They differ from the theory on how organizations attract different strength of punishment because this type of theory considers circumstances that are more weakly associated with organizational characteristics, focusing instead on the form of misconduct and the environment. These conditions can be categorized as affecting the perception of misconduct and are shown in the "Misconduct" box in Figure 13.1.

The assumption of bounded rationality in both the organizations that may engage in misconduct and the organizations that act as social control agents suggest that information distribution is an important part of the environment around potential misconduct. Here there is growing work on the issue of what type of surveillance is most effective, governmental surveillance or self-regulation through the voluntary associations (Short and Toffel 2010). A key difference lies in the potential for decoupling when organizations are subject to governmental regulation (Meyer and Rowan 1977), based on the assumption that state actors will not fully follow up rules, so superficial compliance is enough. There is some evidence that self-regulation is effective in general, but ineffective in regulating the actions of organizations with a record of misconduct, suggesting that decoupling can occur also within voluntary systems of compliance (Short and Toffel 2010). This matches evidence that state surveillance and voluntary self-regulations have separate and additive effects on compliance (Potoski and Prakash 2005). Indeed, it is worth considering how the assurance measures of organizations can play a role in shaping the institutional environment through which they interact with social control agents, particularly the state.

Despite the efforts of social control agents such as voluntary organizations and regulatory agencies, organizational misconduct is present and sometimes even deemed as systemic (Krastev 2000). An important consequence of organizational misconduct is that it perpetrates future wrongdoing; organizational misconduct that fails to be sufficiently punished encourages future decoupling (Earle, Spicer, and Peter 2010). Misconduct becomes normalized and entrenched in organizational processes as individuals engage in sense-making to rationalize deviant practices, and as new individuals entering the system become socialized to adopt these assumptions and norms (Ashforth and Anand 2003; Palmer 2008; Trevino and Weaver 2003). Over time, the normalization of organizational misconduct limits actors' capacity to recognize misconduct and the ability of social control agents to take effective action against offenders. Indeed, extant work has shown how the prevalence of misconduct reduces the likelihood of wronged actors, such as employees, to take action against wrongdoers (Earle et al. 2010). Similarly, anticorruption campaigns have been found to be effective only when they address the underlying taken-for-granted beliefs that individuals have (Misangyi, Weaver, and Elms 2008). These studies highlight the role of the institutional environment and communities in shaping how actors interpret and respond to misconduct. In fact, the institutional environment is likely to have bearing on the level of ambiguity that social control agents experience when confronted with information about potential misconduct. The work thus underscores the importance of taking into account a multitude of different actors, the social relationships between these actors, and the context they are interacting in when understanding the consequences to misconduct.

Discussion

Misconduct and reactions to misconduct are phenomena of practical importance, and they also have clear links to important theories of how organizations relate to other organizations and to individuals. In addition to this broad rationale, the motivation for conducting misconduct research is linked to three surprising observations. First, the extent of punishment varies widely and includes cases of non-punishment. The work on punishment scope and attraction of punishment has examined different variables indicating punishment extent and has clearly shown that the extent is determined both by the relation of the organization associated with misconduct and the potential punisher and by a range of organizational characteristics. The theoretical account that best explains the current findings on punishment extent is institutional theory, which underlies mechanisms such as salience, association, and status. However, this central role of institutional theory could be a result of inattention from other theoretical perspectives, as power theory explains punishment well when it is applied, and social identity theory seems to have unexploited potential.

Second, the social control agents who do the punishment vary and include actors who might be indifferent because they experienced low or no consequences of the wrongdoing. Thus, many papers have shown punishment by actors that were not affected by the misconduct or were affected at minor levels. This contradicts the agency theory explanation of misconduct punishment as a way of controlling the value provision of an agent to a principal. In contrast, institutional theory supports the perspective of punishment as the result of actions by actors avoiding others that have been made illegitimate due to their association with misconduct. Indeed, the key point is that the organization being punished is *associated* with misconduct, in the sense of being *cognitively* associated, which is different from being an actual culprit. Such associations can also determine the behaviors of actors that would not have been harmed by the misconduct in question. This also explains the third surprising observation that the range of organizations that gets punished is broad and includes organizations that are unrelated to the original misconduct. Thus, just as there is a range of punishing actors, unlike that proposed by economic theory, mechanisms related to association and legitimacy loss result in a range of punished organizations.

The strong role of cognition in creating associations between organizations and acts of misconduct suggests that social processes that affect cognition have a key role in explaining misconduct reactions. Just as institutional theory has had an early and strong record in explaining institutionalization through diffusion processes, the converse has been found; research on misconduct punishment has found evidence for the diffusion of punishment. These results demonstrate that social similarity guides the diffusion of punishment, but less that social networks channel the diffusion process. This is not surprising, as the diffusion of the judgments underlying reactions to misconduct is still in an early phase of research. Nevertheless, it seems to be an important and neglected area of research as it is important to understand the effects of social networks between social control agents and the punished organization, among the social control agents, and between organizations involved in misconduct and other organizations. Such research would involve considerations of social learning among social control agents and stigma spread among punished organizations (some of which could be innocent).

Perhaps most importantly, such research could explore further the social relationship between the organization associated with misconduct and the actors reacting to the misconduct. Work on economic ties and the relative power of the two organizations has already produced promising findings and should be extended to give a more thorough examination of whether resource dependence relations affect punishment. Social ties are also important because they may speak to the fourth theoretical perspective with potential for informing work on misconduct punishment: social identity theory. The potential to learn more from this theoretical perspective seems clear: agency theory relies on a purely rational model of punishment in the target selection and extent, while institutional theory relies on loss of legitimacy as the source of actions that become (and could be intended as) punishment. Neither of these theoretical conceptions is strongly relational, and neither takes into account the potential for misconduct to become a greater source of identity threat when the organization responsible for the misconduct is highly similar to the organization reacting, or is closely linked to it socially. Further investigation of the two relational perspectives of resource dependence theory and social identity theory is important because each speaks to an important dimension of how the punisher is related to the organization associated with misconduct.

A central part of research on punishment of misconduct is that the misconduct is not always actual misconduct, just perceived misconduct, and that the punishment is not always actual punishment, but reactions to legitimacy loss or identity changes that result in losses for the "punished" organization. These observations are theoretically important and well supported empirically and suggest that research on misconduct punishment should take a broad view of the organizational field in which misconduct occurs, is detected, and is reacted to. There is interesting early work on the effect of ambiguity, and of media as a resolver of ambiguity, but much more work seems possible. There can be different levels of ambiguity in whether an action actually is misconduct, and what type of misconduct it is. There can be different levels of ambiguity in how an organization is socially related to the organization responsible for the misconduct, and thus whether it will be affected by legitimacy loss or not. For organizations highly dependent on exchanges with an organization that is associated with (but not responsible for) misconduct, there can be ambiguity on how much the environment can observe and react to continued exchange with the organization associated with misconduct. Suppliers involved in labor or environmental misconduct can raise this issue.

We started by characterizing work on the consequences of misconduct as being in such an early stage that our chapter could not provide secure answers, only a map of the issues involved and some early results. We hope that this mapping is still useful in showing where the main opportunities are. It seems clear from the treatment so far that the topic most in need of theoretical contributions as well as empirical work is organizational responses to misconduct. Although it is easy to document that organizations seek to avoid punishment and to argue that responses with such effects are reasonable, the work would benefit from a much closer association with the main theoretical perspectives. What are the responses predicted from agency theory, institutional theory, resource dependence theory, and social identity theory? Two dimensions should be prominent in outlining the theory. The first is a focus on economic versus social responses, with agency theory and resource dependence theory (through the dependence relation) being more focused on economic responses, while institutional theory and social identity theory are more focused on social ones. The second is a focus on dyadic versus general responses, where resource dependence theory and social identity theory are much more focused on how the organization associated with misconduct relates to the potential punisher. Based on those two dimensions, it should be easy to distinguish predictions associated with each perspective and test them empirically. It would let work on organizational responses catch up with work on punishment scope and punishment attraction in the theory-evidence mapping.

The remaining areas of work have a stronger theoretical foundation currently, but the work is fairly unevenly distributed across the theoretical perspectives. The clearest gap is that the two relational theories, resource dependence theory and social identity theory, have done less than the other theories. This could mean that they simply are less promising lenses for examining consequences of misconduct, but it seems to us that the research is not mature enough to draw this conclusion. Agency theory and institutional theory have better track records empirically, and it is becoming clear that institutional theory is needed to explain many empirical patterns such as the surprises that started the chapter. Key future contributions from institutional theory would involve drawing lines between cognitive institutional effects and related theory such as categorization theory and status theory.

In work on the consequences of misconduct there is research in place showing significant progress and interesting findings. The work typically covers events that are important for the organizations being punished, and often the misconduct has consequences for other actors so that the social control feature of punishment is important as well. However, all areas of research covered in this chapter appear receptive to further work. Just as misconduct research overall is a relatively young stream of work, the specific area of misconduct punishment and the behavior of social control agents and punished organizations still have much work to do.

References

Adut, A. 2005. "A theory of scandal: Victorians, homosexuality, and the fall of Oscar Wilde," *American Journal of Sociology* 111(1): 213–248.

Alexander, C. R. 2008. "On the nature of the reputational penalty for corporate crime: Evidence," *Journal of Law & Economics* 42(1): 489–526.

Ashforth, B. E. and Anand, V. 2003. "The normalization of corruption in organizations," *Research in Organizational Behavior* 25: 1–52.

Barnett, M. L. and King, A. A. 2008. "Good fences make good neighbors: A longitudinal analysis of an industry self-regulatory institution," *Academy of Management Journal* 51(6): 1150–1170.

Bartley, T. 2003. "Certifying forests and factories: States, social movements, and the rise of private regulation in the apparel and forest products fields," *Politics & Society* 31(3): 433–464.

Bartley, T. and Child, C. 2011. "Movements, markets and fields: The effects of anti-sweatshop campaigns on US firms, 1993–2000," *Social Forces* 90(2): 425–451.

Campbell, J. L. 2007. "Why would corporations behave in socially responsible ways? An institutional theory of corporate social responsibility," *Academy of management Review* 32(3): 946–967.

Carberry, E. J. and King, B. G. 2012. "Defensive practice adoption in the face of organizational stigma: Impression management and the diffusion of stock option expensing," *Journal of Management Studies* 49(7): 1137–1167.

Coleman, J. S. 1988. "Social capital in the creation of human capital," *American Journal of Sociology* 94: S95–S120.

Creed, W. D., Hudson, B. A., Okhuysen, G. A., and Smith-Crowe, K. 2014. "Swimming in a sea of shame: incorporating emotion into explanations of institutional reproduction and change," *Academy of Management Review* 39(3): 275–301.

Davis, G. F., Morrill, C., Rao, H., and Soule, S. A. 2008. "Introduction: Social movements in organizations and markets," *Administrative Science Quarterly* 53(3): 389–394.

Davis, G. F. and Thompson, T. A. 1994. "A social movement perspective on corporate control," *Administrative Science Quarterly* 39(1): 141–173.

Deephouse, D. L. and Suchman, M. 2008. "Legitimacy in organizational institutionalism," in R. Greenwood, C. Oliver, R. Suddaby, and K. Sahlin-Andersson (eds.), *The Sage Handbook of Organizational Institutionalism*: 49–77. Thousand Oaks, CA: Sage.

Diestre, L. and Rajagopalan, N. 2014. "Toward an input-based perspective on categorization: Investor reactions to chemical accidents," *Academy of Management Journal* 57(4): 1130–1153.

DiMaggio, P. J. and Powell, W. W. 1983. "The iron cage revisited: Institutional isomorphism and collective rationality in organizational fields," *American Sociological Review* 48: 147–160.

Earle, J. S., Spicer, A., and Peter, K. S. 2010. "The normalization of deviant organizational practices: Wage arrears in Russia, 1991–98," *Academy of Management Journal* 53(2): 218–237.

Elsbach, K. D. 1994. "Managing organizational legitimacy in the California cattle industry: The construction and effectiveness of verbal accounts," *Administrative Science Quarterly* 39(March): 57–88.

Elsbach, K. D. and Kramer, R. M. 1996. "Members' responses to organizational identity threats: Countering the Business Week rankings." *Administrative Science Quarterly* 41(September): 442–476.

Elsbach, K. D. and Sutton, R. I. 1992. "Acquiring organizational legitimacy through illegitimate actions: A marriage of institutional and impression management theories," *Academy of Management Journal* 35(4): 699–738.

Elsbach, K. D., Sutton, R. I., and Principe, K. E. 1998. "Averting expected challenges through anticipatory impression management: A study of hospital billing," *Organization Science* 9(1): 68–86.

Fiss, P. C. and Zajac, E. J. 2006. "The symbolic management of strategic change: Sensegiving via framing and decoupling," *Academy of Management Journal* 49(6): 1173–1193.

Godfrey, P. C., Merrill, C. B., and Hansen, J. M. 2009. "The relationship between corporate social responsibility and shareholder value: An empirical test of the risk management hypothesis," *Strategic Management Journal* 30(4): 425–445.

Gomulya, D. and Boeker, W. 2014. "How firms respond to financial restatement: CEO successors and external relations," *Academy of Management Journal* 57(6): 1759–1785.

Graffin, S. D., Bundy, J., Porac, J. F., Wade, J. B., and Quinn, D. P. 2013. "Falls from grace and the hazards of high status: The 2009 British MP expense scandal and its impact on Parliamentary elites," *Administrative Science Quarterly* 58(3): 313–345.

Graffin, S. D., Carpenter, M. A., and Boivie, S. 2011. "What's all that (strategic) noise? anticipatory impression management in CEO succession," *Strategic Management Journal* 32(7): 748–770.

Greve, H. R., Kim, J.-Y., and Teh, D. 2016. "Ripples of fear: The diffusion of a bank panic," *American Sociological Review* 81(2): 396–420.

Greve, H. R., Palmer, D., and Pozner, J. E. 2010. "Organizations gone wild: The causes, processes, and consequences of organizational misconduct," *Academy of Management Annals* 4: 53–107.

Hennes, K. M., Leone, A. J., and Miller, B. P. 2014. "Determinants and market consequences of auditor dismissals after accounting restatements," *Accounting Review* 89(3): 1051–1082.

Hiatt, S. and Park, S. 2012. "Lords of the harvest: Third-party influence and regulatory approval of genetically modified organisms," *Academy of Management Journal* 56(4): 923–944.

Hirsch, P. and Pozner, J. E. 2005. "To avoid surprises, acknowledge the dark side: Illustrations from securities analysts," *Strategic Organization* 3(2): 229–238.

Holmstrom, B. 1979. "Moral hazard and unobservability," *Bell Journal of Economics* 10: 74–91.

Jensen, M. 2006. "Should we stay or should we go? Accountability, status anxiety, and client defections," *Administrative Science Quarterly* 51(1): 97–128.

Jonsson, S., Greve, H. R., and Fujiwara-Greve, T. 2009. "Undeserved loss: The spread of legitimacy loss to innocent organizations in response to reported deviance," *Administrative Science Quarterly* 54(June): 195–228.

Kang, E. 2008. "Director interlocks and spillover effects of reputational penalties from financial reporting fraud," *Academy of Management Journal* 51(3): 537–555.

Karpoff, J. M., Lee, D. S., and Vendrzyk, V. P. 1999. "Defense procurement fraud, penalties, and contractor influence," *Journal of Political Economy* 107(4): 809–842.

King, B. G. and Pearce, N. A. 2010. "The contentiousness of markets: Politics, social movements, and institutional change in markets," *Annual Review of Sociology* 36: 249–267.

King, B. G. and Soule, S. A. 2007. "Social movements as extra-institutional entrepreneurs: The effect of protests on stock price returns," *Administrative Science Quarterly* 52(3): 413–442.

Koh, P.-S., Qian, C., and Wang, H. 2013. "Firm litigation risk and the insurance value of corporate social performance," *Strategic Management Journal* 35(10): 1464–1482.

Krastev, I. 2000. "The strange (re)discovery of corruption," in R. Dahrendorf (ed.), *The Paradoxes of Unintended Consequenes*: 23–41. Budapest: Central European University Press.

Lambert, R. A. 2001. "Contracting theory and accounting," *Journal of Accounting and Economics* 32(1–3): 3–87.

March, J. G. 1978. "Bounded rationality, ambiguity, and the engineering of choice," *Bell Journal of Economics* 9: 587–608.

March, J. G. 1994. *A Primer On Decision Making: How Decisions Happen.* New York: Free Press.

Marcus, A. A. and Goodman, R. S. 1991. "Victims and shareholders: The dilemmas of presenting corporate policy during a crisis," *Academy of Management Journal* 34(2): 281–305.

Martin, J. A. and Combs, J. G. 2011. "Does it take a village to raise a whistleblower?" *Academy of Management Perspectives* 25(2): 83–85.

McAdam, D., McCarthy, J. D., and Zald, M. N. 1996. *Comparative Perspectives on Social Movements: Political Opportunities, Mobilizing Structures, and Cultural Framings*. Cambridge University Press.

McDonnell, M.-H. and King, B. 2013. "Keeping up appearances: Reputational threat and impression management after social movement boycotts," *Administrative Science Quarterly* 58(3): 387–419.

Meyer, J. W. and Rowan, B. 1977. "Institutionalized organizations: Formal structure as myth and ceremony," *American Journal of Sociology* 83: 340–363.

Mezias, J. M. 2002. "How to identify liabilities of foreignness and assess their effects on multinational corporations," *Journal of International Management* 8(3): 265–282.

Miller, S. R. and Parkhe, A. 2002. "Is there a liability of foreignness in global banking? An empirical test of banks' X-efficiency," *Strategic Management Journal* 23(1): 55–75.

Misangyi, V. F., Weaver, G. R., and Elms, H. 2008. "Ending corruption: The interplay among institutional logics, resources, and institutional entrepreneurs," *Academy of Management Review* 33(3): 750–770.

Nagin, D. S. 1998. "Criminal deterrence research at the outset of the twenty-first century," *Crime and Justice* 23: 1–42.

Oliver, C. 1991. "Strategic responses to institutional processes," *Academy of Management Review* 16(1): 145–179.

Palmer, D. 2008. "Extending the process model of collective corruption," *Research in Organizational Behavior* 28: 107–135.

Paruchuri, S. and Misangyi, V. F. 2015. "Investor perceptions of financial misconduct: The heterogeneous contamination of bystander firms," *Academy of Management Journal* 58(1): 169–194.

Peak, M. H. 1990. "The Alaskan oil spill: Lessons in crisis management," *Management Review* 79(4): 12–21.

Pfeffer, J. and Salancik, G. R. 1978. *The External Control of Organizations*. New York: Harper and Row.

Pierce, L. and Toffel, M. W. 2013. "The role of organizational scope and governance in strengthening private monitoring," *Organization Science* 24(5): 1558–1584.

Podolny, J. M. 1993. "A status-based model of market competition," *American Journal of Sociology* 98(4): 829–872.

Potoski, M. and Prakash, A. 2005. "Green clubs and voluntary governance: ISO 14001 and firms' regulatory compliance," *American Journal of Political Science* 49(2): 235–248.

Pozner, J. E. 2008. "Stigma and settling up: An integrated approach to the consequences of organizational misconduct for organizational elites," *Journal of Business Ethics* 80(1): 141–150.

Ramirez, F. O., Soysal, Y., and Shanahan, S. 1997. "The changing logic of political citizenship: Cross-national acquisition of women's suffrage rights, 1890 to 1990," *American Sociological Review* 62(5): 735–745.

Rao, H. 1998. "Caveat emptor: The construction of nonprofit consumer watchdog organizations 1," *American Journal of Sociology* 103(4): 912–961.

Rehg, M. T., Miceli, M. P., Near, J. P., and Van Scotter, J. R. 2008. "Antecedents and outcomes of retaliation against whistleblowers: Gender differences and power relationships," *Organization Science* 19(2): 221–240.

Rhee, E. Y. and Fiss, P. C. 2014. "Framing controversial actions: Regulatory focus, source credibility, and stock market reaction to poison pill adoption," *Academy of Management Journal* 57(6): 1734–1758.

Rhee, M. and Haunschild, P. R. 2006. "The liability of a good reputation: A study of product recalls in the U.S. automobile industry," *Organization Science* 17(1): 101–117.

Rindova, V. P., Pollock, T. G., and Hayward, M. L. A. 2006. "Celebrity firms: The social construction of market popularity," *Academy of Management Review* 31(1): 50–71.

Sappington, D. E. M. 1991. "Incentives in principal–agent relationships," *The Journal of Economic Perspectives* 5(2): 45–66.

Schlenker, B. R. 1980. *Impression Management: The Self-Concept, Social Identity, and Interpersonal Relations*. Monterey, CA: Brooks/Cole Publishing Company.

Schurman, R. 2004. "Fighting 'Frankenfoods': Industry opportunity structures and the efficacy of the anti-biotech movement in Western Europe," *Social Problems* 51(2): 243–268.

Scott, W. R. 2001. *Institutions and Organizations*. Thousand Oaks, CA: Sage.

Sharkey, A. J. 2014. "Categories and organizational status: The role of industry status in the response to organizational deviance," *American Journal of Sociology* 119(5): 1380–1433.

Short, J. L. and Toffel, M. W. 2010. "Making self-regulation more than merely symbolic: The critical role of the legal environment," *Administrative Science Quarterly* 55(3): 361–396.

Suddaby, R. and Greenwood, R. 2005. "Rhetorical strategies of legitimacy," *Administrative Science Quarterly* 50(1): 35–67. .

Sullivan, B. N., Haunschild, P., and Page, K. 2007. "Organizations non gratae? The impact of unethical corporate acts on interorganizational networks," *Organization Science* 18(1): 55–70.

Tajfel, H. and Turner, J. C. 1979. "An integrative theory of intergroup conflict," in W. G. Austin and S. Worchel (eds.), *The Social Psychology of Intergroup Relations*. Monterey, CA: Brooks-Cole.

Tajfel, H. and Turner, J. C. 1986. "The social identity theory of intergroup behavior," in W. G. Austin and S. Worchel (eds.), *The Social Psychology of Intergroup Relations* (2nd edn). Chicago: Nelson-Hall.

Trevino, L. K. and Weaver, G. R. 2003. *Managing Ethics in Business Organizations: Social Scientific Perspective*. Stanford: Stanford University Press.

Vergne, J.-P. 2012. "Stigmatized categories and public disapproval of organizations: A mixed-methods study of the global arms industry, 1996–2007," *Academy of Management Journal* 55(5): 1027–1052.

Weber, K., Rao, H., and Thomas, L. G. 2009. "From streets to suites: How the anti-biotech movement affected German pharmaceutical firms," *American Sociological Review* 74(1): 106–127.

Westphal, J. D. and Bednar, M. K. 2008. "The pacification of institutional investors," *Administrative Science Quarterly* 53(1): 29–72.

Westphal, J. D. and Khanna, P. 2003. "Keeping directors in line: Social distancing as a control mechanism in the corporate elite," *Administrative Science Quarterly* 48(3): 361–398.

Westphal, J. D., Park, S. H., McDonald, M. L., and Hayward, M. L. A. 2012. "Helping other CEOs avoid bad press," *Administrative Science Quarterly* 57(2): 217–268.

Westphal, J. D. and Zajac, E. J. 1995. "Who shall govern? CEO/board power, demographic similarity, and new director selection," *Administrative Science Quarterly* 40(1): 60–83.

Yiu, D. W., Xu, Y., and Wan, W. P. 2014. "The deterrence effects of vicarious punishments on corporate financial fraud," *Organization Science* 25(5): 1549–1571.

Yu, T., Sengul, M., and Lester, R. 2008. "Misery loves company: The spread of negative impacts resulting from an organizational crisis," *Academy of Management Review* 33(2): 452–472.

14 | Who bears the brunt? A review and research agenda for the consequences of organizational wrongdoing for individuals

JO-ELLEN POZNER AND JARED D. HARRIS

The subject of corporate misconduct has become a topic of particular interest for scholars in accounting, finance, and organizational studies. Corporate misconduct is broadly defined as "the organizational pursuit of any action considered illegitimate from an ethical, regulatory, or legal standpoint" (Harris and Bromiley 2007: 351). Scholars have investigated the antecedents of misconduct (e.g., Larkin and Pierce, this volume; Palmer and Moore, this volume; Ashforth and Lange, this volume), and to a lesser degree, its immediate consequences for guilty organizations and other firms to which they are linked (e.g., Greve and Teh, this Volume). Significant gaps in this literature are still ripe for exploration, particularly as concerns the longer-lasting effects that organizational wrongdoing can have on individuals employed by those organizations, to whom consequences might adhere, and the consequences of illegitimate behavior for employees below the level of the top management team. That is, although scholars have demonstrated that revelations of financial misconduct lead to immediate consequences for organizational elites, we have scant theory explaining the mechanisms through which the taint of fraud is transferred from organizations to individuals – especially the non-elite – or what the lasting impact for any of those individuals might be.

The link between misconduct at the macro-level and consequences for the individuals who are implicated, either directly or indirectly, seems like an area ripe with opportunity for meso-level theorizing. Furthermore, extending this line of inquiry to employees of

The authors express gratitude to S. Travis Elliott for research assistance on this project, and thank Don Palmer and Kristin Smith-Crowe for helpful, constructive feedback on earlier drafts.

organizations who have no plausible connection to wrongdoing save the source of their paycheck – for example, entry-level employees, those at satellite offices, those in completely unconnected business units or operating divisions – remains unexplored. How can what we know about individual psychology, biases, and behavior inform the process through which organizational misconduct leeches into individuals' lives? What can our knowledge of organizational learning, routines, roles, norms, and culture tell us about the ways in which individuals are likely to react to wrongdoing within the organizations they inhabit? Despite the abundance of fertile ground for theorizing, almost none of this research has been published.

Indeed, what we know about the consequences of organizational wrongdoing on individuals is limited to a narrow set of about three dozen studies, roughly evenly distributed among the fields of organizational theory, finance, and accounting, with very little input from researchers in social psychology or organizational behavior. Although researchers have studied a wide range of misconduct at the organizational level, from environmental violations (e.g., McKendall and Wagner 1997) to deceptive sales practices (e.g., MacLean 2002), they have so far neglected the impact of such wrongdoing on individuals. Instead, our knowledge in this particular domain comes from a group of papers that focus primarily on financial misconduct at the corporate level, and the only individuals under observation are C-suite executives and directors, who themselves are generally C-suite executives at their home firms. In contrast, almost nothing is known about the effects of misconduct on the organizational rank and file. How do they adapt? How are turnover rates affected, and for how long? Are lower-level employees' labor outcomes on the external labor market impacted? How are the careers and outcomes of individuals outside of the organization, but whose work impinges upon misconduct – the regulators and auditors who failed to uncover or sanction wrongdoing, for example – altered by this association?

In addition, even the research on upper echelons tends not to reveal much about the lasting impact on top managers' future careers. While work tends to study executive turnover, questions about second- and third-order effects remain unexplored. Finally, this research focuses on cases of misconduct that have been detected and made public, which represents only a small portion of the wrongdoing that goes on in organizational life.

The focus on the first-order consequences of detected financial misconduct for individuals within the upper echelons of the implicated organizations is understandable, considering the challenges of empirical analysis and research design, more on which below. Nevertheless, this myopia also demonstrates the relative vacuum in theorizing about much broader phenomena, which are without doubt highly consequential for untold numbers of individuals. As such, we will attempt to use what we do know to generate research questions about the consequences of organizational misconduct for individuals in the hopes of inspiring a new way of thinking about organizational wrongdoing and opening up some promising new avenues of research.

We first review the existing literature on the consequences of being associated with financial misconduct at the organizational level for organizational elites. After defining the relatively limited accumulated knowledge of what is already known, we discuss the challenges of conducting research in this particular area, and propose a set of questions that has yet to be addressed but which has the potential to be studied in an empirically rigorous way. In this way, we attempt to define an agenda for future research that goes beyond the examination of immediate consequences to top managers of firms revealed to have engaged in misconduct, which marks most of our research to date, and aims to explore the deeper consequences of wrongdoing on individuals, which feed back to longer-term implications for organizational life.

Accounting for the consequences of organizational misconduct for individuals

Two primary streams of research address the accrual of consequences of organizational misconduct to top managers and directors. One account, deriving from assumptions of economic rationality, argues that misconduct is a signal of manager and director quality. The other, which takes an institutional perspective, argues that consequences arise from attempts to avoid stigmatization on the part of both organizations and individuals.

While a subset of these papers deals explicitly with organizational wrongdoing, many deal with the related phenomenon of organizational failure, which often results from managerial negligence. For the sake of inclusivity, we have chosen to review this stream of literature, essentially broadening our definition of misconduct to include performance- and legitimacy-compromising mismanagement.

The signaling account

The canonical work on the consequences of negative organizational outcomes for individuals comes from the finance literature, and in particular the Nobel Prize-winning work of Eugene Fama. Fama (1980) and Fama and Jensen (1983) argue that the labor markets for managers and directors help solve the agency problem by providing an *ex post* settling-up mechanism: poor organizational performance signals to markets that managers are of relatively poor quality, and subjects them to discipline both within the firm and on external labor markets in the form of turnover and reduced compensation (Fama 1980). Similarly, directors are incentivized to maintain their reputation for vigilance and managerial oversight and are penalized when they allow or fail to sanction managerial action that jeopardizes firm performance (Fama and Jensen 1983).

Signaling theory holds that, because of uncertainty and asymmetric information inherent in interpreting organizational processes, information about quality, expectations, and performance can be inferred only through the concrete actions and objective outcomes that serve as signals (Milgrom and Roberts 1982; Shapiro 1982; Spence 1973). Thus, just as managers and directors are rewarded for strong firm performance, so are they penalized for negative organizational outcomes. By this logic, organizational leaders will face labor market penalties for organizational misconduct because the actions of the firms they oversee reflect their inadequacies (Lorsch and MacIver 1989). Underlying this mechanism, of course, are the assumptions that (1) firm performance is a direct and accurate signal of leader quality, (2) firm performance reflects an underlying truth about leaders' skills, and (3) labor markets are rational, efficient information processors (Fama 1980: 296).

As quality managers are valuable because of their social capital (Mizruchi 1996) and human capital – which are signals of legitimacy (Deutsch and Ross 2003; Pfeffer and Salancik 1978; Selznick 1949) – as well as their performance (Herman 1981; Mace 1986), poor performers are devalued (Baum and Oliver 1991; Elsbach 1994; Elsbach and Sutton 1992; Jensen 2006) because they present unfavorable signals of firm quality. Organizations are, in essence, reflections of their top managers (Hambrick and Mason 1984), and evidence of poor managerial and director oversight ability reflects badly on the organization itself; when director and executive reputations are tarnished, the stain therefore leeches onto the organization, whose reputation is similarly diminished. *Ex post* settling up therefore implies that individuals who might be responsible for setting the tone of the organization or providing oversight, and who are therefore technically accountable for misconduct at the organizational level, may lose both their positions within the misconduct firm and their appointments on other corporate boards.

It is worth noting that this account takes seriously the idea that labor markets are rational and process information efficiently and accurately. That is, this account focuses on markets as abstract actors capable of fulfilling a corporate governance and oversight role. Markets are often described as if they were discrete actors, without real consideration of the sociological forces that distort market efficiency, the social psychological phenomena that interfere with individual judgment, or the possibility that observables can differ in any significant way from underlying realities. This stands in stark contrast to the symbolic management approach, which views the world through a very different set of assumptions.

The symbolic management account

Whereas rational calculations and signaling underlie the signaling account, many scholars argue that the apportionment of the consequences of organizational misconduct to individuals may be a symbolic act driven by concerns tied to legitimacy, status, and social connections. The symbolic management account therefore emphasizes the need for organizational actors to prevent their social identities from being diminished through association with discrediting characteristics or discredited actors, which ultimately leads to the loss of social ties (Goffman 1963; Pozner 2008; Wiesenfeld, Wurthmann, and Hambrick 2008). In the organizational context, this might imply the loss of investors, suppliers, customers, alliance partners, and public support, while for individuals stigmatization implies the loss of network ties and lower-quality labor market outcomes.

Unlike the signaling story provided by the *ex post* settling-up hypothesis, this school of thought does not assume that firm performance is a direct or accurate signal of leader quality or that markets are rational actors. Instead, it assumes that markets comprise a broad set of individual social actors subject to sociological and social psychological influence. This implies that observables are likely to be disconnected from underlying truths about leaders' skills and that labor markets are collectives of largely irrational, inefficient, individual information processors. Individual and organizational outcomes cannot therefore be related to each other in a deterministic way, leading this line of thinking to take seriously the exploration of the conditions under which organizational misconduct might imply consequences for individuals, and the factors that add nuance to this relationship.

Given these assumptions, to avoid stigmatization and to maintain legitimacy and status, with all the benefits and resources they entail (Pfeffer and Salancik 1978; Suchman 1995), organizations may sever ties with actors that might be responsible for misconduct. Likewise, individuals may dissociate from the misconduct firm in an effort to avoid stigma by association. Both types of symbolic action, which are empirically indistinguishable from one another (Pozner 2008), lead to outcomes similar to those predicted by Fama (1980) and Fama and Jensen (1983), but are driven by concerns for actors' legitimacy, status, and social connectedness rather than by signals of underlying quality. Dissociation from potentially tainted interaction partners allows organizational actors to distance themselves from those that might be labeled bad influences (Pozner 2008; Suchman 1995). Such actions might also be used to indicate organizational commitment to change or the undertaking of substantial governance reform to prevent the same kinds of mistakes from happening again, and as such "symbolize contrition" to external stakeholders (Suchman 1995: 598).

Reviewing the findings

There is abundant evidence establishing that directors and top managers of firms found to engage in misconduct suffer penalties; unsurprisingly, both the signaling and symbolic management accounts are supported. Upon reviewing the findings, however, it becomes clear that the different conclusions drawn are not the result of differences in methodology, data, or analysis, but rather stem from the fundamentally different theoretical approaches to the problem and concomitant articulations of the research question taken by various scholars. In the following sections, we review the research that promotes the signaling account, followed by work that offers mixed accounts, and finally research that suggests a purely symbolic account.

Support for the signaling account

A number of studies provide evidence that is consistent with a strong-form signaling account. In this tradition, markets readily penalize executives identified as most closely associated with misconduct, while going easy on their peers, and outcomes suggest that organizational performance reflects stakeholders' assessments of and information about managerial effectiveness. This research convincingly establishes that penalties do accrue to top managers and directors of firms found to have engaged in financial misconduct and its close cousin, lax corporate governance.

For example, Coughlan and Schmidt (1985) find that board compensation committees exert control over managers by changing the CEO when stock price performance is poor and by altering executive compensation. Warner, Watts, and Wruck (1988) find that extremely poor stock price performance – even in the absence of allegations of wrongdoing – is associated with substantially higher levels of turnover among top managers, including the CEO, President, and Chairman of the Board. Weisbach (1988) presents a similar finding, whereby CEO turnover is predicted by poor stock and earnings performance; this result is particularly strong for those firms whose boards are dominated by outsiders, rather than insiders.

Gilson (1989) finds that more than 50 percent of those firms that are in default on corporate debt, going through bankruptcy proceedings, or privately restructuring debt so as to avoid bankruptcy in any given year experience managerial turnover. When managers of these firms lose their positions, they are unable to find employment at another exchange-listed firm for at least three years. Feroz, Park, and Pastena (1991) similarly find that 72 percent of firms subject to Securities and Exchange Commission (SEC) Accounting and Auditing Enforcement Releases between 1982 and 1989 lost at least one top manager.

Kaplan and Reishus (1990) find that managers who reduce the dividend payout at their own firms are only half as likely to receive new board appointments and more likely to resign from or lose existing external board appointments as are executives of firms that maintain constant dividend streams. Poor home firm performance, it seems, is perceived as a signal of poor management and oversight ability.

Farrell and Whidbee (2000) find that directors' labor market outcomes are influenced by their decision-making with respect to CEO turnover. Outside director turnover increases significantly after a forced CEO ousting, particularly among directors who have little equity, make poor replacement decisions, and are aligned with the departing CEO. Outside directors who own larger equity stakes and who are more independent of the CEO are rewarded when they oust a poorly performing CEO and replace him with a more successful CEO, improving firm performance, and directors that stay on the board are more likely to gain other directorships than those that stay on the board of a matched sample firm. These findings provide evidence that the market for directors takes into consideration directors' responses to organizational crisis in determining the skill level and suitability of an individual to oversight positions.

Coles and Hoi (2003) investigate the relationship between signals of boards' commitment to strong corporate governance and directors' outcomes on external labor markets. They find that firms with directors serving on the boards of Pennsylvania companies that rejected anti-takeover provisions were three times more likely than those that accepted at least some of those provisions to add seats on additional boards. Those directors were also 30 percent more likely to remain on the board of the focal company.

Along the same lines, Wu (2004) finds that, among firms named by CalPERS as having poor corporate governance practice, a large proportion of departing inside directors remain full-time employees. That is, although insiders are removed from boards, they are not fired from their positions at the named firm. Those insiders that are removed from the board, however, are far less likely than a matched sample to receive new board appointments. Taken together, these results indicate that board turnover following misconduct might be an effort to improve governance practice.

Likewise, Fich and Shivdasani (2005) find that while outside directors do not depart the boards of firms sued by shareholders following financial fraud at an accelerated rate, they do lose seats on the boards of other firms. The loss of director positions is greater for more severe frauds and when outside directors are members of the audit committee, who have greater responsibility for monitoring against fraud. These directors are most likely to lose seats on boards with stronger corporate governance, and their departure from those firms is associated with increased firm value. This suggests that markets attribute negative organizational outcomes to directors' poor oversight capabilities and punish them accordingly.

Srinivasan (2005) finds that although the penalties suffered by directors from lawsuits and SEC enforcement actions following financial fraud are small, the labor market penalties are significant. Within three years of a downward restatement, 48 percent of directors turn over compared to 33 percent of directors of a performance-matched sample of firms, 28 percent of directors of firms that restate earnings upward, and 18 percent of those involved in restatements for technical reasons. Among firms restating earnings downward, director turnover increases with restatement severity, particularly for audit committee members. Finally, directors lose a full 25 percent of their seats on other boards, with greater losses for more severe restatements and audit committee members. The discernment among those more and less accountable for the initial misconduct, and the differentiation of consequences by severity of the misconduct, supports the signaling story.

Desai, Hogan, and Wilkins (2006) find that 59 percent of firms that restate earnings replace their CEO or President within two years, compared with 35 percent of matched-sample firms. Moreover, the future employment prospects of managers associated with restatements are worse than those of the control sample firms, with both corporate boards and external labor markets imposing private penalties, which the authors suggest to replace public enforcement mechanisms. Karpoff, Lee, and Martin (2008) also provide evidence that markets react to signals of managerial competence, finding that 93 percent of those managers identified as "responsible parties" according to enforcement actions brought by the SEC and Department of Justice (DOJ) eventually lose their positions, with the majority being explicitly fired; this compares to 23 percent of executives that are not targeted by the SEC and DOJ, and 20.5 percent of executives within a matched sample of control firms. Targeted executives are also likely to lose their shares in the focal firm, are subject to SEC fines, and lose future employment opportunities, and 28 percent of them face criminal charges and penalties. The likelihood of being fired also increases with the cost of the misconduct to shareholders and the quality of the misconduct firm's corporate governance.

Hennes, Leone, and Miller (2008) find that markets are able to interpret financial misconduct in a relatively nuanced way. They find that firms with restatements driven by true accounting irregularities – indicating wrongdoing by commission or omission – are seven times more likely to encounter CEO turnover than firms with restatements driven by errors. In firms with true accounting irregularities at the parent (rather than subsidiary) organization, 67 percent of CEOs and 85 percent of CFOs turn over, with at least one of those managers departing the restating firm in 91 percent of cases. That labor market reactions to misconduct are guided by characteristics of the wrongdoing itself suggests that the signaling mechanism is indeed at work.

Additional support for the signaling account is given by Peterson's (2012) finding that accounting complexity in the area of revenue recognition moderates the consequences of earnings restatements, including the incidence of post-restatement CEO turnover. Whereas accounting complexity – a function of the number of words and revenue recognition methods included in the relevant disclosure sections of a firm's annual 10-K financial filing – increases the probability of an earnings restatement, it is also associated with a decreased rate of CEO turnover following the restatement. This evidence that markets consider the complexity of a firm's accounting situation in allocating punishments suggests that they respond to signals of actual managerial capability, rather than symbols of managerial oversight and skill.

Wu (2004) finds that the likelihood of CEO dismissal increases when firms are named by CalPERS as suffering from poor governance, and that the relationship between CEO dismissal and firm performance is strengthened after companies are named by CalPERS, suggesting that firms and markets hold executives directly responsible for negative firm outcomes.

Hazarika, Karpoff, and Nahata (2012) find that forced CEO turnover, but not voluntary turnover, is more likely and comes more quickly at firms that manipulate and subsequently restate earnings. Forced turnover is highest when the earnings manipulation is substantial, making market disciplinary action most likely when the scope of the misconduct is extreme. CEOs ousted because of earnings management are found to lose their seats on the boards of both the misconduct firm and other firms and are more likely to be sued for misconduct than their peers at non-restating firms. CFOs experience similar penalties, as their forced departure, but not voluntary departure, is accelerated at firms found to be managing earnings. The authors conclude that these results suggest that boards are enacting *ex post* settling-up, disciplining unethical executives in anticipation of market responses.

Finally, Efendi, Files, Ouyang, and Swanson's (1988) study finds that CEOs, CFOs, and General Counsel are forced out at 36 percent of firms accused of backdating options. This is several times higher than the rate of forced turnover among matched sample firms, and the executives fired in the wake of these scandals are substantially less likely than their peers at matched firms to find comparable employment on the external labor market. In addition, to signal a commitment to corporate governance reform, boards tend to change CEO compensation to minimize the component of stock options in overall remuneration.

Moving from signaling to symbolic management

The studies above begin by painting markets as abstract but unified actors, and focus on characteristics of the firm, details of the misconduct, and traits of top managers and directors. Because individual and firm behaviors and social forces do not impinge on this research, any finding of an individual penalty for firm wrongdoing provides support for the signaling account. Once researchers begin to incorporate the behaviors of stakeholders into their analysis, they move away from a pure signaling account and toward a symbolic management account. In these studies, internal and external stakeholders take purposive action to affect the interpretation of signals of firm, manager, and director quality. While these studies do not represent a symbolic management perspective, their approach and findings straddle the line between markets rationally interpreting signals and stakeholders intentionally manipulating interpretations of actions and outcomes.

For example, Klein and Rosenfeld's (1988) study of dubious corporate governance practices finds that, when firms pay greenmail – repurchase a block of stock from a particular shareholder group on favorable terms – they experience above-average turnover within one year. This seems not to be related exclusively to poor stock performance, as greenmail tends to increase stock returns. Rather, it seems that the greenmail payment is associated with heightened conflict between shareholders and management, as evidenced by the lawsuits and proxy fights that accrue to those firms that lose managers after the greenmail payment relative to those that do not. This suggests that internal mechanisms are at work to monitor top management activity, with directors and large blockholders sanctioning poor managers directly; their motivation stems at least in part from the desire to distance themselves from sanctioning by external stakeholders.

Likewise, while Hilger, Mankel, and Richter (2013) find that poor individual and firm performance accelerate the pace of executive dismissal, they also find that a CEO's power base and effective ownership and governance structures diminish CEO replacement rates, providing evidence that there may be more at work than a straightforward signaling story. Wiersma and Zhang (2011) also find that negative analyst recommendations are associated with a greater likelihood of CEO dismissal, suggesting that it is not objectively rational markets but, to a certain extent, subjective market participants that adjudicate consequences.

Similarly, Harris (2008) finds that the diminished performance consequences associated with earnings restatements are moderated by specific firm responses such as CEO replacement and increased board independence. Although this finding could certainly be interpreted as support for the idea that poor oversight and managerial skill may have led to the initial misconduct, the study also demonstrates that *ex ante* board independence had no dampening effect on that initial misconduct, suggesting that certain governance practices may be primarily effective only as symbolic responses.

Gomulya and Boeker (2014) find that, among firms that experience CEO turnover following restatement, those with more severe restatements are more likely to name successors with prior turnaround experience and elite education. These appointments, which telegraph a commitment to organizational change and an attempt to rectify underlying organizational issues, are likely to result in more positive reactions from stock markets, financial analysts, and the media.

Directors of firms involved in the options backdating scandal of 2006–2007 also faced significant market penalties, particularly those who served on the board's compensation committee during the back-dating period, according to Ertimur, Ferr, and Maber (2012). These directors received fewer votes when up for election, and turned over at higher rates than those of matched sample firms, particularly in more egregious instances of backdating, although those directors did not lose seats on boards that were not associated with options backdating; the latter finding in particular supports the idea that directors might be distancing themselves agentically, rather than being acted on by invisible market forces.

Farber (2005) finds that restating firms have poorer governance practices relative to a control sample in the year before a restatement is issued, with fewer audit committee meetings, fewer financial experts on the audit committee, a smaller percentage of Big four accountants, a higher percentage of dual CEO/Chairmen, and a smaller number and percentage of outside directors. Three years after the restatement, however, the numbers and percentage of outside directors at restating firms rival those of control firms, and restating firms have more audit committee meetings than at control firms. While this study does not find that improvements to corporate governance practice increase or improve analyst coverage or institutional holdings, it does find that such reforms boost stock returns, controlling for earnings performance. This suggests that organizations proactively take steps to influence market reactions, enacting structural changes that symbolize a commitment to correcting firm behavior.

Support for the symbolic management account

A reasonable body of research in the symbolic management tradition focuses not on establishing that consequences accrue to top managers and directors, but rather on how and why they accrue. By taking into consideration the variation in the distribution of consequences, research in this area provides insight into the sociological forces that impinge on the process of penalization. Moreover, it assumes that individuals are actors with agency, motivations, and cognitions, with which they can intentionally manipulate signals and outcomes; penalties, under this regime, may have little to do with signals of underlying quality or culpability, and everything to do with actors' interests in maintaining their status, legitimacy, and social connections.

Some of the earliest support for the symbolic management account comes from a lack of findings in support of the signaling account. Beneish (1999) finds that, following earnings overstatements that lead to SEC enforcement actions, managers do not lose employment at a higher rate than those not involved in financial misconduct, and that the SEC tends only to impose trading sanctions on those managers who sell their own shares as part of a firm security offering.

Agrawal, Jaffe, and Karpoff (1999) similarly find that senior managers do not experience higher turnover than others following discovery of fraud, based on a sample of fraud firms identified in the "fraud" and "crime" listings in the general section of the *Wall Street Journal Index*. What these studies fail to investigate is the impact of being included in the *Wall Street Journal Index*, which implies a level of public and media attention, or being the subject of SEC enforcement actions, which tend to target highly visible firms to maximize the deterrence effect of their actions. Taken together with the robust findings summarized in the previous section, we might infer that there is less variation in outcomes among individuals associated with highly visible firms – most likely large, high-status organizations – than there is between those highly visible firms and their less visible peers. This, in turn, provides support for the symbolic management account.

Social connections.   An important mechanism that links individual consequences to organizational misconduct is stigma, or the loss of social ties through discredited social identity. Because managers and directors in place at the time of the misconduct are symbolically yet inextricably linked to it due to their presumed authority (Cannella et al. 2002; Goffman 1963; Tetlock 1985), they are discredited by association with the misconduct, a fact that can be strategically exploited by organizations interested in preserving their own identities and legitimacy (Arthaud-Day et al. 2006). In addition, high-profile individuals are more likely to be targeted by the press and other public watchdogs, making them more prone to scandal – or scapegoating – than their lower-status peers (e.g., Graffin et al. 2013; Warren 2007). Organizations may therefore dismiss managers and directors in an attempt to symbolically lay blame on those individuals and remove the possibility of them asserting a negative influence in the future (Pfeffer and Salancik 1978; Suchman 1995; Sutton and Callahan 1987).

Studies in this tradition show that managers are stigmatized by association with firms experiencing poor financial performance, leading to deleterious effects on managerial careers (D'Aveni 1989; Daily and Dalton 1995; Hambrick and D'Aveni 1992). CEO turnover is much higher in firms undergoing poor performance (Gilson and Vetsuypens 1993; Schwartz and Menon 1985; Warner et al. 1988; Weisbach 1988), and stock markets respond quite favorably to managerial changes in firms experiencing unusually poor performance (Bonnier and Bruner 1989; Davidson, Worrell, and Dutia 1993). Arthaud-Day et al. (2006) extended this perspective to the realm of organizational misconduct, and find that CEOs, CFOs, outside directors, and audit committee members leave restating firms up to 70 percent more frequently than they do a matched sample of non-restating firms; they build a convincing case for this being a reasonable symbolic reaction to the threat that restatement poses to organizational legitimacy.

Kang (2008) also finds that reputational penalties accrue to organizations that share connections to misconduct firms through interlocking directorates. This study shows that over 18 percent of firms that share directors with a sample of companies accused of reporting fraud experience abnormally low stock returns. Moreover, these penalties are more severe when the directors serving as links between the tainted and untainted firms served as the chair of the audit or governance committee at the restating firm, but less severe when observable governance structures at the restating firm signal high-quality corporate governance. This suggests that individuals, and by extension, the firms with which they associate, are tainted by their relationships with the misconduct firm. In this case it is the symbolic attachment that provides the primary trigger of reputational penalties, although this effect is moderated by signals of director quality.

Status and legitimacy. Other research illuminates the link between symbolic responses to misconduct and threats to both individual and organizational status and legitimacy. When threats to an actor's social standing are indicated, that actor is far more likely to distance himself from the source of the threat. In other words, if we reinterpret the findings from the signaling account in light of substantive threats to status and legitimacy, we find a very different pattern of results.

Consistent with this line of thinking, Persons (2006) provides evidence that individuals suffer greater consequences when their dirty laundry is aired in the *Wall Street Journal*. Compared to a matched sample of firms, those whose fraud and lawsuits were reported in that newspaper experienced significantly higher managerial turnover, as well as smaller increases in managerial compensation. Evidence of an amplifying effect of the media suggests that markets are not rational, detached interpreters of events, but rather are influenced by the actions of other stakeholders. Leone and Liu (2010), in turn, highlight the importance of individual status in directing the allocation of individual consequences of misconduct. They find that the probability of CEO turnover is lower, whereas the probability of CFO turnover is higher, following restatements when the offending organization is a newly public firm and the CEO is the founder, compared to a control sample; non-founder CEOs turn over at a rate of 49 percent following restatement, compared to founder CEOs, who turn over at a rate of 29 percent. This suggests that both boards of directors and external labor markets are influenced not only by rational estimations of culpability but also by the costs associated with divorcing an organization from its primary source of legitimacy and identity: its founder. That individual identities and the durability of an organization's legitimacy play such an important role in determining the allocation of consequences strongly implies that symbolic factors are at play.

Wiersema and Zhang (2013) find that firms accused of backdating stock options later in the scandal's history were less likely to experience executive turnover than those involved earlier. They argue that the heightened media attention associated with early identification with the scandal moderates the rate of managerial turnover. Additional attention drivers, including SEC and DOJ investigations, also amplify the effects of timing and media on executive turnover. Taken together, these findings suggest that increased attention drives the need for symbolic management in a way that is disconnected from rational assessments of managerial skill.

Similar forces seem to be at play in Burks's (2010) study, which provides evidence that the signaling effect of managerial turnover may diminish after the passage of Sarbanes-Oxley. His findings show that, although boards are able to demonstrate their commitment to improving corporate governance following earnings restatements, the highly visible step of firing the CEO is unattractively costly. After Sarbanes-Oxley, when he argues restatements may be less severe, boards move away from CEO termination and instead penalize CEOs through lower bonuses. At the same time, his findings indicate that boards are more likely to fire CFOs after the enactment of Sarbanes-Oxley. This mismatch between the severity of the infraction and the magnitude of the consequence for top managers suggests that the signaling effect of managerial discipline may be secondary to the symbolic effect of board action.

In contrast, Cowen and Marcel (2011) find that the consequences of misconduct on director outcomes are largely the result of the impact of stakeholder attention. Their study finds that non-restating boards are more likely to fire directors associated with misconduct when the percentage of public pension fund ownership is high, more securities analysts cover the firm, and coverage by independent governance rating agencies is present. From the finding that outside stakeholder attention is a primary driver of director consequences, we can infer that it is the need to defend organizational status and legitimacy – symbolic concerns – rather than rational assessments of director quality that influences organizational decision-making.

A complementary perspective is promoted by Boivie, Graffin, and Pollock (2012), who find that directors voluntarily dissociate from firms experiencing shareholder lawsuits and restatements because they endanger director reputation, whereas their motivation for joining corporate boards was to increase their own visibility and improve their reputations. Negative events are more likely to lead to director defection when the firms on whose boards they serve are high-performing and highly visible in the media – characteristics that are generally negatively correlated with director turnover – suggesting that those directors most concerned about defending their reputations are, in fact, most likely to desert in times of trouble. This argument is bolstered by Withers, Corley, and Hillman's (2012) theory that the prestige of serving on a board is diminished when the firm's reputation is tarnished by misconduct, increasing directors' willingness to exit.

Finally, Rider and Negro (2015) find that partners departing a failed law firm generally find new jobs at lower-status firms. Moreover, this status loss increases with partners' tenure in the failed firm's partner structure, but is decreased with educational prestige, independent of demonstrated partner productivity. These results suggest that status characteristics such as education can protect individuals associated with negative organizational outcomes from status loss, lending further support to the symbolic management story.

Moving beyond turnover

Having reviewed the literature dealing with the consequences of organizational misconduct for individuals, it is clear that many gaps remain. Not only is our knowledge confined largely to the realm of financial misconduct within publicly traded companies, it also addresses a limited group of top managers and directors. This indicates substantial space for further theorizing and empirical research.

This lacuna is an artifact of the difficulty in studying misconduct, which suffers more than most areas of inquiry from the problem of proper identification. The majority of wrongdoing is never revealed – or, at least, this is our assumption as a field – which makes drawing inferences based only on observable cases of organizations that got caught difficult, particularly in light of recent research indicating that firms that get away with financial fraud experience better outcomes than those that do not cheat (Stuart and Wang 2014). Given these limitations, what can we learn from the assumed small population of firms that are insufficiently skilled to hide their wrongdoing in the first place? What factors differentiate firms that are caught from those that are not, and how can we possibly correct for selection bias in running statistical analyses? If fundamental organizational social characteristics such as status, reputation, and performance influence the likelihood of being found out, is it reasonable to draw meaningful inferences about the effect of those characteristics on the outcomes realized by relevant organizational actors? Is it ever possible to pinpoint where accountability for misconduct lies with any degree of accuracy, or are all observable consequences that accrue to individuals possibly the result of scapegoating and impression management? These conundrums make it both risky and intriguing for scholars to enter into the serious study of organizational misconduct.

Because of the challenges associated with conducting high-quality empirical research on organizational misconduct in general, the ability to bring the study of individuals into this research stream is similarly limited. Consequently, research in this area has tended to focus on a few easily identifiable types of misconduct for which data are publicly available and which have clear connections to immediate individual outcomes. The cluster of studies around financial misconduct, options backdating, and questionable corporate governance practices exist because these empirical settings are advantaged by public reporting requirements, easily accessible records, and multiple empirically measurable outcomes.

The consequences for some highly identifiable groups of individuals associated with these forms of misconduct are also relatively easily traceable, particularly as regards corporate executives, directors, and other public figures; the media, regulatory agencies, and corporate disclosures provide a paper trail for most of these individuals, and those that "drop out" of public life provide similarly useful data on organizational exit, a relevant outcome in this research setting. Thus the majority of what we know about individual consequences of organizational wrongdoing therefore stems from a set of studies in this particular empirical domain.

Nevertheless, the almost exclusive focus on a few particular types of organizational misconduct leaves many questions unexplored. What can we say about organizational corruption or other types of fraud, for example? What lessons might we learn about large-scale, organizationally induced crises – the financial crisis of 2007–2008, for example – if we could access information about the responsible decision-makers, their decision processes, and private allocation of blame? What questions might we ask if we could properly identify a population – or even a truly representative sample – of organizations and individuals engaged in different types of misconduct, such as cutting corners in regulatory compliance, failing to disclose conflicts of interest or outright wrongdoing, or endangering consumers through product defects?

New directions for research

As we have demonstrated, most of what we know about the individual consequences of organizational wrongdoing focuses on the outcomes for executives and directors, which barely scratches the surface of what is possible. As Greve, Palmer, and Pozner (2010) suggest, future research must address how organizational misconduct affects organizational members outside the C-suite and boardroom. We know that failures at the organizational level have a trickle-down effect through the rank and file. For example, the perceived failure of an organization to behave in a pro-social way engenders strong reactions from organizational members (Dutton and Dukerich 1991); we must anticipate that an identity-threatening and potentially stigmatizing act such as organizational misconduct would engender similarly strong responses from ordinary organizational employees. In addition, we propose further study of the long-term and second-order effects of organizational misconduct on top management teams and directors. Below, we enumerate a research agenda focusing on both of these areas of inquiry. Because the availability of reliable data sufficient to address these questions is limited, we suggest multiple methods though which such research might be conducted.

Long-term implications for executives and directors. Although much of the literature addresses manager or board turnover as a first-order result of organizational misconduct, we know very little about how the fallout from organizational wrongdoing follows upper echelons throughout their careers. In other words, what happens after the immediate aftermath of a corporate scandal arising from misconduct? Further study of these effects could shed light on four specific areas of research inquiry.

1. *Longer-term employment and compensation effects.* For example, executives and board members known to be associated with misconduct could be tracked over time, particularly when they remain involved with public organizations. Given the more advanced ages of many senior executives and board members who achieve and maintain these high-status positions during late career, do these individuals retire earlier than peers who are not implicated or associated with wrongdoing? Are their long-term salaries and bonuses affected, and is the performance-contingent component of their compensation affected?

   Studying longer-term effects on a set of specific individuals may simply be a matter of following them over time, identifying employment changes via media accounts and public filings. Supplementing a quantitative and archival approach, future research might pursue in-depth case studies of individuals, including direct interviews. Richer qualitative data on specific individuals' experiences, while not necessarily generalizable, would likely provide deeper insight into the personal and professional toll imposed by association with corporate misconduct.

2. *Decision processes.* Another research opportunity involves the processes through which decisions about consequences for individuals get made. Whether the consequences involve turnover (who stays and who leaves), compensation structure, or other types of organizational sanctions, we know very little from a process standpoint about how these decisions get made. For instance, while several studies we have reviewed have investigated who stays and who goes, the specific mechanisms and managerial processes behind these decisions are not fully understood.

A better understanding of the decision-making process behind the outcomes we observe would be best achieved either through qualitative, ethnographic means, or through the study of board or top management team meeting minutes. Both these research approaches represent significant access challenges, as firms may be reluctant to give a researcher access to such sensitive meetings. Nevertheless, it may be possible to observe these decision-making processes directly as part of an intervention aimed at helping the organization respond to the crisis of discovered misconduct.

3. *Status effects.* Future research might also investigate the status-enhancing versus status-destroying effect of director involvement in misconduct. That is, are high-status directors tainted by wrongdoing relegated to lower-status boards later on, or do they maintain the elite nature of their connections? It would be interesting to observe how these relationships might be moderated by the director's role on the board, and whether or not they remain at or depart from the stigmatized organization. Do executives and board members associated with a corporate scandal continue to be invited to prestigious gatherings of other elites like exclusive conferences or professional society/policy meetings? Are political and other social ties affected (lobbying activity, access to political and government leadership, etc.)? Research might also simply study the effect of being associated with corporate misconduct on an individual's media prominence. Controlling for coverage that directly results from the misconduct, do these individuals experience changes in the number of media mentions, appearances, or quotes?

One stumbling block to this research is that it is difficult to measure director and manager status and reputation effectively, particularly in such a way as to be able to compare status before and after misconduct. To resolve this, well-known executives and directors might be subjects of existing ongoing opinion polls (similar to job approval ratings for politicians throughout their tenure), which might be conducted by survey researchers and social scientists.

4. *Disclosure effects.* Finally, we believe that an interesting follow-on from the study of top managers' reactions to misconduct might involve changes in disclosure practices in the wake of corporate misconduct. One effect of misconduct-associated stigma might be a change in how organizations and affected individuals approach publicity and media. For example, stigmatized executives might

engage in potential retaliation against the social control agents that label and publicize the wrongdoing by granting them less access to interviews. How do organizational elites' relationships with regulatory agencies, reporters, analysts, and other watchdogs change after misconduct is revealed? Whether they remain at the stigmatized organization or move to a new one, executives associated with corporate misconduct may become more closed, revealing less information at quarterly earnings calls, for example. Alternatively, the stigmatized firm may change its disclosure practices as well; subsequent organizational disclosure (e.g., public filings, shareholder letters) may change in scope, tone, or character as a result of the misconduct. A better understanding of how disclosure practices of both organizations and affected individuals change in response to wrongdoing could provide insight into the group dynamics among organizational elites, the ways in which they make sense of negative events, and the relationships among different corporate stakeholder groups.

Impact of misconduct on the organizational rank and file. Building on our results with respect to top management teams and directors, future research might ask questions about the impact of organizational wrongdoing on lower-level employees. In other words, what happens to non-elite individuals also associated with the misconduct? Four specific areas of research inquiry in this area seem particularly fruitful.

1. *Rank-and-file turnover.* One potentially productive stream of research might focus on employee turnover as an indicator of stigma-by-association at all levels of the organization. Turnover effects on elites are relatively well understood; less well understood is the effect further down the organization. Are middle managers and lower-level employees more likely to seek other employment following instances of organizational misconduct, even if they weren't directly involved? How are they received on external labor markets: do they move to lower-status firms and are they paid less than they were at their starting positions?

   Whereas the questions above might be answered through archival research, another set of questions might be better suited to laboratory experiments or audit studies. For example, researchers could study how potential employers interpret job applicants' prior history with misconduct firms. Research in this area might even provide a setting in which it is possible to distinguish the signaling and symbolic accounts; by asking experimental subjects questions about their attributions, researchers might be able to disentangle the effects of signaling proposed by the *ex post* settling up mechanism from those of stigma avoidance forwarded by the symbolic management mechanism.

2. *Identity management.* Researchers could approach the study of individual stigmatization by taking a cue from the research on normalizing dirty work. Ashforth et al. (2007) study the way managers handle both being tainted themselves and the tainting of their subordinates. Following this logic, future research might seek to better understand the effects of misconduct on lower-level organizational employees by exploring the cognitions through which managers and employees process and make sense of working for an organization that has transgressed.

   Another related approach might be to focus on group-level strategies for confronting stigma through identity management, building on the work of Blanz et al. (1998), or what Schwalbe and Mason-Schrock (1996) refer to as "oppositional identity work." Both individual- and group-level cognitive processes for dealing with transgressions could be explored from the perspective of actors actively dealing with transgressions, rather than those dealing with inherently tainted identities. In other words, what difference does it make if the stigma is unexpected and arises from organizational misconduct, as opposed to the stigma generally associated with a particular profession or sector? In particular, a promising line of inquiry might start with exploring voluntary manager and employee turnover following transgressions relative to those before the misconduct was uncovered.

3. *Workplace motivation.* Relatedly, further research might specifically address how organizational misconduct impacts prosocial behavior and individual job performance (Grant 2007; Spreitzer and Sonenshein 2004). Are the employees that stay with a tainted firm more likely to engage in positive changes to set the organization on a path of righteousness, or do they "check out" and stick strictly to their job descriptions? In performing their daily tasks, do they strive for constant improvement, with the goal of improving overall organizational performance and rebuilding firm reputation? What are the individual characteristics that lead to these differential

responses? These questions might be addressed experimentally, through vignette studies, or ethnographically, following Petriglieri (2011).

4. *Different misconduct, different effects.* Finally, we propose that organizational performance and the differing character of the misconduct itself might moderate many of the relationships proposed here, especially on lower-level employees. For example, the likelihood of employee turnover may vary depending on the type of misconduct the firm has been involved in. Misconduct stemming from attempts to hide poor performance might impact lower-level employees differently than misconduct that is more easily associated with opportunistic behavior of the firm's top managers. Furthermore, employee commitment may be attenuated when organizational problems only begin to emerge once the misconduct has been revealed, and these tensions may be exacerbated by the structural changes enacted in response to the misconduct and its aftermath. These research topics could be addressed through a mix of experimental studies and survey research.

Conclusion

Our goal in this chapter is twofold: first, to summarize the state of the literature linking individual outcomes to organizational misconduct, and second, to propose areas of inquiry that move us beyond the well-trodden soil of organizational elites' labor market penalties, and the tension between the signaling and symbolic management accounts of the process through which such consequences are allocated. The body of work on organizational misconduct is substantial and wide-reaching, yet the most thoroughly studied aspects of the consequences of organizational wrongdoing for individuals deal predominantly with financially oriented misconduct and its effects on top managers and directors, with a particular focus on turnover and compensation. Most studies focus on the signaling account or the symbolic management account in isolation, whereas most likely, there is an element of both processes at work in the allocation of consequences for the majority of individuals; achieving a research design that can identify each discrete effect is challenging.

Significant opportunities for the advancement of knowledge include the effects (both first order and beyond) on rank-and-file individuals (essentially all individuals outside the top management team and the board) who have been associated with or affected by organizational wrongdoing, and on the second-order (and beyond) consequences to all individuals including top managers and board members as well as the rank and file. These two broad research avenues indicate promising areas of inquiry in this field. We believe that there is tremendous room for theorizing and empirically testing the interplay between individual-level cognitive and motivational processes, for example, and negative events at the organizational level. How employees react to the revelation that they have been working among unethical colleagues – or worse, for ethically challenged organizations – seems ripe for informative and relevant meso-level research. Moving beyond what we have suggested here, one can imagine studying the long-term performance consequences of organizational misconduct, mediated by the individual-level reactions we have proposed.

In addition, we hope to inspire further research into the consequences of misconduct for organizational elites. Whether the mechanism at play is one of signaling or symbolism, the implications are real. People's careers are likely to be affected, with spillover effects to the organizations with which these elites engage. We call for rigorous investigation of these pragmatic yet theoretically interesting phenomena.

References

Agrawal, A., Jaffe, J. F., and Karpoff, J. M. 1999. "Management turnover and governance changes following the revelation of fraud," *Journal of Law and Economics* 42(1): 309–342.

Arthaud-Day, M. L., Certo, S. T., Dalton, C. M., and Dalton, D. R. 2006. "A changing of the guard: Executive and director turnover following corporate financial restatements," *Academy of Management Journal* 49 (6): 1119–1136.

Ashforth, B. E., Kreiner, G. E., Clark, M. A., and Fugate, M. 2007. "Normalizing dirty work: Managerial tactics for countering organizational taint," *Academy of Management Journal* 50 (1): 149–174.

Baum, J. A. C. and Oliver, C. 1991. "Institutional linkages and organizational mortality," *Administrative Science Quarterly* 36(2): 187–218.

Beneish, M. D. 1999. "Incentives and penalties related to earnings overstatements that violate GAAP," *Accounting Review* 74(4): 425–457.

Blanz, M., Mummendey, A., Mielke, R., and Klink, A. 1998. "Responding to negative social identity: A taxonomy of identity management strategies," *European Journal of Social Psychology* 28(5): 697–729.

Boivie, S., Graffin, S. D., and Pollock, T. G. 2012. "Time to fly: Predicting director exit at large firms," *Academy of Management Journal* 55(6): 1334–1359.

Bonnier, K. and Bruner, R. F. 1989. "An analysis of stock price reaction to management change in distressed firms," *Journal of Accounting and Economics* 11(1): 95–106.

Burks, J. J. 2010. "Disciplinary measures in response to restatements after Sarbanes-Oxley," *Journal of Accounting and Public Policy* 2(3): 195–225.

Cannella, Jr. A., Fraser, D., Lee, D. S., and Semadeni, M. 2002. "Fight or flight: Managing stigma in executive careers," *Academy of Management Proceedings and Membership Directory* N1–N6.

Coles, J. L. and Hoi, C. K. 2003. "New evidence on the market for directors: Board membership and Pennsylvania Senate Bill 1310," *Journal of Finance* 58(1): 197–230.

Coughlan, A. T. and Schmidt, R. M. 1985. "Executive compensation, management turnover, and firm performance: An empirical investigation," *Journal of Accounting and Economics* 7(1): 43–66.

Cowen, A. P. and Marcel, J. J. 2011. "Damaged goods: Board decisions to dismiss reputationally compromised directors," *Academy of Management Journal* 54(3): 509–527.

D'Aveni, R. 1989. "The aftermath of organizational culture: A longitudinal study of the strategic and managerial characteristics of declining firms," *Academy of Management Journal* 32(3): 577–605.

Daily, C. M. and Dalton, D. R. 1995. "CEO and director turnover in failing firms: An illusion of change," *Strategic Management Journal* 16(5): 393–400.

Davidson III, W. N., Worrell, D. L., and Dutia, D. 1993. "The stock market effects of CEO succession in bankrupt firms," *Journal of Management* 19(3): 517–533.

Desai, H., Hogan, C. E., and Wilkins, M. S. 2006. "The reputational penalty for aggressive accounting: Earnings restatements and management turnover," *Accounting Review* 81(1): 83–112.

Deutsch, Y. and Ross, T. W. 2003. "You are known by the directors you keep: Reputable directors as a signaling mechanism for young firms," *Management Science* 49(8): 1003–1017.

Dutton, J. E. and Dukerich, J. M. 1991. "Keeping an eye on the mirror: Image and identity in organizational adaptation," *Academy of Management Journal* 34(3): 517–554.

Efendi, J., Files, R., Ouyang, B., and Swanson, E. P. 1988. "Executive turnover following option backdating allegations," *Accounting Review* 88(1): 75–105.

Elsbach, K. D. 1994. "Managing organizational legitimacy in the California cattle industry: The construction and effectiveness of verbal accounts," *Administrative Science Quarterly* 39(1): 57–88.

Elsbach, K. D. and Sutton, R. I. 1992. "Acquiring organizational legitimacy through illegitimate actions: A marriage of institutional and impressions management theories," *Academy of Management Journal* 35(4): 699–738.

Ertimur, Y., Ferri, F., and Maber, D. A. 2012. "Reputation penalties for poor monitoring of executive pay: Evidence from option backdating," *Journal of Financial Economics* 104(1): 118–144.

Fama, E. F. 1980. "Agency problems and the theory of the firm," *Journal of Political Economy* 88(2): 288–307.

Fama, E. F. and Jensen, M. C. 1983. "Separation of ownership and control," *Journal of Law and Economics* 26(2): 301–326.

Farber, D. B. 2005. "Restoring trust after fraud: Does corporate governance matter?" *Accounting Review* 80(2): 539–561.

Farrell, K. A. and Whidbee, D. A. 2000. "The consequences of forced CEO succession for outside directors," *Journal of Business* 73(4): 597–627.

Feroz, E. H., Park, K., and Pastena, V. S. 1991. "The financial and market effects of the SEC's accounting and auditing enforcement releases," *Journal of Accounting Research* 29(3): 107–142.

Fich, E. M. and Shivdasani, A. 2005. "The impact of stock-option compensation for outside directors on firm value," *Journal of Business* 78(6): 2229–2254.

Gilson, S. C. 1989. "Management turnover and financial distress," *Journal of Financial Economics* 25(2): 241–262.

Gilson, S. C. and Vetsuypens, M. R. 1993. "CEO compensation in financially distressed firms: An empirical analysis," *Journal of Finance* 48(2): 425–458.

Goffman, E. 1963. *Stigma: Notes on the Management of Spoiled Identity.* Englewood Cliffs, NJ: Simon and Schuster, Inc.

Gomulya, D. and Boeker, W. 2014. "How firms respond to financial restatement: CEO successors and external reactions," *Academy of Management Journal* 57(2014): 1759–1785.

Gove, S. and Janney, J. J. 2004. "The effect of director linkages to stigmatized firms: Market reaction to bankruptcy," *Annual meeting of the Academy of Management.*

Graffin, S. D., Bundy, J., Porac, J. F., Wade, J. B., and Quinn, D. P. 2013. "Falls from grace and the hazards of high status: The 2009 British MP expense scandal and its impact on Parliamentary elites," *Administrative Science Quarterly* 58(3): 313–345.

Grant, A. M. 2007. "Relational job design and the motivation to make a prosocial difference," *Academy of Management Review* 32(2): 393–417.

Greve, H. R., Palmer, D., and Pozner, J. 2010. "Organizations gone wild: The causes, processes, and consequences of organizational misconduct," *Academy of Management Annals* 4(1): 53–107.

Hambrick, D. C. and D'Aveni, R. A. 1992. "Top team deterioration as part of the downward spiral of large corporate bankruptcies," *Management Science* 38(10): 1445–1466.

Hambrick, D. C. and Mason, P. A. 1984. "Upper echelons: The organization as a reflection of its top managers," *Academy of Management Review* 9(2): 193–206.

Harris, J. D. 2008. "Financial misrepresentation," *Business and Society* 47(3): 390–401.

Harris, J. D. and Bromiley, P. 2007. "Incentives to cheat: The influence of executive compensation and firm performance on financial misrepresentation," *Organization Science* 18(3): 350–367.

Hazarika, S., Karpoff, J. M., and Nahata, R. 2012. "Internal corporate governance, CEO turnover, and earnings management," *Journal of Financial Economics* 104(1): 44–69.

Hennes, K. M., Leone, A. J., and Miller, B. P. 2008. "The importance of distinguishing errors from irregularities in restatement research: The case of restatements and CEO/CFO turnover," *Accounting Review* 83(6): 1487–1519.

Herman, E. S. 1981. *Corporate Control, Corporate Power.* Cambridge University Press.

Hilger, S., Mankel, S., and Richter, A. 2013. "The use and effectiveness of top executive dismissal," *Leadership Quarterly* 24(1): 9–28.

Jensen, M. 2006. "Should we stay or should we go? Status accountability anxiety and client defections," *Administrative Science Quarterly* 51(1): 97–128.

Kang, E. 2008. "Director interlocks and spillover effects of reputational penalties from financial reporting fraud," *Academy of Management Journal* 51(3): 537–555.

Kaplan, S. N. and Reishus, D. 1990. "Outside directorships and corporate performance," *Journal of Financial Economics* 27(2): 389–410.

Karpoff, J. M., Lee, D. S., and Martin, G. S. 2008. "The consequences to managers for financial misrepresentation," *Journal of Financial Economics* 88(2): 193–215.

Klein, A. and Rosenfeld, J. 1988. "Targeted share repurchases and top management changes," *Journal of Financial Economics* 20(1–2): 493–506.

Leone, A. J. and Liu, M. 2010. "Accounting irregularities and executive turnover in founder-managed firms," *Accounting Review* 85(1): 287–314.

Lorsch, J. W. and MacIver, E. 1989. *Pawns or Potentates: The Reality of America's Corporate Boards*. Boston: Harvard Business School Press.

Mace, M. L. 1986. *Directors: Myth and Reality*. Boston: Harvard Business School Press.

MacLean, T. 2002. "Reframing organizational misconduct: A study of deceptive sales practices at a major life insurance company," *Business & Society* 41(2): 242–250.

McKendall, M. A. and Wagner, J. A. 1997. "Motive, opportunity, choice, and corporate illegality," *Organization Science* 8(6): 624–647.

Milgrom, P. and Roberts, J. 1982. "Predation, reputation and entry deterrence," *Journal of Economic Theory* 27(2): 280–312.

Mizruchi, M. S. 1996. "What do interlocks do? An analysis, critique, and assessment of research on interlocking directories," *Annual Review of Sociology* 22: 271–298.

Persons, O. 2006. "The effects of fraud and lawsuit revelation on U.S. executive turnover and compensation," *Journal of Business Ethics* 64(4): 405–419.

Peterson, K. 2012. "Accounting complexity, misreporting, and the consequences of misreporting," *Review of Accounting Studies* 17(1): 72–95.

Petriglieri, J. L. 2011. "Under threat: Responses to and the consequences of threats to individuals' identities," *Academy of Management Review* 36(4): 641–662.

Pfeffer, J. and Salancik, G. R. 1978. *The External Control of Organizations: A Resource Dependence Perspective*. New York: Harper and Row.

Pozner, J. 2008. "Stigma and settling up: An integrated approach to the consequences of organizational misconduct for organizational elites," *Journal of Business Ethics* 80(1): 141–150.

Rider, C. I. and Negro, G. 2015. "Organizational failure and intraprofessional status loss," *Organization Science*, Published online in *Articles in Advance* January 15, 2015.

Schwalbe, M. L. and Mason-Schrock, D. 1996. "Identity work as group process," *Advances in Group Processes* 13: 113–147.

Schwartz, K. B. and Menon, K. 1985. "Executive succession in failing firms," *Academy of Management Journal* 28(3): 680–686.

Selznick, P. 1949. *TVA and the Grass Roots: A Study of Politics and Organization*. Berkeley, Los Angeles, London: University of California Press.

Shapiro, C. 1982. "Consumer information, product quality, and seller reputation," *Bell Journal of Economics* 13(1): 20–35.

Spence, M. 1973. "Job market signaling," *Quarterly Journal of Economics* 87(3): 355–374.

Spreitzer, G. M. and Sonenshein, S. 2004. "Toward the construct definition of positive deviance," *American Behavioral Scientist* 47(6): 828–847.

Srinivasan, S. 2005. "Consequences of financial reporting failure for outside directors: Evidence from accounting restatements and audit committee members," *Journal of Accounting Research* 43(2): 291–334.

Suchman, M. C. 1995. "Managing legitimacy: Strategic and institutional approaches," *Academy of Management Review* 20(3): 571–610.

Sutton, R. I. and Callahan, A. L. 1987. "The stigma of bankruptcy: Spoiled organizational image and its management," *Academy of Management Journal* 30(3): 405–436.

Stuart, T. and Wang, Y. 2014. "Who cooks the books in China, and does it pay?" Available at *SSRN 2391744*.

Tetlock, P. E. 1985. "Accountability: The neglected social context of judgment and choice," *Research in Organizational Behavior* 7: 297.

Warren, D. E. 2007. "Corporate scandals and spoiled identities: How organizations shift stigma to employees," *Business Ethics Quarterly* 17(3): 477–496.

Warner, J. B., Watts R. L., and Wruck, K. H. 1988. "Stock-prices and top management changes," *Journal of Financial Economics* 20(1–2): 461–492.

Weisbach, M. S. 1988. "Outside directors and CEO turnover," *Journal of Financial Economics* 20(1–2): 431–460.

Wiersema, M. F. and Zhang, Y. 2011. "CEO Dismissal: The role of investment analyst," *Strategic Management Journal* 32(11): 1161–1182.

Wiersema, M. F. and Zhang, Y. 2013. "Executive turnover in the stock option backdating wave: The impact of social context," *Strategic Management Journal* 34(5): 590–609.

Wiesenfeld, B. M., Wurthmann, K. A., and Hambrick, D. C. 2008. "The stigmatization and devaluation of elites associated with corporate failures: A process model," *Academy of Management Review* 33(1): 231–251.

Withers, M. C., Corley, K. G., and Hillman, A. J. 2012. "Stay or leave: Director identities and voluntary exit from the board during organizational crisis," *Organization Science* 23(3): 835–850.

Wu, Y. 2004. "The impact of public opinion on board structure changes, director career progression, and CEO turnover: evidence from CalPERS' corporate governance program," *Journal of Corporate Finance* 10(1): 199–228.

15 | *Organizational wrongdoing and media bias*

MARCO CLEMENTE, RODOLPHE DURAND,
AND JOSEPH PORAC

Introduction

A social constructivist view of wrongdoing conceives organizational transgressions as the result of a two-way interaction between organizations and observers (Becker 1963; Greve, Palmer, and Pozner 2010). This view suggests that judgment determines whether organizational actors have crossed a fuzzy line separating right from wrong. This requires collecting, interpreting, and evaluating information that is sometimes ambiguous and conflicting, from many sources with varying credibility. Observers include governmental bodies, the state, professional associations, and organizational managers acting as authoritative social control agents that have formal authority to monitor individual and organizational behavior, evaluate transgressions, and impose sanctions when appropriate. Observers may also be stakeholders and members of the public who have little formal authority, yet have a direct or indirect interest in an organization's activities. These include interest groups, rival organizations, customers, suppliers, and informed private citizens. These groups form an expansive audience that consumes information about transgressions, and formally and informally influences opinions, decisions, and even the rules of social control agents who depend on the public for legitimacy. A constructivist view of wrongdoing thus recognizes that major organizational transgressions involve complex webs of public and private orderings.

Media organizations help coalesce these groups by serving as information intermediaries, collecting, interpreting, and distributing

We thank the Society and Organization Research Center for providing funds to collect data for this project, and research assistant Giao Le for her outstanding work.

information among transgressors, social control agents, and other publics (Deephouse and Heugens 2008). Investigative media unearth concealed and oblique activities, reframe activities that challenge benign interpretations, and publicly broadcast these framings across temporal and spatial boundaries. Bureaucratic routines can filter organizational deviance and shield transgressions from public view and even use bureaucratic definitions to frame behaviors as legitimate (Becker 1963; Greve et al. 2010; Wheeler, Weisburd, and Bode 1982). Even when transgressions become public, fear of retribution and contamination serve as strong incentives to avoid correcting them (Adut 2005). An important role for investigative media organizations is to penetrate these filters and framings and to find and publicize controversial behaviors. In this way, private and public orderings become commingled, contested, and reformulated if necessary.

Nowhere is the role of the media more apparent than when organizational transgressions become full-blown public scandals. Scandals are triggered when suspect behaviors are exposed, framed, and broadcast in a way that causes general moral outrage (Adut 2005). Not all transgressions become public scandals and strong inertia often hides major transgressions from public view (Adut 2008; Entman 2012). However, when a transgression is exposed and resonates with moral sentiments, engagement of the media transforms a transgression from a local event, contained within face-to-face networks, to an event that attracts a broad audience, beyond local interactions and word-of-mouth transmissions. Thompson (2000) called this transformation a movement from "local publicness" to "global publicness" and suggested that scandals are prototypical "mediated events," controlled in large part by media accounts. Entman (2012) further suggested that scandalous transgressions, once exposed, take on a mediated life of their own that may be several times more significant than the magnitude of the wrongdoing per se.

Organizational theorists recognize the important role of the media in organizational fields (Clemente and Roulet 2015; Durand 2014; Kennedy 2008; Pollock and Rindova 2003) but have generally had a benign view of how media shape and influence organizational activities. They usually view media as simple mediators between organizational actions and other audiences, with much of their power and credibility coming from the strict ethical codes of accuracy and neutrality imposed by journalists' professional associations. Reputation and credibility are valuable resources in the media market. Yet, media organizations operate in competitive markets and face profit and survival imperatives. Media outlets must balance the supply of news with demands of their readers (Baron 2006). Each media outlet has a subscriber base, and in domains such as sports, politics, and local economic affairs, subscribers often hold strongly partisan beliefs, with definite loyalties and points of view (Surface 1972). When reporting in these domains, media outlets must navigate between neutrality and the partisan interests of their subscribers.

Puglisi and Snyder (2011) suggested that the media manifest bias in the reporting of wrongdoing in three ways. First, journalists can enact explicitly partisan positions by advocating a particular point of view in their reports. In politics, a newspaper might explicitly endorse an office holder's resignation, or call for a formal investigation of questionable events. Second, media accounts can frame or interpret questionable events and behaviors in ways that amplify or modulate their partisan implications. The morality of suspect behaviors can be recast into rhetorical arguments by suggesting, for example, that "everyone does this" or that such behaviors are simply "opportunistically taking advantage of rule ambiguities." Finally, media can bias their accounts by allocating more or less coverage to the transgression in question. They can omit or underreport important details of a transgression when they impugn partisan interests, or they can extensively discuss and highlight it when they want to reinforce these interests.

The possibility of biases associated with reporting organizational transgressions significantly complicates the study of wrongdoing, its explanation, and its theoretical role in organizational fields. Media outlets, particularly those in specialized domains, are not neutral information brokers when covering organizational transgressions, and they do not simply passively connect existing private interests with their publics. Rather, media are endogenous to organizational transgressions, as they actively interpret and shape interests by highlighting some behaviors and minimizing others, frame interpretations of events to accommodate their respective publics, and take a stand on issues when it is in their best interests to do so. Often this endogeneity may be benign, but it becomes controversial in cases of organizational wrongdoing because it diffuses and scatters interpretations of wrongdoing in many directions. In particular partisan contexts, this refraction undermines the media's role as arbiters of organizational behaviors – a role organizational theorists often confer on the media. In extreme cases, refraction can disconnect organizational transgressions from the outcomes they incite, leading to disproportionate sanctions.

These complications suggest that there are good theoretical and empirical reasons to explore media bias in accounts of organizational wrongdoing: media play a fundamental role at key junctures of the scandal process, biasing observers' sympathy regarding scandalized individuals or organizations. In this chapter, we strive to initiate a conversation on these matters. Given media's acknowledged role in the construction of scandals, we focus on media bias of events that developed into full-blown organizational scandals. We begin the chapter by describing a process model of scandals and media, which forms the foundation for our arguments. We then briefly review key findings from the extensive research literature on media bias and summarize them in a framework, organizing what is known about the forms, causes, and consequences of bias in media accounts. We then superimpose these insights onto our model of scandal and media and develop an integrated model that systematizes the ways in which media bias becomes embedded and shapes a scandal. To concretize these insights, we discuss one particular scandal, the Calciopoli scandal, which wreaked havoc on Italian Serie A football during and after 2006. We conclude the chapter by discussing the implications of our arguments and suggesting promising avenues for future research.

Representing scandals as "mediated events"

Scandals are intriguing events because they violently shock social systems, have a relatively clear beginning, and have temporal dynamics which allow researchers to track their implications and consequences (Adut 2008). In recent years, a constructivist perspective has become dominant within the scandal literature (Adut 2005; Entman 2012; Thompson 2000). This perspective conceives scandals as cultural and social events, where a transgression is neither a necessary nor a sufficient condition to trigger a scandal. A transgression is not a necessary condition because some scandals are based on presumed transgressions that are never proved. It is not a sufficient condition because similar misconduct may or may not become a scandal.

This perspective instead focuses on the public reaction to a transgression (Adut 2005), which is usually relative to the level of news coverage a transgression receives. Media attention is the main variable that distinguishes many transgressions that remain concealed from those that society labels as "scandals." Entman (2012: 4) distinguishes between a scandal and a "potential scandal," which is a "misconduct that the media could reasonably be expected to treat as a scandal because the bad deeds resemble previously publicized scandals in key respects," but which received minimal or no media coverage. Therefore, the constructivist perspective holds greatly on the role of the media to the extent that Thompson (2000) explicitly refers to scandals as "mediated events." Researchers have demarcated several stages of a scandal, and media play a distinctive role in each of them.

Pre-scandal stage: discovery and publicity

Transgressions become scandalous when they elicit public expressions of disapproval (Thompson 2000). This is possible only when transgressions are discovered and when they receive enough publicity. The pre-scandal stage can last many years or even decades. Some transgressions are kept secret for a long time, and when they are discovered they are not publicized immediately (see the Watergate scandal as an example). Discovery occurs when a whistle-blower or a social control agent, such as a state agency or an independent watchdog, makes a behavior known outside the community that kept it secret.

While this can happen through the ruling of a judge, a website, a blog, or in other forms, a transgression does not truly enter the public domain and it cannot generate significant public disapproval until it reaches the media, and in particular traditional newspapers (Entman 2012). Hence the common saying in the scandal literature: No media, no scandal (Adut 2008; Entman 2012). Media can also unearth transgressions through their investigations, but their main effect is publicity and diffusion (Adut 2008). A scandal originates when media publicize a transgression that causes public disapproval and does not go by with the mass of daily news.

During the scandal: social construction, stigmatization, and image repairing

When publicized, a transgression at the core of a scandal becomes common knowledge. At this stage, transgressors can no longer seek help from their personal networks; friends, even high-status and powerful ones, tend to distance themselves from actors involved in scandals for fear of contamination by association (Jonsson, Greve, and Fujiwara-Greve 2009). For example, this ostracism may explain why Oscar Wilde was condemned and died in exile, despite the fact that homosexual behaviors were common among other high-status figures in the Victorian age (Adut 2005). Once allegations of his homosexuality became public and the media closely reported his subsequent trial, Oscar Wilde's extensive and powerful network was inoperative.

Prior to a verdict regarding the protagonists involved in a scandal, media critically disseminate information and shape events surrounding the scandal. Media contribute to the social construction of a scandal and help shape three crucial components: (1) nature of a potential transgression – did the identified behavior break any social or legal norms? (2) gravity of transgression – how severe was the transgression? and (3) responsibility – who was responsible for the transgression? The combination of these three components can highly stigmatize the actors involved in scandals. Therefore, actors strive to offset any responsibility by detaching themselves from scandals, and attempting to preserve or repair their damaged reputations (Durand and Vergne 2015; Jonsson et al. 2009). The process of stigmatization and attempts of image repair carry over the post-scandal stage.

Post-scandal stage: collective memory and reconstruction

While it is relatively easy to identify when a scandal starts (usually by looking at the date of the first published reports), it is harder to define when a scandal ends. However, at some point, a scandal moves into a different phase as media articles wane, discovery of new evidence abates, and transgressors are identified. This usually happens when a social control agent announces a verdict, which identifies responsibility, issues sanctions, or acquits the actors involved. Frequently, the appropriate social control agent is easily identified; it is the criminal court judge or similar state entities. For example, many would agree that the Oscar Wilde scandal finished with his sentencing, and that the Clinton–Lewinsky scandal ended when the Senate voted against Clinton's impeachment.

In other cases, it may be more problematic to identify a specific verdict that signals the end of a scandal. First, several social control agents may investigate and issue different rulings. A transgression can cut across different juridical boundaries, such as national and international legal bodies. It also happens when a sector has its own statute and internal regulations, such as within sport, which allows sports bodies to impose sanctions on transgressions before any civil or criminal law investigations transpire. Second, investigations can last years and involve multiple rulings, because most countries allow actors to lodge many appeals against a court's decision. These lengthy processes complicate the analysis and the determination of the exact moment when a scandal moves to a different phase. Therefore, there are no general rules to identify a clear cut-off point that demarcates the post-scandal stage; each case has its own specific point.

Several processes occur in the post-scandal stage. For actors, stigmatization can intensify (Roulet 2015), especially if the verdict found them guilty. In the case of acquittal, or simply with the passing of time, the actors' image improves eventually. At a societal level, morally intense scandals often become embedded in society's collective memory, are milestones in its history, and exert a lasting influence (Adut 2005). The media contribute to the creation of a collective memory by repeatedly referring to the scandal over time. During the Clinton–Lewinsky scandal, many articles contrasted it with the Nixon–Watergate scandal, thus refreshing the collective memory of the Watergate scandal and passing it on to a new generation.

As part of a collective memory, the revelation of further details about events may facilitate the reconstruction of scandals. The media play a crucial role in collecting new facts and disseminating them to the public, favoring alternative interpretations and a potential reconstruction of the scandal. Given the public interest around such events, scandals can also turn into a lucrative business for the protagonists, who often write books or grant interviews in which they disclose new facts and provide their own version.

Organizational responses

Organizations under scrutiny can influence all stages of a scandal. In the pre-scandal stage, many organizations strive to prevent a scandal from erupting. Organizations try to keep transgressions concealed, thus preventing the media from investigating or publicizing information. They can deter potential whistle-blowers, use private legal settlements, such as litigation, to assure non-disclosure of information, or exert pressure on the media not to publish some information. Entman (2012) shows that such interventions are able to stifle political scandals because the media and political spheres are interwoven. Alternatively, in some cases organizations proactively and voluntarily decide to disclose misdemeanors in the hope of reducing negative consequences. This situation is known as "stealing thunder" (Arpan and Pompper 2003).

During the social construction stage of a scandal, organizations have several ways to influence public perception. They can strategically select which information to disclose and when to disclose it. Space in newspapers is limited and information comes in waves, so a timely disclosure of new information by organizations influences media coverage on a given day. Organizations can shape the social construction of scandals by deciding which actors to save and which to blame. For example, Dennis Kozlowski, the CEO of Tyco, argued that the board knew about the activities he was then convicted for, but the board denied it during the trial. In contrast, when Jack Welch, GE's CEO, faced similar charges, the board supported him and helped his case (Neal 2014). Organizations can also modify their activities and affiliations to deflect media and public attention away (Durand and Vergne 2015; Durand 2014).

Finally, during the post-scandal stage, organizations continue to influence messages, images, and narratives related to past scandal events. Organizations may make multiple appeals against a verdict, which can take years. Finding new evidence and facts contributes to reconstructing the meaning of a scandal. A key decision for organizations is whether to keep or re-integrate the individuals tainted by the scandal, even if a court found them innocent. Alternatively, organizations may distance themselves from such individuals and signal a rupture from the past and the culture that originated the scandal.

Figure 15.1 illustrates the process model of scandals that we have discussed, and it shows the roles played by the media.

Research on media bias

Because media publicize transgressions and affect scandal history, media are active participants in the construction of scandals. It is

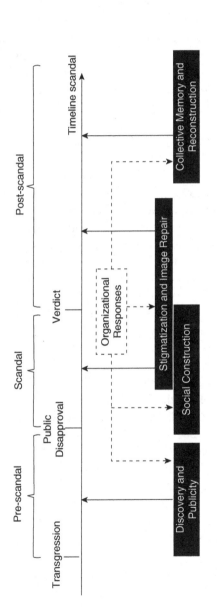

Figure 15.1 Representing scandal stages and the roles played by media

therefore essential to understand how media cover events. Few people today perceive the media as neutral or objective. Complaints that "news media are partisan or 'politically biased' are common. They can be heard almost daily on radio and television talk shows, and found on the internet, in articles and letters to editors in countless newspapers and newsmagazines, as well as in a variety of popular books, reports on media watchdog organizations, and in scholarly publications" (Covert and Wasburn 2009: xiii). Recently, there has been significant academic research in this area, including some review works that have focused on media bias in a political context (Covert and Wasburn 2009; D'Alessio and Allen 2000; Groeling 2013; Niven 2002). However, it seems that there is less research that connects media bias with organizational literature, especially in relation to organizational wrongdoing.

We used bibliometrics to conduct an initial systematic review of media bias and organizational wrongdoing. After a qualitative inspection of the literature, we identified the following keywords: "media" (and alternative terms such as "news/newspapers" and "press") together with "bias" (and alternative terms such as "slant," "partisanship," or "frames/framing"). We ran our search of keywords on articles' titles and abstracts published until December 2014 using the Institute Scientific Information Web of Knowledge (ISI), a commonly used database for retrieving journal articles (Goodall 2008). After eliminating articles that produced false hits, we analyzed 1,356 articles for general patterns. A detailed explanation of the methodology used is available from the authors.

We first grouped articles according to their year of publication (Figure 15.2). Academic interest in media bias has been increasing steadily since 1993. Until then the number of articles was less than six a year, but rose to 172 articles in 2013 and to 193 in 2014. Second, we analyzed the results based on the Web of Science Categories. While interest in media bias has been growing, there is considerable variation among different disciplines. The vast majority of articles on media bias fall within communication research (47 percent), followed by political science literature (20 percent), and sociology and economics (7 percent and 6 percent, respectively). Business and management[1] ranked sixth,

---

[1] Business and Management are two distinct categories in ISI. We combine them as in Goodall (2008).

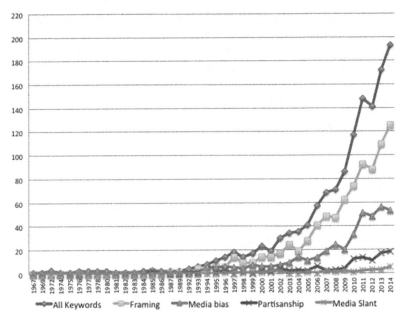

Figure 15.2 Articles on media bias over the years (overall and by keyword)

with fifty-two articles (4 percent) mentioning media bias. In the same period, the top thirty business and management journals mentioned media 1,618 times,[2] which suggests that there is considerable potential for more research on media bias within business and management literature.

Finally, we looked at how many articles on media bias dealt with organizational wrongdoing. We created a list of sixty-three keywords related to wrongdoing and ran a search within the articles on media bias. We found only twentyone articles on organizational wrongdoing per se, plus eighteen related to political scandals. Out of the twentyone articles on organizational wrongdoing, fourteen concerned corporations (e.g., three articles on the British Petroleum Deepwater Horizon explosion), three sports and athletes, three scientific contexts (e.g., ClimateGate), and one religious organizations. When we analyzed these twenty-two articles in more detail (see Appendix 15.1), we found that most of the

---

[2] We took the list of the top thirty journals in business and management from Goodall (2008).

articles focused on the social construction stage of a scandal (eighteen articles), and on few types of media bias. All this evidence suggests there is an opportunity for a more detailed understanding on the effect of media bias in relation to organizational wrongdoing.

Despite some limitations of bibliometric method (Goodall 2008), this analysis revealed the following:

1. Media bias is an established field of research and the number of articles has soared in the last two decades
2. Media bias has been under-represented in literature on business and management
3. Media bias has been under-represented in literature on organizational wrongdoing

Therefore, while scholars have expressed some interest in the connection between media bias and organizational wrongdoing, it seems we are at the very beginning of this effort. Before exploring this connection in detail, we describe the main concepts found in media bias literature.

A framework to understand media bias research

Literature on media bias is broad and fragmented, and no agreement exists on its definition, operationalization, or even findings (Groeling 2013; Niven 2002; Nyhan 2012). We present a preliminary framework of media bias, which suggests insights for organizational wrongdoing research (Figure 15.3). Our objective is to provide a snapshot of the media bias literature and present key concepts in a way that will be helpful in developing an integrated model that links media bias and organizational wrongdoing.

Media bias can be defined as media's "portrayal of reality that is significantly and systematically (not randomly) distorted"[3] (Groeling 2013: 133). The idea underlying media bias is that media provide filters "through which information must pass before it appears in the media as news" (Covert and Wasburn 2009: 11) and that these filters distort the information in a non-random way. Groeling (2013) distinguishes two forms of distortion: selection and presentation bias (see D'Alessio

---

[3] The reference to reality is often a disputed topic among media scholars (Nyhan 2012). Groeling (2013) provides an overview of other definitions of media bias, e.g., Entman (2007).

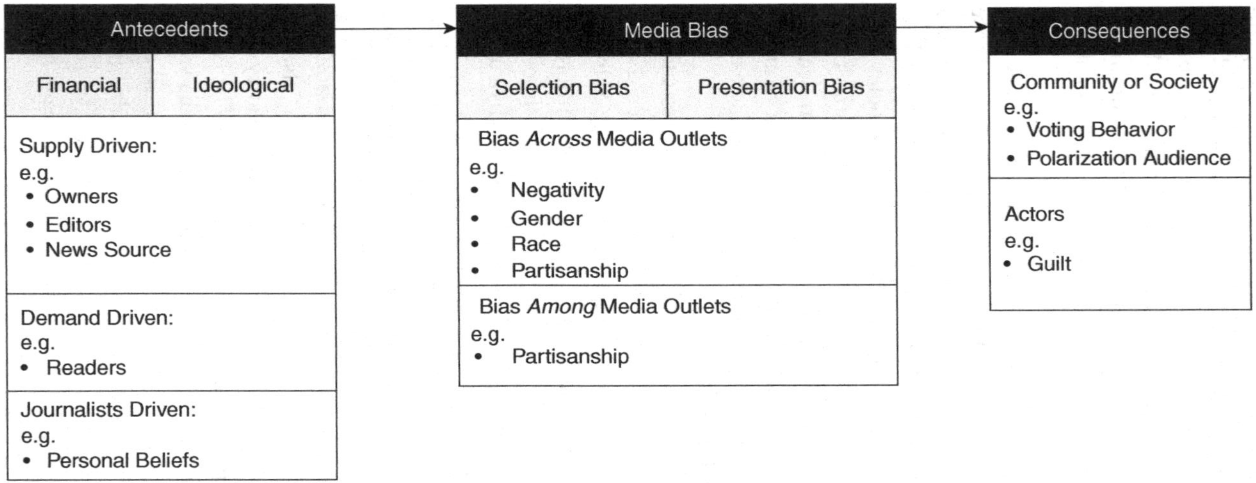

Figure 15.3 A summative framework of media bias literature

and Allen [2000] for an alternative approach). First, selection bias occurs when "not all units in the target population are equally likely to be included, either because they are not sought out by news organizations or are not published when available" (Groeling 2013: 134). Second, there is presentation bias, which is "the focus of the vast majority of the media bias literature" (Groeling 2013: 134). Presentation bias refers to the way journalists distort content, and it includes the "sources present, tone, framing, issues, visual dimension, length, ordering, etc." (Groeling 2013: 134).

Articles on media bias can be divided into two groups. The first group, which we name "bias *across* media outlets," includes those articles that look at media bias as a general tendency of all media outlets. The second group encompasses articles that link media bias to the specific features of individual media outlets. These articles typically compare how media outlets with different characteristics cover the same event, e.g. how Democratic-leaning and Republican-leaning newspapers report a political campaign. Given that this type of article looks at the variation in news coverage among media outlets, we name this group "bias *among* media outlets."

Articles in the first group have typically investigated biases such as negative bias – favoring negative news over positive (Niven 2002), gender bias – favoring men over women (Konrath and Schwarz 2007), or racial bias – framing white and black people differently (Niven 2002). Partisan bias needs separate attention, as it is one of the most popular forms of bias studied in the literature, particularly within the second group ("bias *among* media outlets").

Groeling (2013: 133) defines partisan media bias "as a significantly distorted portrayal of reality that systematically and disproportionately favors one party over the other." This "party" is usually a political party, such as Democratic versus Republican, or a political ideology, such as liberal versus conservative, but it can also be a country (Storie, Madden, and Liu 2014) or a team (Raney and Bryant 2009). In an early and classic study of media bias – *The News Twisters* – Edith Efron (1971) demonstrates how partisan media works in practice, by scrutinizing CBS's coverage of the 1968 political campaigns. She concluded that "in virtually all areas, the elitist-liberal-left line in all controversies was given major play on the air, while the voices speaking for a different view received substantially less coverage or no coverage at all" (Efron 1972: ix).

Over the years, many studies have attempted to prove that US media have a liberal or conservative bias across media outlets; however, the results are inconsistent (Covert and Wasburn 2009; D'Alessio and Allen 2000; Lundman, Douglass, and Hanson 2004; Niven 2002). While there is no ultimate evidence of partisan media bias within the entire media population, this does not imply that individual media outlets are unbiased; individual biases tend to cancel each other out at the aggregate level. As D'Alessio and Allen (2000: 148) noticed, "[the absence of overall partisan media bias] is not to say that every reporter and every newspaper is unbiased. Quite the opposite: A wide variety of data . . . indicates that specific newspapers or specific reporters and editors can show substantial (and substantive) ideological bias."

Antecedents of media bias involve two main motives – financial and ideological. Financial motives refer to simple cost–benefit analyses; most media outlets are profit-oriented. Ideological motives usually refer to political convictions, but can also refer to national, cultural, religious, or other types of beliefs.

Media bias can come from the supply side. Owners (Andon and Free 2014), and editors (Puglisi and Snyder 2011), among others, may exert pressure on journalists to report favorably biased information. Alternatively, media bias can come from the demand side. Media exist both symbolically and financially only for and through their readers, viewers, and listeners. Media consumers assure a significant stream of revenue, and, more importantly, allow media organizations to sell advertising space to companies. Thus, the media have incentives to publish news that coincides with their readers' opinions in order to increase their profits (Gentzkow and Shapiro 2010; Mullainathan and Shleifer 2005).

Finally, the simplest reason for media bias is that journalists have opinions and beliefs themselves and bias news accordingly. Traditional accusations of liberal bias in the US media were supported on the basis of surveys that showed that, compared with the overall population, journalists have more liberal views on many issues (Groseclose 2011). The implication of this evidence is controversial. Some authors state that the liberal bias in the news proceeds from journalists' liberal orientation (Watson 2014). Other researchers suggest that this liberal orientation has no effect, or even the opposite effect, as journalists would write conservative-leaning articles because they do not want their writing to reveal their personal beliefs.

The political and communication literature produced many studies about the societal consequences of media bias, such as voting behaviors or polarization of viewers along political ideologies (Levendusky 2013). Few studies have analyzed the consequences of media bias for actors. Media slant can influence jurors' decisions (Kovera 2002) and even sanction people "guilty without a trial" (Yang 2014: 87). Graffin et al. (2013) showed that in the 2009 scandal about British parliamentarians' annual expense claims, the media targeted elite MPs more than their lower-status counterparts, with dramatic consequences for their reelection. In contrast, the media might favor a person embroiled in a scandal. For example, Shah et al. (2002) reasoned that media framing explains why Clinton maintained high levels of popular approval during the Lewinsky scandal.

The framework developed in Figure 15.3 displays the different dimensions of media bias. In the remainder of the chapter, we propose a model of how media bias can intersect and enrich research on organizational wrongdoing and scandals.

Linking media bias and organizational wrongdoing: Calciopoli example

In this section, we integrate the process model of scandals and media (Figure 15.1) with the framework of media bias (Figure 15.3). We do so by illustrating how media bias operated within the 2006 scandal known as Calciopoli – the Italian term for FootballGate – which involved teams in the Italian football top league – Serie A. We track the roles and actions of specialized media (sports newspapers) before, during, and after the scandal and examine their tendency, or lack thereof, toward bias.

Figure 15.4 integrates Figures 15.1 and 15.3. The upper part of the figure represents the main stages identified in literature on scandals. The central part represents the role of the media in each stage and symbolically shows the attempts of embroiled organizations to influence these events and stages. The lower part shows the effect of media bias, especially the two most common biases (selection and presentation) in the overall process of a scandal. We do not aim to cover all possible relationships, but to use Calciopoli to illustrate how and where media bias participates in the construction of a public transgression of norms.

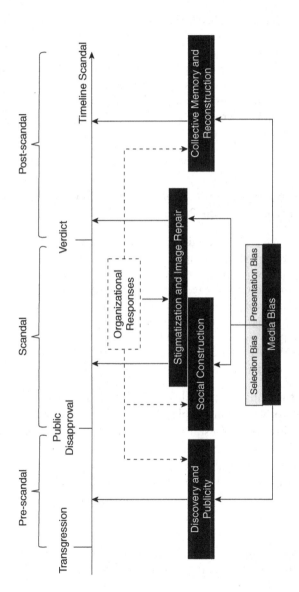

Figure 15.4 Integrating the scandal stages with the media bias framework

Setting

Italian football – *calcio* – is an ideal context to study media bias given the emotional intensity of football in Italy and the liberties taken in this sport with what might be considered moral violations. As the British historian John Foot (2007: xii) notes:

> Calcio is no longer a game . . . A better way to see calcio is a kind of fanatical civic religion – where loyalty is total and obsession the norm. Fair play seemed to me to be a concept absent from Italian football discourse. Diving was common and not particularly frowned upon – as long as it worked. In fact, commentators often praised the "craftiness" of non-sportsmanship. There was no moral code here. Winners were always "right", losers always wrong.

Maurilio Prioreschi was the defense lawyer for Luciano Moggi, the administrator and general director of Juventus and the main individual accused in the scandal. During the criminal trial, Prioreschi provided more evidence of the pre-scandal ethos related to football, which prevailed in Italy at that time (Prioreschi 2012: 1314):

> Football is the environment where bragging is the rule, where discussions with friends over morning coffee are obligatory, where everyone is coach of the national team, [. . .] where people tease each other from morning to night about their team, where the referee is good if your team wins, and he is an ass if it loses; where if you read the sports newspaper of Rome on Lazio-Inter, it tells you that the referee has refereed badly because the Roman team [Lazio] has lost and if you read the sports newspaper of Milan you discover that the referee has refereed well because the team from Milan won [Inter]. (Our translation)

In a context where suspicion reigns and the "civic religion" does not establish what is right or wrong, media play a crucial role in discerning fair from unfair, and just from unjust. Prioreschi's quote indicates that media bias is present in this context: media interpret facts in a partisan way, even in the absence of a public transgression.

Italian football has experienced several scandals throughout its history. As early as 1927, Torino faced charges of allegedly bribing a player from the opposite team in order to win a match (Felici 2011). However, the Calciopoli scandal differs from others because it represents "a systemic corruption," according to the state's trial attorney, Giuseppe Narducci. This system included "referees, the selectors of referees, journalists, slow-motion replay experts, policemen, agents, tax police, carabinieri [Italian police], members of the Agnelli family [the owner of Juventus and FIAT, the automotive company] and even the manager of the national team, Marcello Lippi" (Foot 2007: 8935). Moggi was the main person accused of manipulating "the entire system of professional football, thanks to blackmail, psychological violence and, above all, cohabitations of all kinds" (Foot 2007: 8915).

After the revelation of facts by the media, the Italian football federation organized an investigation. Juventus, Lazio, Fiorentina, and Milan were the subjects of the main investigation, which ended with two rulings in July 2006 and an appeal in October 2006. A follow-up investigation announced rulings for the Reggina and Arezzo teams in August and in December 2006. The investigations declared all the teams were guilty and imposed sanctions on some referees and club managers. The ruling was particularly severe for Juventus; it relegated them to play the following season in the lower division (Serie B) for the first time in history and stripped them of two *scudetti* – Serie A titles. The other teams started the 2006–2007 season with penalty points but were not relegated to the lower division. In the meantime, a criminal trial started (it continued until 2015) and revealed new details.

Calciopoli and the role of specialized media

In this section, we follow the integrated model illustrated in Figure 15.4 and study how media outlets – more precisely sports newspapers – reported the scandal. All media covered the scandal: national and local dailies, generalist and specialized (sports) newspapers. We follow how national sports newspapers reported the scandal and look for evidence of partisan bias. *Gazzetta dello Sport* (hereafter *Gazzetta*), *Corriere dello Sport* (hereafter *Corriere*), and *Tuttosport* are the three main Italian sports dailies, headquartered in different cities – Rome, Turin, and Milan respectively – and with different distributions nationally, skewed toward the region where they are located. It is common in Italy to refer to *Corriere* as "the sports newspaper of Rome," *Tuttosport* as "the sports newspaper of Turin," and *Gazzetta* as "the sports newspaper of Milan."

Each of the three city hosts two teams: Roma and Lazio play in Rome, Juventus and Torino play in Turin, and Milan and Inter play in Milan. These different geographic locations and readership

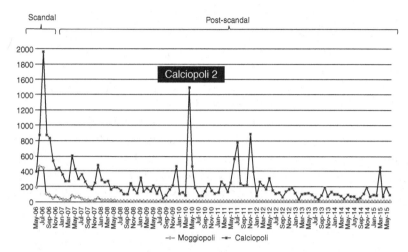

Figure 15.5 Frequency of the words Calciopoli and Moggiopoli in media articles in Italian language (from May 2006 to June 2015)

characteristics allow us to scrutinize if and by how much these news-papers biased their reports in favor of their local teams. We hypothesize a partisan bias due both to readership taste (demand driven) and the relationship with the teams (supply driven). Note that *Tuttosport* has a special status in this research because of its ties with the main actor in the scandal – Juventus. We define *entanglement* as the social and/or economic proximity of media to a key actor involved in a scandal and consider whether entangled media behave differently than those that are not entangled.

We start our analysis of media bias by drawing the timeline for Calciopoli. Figure 15.5 shows the frequency of the word Calciopoli and Moggiopoli (MoggiGate), the two main keywords used to identify the scandal, in Italian media articles from May 2006 to June 2015 (source Factiva). The scandal suddenly hit the headlines in May 2006, and we consider that it ended in December 2006, when the sports bodies issued their last rulings on Reggina and Arezzo. By then, the sports bodies had released their final sanctions (relegation and points penalization) and media articles had diminished substantially, although the criminal trial continued until 2015. The various peaks in media articles often coincided with particular events during the criminal trial. A significant peak occurred in April 2010, when the

Moggi defense lawyers presented new evidence that involved another team, Inter, which had escaped the scandal so far.

Media bias in the Calciopoli scandal stages

We look at how partisan media bias materializes in the pre-scandal, scandal, and post-scandal stages, and we investigate both coverage and presentation bias.

Pre-Calciopoli stage: discovery and publicity. Before the scandal erupted, rumours about criminal investigations and the existence of phone tapes involving powerful actors in the football world had probably been around for months, if not years, among insiders (Bartolozzi and Mensurati 2007). However, this information hit the headlines only in May 2006. *Gazzetta* and *Corriere* published the first news of the scandal on their front pages on May 3, although not as their headlines. *Tuttosport*, the entangled newspaper, published the news on May 4, in a small article on the front page. Starting on May 5 until the end of the month, the story became big news and all three newspapers had their headlines on Calciopoli on May 5. During May 2006, we counted the front-page articles about the scandal or some related aspect of it: *Gazzetta* had 79 articles, *Corriere* had 57 and *Tuttosport* had 104.[4] The difference in absolute numbers can be misleading given that it depends on the layout of each newspaper, though a visual inspection of the newspapers does not reveal a significant difference in the way the three newspapers presented the scandal. Calciopoli was undoubtedly the most important front-page news of these Italian newspapers throughout May.

A generalist newspaper – *la Repubblica*, headquartered in Rome – played a key role in exposing the scandal by publicizing the existence of phone tapes. Marco Travaglio, a well-known Italian journalist, recalls how, thanks to a "stroke of luck" (Narducci 2012: 9), he succeeded in obtaining the phone tapes and started publishing them early in May. On May 22 and 29, the weekly magazine *l'Espresso*, which belongs to the same editorial group as *la Repubblica*, published the majority of the content of the phone tapes in two supplements.

---

[4] In this period, we have two missing days for *Gazzetta* and *Corriere* and one for *Tuttosport*. Also, on May 2 none of the newspapers were published because it was a national holiday on May 1.

It remains vague whether sports journalists knew about Juventus' wrongdoing and kept silent. What is surprising is that a non-sports journalist from a generalist newspaper, not a sports newspaper, obtained the phone tapes. While this may have been due simply to "luck," an alternative explanation is that sports journalists were too embedded to proactively investigate or disclose such behaviors. A few years before, Travaglio co-authored a critical biography of Moggi and stated that other authors – sports journalists – wanted to remain anonymous because they feared the "vindictive character of Moggi" (Ala Sinistra and Mezzala Destra 2006: 10). Initially, it was unclear whether the scandal involved teams other than Juventus. Later, however, evidence also implicated Lazio and Milan – the local teams of *Corriere* and *Gazzetta* respectively – as well as Fiorentina, Reggina, and Arezzo. The uncertainty about who is guilty (or guiltier) and who is not characterizes the early stage of a scandal and may help explain the potential reluctance of sports newspapers to report and inflate a scandal.

To summarize the pre-scandal stage of Calciopoli, a generalist newspaper and magazine – *la Repubblica* and *l'Espresso* – played a leading role in exposing the scandal. Among the specialized newspapers, the most entangled newspaper – *Tuttosport* – was the last to mention the scandal on its front page. However, when the scandal erupted, the three sports newspapers aligned quickly and presented similar coverage of the scandal.

During Calciopoli: social construction and stigmatization. Media played a key role in socially constructing Calciopoli and, probably, in influencing the final rulings of the sports bodies. An important element in the development of the Calciopoli scandal was the publication of phone tapes. Phone tapping is a key explanation of the escalation of scandals in the modern age (see, for example, the Watergate scandal). *L'Espresso* published two supplements that detailed a large part of the content of the Calciopoli conversations, revealing the extent of the manipulations. Thus, everyone had access to this information, in print or on the Internet.

The public seemed to reach their verdicts much more quickly than the sports and legal bodies. Prioreschi, the defense attorney for Moggi, argued that, in 2006, "the mere fact of having been intercepted and published in the two supplements by l'Espresso already constituted a criminal offence in the world of sport. If not, you were considered to be absolved by God himself" (Prioreschi 2012: 246). To some observers, negative public opinion influenced the ruling of the Italian football federation (Prioreschi 2012). One of the council members of the Court of Federal Appeal – Mario Serio – in an interview (July 27, 2006), commented on the second ruling published on July 25, 2006:

> We tried to interpret a *collective feeling*; we tried to hear the common people and tried to put ourselves on the same wavelength. (Our translation, italics added)

Three sports newspapers participated in socially constructing the scandal through the selection and presentation of the events they reported. In May, all three newspapers gave similarly high levels of attention to the scandal, although they varied in the way they presented it. Many observers argued that *Gazzetta* tended to charge Juventus and Moggi for the scandal in order to protect its two local teams: Milan, which was already involved in the scandal, and Inter, which would benefit from the penalization of Juventus. In an interview, Moggi publicly criticized *Gazzetta* as "a newspaper, co-owned by one of the shareholders of Inter, which is conducting a hypocritical ethics campaign that has transformed the football scandal into Moggiopoli" as if "Luciano Moggi has created all the dirt [in Italian football]" (Bellato and Monti 2007: 30, our translation).

It is a fact that *Gazzetta* tended to use the term Moggiopoli instead of Calciopoli. Between May 2006 and December 2006 (the duration of the scandal), we found 6,348 hits for the word Calciopoli in the Italian newspapers, while the word Moggiopoli counted only 1,456 hits (source Factiva). Notably, *Gazzetta* used Calciopoli in 219 articles and Moggiopoli in 1,007. This evidence supports Moggi's allegation that *Gazzetta* tended to discuss the events with a presentation bias.

An analysis of the way the three newspapers reported the rulings of the sports bodies provides more evidence of presentation bias. (All headlines cited in this analysis are a translation of the Italian version.) All three newspapers seemed disappointed by the first ruling, although their focus was different. *Corriere* used the headline "What a scandal" and in the sub-headline noted "Lazio [*Corriere*'s local team] and Fiorentina are guiltier than Milan." *Tuttosport* used the headline "Juventus is furious" and published an editorial titled "Total opposition," in which it criticized the fact that Milan was less penalized than Juventus. *Gazzetta* opted for a more general headline, "Big sting," without commenting on which team received more or less penalization (Milan is *Gazzetta*'s local team). Newspapers maintained a similar attitude when commenting on the second ruling. *Corriere's* headline was "Only Juventus in Serie B/Milan given too much grace." *Tuttosport's* headline was much more scathing: "Shame on football – Juventus is relegated while Milan go to the Champions League [a prestigious international competition]." Finally, *Gazzetta* again chose a more neutral title, "Little sting," without arguing for any difference in punishment among the teams in the headlines.

Post-Calciopoli stage: reconstruction. Since the sports bodies concluded their investigation and during the criminal trial, *Tuttosport* actively reported on Calciopoli and tried to restore the tainted image of Juventus. *Tuttosport* became the reference newspaper for the Juventus fans, who resented how official sports bodies and other media treated Juventus. Among others, two Juventus fans – Emanuele Bellato and Francesca Monti – started a blog in September 2006 – www .juventus2006.ilcannocchiale.it – to defend the Juventus team. One year later, in August 2007, they published a book in order to "understand why Juventus ... had been the team that paid for everyone, while the other teams involved had been cleared of charges" (Bellato and Monti 2007: xvii, our translation). In the book's preface, the director of *Tuttosport*, Giancarlo Padovan, wrote:

> I believe that the authors' testimony *validates our editorial choice.* For sure I know that *we [Tuttosport] are not alone anymore* ... we feel that we are accomplices, if not the protagonists, of a little cultural revolution: one which does not simply accept things on face value, but which also does not proclaim innocence without justification. (Bellato and Monti 2007: xiii, our translation, italics added)

The role of *Tuttosport* continued to be important over the years. Journalists at *Tuttosport* actively followed the trial and keenly reported any new developments, especially those that favored Juventus's and Moggi's image. A key moment came when Moggi's defense lawyers discovered new phone tapes involving Inter, which had emerged unscathed from earlier investigations.

We analyze the way the three newspapers reported this new important revelation in March and April 2010.[5] In March 2010,

---

[5] For March, front pages are missing for the following days: *Tuttosport* on March 28; *Gazzetta* on March 30 and 31. For April, front pages are missing for the following days: *Tuttosport* on April 4, 18, 23, 25; *Gazzetta* on April 2; *Corriere* on April 22 and 24. Furthermore, on April 5 the three newspapers were not published.

Tuttosport was the only newspaper that covered Calciopoli on the front page and it did it twice, on March 25 and 31. On April 1, *Tuttosport* dedicated the headline to the news that Moggi's defense lawyers were about to release new evidence at the trial. In contrast, *Corriere* and *Gazzetta* covered Calciopoli as a secondary headline on the front page two days later, on April 3. During April 2010, we counted thirty-five related articles on the front page of *Tuttosport*, while *Gazetta* had only sixteen, and *Corriere* had thirteen. This difference became even more significant when analyzing the headlines. *Tuttosport* had sixteen headlines on this topic, followed by *Corriere* with three and *Gazzetta* with only one. From a coverage perspective, *Tuttosport* was the newspaper that gave the most emphasis to the new revelations. *Gazzetta* and *Corriere* each published a comparable number of articles, but *Corriere* gave the topic more emphasis in terms of headlines.

Not only was the coverage different, but also its presentation. *Tuttosport* used emotionally charged words such as "revenge," "justice," and "showdown" (our translation), while *Gazzetta* and *Corriere* seemed to use more factual and neutral language. In contrast to Gazzetta, which used the word Moggiopoli a few years earlier, *Tuttosport* coined the word Morattopoli, in reference to the owner of Inter, Massimo Moratti, who was now in the eye of the storm. *Tuttosport* encouraged Juventus fans to petition the Italian football federation to re-assign the revoked 2006 title and even published a facsimile of the petition on the front page of the newspaper (on April 8, 2015).

In the post-scandal stage, *Tuttosport* emerged clearly as the most active newspaper: it followed the criminal trial closely and revealed important facts. This contrasts with the newspaper's attitude during the beginning of the scandal, when *Tuttosport* delayed reporting news. In the post-scandal stage, the three newspapers tended to diverge much more in the coverage of the scandal than in the early stage, when they harmonized quite quickly. This evidence suggests that entangled media become extremely partisan when a scandal erupts. Both *Gazzetta* and *Corriere* announced the news after *Tuttosport* and gave much less coverage to it, but *Gazzetta* gave the least emphasis on the front page (fewer headlines). Since the revelations involved Inter, its local team, *Gazzetta* became entangled too, which could explain its behavior.

Discussion and conclusion

We had four goals for this chapter. Our first objective was to cover the vast volume of literature on scandals and media bias. We observed that while research on media bias has proliferated over the last two decades (with more than 1,300 academic articles), research on the combination of media bias, organizational wrongdoing, and scandal remains far less established with only twenty-one articles addressing this area. Scandals emerge from publicity about a transgression and it is the media that create this publicity. Hence, this chapter highlights an area of research that needs more investigation.

A second objective was to lay the foundations for a detailed study of media accounts of organizational wrongdoing. Unlike other disciplines, we have long considered media accounts as neutral, or that multiple media sources were enough to control for media bias. In the case of organizational wrongdoing and scandals, the media participate in different stages that create scandals, and their roles and actions vary depending on the stage and their relationship with protagonists. There are many ways to characterize relationships between the media and organizations involved in scandals: resource-dependence, network, communication, political science, and so forth. Complementary research concerns online media, and the influence of social networks, which make and unmake organizational reputations and determine individuals' fates (Graffin et al. 2013).

A third objective strove to integrate the process model describing the stages of scandal development and the location of where media bias influences each stage independently. This integrated model, presented in Figure 15.4, can help future research to combine new findings on organizational wrongdoing.

Finally, we contextualized our integrated model by drawing on the famous Italian scandal, Calciopoli. This case description identifies different media actors who had different degrees of bias in their accounts, depending on their interests and closeness to the scandal's protagonists. We emphasized the role played by main generalist Italian media outlets – *la Repubblica* and *l'Espresso* – that led the revelation of the phone tapping, and by the specialist newspaper *Tuttosport*, entangled with the main protagonists (individual: Moggi; organization: Juventus), and which attempted to restore the damaged identity of its local team. In this effort, we defined partisan bias and associated it with the degree of media entanglement.

Linking organizational wrongdoing and media bias: future research

This chapter calls for an increased understanding of multiple cognitive, social, and institutional processes that take place before, during, and after a scandal. Scandals are publicized transgressions with powerful consequences at emotional, normative, and political levels. After a scandal, "things will never be as before." Is this adage true? Testing its veracity calls for more studies. What are the forces that prevent organizations embroiled in a scandal from acting as before, or avoiding the stigmatization associated with a scandal? What role do media play in stoking or stifling news? How do audiences react to scandals that involve organizations? Do they boycott those organizations? Do nothing? Ignore them? Do the media act the same way before, during, and after a scandal? How do scandals influence media selection and presentation biases? Many future organizational studies could incorporate existing literature from communication and reputation research, institutional theory, sociology of norms and social movements, and political science both to enrich organization studies and to contribute to other fields.

References

*Articles on organizational misconduct and media bias

Adut, A. 2005. "A theory of scandal: Victorians, homosexuality, and the fall of Oscar Wilde," *American Journal of Sociology* 111: 213–248.

Adut, A. 2008. *On Scandal*. Cambridge University Press.

*An, S.-K. and Gower, K. K. 2009. "How do the news media frame crises? A content analysis of crisis news coverage," *Public Relations Review* 35: 107–112.

*Andon, P. and Free, C. 2014. "Media coverage of accounting: The NRL salary cap crisis," *Accounting, Auditing and Accountability Journal* 27: 15–47.

*Arpan, L. M. and Pompper, D. 2003. "Stormy weather: testing 'stealing thunder' as a crisis communication strategy to improve communication flow between organizations and journalists," *Public Relations Review* 29: 291–308.

Baron, D. P. 2006. "Persistent media bias," *Journal of Public Economics* 90: 1–36.

Bartolozzi, B. and Mensurati, M. 2007. *Calciopoli. Collasso e restaurazione di un sistema corrotto*. Milano Baldini Castoldi: Dalai Editore Spa.

Becker, H. S. 1963. *Outsiders: Studies in the Sociology of Deviance*. New York: Free Press.

Bellato, E. and Monti, F. 2007. *Juventus. La meglio gioventù*. Reggio Calabria: Città del Sole Edizioni.

*Bowe, B. J., Oshita, T., Terracina-Hartman, C., and Chao, W.C. 2014. "Framing of climate change in newspaper coverage of the East Anglia e-mail scandal," *Public Understanding of Science* 23: 157–169.

*Brown, J., Chapman, S., and Lupton, D. 1996. "Infinitesimal risk as public health crisis: News media coverage of a doctor-patient HIV contact tracing investigation," *Social Science and Medicine* 43: 1685–1695.

*Clayton, S., Koehn, A., and Grover, E. 2013. "Making sense of the senseless: Identity, justice, and the framing of environmental crises," *Social Justice Research* 26: 301–319.

Clemente, M. and Roulet, T. J. 2015. "Public opinion as a source of deinstitutionalization: A "Spiral of Silence" approach," *Academy of Management Review* 40: 96–114.

Covert, T. and Wasburn, P. C. 2009. *Media Bias?: A Comparative Study of Time, Newsweek, the National Review, and the Progressive Coverage of Domestic Social Issues, 1975–2000*. Lanham, MD: Lexington Books.

CF Judge Mario Serio stated in an interview in "La Repubblica," http://ricerca .repubblica.it/repubblica/archivio/repubblica/2006/07/27/salvati-perche-la-gente-voleva-cosi.html.

D'Alessio, D. and Allen, M. 2000. "Media bias in presidential elections: A meta-analysis," *Journal of communication* 50: 133–156.

Deephouse, D. L. and Heugens, P. P. M. A. R. 2008. "Linking social issues to organizational impact: The role of infomediaries and the infomediary process," *Journal of Business Ethics* 86: 541–553.

*Djerf-Pierre, M., Ekstrom, M., and Johansson, B. 2013. "Policy failure or moral scandal? Political accountability, journalism and new public management," *Media, Culture and Society* 35: 960–976.

Durand R. 2014. *Organizations, Strategy, and Society: The Orgology of Disorganized Worlds*. Oxford, UK: Routledge.

Durand R. and Vergne J. P. 2015. "Asset divestment as a response to media attacks in stigmatized industries," *Strategic Management Journal* 36: 1205–1223.

*Dyck, A., Volchkova, N., and Zingales, L. 2008. "The corporate governance role of the media: Evidence from Russia," *Journal of Finance* 63: 1093–1135.

Efron, E. 1971. *The News Twisters*. Los Angeles: Nash Pub.

Efron, E. 1972. *How CBS Tried to Kill a Book*. Los Angeles: Nash Pub.

Entman, R. M. 2007. "Framing bias: Media in the distribution of power," *Journal of Communication* 57:163–173.

Entman, R. M. 2012. *Scandal and Silence*. United Kingdom: Polity.

*Fan, D. R., Wyatt, R. O., and Keltner, K. 2001. "The suicidal messenger – How press reporting affects public confidence in the press, the military, and organized religion," *Communication Research* 28: 826–852.

Felici, A. 2011. *Le pagine nere del calcio*. Guidonia, RM: Iacobellieditore.

Foot, J. 2007. *Winning at All Costs*. New York: Nation Books.

*Garcia, M. M. 2011. "Perception is truth: How U.S. newspapers framed the "Go Green" conflict between BP and Greenpeace," *Public Relations Review* 37: 57–59.

Gentzkow, M. and Shapiro, J. M. 2010. "What drives media slant? Evidence from US daily newspapers," *Econometrica* 78: 35–71.

Goodall, A. H. 2008. "Why have the leading Journals in management (and other social sciences) failed to respond to climate change?" *Journal of Management Inquiry*, 17(4): 408–420.

Graffin, S. D., Bundy, J., Porac, J. F., Wade, J. B., and Quinn, D. P. 2013. "Falls from grace and the hazards of high status: The 2009 British MP expense scandal and its impact on parliamentary elites," *Administrative Science Quarterly* 58(3): 313–345.

Greve, H. R., Palmer, D., and Pozner, J. E. 2010. "Organizations gone wild: The causes, processes, and consequences of organizational misconduct," *The Academy of Management Annals* 4: 53–107.

Groeling, T. 2013. "Media bias by the numbers: Challenges and opportunities in the empirical study of partisan news," *Annual Review of Political Science* 16: 129–151.

Groseclose, T. 2011. *Left Turn*. New York: St. Martin's Press.

*Hannah, D. R. and Zatzick, C. D. 2008. "An examination of leader portrayals in the US business press following the landmark scandals of the early 21st century," *Journal of Business Ethics* 79: 361–377.

*Honess, T. M., Charman, E. A., and Levi, M. 2003. "Factual and affective/ evaluative recall of pretrial publicity: Their relative influence on juror reasoning and verdict in a simulated fraud trial," *Journal of Applied Social Psychology* 33: 1404–1416.

Jonsson S., Greve H., and Fujiwara-Greve T. 2009. "Undeserved loss: The spread of legitimacy loss to innocent organizations in response to reported corporate deviance," *Administrative Science Quarterly* 54: 195–228.

Kennedy, M. T. 2008. "Getting counted: Markets, media, and reality," *American Sociological Review* 73: 270–295.

*Kim, H. J. and Cameron, G. T. 2011. "Emotions matter in crisis: The role of anger and sadness in the publics' response to crisis news framing and corporate crisis response," *Communication Research* 38: 826–855.

*Kjaergaard, R. S. 2011. "Stem-cell spin: Covering the Hwang affair in science and nature," *Science as Culture* 20: 349–373.

Konrath, S. H. and Schwarz, N. 2007. "Do male politicians have big heads? Face-ism in online self-representations of politicians," *Media Psychology* 10: 436–448.

Kovera, M. B. 2002. "The effects of general pretrial publicity on juror decisions: An examination of moderators and mediating mechanisms," *Law and Human Behavior* 26: 43–72.

Levendusky, M. S. 2013. "Why do partisan media polarize viewers?" *American Journal of Political Science* 57: 611–623.

Lundman, R. J., Douglass, O. M., and Hanson, J. M. 2004. "News about murder in an African American newspaper: Effects of relative frequency and race and gender typifications," *Sociological Quarterly* 45: 249–272.

*Miller, E. A., Tyler, D. A., Rozanova, J., and Mor, V. 2012. "National newspaper portrayal of US nursing homes: Periodic treatment of topic and tone," *Milbank Quarterly* 90: 725–761.

Mullainathan, S. and Shleifer, A. 2005. "The market for news," *American Economic Review* 95: 1031–1053.

Narducci, G. 2012. *Calciopoli. La Vera Storia.* Roma: Edizioni Alegre.

Neal, C. S. 2014. *Taking Down the Lion.* New York: St. Martin's Press.

Niven, D. 2002. *Tilt? The Search of Media Bias.* Santa Barbara, CA: Praeger.

Nyhan, B. 2012. "Does the US media have a liberal bias?" *Perspective on Politics* 10:767–771.

Pollock, T. G. and Rindova, V. P. 2003. "Media legitimation effects in the market for initial public offerings," *Academy of Management Journal* 46: 631–642.

Prioreschi, M. 2012. *Trenta sul campo*. Milano: Dalai Editore.

Puglisi, R. and Snyder, J. M. 2011. "Newspaper coverage of political scandals," *Journal of Politics* 73: 931–950.

Raney, A. A. and Bryant, J. 2009. *Handbook of Sports and Media*. New York: Routledge.

Roulet, T. 2015. "What good is Wall Street? Institutional contradiction and the diffusion of the stigma over the finance industry," *Journal of Business Ethics* 130: 389–402.

*Schultz, F., Kleinnijenhuis, J., Oegema, D., Utz, S., and van Atteveldt, W. 2012. "Strategic framing in the BP crisis: A semantic network analysis of associative frames," *Public Relations Review* 38: 97–107.

Shah, D. V., Watts, M. D., Domke, D., and Fan, D. P. 2002. "News framing and cueing of issue regimes – Explaining Clinton's public approval in spite of scandal," *Public Opinion Quarterly* 66: 339–370.

Sinistra, A., and Destra, M. 2006. *Lucky Luciano*. Milano: Kaos.

*Stepanova, E. V., Strube, M. J., and Hetts, J. J. 2009. "They saw a triple Lutz: Bias and its perception in American and Russian newspaper coverage of the 2002 Olympic figure skating scandal," *Journal of Applied Social Psychology* 39: 1763–1784.

Storie, L. K., Madden, S. L., and Liu, B. F. 2014. "The death of bin Laden: How Russian and US media frame counterterrorism," *Public Relations Review* 40: 429–439.

Surface, B. 1972. "The shame of the sports beat," *Columbia Journalism Review* 10: 48–55.

Thompson, J. B. 2000. *Political Scandal. Power and Visibility in the Media Age*. Cambridge: Polity.

*Wachs, F. L., Cooky, C., Messner, M. A., and Dworkin, S. L. 2012. "Media frames and displacement of blame in the Don Imus/Rutgers women's basketball team incident: Sincere fictions and frenetic inactivity," *Critical Studies in Media Communication* 29: 421–438.

*Watson, B. R. 2014. "Assessing ideological, professional, and structural biases in journalists' coverage of the 2010 BP oil spill," *Journalism and Mass Communication Quarterly* 91: 792–810.

Wheeler, S., Weisburd, D., and Bode, N. 1982. "Sentencing the white-collar offender: Rhetoric and reality," *American sociological Review* 47: 641.

*Yang, M. M. 2014. Guilty without trial: state-sponsored cheating and the 2008 Beijing Olympic women's gymnastics competition. *Chinese Journal of Communication* 7, 80–105.

*Yang, J., Xu, K., and Rodriguez, L. 2014. "The rejection of science frames in the news coverage of the golden rice experiment in Hunan, China," *Health Risk and Society* 16: 339–354.

Appendix 15.1 Summary of articles on media bias and organizational wrongdoing

Author Year *Method*	Transgression details	Actors involved	Type of media bias	Scandal stage
An and Gower 2009 *Quantitative*	Corporate: Top 10 crises in 2006 Annual Crisis Report by Institute for Crisis Management + 25 others	Enron, HP, Microsoft, Wal-Mart, Northwest Airlines, Merck, Computer Associate, Goodyear Tire, Boeing, and Delta Airline (Top 10) and Diamond Pet Food Company, WorldCom, Dell, Sony, Apple, Crown Princess, Freddie Mac, Pfizer, Bristol-Myers Squibb, Anderson Guest House (a Missouri group home), CAI Inc. (Danvers, Mass.), Methodist Hospital, Mizpah Hotel (Reno, Nev.), Falk Corp. (Milwaukee), and Tenet Healthcare.	Across outlets (*New York Times, Washington Post, USA Today*)	DS
Andon and Free 2014 *Mixed method: qualitative and quantitative*	Sport: NRL salary cap crisis	National Rugby League (NRL) in Australia	Among outlets (*News Limited vs. Fairfax Media Limited*)	DS
Arpan and Pompper 2003 *Quantitative*	Corporate: Hypothetical scenario: toxic chemical spill into Chicago River	A hypothetical clothing company	Across outlets (experiment)	PreS DS

Appendix 15.1 (*cont.*)

Author Year *Method*	Transgression details	Actors involved	Type of media bias	Scandal stage
Bowe et al. 2014 *Quantitative*	Scientific: East Anglia email scandal	University of East Anglia Climate Research Unit	Among outlets (UK: *The Guardian* and *The Independent* vs. US: *The New York Times* and *The Washington Post*)	DS
Brown, Chapman, and Lupton 1996 *Qualitative*	Corporate: Doctor-patient HIV contact tracing investigation	An HIV-positive hospital obstetrician and New South Wales Health Department	Across outlets (All Sydney and national newspapers, television and radio stations covering the story)	DS
Clayton, Koehn, and Grover 2013 *Quantitative*	Corporate: Deepwater Horizon and general global climate change problem	BP and others	Across outlets (hypothetical articles)	DS
Djerf-Pierre, Ekstrom, and Johansson 2013 *Qualitative*	Corporate: Carema Case	Carema and other private health care corporations in Sweden	Across outlets (*Dagens Nyheter, Aftonbladet, Rapport,* and *Nyheterna*)	DS

Study (method)	Topic	Entities	Outlets	Code
Dyck, Volchkova, and Zingales 2008 *Quantitative*	Corporate: Various corporate governance violations	Hermitage Fund and various organizations listed by Troika Dialogue	Across outlets (*Wall Street Journal* and *FT* (in English); *Kommersant, Izvestia,* and *Vedemosti* (in Russian))	PreS
Fan, Wyatt, and Keltner 2001 *Quantitative*	Religious and others: Televangelists scandals Persian Gulf War,	US press, military, and organized religion	Across outlets (*Associated Press* and *Washington Post*)	PostS
Garcia 2011 *Qualitative*	Corporate: "Go Green" conflict	BP, Greenpeace	Across outlets (*The New York Times, The Washington Post, The Houston Chronicle, The San Francisco Chronicle, St. Louis Post-Dispatch, The Oregonian, San Jose Mercury News, Seattle Post-Intelligencer, The Washington Times*)	DS
Hannah and Zatzick 2008 *Quantitative*	Corporate: Landmark corporate scandals in the early twenty-first century	Enron, WorldCom	Across outlets (*Fortune, Forbes,* and *Business Week*)	PostS

Appendix 15.1 (cont.)

Author Year Method	Transgression details	Actors involved	Type of media bias	Scandal stage
Honess, Charman, and Levi 2003 *Quantitative*	Corporate: Hypothetical Maxwell fraud case	Maxwell family and business	Across outlets	DS
Kim and Cameron 2011 *Quantitative*	Corporate: Technical error accident (cell phone battery explosion)	A fictious cell phone company, GeoTech	Across outlets	DS
Kjaergaard 2011 *Qualitative*	Scientific: Hwang Affair	South Korean cloning expert Woo Suk Hwang	Among outlets (*Science* vs. *Nature* Journal)	DS
Miller et al. 2012 *Quantitative*	Corporate: Nursing home scandals	Various nursing homes in the US	Across outlets (*The New York Times, Washington Post, Chicago Tribune, and Los Angeles Times*)	PostS
Schultz et al. 2012 *Quantitative*	Corporate: BP oil spill	BP	Among outlets (US: *New York Times, USA Today, Wall Street Journal* vs. UK: *Sunday Times, Times, FT*)	DS

| Stepanova, Strube, and Hetts 2009 *Quantitative* | Sport: 2002 Olympic figure skating scandal | Canadian and Russian competing pairs of skaters, French judge Marie-Reine Le Gougne | Among outlets (US: *USA Today, New York Times, Washington Post, Daily News, Chicago Sun-Times, Boston Globe, Denver Post,* and *Boston Herald*) vs. (Russia: *Moskovskii Komsomolets, Komsomol'skaia Pravda, Trud, Rossiiskaia Gazeta,* and *Argumenty i Facty, Kommersant-Daily, Vremia MN, Moskovskaia Pravda, Izvestiia, Novye Izvestiia, SPB Vedomosti, Vremia Novostei, Vedomosti, Sovetskaia Rossiia, Vecherniaia Moskva, Krasnaia Zvezda, Novaia Gazeta, Slovo, Nezavisimaia Gazeta, Rossiiskie Vesti,* | DS |

Appendix 15.1 (*cont.*)

Author Year *Method*	Transgression details	Actors involved	Type of media bias	Scandal stage
			ObschaiaGazeta, Itogi, Moskovskie Novosti, Expert, Vek, Ekho Planety, and Profil)	
Wachs et al. 2012 *Qualitative*	Corporate: Don Imus/Rutgers women's basketball team	Self-proclaimed media "bad boy" Don Imus, Rutgers University Scarlett Knights, National Collegiate Athletic Association (N.C.A.A.) women's basketball championship runners up	Across outlets (*The New York Times, The Los Angeles Times, The Washington Post, USA Today* and nine regional papers selected from top twenty-five newspapers based on circulation rates, including a local paper for Rutgers University, *The Star Ledger*)	DS
Watson 2014 *Quantitative*	Corporate: BP oil spill	BP	Across outlets (America's News Database)	DS

Yang, Xu, and Rodriguez 2014 *Qualitative*	Scientific: The golden rice experiment in Hunan	Researchers from Tufts University and the Chinese Centre for Disease Control and Prevention, Greenpeace	Across outlets. Among outlets (*Sina, Sohu, Netease,* and *21 CN,* government-sponsored news websites, popular science websites and Greenpeace website)	DS
Yang 2014 *Qualitative*	Sport: 2008 Beijing Olympics gymnastics competition	Several Chinese female gymnasts	Across outlets (*New York Times* and *Washington Post*)	DS

PreS= Pre-scandal: discovery and publicity, DS=During scandal: social construction, PostS=Post-scandal: collective memory and re-construction

16 | Ethical learning: releasing the moral unicorn

DOLLY CHUGH AND MARY C. KERN

Of all the legendary animals of art, folklore, and literature, the Unicorn is the one with the greatest hold on our imaginations. Other fabulous beasts are clearly inventions, existing only in a mythical landscape of our own collective creation. But the Unicorn strikes us as more than imaginary. It seems possible, even probable – a creature so likely that it ought to exist.

(Nancy Hathaway 1987: 3)

Unbounded ethicality and unbounded rationality are the unicorns of social science: persistent in our imaginations and representative of the beauty we crave in the world, but lacking empirical support. Like the unicorn, such behavioral elegance feels like it "ought to exist." The concepts of bounded rationality (Simon 1957) and bounded ethicality (Chugh, Bazerman, and Banaji 2005; Chugh and Kern, working paper) offer more empirically valid representations of reality, reminding us not only that we and others are prone to departures from rationality and ethicality in our behavior but that these departures are the outcome of systematic and ordinary psychological processes.

Still, despite the reveal of the illusion of the moral unicorn, we cling to what it offers, an alternate reality in which good people are ethically infallible, and in which we (all of us) are among the good. Many people care about being ethical (Aquino and Reed 2002; Higgins 1987; Mazar, Amir, and Ariely 2008; Nisan 1991). And, not only do people care about being ethical, they also believe that they are ethical (Tenbrunsel 1998). Despite caring about ethicality and believing in their own ethicality, ample evidence suggests that there is a significant

We thank Max Bazerman, Arthur Brief, Jonathan Haidt, Frances Milliken, and Batia Wiesenfeld for generously sharing feedback on earlier drafts of this work, as well as Don Palmer and Kristin Smith-Crowe for their insightful and developmental reviews. We are also grateful to Krishna Savani and Xi Zou for including our work in their AOM symposium and for the excellent research assistance of Julia Turret.

gap between how people view their own ethicality and how ethically people actually behave (Bazerman and Tenbrunsel 2011). But, our "bounded ethicality" is often outside of awareness (Chugh et al. 2005; Tenbrunsel and Smith-Crowe 2008), allowing for the illusion of the unicorn to persist despite evidence contradicting its existence.

The evidence for this gap is significant. Most of us believe that we are more ethical than the majority of our peers, which is a statistically untenable belief for at least some of us (Tenbrunsel 1998). We tend to mispredict our future behavior, overestimating the likelihood that we would behave in socially desirable ways (Epley and Dunning 2000). We overclaim credit for group work (Caruso, Epley, and Bazerman 2006). We hold others to high moral standards while falling short of those standards in our own behavior (Batson et al. 1997; Batson et al. 1999; Lammers, Stapel, and Galinsky 2010). We hold implicit biases that directly contradict our self-reported intentions about equality (Greenwald and Banaji 1995; Nosek et al. 2007). In short, we stubbornly hold on to an ethical self-view, even though our actual behavior may sometimes contradict this self-view.

Descriptive research documenting this gap has proliferated in recent years, perhaps leaving some readers of such scholarship yearning for even the fictional and hopeful hint of a unicorn. In this chapter, we cannot deliver a normatively attractive but empirically unsupported unicorn in the face of the massive evidence revealing that the moral unicorn is an illusion. But we do strive toward prescription. We hope to point both individuals and organizations toward a path which both acknowledges the descriptive reality of bounded ethicality and leverages this reality toward a prescriptive vision of how to close the gap between our self-view and our actual behavior. In other words, we advise individuals and organizations on how to close this gap in a world in which unicorns do not exist.

To this end of closing the gap, we propose a framework for facilitating the emergence of *ethical learning* and *ethical learners* in organizations. We define ethical learning as the active engagement in efforts to close the gap between one's self-view and one's actual behavior, and we define ethical learners as those engaged in closing this gap. The reality of bounded ethicality is that ethical perfection is psychologically infeasible, and thus, we are intentional in speaking of efforts to close the gap, rather than the actual and complete closing of the gap. In other words, ethical learning is not an outcome, but a process. Furthermore, consistent with recent conceptualizations of bounded ethicality as a dynamic and cyclical process (Chugh and Kern, working paper), ethical learning is a process that is ongoing and lacking in a distinct start or end point.

Ethical learners are actively engaged in this ongoing process, which draws on three attributes, each of which can be cultivated by the individual. First, ethical learning is more likely to occur when the individual places great importance on being ethical (known as having a central moral identity [Aquino and Reed 2002]). Second, ethical learning is more likely to occur when individuals understand and accept that a gap exists between how we see ourselves and our actual ethical behavior, because of the small ethical lapses to which we are all prone (an understanding that we refer to as "psychological literacy"). Third, ethical learning is more likely to occur when individuals – having acknowledged the realities of their ethical lapses – believe that effort will enable them to behave and become more ethical (known as having a growth mindset [Dweck 2006] in ethics). In this chapter, we will argue that with these three (necessary, though not independently sufficient) qualities of a central moral identity, psychological literacy, and a growth mindset, individuals will be better able to close the gap between their self-view and ethical behaviors. Furthermore, we will use the organization as the context for our framework of ethical learning, in which psychological safety (Edmondson 1999) is the critical condition needed for ethical learners to actually improve their ethical behavior.

Self-threat and the gap

How can we help people act as ethical learners? Our goal in this section of the chapter is to demonstrate how self-threat[1] is a formidable obstacle to acknowledging and closing the gap and therefore to ethical learning. By establishing the relevance of self-threat, we lay the foundation for our ethical learning framework, which focuses on the reduction of self-threat, both at the individual and team levels.

---

[1] Self-threat (Campbell and Sedikides 1999) and ego-threat (Baumeister, Heatherton, and Tice 1993; Baumeister, Smart, and Boden 1996) are often used to describe similar concepts. For parsimony, we use the term self-threat but make reference to research about both self- and ego-threat.

Self-view and self-threat

A fundamental tenet of the self literature is that we are not neutral or indifferent with regard to our self-view; rather, we care deeply about our self-concept and self-esteem – known collectively as our self-view (Sedikides 2012) – so much so that self-esteem boosts are valued more than eating a favorite food, engaging in a favorite sexual activity, drinking alcohol, receiving a paycheck, or seeing a best friend (Bushman, Moeller, and Crocker 2011). We are motivated to both protect and enhance our self-view (Alicke and Sedikides 2009).

A self-threat challenges this self-view (Baumeister et al. 1996; Campbell and Sedikides 1999; Leary et al. 2009). Because most people have a strong desire to see themselves and be seen by others as ethical (Higgins 1987; Mazar et al. 2008; Nisan 1991), any challenge to this ethical self-view is a threat. For example, self-threat can be an actual or feared failure experience, such as when I do something unethical, or even when I am tempted to do something unethical (and the real or imagined experience of committing this unethical act contradicts and therefore challenges my self-view of being ethical). Self-threat can be a perceived or real devaluation of one's self-view; this occurs when I think, either accurately or inaccurately, that others no longer view me as ethical. Or, self-threat might be an internally felt doubt, such as when I wonder if I am as ethical as others or when a moral exemplar behaves far more ethically than I am, again challenging my self-view.

Self-enhancement and self-protection processes

Whether real or perceived, self-threats instantiate strivings to counter-act the threat through a variety of behavioral and cognitive mechanisms (Sedikides 2012) which are collectively known as self-protection. Even in the absence of self-threat, self-enhancement processes are continually ensuring that one's self-view is sustained on an ongoing basis (Alicke and Sedikides 2009). Together, self-protection and self-enhancement processes play a critical role in restoring and sustaining one's self-view.

How self-protection and self-enhancement do this work relies on an important distinction between primary and secondary control (Alicke and Sedikides 2009; Rothbaum, Weisz, and Snyder 1982). This distinction might be summarized as the difference between "being ethical" and "feeling ethical," respectively. For example, a consultant can self-protect and self-enhance an ethical self-view through a primary control strategy of alerting a client to the fact that they have overpaid for a service; this is "being ethical" and "feeling ethical." Or, a consultant can utilize a secondary control strategy of quietly accepting the overpayment under the reasoning that the client benefited from a great deal of unbilled time and may have intended the additional payment, making the cashing of the check an appropriate act; this is "feeling ethical" without the accompanying "being ethical." In these examples, we see how self-enhancement and self-protection of the self-view may occur through ethical behavior, but alternatively, the ethical self-view can be enhanced and protected even in the absence of ethical behavior.

The emergence of the self in ethics research

The impact of self-view and self-threat on ethical behavior has been made more evident through several recent perspectives on ethical decision-making: moral credentials (Monin and Miller 2001); egocentric ethics (Epley and Caruso 2004); bounded ethicality (Chugh et al. 2005); the "moral individual" (Reynolds and Ceranic 2007); self-concept maintenance (Mazar et al. 2008); dynamic moral self (Monin and Jordan 2009); moral self-regulation (Zhong, Liljenquist, and Cain 2009); compensatory ethics (Zhong et al. 2010); the temporal want versus should self-perspective (Tenbrunsel et al. 2010); and moral self-completion theory (Jordan, Mullen, and Murnighan 2011). In each of these perspectives of modern ethics research, self-threat varies from situation to situation and time to time and ethical behavior fluctuates around the degree of self-threat. For example, one interpretation of the dynamic moral self model (Monin and Jordan 2009) is that when the self-threat of feeling unethical is high due to a recent ethical lapse, an individual reduces this self-threat through a more ethical act in the present. Similarly, the other perspectives rely on self-view and self-threat (though sometimes using alternate terminology) in explaining variations in ethical behavior. Together, these perspectives on ethical decision-making have placed self-view and self-threat in a central role.

The emergence of automaticity in ethics research

The limitations of the conscious mind and the power of the unconscious mind – the "illusion of conscious will" (Wegner 2002) and the "unbearable automaticity of being" (Bargh and Chartrand 1999) – have become evident in virtually every cognitive process studied by psychologists (Greenwald and Banaji 1995; Wegner and Bargh 1998). Within the study of ethics, unconscious and/or automatic processes have also emerged as an important aspect of both our own ethical lapses (Chugh et al. 2005; Dane and Pratt 2007; Greenwald and Banaji 1995; Reynolds 2006; Reynolds, Leavitt, and DeCelles 2010; Sonenshein 2007) as well as our moral judgments of others (Haidt 2001). Bounded ethicality (Chugh et al. 2005; Chugh and Kern, working paper) is the ethical manifestation of those unconscious and automatic processes which contribute to the gap between our self-view and our behavior.

The ethics literature is rife with evidence of psychological mechanisms that are likely to emerge automatically. For example, moral disengagement (Bandura 1986) is a process by which individuals engage in unethical behavior without the guilt and shame such behavior might bring by diminishing the impact of their actions on the victim or blaming the victim. Mechanisms like moral disengagement, in its automatic form, allow for a dizzying array of ethical consequences, not at all limited to moral hypocrisy (Valdesolo and DeSteno 2008), the ethical framing effect (Kern and Chugh 2009), the ethical effects of non-secure attachment (Chugh et al. 2014), and motivated forgetting (Shu and Gino 2012; Shu, Gino, and Bazerman 2011), to name just a very few. In all of these examples, it is likely that even individuals motivated to be ethical will be unaware of the gap between their self-view and their actual behavior. Thus, it is unlikely that these individuals will be naturally led to acknowledge and close the gap.

The original conception of bounded ethicality (Chugh et al. 2005) proposed that much of our unethical behavior occurs through automatic psychological processes. In an updated conception of bounded ethicality (Chugh and Kern, working paper), self-threat assessment determines whether self-enhancement or self-protection will follow. When self-threat is low, the continual and automatic process of self-enhancement maintains its orientation toward the goal of a positive ethical self-view; when self-threat is not low, self-enhancement yields to the more episodic and less automatic process of self-protection.

Similarly, recent advances in behavioral ethics explore the role of automaticity in ethical decision-making and thus challenge rationalist models. Several other models highlight the role of automaticity, such as a neurocognitive model which includes automatic pattern matching (Reynolds 2006), a sensemaking model which captures the automatic processes inherent in both issue construction and intuitive judgment (Sonenshein 2007), an intuitionist model which upends the rationalist sequence of reason and intuition (Haidt 2001), and an associationist model in which normative associations between business and ethics are automatically enacted (Reynolds et al. 2010).

To summarize, we have described the relevance of self-threat to the gap that lies between an individual's self-view and actual ethical behavior. Through self-enhancement and self-protection, individuals are able to hold an ethical self-view of themselves, despite this gap. But, as long as the gap persists, and especially as long as the gap persists outside of an individual's awareness, it is unlikely that ethical behavior will improve. For this to happen, individuals must intentionally engage in ethical learning.

Ethical learning

Argyris described the individual who is highly successful and thus, having failed very little, as unable to learn from failure (Argyris 1977, 1991; Argyris and Schön 1999). This "myopia of failure" leads individuals to generalize their success, and exaggerate its likelihood (Levinthal and March 1993). Should failure occur, the individual "become(s) defensive, screen(s) out criticism, and put(s) the 'blame' on anyone and everyone but themselves. In short, their ability to learn shuts down precisely at the moment when they need it most" (Argyris 1991: 1).

The phenomenon of learning shutting down at precisely the moment "when we need it most" can be translated into the language of self-threat. Real, potential, or perceived failure (particularly for those not accustomed to failure) is a self-threat leading to the enactment of self-protective processes which have the unfortunate byproduct of shutting down learning. We can place this pattern into the ethics context. Most of us believe we are more ethical than others (Baumhart 1968; Messick and Bazerman 1996; Tenbrunsel 1998), and thus we consider ourselves to be ethically successful people. Because of our bounded ethicality, we have unconsciously created a long track record of ethical success. Should we experience a small ethical lapse, we enact the self-protecting and self-enhancing secondary processes necessary to ensure that the lapse is minimized and any necessary adjustments in our subsequent behavior bring our self-view back into equilibrium. Again, our ability to engage in ethical learning shuts down precisely at the moment when we need it most. The potential learning utility of a small ethical lapse is lost. In contrast, we propose that the small ethical lapse is a useful opportunity for ethical learning.

Our framework of ethical learning is designed to address the challenges of self-threat. First, individuals strive to protect an ethical self-view, in which any ethical lapse is a self-threat. We will address this by reframing moral identity. Second, many people have the lay assumption that the gap does not exist in their own behavior and thus that they are not prone to the ethical lapses and automatic psychological processes of bounded ethicality. We will address this through the advancement of psychological literacy. Third, when individuals assume that their ethicality is a fixed trait, an ethical lapse is a potential self-threat. We will address this through the adoption of a growth mindset.

Thus, in our framework, ethical learners have three qualities: a central moral identity, psychological literacy, and a growth mindset about ethics. Each of these qualities is necessary but not independently sufficient for ethical learning. All three qualities, together, are necessary for ethical learning to occur. We next present each of these qualities in more detail, followed by a discussion of how the three qualities relate to each other.

Moral identity

We began this chapter by describing a gap between an individual's ethical self-view and his or her actual behavior. This gap would not exist, of course, if the individual did not have the desire for an ethical self-view in the first place. This desire for an ethical self-view is equivalent to what researchers describe as moral identity. Moral identity refers to an individual's self-concept and the extent to which it is organized around moral traits (Aquino and Reed 2002; Blasi 2004; Shao, Aquino, and Freeman 2008), and it is one of the many social identities that an individual might hold. Individuals who hold a more central (versus peripheral) moral identity are more likely to engage in what they consider to be moral behavior (Erikson 1964). This consistency arises because actions that are inconsistent with one's self-view can generate emotional distress and cognitive dissonance (Blasi 1999; Festinger 1957).

Moral identity has been shown to motivate more ethical behavior (Barclay et al. 2013; Damon 1984; Damon and Hart 1992; Reynolds and Ceranic 2007). However, this relationship between moral identity and behavior may be nuanced. For example, Reynolds and Ceranic (2007) find that individuals with more central moral identities show a pattern of extreme behaviors (either unethical or ethical) when social consensus about right or wrong is low. We will also argue that the effects of moral identity are not straightforward. That is, a more central moral identity may also have the potential to generate less ethical behavior, while the individual continues to maintain an ethical self-view. An indication of this nuance can be found in the identity literature, in which identity threats lead to individuals engaging in coping responses that may prevent the threat from having impact (Lazarus and Folkman 1984; Major and O'Brien 2005; Petriglieri 2011). Similarly, we will propose that threats (ethical lapses) to an individual's moral identity (ethical self-view) will lead the individual to engage strategies of protecting himself or herself from information which contradicts his or her ethical self-view. We delineate this proposed unintended effect of moral identity below.

We know that all individuals, even those with central moral identities, are prone to the everyday ethical lapses of bounded ethicality (Chugh et al. 2005), so the important question is what happens when individuals with central moral identities engage in an ethical lapse? Our earlier distinction between being ethical and feeling ethical becomes relevant as individuals with a more central moral identity place a high premium on feeling ethical (that is, an ethical self-view). The situation in which an individual experiences his or her own ethical lapse is a tremendous self-threat for individuals with more central moral identities. This self-threat must be reduced, and secondary control strategies are likely to be engaged to restore the ethical self-view. The unintended result of this process is the gap between self-view and actual behavior grows but remains out of sight for the individual. That is, the individual with the central moral identity feels ethical despite behaving less ethically. Being ethical is subordinated to feeling ethical. Because of this perverse sequence of psychological processes, individuals with central moral identities face unique challenges in reducing their gaps between self-view and actual behavior.

A relatively central moral identity is the pre-existing condition of our framework; that is, our framework of ethical learning is most applicable to individuals with a more central moral identity. We focus our framework of ethical learning on individuals motivated to be (or at least, feel) ethical. After all, individuals who lack a relatively central moral identity are unlikely to be ethical learners, because they are less motivated to maintain an ethical self-view. Yet, the desire for an ethical self-view is not the same as improving one's ethical behavior. Thus, we also claim that our framework of ethical learning is not simply most applicable to those with a more central moral identity; ironically, this framework is also most needed by them.

Psychological literacy

We next describe a second quality needed for ethical learning: psychological literacy. We define psychological literacy as the understanding that the gap exists, often outside of our own awareness. This literacy is especially powerful because psychology is a discipline that carries an unusual burden. It appears accessible and knowable via lay beliefs and intuitions to all those who inhabit its realm (all humans) while simultaneously being an area of scientific study whose findings often contradict lay beliefs and intuitions. As a result, most of us are regularly using flawed operating instructions in our daily activities. Psychological literacy refers to a more accurate set of operating instructions, grounded in the clear findings of psychological science. The application of common lay beliefs to everyday living characterizes the absence of psychological literacy.

In the domain of ethics, a prevalent lay belief lies in the conviction that we do not have a gap between our intended and actual ethical behavior. When I am psychologically literate, I can see the gap and thus, I know that I am not as ethical as I think I am, as often as I think I am, and despite all that, I know that I still have a fundamental and automatic tendency to enhance and protect my self-view as an ethical person. When I can see the gap, I know that feeling ethical is even more important to me than being ethical, and I know that I am not always aware of how powerful this need is in my thinking and behavior. Said simply, psychological literacy is the awareness of the gap's existence.

While psychological literacy is far from prevalent today, it is very conceivable that this could change. Precedents exist in other domains in which society has undergone a fundamental shift from lay beliefs to basic literacy. For example, awareness about the risks of smoking has contributed to less smoking, yet few of us understand the actual ratio- nale for why tobacco is harmful to our health (National Cancer Institute 2008; Peto et al. 2000). Basic literacy about an effect should not be confused with a sophisticated or nuanced fluency about the mechanisms underlying the effects. Similarly, we propose that psycho- logical literacy can emerge and lead to changes in behavior. One need simply accept that normal psychological functioning leads to a gap, but need not understand the scientific mechanisms that cause the gap and its underlying processes.

Thus far, we have proposed that moral identity and psychological literacy are two necessary, but not sufficient, qualities needed to engage in ethical learning. In the next section, we present the final quality needed to engage in ethical learning: growth mindset. We begin by describing mindset and its relationship to self-threat.

Growth mindset

"Mindset" refers to the belief an individual has about whether perfor- mance in a specific domain can be improved with effort and engage- ment (Dweck and Leggett 1988; Dweck 2000, 2006). In a fixed mindset, one views performance as non-malleable and one's abilities to be finite and fixed; one focuses on how one will be judged (not only by others but also self-judged). In a growth mindset, one views improvement as possible and believes that one's current abilities are a starting point for improvement fueled by effort; one focuses on how one can improve.

In the context of ethics, an individual with a fixed mindset believes that "character" is set and immutable. Because a fixed mindset suggests that one only has a certain level of morality and because a central moral identity suggests that individuals value an ethical self-view, it is essen- tial to the individual with a more fixed mindset that this self-view be highly ethical. Anything that challenges this self-view is a self-threat. When the self-threats of temptation or ethical failure occur, the only possible response is to generate psychological cover via secondary control mechanisms such as moral disengagement – which might reframe the temptation or ethical failure as being morally acceptable or someone else's fault – rather than to gather information about one's own ethicality and to learn from it. In a fixed mindset, a gap does not exist, which is a psychologically non-literate belief.

Fixed mindsets are psychological minefields of self-threat. In a fixed mindset, the worst possible scenario is to try and fail, because failure is viewed as diagnostic of one's finite ability and thus leaves no possibility of rescuing one's self-view. Failure, and even effort, in and of itself, is a self-threat. Thus, in a fixed mindset, one expects perfection quickly, whereas in a growth mindset, one expects learning over time. Said another way, in the fixed mindset, self-threat poses a dichotomous question: is my moral self-view right or wrong – yes or no? In the growth mindset, self-threat poses a non-dichotomous question: how can I update and improve upon my self-view – in what ways is my self-view right or wrong? In terms of ethicality, the question shifts from "am I ethical?" to "what can I learn from this?" and "how can I behave more ethically over time?"

Furthermore, in a fixed mindset, people are also less accurate at estimating their own abilities (Dweck 2006), while people with a growth mindset are more accurate in estimating their own performance (Ehrlinger 2008). This difference in self-assessment can be traced to a difference in how individuals allocate their attention to feedback and past performance. Negative feedback acts as a particularly dangerous self-threat to those in fixed mindsets and thus is avoided. This is accomplished when individuals with fixed mindsets rely on data from less challenging performance situations when self-assessing their abilities, which results in overconfident self-assessments, whereas those with growth mindsets pay attention to data points from both more and less challenging situations (Ehrlinger 2008).

In the ethics domain, this difference in accuracy and response to self-threat has important implications for an individual's psychological literacy. An individual who makes overconfident self-assessments of his or her ethicality based on a narrow sub-set of observations will underestimate the gap. In essence, through this motivated allocation of attention, people with a fixed mindset corner themselves into a context with little chance of ethical learning, one which lacks negative feedback and is devoid of the challenging situations that are useful for learning (Ehrlinger 2008). In contrast, an individual with psychological literacy accepts the reality that a gap likely exists and an individual with a growth mindset is less likely to view the gap as a self-threat.

A particularly pernicious aspect of the fixed mindset is the tendency to equate high effort with low ability and vice versa (Dweck and Leggett 1988). There is little evidence of unicorn-like individuals who display effortless resistance to temptation and infallibly superior character, but even their potential existence does not pose a challenge to our argument. It is faulty and dangerous logic to conclude that just because this rare person can be highly ethical with minimal effort, the rest of us should not expect to exert effort. Unfortunately, that is exactly the conclusion that emerges from a fixed mindset. This conclusion leads us to the psychologically non-literate belief the gap does not exist, or can be reduced without effort. Thus, individuals with a fixed mindset in ethics are not only incorrect in their beliefs but more likely to self-enhance and self-protect so that their ethical failures do not pose a self-threat; these individuals are more likely to withhold effort from ethical learning, and thus, are highly prone to ethical lapses.

Ethical learning and self-threat

Each of the three components of our ethical learning framework affects self-threat independently and reinforces each other collectively. That is, each quality is necessary, but not sufficient, for ethical learning to occur; all three qualities working in conjunction will lead to ethical learning. But how does this learning translate to actual ethical behavior in an organizational context? We move to this question next and for this a team- and organization-level perspective is critical. We first consider the attributes of organizations that pose particular challenges for ethical behavior and then introduce the team-level construct of psychological safety into our framework.

Psychological safety and ethical behavior in organizations

In our proposed framework of ethical learning, the reduction of self-threat within the individual allows him or her to see the gap between self-view and actual behavior. However, seeing the gap is not the same as reducing the gap; in other words, ethical learning is not necessarily the same as an improvement in ethical behavior. We will propose that psychological safety is needed in order for the ethical learning to generate actual improvements in ethical behavior.

The challenges of organizational life

Organizations are "moral microcosms" (Brief, Buttram, and Dukerich 2001) in which multiple complex processes can generate unethical behavior (Ashforth and Anand 2003; Jackall 1988). Kish-Gephart, Harrison, and Treviño (2010) use meta-analytic methods to make a convincing argument for the necessity of integrating individual (bad apple), moral issue (bad case), and organizational (bad barrel) variables in the study of ethical decision-making, while Treviño, Weaver, and Reynolds (2006) offer a comprehensive review of behavioral ethics research in organizations. In this spirit, while ethical learning can be facilitated at the individual level, ethical learning in individuals cannot be studied solely at the individual level, nor can ethical learning in organizations be studied solely at the organizational level. As examples, factors such as ethical climate (Victor and Cullen 1988) are shaped at the organizational level and influence individual ethical decision-making. Stakeholder culture describes how managers address the tensions between their own interests and the often competing interests of other organizational actors (Jones, Felps, and Bigley 2007). Thus, in order to understand ethical decision-making in organizations, we must incorporate a non-individual level of analysis in examining the role of self-threat.

Organizations are ethically challenging contexts due to the volume of ethical decisions embedded in daily work, the frequent ambiguity of what is more or less ethical, and the stigmatization of ethical failure. Work is an ethically charged domain. Expense reports are padded, inventory is borrowed, supplies are carried home, budgets are finessed, sales are inflated, negotiations are misleading, hiring is biased, advice is ignored, quality is short-cutted, inspections are delayed, audits are friendly, information is leaked, statistics are refined, executive directives are followed, friends are alerted, favors are exchanged, gifts are accepted, and competitors are monitored.

Thus, the volume of ethical decisions is the first significant ethical challenge of organizational life. Decisions which involve other parties often have ethical ramifications and the collective nature of work in organizations generates a greater volume of "tricky" ethical situations. For example, group norms exert influence on individual ethical behavior (Greenberg 1997; Litzky, Eddleston, and Kidder 2006) and norm violations are, thus, a powerful source of self-threat in an organization.

Responsibility is diffused when individuals perceive that others might take responsibility, reducing the probability of individuals intervening in situations when they might otherwise, in part due to the self-threat of potential embarrassment of not being the best equipped to assist (Darley and Latané 1968). Groups lie more than individuals when lying will clearly maximize economic outcomes, suggesting that individuals in groups face a self-threat perhaps due to competing interests at the individual, group, and organizational levels (Cohen et al. 2009). Corruption can spread efficiently in organizations via self-directed moral emotions, creating "collective corruption" (Smith-Crowe and Warren 2014). Groupthink (Janis 1972, 1982) describes unproductive levels of conformity and harmony at the expense of sound decision-making in groups, which may be due to the heightened self-threat that individuals feel about voicing concerns or contrary views. Finally, the ubiquity of impression management (Leary and Kowalski 1990; Schlenker 1980) in organizations is a persistent self-threat. In sum, there is much evidence that groups generate self-threats to the individual.

The second ethical challenge of organizational life is the ambiguity of many of these decisions. The examples just offered are ubiquitously enmeshed in organizational life and are not necessarily characterized as ethical issues (Sonenshein 2009; Tenbrunsel and Smith-Crowe 2008). Furthermore, what is more or less ethical in these situations is not self-evident, nor is it necessarily viewed the same across individuals (Ford and Richardson 1994; Lewicki and Robinson 1998; Warren and Smith-Crowe 2008). In an interdependent organization with competing interests among multiple stakeholders, right and wrong are not always obvious, and this "pervasive ambiguity" has implications for ethical learning (Sonenshein 2007; Warren and Smith-Crowe 2008). While these "right versus wrong" decisions (versus "right versus right") are prevalent, they can also be fraught with ambiguity and framed in business or legal terms, rather than in ethical terms.

The third ethical challenge of organizational life is the stigmatization of failure, which generates significant potential for self-threat. Organizations strive for success and effectiveness, not failure. Similarly, organizational learning "oversamples successes and under-samples failures" (Levinthal and March 1993: 110). This bias toward success is not surprising, but it creates a stereotype around failure that is stigmatizing. When presented with a spectrum of reasons for failure, ranging from the most blameworthy to the most praiseworthy, executives estimated that 2–5 percent of the failures in their organization are due to blameworthy causes, but that 70–90 percent of failures are treated as if they emerged from blameworthy causes (Edmondson 2012).

In other words, most failures are treated the same, as bad failures. This assumption about failures all being the same ignores the benefits of failure. "Smart failures" (Seiken 2013) allow organizations to grow, improve, and innovate (Weick 1993). Some failures can serve as early warning signals to help organizations avoid disastrous failures down the road. Organizations which can see and respond to these warning signs will learn from and recover from these failures.

Similarly, ethical failures are not all the same. For example, everyday "ordinary" ethical lapses are generally lower in moral intensity (Jones 1991) (less impact on others), in contrast to the high moral intensity of headline failures. For example, I might expense a dinner with an old friend visiting town who reached out to reconnect socially but who showed interest in engaging my firm during our conversation. My behavior is ethically ambiguous, and if judged to be an ethical failure, it is not a catastrophically large ethical failure. But it could be the type of small ethical lapse that could lead to a more serious problem in which I systematically use corporate funds for personal benefit. Larger headline failures can begin with small ethical failures (Gino and Bazerman 2009), and thus, these small failures are critical moments for both learning and intervention. In the context of an ethical failure, an individual may see his or her lapse (the gap) but feel that others will negatively view his or her acceptance of the blame for this lapse (self-threat), and thus, they do not publicly discuss the potential lapse. Being a failure and being unethical are both stigmatized identities in which a person is "tainted" (Major and O'Brien 2005), and these self-threats are sufficient to ensure that individuals keep their questions about ambiguous ethical situations to themselves. However, while people tend to infrequently take the blame for a failure, when they do so, others view this in a positive light and as a positive sign of the individual's character (Gunia 2011). It is possible that even the ethical learner, who has reduced self-threat at the individual level, overestimates the self-threat inherent at the team or organizational levels, and thus is unlikely to look for opportunities to learn and grow.

This heightened self-threat makes ethical learning in organizations particularly challenging, even for those who do not want a gap (due to central moral identity), those who believe that a gap exists (due to psychological literacy), and those who try to believe they can address the gap (due to a growth mindset). But if this individual is interdependent with others who do not share these qualities, he or she will have strong incentives to protect his or her ethical self-view, especially in the eyes of others, and to deny the existence of a gap. Operationally, this means that the individual will not reveal ethical lapses, engage others in developing approaches to reducing ethical lapses, or share their strategies of learning from ethical lapses. It is clear that work is a domain filled with ethical decision-making, but it is less clear if it is a domain that encourages ethical learning. The self-threats that specifically emerge within organizations are significant barriers to converting ethical learning into improved ethical behavior, and therefore, a reduction of self-threat at the organization and team levels is necessary. We next propose that psychological safety is the condition necessary for ethical learning to lead to actual improvements in ethical behavior.

Psychological safety

Many of these challenges relate to the perceived risks related to speaking up, asking for help, admitting mistakes, proposing an idea, taking blame, confessing uncertainty about right versus wrong, and/or confessing inability, all of which are examples of interpersonal risk-taking. Psychological safety refers to the shared beliefs that a team is safe for these types of interpersonal risk-taking (Edmondson 1999). In a psychologically safe team, self-threat is reduced at the team level and thus individuals are more willing to disclose and discuss failure. For example, psychological safety was originally studied in hospitals where human errors (such as confusing two different medications which were labeled similarly) were less likely to be reported under conditions of low psychological safety, and thus, the opportunity to prevent the same error from recurring was lost; when psychological safety was higher, more errors were reported, allowing for safety to improve in the long term (Edmondson 1999). The self-threat associated with admitting failure was reduced through psychological safety in order for the learning and improvement to occur.

Similarly, the self-threat of ethical learning can be reduced at the team level through greater psychological safety, thus facilitating more ethical behavior. In a psychologically safe team, individuals feel that ethically ambiguous situations can be discussed, ethical lapses can prompt reflection and change, and blameworthiness is not an inevitable, fatal self-threat if it accompanies learning. These individuals, whose self-threat is reduced through psychological safety, can improve their ethical behavior.

Increasing psychological safety should not be confused with a lowering of ethical standards. Acknowledgment of the reality of small ethical failures is not the same as endorsing the failure or lowering standards. In fact, it sends the message that expectations are high and thus, failure is possible, but progress must continually be made. This approach is aspirational, forsaking the blind eye to the small ethical lapses which will inevitably occur due to the gap, and positioning each individual as an ethical learner.

Discussion

Currently, the conditions of typical organizations are those in which employees are uniquely unlikely to engage in ethical learning, and thus, unethical behavior will not only occur but will recur. However, these conditions have the potential to be shaped such that ethical behavior is facilitated by the organizational context rather than inhibited by it. Individuals in organizations face a minefield of ethical self-threat, thus setting these individuals up for exactly the opposite conditions required for ethical learning. The result is extreme ethical self-threat in which the process of learning from a small but empirically inevitable ethical lapse ends before it begins. The self-threat associated with ethical learning is high, making ethical learning less likely to occur.

In this chapter, we leverage descriptive, empirical research about the gap between intended and actual ethical behavior to develop a theoretically motivated prescriptive framework of how to generate ethical learning and improvements in ethical behavior in organizations. Our framework is preliminary and beckons future testing and refinement. But it provides a starting point to building on what we know happens (descriptive) and what we wish happened (normative), toward what we recommend (prescriptive). While excellent ethics research has been produced at unprecedented rates in recent years (Tenbrunsel and

Smith-Crowe 2008), most of this work is descriptive in nature. By generating a framework that offers a path toward a positive outcome (ethical learning, improved ethical behavior), we respond directly to the opportunity for researchers to integrate the scientific study of positive outcomes with the study of business ethics (Sonenshein 2005). Also, by generating a prescriptive framework of how to improve ethical behavior that is grounded in "psychological pragmatism" (Margolis 1998), we respond directly to an acknowledged need for researchers to provide more direction to individuals and organizations who want to improve their ethical behavior but do not know how to do so (Bazerman 2005).

Within organizations, each component of our framework falls directly under the scope of influence of the senior leadership of most organizations. We propose that the approach that many organizations take toward teaching and the enforcement of ethics (e.g., compliance) may benefit from a new emphasis on leveraging moral identity, building psychological literacy, generating a growth mindset, and facilitating psychological safety. While the instituting of compliance and ethics programs has been found to correlate with a variety of improved ethics-oriented measures (Basran 2012; Ethics Resource Center 2011; McCabe, Treviño, and Butterfield 1996), these results are not unambiguous (Badaracco and Webb 1995) nor is it clear how these programs affect ethical behavior over the longer term.

In fact, it is possible that programs that are not grounded in psychological literacy, and thus ignore the gap, may actually foster an unintended fixed mindset about ethics. This fixed mindset will generate self-threat when an ethical lapse occurs, and thus, we worry that such programs may lead to short-term compliance via primary control activities (being ethical) on clearly defined issues but also might lead to greater use of some secondary control activities (feeling ethical but not being ethical) over time, thus cultivating the conditions for an eventual headline failure. More specifically, an ethics program might simultaneously prevent immediate headline failures but actually facilitate small ethical lapses, primarily due to the lack of a psychological literacy that makes this pattern obvious. As a result, we are concerned that compliance programs that are not grounded in psychological literacy will heighten self-threat, and thus, be self-defeating. Our concern echoes the possibility of unintended consequences of ethics programs that has been raised by others (Killingsworth 2012; Tenbrunsel and Messick 1999; Treviño and Weaver 2003) and runs parallel to our concern that individuals with more central moral identities face a surprising risk of behaving less ethically over time, perhaps leading to eventual headline failures for some.

Using the ethical learning approach, organizations can consider how to reduce self-threat throughout the "rock" (formal elements) and "sand" (informal elements) of their ethical infrastructures (Tenbrunsel, Smith-Crowe, and Umphress 2003). That is, the formal elements of an organization include what many compliance programs include: rules, regulations, sanctions, and communications, much of which may convey a fixed mindset. Similarly, the informal elements of an organization, such as its culture, are opportunities to shift the dialogue about what is valued and what is stigmatized from a fixed mindset to a growth mindset.

Another practical parallel between individuals and organizations lies in the fact that just as the gap exists for individuals, it also exists for organizations. That is, just as bounded ethicality suggests that all individuals will have some ethical lapses, it also suggests that all organizations will have ethical lapses. Thus, organizations and their leaders need to expect that some unintended ethical failures will occur; these are "predictable surprises" (Bazerman and Watkins 2004). For both organizations and individuals, smaller ethical failures are easier to learn from, as they do not attract the public attention that high moral intensity, headline public failures are likely to attract. Once headline ethical failures occur, ethical learning becomes secondary to necessary public relations and legal protections. So, the time for ethical learning is before small ethical failures become headline failures, and given that small ethical failures are inevitable, organizations can plan accordingly for such occurrences.

Models of this approach can be found. The airline industry collects and analyzes data on "near misses"; hospitals conduct mortality and morbidity conferences in which cases which have not risen to the level of a malpractice suit are analyzed; the mountain-climbing community, led by the American Alpine Club, publishes an annual report with significant climbing incidents, as well as the most teachable incidents (Leviss 2011). And, some Australian companies are using an approach toward "restorative justice" (versus "punitive justice") where stakeholders connected to a misdeed gather together to discuss the incident and agree on reforms to prevent future incidents (Braithwaite 2012).

Confidentiality within the organizational context is critical for these types of initiatives to be successful. The tendency for "public shaming" on the Internet challenges the psychological safety within a team and threatens the ethical learning potential. For example, companies with whistle-blower hotlines might consider how this approach to confidentiality can be expanded to allow individuals to call to seek advice with very limited punitive potential, in an attempt to address their own ethical lapses in a constructive, forward-looking fashion, rather than simply reporting others. Other means of limiting the broad exposure of small lapses are worthy of exploration.

Our framework also challenges the heavy reliance that some organizations place on integrity tests within selection processes. These tests, which come in a variety of forms (Barrett 2003), are designed to help organizations screen out individuals based on the assumption that unicorn-type qualities like honesty and trustworthiness are predictive of who is more likely to behave dishonestly on the job. While these methods may be useful for screening out extreme instances of deliberate unethical behavior, our knowledge of bounded ethicality suggests a large portion of an applicant pool will "pass" such a test. Yet, these individuals will remain highly susceptible to self-threat. Thus, these individuals are unlikely to engage in ethical learning, but the tests will give both the individuals and organizations a false sense of ethical security.

Our work also has important implications for ethics courses in business and other professional schools. A perpetual debate continues regarding whether, how, and when ethics should be taught to adults. We propose that teaching ethics is different, and less productive, than teaching ethical learning. The traditional, value-based approach to teaching ethics does not deepen a student's psychological literacy, potentially fosters a fixed, rather than growth, mindset, and makes moral identity more salient, but not necessarily more central. As a result, such a course may generate a false sense of security, in which students believe they are more likely to behave ethically, but without equipping the students to be true ethical learners. And, many of these individuals will lead teams and organizations, with tremendous impact on the degree of psychological safety. By shifting from teaching ethics to teaching ethical learning, professional schools can play a critical role in shaping the trajectory of ethical learning in organizations. Courses can be designed to foster all three elements and, potentially, to deepen our understanding of how to sequence these elements. For example, fostering a growth mindset first might ease the deepening of psychological literacy, which forces the student to confront the self-threat of their own bounded ethicality.

Conclusion

If we accept the reality of bounded ethicality, we must consider a novel approach to improving ethical behavior, perhaps through ethical learning. Our goal in this chapter was to leverage the tremendous insights from research on the self and on ethics in service of a new approach of improving ethical behavior. We hope to have taken a step toward releasing the illusion of the unicorn, and bringing us closer to the beauty and elegance of our own ethical aspirations through ethical learning.

References

Alicke, M. D. and Sedikides, C. 2009. "Self-enhancement and self-protection: What they are and what they do," *European Review of Social Psychology* 20: 1–48.

Aquino, K. and Reed, A. 2002. "The self-importance of moral identity," *Journal of Personality and Social Psychology* 83:1423–1440.

Argyris, C. 1977. "Organizational learning and management information systems," *Accounting, Organizations and Society* 2(2): 113–123.

Argyris, C. 1991. "Teaching smart people how to learn," *Harvard Business Review* 69(3): 99–109.

Argyris, C. and Schön, D. A. 1999. *On Organizational Learning*. Oxford: Blackwell.

Ashforth, B. and Anand, V. 2003. "The normalization of corruption in organizations," *Research in Organizational Behavior* 25: 1–52.

Badaracco Jr, J. L. and Webb, A. P. 1995. "Business ethics: A view from the trenches," *California Management Review* 37(2): 8–28.

Bandura, A. 1986. *Social Foundations of Thought and Action: A Social Cognitive Theory*. Englewood Cliffs, NJ: Prentice Hall.

Barclay, L. J., Whiteside, D. B., and Aquino, K. 2013. "To avenge or not to avenge? Exploring the interactive effects of moral identity and the negative reciprocity norm," *Journal of Business Ethics* 121: 1–14.

Bargh, J. A. and Chartrand, T. L. 1999. "The unbearable automaticity of being," *American Psychologist* 54(7): 462–479.

Barrett, P. T. 2003. "Beyond psychometrics: Measurement, non-quantitative structure, and applied numerics," *Journal of Managerial Psychology* 18 (5): 421–439.

Basran, S. 2012. *Employee Views of Ethics at Work: 2012 Continental Europe Survey.* London: Institute of Business Ethics.

Batson, C. D., Kobrynowicz, D., Dinnerstein, J. L., Kamf, H. C., and Wilson, A. D. 1997. "In a very different voice: Unmasking moral hypocrisy," *Journal of Personality and Social Psychology* 72(6): 1335–1348.

Batson, C. D., Thompson, E. R., Seuferling, G., Whitney, H., and Strongman, J. A. 1999. "Moral hypocrisy: Appearing moral to oneself without being so," *Journal of Personality and Social Psychology* 77: 525–537.

Baumeister, R. F., Heatherton, T. F., and Tice, D. M. 1993. "When ego threats lead to self-regulation failure: Negative consequences of high self-esteem," *Journal of Personality and Social Psychology* 64(1): 141–156.

Baumeister, R. F., Smart, L., and Boden, J. M. 1996. "Relation of threatened egotism to violence and aggression: The dark side of high self-esteem," *Psychological Review* 103(1): 5–33.

Baumhart, R. 1968. *Ethics in Business.* New York: Holt, Rinehart and Winston.

Bazerman, M. H. 2005. "Conducting influential research: The need for prescriptive implications," *Academy of Management Review* 30(1): 25–31.

Bazerman, M. H. and Tenbrunsel, A. E. 2011. *Blind Spots: Why We Fail To Do What's Right and What To Do About It.* Princeton University Press.

Bazerman, M. and Watkins, M. 2004. *Predictable Surprises.* Boston, MA: Harvard Business School Press.

Blasi, A. 1999. "Emotions and moral motivation," *Journal for the Theory of Social Behavior* 29: 1–19.

Blasi, A. 2004. "Moral functioning: Moral understanding and personality," in D. K. Lapsley and D. Narvaez (eds.), *Moral Development, Self, and Identity*: 335–347. Mahwah, NJ: Lawrence Erlbaum Associates Publishers.

Braithwaite, J. 2012. "Flipping markets to virtue with qui tam and restorative justice," *Accounting, Organizations and Society* 38(6): 458–468.

Brief, A. P., Buttram, R. T., and Dukerich, J. M. 2001. "Collective corruption in the corporate world: Toward a process model," in M. E. Turner (ed.),

Groups at Work: Theory and Research: 471–499. Mahwah, NJ: Lawrence Erlbaum Associates.

Bushman, B. J., Moeller, S. J., and Crocker, J. 2011. "Sweets, sex, or self-esteem? Comparing the value of self-esteem boosts with other pleasant rewards," *Journal of Personality* 79(5): 993–1012.

Campbell, W. K. and Sedikides, C. 1999. "Self-threat magnifies the self-serving bias: A meta-analytic integration," *Review of General Psychology* 3: 23–43.

Caruso, E., Epley, N., and Bazerman, M. H. 2006. "The costs and benefits of undoing egocentric responsibility assessments in groups," *Journal of Personality and Social Psychology* 91: 857–871.

Chugh, D., Bazerman, M. H., and Banaji, M. R. 2005. "Bounded ethicality as a psychological barrier to recognizing conflicts of interest," in D. Moore, D. Cain, G. Loewenstein, and M. Bazerman (eds.), *Conflicts of Interest: Challenges and Solutions in Business, Law, Medicine, and Public Policy*: 74–80. Cambridge University Press.

Chugh, D. and Kern, M. C. "Bounded ethicality at work." Working paper under review.

Chugh, D., Kern, M. C., Zhu, Z., and Lee, S. 2014. "Withstanding moral disengagement: Attachment security as an ethical intervention," *Journal of Experimental Social Psychology* 51: 88–93.

Cohen, T. R., Gunia, B. C., Kim-Jun, S. Y., and Murnighan, J. K. 2009. "Do groups lie more than individuals? Honesty and deception as a function of strategic self-interest," *Journal of Experimental Social Psychology* 45(6): 1321–1324.

Damon, W. 1984. "Self-understanding and moral development from childhood to adolescence," in W. Kurtines and J. Gewirtz (eds.), *Morality, Moral Behavior and Moral Development*: 109–127. New York: Wiley.

Damon, W. and Hart, D. 1992. "Self-understanding and its role in social and moral development," in M. Bornstein and M. E. Lamb (eds.), *Developmental Psychology: An Advanced Textbook*: 421–464. Hillsdale, NJ: Erlbaum.

Dane, E. and Pratt, M. G. 2007. "Exploring intuition and its role in managerial decision making," *Academy of Management Review* 32(1): 33–54.

Darley, J. M. and Latané, B. 1968. "Bystander intervention in emergencies: Diffusion of responsibility," *Journal of Personality and Social Psychology* 8(4): 377–383.

Dweck, C. S. 2000. *Self-theories: Their Role in Motivation, Personality, and Development*. Philadelphia, PA: Psychology Press.

Dweck, C. S. 2006. *Mindset: The New Psychology of Success.* New York: Random House Digital, Inc.

Dweck, C. S. and Leggett, E. L. 1988. "A social-cognitive approach to motivation and personality," *Psychological Review* 95: 256–273.

Edmondson, A. 1999. "Psychological safety and learning behavior in work teams," *Administrative Science Quarterly* 44: 350–383.

Edmondson, A. C. 2012. *Teaming: How Organizations Learn, Innovate, and Compete in the Knowledge Economy.* San Francisco, CA: John Wiley & Sons.

Ehrlinger, J. 2008. "Skill level, self-views and self-theories as sources of error in self-assessment," *Social and Personality Psychology Compass* 2(1): 382–398.

Epley, N. and Caruso, E. M. 2004. "Egocentric ethics," *Social Justice Research* 17(2): 171–187.

Epley, N. and Dunning, D. 2000. "Feeling 'holier than thou': Are self-serving assessments produced by errors in self or social prediction?," *Journal of Personality and Social Psychology* 79(6): 861–875.

Erikson, E. H. 1964. *Insight and Responsibility.* New York: Norton.

Ethics Resource Center. 2011. *NBES-CI key findings.* www.ethics.org/nbes/findings.html [First accessed: December 10, 2013].

Festinger, L. 1957. *A Theory of Cognitive Dissonance.* Stanford University Press.

Ford, R. C. and Richardson, W. D. 1994. "Ethical decision making: A review of the empirical literature," *Journal of Business Ethics* 13 (3): 205–221.

Gino, F. and Bazerman, M. H. 2009. "When misconduct goes unnoticed: The acceptability of gradual erosion in others' unethical behavior," *Journal of Experimental Social Psychology* 45: 708–719.

Greenberg, J. 1997. "A social influence model of employee theft: Beyond the fraud triangle," in R. J. Lewicki, R. J. Bies, and B. H. Sheppard (eds.), *Research on Negotiation in Organizations* 6: 29–51. Greenwich: Jai Press Inc.

Greenwald, A. G. and Banaji, M. R. 1995. "Implicit social cognition: Attitudes, self-esteem, and stereotypes," *Psychological Review* 102: 4–27.

Gunia, B. C. 2011. "The blame-taker's dilemma," *Academy of Management Best Chapter Proceedings* 1: 1–6.

Haidt, J. 2001. "The emotional dog and its rational tail: A social intuitionist approach to moral judgment," *Psychological Review* 108(4): 814–834.

Hathaway, N. 1987. *The Unicorn.* New York: Random House Value Publishing.

Higgins, E. T. 1987. "Self-discrepancy: A theory relating self and affect," *Psychological Review* 94(3): 319–340.

Jackall, R. 1988. *Moral Mazes: The World of Corporate Managers*. New York: Oxford University Press.

Janis, I. L. 1972. *Victims of Groupthink: A Psychological Study of Foreign-policy Decisions and Fiascoes*. Oxford: Houghton Mifflin.

Janis, I. L. 1982. *Groupthink: A Psychological Study of Foreign Policy Decisions and Fiascoes*. Oxford: Houghton Mifflin.

Jones, T. M. 1991. "Ethical decision making by individuals in organizations: An issue-contingent model," *Academy of Management Review* 16(2): 366–395.

Jones, T. M., Felps, W., and Bigley, G. A. 2007. "Ethical theory and stakeholder-related decisions: The role of stakeholder culture," *Academy of Management Review* 32(1): 137–155.

Jordan, J., Mullen, E., and Murnighan, J. K. 2011. "Striving for the moral self: The effects of recalling past moral actions on future moral behavior," *Personality and Social Psychology Bulletin* 37: 701–713.

Kern, M. C. and Chugh, D. 2009. "Bounded ethicality: The perils of loss framing," *Psychological Science* 20(3): 378–384.

Killingsworth, S. 2012. "Modeling the message: Communicating compliance through organizational values and culture," *Georgetown Journal of Legal Ethics* 25: 961–987.

Kish-Gephart, J. J., Harrison, D. A., and Treviño, L. K. 2010. "Bad apples, bad cases, and bad barrels: Meta-analytic evidence about sources of unethical decisions at work," *Journal of Applied Psychology* 95: 1–31.

Lammers, J., Stapel, D. A., and Galinsky, A. D. 2010. "Power increases hypocrisy moralizing in reasoning, immorality in behavior," *Psychological Science* 21(5): 737–744.

Lazarus, R. S. and Folkman, C. 1984. *Stress Appraisal and Coping*. New York: Springer-Verlag.

Leary, M. R. and Kowalski, R. M. 1990. "Impression management: A literature review and two-component model," *Psychological Bulletin* 107: 34–47.

Leary, M. R., Terry, M. L., Allen, A. B., and Tate, E. B. 2009. "The concept of ego threat in social and personality psychology: Is ego threat a viable scientific construct?," *Personality and Social Psychology Review* 13(3): 151–164.

Levinthal, D. A. and March, J. G. 1993. "The myopia of learning," *Strategic Management Journal* 14(S2): 95–112.

Leviss, J. 2011. "HIT or miss – Studying failures to enable success," *Applied Clinical Informatics* 2(3): 345–349.

Lewicki, R. J. and Robinson, R. J. 1998. "Ethical and unethical bargaining tactics: An empirical study," *Journal of Business Ethics* 17(6): 665–682.

Litzky, B. E., Eddleston, K. A., and Kidder, D. L. 2006. "The good, the bad, and the misguided: How managers inadvertently encourage deviant behaviors," *The Academy of Management Perspectives* 20(1): 91–103.

Major, B. and O'Brien, L. T. 2005. "The social psychology of stigma," *Annual Review of Psychology* 56: 393–421.

Margolis, J. D. 1998. "Psychological pragmatism and the imperative of aims: A new approach for business ethics," *Business Ethics Quarterly* 8(3): 409–430.

Mazar, N., Amir, O., and Ariely, D. 2008. "The dishonesty of honest people: A theory of self-concept maintenance," *Journal of Marketing Research* 45: 633–644.

McCabe, D. L., Treviño, L. K., and Butterfield, K. D. 1996. "The influence of collegiate and corporate codes of conduct on ethics-related behavior in the workplace," *Business Ethics Quarterly* 6(4): 461–476.

Messick, D. M. and Bazerman, M. H. 1996. "Ethical leadership and the psychology of decision making," *Sloan Management Review* 37: 9–22.

Monin, B. and Jordan, A. H. 2009. "The dynamic moral self: A social psychological perspective," in D. Narvaez and D. Lapsley (eds.), *Personality, Identity, and Character: Explorations in Moral Psychology*: 341–354. New York: Cambridge University Press.

Monin, B. and Miller, D. T. 2001. "Moral credentials and the expression of prejudice," *Journal of Personality and Social Psychology* 81: 33–43.

National Cancer Institute. 2008. "The role of the media in promoting and reducing tobacco use," Tobacco Control Monograph No. 19. NIH Pub. No. 07-6242, Bethesda MD: National Institutes of Health, National Cancer Institute.

Nisan, M. 1991. "The moral balance model: Theory and research extending our understanding of moral choice and deviation," in W. M. Kurtines and J. L. Gewirtz (eds.), *Handbook of Moral Behavior and Development*: 213–249. Hillsdale, NJ: Erlbaum.

Nosek, B. A., Smyth, F. L., Hansen, J. J., Devos, T., Lindner, N. M., Ranganath, K. A., Smith, C. T., Olson, K. R., Chugh, D., Greenwald, A. G., and Banaji, M. 2007. "Pervasiveness and correlates of implicit attitudes and stereotypes," *European Review of Social Psychology* 18: 36–88.

Peto, R., Darby, S., Deo, H., Silcocks, P., Whitley, E., and Doll, R. 2000. "Smoking, smoking cessation, and lung cancer in the UK since 1950: Combination of national statistics with two case-control studies," *British Medical Journal* 321(7257): 323–329.

Petriglieri, J. L. 2011. "Under threat: Responses to and the consequences of threats to individuals' identities," *Academy of Management Review* 36(4): 641–662.

Reynolds, S. J. 2006. "Moral awareness and ethical predispositions: Investigating the role of individual differences in the recognition of moral issues," *Journal of Applied Psychology* 91(1): 233–243.

Reynolds, S. and Ceranic, T. L. 2007. "The effects of moral judgment and moral identity on moral behavior: An empirical examination of the moral individual," *Journal of Applied Psychology* 92: 1610–1624.

Reynolds, S. J., Leavitt, K., and DeCelles, K. A. 2010. "Automatic ethics: The effects of implicit assumptions and contextual cues on moral behavior," *Journal of Applied Psychology* 95(4): 752–760.

Rothbaum, F., Weisz, J. R., and Snyder, S. S. 1982. "Changing the world and changing the self: A two-process model of perceived control," *Journal of Personality and Social Psychology* 42: 5–37.

Schlenker, B. R. 1980. *Impression Management: The Self-concept, Social Identity, and Interpersonal Relations*. Monterey, CA: Brooks/Cole Publishing Company.

Sedikides, C. 2012. "Self-protection," in M. R. Leary and J. P. Tangney (eds.), *Handbook of Self and Identity*: 327–353. New York: The Guilford Press.

Seiken, J. 2013. *How I got my team to fail more*. http://blogs.hbr.org/2013/09/how-i-got-my-team-to-fail-more/ [First accessed: December 10, 2013].

Shao, R., Aquino, K., and Freeman, D. 2008. "Beyond moral reasoning," *Business Ethics Quarterly* 18(4): 513–540.

Shu, L. L. and Gino, F. 2012. "Sweeping dishonesty under the rug: How unethical actions lead to forgetting of moral rules," *Journal of Personality and Social Psychology* 102: 1164–1177.

Shu, L. L., Gino, F., and Bazerman, M. H. 2011. "Dishonest deed, clear conscience: When cheating leads to moral disengagement and motivated forgetting," *Personality and Social Psychology Bulletin* 37: 330–349.

Simon, H. A. 1957. *Models of Man; Social and Rational*. Oxford: Wiley.

Smith-Crowe, K. and Warren, D. E. 2014. "The emotion-evoked collective corruption model: The role of emotion in the spread of corruption within organizations," *Organizational Science* 25(4): 1154–1171.

Sonenshein, S. 2005. "Positive organizational scholarship and business ethics,"
in P. H. Werhane and R. E. Freeman (eds.), *The Blackwell Encyclopedia of Management: Business Ethics:* 410–414. Malden, MA: Blackwell Publishing.

Sonenshein, S. 2007. "The role of construction, intuition, and justification in responding to ethical issues at work: The sensemaking-intuition model," *Academy of Management Review* 32(4): 1022–1040.

Sonenshein, S. 2009. "Emergence of ethical issues during strategic change implementation," *Organization Science* 20(1): 223–239.

Tenbrunsel, A. E. 1998. "Misrepresentation and expectations of misrepresentation in an ethical dilemma: The role of incentives and temptation," *Academy of Management Journal* 41(3): 330–339.

Tenbrunsel, A. E., Diekmann, K. A., Wade-Benzoni, K. A., and Bazerman, M. H. 2010. "The ethical mirage: A temporal explanation as to why we are not as ethical as we think we are," *Research in Organizational Behavior* 30: 153–173.

Tenbrunsel, A. E. and Messick, D. M. 1999. "Sanctioning systems, decision frames, and cooperation," *Administrative Science Quarterly* 44(4): 684–707.

Tenbrunsel, A. E. and Smith-Crowe, K. 2008. "Ethical decision making: Where we've been and where we're going," *The Academy of Management Annals* 2: 545–607.

Tenbrunsel, A. E., Smith-Crowe, K., and Umphress, E. E. 2003. "Building houses on rocks: The role of the ethical infrastructure in organizations," *Social Justice Research* 16(3): 285–307.

Treviño, L. K. and Weaver, G. G. R. 2003. *Managing Ethics in Business Organizations: Social Scientific Perspective.* Palo Alto, CA: Stanford University Press.

Treviño, L. K., Weaver, G. R., and Reynolds, S. J. 2006. "Behavioral ethics in organizations: A review," *Journal of Management* 32(6): 951–990.

Valdesolo, P. and DeSteno, D. 2008. "The duality of virtue: Deconstructing the moral hypocrite," *Journal of Experimental Social Psychology* 44: 1334–1338.

Victor, B. and Cullen, J. B. 1988. "The organizational bases of ethical work climates," *Administrative Science Quarterly* 33(1): 101–125.

Warren, D. E. and Smith-Crowe, K. 2008. "Deciding what's right: The role of external sanctions and embarrassment in shaping moral judgments in the workplace," *Research in Organizational Behavior* 28: 81–105.

Wegner, D. M. 2002. *The Illusion of Conscious Will.* Cambridge, MA: MIT Press.

Wegner, D. M. and Bargh, J. A. 1998. "Control and automaticity in social life," in D. Gilbert, S. Fiske, and G. Lindzey (eds.), *Handbook of Social Psychology, 4th edition*: 446–496. Boston: McGraw-Hill.

Weick, K. E. 1993. "The collapse of sensemaking in organizations: The Mann Gulch Disaster," *Administrative Science Quarterly* 38: 628–652.

Zhong, C. B., Ku, G., Lount, R. B., and Murnighan, J. K. 2010. "Compensatory ethics," *Journal of Business Ethics* 92: 323–339.

Zhong, C. B., Liljenquist, K. A., and Cain, D. M. 2009. "Moral self-regulation," in D. DeCremer (ed.), *Psychological Perspectives on Ethical Behavior and Decision Making*: 75–89. Charlotte: Information Age Publishing.

Index

Printed in the United States
By Bookmasters